Private Martin, going to battle, stuffs his shirt full of bread ration . . .

Sixteen-year-old James Collins subdues his fears before his first battle . . .

Mrs. Theodore Bland goes riding at Morristown with the Washingtons and tells a friend that the General is "downright impudent sometimes, such impudence . . . as you and I like."

Here is an on-the-spot report by the commanders, foot soldiers, clay-pipe politicians and civilians who fought in America's epic struggle for independence . . . their lively commentary explained and dramatized by Hugh F. Rankin and George F. Scheer's colorful narrative.

Shown in their moments of defeat and triumph, here are the men and women who made victory possible. Roistering, complaining, deserting, fighting, trading shots and chews of tobacco with their British counterparts, they come alive again through their letters, diaries and journals.

"I know of no book where, within a single pair of covers either the professional student or the general reader can attain, in one vivid apprehension, a more stimulating sense of what it truly was to have been there . . ."

Other MENTOR Books of Special Interest

The Federalist Papers
with an Introduction by Clinton Rossiter

Political essays by Alexander Hamilton, James Madison, and others, which influenced the acceptance of our Constitution and remain prime examples of political theory. (#MQ556—95¢)

The Living U. S. Constitution
edited by Saul K. Padover

Complete text of one of the world's greatest documents, the basis of American democracy. The story of its making and the men who framed it.
(#MP412—60¢)

The United States Political System and How It Works *by David Cushman Coyle*

A guidebook for the student and general reader, to the mechanics of national, state, and local politics.
(#MP487—60¢)

The Democratic Way of Life
by T. V. Smith and E. C. Lindeman

A challenging book which examines the democratic ideal and how it works in practical application.
(#MP356—60¢)

REBELS
and
REDCOATS

by
GEORGE F. SCHEER
and
HUGH F. RANKIN

A MENTOR BOOK

Published by THE NEW AMERICAN LIBRARY,
New York and Toronto

MAPS DRAWN BY AVA WEISS

COPYRIGHT © 1957 BY THE WORLD PUBLISHING COMPANY

This is an authorized reprint of a hardcover edition published by The World Publishing Company.

FIFTH PRINTING

MENTOR TRADEMARK REG. U.S. PAT. OFF. AND FOREIGN COUNTRIES
REGISTERED TRADEMARK—MARCA REGISTRADA
HECHO EN CHICAGO, U.S.A.

MENTOR BOOKS are published *in the United States* by The New American Library, Inc., 1301 Avenue of the Americas, New York, New York 10019, *in Canada* by The New American Library of Canada Limited, 295 King Street East, Toronto 2, Ontario

Contents

List of Maps

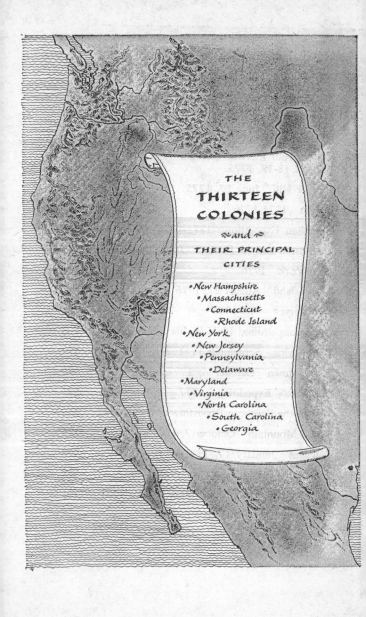

THE
**THIRTEEN
COLONIES**
~and~
**THEIR PRINCIPAL
CITIES**

· New Hampshire
· Massachusetts
· Connecticut
· Rhode Island
· New York
· New Jersey
· Pennsylvania
· Delaware
· Maryland
· Virginia
· North Carolina
· South Carolina
· Georgia

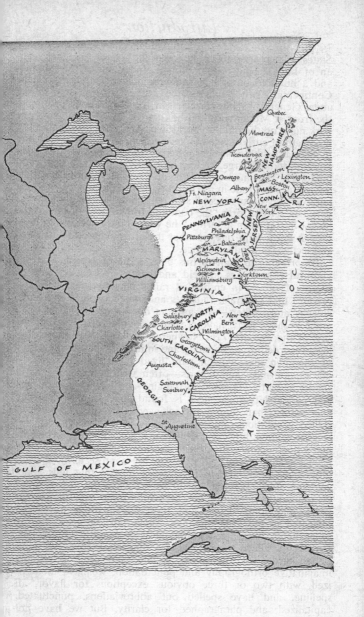

Introduction

In the fifty-fourth year of the Independence of the United States, as they used to say in copyright notices, an aging veteran of Long Island, Germantown, Valley Forge, Monmouth, and a hundred other engagements and encampments of the Continental Army published the story of his life as a soldier under General Washington. He saw the General once, riding to the front at Monmouth, and he thought he saw him again one dark night on the lines at Yorktown. And once he saw and felt the wrath of curly-headed Israel Putnam, when Put caught him in company with comrades pilfering wine from a civilian's cellar. But, by and large, he had little intercourse with high command. He remained a private for five years, until at last he moved up one grade in the military scale. His book of "nothing but everyday occurrences," said he, "contained no alpine wonders." In setting forth "the common transactions of one of the lowest in station in an army," he wished only to "give an idea, though but a faint one, of what the army suffered that gained and secured our independence."

By bringing to light in this book some of Joseph Martin's youthful experiences in field and camp, as well as those of scores of others in embattled ranks or threatened homes—privates and generals, redcoats and rebels, women and men, citizens and soldiers—the authors hope that they also, on a much broader scale, have created a contemporaneous impression of the war of 1776. Nowhere, we think, have those days been recorded more humanly and intimately than in the words of the men and women who lived them. In their letters, diaries, journals, and reports—often written while the acrid smoke of battle yet stood in the air—and in their newspapers and personal reminiscences is found a sense of immediacy and reality that cannot be achieved by a writer, however skilled, generations removed.

This volume, however, is neither a collection of documents nor a documentary history; it was not conceived to meet the need for such a work. Instead, to use a prose term, the authors have attempted to fabricate a mosaic that tells a developing story. In order to do so, we have omitted portions of individual accounts not germane, some repetitious material, and some detail, and those emendations have been indicated in the usual manner. Those portions used, on the other hand, have been tampered with as little as possible. Hoping to relieve the reader of a long book from the additional burden of translating archaic and often puzzlingly imaginative orthography and punctuation, we have modernized, with two or three obvious exceptions for flavor, all spelling, and have spelled out abbreviations, punctuated, capitalized, and paragraphed for clarity. But we have not changed the original text to correct grammatical or minor factual errors or infelicities of style. We have allowed trivial factual errors to stand as the lapse of memory or the simple mistake of a contemporary; more serious ones have been pointed out and corrections made and indicated either in the quotation or in our own interpolations.

We are aware that many aspects of the war—the naval, the diplomatic, the political, to mention three—have not been treated. Space limitations alone would have ruled them out, but also our primary interest has been to tell anew the story of the land war, which was the major event in the lives of most Americans from 1776 to 1782. We have limited that story particularly to the main fighting force, the Continental Army. The fascinating Southern Campaign has been abbreviated because it consisted of a number of smaller engagements in places often obscure and of strategy and maneuvers often difficult for the nonspecialist to follow. Too, the engagements that did much to win the war in the South were often spontaneous actions by relatively local forces who made few personal records.

In assembling materials the authors made no special effort to locate unknown or unpublished documents, though several interesting ones came their way. Rather we chose to sift the tremendous wealth of Revolutionary material to be found in newspapers; numerous biographies containing letters and documents of much interest; the long runs of early American historical periodicals; such remarkable depositories as Peter Force's *American Archives* and Benjamin F. Stevens' *Facsimiles;* the multi-volume writings of Washington, John Adams, Jefferson, Hamilton, and others; and especially the rich publications of the great historical societies. The laborious process of turning page by page through hundreds upon hundreds of such volumes revealed again the truth of the observation that in print is an unbelievably vast body of contemporary documents unknown to the general reader, often unfamiliar to the specialist, and far from exhausted. Many of these unexploited documents in trustworthy printed form qualify as almost unused primary sources. The late Douglas Southall Freeman, after many years of work on his life of Washington, remarked that long handling of source material for the American Revolution "never quite prepares one for the volume and variety of what one finds in print."

The greatest part of the research for this volume was done at The University of North Carolina Library, where through the interested co-operation of Olan V. Cook and the late George F. Bentley the authors were provided facilities and services for many months. To the friendly staffs of every department of that institution, from Circulation to Photo-duplication, we are immeasurably indebted. Other institutions have been similarly generous, notably The New-York Historical Society and especially Miss Dorothy C. Barck,

Wayne Andrews, Wilmer C. Leech; The New York Public Library and Robert W. Hill and Edward B. Morrison; The Historical Society of Pennsylvania and Richard N. Williams, 2nd, J. H. Givens, Miss Catherine H. Miller; the William L. Clements Library and Howard Peckham, William S. Ewing, Colton Storm; the Chicago Historial Society and Paul M. Angle and Miss Margaret Scrivon; the Princeton University Library and Alexander P. Clark; The Library of Congress and David C. Mearns, C. Percy Powell, and the informed librarians of the Main Reading Room; the Virginia Historical Society and John M. Jennings, Miss Ellen B. Wooldridge, Miss Katherine Marks; the Virginia State Library and William J. Van Schreeven; the Duke University Library and Thomas M. Simkins, Jr.; The Mount Vernon Ladies' Association of the Union and Charles C. Wall; The Rutherford B. Hayes Library and Watt P. Marchman.

At least one of the authors has visited every Revolutionary field now preserved as a state or national historical site, where uniformly our guides have been liberal with their time and extremely helpful. Often at locales where the historical site has been almost entirely lost, we have found an antiquarian ready to help establish a base line for our sketch maps or to find some identifying point which might have been missed. At Morristown National Historical Park, Melvin J. Weig devoted many hours to our problems, and Francis S. Ronalds holds a special place in our affections for generosities beyond mention and far outside his official domain.

Numerous others, through their counsel and the loan of materials, have enriched the work, lightened the labors, and gladdened the hours of the authors: Julian P. Boyd, the late Douglas Southall Freeman, Arthur Swann, Harold Easterby, Richard A. Maass, Nathaniel E. Stein, Mrs. Ben Sheldon, E. A. Daube, the late Homer M. Pace, Robert M. Meriweather, Samuel Galliard Stoney, Leon DeValinger, the late Allen French, Mrs. Joseph Carson, Forest H. Sweet, James T. Flexner, and Manly Wade Wellman.

Hugh F. Rankin is especially indebted to Hugh T. Lefler, Fletcher M. Green, and the Trustees of the Morehead Foundation for endorsing his participation in this project.

Perhaps this book would not have been undertaken but for the enthusiasm, imagination, and faith of Earl Schenck Miers, who held it together on more than one occasion when it threatened to fall apart. No expression of gratitude can satisfy the debt the authors owe him.

And we are confident that the volume never could have existed without the patience and understanding of Genevieve Yost Scheer and Betty Bursley Rankin, who endured four years of General Washington's war and typed and retyped. Genevieve Scneer, in addition, for months tracked down references, checked notes and citations, and prepared the footnotes and bibliography.   GEORGE F. SCHEER & HUGH F. RANKIN

"MY NAME IS REVERE"

Lexington

APRIL 19, 1775

No ONE knows who knocked on the door of Paul Revere's house, jammed between the Holyokes' and the Barnards', on Boston's North Square. It was night, about ten o'clock. The date was Tuesday, the eighteenth of April, 1775.

When the door opened, letting light into the shadows under the second-story overhang, the messenger must have whispered a name: Dr. Warren.

Moments later, brawny Mr. Revere was hurrying along the dark cobbles toward fashionable Hanover Street. It did not take him long to reach Dr. Joseph Warren's, where he was probably admitted by the doctor himself. The doctor was thirty-four, tall and fair and blue-eyed, rather handsome. He was genial and kind and always dapper, with much charm of manner. He was a good doctor and extremely popular with Boston's fifteen thousand citizens. Recently he had come to be recognized as third only to violent Samuel Adams and zealous John Hancock as a political leader of the radical Whig party. He was as much a marked man as they in the eyes of the British, and at the moment in even greater personal danger.

When the Provincial Congress of Massachusetts had adjourned in Concord last Saturday, Adams and Hancock had not dared return to Boston, but had taken residence in the comparative safety of Lexington, twelve miles away, at the home of Hancock's kinsman, the Reverend Jonas Clark. There, until they should depart for the Continental Congress in Philadelphia next month, they felt secure from the colony's military governor, who might at any time during the existing tension decide to snatch up the rebel leaders. Warren, however, ignoring muttered threats of hanging, had returned to town to serve as a link between them and the Whigs in Boston. Suddenly a time for action had come, and he had summoned Paul Revere.

On the face of it, Dr. Warren and Paul Revere seemed unlikely associates. Burly, forty-year-old Revere was the town's most gifted artificer, a ruddy-faced, plain man with a wide, generous mouth, a substantial flaring nose, and quizzical brows arching over warm, dark eyes. His blunt, capable hands had fashioned the most beautiful silver pieces in America, and that spring, in his oft-exercised role of surgeon-dentist, he had contrived and fitted for Dr. Warren two artificial ivory teeth. His skill, good taste, and sensibility ordinarily would not have been sufficient to break down the social barrier that existed between the world of the mechanic and the circle of the well-born, Harvard-bred Joseph Warren, but between these two had grown a genuine affection, born of political rebellion and bonded by common cause and common peril.

That there was something special about the man Revere his nominal social superiors recognized; they accepted him graciously into the exclusive Long Room Club, made up of Harvard graduates, scholars, and men of affairs. Fashionable, vain, wealthy John Hancock and strange, gifted Dr. Benjamin Church were members, and fine, delicate Josiah Quincy, and Thomas Melville, and a few others, and of course Sam Adams. In the heated discussions of the secret Long Room Club, in the work of the Masonic Order, in noisy taprooms, the friendship of Revere and Warren had grown apace with their radicalism. Together, two years past, they had blacked their faces and joined the silent "Mohawks" when they dumped the East India Company tea off the tea ships into the tide of Boston Harbor. The next day their names were linked in a street ballad that ran:

> Our Warren's there and bold Revere
> With hands to do and words to cheer
> For liberty and laws . . .

More and more Warren had come to rely upon the judgment and abilities of his friend Revere, who worked closely with the Whig committees, mostly doing what he loved— "outdoor work" he called it—riding courier from the Boston committee to others as far away as Philadelphia.

During the past winter, about thirty mechanics, most likely all North Enders and friends of Revere, had formed themselves into a vigilance committee to keep an eye on the activities of the Tories and the movements of the British troops quartered in the town. Ever since General Thomas Gage, a plain, sensible man, had returned from England in the spring of 1774 as the colony's first military governor, supported by nearly four thousand regular troops "to keep order," the Whigs had been expecting him to take some sort of punitive action against them and their leaders. In pairs the mechanics patrolled the streets all night.

Not only the Whig leaders were in jeopardy, but also a

certain valuable cache in the town of Concord, about seventeen miles to the northwest. There, with typical New England prudence and foresight, the radicals already had stockpiled and concealed against the day of need muskets and cannon, musket balls and cartridges, hundreds of barrels of gunpowder, reams of cartridge paper, spades, axes, medicine chests, tents, hogsheads of flour, pork, beef, salt, boxes of candles, wooden spoons, dishes, canteens, casks of wine and raisins, and other supplies for war.

On Saturday night, April 15, three nights ago, the patrolling mechanics began to suspect that General Gage meant to move his troops, perhaps in a raid on the party chiefs and the supplies at Concord. The rowboats which belonged to the British naval ships anchored in the harbor had previously been hauled up for repairs, but about midnight they all were launched and moored under the sterns of the men-of-war. The surreptitious launching of the boats reminded the patrol that Gage's crack Grenadier companies, his biggest men, his heavy-duty troops, and the Light Infantry companies, his fast active troops trained as flankers, had been detached from their regiments earlier in the day on undesignated special duty. The two facts together suggested that something was astir.

When the general marched his troops into the country for exercise, it was usually from the southward across Boston Neck and through the hamlet of Roxbury, or northward across the Charles River by ferry and through Charlestown. He would know that any expedition through these towns was sure to be detected. Was he now shrewdly planning to move troops swiftly one night by boat across Back Bay to East Cambridge and steal a march on the unsuspecting patriots by lonely country lanes that led into the road to Concord?

Nothing more happened that Saturday night, the fifteenth.

On Sunday morning, sent by Dr. Warren, Paul Revere rode to Lexington to warn Sam Adams and John Hancock that Gage soon might make a sudden march to seize both them and the Concord stores.

Riding back to Boston, Revere wondered if Gage, when he marched, would post extra guards at the Charlestown Ferry and the town gates on Boston Neck to prevent couriers from leaving Boston to alert the countryside. So he turned toward Charlestown. From there, across the broad mouth of the Charles, Boston was plainly visible, its steeples pricking the sky. Revere hunted up Colonel William Conant, a high Whig, and several "other gentlemen" and with them he arranged signals: If General Gage should leave Boston by water, Revere would show two lanterns in the North Church

tower; if the redcoats marched over Boston Neck and out of
town by land, he would show one lantern. He himself would
endeavor to reach Charlestown with details, but if he should
fail, the lanterns would tell the colonel what warning he must
send into the countryside.

Monday, the seventeenth, dreary and threatening rain, and
this Tuesday, the eighteenth, showery but turning clear and
cold, were taut with rumors. Many of the British regulars
were billeted in private houses. Profane, honest, likable old
Major John Pitcairn of the Marines was quartered almost
next door to the Reveres in North Square. Officers of the
Royal Irish and the Forty-third were in Back Street close by.
Scarcely a house with an extra bed but quartered one or
more of His Majesty's troops. And it was obvious to anyone
that they were going on active duty.

With the approach of dark, tension in town became almost
unbearable. Each hour produced more rumor. Mrs. John Stedman, in Winter Street, said that a soldier in full uniform
had come by and told her serving-girl that the girl's soldier-
husband must be on the Common by eight o'clock with a
day's provisions and thirty-six rounds of ammunition. A gunsmith in Hatter's Square revealed that a sergeant major quartered on him had said that the troops were about to move.
Several people reported with some excitement that a Light
Infantry soldier in full field accouterments was seen in a
retail shop.

So by ten o'clock, when the unknown messenger brought
Dr. Warren's summons to North Square, Paul Revere was
waiting for it. What took place at Dr. Warren's house that
Tuesday night is Revere's own recollection:

. . . Dr. Warren . . . begged that I would immediately
set off for Lexington, where Messrs. Hancock and Adams
were, and acquaint them of the movement and that it was
thought they were the objects. . . . I found he had sent an
express by land to Lexington, a Mr. William Dawes. . . .

I left Dr. Warren, called upon a friend and desired him
to make the signals. I then went home, took my boots and
surtout, went to the north part of the town, where I had
kept a boat. Two friends rowed me across Charles River,
a little to the eastward where the *Somerset* man-of-war lay.
It was then young flood, the ship was winding, and the moon
was rising.

They landed me on the Charlestown side. When I got into
town I met Colonel Conant and several others. They said
they had seen our signals. I told them what was acting and
went to get me a horse. I got a horse of Deacon [John]
Larkin. While the horse was preparing, Richard Devens, Es-

quire, who was one of the Committee of Safety, came to me and told me that he came down the road from Lexington after sundown that evening, that he met ten British officers, all well mounted and armed, going up the road.[1]

The British patrol, muffled in their long blue cloaks, had asked Devens where "Clark's tavern" was, leading him to suspect that the men knew that Adams and Hancock were at Clark's but were unaware that Clark's was a parsonage, not a public house. Devens had sent a warning to the Reverend Jonas Clark that the patrol evidently was seeking his residence and his guests.

Revere mounted Deacon Larkin's horse and, with Devens' warning of the British troop in mind, spurred through slumbering Charlestown and out over Charlestown Neck, with the Mystic on his right and the Charles glistening on his left. It was now about eleven o'clock. The night was chill but pleasant, and the moon shone bright.

Through the desolate salt marshes, clay pits, and scrub, where the smell of the sea rose strong and rank, Revere bore left, taking the short road through Cambridge to Lexington. He came in sight of the awesome gibbet where the mummified body of Captain Codman's Mark, who had conspired in poisoning his master, had hung in chains for twenty years as a warning against insurrection. The sandy road narrowed where it approached woods. Suddenly, Revere saw two horsemen ahead, close in the shadow of a spreading tree. He was near enough to recognize their British holsters and cockades. One started toward him, and the other trotted up the road to head him off. Revere spun short about, raked his horse's flanks, and "rode upon a full gallop for Mystic Road." Over his shoulder he saw his pursuer's heavy charger stumble into a clay pond.

"I got clear of him," Revere told later, "and went through Medford, over the bridge, and up to Menotomy. In Medford I awaked the captain of the minutemen. And after that I alarmed almost every house till I got to Lexington."

Lexington was a cluster of pleasant, roomy country houses, where the road from Boston forked left to Concord and right to Bedford. On the triangular village common stood a big, barnlike meetinghouse with an awkward detached wooden belfry in the yard. Across the road was John Buckman's popular tavern, strangely alight at this late hour, while the large dwellings on the other side of the green slept quietly in the moonlight.

Revere flanked the common and turned down the Bedford

Road about a quarter of a mile to Clark's rambling frame house, snuggled in a grove of trees.

To his surprise, he found a military guard at the door! Earlier in the evening, a townsman returning from the Boston market had told Orderly Sergeant William Munroe of the Lexington minutemen that he had seen the patrol of British officers on the road. The sergeant, sensitive to the temper of the day, assumed they were out for no good; he guessed that the important visitors at Clark's, for whom he as militia officer felt responsible, might be the object of a raid. To protect them from molestation, he posted himself and eight other minutemen around the parsonage as a guard.

When Revere trotted up and demanded entrance, Sergeant Munroe said the family had retired. Adams and Hancock, after receiving Devens' warning that a British patrol was asking for "Clark's" and appeared to be headed toward Lexington and perhaps Concord, had sent a warning to leaders in Concord, and then had settled down for the night, asking Munroe not to disturb them by any noise in the yard.

"Noise!" shouted Revere. "You'll have noise enough before long. The regulars are coming out!"

John Hancock heard the commotion in the yard and recognized Revere's hearty voice. From the house he called, "Come in, Revere. We are not afraid of *you*!"

Both Hancock and Sam Adams ushered him in, eager to know what tidings had brought him to their door at midnight. His news shattered the peace of the household. John Hancock's formidable old aunt and his fiancée, pert, pretty Dorothy Quincy, were also guests of the minister and his wife. They all crowded noisily about Revere, while frail, dandified John theatrically proclaimed he would take up a gun and join the Lexington minutemen if they opposed the British march. Sam Adams tried to persuade him not to act foolishly, but Hancock was insistent; somewhere in this compulsive fervor was the key to one of Hancock's weaknesses as a revolutionary.

Revere, who knew both Hancock and Adams well, must have been faintly amused by the contrast between them at this moment when their dissimilarities were thrown into bold relief. Sam Adams at fifty-two appeared to be an old man. Although his gray eyes were clear and his thin mouth and thick jaw were firm and often stern, his hair was a thinning gray and his voice and hands shook with palsy. In the rusty, patched clothes he wore, he looked like a seedy failure, and by economic standards he was one. He had run indifferently through a modest inheritance because he simply could not manage business or money. He actually despised money

for the overbearing power it gave those who possessed it; he
had devoted his life instead to the political cause of the vast
majority who did not. For years he had been no more successful in politics than in commerce. Very slowly he had
elevated himself from "town scavenger" to tax collector, an
office that came near being his undoing. He was so easy-going, soft-hearted, and impractical that what with dipping
into his collections for small personal sums, ignoring de-
linquencies, and neglecting his records, he was discovered at
the end of ten years to be in arrears nearly seven thousand
pounds.

Fortunately, just as he faced jail for defalcation, passage
of the Stamp Act diverted attention from his shortages, and
he swept into power as a radical member of the Massachusetts
House of Representatives and quickly rose from an obscure
workhorse of the radical wing of the Whig party to its supreme leadership. Eschewing personal glory, he became a
self-effacing, single-minded man, unwavering in his devotion
to republican principles and content to stand behind the
scene and maneuver more colorful men into rebellion. At
last he found success in the specialized field of political revolution. He was a dedicated, realistic revolutionary, who did
not waste himself in gestures, histrionics, or in courting personal popularity.

John Hancock was one of his political protégés and he
was everything Sam Adams was not. By inheritance, the merchant, shipowner, and smuggler was the wealthiest man in
New England. Adams had recruited him for the party when
he was twenty-eight and had but recently inherited the
mighty fortune of his uncle, Thomas Hancock. Someone described him then as a young man whose "brains were shallow
and pockets deep." Adams saw in this combination an opportunity to make a powerful friend who might rescue him
from his own troubles and at the same time might bring to
the party what no other member could offer: both money and
prestige. The two men never developed any real affection such
as that which grew between Revere and Warren, for their
moral concepts were completely different: Hancock dreamed
of snatching leadership from Adams, the rabble-rouser, and
Adams, who was pleased to have Hancock as a figurehead
and financier, distrusted him intellectually and emotionally,
suspecting quite rightly that Hancock hoped to head a new
aristocracy. Nevertheless, through Hancock—vain, petulant,
vacillating, selfish—ran a strain of idealism not unlike Sam
Adams': a sense of charity, and a notion of fair play. It
was only characteristic of him now to be contending wildly
in Clark's parlor that he should arm himself and sally forth.

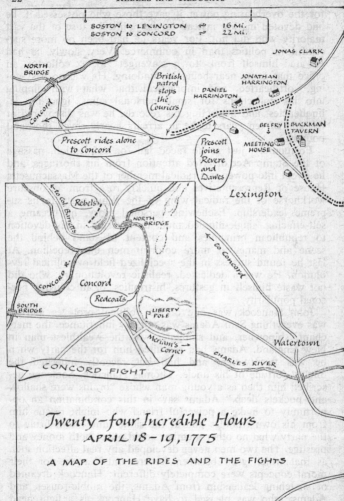

BOSTON to LEXINGTON ≈ 16 Mi.
BOSTON to CONCORD ≈ 22 Mi.

NORTH BRIDGE

JONAS CLARK

British patrol stops the Couriers

JONATHAN HARRINGTON

DANIEL HARRINGTON

Concord

Prescott rides alone to Concord

Prescott joins Revere and Dawes

BELFRY

BUCKMAN TAVERN

MEETING HOUSE

Lexington

to Col. Barretts

Rebels

NORTH BRIDGE

to Concord

CONCORD R.

Concord

Redcoats

SOUTH BRIDGE

LIBERTY POLE

Meriam's Corner

Watertown

CHARLES RIVER

CONCORD FIGHT

Twenty-four Incredible Hours
APRIL 18-19, 1775

A MAP OF THE RIDES AND THE FIGHTS

But shrewd, level-headed Sam Adams had brought his revolution too far along to lose one of its potential leaders. Both he and Hancock were representatives-elect to the Second Continental Congress to be held in May. Calmly he reasoned with the younger man that it was their duty to flee and save themselves for the important work of the cabinet.

John was still holding out a half-hour later when William

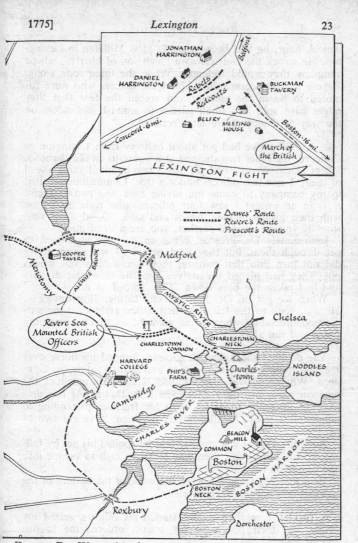

JONATHAN HARRINGTON

DANIEL HARRINGTON

Rebels

Redcoats

BUCKMAN TAVERN

BELFRY

MEETING HOUSE

Concord·6mi.

Boston·16mi.

March of the British

LEXINGTON FIGHT

Dawes' Route
Revere's Route
Prescott's Route

COOPER TAVERN

Medford

Menotomy

ALEWIFE BROOK

MYSTIC RIVER

Chelsea

Revere Sees Mounted British Officers

CHARLESTOWN COMMON

CHARLESTOWN NECK

HARVARD COLLEGE

PHIP'S FARM

Charles-town

NODDLES ISLAND

Cambridge

CHARLES RIVER

BEACON HILL

COMMON

Boston

Boston Harbor

BOSTON NECK

Roxbury

Dorchester

Dawes, Dr. Warren's other messenger, who had come out of Boston over Boston Neck, arrived at Clark's. He and Revere had no time to lose on senseless heroics. They took a bite together, rested a few minutes, and then departed to ride on to Concord to arouse more of the countryside.

As the two couriers cantered out of Lexington, they were joined by Dr. Samuel Prescott of Concord. Until this one-o'clock hour, he had been courting Miss Milliken in Lexington. He struck the couriers as a "high son of liberty," whose company they would welcome. While the three rode along, Revere told his companions about the officers who were rumored to be in the vicinity and voiced the fear that they might have split into small parties to ambush any riders on the way to Concord. He later recalled:

> . . . When we had got about halfway from Lexington to Concord, the other two stopped at a house to awake the man. I kept along. When I had got about two hundred yards ahead of them, I saw two officers under a tree. I immediately called to my company to come up, saying here was two of them. . . . In an instant I saw four officers, who rode up to me with their pistols in their hands and said, "G—d d—n you, stop! If you go an inch further, you are a dead man!"

Immediately Dr. Prescott came up . . . we attempted to get through them, but they kept before us and swore if we did not turn into that pasture, they would blow our brains out. They had placed themselves opposite to a pair of bars and had taken the bars down. They forced us in.

When we got in, Dr. Prescott said to me, "Put on!" . . . He . . . took to the left. I turned to the right . . . towards a wood, intending when I had gained . . . that to jump my horse and run afoot.[2]

The doctor, who knew the ground, jumped his horse over the low stone wall of the pasture and headed safely for Concord. William Dawes also escaped. There was much of the amateur actor in merry, blue-eyed Billy Dawes. At this dramatic moment he made his dash for freedom pretending to command a troop. "Hallo, boys!" he cried. "I've got two of 'em!"

But Billy Dawes was no Garrick; he spoiled his act by falling off his horse, and then was lucky enough to escape into the woods on foot.

Paul Revere, dashing toward the wood at the bottom of the pasture, was not that fortunate:

> Just as I reached it, out started six officers, seized my bridle, put their pistols to my breast, ordered me to dismount, which I did. . . .
> One of them, who appeared to have command there and much of a gentleman, asked where I came from. I told him. He asked what time I left. . . . I told him. He seemed surprised. He said, "Sir, may I crave your name?"
> I answered, "My name is . . . Revere."
> "What?" said he. . . . "Paul Revere?"
> I answered, . . . "Yes."

The others abused me much, but he told me not to be afraid, no one . . . should . . . hurt me.[3]

Revere then glibly told the officers that the British would "miss their aim," because he had alarmed "the country all the way up" from Boston. Hoping to confuse the patrol and convince it to release him, and thus to gain time for the men who were being called out, he blandly lied that the British boats had run aground; by the time the delayed troops reached Lexington, he warned, five hundred men would fall upon them.

The patrol, seeming very agitated, grilled him closely. They already had rounded up four countrymen who had been found riding in the night. The commanding officer herded his prisoners together and turned back toward Lexington. To Revere he announced, "We are now going toward your friends, and if you attempt to run, or we are insulted, we will blow your brains out."

Revere coolly told him he might do as he pleased. According to Revere:

> We rode down towards Lexington a . . . pretty smart pace. . . . I was often insulted by the officers . . . calling me damned rebel, etc., etc. The officer who led me said I was in a d—m—d critical situation. I told him I was sensible of it. After we had got about a mile I was delivered . . . to . . . a sergeant to lead, . . . who was ordered to take out his pistol . . . and . . . should I run to execute the major's sentence. When we got within about half a mile of the Lexington Meeting House, we heard a gun fired. The major asked me what . . . that was for. I told him to alarm the country.[4]

The major must have figured that there was little time to lose if he was to join the advancing British main force and inform its officers that the rebels were awake and waiting. He ordered the girths and bridles on the four countrymen's horses to be cut and the horses driven afield, and told the men to go home afoot. For a short distance, he refused to dismiss Revere. Then he commandeered Deacon Larkin's horse from Revere for the use of the sergeant, whose mount was tired. The sergeant's horse was stripped and turned loose. The patrol rode away and, ironically, Deacon Larkin's gallant little horse that had borne Revere and his news to every Middlesex village and farm carried a British soldier off on the King's business and forever disappeared into the British army. Revere was left to make his way afoot through the fields in what he guessed was the direction of Jonas Clark's:

> I went across the burying ground and some pastures and

came to the Reverend Mr. Clark's house, where I found
Messrs. Hancock and Adams. I told them of my treatment,
and they concluded to go . . . towards Woburn. I went with
them and a Mr. Lowell, who was a clerk to Mr. Hancock.
When we got to the house where they intended to stop, Mr.
Lowell and myself returned to Mr. Clark's to find what was
going on.[5]

By now, a great many men of the neighborhood were doing the same thing. At Lexington, an hour or more earlier,
Revere's alarm had brought out the captain of the minutemen, John Parker. He lost no time in assembling his company. From warm beds his men hurried in their workaday
clothes to the Common before Buckman's Tavern "to consult
what to do."

Captain Parker, "a great tall man with a large head and a
high, wide brow," did not think his handful of rustics could
halt the regulars, but he determined to protect the town and
its women and children if the redcoats grew mischievous
there on the way to Concord. He and his men had stood
waiting for a time in the clear, cold moonlight, stamping their
chilled feet and blowing on their stiff fingers. When the British failed to appear and riders sent toward Boston to spy
them out failed to return, Captain Parker assumed Revere's
report was false or exaggerated. After about an hour, he dismissed the company, but he warned the men they should re-
assemble instantly at the call of the drum. Those who lived
nearby straggled home, muttering to their wives as they
crawled back into bed that some tarnal fool was making another false alarm. A number of them sought the warmth and
conviviality of Buckman's Tavern to while away the rest of
the uneasy night. It was already far spent; darkness was
about to flee before the misty gray shadows of dawn.

Had everything gone as smoothly for General Gage's ex-
peditionary force as he had planned, it would probably have
passed through Lexington by this time. From the beginning,
however, it seemed doomed to irritating failures. Before Gage
marched his men to the Boston Common, he knew that his
secret was out.

In the evening he informed Hugh, Earl Percy, the young
but battle-tested commander of the Fifth Regiment, that Lieutenant Colonel Francis Smith was to command a force of
seven hundred to be sent to seize the stores at Concord.
Very likely because he was senior field officer in town, Colonel Smith was chosen to head the force. Although a friend
called him "a gallant old officer," most of the army knew
him to be grossly fat, slow thinking, and often tardy. Perhaps that is why Gage had named Major Pitcairn of the Ma-

rines second in command. The major was a portly, comfortably middle-aged, devout Scotsman, an old army man who was a rigorous disciplinarian, but who tempered his strict demands with humanity, patience, and tact—the kind of man General Gage would want on a difficult command such as this. Lord Percy was told he would command reserves which would be ordered up to support Smith if the colonel should run into trouble. But the general added he probably would not have to call them out, for he "did not think the damned rebels would . . . take up arms against His Majesty's Troops." Percy rather agreed. He had come to Boston only a short time after Gage's return last spring, and although Whig-principled, he quickly had decided "the people here are a set of sly, artful, hypocritical rascals, cruel and cowards."

At dusk, Lord Percy left the general's office at Province House for his own quarters. He walked unrecognized up to a group of eight or ten men on the Common. One of them said, "The British have marched, but they will miss their aim."

"What aim?" Percy asked.

"Why, the cannon at Concord," said the loiterer.

Percy quickly retraced his steps to Gage's headquarters and repeated what he had heard, much to the general's consternation. But it was too late to abandon the enterprise. Gage, hoping his plans were not too widely known, decided to proceed.

A staunch Whig a few weeks later recorded in his diary a British deserter's account of their start:

. . . they took every imaginable precaution to prevent a discovery. Their meat was dressed on board a transport ship in the harbor. Their men were not apprised of the design till just as it was time to march they were waked up by the sergeants putting their hands on them and whispering gently to them, and were even conducted by a back way out of the barracks without the knowledge of their comrades and without the observation of the sentries.

They walked through the street with the utmost silence. It being about ten o'clock, no sound was heard but of their feet. A dog, happening to bark, was instantly killed with a bayonet. They proceeded to the beach under the new powder house, the most unfrequented part of the town, and there embarked on board the boats, which had their oars muffled to prevent a noise.[6]

Lieutenant John Barker, of the King's Own Regiment, a peevish, carping young man who was a little contemptuous of his superiors, kept a diary in which he described the landing at Phip's Farm on Cambridge Marsh. The heavily loaded boats could not get close in. The men dropped overboard into shallow water.

After getting over the marsh, where we were wet up to the knees, we were halted in a dirty road and stood there till two o'clock in the morning waiting for provisions to be brought from the boats and to be divided, and which most of the men threw away, having carried some with them. At two o'clock we began our march by wading through a very long ford up to our middles.[7]

The cold, wet, miserable march was not long under way when Colonel Smith, doubtless dissatisfied with his slow progress, dispatched Major Pitcairn ahead with six companies as an advance corps to secure the two bridges beyond Concord.

Pitcairn took every precaution to prevent any warning of his approach from reaching Lexington. By marching a small advance guard as flankers, he swallowed up all but one of Captain John Parker's Lexington scouts. Finally, he was met by the patrol that had taken Revere, and was told that at least five hundred men stood ready at Lexington to oppose his advance. The major slowed his march to allow Colonel Smith to draw closer. Revere's ruse had succeeded.

Colonel Smith, meanwhile, already had sent back to Boston for reinforcements. Major Pitcairn had scarcely left him when he had become aware, by the sound of an occasional, distant musket shot and the faraway ring of bells, that the countryside was astir.

The colonel had cause for concern. Few men slept that night in the towns and on the farms along the British route. Among those aroused by the excitement was twenty-three-year-old Sylvanus Wood of Woburn, three miles from Lexington. The sharp, shrill tolling of the Lexington bell had suggested to the sleepy youth that "there was difficulty" there.

I immediately arose, took my gun, and with Robert Douglass went in haste to Lexington. . . . When I arrived there, I inquired of Captain Parker . . . the news. Parker told me he did not know what to believe, for a man had come up about half an hour before and informed him that the British troops were not on the road. But while we were talking, a messenger came up and told the captain that the British troops were within half a mile.

Parker immediately turned to his drummer . . . and ordered him to beat to arms. . . .[8]

Captain Parker asked Sylvanus Wood and his companion if they would parade with his company. As the men gathered, Parker called out, according to Wood's account:

"Every man of you who is equipped, follow me. And those of you who are not equipped, go into the meetinghouse and furnish yourselves from the magazine and immediately join the company."

Parker led those of us who were equipped to the north end of Lexington Common, near the Bedford Road, and formed us in single file. I was stationed about in the center of the company.

While we were standing, I left my place and went from one end of the company to the other and counted every man who was paraded, and the whole number was thirty-eight and no more. Just as I had finished and got back to my place, I perceived the British troops had arrived on the spot between the meetinghouse and Buckman's, near where Captain Parker stood when he first led off his men.[9]

Paul Revere also happened to see the British ranks march into sight. At John Lowell's request he had accompanied him to Buckman's to help carry off a trunk of Hancock's papers, lest they fall into the hands of the British authorities. By the time the two men neared Buckman's, a strong east wind was rising, and the sky was paling with first morning light. They passed through the groups of minutemen as they were reassembling, and entered the tavern. Revere, glancing from a second-floor window, saw the approaching column of soldiers. He and Lowell hastened from the tavern with their burden.

Captain Parker did not intend to meet the British regulars with force. He planned only to stand and resist any overt act. But he chose to stand in a position and at a place that dared the redcoats to pursue the road they had determined to take.

On the far side of the Common at this instant, Thomas Willard watched from a window in Daniel Harrington's house as Major Pitcairn took the rebel dare. Willard testified later:

I . . . saw . . . about four hundred of Regulars in one body coming up the road and marched toward the north part of the Common back of the meetinghouse. . . .

As soon as said Regulars were against the east end of the meetinghouse, the commanding officers said something, what I know not. But upon that, the Regulars ran till they came within about eight or nine rods of about a hundred of the militia . . . at which time the militia of Lexington dispersed. Then the officers made a huzza, and the private soldiers succeeded them. Directly after this, an officer rode before the Regulars to the other side of the body and hallooed after the militia . . . and said, "Lay down your arms, damn you! Why don't you lay down your arms?"[10]

These were practically the same words that rang in the

ears of Sylvanus Wood, just as the little five-footer regained
his place in the minuteman line:

The officer . . . swung his sword and said, "Lay down
your arms, you damned rebels, or you will all be dead men!
Fire!"

Some guns were fired by the British at us from the first
platoon, but no person was killed or hurt, [the guns] being
probably charged only with powder. Just at this time, Captain Parker ordered every man to take care of himself. The
company immediately dispersed, and while the company was
dispersing and leaping over the wall, the second platoon of
the British fired and killed some of our men.

There was not a gun fired by any of Captain Parker's company within my knowledge. I was so situated that I must
have known it, had anything of the kind taken place before a
total dispersion of our company.[11]

When the strong east wind swept away the cloud of acrid
gunsmoke that for moments shrouded Lexington Common, it
revealed mad disorder. In every direction minutemen dashed
from the protection of trees and walls. The redcoats, contrary to Pitcairn's orders, pursued them viciously with ball
and bayonet.

Jonas Parker, an older cousin of the captain, stood his
ground. In his hat at his feet he had tossed bullets, wadding,
and spare flints. When a British ball buckled his knees, he
tried vainly to reload his piece, but a redcoat's bayonet finished him. Jonathan Harrington, with a ball in his body,
dragged himself from the Common almost to his own door-
step, but he died before his anguished wife, bursting from
the house, could reach him. John Brown fell on the edge
of a swamp a little to the north of the Common. Another
man slumped dead behind the wall in John Buckman's garden.

The regulars went entirely out of hand, much to the disgust of Lieutenant Barker: "The men were so wild they could
hear no orders." Major Pitcairn was furious, chagrined and
mortified; one of his subordinates had shouted the order to
fire. His own cease-fire order went unheeded. He was finally
able to form his unruly ranks, just as Colonel Smith came
into sight with the main body.

The Common was deserted now, except for the redcoats
and the rebel dead and wounded. In those few minutes of
fire, eight Massachusetts men had been killed and ten
wounded. One regular had suffered a slight leg wound, and
Major Pitcairn's horse had been struck lightly twice.

Regrouped, the British fired a volley to celebrate their victory, struck up their music, and marched briskly for Concord. Sylvanus Wood reported:

After the British had begun their march to Concord I returned to the Common and found Robert [Munroe] and Jonas Parker lying dead . . . near the Bedford Road, and others dead and wounded. I assisted in carrying the dead into the meetinghouse. I then proceeded toward Concord with my gun. . . .[12]

2

"THEIR BALLS WHISLED WELL"

Concord

APRIL 19, 1775

MANY A tanner, farmer, wheelwright, and clerk was proceeding that morning toward Concord with his gun. By the time the fresh April sunlight flooded down on the bloody Common at Lexington, the alarm set off by Dr. Warren had spread far and wide.

Colonel Conant and his Charlestown friends, signaled by Paul Revere's lanterns, had roused their neighborhood, and as Revere and Dawes awakened house after house and village after village on the roads to Concord, other riders swung into the saddle and galloped to spread the warning that the regulars were marching into the country. Lynn, ten miles northeast of Boston, was awakened early in the morning. Woburn was out an hour before day, when Sylvanus Wood scrambled from bed. Billerica, seventeen miles northwest of Boston, was aroused by two in the morning, and Acton, about five miles west of Concord, soon after. Reading heard alarm guns at sunrise. At Danvers it was a little later. At Tewksbury, twenty miles northwest of Boston, a messenger awoke Captain John Trull about two o'clock in the morning: on a prearranged signal, he fired his gun to alert Dracut across the Merrimack River. Andover heard at about sunrise. Bedford was aroused soon after Lexington. Southwestward, too, rode the messengers to Dedham ten miles, and westward to Framingham and Sudbury, and on to Worcester before noon. From every direction in Essex, Middlesex, Norfolk, and Worcester counties, militiamen and minutemen were on the march to Concord.

Over their shoulders or cradled in their arms, they carried the muskets that their English law required each of them to own. Every one of them, from sixteen to sixty, was enrolled in the Crown militia, liable to be called out en masse or by a draft in time of danger. Each was expected to possess a firelock, a bayonet, and a quantity of ammunition. By now, many of them belonged also to secret minuteman companies, recently formed to march *against* Crown forces at a minute's notice from watchful Whig committees of safety.

Concord stood alerted. Harness-maker Reuben Brown had been sent down toward Lexington before light to learn the truth of Dr. Prescott's panted warning that the British were out in force. He had arrived in sight of the Lexington Common just as the regulars drew up before the minutemen and the firing started. He reined in long enough to take in what was happening, then he wheeled his horse and dashed for home to tell what he had seen. There the two local minuteman companies and one from Lincoln already were assembled, about two hundred men in all.

Corporal Amos Barrett of David Brown's Concord minuteman company expected to celebrate his twenty-third birthday in a few days; his recollection of the morning of the nineteenth was far more accurate than his orthography:

the Beel Rong at 3 o Clock for alarum. as I was then a minnit man I was soon in town and found my Capt and the Rest of my Company at the post. it wont Long Before thair was other minit Compneys. one Compney I believe of minnit men was Rais[d] in a most every town to Stand at a minits warning. before Sunrise thair was I beleave 150 of us and more of all that was thair. we thought we wood go and meet the Britsh. we marched Down to wards L[exington] about a mild or mild half and we see them acomming. we halted and stay[d] till they got within about 100 Rods. then we was ordered to the about face and march[d] before them with our Droms and fifes agoing and allso the B[ritish]. We had grand musick.[1]

About a mile from Concord, a sharp ridge rose abruptly from the plain and flanked the Lexington Road all the way to the Concord town square. At the square, the road turned sharply right and followed another ridge to the wide wet meadows on the bank of the Concord River, where it turned squarely to the left and crossed the North Bridge across the stream. Thence it followed the graceful curve of the river, skirting a hill, and arrived after about two miles at the farm buildings of Colonel James Barrett, commander of the Concord militia. Not far beyond the bridge a short road struck right off the main road to Barrett's and climbed to the top of the hill north of the river. Colonel Barrett's buildings were one of the main objectives of the British, who knew that a quantity of the stores was concealed around them.

Lieutenant Barker described the British approach to Concord:

We met with no interruption till within a mile or two of the town, where the country people had occupied a hill which commanded the road. The Light Infantry were ordered away to the right and ascended the height in one line, upon which the Yankees quitted it without firing, which they did likewise for one or two more successively. They then crossed the river beyond the town, and we marched into the town, after taking possession of a hill with a liberty pole on it and a flag flying which was cut down. The Yankees had that hill but left it to us. We expected they would have made a stand there, but they did not choose it.[2]

Upon occupying Concord, the British troops systematically searched for stores to destroy. Observed Corporal Barrett:

Thair was in the town House a number of intrenchen tools witch they Caried out and Burnt them. at last they said it was Best to Burn them in the house and Sat fire to them in the house, but our people Beg[d] of them not to Burn the house and put it out. it wont Long before it was Set fire again but finaily it warnt Burnt. their was about 100 Barrels of flower in Mr Hubbards malt house, they Rold that out an nock[d] them to peces and Rold some in the mill pond.[3]

While the Grenadiers went about their work and the officers refreshed themselves in the local taprooms, advance companies marched to secure the bridges across the river beyond which the minutemen and militia were retiring. Captain Munday Pole marched left from the square past Jones's tavern and posted his company at the South Bridge, but it was along the road that crossed the North Bridge that trouble promised. Colonel Smith ordered seven companies of Light Infantry in that direction, under command of Captain Lawrence Parsons of the Tenth Regiment. Captain Walter Sloane Laurie of the Light Company of the Forty-third recalled:

As we advanced to the bridge a large body of people under arms, assembled on the hills near the bridge, immediately retreated over it and took post on the rising grounds on the other side. As soon as we got possession of the bridge, Captain Parsons ordered my company and the company of the Fifth Regiment to remain at the bridge, whilst he and the other four proceeded [toward Barrett's farm]. On his advancing towards the heights the country people retired at a great distance to the woods.[4]

The Light Company of the Twenty-third, accompanied by two officers jouncing along in a chaise, passed Laurie's handful of men a few minutes later and crossed the bridge to overtake Parsons. A courier came back from Parsons with orders for Laurie to advance the Light Company of the Fifth, leaving only Laurie's men at the bridge.

The "large body of people under arms" on the height overlooking Laurie's position steadily increased in numbers. From Acton came thirty-eight minutemen under a gunsmith, Isaac Davis, and two companies of militia. Several score from Bedford were there. Men from Lincoln came, and other small groups. The force of aroused rebels grew to about four hundred and fifty strong, standing menacingly on the hill. Colonel Barrett was on the field among them consulting a group of citizens of the town.

There was uneasy waiting on both sides.

Captain Laurie passed a tense hour. Although there were about seven hundred British troops in and about the town, his company of thirty-odd men, advanced about a half-mile beyond town, alone facing the mass of rebels, was piteously outweighed. The rebels shifted a little closer. Laurie reported:

. . . as they came nearer, the Light Company of the Fourth Regiment posted on a height immediately retreated to me at the bridge as did likewise the Light Company of the Tenth Regiment, who also had been at no great distance.

Upon this, I sent Lieutenant [Alexander] Robertson . . . to acquaint Colonel Smith of my situation, desiring he would send some of the Grenadiers to support me in case of their attacking. Mr. Robertson brought for answer that two companies would be sent me. By this time the body of the country people arrived on the heights which the company of the Fourth Regiment had occupied, and there drew up with shouldered arms. . . .

They halted for a considerable time looking at us and then moved down upon me in a seeming regular manner. . . . I determined to repass the bridge with the three companies, retreating by divisions to check their progress, which we . . . did, lining the opposite side of the river with one company to flank the other two in case of an attack. By this time they were close upon us.[5]

Both sides were moving cautiously, neither eager to be guilty of opening fire. It was now nine-thirty, or a little later, of a bright, cool morning. The rising smoke from the fires in town inspired Colonel Barrett and the rebel officers assembled on the hill to advance to the town and defend it. The troops, commanded by Major John Buttrick with Captain Davis of Acton at the head of the column and Colonel John Robinson as a volunteer aide, formed in a column of twos and started down the hill toward the British. Colonel Barrett, who remained at the crest of the hill, ordered the column not to fire unless fired upon. The two Acton fifers struck up "The White Cockade," and the rebels strode resolutely forward. The road off the hill met at right angles the road that led to the bridge. Major Buttrick's men turned toward the British soldiers and formed up on the causeway that led over a meadow to the bridge. At the bridge a small detail of redcoats left by Laurie were pulling up the planks.

Corporal Amos Barrett marched in the third company of minutemen; this is the way the next moments appeared to him:

Mager Buttrick said if we wair all of his mind he would Drive them away from the Bridge. they should not tair that up. we all said we wood go. We then warnt Loded. we wair all orded to Load and had stricked order not to fire till they fir^d firs, then to fire as fast as we could. we then marche^d on . . . 2 Deep. It was a long Corsay. . . . Capt Davis had got, I Be leave, within 15 Rods of the B[ritish] when they fir^d 3 gons one after the other. I see the Balls strike in the River on the Right of me. as soon as they fir^d them, they fir^d on us. their balls whisled well. we then was all orded to fire . . . it is Straing that their warnt no more kild but they fird to high. Capt Davis was kild and mr osmore and a number wounded. we soon Drove them from the Bridge.[6]

Three regulars were killed, four officers and four privates were wounded, before Laurie's men fled from the bridge back toward town. The Americans did not pursue them far beyond the bridge, but withdrew to the hill from which they had marched.

The regulars, falling pell-mell back to town, collided with two belated companies of reinforcements under Colonel Smith himself. Lieutenant Barker bitterly accused the colonel of being responsible for their tardiness: the elephantine commander had insisted on bringing them up himself, which, said Barker, "stopped 'em from being [in] time enough, for being a very fat heavy man he would not have reached the bridge in half an hour, though it was not half a mile. . . ." Colonel Smith, instead of re-forming the retreating troops and driving back across the bridge to succor Parsons, who had not yet returned from Barrett's, abandoned him and joined the retreat to town. As it happened, however, Parsons and his three companies were allowed by the colonials to recross the bridge without interference.

Colonel Smith, rejoined in the heart of the sprawling village by his scattered detachments, faced a rapidly swelling hostile force that threatened his escape. Nevertheless, he dallied an unconscionably long time. Eyewitness Parson Emerson considered it "gt Feekelness and Inconstancy of Mind, sometimes advancing, sometimes returning to yᵉ former Posts, till at Lenth they quitted ye Town, & retreated by yᵉ Wa yy came."

The rebels allowed the British to retire in order for about a mile out of town. Then, as the sparkling red ranks, all aglitter in the sun, came to a bridge where the road narrowed, the angry men of the Massachusetts towns swarmed down on them. Of a sudden, Corporal Amos Barrett said, "a grait many Lay dead and the Road was bloddy." For Lieutenant Barker, of the King's Own Regiment, a nightmare had begun:

. . . we were fired on from all sides, but mostly from the rear, where people had hid themselves in houses till we had passed and then fired. The country was an amazing strong one, full of hills, woods, stone walls, etc., which the rebels did not fail to take advantage of, for they were all lined with people who kept an incessant fire upon us, as we did too upon them, but not with the same advantage, for they were so concealed there was hardly any seeing them. In this way, we marched . . . miles, their numbers increasing from all parts, while ours was reducing by deaths, wounds, and fatigue; and we were totally surrounded with such an incessant fire as it's impossible to conceive; our ammunition was likely near expended.[7]

Lieutenant Colonel Smith, now nursing a painful leg wound, prayed desperately for the relief column he had ordered so many long hours before, at two or three o'clock in the morning, when he had found the night filled with rebel alarms. General Gage had not waited for his request; on his own initiative he had ordered out Lord Percy's force at four in the morning, but a series of stupid blunders and misunderstandings had delayed its start until nine. About that hour a thousand troops under Percy had swung out of Boston, toward Roxbury, their fifes and drums impudently shrilling "Yankee Doodle."

With the relief force marched Frederick Mackenzie, a serious, methodical lieutenant of the Royal Welsh Fusiliers. In his diary he wrote that when the column neared Lexington a little after midday, "some persons who came from Concord informed that the Grenadiers and Light Infantry were at that place and that some persons had been killed and wounded by them early in the morning at Lexington." It was about two o'clock when Mackenzie heard some straggling shots fired about a mile in front.

As we advanced we heard the firing plainer and more frequent, and at half after two, being near the church at Lexington and the fire increasing we were ordered to form the line, which was immediately done by extending on each side of the road. But by reason of the stone walls and other obstructions, it was not formed in so regular a manner as it should have been.

The Grenadiers and Light Infantry [under Smith] were at this time retiring towards Lexington, fired upon by the rebels who took every advantage the face of the country afforded. . . . As soon as the Grenadiers and Light Infantry perceived the First Brigade drawn up for their support, they shouted repeatedly, and the firing ceased for a short time.

The ground we first formed upon was something elevated and commanded a view of that before us for about a mile, where it was terminated by some pretty high grounds covered with wood. The village of Lexington lay between both parties. We could observe a considerable number of the rebels, but they were much scattered, and not above fifty of them to be seen in a body in any place. Many lay concealed behind the stone walls and fences. They appeared most numerous in the road near the church and in a wood in the front, and on the left flank of the line where our regiment was posted. A few cannon shot were fired at those on and near the road which dispersed them. The flank companies now retired and formed behind the brigade which was soon fired upon by the rebels most advanced. A brisk fire was returned but without much effect.

As there was a piece of morassy ground in front of the left of our regiment, it would have been difficult to have passed it under the fire of the rebels from behind the trees and walls on the other side. Indeed, no part of the brigade was ordered to advance. We, therefore, drew up near the morass in expectation of orders how to act, sending an officer for one of the six-pounders. During this time the rebels endeavored to gain our flanks and crept into the covered ground on either side and as close as they could in front, firing now and then in perfect security. We also advanced a few of our best marksmen, who fired at those who showed themselves. About a quarter past three, Earl Percy having come to a resolution of returning to Boston, and having made his disposition for that purpose, our regiment received orders to form the rear guard. We immediately lined the walls and other cover in our front with some marksmen and retired from the right of companies by files to the high ground a small distance in our rear, where we again formed in line and remained in that position for near half an hour, during which time the flank companies and the other regiments of the brigade began their march in one column on the road towards Cambridge. . . .

Lord Percy, judging that the returning to Boston by way of Cambridge (where there was a bridge over the Charles River which might either be broken down or required to be forced) and Roxbury might be attended with some difficulties and many inconveniences, took the resolution of returning by way of Charlestown, which was the shortest road and which could be defended against any number of the rebels. . . .

During the whole of the march from Lexington the rebels kept an incessant irregular fire from all points at the column, which was the more galling as our flanking parties which at first were placed at sufficient distances to cover the march of it were at last, from the different obstructions they occasionally met with, obliged to keep almost close to it.

Our men had very few opportunities of getting good shots at the rebels, as they hardly ever fired but under cover of a stone wall, from behind a tree, or out of a house, and the moment they had fired, they lay down out of sight until they had loaded again or the column had passed. In the road indeed in our rear, they were most numerous and came on pretty close, frequently calling out "King Hancock forever!" Many of them were killed in the houses on the roadside from whence they fired; in some of them seven or eight men were destroyed. Some houses were forced open in which no person could be discovered, but when the column had passed, numbers sallied out from some place in which they had lain concealed, fired at our rear guard and augmented the numbers which followed us. If we had had time to set fire to those houses, many rebels must have perished in them, but as night drew on Lord Percy thought it best to continue the march. Many houses were plundered by the soldiers, notwithstanding the efforts of the officers to prevent it. I have no doubt this inflamed the rebels and made many of them follow us farther than they would otherwise have done. By all accounts some soldiers who stayed too long in the houses were killed in the very act of plundering by those who lay concealed in them. We brought in about ten prisoners, some of whom were taken in arms. One or two more were killed on the march while prisoners by the fire of their own people.

Few or no women or children were to be seen throughout the day. As the country had undoubted intelligence that some troops were to march out and the rebels were probably determined to attack them, it is generally supposed they had previously removed their families from the neighborhood.[8]

Although Mackenzie had seen few women or children, many were involved in the actions of the day. A man from

the British ships in Boston Harbor wrote to England about
the fury of the rebel attacks:

> . . . even women had firelocks. One was seen to fire a
> blunderbuss between her father and husband from their win-
> dows. There they three, with an infant child, soon suffered
> the fury of the day. In another house which was long de-
> fended by eight resolute fellows, the grenadiers at last got
> possession, when after having run their bayonets into seven,
> the eighth continued to abuse them with all the [beastlike
> rage] of a true Cromwellian, and but a moment before he
> quitted this world applied such epithets as I must leave un-
> mentioned. . . .[9]

The British column had been on the march about an hour
under heavy, scattered rebel fire, when a little more than two
miles from Lexington, it descended the high road to the
"Foot of the Rocks" at Menotomy. In the long street of the
village, nearly eighteen hundred fresh rebels descended
upon the harassed Britons, and it was here that most of the
fierce, bloody, close-quarter and house-to-house fighting of
the day occurred. Lord Percy turned his fieldpieces on his
pursuers, but the cannon balls only tore up the road, toppled
stone walls, and crashed into houses, causing few casualties.
The redcoats fought as wildly as cornered game; their officers
lost all control of their frenzied men, especially the flankers
and the inevitable freebooters. From one house, Deacon
Joseph Adams had fled to a nearby barn and was now hidden
in the hay. In the house in bed lay his wife Hannah, who
later declared:

> . . . divers of them entered our house by bursting open
> the doors, and three of the soldiers broke into the room in
> which I then was laid on my bed, being scarcely able to walk
> from my bed to the fire and not having been to my chamber
> door from my being delivered in childbirth to that time. One
> of said soldiers immediately opened my [bed] curtains with
> his bayonet fixed and pointing . . . to my breast. I immedi-
> ately cried out, "For the Lord's sake, don't kill me!"
> He replied, "Damn you."
> One that stood near said, "We will not hurt the woman if
> she will go out of the house, but we will surely burn it."
> I immediately arose, threw a blanket over me, went out,
> and crawled into a corn-house near the door with my infant
> in my arms, where I remained until they were gone. They im-
> mediately set the house on fire, in which I had left five chil-
> dren and no other person; but the fire was happily extin-
> guished when the house was in the utmost danger of being
> utterly consumed.[10]

Farther on, at Cooper's Tavern, two idle men, thirty-nine and forty-five years old, were calmly drinking flips. When one suggested that the fighting was getting too close for comfort, the other replied, "Let us finish the mug. They won't come yet." Before the cups were drained, some redcoats crowded into the taproom. An altercation broke out, and the soldiers shot down the drinking companions. A few days later the owners of the tavern, swept away by the hysteria of the day's events, deposed for the Provincial Congress a colorful tale of terror:

> The King's Regular troops . . . fired more than one hundred bullets into the house where we dwell, through doors, windows, etc. Then a number of them entered the house where we and two aged gentlemen were, all unarmed. We escaped for our lives into the cellar. The two aged gentlemen were immediately most barbarously and inhumanly murdered by them, being stabbed through in many places, their heads mauled, skulls broke, and their brains beat out on the floor and walls of the house.[11]

Lord Percy continued to hold his force together and astutely made a feint as if to enter Boston by way of Cambridge, then wheeled left in North Cambridge and marched for Charlestown. "We threw them!" exulted Lieutenant Barker.

At sunset, half past six, the exhausted column stumbled its last mile across Charlestown Neck toward the comforting safety of Bunker Hill, rising a hundred feet above the surrounding country. Darkness fell fast and musket flashes showed as bright as fireworks when the footsore, hungry, thirsty regulars—after some thirty-five miles of marching, half of it fighting an enraged and merciless foe—flung themselves down to rest on Bunker's slope.

As the redcoats crowded across the narrow isthmus that connected Charlestown with the mainland, "the rebels ceased fire," charged Ensign Lister, "they not having it in their power to pursue us further in their skulking way behind hedges and walls." Actually, the greenest military novice among the New Englanders recognized that further pursuit would be disastrous. Once the redcoats had crossed Charlestown Neck they were in an almost unassailable position. Bunker Hill commanded the Neck, and if the rebels dared advance on so narrow a front they would be met by overwhelming fire from the hill and could be enfiladed by the warship *Somerset*, anchored in the Charles. Fresh reinforcements from Boston, which could flow unmolested across the Charles into Charlestown, would further increase the odds against the rebels' driving beyond the line Percy established facing

Charlestown Neck. As the descending darkness gave the redcoats cover, the last popping musket fire died away; rebels
and redcoats settled down for an uneasy night.

To the haphazardly assembled citizens' army that had
risen from the farms and shops, command had come late in
the day. Militia General William Heath had come into the
field for a brief hour of glory. The general, a native of Roxbury, was a farmer who candidly described himself as a man
"of middling stature, light complexion, very corpulent, and
bald-headed." An old-time militia officer, and a member of
the Committee of Safety, he was one of five general officers
appointed sixty days earlier to command the colony's troops
in case of hostilities.

At daybreak the morning of the nineteenth, Heath had
been awakened and told that a British detachment was on
the march for Concord. He consulted briefly with members of
the Committee of Safety and then struck out for Lexington.
On the way he met Dr. Joseph Warren. The doctor, on hearing
that morning from one of his messengers of the clash at Lexington, had crossed the Charlestown Ferry for the scene. He
and Heath reached Lexington a few minutes after Percy's relief column had arrived there. Heath had gathered together
a regiment of rebels, which he commanded in the pursuit,
and Warren had stuck with him.

Now as senior officer on the field, Heath ordered the militia, which converged about three thousand strong on Charlestown Common, just outside Charlestown Neck, "to halt
and give over the pursuit, as any further attempt upon the
enemy in that position would have been futile." He ordered a
guard posted close to the Neck to watch the redcoats, and
then ordered the militia "to march to the town of Cambridge,
where, below the town, the whole were ordered to lie on
their arms."

Thus ended an unbelievable April day. About eighteen hundred British regulars had marched to destroy some secreted
rebel stores: seventy-three of them had been killed, two hundred were wounded or missing. Probably an equal number
of Americans had been engaged during the day, but no one
could count accurately the men who came, shot at the red
column, and then either came to Cambridge or hiked home.
Forty-nine of them had died and forty-six were wounded or
missing.

At Lexington it had grown strangely quiet in the late afternoon. The Reverend Mr. Clark, his wife, small daughter, and
baby went to the meetinghouse where the eight dead lay,
Elizabeth Clark remembered years later, "all in boxes made
of four large boards nailed up." The body of Asahel Porter

of Woburn was sent home, but the others "after Pa had prayed" were loaded into two horse carts and taken into the graveyard, where they were buried in a long trench "as near the woods as possible." It was a little rainy, but the burial party waited until the coffins were "covered up with the clods," and then "for fear the British should find them" the common grave was covered with pine and oak boughs and spread to look like a heap of brush.

That night at Acton, Hannah Davis sat bereft in her bedroom, where the body of her husband lay, his countenance composed in death; he seemed so "little altered" to the woman who loved him and could not yet believe he was no more. It mattered little that the men who brought him home a corpse that afternoon told Hannah that when Major Buttrick asked Captain Davis if he were afraid to lead the march to the bridge, he had replied, "No, I am not; and there isn't a man in my company that is."

Grief-torn homes in Lexington, Acton, Woburn, and a dozen more towns, and redcoats hastily buried across the road from Josiah Nelson's boulder-strewn yard in Lincoln and in other spots along the roadside—these were more than statistics. They were the evidence that an intellectual rebellion had become a rebellion in arms.

A man named John Jones arrived at Concord too late for the fighting, but soon his company was in Cambridge, billeted in Harvard College, and he was writing his "Loving Wife" the only universal truth of the day: " 'Tis uncertain when we shall return. . . . Let us be patient & remember that it is ye hand of God."

3

"WHEN THE SWORD OF REBELLION IS DRAWN"

Cambridge Camp and Ticonderoga

APRIL–MAY 1775

THE NIGHT of the nineteenth was long and agonizing for the bone-tired redcoats. In Boston, General Gage had waited tensely all day for the return of his expedition, and as it entered Charlestown in flight, he had sent relief troops across the Charles to throw up and hold a "sort of Redoubt" on Bunker Hill. "My Lord," he had sent word to Percy, "Gen. Pigot will pass over with a Reinforcement and fresh ammunition. The Boats which carry him may return with the Grenadiers and Light Infantry who must be most fatigued and the wounded. . . ." How welcome these words sounded to the hard-fighting young nobleman, who in the thick of it during the day had lost a waistcoat button to a rebel musket ball.

For the rebels the night did not end. Their campfires shone all night in a great circle from the Mystic to Cambridge until they paled at last against the thinning dawn. When light came, the redcoats discovered that yesterday's nightmare had not been just a bad dream. The incredible Yankees had not vanished in the night. There they crouched around their breakfast fires, muttering about yesterday's bloody work, remembering what their women had said when they left home, remarking how it looked like it was going to be a dry spring, and shaking their heads over what they reckoned would happen next. They were not going home. They did not intend to go home until something was decided. It was as preposterous as General Gage must have thought it was, but these men seemed to understand that they had started a war, and they intended to sit right where they were until their adversary made terms.

There was some dissension among them, to be sure. Tall, beak-nosed Timothy Pickering of Salem considered himself as much a Whig as the best of them and perhaps more of a military man. Was he not the author of *Easy Plan of Discipline for a Militia?* But when news of the fight at Lexington had been brought to him in his office at the Registry of Deeds between eight and nine on the morning of the nineteenth, he had not shown enough imagination or spirit to bring his men into the field in time to reach Charlestown before the last of the regulars was ascending Bunker Hill. Now, on the morning of the twentieth, he was called to a meeting of militia officers at which Dr. Warren was present.

> They were consulting on the formation of an army [Pickering recalled]. To me the idea was new and unexpected. I expressed the opinion which at the moment occurred to me—that the hostilities of the preceding day did not render a civil war inevitable: that a negotiation with General Gage might probably effect a present compromise and therefore that the immediate formation of an army did not appear to me to be necessary.[1]

The majority were not of Pickering's mind. General Heath accepted the fact that a state of war already existed and realistically went about putting first things first. "How to *feed* the assembled and assembling militia was now the great object," he thought. Even those men who had been foresighted enough to snatch a slab of bread or some cured meat when they dashed from their homes the day before were long out of food. Heath's sergeants collected all the edibles around Cambridge, including the carcasses of beef and pork prepared for the Boston market and some ship's bread at Roxbury belonging to the Royal Navy. The kitchen of Harvard College provided pots, kettles, and utensils, and soon the informal "army" was fed.

In the afternoon, General Artemas Ward, Massachusetts militia commander-in-chief, arrived. A bluff, fat, "middle-aged man afflicted with bladder-stone," he had been lying ill in bed when an express rider had galloped through his town of Shrewsbury with the news of the fighting at Lexington; at daybreak on the twentieth, he had pulled himself into the saddle and ridden to Cambridge.

Ward was a slow, deliberate man with little or no imagination, but he was dependable and well liked and acted now with decision. He promptly called a council of war to fix upon guard posts, distribution of troops, fortifications, recruiting, and other matters. He sent out parties to bury yesterday's dead and ordered earthworks thrown up to bar the roads from Boston and to protect the central rebel position at Cambridge. He discussed extending his lines to Chelsea on the North, and ordered General Heath to march reinforcements to General John Thomas' position on the right at Roxbury.

A number of families who had fled from Charlestown early on the nineteenth returned to their houses, but others like Hannah Winthrop and her ailing husband recognized that the peninsula, now lying between two armed forces, was a dangerous place. Mrs. Winthrop wrote her friend Mercy Warren, political satirist and wife of Plymouth merchant James Warren, that she and her husband and some eighty fellow refugees spent an uncomfortable night, the nineteenth, at a house a mile from town, "some nodding in their chairs, others resting their weary limbs on the floor."

   To stay in this place [on the twentieth] was impracticable. . . . Thus with precipitancy were we driven to the town of Andover, following some of our acquaintance, five of us to be conveyed with one poor tired horse and chaise. Thus we began our pilgrimage, alternately walking and riding, the roads filled with frightened women and children, some in carts with their tattered furniture, others on foot fleeing into the woods. But what added greatly to the horror

. . . was our passing through the bloody field at Menotomy, which was strewed with the mangled bodies. We met one affectionate father with a cart looking for his murdered son and picking up his neighbors who had fallen in battle in order for their burial.[2]

While the citizens of Charlestown puzzled where to seek refuge, and the Massachusetts Committee of Safety entreated the Massachusetts towns to enlist and sent forward men to form an army at Cambridge and asked Connecticut and New Hampshire to come to their aid, the story of Lexington and Concord swept like a timber blaze through all New England and down the coast. Only a few hours after the firing between the British and the minutemen at Lexington, Israel Bissel, one of the regular post riders from Boston to New York, was thundering down the coast carrying an official report to each of the committees of safety of the other colonies. Bissell made it all the way to Philadelphia in only five days and a few hours, beating the stagecoach time some three days, a remarkable feat of endurance for a single rider. From Philadelphia the news flew southward; other riders were urged to stay in the saddle night and day until the news spread to Georgia and westward across the mountains. Everywhere the "momentous intelligence" went, a spirit of resistance sprang up: meetings were held, arms and powder were seized, and men prepared to fight.

While the American council was sitting, the British troops on Bunker Hill were withdrawn to Boston. Like General Gage himself, few British officers serving in the colonies had believed that Americans ever would resist royal armed force, but the one day of the nineteenth changed many minds. Lord Percy was first to express his revised opinion in a letter to Adjutant General Edward Harvey, in England, the morning after he returned from Charlestown to Boston:

Whoever looks upon them as an irregular mob will find himself much mistaken. They have men amongst them those who know very well what they are about, having been employed as Rangers against the Indians and Canadians, and this country being much covered with wood and hilly is very advantageous for their method of fighting.

Nor are several of their men void of a spirit of enthusiasm, as we experienced yesterday, for many of them concealed themselves in houses and advanced within ten yards to fire at me and other officers, though they were morally certain of being put to death themselves in an instant.

You may depend upon it, that as the rebels have now had time to prepare, they are determined to go through with it, nor will the insurrection here turn out so despicable as it is perhaps imagined at home. For my part, I never believed, I confess that they would have attacked the King's troops or have had the perseverance I found in them yesterday.[3]

These rebels moved swiftly to gain the advantage in propaganda. The Second Continental Congress would not convene until May 10; the Provincial Congress of Massachusetts, convening on April 22, decided that news of the hostilities of the nineteenth should be given to the English people as quickly as possible and from the viewpoint of the colonists. Without waiting to consult the general Congress, the Massachusetts body within three days took depositions from scores of participants who avowed that the British troops fired first. These depositions, accompanied by a letter addressed "To the Inhabitants of Great Britain," were directed to Benjamin Franklin, agent for the colony in London, who was requested to "print and disperse" the story.

Four days before the papers were dispatched to Franklin, General Gage's official British account had been started to London aboard a British vessel, the *Sukey*. But Captain John Derby of Salem, crowding sail on his light schooner *Quero*, reached England twelve days ahead of the *Sukey*. Franklin, meantime, had sailed for home; Derby placed his papers in the hands of Arthur Lee, Franklin's successor, and on the twenty-ninth of May the news was all over London.

The King was not disturbed. He thought no reliance could be placed on the American account, and he was willing to await more authentic intelligence. If the game were opened, however, he was ready to play it. Thirty-seven-year-old George III was accustomed to fighting Whigs at home and prepared to crush them in the colonies. From the day he had come to the throne at the age of twenty-one, full of piety, a personal purity new to his Hanoverian line, and a consuming ambition, he had determinedly maintained a Tory government that supported his absolute personal rule. Through the years he had forced the great William Pitt from office, had successfully withstood the assaults of John Wilkes and his howling supporters, had formed ministry after ministry—until he had found in Frederick, Lord North a Prime Minister to do his bidding. The opposition of such powerful Whigs as Pitt, Edmund Burke, Charles James Fox, and others had failed to shake his government, which preferred a strong, reactionary king to a government controlled by liberals. That the American colonists had found friends among the men who opposed him did not faze the strong-willed King. Long months since, his mind had been made up. Insubordination

in his subjects he would not tolerate, and during the sitting of
the First Continental Congress he had written to Lord North,
"The die is now cast, the Colonies must either submit or
triumph; I do not wish to come to severer measures, but we
must not retreat." Now, eight months later, he would employ "every means of distressing America" until his deluded
subjects "felt the necessity of returning to their duty."

The Whig press in London accepted the news from New
England largely as it came, making reasonable allowances for
hysteria and exaggeration. An American sympathizer reported:

> Administration were alarmed at the unexpected success
> of the Provincials and were at a loss what lies to fabricate
> which would destroy the force of the qualifications which
> accompanied the intelligence. Runners were sent to every
> part of the city, who were authorized to deny the authenticity
> of the facts, and so distressed was Government that they
> officially requested a suspension of belief until dispatches
> were received from General Gage.[4]

The Tory press, on the other hand, ridiculed the provincials, their claims, and their charges of barbarities committed by the British regulars. *Mercator Americus* was the
signature to a letter published in the *Gazeteer and New Daily
Advertiser*:

> We may expect to hear that Mr. Samuel Frost and Mr.
> Seth Russell, the two militia gentlemen who are missing, have
> been eaten up by these cannibal regulars and that an affi-
> davit will be made by some persons that they saw Lord Percy
> and Colonel Smith make a hearty meal of them.[5]

When General Gage's official account reached London on
June 10 and was published in a rewritten version, which
evoked contempt from the Whigs, it stirred England profoundly. The King now reluctantly admitted that a state of
rebellion did exist and that a vast army would be required for
America. Conscious that Great Britain was not likely to provide sufficient manpower, he considered a scheme for hiring twenty thousand Russian mercenaries, but Catherine of
Russia refused to make a deal. The Government began to
strip "desks, counting-houses and public offices" of their
"peaceful occupiers to supply a new race of commanders and
generals" and soldiers for the field.

From England the news sped across the channel and elec-
trified the Continent. John Singleton Copley, Boston painter
whose subjects included Paul Revere and Samuel Adams, was
traveling in Italy when the news reached him. Writing home

to his Tory half brother to persuade him to leave the country and the war to others, he made a prediction:

> The flame of civil war is now broke out in America, and I have not the least doubt it will rage with a violence equal to what it has ever done in any other country at any time. You are sensible also by this time of the determined resolutions of Government to persevere in vigorous measures, and what will keep them firm in this determination is that they act as (at least) four-fifths of the people would have them, they so resent the outrage offered to them in the destruction of the tea. . . .
>
> You must also know, I think that the people have gone too far to retract and that they will adopt the proverb which says, "When the sword of rebellion is drawn, the sheath should be thrown away." And the Americans have it in their power to baffle all that England can do against them. I don't mean to ward off the evils attendant on civil war, but so far as never to be subdued, so that oceans of blood will be shed to humble a people which they never will subdue. And the Americans, from the idea that England would not act against them, have tempted its power to the extreme and drawn all its weight of rage upon them, and after they have, with various success, deluged the country in blood, the issue will be that the Americans will be a free independent people.[6]

John Singleton Copley understood his former neighbors. On the outskirts of Boston a miracle was in the making. From several thousand amateur citizen-soldiers who poured into the camp around Boston, General Ward was creating an army. Regimental organization, where it existed at all, was crude; leadership was largely incompetent and in the hands of men of local prominence rather than ability; and no strong authority prevented men from coming and going at will. Yet the conscientious, Bible-quoting militia general from Shrewsbury steadily increased and strengthened his force.

Ward's heterogeneous assemblage derived much of its inspiration from the vibrant presence of Dr. Warren. John Hancock, Sam Adams, and Sam's younger cousin, John, had set out for the Congress at Philadelphia, leaving to Warren almost sole management of Massachusetts civil affairs.

On the twentieth, Warren established headquarters at Jonathan Hastings' house in Cambridge with General Ward. The Provincial Congress, through its Committee of Safety, maintained iron control over the military as well as the civil situation. And as Chairman of the Committee of Safety and then as President of the Provincial Congress, Warren labored endless hours to bring order to the undisciplined troops at hand and to call more into the field. He engaged Paul Revere, now at Cambridge and unable safely to return home, "as a messenger to do the outdoor work for the committee" and turned over to him two of the colony's horses. The next month Revere filed a bill for seventeen days' riding as courier at five shillings a day, expenses for "Self & horse," and for keeping two horses; then he went on to other work for the provisional government at its later capital in Watertown.

The rude rebel army lacked supplies of all kinds. Most of the men carried their own arms, every variety of musket and rifle, but few had much ammunition—at most, a flask or horn of powder and a pocket or pouch of balls—and fewer still had blankets, tents, utensils, or provisions. Despite the old Crown militia requirements, there were practically no bayonets, and uniforms did not exist. The public supply of gunpowder was only a few score barrels, and in cannon, that most essential article for a siege, the army was weakest of all: a mere handful of guns was assembled.

It was a New England volunteer force with its good and its bad and its rock-ribbed individualism, but it doggedly cut off Boston from all communication with the rest of the country and forced a military stalemate. It had no way to drive into Boston, but it kept General Gage from breaking out. As long as British ships could move freely in and out of the harbor, Gage was not truly besieged, but he was dependent upon the country around for food and fuel, and that he could not reach by water. "The rebels certainly block up our town and cut off our good beef and mutton . . . ," moaned Captain Harris of the Fifth Regiment. "At present we are completely blockaded and subsisting almost on salt provisions." Many Whigs had fled from town on the nineteenth, the minute that fighting became a certainty. But the thousands of citizens remaining—Whigs who either had no place to go or were not yet ready to leave, Tories who lived in town or who had come in from the country for the protection of the troops, and moderates who chose to stay—also were now entrapped and suffered privations as severe as those of the grumbling regulars.

Although the chain of fortifications General Ward was throwing up could mount few guns and his army was powerless to assault the fortified regulars, perceptive Lieutenant Mackenzie recognized Gage's uneasiness. On the twenty-third he wrote in his journal:

From all the measures which have been taken since the nineteenth instant, it appears that the general is apprehensive

the rebels will make some desperate attempt on the town.
The numbers which are assembled round it and their violent
and determined spirit make it prudent to guard against what
they may do.[7]

General Gage's "measures" were to increase the guards and
sentries at the posts around town, to enjoin his officers "to
lay at their barracks" for easy accessibility in case of alarm,
and especially to expand his fortifications. The weather
turned fair and mild for the next few days. Construction progressed rapidly.

Gage also took steps to forestall an underground revolt. On
April 28 he drove a bargain with the inhabitants, which Lieutenant Barker noted in his diary:

The townspeople have today given up their arms to the
selectmen, who are to deliver them over to the general. I
fancy this will quiet him a little, for he seemed apprehensive
that if the lines should be attacked, the townspeople would
raise and assist. They would not give up their arms without
the general promising that they should have leave to quit the
town, as many as pleased. Ever since the nineteenth we have
been kept in constant alarm. . . . We are in daily expectation of the troops [from England] coming here with General Howe, etc. We then expect some alterations of affairs.[8]

Meanwhile, snorted British Lieutenant John Barker, the
rebels had raised a standard at Cambridge: "They call themselves the King's troops and us the Parliament's. Pretty burlesque!"

While Gage peered fearfully from Boston's forts toward the
growing rebel lines, Ward's troops toiled manfully building entrenchments and redoubts, and Dr. Warren's committee set
afoot a secret expedition in the northern wilderness of New
York in the hope of obtaining heavy guns for the siege. It
was an odd adventure that had started in Connecticut when
Israel Bissel, the post rider, had aroused New Haven. There
an ambitious, bustling thirty-four-year-old apothecary and
merchant named Benedict Arnold commanded the local militia company, an elite outfit called the Governor's Foot
Guard, smartly uniformed in scarlet, white, and black. Bissel's news precipitated a town meeting, in which the conservatives carried a vote against sending armed aid to the
Massachusetts rebels. But the hot-blooded captain, whose men
were spoiling to fight, would have none of that decision. He
demanded power and ball from the town powder house. When
the selectmen refused it, the truculent captain sent a message to the town fathers that if they did not deliver him the

keys to the powder house in five minutes, he would order his
men to break open the door and help themselves. That was
Benedict Arnold's way: arrogant, explosive, and ruthless. The
selectmen released the keys, and on the next morning, a shining Saturday, the twenty-second, the short, swarthy captain
led his fifty-odd men swinging up the road toward Cambridge.

On the road, Captain Arnold met Colonel Samuel Parsons,
returning from Cambridge to Connecticut to recruit more
men. Colonel Parsons expressed concern over the lack of cannon on the lines at Cambridge, and at once Arnold thought of
a source of supply. On trips to Canada, where he often had
traded in horses and merchandise, he told Colonel Parsons,
he had become familiar with the rotting, old British-held
fort, Ticonderoga, at the southern end of Lake Champlain.
It contained, he guessed, eighty pieces of heavy cannon,
twenty brass guns, and ten to twelve mortars with small arms
and other supplies in proportion, and its peacetime British
garrison was insignificant.

By the time Arnold reached Cambridge, he was ready to
propose the capture of Fort Ticonderoga to the Committee of
Safety. Because the fort was in New York territory, the committee sent Arnold's information to the New York committee,
rather than launch an armed expedition into New York's
jurisdiction. But impulsive Dr. Warren could not wait. On the
third of May, he persuaded his committee to appoint Arnold
a colonel for "a secret service," for which he was to enlist
not over four hundred men in western Massachusetts and
neighboring colonies. Arnold's instructions were to take the
fort, leave a garrison, and bring away the cannon and stores.

The energetic Arnold set out at once. When he reached
Stockbridge, he learned to his angry astonishment that another expedition was on the march against the fort. Colonel
Parsons, after his meeting with Arnold, had conferred with
several prominent Hartford citizens, who had decided to commission capture of the fort by the giant outlaw chief of the
New Hampshire Grants, Ethan Allen, and his Green Mountain
Boys, a powerful vigilante force that had been battling for
five years against New York authority to uphold land rights
of Hampshire citizens.

Colonel Arnold, fearing a rival might outrace him to glory,
did not wait for the men he had recruited to join him, but
galloped north with a single servant on the trail of the Green
Mountain Boys.

At Castleton, twenty miles below Ticonderoga, in a smoky
taproom, he found the Boys and the Connecticut men and
their followers, idling away time before joining their elected

leader, Ethan Allen, who had gone ahead to a rendezvous point a few miles north, on the east shore of Lake Champlain.

The newly commissioned Colonel Arnold coldly demanded recognition as commander of the force. At first, the woodsmen, flushed with that Green Mountain concoction of rum and rock-hard cider called a "stonewall," laughed at the gaudy, choleric little stranger. But when he set out to overtake Allen to argue the superiority of his commission, the Boys raged after him, threatening to mutiny if Allen gave in to him.

When Arnold reached the rendezvous after midnight, he argued violently with Allen, but the giant Hampshireman remained unmoved.

"What shall I do with the damned rascal?" he asked one of his boys. "Put him under guard?"

"Better go side by side," one of them said.

Arnold reluctantly agreed to a compromise—to march with Allen at the head of the column, but to issue no orders.

The problem now was to get across the dark, squall-ruffled waters of Lake Champlain to the western shore. Allen had sent men to commandeer boats from the head of the lake, but hours passed and they did not come. Finally, accompanied by Arnold, Allen started across with two boats that were at hand. It was nearly three o'clock in the morning of May 10 when he landed his first contingent of eighty-three men north of the fort. The eastern sky was beginning to pale. Reluctant to lose the element of surprise, he dared not wait for the rest of the men to ferry across, and left them on the eastern shore. He led his eighty-three down a road through thick forest skirting the lake and the east wall of the fort, to an open wicket gate on the south side.

Allen and Arnold stormed through the gate, each trying to outpace the other. A drowsing sentry jerked to life, and aimed his musket. When it flashed in the pan, he flung it away and fled through the covered way into the fort. The American commanders were hard at his heels as he shrieked an alarm. Another sentry came at them with his bayonet. Tall, powerful Allen slashed at him with his sword and disarmed him; he "demanded of him the place where the commanding officer kept." The Green Mountain Boys crowded through the gate and formed, back to back, on the parade ground, whooping like redmen.

Only forty-five redcoats garrisoned the fort, five described by their own officers as "old, wore out, & unserviceable," others sick. Twenty-four of their women and children lived in the barracks, and all were fast asleep. Lieutenant Jocelyn Feltham, of His Majesty's Twenty-sixth Foot, second in com-

mand of the garrison, slept soundly on the upper floor of the
barracks, until, he reported later, about half past three:

I was awakened by numbers of shrieks and the words,
"No quarter, no quarter," from a number of armed rabble. I
jumped up, . . . ran undressed to knock at Captain Delaplace's door and to receive his orders or wake him. The door
was fast. The room I lay in being close to Captain Delaplace's, I stepped back, put on my coat and waistcoat and
returned to his room, there being no possibility of getting
to the men, as there were numbers of the rioters on the
bastions of the wing of the fort on which the door of my
room and back door of Captain Delaplace's room led.

With great difficulty I got into his room . . . from which
there was a door down by stairs into the area of the fort. I
asked Captain Delaplace, who was now just up, what I
should do and offered to force my way, if possible, to our
men. On opening this door, the bottom of the stairs was filled
with the rioters and many were forcing their way up, knowing the commanding officer lived there. . . .

From the top of the stairs I endeavored to make them hear
me, but it was impossible. On making a signal not to come
up the stairs, they stopped and proclaimed silence among
themselves. I then addressed them, but in a style not agreeable to them. I asked a number of questions, expecting to
amuse them till our people fired, which I must certainly own
I thought would have been the case. After asking them the
most material questions I could think, viz. by what authority
they entered His Majesty's fort, who were the leaders, what
their intent, &c., I was informed by one Ethan Allen and one
Benedict Arnold that they had a joint command, Arnold
informing me he came from instructions received from the
Congress at Cambridge, which he afterward showed me.

Mr. Allen told me his orders were from the province of
Connecticut and that he must have immediate possession of
the fort and all the effects of George, the Third (those were
his words), Mr. Allen insisting on this with a drawn sword
over my head and numbers of his followers' firelocks presented at me, alleging I was commanding officer and to give
up the fort, and if it was not complied with, or that there
was a single gun fired in the fort, neither man, woman, or
child should be left alive. . . .

Mr. Arnold begged it in a genteel manner, but without success; it was owing to him they were prevented getting into
Captain Delaplace's room, after they found I did not command.

Captain Delaplace, being now dressed, came out. . . .

Lieutenant Feltham, his breeches in his hand, was hustled
into the captain's room under guard. The captain was

trotted downstairs. When he realized to his mortification that all his men had been caught in bed, he surrendered the fort.

The next day, the Americans took the little British post at Crown Point, farther north, and a few days later, Arnold, supported by his own men who now joined him, took the post at St. John's, on the Richelieu River.

Ethan Allen, reporting the capture of Ticonderoga to New York, wrote that he and Arnold had entered the fort side by side. Before Allen could write his report to the Massachusetts Committee, Arnold loudly renewed his demand for supreme command, and Allen then wrote to the Massachusetts Committee as if Arnold were not even present.

The dispute over command continued, until Allen gained an upper hand, and, Arnold, enraged, wrote to Cambridge for a decision.

But the decision no longer rested with the Massachusetts Congress. The northern colonies, alarmed by reports that in Canada an expedition to retake the forts was contemplated and that the British commander there was soliciting the Six Nations of Indians to join forces with him, had persuaded the Continental Congress to assume responsibility for Crown Point and Ticonderoga. On the first of June, the Continental Congress accordingly called upon New York and Connecticut to furnish troops for the defense of the posts and authorized the rebel governor of Connecticut to appoint a commander. The Massachusetts Congress, meanwhile, sent a commission to Ticonderoga to investigate the command situation. Arnold considered this action a reflection upon his rectitude and abilities and promptly left the service in disgust while the argument over who first had entered the fort and who was in command still swirled about him.

Ethan Allen had the final word four years later in an autobiographical account. Writing with careless regard for detail, confusing the dishabille of captain and lieutenant, he did not even mention Arnold as being with him the morning of the capture, May 10, but his account of who said what when the fort was entered is the one that generations remember:

I . . . ordered the commander, Captain Delaplace, to come forth instantly or I would sacrifice the whole garrison; at which the captain came immediately to the door with his breeches in his hand; when I ordered him to deliver me the fort instantly, he asked me by what authority I demanded it. I answered him, "In the name of the great Jehova and the Continental Congress."[10]

"I BEAT TO 'YANKEE DOODLE'"

Bunker Hill

JUNE 17, 1775

ALLEN'S AND Arnold's roistering exploits at Ticonderoga and
Crown Point did not immediately change the situation before
Boston. For lack of transport the cannon and stores could not
be moved, and although the capture of the two strategic
points on the lake had the very important effect of discouraging for some time an English thrust from Canada, this advantage was to be lost through American lack of foresight.

At Cambridge every energy was consumed in making an
army of the force gathered there. The men who had come on
the alarm of the nineteenth of April were militia and minutemen from sixteen to sixty, married and single, strong and
feeble. Many of them were impossible soldier material, without regimental organization, serving under elected local captains, and feeling no obligation to remain but that of moral
suasion. They could not be expected to linger long. Many went
home for additional clothing, or to settle personal affairs,
or to sow crops. The Committee of Safety called for substi-
tutes from the towns, and a few came. Probably twenty thousand men traveled to Cambridge, but only part of them
stayed after the first few days. Those who did remain were
not an army but rather, as one man described them, "such a
confused Company as small detachments from every quarter
composes."

A new army had to be created, and within three days the
Provincial Congress authorized the enlistment of troops for
the rest of the year, to be paid by the Congress, and promised
to issue commissions to officers who raised regiments. But in-
decisions and red tape slowed down the development of a
firm plan of organization, while the men at hand drifted
away. By the twenty-fourth of April, Artemas Ward warned
Congress:

Gentlemen: My situation is such that if I have not enlisting orders immediately I shall be left all alone. It is impossible to keep the men here, excepting something be done.

I, therefore, pray that the plan may be completed and handed to me this morning, and that you, gentlemen of the Congress, issue orders for enlisting men.[1]

Even though the Congress responded instantly and sent him that day printed enlisting orders for twenty regiments, recruiting went slowly. From six thousand, Thomas' force at Roxbury evaporated to twenty-five hundred, and on May 8, General Ward wrote him that his own camp at Cambridge was so thin of men that he could send no more to the crucial Roxbury lines.

Such men as Joseph Warren were not blind to another danger. General Gage's royal government had all but ceased to exist in Massachusetts months ago, yet the Provincial Congress which superseded it was not an instrument of a legally constituted government. Its members were haunted by the fear that without a legal civil government "with all its parts" in the colony, the armed mass now forming might take to itself anarchic control of Massachusetts. Therefore, the Provincial Congress appealed to the Continental Congress to advise it upon the establishment of government and to take over regulation and direction of the army. Although the Continental Congress could claim even less legality than the Massachusetts Congress, it was regarded with respect and considered able to speak authoritatively. However, without waiting for the decision of the Continental Congress, General Ward insisted that the Provincial Congress commission officers for the new army and get on with the filling of it. Again the Cambridge body responded, named him commander-in-chief of the New England forces, and began commissioning regiments.

By June, about seventy-five hundred men, not only from Massachusetts, but also from New Hampshire, Rhode Island, and Connecticut, were enlisted and settled in a ring west of Boston from Charlestown on the north to Roxbury on the south, and the force was growing steadily.

Its only military activity, aside from entrenching and standing guard, was sniping at British sentries, skirmishing occasionally with small parties that ventured ashore from boats, and firing on British guard boats. The rebels sometimes paraded at an exposed place to show themselves to the redcoats, as at Charlestown where "after giving the warhoop," they returned to camp, satisfied they had impressed the regulars with their daring. An occasional cannon shot thudded into the American lines. John Trumbull, a delicate, introverted youth, who celebrated his nineteenth birthday soon after reaching camp, was stationed with General Joseph

Spencer's Connecticut troops at Roxbury; he kept a full account of his army life in which he recorded some of the
earliest lessons of that May and June:

Nothing of military importance occurred for some time;
the enemy occasionally fired upon our working parties, whenever they approached too nigh to their works; and in order
to familiarize our raw soldiers to this exposure, a small reward was offered in general orders for every ball fired by the
enemy, which should be picked up and brought to headquarters. This soon produced the intended effect—a fearless
emulation among the men; but it produced also a very unfortunate result; for when the soldiers saw a ball, after having struck and rebounded from the ground several times (*en
ricochet*), roll sluggishly along, they would run and place a
foot before it, to stop it, not aware that a heavy ball long
retains sufficient impetus to overcome such an obstacle. The
consequence was that several brave lads lost their feet, which
were crushed by the weight of the rolling shot. The order
was of course withdrawn, and they were cautioned against
touching a ball, until it was entirely at rest. One thing had
been ascertained by this means, the caliber of the enemy's
guns—eighteen pounds. Thirteen inch shells were also occasionally fired, some of which exploded, at first, to our no
small annoyance and alarm; but some of these also being
picked up (having failed of igniting) were carried to headquarters, and by this means their dimensions were also ascertained.[2]

Isolated houses were burned by raiding parties from both
sides, and one hearty skirmish took place when the British attempted to prevent the rebels from taking cattle from
Noodle's Island, but generally the camps were quiet.

The first reinforcements for Gage's army began to arrive in
late May. On the twenty-fifth, the *Cerberus* dropped anchor
in the harbor, bringing three major generals to assist the
entrapped commander at Boston: William Howe, Henry Clinton, and John Burgoyne.

General Howe was the senior of them in service and the
only one who had served in America. He had been at the
second taking of Louisbourg in 1758 and had commanded
the light infantry that led the way for Wolfe's army, the next
year, up the heights to the Plains of Abraham. Although he
had been re-elected to Parliament in 1774 on his promise to
the liberals of the town of Nottingham that he would refuse
a command against the Americans, when his orders came for
America he accepted them. He was a large man, still soldierly and handsome in a dark, overbearing way, though softened by years of peace and coarsened by the indulgence of

an insatiable appetite for high living. Troops loved him for his heartiness and his great animal courage, and with them he might have done anything, but he was almost reluctant to come to battle, often negligent in preparing for it, and seldom pursued it to victory.

Compared to Howe, Henry Clinton was colorless. He was short and paunchy with a plain, round face whose prominent feature was a large nose. In manner he appeared distant though polite, but his punctilious air concealed a stubborn irascibility and an extreme sensitiveness to criticism. Although he had served with some distinction in the Seven Years' War, he seemed to have bad luck which made his talents appear less than they really were. Like so many men of dark, suspicious nature, he distrusted himself; his solid military acumen surrendered to his own timidity, and he was his own worst enemy.

The most theatrical of the three was John Burgoyne, worldly, graceful, and vivacious. At fifty-three he was the eldest of the trio but the junior in service. He had won lasting recognition in the Spanish campaign of the Seven Years' War, in which he had commanded the Sixteenth Dragoons, called "Burgoyne's Light Horse," and his concept of the duties of an officer was sound and far advanced for his time. Although he had been out of military life during the dozen years since, he had remained prominent in London circles as a member of Commons, a man of fashion, a fabulous gambler, a litterateur, and a fairly popular dramatist. An intriguer, he now came to Boston determined to elevate his position among the British generals in America.

Gossip soon had it that Burgoyne, upon entering the harbor and hearing that the British were cooped up in Boston, exclaimed, "Well, let us in, and we shall make elbow room." His expression quickly was picked up and Clinton, suddenly nervously afire, echoed, "our elbows must be eased." The trio of newcomers, all bluster and advice, urged Gage to take the offensive at once against the rebels.

Following instructions from Lord Dartmouth, Secretary of State for the Colonies, Gage first issued a proclamation, dressed in the verbose prose of John Burgoyne, declaring martial law and offering amnesty to all rebels, except Adams and Hancock. Among the Americans it aroused more ridicule and indignation than dismay. As soon as Gage recognized that such an overture was not going to affect "the present troubles and disorders," he at last laid plans for aggressive military action.

An attempt to destroy the American army lying outside Boston could not be seriously considered, for even if it were successful, Gage's forces were too weak to penetrate into the interior of New England. However, he decided, now was the time to occupy and fortify the outlying heights of Dorchester and Charlestown which, if seized by the rebels, would make Boston untenable. From the hills of Dorchester, rebel cannon could sweep all of Boston and its main anchorage; from those of Charlestown they could bombard Boston's North End and the northern anchorages. Accordingly, he prepared to move a detachment to Dorchester on June 18 and another as soon as possible to cover Bunker Hill and Breed's Hill on Charlestown peninsula.

But Gage's headquarters was talkative, and by the fourteenth his plans were known in the rebel camp. The Committee of Safety moved to check-mate them by recommending that General Ward take and hold Bunker Hill; the Committee confessed its ignorance of "the particular situation" of Dorchester peninsula and left to a council of war the decision as to what steps to pursue respecting it. The council decided, at least for the time, to ignore Dorchester and turned its whole attention to Bunker Hill.

In tall, broad-shouldered Colonel William Prescott's Massachusetts regiment, Private Peter Brown was a company clerk. He had fought at Concord and had come from his home in Westford to the siege. The lad knew nothing of the strategic value of hills and cared less, but he soon was writing about them to his mother:

Friday, the sixteenth of June we were ordered to parade at six o'clock with one day's provisions and blankets ready for a march somewhere, but we did not know where. So we readily and cheerfully obeyed . . . these three: Colonels Prescott's, Frye's, and Nickson's Regiments. . . . About nine o'clock at night we marched down to Charlestown Hill.[3]

There were three hills on Charlestown peninsula: Bunker Hill, Breed's Hill, and Morton's Hill. Bunker Hill, a round, smooth eminence, was considerably the highest, one hundred and ten feet, just inside Charlestown Neck. Connected to it on the southeast by a ridge was steep Breed's Hill, seventy-five feet. East of Breed's lay brick kilns and clay pits and sloughy land; west was the most settled part of Charlestown. In the southeast corner of the mile-long peninsula, where it widened to a half-mile, was Morton's Hill, about thirty-five feet high, sloping down to Morton's Point. A highway, varying from sixteen to thirty feet wide, ascended from Morton's Point, traversed Breed's and Bunker hills, and ran out the Neck, which the tides occasionally overflowed. Another road branched from the highway to the left, circled the base of Breed's Hill and joined the road from Charlestown, meeting the highway at the Neck.

For a reason never satisfactorily explained, the American detachment, which included Captain Samuel Gridley's artillery company with two field pieces and a fatigue party of two hundred Connecticut troops under Captain Thomas Knowlton, marched over Bunker Hill to Breed's Hill, nearer the enemy, where Colonel Richard Gridley, chief engineer, laid out a plan of fortification. Here every advantage of the higher Bunker Hill was lost, for Breed's commanded neither the water nor its own flanks. It's only advantage was that it was so much nearer to Boston that even small cannon from its top could threaten the town and the shipping. Peter Brown wrote:

. . . we entrenched and made a fort of about ten rod long and eight wide, with a breastwork of about eight more. We worked there undiscovered till about five in the morn, and then we saw our danger, being against eight ships of the line and all Boston fortified against us. (The danger we were in made us think there was treachery and that we were brought there to be all slain, and I must and will venture to say that there was treachery, oversight, or presumption in the conduct of our officers.)

And about half after five in the morn, we not having about half the fort done, they began to fire (I suppose as soon as they had orders) pretty briskly a few minutes, and then stopped, and then again to the number of about twenty or more. They killed one of us, and then they ceased till about eleven o'clock, and then they began pretty brisk again; and that caused some of our young country people to desert, apprehending the danger in a clearer manner than the rest, who were more diligent in digging and fortifying ourselves against them. We began to be almost beat out, being tired by our labor and having no sleep the night before, but little victuals, no drink but rum. . . .

They fired very warm from Boston and from on board, till about two o'clock, when they began to fire from the ships in the ferryway [between Boston and Charlestown] and from the ship that lay in the river against the Neck to stop our reinforcements, which they did in some measure. One cannon cut off three men in two on the neck of land. Our officers sent time after time after the cannon from Cambridge in the morning and could get but four, the captain of which fired but a few times and then swang his hat round three times to the enemy, then ceased to fire.

It being about three o'clock, there was a little cessation of the cannons roaring. Come to look, there was a matter of forty barges full of regulars coming over to us. It is supposed

there were about three thousand of them and about seven
hundred of us left not deserted, besides five hundred reinforcement that could not get so nigh to us as to do any good
hardly, till they saw that we must all be cut off, or some of
them, and then they advanced.

When our officers saw that the regulars would land, they
ordered the artillery to go out of the fort and prevent their
landing if possible, from which the artillery captain took his
pieces and went right off home to Cambridge as fast as he
could, for which he is now confined and we expect will be
shot for it.

But the enemy landed and fronted before us and formed
themselves in an oblong square, so as to surround us which
they did in part, and after they were well formed, they advanced towards us in order to swallow us up. But they found
a chokey mouthful of us, though we could do nothing with
our small arms as yet for distance and had *but two cannon
and nary gunner*. And they from Boston and from the ships
a-firing and throwing bombs keeping us down till they got
almost round us.[4]

The booming of the ships' guns in Boston before sunrise
on the morning of the sixteenth, followed almost instantly by
the crash of guns from a battery on Copp's Hill, was General
Gage's first notice that the rebels had stolen a march on him,
and were entrenching on Breed's Hill. In a few minutes the
other generals arrived, and to a window-shaking cannonade
sat down to a council of war. Obviously the rebels must be
driven at once from Charlestown peninsula. General Clinton
proposed that while an attack be made on the hill, troops
should also be sent at once to cut off Charlestown Neck, "not
a stonethrow across," but General Howe argued that a direct
frontal attack on the new rebel redoubt would be sufficient.
Howe prevailed. Then hours passed, while bread was baked,
meat boiled, and officers waited upon tides; finally a main
body of fifteen hundred and fifty men and a reserve of seven
hundred under Howe landed at Morton's Point and formed
on that hill.

By now the rebels had extended an earthwork left of their
redoubt about a hundred yards. To the rear, beyond a patch
of swampy ground, another breastwork extended leftward to
the bank of the Mystic; it "consisted of two fence rails, the
intervals filled with bushes, hay and grass which they found
on the spot ready cut." Along this rail fence lay Knowlton's
detachment, strengthened by Colonel John Stark's New
Hampshire regiment and some of James Reed's.

Howe himself, with the Light Infantry, commanded the
British right, facing the fence, expecting to turn the rebel

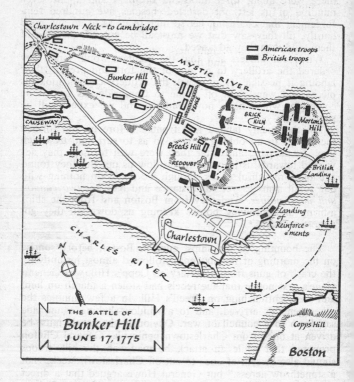

Charlestown Neck - to Cambridge

☐ American troops
■ British troops

MYSTIC RIVER

Bunker Hill

FENCE

BRICK KILN

Morton's Hill

CAUSEWAY

Breed's Hill

REDOUBT

British Landing

Landing of Reinforcements

Charlestown

CHARLES RIVER

N

THE BATTLE OF
Bunker Hill
JUNE 17, 1775

Copp's Hill

Boston

flank, while General Robert Pigot, commanding the left, was to assault the redoubt.

As Private Peter Brown continued to work feverishly on the American earthwork, the red lines moved forward. A British officer, advancing with Howe's troops, later described the redcoat advance that hot afternoon:

Our troops advanced with great confidence, expecting an easy victory. As they were marching up to attack, our artillery stopped firing. The general on inquiring the reason was told they had got twelve pound balls to six pounders, but that they had grape shot. On this, he ordered them forward and to fire grape.

As we approached, an incessant stream of fire poured from the rebel lines. It seemed a continued sheet of fire for near thirty minutes. Our Light Infantry were served up in companies against the grass fence without being able to penetrate. Indeed, how could we penetrate? Most of our Grenadiers and Light Infantry the moment of presenting themselves lost three-fourths, and many nine-tenths, of their men. Some had only eight and nine men a company left, some only three, four, and five.

On the left, Pigot was staggered and actually retreated. Observe, our men were not driven back; they actually retreated by orders.[5]

Across the Charles, Howe's colleagues, Burgoyne and Clinton, stood in a battery overlooking Charlestown. Spread before them, as in a vast amphitheater, was the fierce defense of Breed's Hill. Upon Burgoyne, no stranger to warfare, the sight of Howe's stubborn assault, broken and flung back, made such an impression that when he wrote a friend in England a few days later, every detail was still burning fresh in his memory:

As his first arm advanced up the hill, they met with a thousand impediments from strong fences and were much exposed. They were also exceedingly hurt by musketry from Charlestown, though Clinton and I did not perceive it till Howe sent us word by a boat and desired us to set fire to the town, which was immediately done. . . . Our battery kept an incessant fire on the height. It was seconded by a number of frigates, floating batteries, and one ship of the line.

And now ensued one of the greatest scenes of war that can be conceived. If we look to the height, Howe's corps ascending the hill in the face of the entrenchments and in a very disadvantageous ground was much engaged. To the left the enemy pouring in fresh troops by thousands over the land, and in the arm of the sea our ships and floating batteries cannonading them. Straight before us, a large and noble town in one great blaze. The church steeples being of timber were great pyramids of fire above the rest. Behind us, the church steeples and heights of our own camp, covered with spectators of the rest of our army which was engaged. The hills round the country covered with spectators. The enemy all in anxious suspense. The roar of cannon, mortars, and musketry, the crash of churches, ships upon the stocks, and whole streets falling together in ruins to fill the ear; the storm of the redoubts with the objects above described to fill the eye, and the reflection that perhaps a defeat was a final loss to the British Empire in America to fill the mind, made the whole a picture and a complication of horror and importance beyond anything that ever came to my lot to be witness to.[6]

About midway of the American entrenchments was Robert

Steele, a drummer boy of Ephraim Doolittle's regiment, which had come up during the day from Cambridge, under command of its major, Willard Moore. The two favorite tunes with fifers and drummers in those first days were "Yankee Doodle" and "Welcome Here." Years later, Robert told a friend, "I beat to 'Yankee Doodle' when we mustered for Bunker Hill that morning," and he related what he recalled of the battle:

> . . . the British . . . marched with rather a slow step nearly up to our entrenchment, and the battle began. The conflict was sharp, but the British soon retreated with a quicker step than they came up, leaving some of their killed and wounded in sight of us. They retreated towards where they landed and formed again . . . came up again and a second battle ensued which was harder and longer than the first, but being but a lad and this the first engagement I was ever in, I cannot remember much more . . . than great noise and confusion. One or two circumstances I can, however, distinctly remember. . . .

About the time the British retreated the second time, I was standing side of Benjamin Ballard, a Boston boy about my age, who had a gun in his hands, when one of our sergeants came up to us and said, "You are young and spry, run in a moment to some of the stores and bring some rum. Major Moore is badly wounded. Go as quick as possible."

We threw down our implements of war and run as fast as we could and passed over the hill . . . down to Charlestown Neck and found there was a firing in that quarter. We heard the shot pass over our heads, which I afterwards understood were thrown from a floating battery in Mystic River and from the shipping on the Boston side of the Neck.

We however immediately passed on and went into a store, but see no one there. I stamped and called out to rally some person and a man answered us from the cellar below. I told him what we wanted, but he did not come up, nor did we see him at all. I again told him what we wanted and asked him why he stayed down cellar. He answered, "To keep out of the way of the shot," and then said, "If you want anything in the store, take what you please."

I seized a brown, two-quart, earthen pitcher and drawed it partly full from a cask and found I had got wine. I threw that out and filled my pitcher with rum from another cask. Ben took a pail and filled with water, and we hastened back to the entrenchment on the hill, when we found our people in confusion and talking about retreating. The British were about advancing upon us a third time. Our rum and water went very quick. It was very hot, but I saved my pitcher and kept it for sometime afterwards.[7]

Twice Howe's men had been driven back; windrows of
British dead and wounded lay crimson in the uncut grass before the rebel lines. As his men were stopped, Howe experienced "*A moment that I never felt before*"; every European
tradition had been shattered by such fire as the British never
had f. ced. Still, the dogged Howe determined to have another
go at the tenacious rebels and formed his men again.

General Pigot had failed so far to dislodge the rebels from
their redoubt. There, as he advanced again, fought the tall,
blue-eyed Pepperell farmer, William Prescott, in homespun
clothes, a sword buckled to his side, a light, loose coat about
his shoulders, and a broad-brimmed hat shading his eyes:

> I was now left with perhaps one hundred and fifty men
> in the fort. The enemy advanced and fired very hotly . . .
> and meeting with a warm reception, there was a very smart
> firing on both sides. After a considerable time, finding our
> ammunition was almost spent, I commanded a cessation till
> the enemy advanced within thirty yards, when we gave them
> such a hot fire that they were obliged to retire nearly one
> hundred and fifty yards before they could rally and come
> again to the attack. Our ammunition being nearly ex-
> hausted, could keep up only a scattering fire. The enemy,
> being numerous, surrounded our little fort, began to mount
> our lines and enter the fort with their bayonets.[8]

On the hill and behind the rebel lines all was confusion.
The Americans had fired time after time at rank after rank
of redcoats; the lines were muffled in smoke; powder was almost gone. Behind them reinforcements had balked at the
Neck, which was swept by cannon fire from the ships, or had
hesitated on top of Bunker Hill, or did not know where they
were expected to support the line.

Howe, concentrating his strength against the earthworks, at
last bore the rebels down. His officers were astonished by
the stubbornness of Prescott's defense of the redoubt on the
right. A lieutenant of the Fifth Regiment reported that "the
oldest officers say they never saw a sharper action." The
rebels kept up this fire until the redcoats were within ten
yards. Said the lieutenant, "There are few instances of regular
troops defending a redoubt till the enemy were in the very
ditch of it, and [yet] I myself saw several pop their heads
up and fire even after some of our men were upon the berm."
Then, of a sudden, American powder was gone—their fire
"went out like an old candle." Peter Brown was among the
last defenders: "I was in the fort till the regulars came in," he
told his mother, "and I jumped over the walls and ran for
about half a mile where balls flew like hailstones and cannons roared like thunder."

Lieutenant Samuel Webb had come up with Captain John Chester's Wethersfield, Connecticut, company, one of the few reinforcing units to mount the hill. Said he:

> We covered their retreat till they came up with us by a brisk fire from our small arms. The dead and wounded lay on every side of me. Their groans were piercing indeed, though long before this time I believe the fear of death had quitted almost every breast. They now had possession of our fort and four fieldpieces, and by much the advantage of the ground; and, to tell you the truth, our reinforcements belonging to this province, very few of them came into the field, but lay skulking the opposite side of the hill. Our orders then came to make the best retreat we could. We set off almost gone with fatigue and ran very fast up [Bunker Hill], leaving some of our dead and wounded in the field.[9]

Among the dead lay the beloved Dr. Joseph Warren. When he had heard the report that the regulars had landed at Charlestown, he set out for the scene of action. Three days before, he had been voted a major-generalcy by the Provincial Congress, but was not yet commissioned. When Warren presented himself at the redoubt on Breed's Hill, Prescott, respecting his new commission, asked him if he had any orders to give. Warren replied, "The command is yours."

Throughout the hard-fought action at the redoubt, the doctor fought side by side with the men, who were heartened by his cold, debonair courage. He fell with a musket ball in the back of his head just as the fort was overrun. He "died in his best cloaths," said a British officer, "everybody remembered his fine, silk fringed waistcoat."

To Captain John Chester defeat was bitter; he remained convinced that only Prescott's men fought well:

> Our retreat . . . was shameful and scandalous and owing to the cowardice, misconduct, and want of regularity of the province troops, though to do them justice there was a number of their officers and men that were in the fort and a very few others that did honor to themselves by a most noble, manly, and spirited effort in the heat of the engagement, and 'tis said many of them, the flower of the province, have sacrificed their lives in the cause. Some say they have lost more officers than men. Good Dr. Warren, God rest his soul, I hope is safe in Heaven! Had many of their officers the spirit and courage in their whole constitution that he had in his little finger, we had never retreated.
> Many considerable companies of their men I saw that said there was not so much as a corporal with them. One in particular fell in the rear of my company and marched with

us. The captain had mustered and ordered them to march
and told them he would overtake them directly, but they
never saw him till next day. . . . If a man was wounded,
twenty more were glad of an opportunity to carry him away
when not more than three could take hold of him to advantage. One cluster would be sneaking down on their bellies
behind a rock, and others behind haycocks and apple trees.
    . . . In short, the most of the companies of this province
are commanded by a most despicable set of officers, and the
whole success of the battle with them depends on their virtue; for almost all from the captain general to a corporal are
afraid to set up proper martial authority and say, as affairs
are situated, they think their people will not bear it. But in
my humble opinion, they are very much in the wrong.[10]

The great American failure that day was behind the lines
before the battle ended, where Ward's staff proved inadequate
to his needs, and his regimental officers unequal to the emergency. In the retreat itself, the officers and men who had arrived in the vicinity of the fighting behaved much better than
brave Captain Chester in his agony of defeat gave them credit
for. It was a fighting retreat; like veteran troops they carried
off most of their wounded, and obstinately fought "from one
fence or wall to another," until, said a British officer, "we entirely drove them off the peninsula of Charlestown." Burgoyne admitted, "The retreat was no flight; it was even covered with bravery and military skill." By not taking the Neck
and cutting off all of Prescott's men, the British failed to win
a crushing victory and to capture innumerable rebel prisoners; only their failure to do so made possible the escape of
the beaten survivors.

At five o'clock on a broiling, summer afternoon, the day
was over. If each army wondered what the other might do, it
tended to its own problems. On Winter Hill, slightly more
than a mile outside the Neck, under vigorous old Israel
Putnam's directions, the rebels steadied and flung up a fort,
while Howe's men began pitching tents on the ground they
had taken. General Clinton, who had come over to Charlestown during the afternoon, entreated Howe to push on. Cambridge was only two miles away, and the Americans were demoralized; Clinton was sure they could be smashed entirely,
although he himself admitted Breed's Hill was "A dear
bought victory, another such would have ruined us." But
Howe's men were far "too much harassed and fatigued to give
much attention to the pursuit of the rebels," he reported to
General Gage. As for the rebels themselves, Captain Peter Co-
burn of Dracut, his clothes bullet-rent, possibly spoke for them
all when he sighed, "I arived at Cambridge About Sunset alive,

Tho much Tired and Feteogued. Blessed be God Theirfor."

Gage had gained an outpost, but it was of little real value, and the cost was disastrous. Of his 2,250 men engaged, 1,054, including 92 officers, had been hit by the fierce rebel fire. Of the total, 226 died. Every one of Howe's twelve staff officers had been struck, and in some of the regiments only three or four men escaped. Among the British dead was Major John Pitcairn, of Lexington infamy, whose son carried him dying from the field. Of the Americans, 140 were killed, and 271 wounded.

One of Gage's own officers made a sound critique of the day's work. Over-confidence, he thought, had led to the "dreadful" British loss, and he charged his commander-in-chief with failure to reconnoiter the rebel position before committing his troops, with failure to use the ships either against the exposed rebel left flank or in cutting them off at the Neck by landing in their rear, and with failure to pursue them in retreat. He blamed Howe for allowing his men to fire as they advanced, and for bringing them up in lines instead of in columns. "The wretched blunder of the over-sized balls," he growled, "sprung from the dotage of an officer of rank in that corps, who spends his whole time in dallying with the schoolmaster's daughters. God knows, he is old enough. He is no Samson, yet he must have his Delilah." "Equally true and astonishing," thought the angry officer, was that Gage knew in May the rebel intention of taking Bunker Hill and yet did nothing himself to secure it. In sum, said the sharp-tongued commentator:

We are all wrong at the head. My mind cannot help dwelling upon our cursed mistakes. Such ill conduct at the first outset argues a gross ignorance of the most common and obvious rules of the profession and gives us for the future anxious forebodings. I have lost some of those I most valued. This madness or ignorance nothing can excuse. The brave men's lives were wantonly thrown away. Our conductor as much murdered them as if he had cut their throats himself on Boston Common. Had he fallen, ought we to have regretted him?[11]

General Gage was indeed solely responsible for the attack and for its blunders. Nevertheless, he blandly overlooked in detail his own responsibility, although a few days later, he admitted to Lord Barrington, Secretary at War, that everything had been done wrong:

You will receive an account of some success against the rebels, but attended with a long list of killed and wounded on our side, so many of the latter that the hospital has hardly hands sufficient to take care of them. These people show a spirit and conduct against us they never showed against the French, and everybody has judged of them from their former appearance and behavior when joined with the King's forces in the last war, which has led many into great mistakes.

They are now spirited up by a rage and enthusiasm as great as ever people were possessed of, and you must proceed in earnest or give the business up. A small body acting in one spot will not avail. You must have large armies, making diversions on different sides, to divide their force.

The loss we have sustained is greater than we can bear; small armies can't afford such losses, especially when the advantage gained tends to little more than the gaining of a post—a material one indeed, as our own security depended on it. The troops are sent out too late. The rebels were at least two months before-hand with us, and your Lordship would be astonished to see the tract of country they have entrenched and fortified. Their number is great, so many hands have been employed.

We are here, to use a common expression, "taking the bull by the horns," attacking the enemy in their strong parts. I wish this cursed place was burned; the only use is its harbor, which may be said to be material, but in all other respects it's the worst place either to act offensively from, or defensively. I have before wrote to your Lordship my opinion, that a large army must at length be employed to reduce these people and mentioned the hiring of foreign troops. I fear it must come to that, or else to avoid a land war and make use only of your fleet. I don't find one province in appearance better disposed than another, though I think if this army was in New York that we should find many friends and be able to raise forces in that province on the side of government.[12]

Gage and Howe had had enough for the present. Clinton argued vainly with them to seize Dorchester Heights. From Foster's Hill there, he said, the rebels could do more harm to Boston than ever they might have done from Charlestown. He insisted, "if we were ever driven from Boston it would be by the enemy batteries at Foster Hill." But Gage determinedly stood on the defensive, and soon it was evident that he would continue to do so. The one battle that never should have been fought for the hill that never should have been defended was all. The British strongly fortified Bunker Hill and then Breed's and remained in possession of the peninsula. The rebels, after fortifying Winter Hill, built works atop Prospect Hill to the eastward, and within a week were strengthening their lines all the way round to Roxbury. And the armies settled to inactivity.

"THE SOUND OF WAR ECHOES FROM NORTH TO SOUTH"

America Finds a General

MAY-JUNE 1775

Philad. July 5, 1775

Mr. Strahan,

You are a member of Parliament and one of that Majority which has doomed my Country to Destruction. You have begun to burn our Towns and murder our People. Look upon your Hands! They are stained with the Blood of your Relations! You and I were long Friends: You are now my Enemy,

and
I am
Yours,
B. Franklin[1]

ANGRY BUT worldly-wise old Ben Franklin, recently returned after eighteen years in London as agent for the colonies, never mailed that letter to his old crony, William Strahan, the great London printer and publisher; but certainly it indicated the way he and many other colonists felt after Lexington and Concord and Bunker Hill. The fight was no longer New England's alone: throughout America, Boston's countrymen began to prepare for war.

In New York, a recent arrival from London "saw nothing but rubbing up arms, enlisting, exercising, and every other preparation, denoting a vigorous resolution in the people to defend themselves against all oppressors to the very last." Citizens of Maryland wore cockades in their hats and stepped to fife and drum. In Virginia, where the people were said to be "even madder than in New England," every member of the House of Burgesses, it was observed, "has clothed himself in homespun and has each on the breast of his coat these words wrote with needlework or painting, LIBERTY OR DEATH; and with this on his breast each member sits in the House of Assembly." Charleston, South Carolina, quickly took on "rather the appearance of a garrison town than a mart for trade." In Benjamin Franklin's Philadelphia: "Every man here without distinction is learning the use of arms, and even the Quakers have their companies. It is a strange sight to see the young ones exercising and to hear the words, 'Shoulder thy fire-lock!' . . . What divisions remained, the measures of Parliament and the affair at Lexington have wholly done away."

By the time the Second Continental Congress convened in the Quaker City early in May, the atmosphere of the Pennsylvania capital was entirely martial. The affluent merchant-delegate from Connecticut, Silas Deane, wrote a long letter to his wife, describing the local militia "constantly out, morning and evening" exercising.

There are already thirty companies in this city in uniform, well armed, and have made a most surprising progress. The uniform is worth describing to you: it is a dark brown (like our homespun) coat, faced with red, white, yellow, or buff, according to their different battalions; white vest and breeches, white stockings, half-boots, black knee-garters. Their coat is made short, falling but little below the waistband of the breeches, which shows the size of a man to very great advantage. Their hats are small (as Jesse's little one, almost) with a red or white or black ribbon, according to their battalion, closing in a rose, out of which rises a tuft of fur of deer, made to resemble the buck's tail as much as possible, of about six or eight inches high. Their cartouche boxes are large, with the word, Liberty, and the number of their battalion wrote on the outside in large white letters.

Thus equipped they make a most elegant appearance, as their cartouche boxes are hung with a broad white wash-leather strap or belt and their bayonet, etc., on the other side with one of the same, which two, crossing on the shoulders diamond-fashion, gives an agreeable appearance viewed in the rear.

The Light Infantry are in green, faced with buff, vests, etc., as the others, except the cap, which is a hunter's cap, or jockey. These are, without exception, the genteelist companies I ever saw.

They have besides a body of irregulars or riflemen, whose dress it is hard to describe. They take a piece of ticklenburgh or tow cloth that is stout and put it in a tanvat until it has the shade of a dry or fading leaf. Then they make a kind of frock of it, reaching down below the knee, open before, with a large cape. They wrap it round them tight, on a march, and tie it with their belt, in which hangs their tomahawk. Their hats, as the others. . . . West of this city is an open square of near two miles each way with large groves each side, in which each afternoon they collect, with a vast number of spectators.[2]

The rifle used by these "irregulars" was practically unknown to the New Englanders, accustomed to the smooth-bore musket and fowling piece. Long in barrel, small in bore, light in weight, and perfectly balanced, it was the weapon of the professional hunter and woodsman, the man who eschewed every ounce of unnecessary burden and who could not afford to waste a single charge. Its barrel was spiral-grooved to give spin to its bullet, and its effective range more than doubled the musket's sixty yards. Its greatest disadvantage was that in order to benefit from its rifling, its bullet had to be fitted so tightly that it had to be forced home with an iron ramrod and a wooden mallet, a slow process. It had other disadvantages for line firing: the weather more easily rendered it useless; it had no bayonet, so that its users could not deliver or stand a charge; and surrounded by the smoke of a battle line, the riflemen could not aim carefully enough to take advantage of their weapon's unbelievable accuracy. But with all its disadvantages—especially its one or two shots a minute to the musket's four or five—it was nevertheless the most respected weapon of its time, and the man who carried it usually matched his gun: a breed unto himself, fit, sharp-eyed, woodswise, seasoned as hickory, superbly self-reliant, and hard to civilize. "What would a regular army of considerable strength in the forests of America do with a thousand of these men," asked a wondering civilian, "who want nothing to preserve their health and courage but water from the spring, with a little parched corn, with what they can easily procure in hunting; and who, wrapped in their blankets, in the damp of night, would choose the shade of a tree for their covering, and the earth for their bed."

The riflemen were called up by the Congress from the frontiers of Pennsylvania, Maryland, and Virginia. Down on the Rappahannock River in Virginia, John Harrower, an indentured servant teaching a plantation school, watched a rifle captain choose his company. The number of volunteers far exceeded the number of men called for, so to avoid offending the men, the captain set up a competition:

He took a board of a foot square and with chalk drew the shape of a moderate nose in the center and nailed it up to a tree at one hundred and fifty yards distance, and those who came nighest the mark with a single ball was to go. But by the first forty or fifty that fired, the nose was all blown out of the board, and by the time his company was up, the board shared the same fate.[3]

In spite of the martial ardor of its surroundings, the Congress did not hasten to adopt the army around Boston. Instead, its first few weeks were spent in the consideration and recommendation of some general measures of defense. When New York requested advice on its defense, should expected British troops arrive, a Congressional committee recommended that New York maintain a defensive attitude as long as possible, but oppose any enemy attempts to erect fortifications, to sever communication between the city and the rest of the country, or to invade private property; specific suggestions for the raising and stationing of troops followed.

Another committee was formed to study "ways and means to supply these colonies with ammunition and military stores," and a third to consider the best means of establishing a postal service. A resolution was passed that no one should supply British troops in America; a committee was set up to borrow £6,000 for the purchase of gunpowder for what was called "the Continental Army," though in truth no such body yet existed; another committee sat to estimate how much money would be needed to defend the colonies; and six companies of riflemen were authorized. But while the muggy summer heat increased, and the New Englanders particularly perspired and fretted, no one moved that Congress should adopt the army outside Boston. The fifty-odd delegates continued to hang back even after the desperate appeal of the Massachusetts Provincial Congress. A strong faction was endeavoring instead to persuade the Congress to send a second "Humble and Dutiful" petition to His Majesty, for negotiation and accommodation of the unhappy disputes between colonies and Crown.

Against the would-be petitioners stood Sam Adams' country cousin, John. John Adams was thirteen years younger and profoundly different: logical, cautious, self-examining, and scrupulously honest. Most of his life had been spent on the family farm in the beautiful, rocky country just outside Braintree, ten miles south of Boston on Boston Bay. He lived, off and on, in Boston, and became much more the successful lawyer than the husbandman, but inevitably he was drawn back to the rugged farmhouse at Braintree.

To his intelligent, knowledgeable wife, Abigail, and his children, he was passionately devoted. Unlike Sam, he could not leave their well-being to chance: providing well for their health, comfort, and schooling was his whole life. He was a thoughtful revolutionary, an architect rather than a destroyer, an adherent of gradual change rather than of sudden upheaval. This partridge-plump, bald, round-faced, snub-nosed little man of thirty-nine was as forthright as he was honest.

This great believer in confederation, this adroit statesman, sat in Philadelphia's muggy June heat, because he had reached his decisions the slow, painful way and was ready for a new world.

And John Adams' new world did not include another petition to the King, more shilly-shallying, more words, words, words. The time for action was come. The country must have its army—the men around Boston should be its nucleus—and the army must have its leader. John Hancock, lately vaulted into especial prominence by his unanimous election to the Presidency of the Continental Congress to succeed retiring Peyton Randolph, was being mentioned as a possible successor to ailing General Ward. Although Hancock had seen no military service, he had cut a pretty figure as Colonel of the Company of Cadets of Boston. He or Ward seemed to be New England's choice for a commander-in-chief, but John Adams was not interested in either of them.

Already he had fixed his eyes upon the one man he was sure was capable of that great trust, the tall, taciturn delegate from Virginia, Colonel George Washington. Day after day, the big, two-hundred-pound, six-foot-three-inch, tidewater planter had sat in the Congress, his head slightly bent to all the debates and arguments, his pleasant, pockmarked face sober, saying little but giving sound advice on military questions. He wore the red-and-blue uniform of the Virginia militia perhaps to remind his colleagues that the time had come to take the field; certainly it was not to remind them of his soldier's background, for his career in the West was famous. Although he had met with less than brilliant success on the frontier during the French and Indian War, he had emerged as Virginia's most distinguished soldier, perhaps the most conspicuous native-born soldier on the continent.

In May, John Adams had written Abby that Colonel Washington "by his great experience and abilities in military matters is of much service to us." Individually, the colonel had failed to impress him in the sessions last fall, although he and his fellow Virginia delegates seemed to Adams "the most spirited and consistent of any delegation." Silas Deane at that time had been attracted by Washington's "soldierlike air and gesture." But perhaps Deane was influenced by the exaggerated stories then current of the Virginia aristocrat's enormous land holdings, slaves, and wealth, not to mention his romantic exploits in the field. An unfounded story was then circulating that upon hearing of the Boston Port Bill, Washington had offered in the Virginia Assembly to raise, arm, and lead a thousand men at his own expense in defense of the country.

A Virginian, who seemed to know Washington well, had described him in 1774:

> Colonel Washington was bred a soldier, a warrior, and distinguished himself in early life before and at the death of the unfortunate but intrepid Braddock. He is a modest man, but sensible and speaks little—in action, cool, like a Bishop at his prayers.[4]

This was John Adams' man. More and more talk about accommodation shortened the temper of the delegate from Braintree, until the idea of Washington as commander-in-chief of a Continental Army became a conviction. He squared the last doubt of his New England conscience by recognizing that a commander-in-chief from the South would clinch adoption of the army: It would be no longer a New England army exclusively, and he knew also that only a Southern general would be able to bring Southern men into the field.

In his diary he later wrote of these days:

> This measure of imbecility, the second petition to the King, embarrassed every exertion of Congress; it occasioned motions and debates without end for appointing committees to draw up a declaration of the causes, motives, and objects of taking arms, with a view to obtain decisive declarations against independence, etc.
>
> In the meantime the New England army investing Boston, the New England legislatures, congresses, and conventions, and the whole body of the people, were left without munitions of war, without arms, clothing, pay, or even countenance and encouragement. Every post brought me letters from my friends, . . . urging in pathetic terms the impossibility of keeping their men together without the assistance of Congress.
>
> I was daily urging all these things, but we were embarrassed with more than one difficulty, not only with the party in favor of the petition to the King and the party who were jealous of independence, but a third party, which was a Southern party against a Northern, and a jealousy against a New England army under the command of a New England General. Whether this jealousy was sincere, or whether it was mere pride and a haughty ambition of furnishing a Southern General to command the Northern army, I cannot say, but the intention was very visible to me that Colonel Washington was their object, and so many of our staunchest men were in the plan, that we could carry nothing without conceding to it.
>
> Another embarrassment, which was never publicly known, and which was carefully concealed by those who knew it,

the Massachusetts and other New England delegates were divided. Mr. Hancock and Mr. [Thomas] Cushing hung back; Mr. [Robert Treat] Paine did not come forward, and even Mr. Samuel Adams was irresolute. Mr. Hancock himself had an ambition to be appointed commander-in-chief. Whether he thought an election a compliment due to him, and intended to have the honor of declining it, or whether he would have accepted, I know not. To the compliment he had some pretensions, for, at that time, his exertions, sacrifices, and general merits in the cause of his country had been incomparably greater than those of Colonel Washington. But the delicacy of his health, and his entire want of experience in actual service, though an excellent militia officer, were decisive objections to him in my mind. In canvassing this subject, out of doors, I found, too, that even among the delegates of Virginia there were difficulties. The apostolical reasonings among themselves, which should be greatest, were not less energetic among the saints of the ancient dominion than they were among us of New England. In several conversations, I found more than one very cool about the appointment of Washington, and particularly Mr. [Edmund] Pendleton was very clear and full against it.

Full of anxieties concerning these confusions, and apprehending daily that we should hear very distressing news from Boston, I walked with Mr. Samuel Adams in the State House yard for a little exercise and fresh air, before the hour of Congress, and there represented to him the various dangers that surrounded us. He agreed to them all, but said, "What shall we do?"

I answered him that he knew I had taken great pains to get our colleagues to agree upon some plan, that we might be unanimous; but he knew that they would pledge themselves to nothing; but I was determined to take a step which should compel them and all the other members of Congress to declare themselves for or against something. "I am determined this morning to make a direct motion that Congress should adopt the army before Boston, and appoint Colonel Washington commander of it."[5]

And so it was that, on June 14, when Congress assembled, John Adams rose in his place:

. . . and in as short a speech as the subject would admit, represented the state of the colonies. . . . I concluded with a motion, in form, that Congress would adopt the army at Cambridge and appoint a general; that though this was not the proper time to nominate a general, yet, as I had reason to believe this was a point of the greatest difficulty, I had no hesitation to declare that I had but one gentleman in my mind for that important command, and that was a gentleman from Virginia who was among us and very well known to all of us, a gentleman whose skill and experience as an officer, whose independent fortune, great talents, and excellent universal character, would command the appro- bation of all America and unite the cordial exertions of all the Colonies better than any other person in the Union. Mr. Washington, who happened to sit near the door, as soon as he heard me allude to him, from his usual modesty, darted into the library-room. Mr. Hancock, who was our Presi- dent, which gave me an opportunity to observe his counte- nance while I was speaking on the state of the Colonies, the army at Cambridge, and the enemy, heard me with visible pleasure; but when I came to describe Washington for the commander, I never remarked a more sudden and striking change of countenance. Mortification and resentment were expressed as forcibly as his face could exhibit them. Mr. Samuel Adams seconded the motion, and that did not soften the President's physiognomy at all.

The subject came under debate, and several gentlemen de- clared themselves against the appointment of Mr. Washing- ton, not on account of any personal objection against him, but because the army were all from New England, had a gen- eral of their own, appeared to be satisfied with him, and had proved themselves able to imprison the British army in Bos- ton, which was all they expected or desired at that time. . . . The subject was postponed to a future day. In the meantime, pains were taken out of doors to obtain a unanimity, and the voices were generally so clearly in favor of Washington, that the dissentient members were persuaded to withdraw their opposition. . . .[6]

The next day, while Washington absented himself, the Congress resolved that a general be appointed to command all the Continental forces raised or to be raised in defense of the colonies. Thomas Johnson of Maryland rose and proposed Washington. No other name was put forward; election was unanimous.

Washington of course had known that he was being advo- cated by some Delegates and, after being championed by John Adams, could not have been surprised when he was ad- dressed at suppertime as "General" and told by the Delegates of his election. He spent the evening preparing a reply to the formal notification of his election he could expect the next day.

When the Congress convened in the morning, John Han- cock, from the chair, informed Washington of his appoint- ment and expressed the hope of the Congress that George Washington, Esquire, would accept their choice of him as

General and Commander-in-Chief of the forces raised and to be raised for the defense of America. The Colonel bowed, took a paper from his pocket and read:

> Mr. President: Though I am truly sensible of the high honor done me in this appointment, yet I feel great distress from a consciousness that my abilities and military experience may not be equal to the extensive and important trust. However, as the Congress desire, I will enter upon the momentous duty, and exert every power I possess in their service, and for the support of the glorious cause: I beg they will accept my most cordial thanks for this distinguished testimony of their approbation.
>
> But, lest some unlucky event should happen unfavorable to my reputation, I beg it may be remembered by every gentleman in the room, that I this day declare with the utmost sincerity, I do not think myself equal to the command I am honored with.
>
> As to pay, sir, I beg leave to assure the Congress that as no pecuniary consideration could have tempted me to have accepted this arduous employment at the expense of my domestic ease and happiness, I do not wish to make any profit from it: I will keep an exact account of my expenses; those I doubt not they will discharge, and that is all I desire.[7]

Washington had sound reasons for doubting his qualifications for supreme command. His military service was limited to five years in a militia company, where he had learned only as much as an intelligent colonel might be expected to master. He had no experience in tactics except those of the wilderness, where field evolutions and deployment were unknown. He had never formulated large strategical plans. He knew nothing of cavalry, had not directed artillery, had never commanded any considerable body of men. He knew nothing of supply or the care of the wounded and the sick. But he did know that discipline was the soul of an army, and he had an infinite patience and a cold, calculating boldness. As a soldier, a man of affairs, and a gentleman, his character was above reproach, his ambition was limitless, and his will was inflexible. These things could be counted upon to carry him and his country a long way, even though no one recognized more clearly than their possessor that for the enormous task ahead they were but minimum requirements. To his friend Patrick Henry, Colonel Washington said sorrowfully, "From the day I enter upon the command of the American armies I date my fall and the ruin of my reputation."

The sentiments he expressed publicly were his most private ones as well. To his beloved Martha he wrote:

My Dearest: I am now set down to write you on a subject which fills me with inexpressible concern, and this concern is greatly aggravated and increased, when I reflect upon the uneasiness I know it will cause you. It has been determined in Congress that the whole army raised for the defense of the American cause shall be put under my care, and that it is necessary for me to proceed immediately to Boston to take upon me the command of it.

You may believe me, my dear Patsy, when I assure you in the most solemn manner that, so far from seeking this appointment, I have used every endeavor in my power to avoid it, not only from my unwillingness to part with you and the family, but from a consciousness of its being a trust too great for my capacity, and that I should enjoy more real happiness in one month with you at home than I have the most distant prospect of finding abroad, if my stay were to be seven times seven years. But as it has been a kind of destiny that has thrown me upon this service, I shall hope that my undertaking it is designed to answer some good purpose. You might, and I suppose did, perceive, from the tenor of my letters, that I was apprehensive I could not avoid this appointment, as I did not pretend to intimate when I should return. That was the case. It was utterly out of my power to refuse this appointment, without exposing my character to such censure as would have reflected dishonor upon myself, and have given pain to my friends. . . . I shall rely, therefore, confidently on that Providence which has heretofore preserved and been bountiful to me, not doubting but that I shall return safe to you in the fall. I shall feel no pain from the toil or the danger of the campaign, my unhappiness will flow from the uneasiness I know you will feel from being left alone. . . .

If it should be your desire to remove into Alexandria (as you once mentioned upon an occasion of this sort) I am quite pleased that you should put it into practice, and Lund Washington may be directed by you to build a kitchen and other houses there proper for your reception. If, on the other hand, you should rather incline to spend a good part of your time among your friends below, I wish you to do so. In short my earnest and ardent desire is that you will pursue any plan that is most likely to produce content, and a tolerable degree of tranquility; as it must add greatly to my uneasy feelings to hear that you are dissatisfied or complaining at what I really could not avoid.

As life is always uncertain, and common prudence dictates to every man the necessity of settling his temporal concerns while it is in his power, and while the mind is calm and undisturbed, I have since I came to this place (for I had not time to do it before I left home) got Colonel Pendleton to draft a will for me, by the directions I gave him, which will I now enclose. . . . P. S. Since writing the above I have received your letter of the fifteenth and have got two suits of what I was told was the prettiest muslin. I wish it may please you. It cost 50/ a suit, that is 20/ a yard.[8]

Next after Washington were named two major generals who were to be his senior subordinates, and an adjutant general to keep headquarters records and perform minor executive duties for the Commander-in-Chief. Artemas Ward, general of the Massachusetts army, was chosen "first major general." The second was Charles Lee, a strange, ugly, gifted British veteran of American and foreign wars, now newly settled in America, who had impressed both Washington and the Congress with his vast military experience, but who accepted his commission only after the Congress agreed to indemnify him for "any loss of property which he may sustain by entering into their service." He had actually seen much more service than the Commander-in-Chief; he was a serious student of warfare and, perhaps, Washington's only military rival. Major Horatio Gates, Washington's acquaintance and another former companion-in-arms, was made adjutant general. Philip Schuyler, rich New York landowner and merchant, and Israel Putnam, unknown to Washington and most of the delegates but renowned in his own New England, were also made major generals. Eight brigadiers were chosen: Seth Pomeroy, William Heath, and Joseph Thomas, of Massachusetts; David Wooster and John Spencer, of Connecticut; John Sullivan, of New Hampshire; Richard Montgomery, of New York; and Nathanael Greene, of Rhode Island. Other grade levels were authorized for appointment.

On June 23, Washington wrote a short note to his "Dearest," and armed with his commission and instructions from the Congress, mounted his horse for the long ride northward to his army. Setting off with him were the generals Charles Lee and Philip Schuyler and two handsome young men, his aide-de-camp, Thomas Mifflin, and his military secretary, Joseph Reed. Rain was falling, but it did not dampen the enthusiasm of the Massachusetts delegates and others in their carriages, nor that of the Philadelphia Light Horse, which with its music escorted the General a distance on his way.

Perhaps it was a let down to see the military party out of sight. John Adams, riding in one of the carriages, suddenly was very bitter, maybe envious, and certainly self-pitying. He himself had always wanted to be a soldier. He returned to his quarters and gave way to one of his frequent depressions; he wrote to Abby:

. . . Such is the pride and pomp of war. I, poor creature, worn out with scribbling for my bread and my liberty,
low in spirits and weak in health, must leave others to wear
the laurels which I have sown; others to eat the bread which
I have earned; a common case.[9]

The new General of the army left behind him in Philadelphia a Congress a little more willing to advance preparations for war. Having at last adopted the army in Massachusetts, the Congress issued for its support Continental currency to be redeemed by the twelve federated colonies, drew
up Articles of War, established secret committees for im-
porting gunpowder, and otherwise girded colonial loins.

It was not an easy business. Many divergent minds had to
be brought to accord. Few delegates shared identical opinions
on the extent to which they should go in opposition to the
Crown; few could agree on the function of the Congress,
which was still undefined. It remained an illegal body whose
power derived only from the consent of the represented colonies to accept its advice, and the delegates were sent with
varying instructions and could commit their colonies only to
varying degrees. Frequently the Congress sat as a committee
of the whole to consider the state of America, and then the
differences of opinion among the delegates were brought into
harmony. It was a hard-working body and kept long hours:
"Our debates and deliberations are tedious," wrote John
Adams to his wife, "from nine to four, five, and once near
six." Silas Deane wrote home one midnight: "The history of
this day is—rose at five, breakfasted and dressed by seven;
at half past, met a Committee in the State House on business,
and never left the house till past five this afternoon, when I
went to dine with a stomach, or appetite, so, so; immediately
after which, other business called. . . ." Another day he
sighed, "eleven hours at a sitting is too much for my constitution."

Despite long hours of exhausting debate and depressing
differences of opinion, by the time the Congress recessed the
first day of August it had provided the colonies with an army,
money, and some of the machinery of war. And it had established for the future that at Philadelphia men would work as
laboriously for the cause of freedom as would soldiers in
the field. To the names of Washington, Lee, Gates, Ward,
Putnam, and others at Boston and others yet to come, must
now be added the Adamses, Franklin, Jefferson, Jay, Dickinson, Richard Henry Lee, Edmund Pendleton, James Wil-
son, Silas Deane, Patrick Henry, Samuel Ward, Roger Sherman.

For a war in defense of their liberties *within the Empire,* they were ready to make every sacrifice, but few if any of them except the Adamses desired independence; it was seldom mentioned, and generally, the people, while making firelocks, molding bullets, making saltpeter, storing provisions, marching, and drilling, clung still to the hope of conciliation. In Maryland a clergyman lamented:

> Unhappy Britain! Unhappy America! Had an angel from Heaven told me but two years ago that your dissolution was to have been hurried on so precipitately, I could not have believed it. . . .

However they may be represented to him, the King has not more affectionate or more loyal subjects in any part of his dominions than the Americans. They desire no other King; they wish not a division from or independence on the Mother Country. They have taken up arms, it is true, in defense of their lives, privileges, and properties, invaded by the machinations of a set of Ministers, at the bottom equally inimical to both countries; but are ready to lay them down, and return within the line of their duty, whenever their just complaints are heard, and grievances redressed.[10]

A Virginian expressed to a Scottish friend his mixed emotions:

> . . . Tears stand in my eyes when I think . . . of this once happy . . . land of liberty. All is anarchy and confusion. . . . We are all in arms. . . . The sound of war echoes from north to south. Every plain is full of armed men. . . . May God put a speedy and happy end to this grand and important contest between the mother and her children. The colonies do not wish to be independent; they only deny the right of taxation in Parliament. They would freely grant the King whatever he pleases to request of their own Assemblies, provided the Parliament has no hand in the disposing of it.[11]

In Virginia, or in Philadelphia, women prepared to grieve and to sacrifice. From Philadelphia one wrote:

> My only brother I have sent to the camp with my prayers and blessings; I hope he will not disgrace me. I am confident he will behave with honor, and emulate the great examples he has before him; and had I twenty sons and brothers they should go. I have retrenched every superfluous expense in my table and family . . . and what I never did before, have learnt to knit and am now making stockings of American wool for my servants, and this way do I throw in my mite for the public good . . .[12]

But the people, in spite of their doubts and fears, and in spite of the studied care with which their leaders avoided any step that might lead irrevocably to independence, worked diligently that summer to arm and to prepare themselves; the tread of marching feet resounded firm and determined. The people were taking liberty fever, for what else could account for Mr. Coggeshall's attitude toward that most sacrosanct of His Majesty's symbols of authority, an armed vessel patrolling Newport harbor? The newspapers told that Coggeshall exposed his sentiments immodestly:

Early last Saturday morning, one Coggeshall, being somewhat drunk or crazy, went on the long wharf and turned up his backside towards the bomb brig in this harbor, using some insulting words, upon which the brig fired two four-pound shot at him; one of which went through the roof of Mr. Hammond's store . . . and lodged in Mr. Samuel Johnston's distill house. . . .[13]

6

"NEW LORDS, NEW LAWS"

Washington Takes Command

SUMMER 1775

On a quiet Sunday afternoon, July 2, 1775, the new Commander-in-Chief and his military family—except Schuyler, who had been left to command in New York—arrived in the beautiful little college town of Cambridge. The commodious house of the President of Harvard College had been prepared as Washington's headquarters. There the General soon met some of the officers commanding the forces around Boston. Before dark, in company with several of them and some of his own staff, he set off for a preliminary view of the fortifications. In the party rode General Ward, saying little and riding easy because of his ailment. Putnam, his farmer's nose enjoying the clean rain-washed air of the quiet Sabbath afternoon, was with them, and caustic, talkative Lee, perched on his horse like a broomstick scarecrow and trailed by the dogs that were his constant companions.

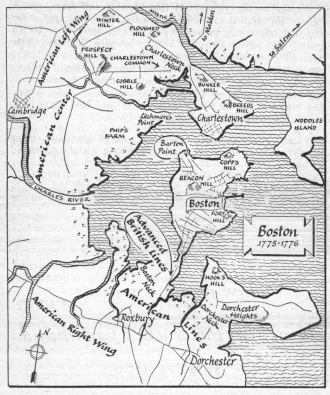

From Prospect Hill, about a mile from Cambridge, Washington could see Boston, whose streets he had last trod nineteen years before when he had journeyed north to present to General William Shirley his claims in a dispute over rank with another soldier-servant of the King. Directly before him, a little more than a quarter of a mile, was a rise his guides called Cobble Hill, an excellent gun position. On all sides, thin woods and cleared fields fell away to salt marshes and open water. About a mile off, east and southeast, stood Bunker Hill, where redcoat sentinels strode. To the southeast, he could see Roxbury, and parts of Dorchester. At a glance he saw that the American redoubts were weak and several of them badly placed, but that some of the positions in this rolling country were naturally strong. By building works well and placing batteries wisely, he could hope to confine the

British to Boston and Charlestown, while he trained an army.

The next morning, without ceremony, he took over command from General Ward. His first orders called for a return of the troops and of the quantity of ammunition in each regiment. For the following two or three days, he toured the lines, appraising his forces, their camps, and their fortifications. General Lee accompanied him around the eight- to nine-mile semicircle and wrote ruefully to his old friend, banker Robert Morris in Philadelphia: "We found everything exactly the reverse of what had been represented. We were assured at Philadelphia that the army was stocked with engineers. We found not one. We were assured that we should find an expert train of artillery. They have not a single gunner, and so on. . . ."

Lack of gunners to handle the few cannon that had been brought to the siege did not disturb Lee half so much as the dearth of officers with engineering training; he realized as well as Washington that the first task of the army must be proper fortification. Two weeks later, he remarked of the army, "I really believe not a single man of 'em is capable of constructing an oven," and soon he himself was trying to fill the need. "I work like ten post horses," he wrote. "Our miserable defect of engineers imposes upon me eternal work in a department to which I am rather a stranger."

But the acidulous Lee, complaining against the exaggerated impression of the army given the officers before they came, was not discouraged: they are "really very fine fellows," he admitted, "and had they fair play would make an invincible army." He was particularly taken by the Rhode Island officers and was doubtless pleased when Washington assigned the Rhode Island troops and New Hampshire and Massachusetts forces under Nathanael Greene and John Sullivan to the left wing of the army, over which he was placed.

Nathanael Greene, the brigadier general in command of the Rhode Island forces, was the youngest of the generals elected by the Continental Congress. He was a pleasant man, moderately tall and well set up, with a rugged, candid face, eyes of bright blue, a full mouth deep-set, and a finely chiseled nose. He was a man of labor, one of the sons of a Quaker preacher who had reared him to run the family flour, grist, and saw-mills and forge. He had educated himself, especially in mathematics, history, and political theory. Although a Quaker, he had come to believe in the necessity for resistance to the Crown and to support it at the cost of expulsion from the Society of Friends for forsaking pacifism. Resolutely he had served the Rhode Island Assembly in setting up militia laws, and had enlisted in a local company.

The husky ironmonger was genial but impetuous, and sensitive. When his friends and neighbors intimated that his stiff left leg, which gave him a decided limp, was a blemish to the company, Nathanael concealed his hurt and graciously volunteered to withdraw, but he was persuaded to stay. Only six months later, when the Assembly voted itself an army and sent it to Cambridge, Nathanael Greene was unanimous choice as brigadier general in command. His talents, though undeveloped, were evidently recognized; he knew how to manage men, to husband resources, to exercise great patience and intelligent caution, and he believed in discipline.

If Nathanael Greene's soldierly qualities impressed General Lee, certainly Lee's own incredible eccentricities did not escape Greene's notice. Lee's first Cambridge residence was at Washington's headquarters. But when Washington moved, a few days after his arrival, to the abandoned house of loyalist John Vassall, Lee's headquarters were transferred to General Royall's place at Medford. He promptly styled it "Hobgoblin Hall," and the moody master of Hobgoblin Hall was soon a familiar figure in the drawing rooms of the neighborhood, as well as upon the lines. Abigail Adams, who met him socially, thought he looked "like a careless, hardy veteran, and by his appearance brought to my mind his namesake, Charles the Twelfth of Sweden. The elegance of his pen far exceeds that of his person."

Lee himself would have agreed. From Philadelphia, he had opened a highflown correspondence with General Burgoyne, with whom he had served years before on the European continent. At Boston he continued communicating through the lines by flag. His letters were pure propaganda, assailing the King and charging that Burgoyne and Howe, who was a Whig, should refuse to serve against the colonies. He published his first letter to Burgoyne before the general had received it. The exchange led to a proposal by Burgoyne that they meet between the lines to renew their old friendship and to allow Burgoyne to deliver letters he brought from Lee's English friends. Lee sent Burgoyne's proposal to the Provincial Congress for its opinion and rejected the offer when the Congress suggested that it might cast doubt upon Lee's fidelity to the cause.

The impression the spindly, ugly soldier made upon all who met him was expressed by Jeremy Belknap, minister and historian, who first met him in August at dinner at the headquarters of Thomas Mifflin. Later Belknap wrote in his journal:

General Lee is a perfect original, a good scholar and soldier; and an odd genius, full of fire and passion and but little good manners; a great sloven, wretchedly profane, and a great admirer of dogs, of which he had two at dinner with him, one of them a native of Pomerania, which I should have taken for a bear had I seen him in the woods.

A letter which he wrote General Putnam . . . is a copy of his odd mind, . . . being a letter of introduction of one Page, a church clergyman:

> Hobgoblin Hall . . .
> Dear General: Mr. Page, the bearer of this, is a Mr. Page. He has the laudable ambition of seeing the great General Putnam. I, therefore, desire you would array yourself in all your majesty and terrors for his reception. Your blue and gold must be mounted, your pistols stuck in your girdle; and it would not be amiss if you should black one half of your face. I am, dear general, with fear and trembling, your humble servant,
>
> Charles Lee[1]

It was in those first days riding the lines with Lee that Washington was introduced to another young man whose promise was as great as that of Nathanael Greene. On their way to Roxbury, they met Henry Knox, a round, fat, convivial young man of twenty-five, with merry gray eyes and nicely modeled features in a face already acquiring its second chin. Knox was a Boston bookseller until the outbreak of hostilities. Since then he had been serving with General Ward as a volunteer, and this morning was bound for Cambridge. But at the request of the generals he turned about and showed them the works facing Boston Neck. He was proud of them, for he had helped lay them out.

Knox was an able guide. His comprehension of the problems of defense was surprising in one so young and obviously inexperienced, but behind it lay a consuming interest, intensive study, and a natural feeling for the problems of warfare. He had grown up a Whig and perhaps had met secretly with Sam Adams' group of plotters at the Green Dragon Tavern, but he had not been vociferous about his politics. He was married to Lucy Flucker, daughter of the royal Secretary of the Province, and his livelihood depended considerably upon the patronage of British officials and soldiers. His bookshop, near the Province House was, according to a customer, a place of "great display and attraction for young and old and a fashionable lounging place," but books did not sell as profitably as shoes, "goloshoes," dry goods, utensils, linens and other necessary commodities, and it behooved a bookseller to keep all the trade he could get. For the British officers he laid in a stock of works on the arts of war, especially artillery, which he himself read and discussed voraciously with them. In his shop Nathanael Greene had purchased military books. Either the jolly bookseller's friendly, innocent manner or his close connection with a leading Tory family had enabled him to publish and sell at least one liberty tract without getting into trouble; *The Other Side of the Question: or, A Defense of the Liberties of North America—In Answer to a late Friendly Address to all Reasonable Americans on the Subject of our Political Confusions, By a Citizen* could be had that spring of Henry Knox in Cornhill.

Although now Knox was serving only as a civilian volunteer, Washington bore him in mind for a future appointment.

The General's tour of the lines was discouraging, a fact he did not hide from Congress in his first report. After outlining the positions held by the British and by the Americans, he set down the disadvantages under which he labored. His excuse for not writing until eight days after his arrival was the failure of the officers to make the returns he had requested. He admitted that he was "drilled on," that is, put off, day after day by them; it was beyond his conception that "what ought, and, in a regular army, would have been done in an hour, would employ eight days," and when the returns finally were on his desk, he was stunned to find the army much smaller than he had been told it was and destitute of all things needed for waging war. But he cautioned that "this unhappy and devoted province has been so long in a state of anarchy and the yoke of ministerial oppression so heavily laid that great allowances are to be made for their troops collected under such circumstances. The deficiencies in their numbers, their discipline, and stores can only lead to this conclusion, that their spirit has exceeded their strength."

The first basic needs were for engineers who could construct proper works, for tools, and for a sufficient number of men to man the works in case of an attack. Although the army had collected all available sails from nearby seaport towns and converted them into tents, the number was far short of needs. Powder had been on the General's mind all the way northward, and now he felt he "must re-echo the former complaints on this subject." What was on hand must be reserved for small arms. Until ammunition arrived, his artillery would be useless. The soldiers already were ragged, and he was told that no clothing was obtainable in Massachusetts; ten thousand hunting shirts, such as riflemen wore, he thought, would be the quickest, cheapest way to supply the army: "I know nothing so trivial in a speculative view that in practice would have a happy tendency to unite the men and abolish those provincial distinctions which lead to jealousy and dissatisfaction." An enlarged general staff, he insisted, must be appointed at once to include a commissary general, a quartermaster general, a commissary of musters, and a commissary of artillery. He reminded the Congress that he "already was much embarrassed for want of a military chest"; money, "this most necessary article," he earnestly requested "as soon as possible."

Before the Congress the General placed another matter of great concern. On the afternoon he reached Cambridge, he had handed to Israel Putnam his commission as one of the four Congress-appointed major generals. But a few hours revealed a situation that prompted Washington to withhold the other Congressional commissions until he could discuss them further with Congress. He discovered that seniority as prescribed by the Congress often did not accord with opinions held by civil and military leaders in New England and had created great "disgusts" among the generals. When he saw General Joseph Spencer—angry because Putnam, whom he outranked in Connecticut service, was named over him—depart the army, "without visiting me or making known his intention in any respect," the General was deeply worried. General Seth Pomeroy had retired in pique even before Washington's arrival, and capable General John Thomas, who had outranked both William Heath and Pomeroy, was determined to withdraw because he was listed junior to them. It was a vexatious problem. Good officers, particularly men with experience, were too valuable to lose. It persisted for a long time and annoyed the General's days and nights until everyone could be accommodated.

These were all problems upon which Washington could expect Congressional aid. One of the worst, the almost entire absence of discipline, he must solve himself. "The abuses in this army, I fear, are considerable," he told Lee. To the Congress he said:

It requires no military skill to judge of the difficulty of introducing discipline and subordination into an army while we have the enemy in view and are in daily expectation of an attack, but it is of so much importance that every effort will be made to this end which time and circumstances will admit.[2]

One of the main troubles was that these volunteers could see no reason why they should not return home to look after private affairs during a period of inactivity. Nor were they willing to submit to onerous duties and rules of behavior they themselves did not formulate. The British seemed helpless enough cooped up in the town, so what was wrong with a fellow's taking a little nap on guard, there were plenty of sentries. And anyway Captain Baldwin, who kept the harness shop across from the meeting at home, was not likely to be hard on the boys who had chosen him their captain. The result was that from the moment of Washington's coming and the beginning of discipline, orderly books were quickly filled with notices of courts-martial for a number of offenses: leaving post while on guard, drunkenness, abusive language to officers, sleeping on post, insulting the sentry, theft, and other offenses.

Infractions of military law were not confined to private soldiers. Washington's first court-martial sat to investigate the charge that the quartermaster of a Massachusetts regiment had drawn "provisions for more men than the regiment consisted of." One captain was found guilty of taking home large quantities of food issued for his troops, and other officers of withholding their men's pay. It was enough to vex any professional soldier, and Charles Lee proved he had not been named "Boiling Water" by the Indians without reason. One day Lieutenant Benjamin Craft scratched in his journal: "Stephen Stanwood for saucy talk to Gen. Lee had his head broke. The General gave him a dollar and sent for the doctor."

The strongest bar to discipline, as Washington saw it, was the "leveling" doctrine that had been at work in New England for generations. The Virginia society of Washington's acquaintance would have none of it. In Virginia it was held impossible, if not downright undesirable, to lessen the gap between the castes: a gentleman remained a gentleman, a person of lower station remained a person of lower station, and each recognized his responsibility toward the other. The New Englanders were full of what colonists farther south called "the leveling spirit," and which John Adams recognized was "very disagreeable to many gentlemen in the colonies."

Joseph Reed wrote his wife:

To attempt to introduce discipline and subordination into a new army must always be a work of much difficulty, but where the principles of democracy so universally prevail, where so great an equality and so thorough a leveling spirit predominates, either no discipline can be established, or he who attempts it must become odious and detestable, a position which no one will choose. . . . You may form some notion of it when I tell you that yesterday morning a captain of horse, who attends the general from Connecticut, was seen shaving one of his men on the parade near the house.[3]

Colonel Stephen Moylan, a hot-blooded Irishman from Pennsylvania, deplored the "spirit of equality which reigns through this country," and considered it reason enough why a person should not be sent on army business to the town in which he was born, because, he said, it "will make him afraid of exerting that authority necessary for the expediting his business. He must shake every man by the hand, and desire, beg, and pray, do brother, do my friend, do such a thing; whereas a few hearty damns from a person who did not care a damn for them would have a much better effect."

After six weeks of patient reasoning with the disgruntled New England officers, of disillusioning courts-martial of officers for cowardice at Bunker Hill, of wearisome efforts to overcome the leveling spirit and make an army of "a mixed multitude," Washington's aristocratic soul poured forth its burden to his brother Lund:

> The people of this government have obtained a character which they by no means deserved; their officers generally speaking are the most indifferent kind of people I ever saw. I have already broke one colonel and five captains for cowardice and for drawing more pay and provisions than they had men in their companies. There is two more colonels now under arrest and to be tried for the same offenses. In short, they are by no means such troops, in any respect, as you are led to believe of them from the accounts which are published, but I need not make myself enemies among them by this declaration, although it is consistent with truth. I daresay the men would fight very well (if properly officered) although they are an exceedingly dirty and nasty people.[4]

A good part of Washington's justifiable wrath stemmed from Ward's easygoing nature. He often neglected to issue orders for days together, and James Warren, President of the Massachusetts Congress since the death of Joseph Warren, judged Ward's camp to be "spiritless, sluggish, confused, and dirty," in contrast to General Thomas', which was "spirited, active, regular, and clean." A frequent visitor to camp was the Reverend William Emerson, Concord minister. On his first trip after the coming of Washington, he wrote to his wife:

> There is great overturning in the camp as to order and regularity. New lords, new laws. The generals Washington and Lee are upon the lines every day. New orders from his Excellency are read to the respective regiments every morning after prayers. The strictest government is taking place and great distinction is made between officers and soldiers. Everyone is made to know his place and keep in it, or be immediately tied up, and receive not one but thirty or forty lashes

according to his crime. Thousands are at work every day from four till eleven o'clock in the morning. It is surprising the work that has been done. . . .[5]

If the camp of huts appeared helter-skelter, unmilitary, and inadequate to Washington, its very bigness and variety appealed to the inexperienced minister, who told Mrs. Emerson:

'Tis also very diverting to walk among the camps. They are as different in their form as the owners are in their dress; and every tent is a portraiture of the temper and taste of the persons that encamp in it. Some are made of boards, some of sailcloth, and some partly of one and partly of the other. Others are made of stone and turf, and others again of birch and other brush. Some are thrown up in a hurry and look as if they could not help it—mere necessity—others are curiously wrought with doors and windows done with wreaths and withes in the manner of a basket. Some are your proper tents and marquees and look like the regular camp of the enemy.[6]

What manner of man made up this army the iron-willed Virginian had come to command? He was Amos Farnsworth, pious young corporal from Groton, a serious, brave Puritan, much more concerned with his salvation than his skin. At Bunker Hill he took two wounds, but proudly recorded in his diary, "I did not leave the entrenchment until the enemy got in." After eight weeks leave to recover, he returned to the field, happy to find "a young gentleman that I could freely converse with on spiritual things."

Washington's soldier was seventeen-year-old David How, leather worker of Methuen. He was a shrewd Yankee trader, who never missed a chance to make a fast shilling and whose curiosity had a decidedly earthy quality. He was interested in such affairs as a drinking bout between two men in Cambridge who "Drinkd So much That one of them Died in About one hour or two after," or the discovery of "a man found Dead in a room with A Woman this morning. It is not known what killed him." He witnessed public punishments with stoic unconcern, although his comrade-at-arms, Amos Farnsworth, on such an occasion commented, "O what a pernitious thing it is for A man to steal and cheat his feller nabors, and how Provocking it is to God!"

Washington's soldier also was Daniel McCurtin, Scotch-Irish from western Maryland, one of Captain Michael Cresap's riflemen, who marched about five hundred and fifty miles to Cambridge in twenty-two days and called over twenty miles a day "a pleasant march." He saw only a few things along the way worth noting: "The barrenness of New Jersey, the rocks at the beginning of New England, the populousness of New England, the unfair number of fine ladies, the stones and walls of stone . . ." He took to soldiering easily, kept a record of the weather, delighted in camp gossip, and laughed at himself. He was stationed at Roxbury and was cannonaded loudly but harmlessly a few days after arriving there. He was breakfasting with three comrades in a dwelling taken over for billet. A British thirty-two-pounder "rushed through the room . . . and filled our dishes with plastering, ceiling and bricks . . . I went down two pairs of stairs of three strides without a fall and as soon as I was out of doors ran to the breastwork in great haste, which is our place of safety, without the least concern about my breakfast."

Another rifleman was Aaron Wright, from Northumberland, Pennsylvania. He and his comrades were sworn into service on June 29. "After this we chose our officers," he noted in the diary he kept of his services. A few days later came orders to march:

> When on parade, our first lieutenant came and told us he would be glad if we would excuse him from going, which we refused. But on consideration we concluded it was better to consent, after which he said he would go; but we said, "You shall not command us, for he whose mind can change in an hour is not fit to command in the field where liberty is contended for." In the evening we chose a private in his place.[7]

Thus were most of the officers selected, in all the army. The regiment in which Wright marched had a thumping good time on its way north. In New York the men frightened a Tory and "sarched" his goods; in Litchfield they "took a girl out of jail, and they tarred and feathered another Tory near Hartford, who said when they marched by that he was sorry to see so many men going to fight the king."

When the boys from Northumberland arrived in camp the effects of their indoctrination began to show strongly in Aaron Wright's diary. Fierce contempt for the enemy marked every page. The British became "redcoated Philistines," parapets were to secure "Sons of Liberty" against "the diabolical rage of the Parliamentary tools on Bunker Hill." Private Wright worked as a carpenter on barracks, dug entrenchments, mounted guard, and occasionally turned out on an alarm; he read newspapers when he could obtain them, walked, visited friends, was amused when "our clargyman preached with his hat on." One day he wrote in his diary, "Peace with our enemy, but disturbance enough with rum, for our men got money yesterday." On another he listened delightedly when

American artillery "made their balls rattle in Boston bravely." And every day he followed orders and served faithfully
but without distinction.

Big Jabez Fitch was another sort, but typical of many of
the men who tramped to Cambridge. He was an old campaigner. He had served in the war against the French in '56
and '57 and then returned to Norwich. In the summer of
1775 he was appointed first lieutenant of the Eighth Company of the Eighth Connecticut Regiment. He was a good
father, great social drinker, fine companion, something of a
wit, and a careless soldier who took things as they came. He
avoided work when he could, but accepted hardships without
complaint. At heart he was a tourist with a taste for oddities
and a talent for enjoying the trivial. In the summer he and
his son, Cordilla, joined the camp at Roxbury, "where money
will not readily command all the conveniences of life." The
company spent its second day in camp "pitching our tents,
&c.," but on the third Jabez obtained leave of the colonel to
go "over to the Neck and down to the Lower Point near
Castle William. . . . We had a very fine prospect of the town
of Boston and also of the ships in the harbor, which make an
appearance like a dry cedar swamp." His party was trapped
by the tides and forced to wade a distance in full view of
the British works, and arrived home in time to complain of
the butter at company dinner.

At most off-duty gatherings "the gin sling passed very
briskly" when Jabez Fitch was around, and banter was light
and constant:

I . . . mentioned among the officers Mr. Beckwith's observation . . . that before he left home he made a covenant with
his eyes concerning women, when Colonel Huntington replied
that there was no need of that here, for he and Mr. Trumbull
were yesterday obliged to use a spy glass to get a sight at
one.[8]

It was on another day that "Pease and I . . . went up beyond the Punch Bowl Tavern to find him some white-stock-
inged women, etc."

Like David How, Jabez Fitch traded, but not nearly so
cleverly. He was fairly free with his money if it would buy
comfort and a satisfying meal; he was tidy and objected
when soldiers were "as dirty as horses." He was social, yet
he enjoyed solitary rambles from which he returned leg-
weary, hungry, and refreshed, and he took considerable time
to write to his wife and to keep his journal.

Less desirable by far than the Farnsworths, Hows, Mc-
Curtins, Wrights, and Fitches, who might be made into sol-

diers by dint of ceaseless labor, were the dregs of New England, the habitual malcontents, who came to the army and left it when they discovered that its life was hard and ordered. Three such were advertised for in the fall of 1775 in the *Essex Gazette:*

Deserted from Colonel Brewer's regiment and Captain Harvey's company, one Simeon Smith, of Greenfield, a joiner by trade, a thin spared fellow about five feet, four inches high, had on a blue coat and black vest, a metal button on his hat, black long hair, black eyes, his voice in the hermaphrodite fashion, the masculine rather predominant. Likewise, one Mathias Smith, a small, smart fellow, gray-headed, has a younger look in his face, is apt to say, "I swear! I swear!" and between his words will spit smart; had on an old red great coat; he is a right gamester, although he wears a sober look. Likewise one John Darby, a long, hump-shouldered fellow, drawls his words, and for "comfortable" says "comfable," had on a green coat, thick leather breeches, slim legs, lost some of his fore teeth. . . . Whoever will take up said deserters and secure or bring them into camp, shall have two dollars reward for each, and all necessary charges paid by me.

Moses Harvey, Capt.[9]

Even the vaunted riflemen of whom Washington and the country expected so much proved to be more noisome than useful. It soon appeared that "the riflemen go where they please and keep the regulars in continual hot water." At first, as special outfits, they were excused from camp duties. With little to do following their triumphant march through the country, they found camp life dull and made sniping their pastime. They conducted one successful night raid on the British lines at Charlestown, creeping Indian style on hands and knees, and brought in prisoners for questioning. Soon, however, as Benjamin Thompson reported, it was realized that "instead of being the best marksmen in the world and picking off every regular that was to be seen, there is scarcely a regiment in camp but can produce men that can beat them at shooting, and the army is now universally convinced that the continual firing which they kept up by the week and month together has had no other effect than to waste their ammunition and convince the King's troops that they are not really so formidable . . . as they wish to be thought. . . . And to be sure, there never was a more mutinous and undisciplined set of villains that bred disturbance in any camp."

The riflemen were given to desertion, were insolent, arrogant, and almost impossible to control. Scarcely a night passed, a Briton observed, that Americans did not desert to the British post at Charlestown or Boston: "They are mostly Irish, and bring in their rifled barrelled guns." Ere long Washington said severely: "There is no restraining men's tongues, or pens, when charged with a little vanity, as in the accounts given of, or rather by, the riflemen." Soon Ward was writing: "They do not boast so much of the riflemen as heretofore. General Washington has said he wished they had never come; General Lee has damned them and wished them all in Boston; General Gates has said, if any capital movement was about to be made the riflemen must be removed from this camp."

Little more than sixty days after the riflemen reached camp, their insubordination reached a climax. Twice they had broken open the guard house and released their companions jailed for small offenses. Once, when a rifleman was brought to the post to be whipped, they damned their officers, and probably only a last-minute pardon of the criminal prevented a mutiny.

Jesse Lukens had come as a volunteer in Colonel William Thompson's battalion of riflemen, one of whose companies had been recruited in Virginia. From Prospect Hill, Lukens wrote an installment letter to a Philadelphia friend, carrying it with him from post to post and writing over a period of days. "I feel myself blush with shame and indignation at what I am forced to relate," he said of a row one Sunday night.

. . . the adjutant having confined a sergeant for neglect of duty and murmuring, the men . . . threatened to take him out. The adjutant, being a man of spirit, seized the principal mutineer and put him in also, and coming to report the matter to the colonel, where we [were] all sitting after dinner, were alarmed with a huzzaing and upon going out, found they had broke open the guard house and taken the man out. The colonel and lieutenant colonel with several of the officers and friends seized the fellow from amongst them and ordered a guard to take him to Cambridge at the Main Guard which was done without any violent opposition, but in about twenty minutes thirty-two of Captain Ross's company with their loaded rifles swore, by God, they would go to the Main Guard and release the man or lose their lives, and set off as hard as they could run. . . . We stayed in camp and kept the others quiet, sent word to General Washington, who reinforced the Guard to five hundred men with fixed bayonets and loaded pieces. Colonel Hitchcock's Regiment (being the one next us) was ordered under arms and some part of General Greene's Brigade. . . .

Generals Washington, Lee, and Greene came immediately, and our thirty-two mutineers, who had gone about half a

mile towards Cambridge and taken possession of a hill and
woods, beginning to be frighted at their proceedings, were
not so hardened but upon the General's ordering them to
ground their arms, they did it immediately. The General then
ordered another of our companies . . . to surround them with
their loaded guns . . . however, to convince our people . . .
that it did not altogether depend upon themselves, he ordered
part of Colonel Hitchcock's and Colonel Little's regiments to
surround them with their bayonets fixed and ordered two of
the ring leaders to be bound.

I was glad to find our men all true and ready to do their
duty except these thirty-two rascals. Twenty-six were conveyed to the Quarter Guard on Prospect Hill, and six of the
principals to the Main Guard. You cannot conceive what disgrace we are all in and how much the General is chagrined
that only one regiment should come from the South and that
set so infamous an example; and in order that idleness shall
not be a further bane to us, the General Orders on Monday
were "that Colonel Thompson's regiment shall be upon all
parties of fatigue and do all other camp duty with any other
regiment."

The men have since been tried by a General Court Martial
and convicted of mutiny and were only fined 20s. each for
the use of the hospital, too small a punishment for so base a
crime and mitigated, no doubt, on account of their having
come so far to serve the cause and its being the first crime.
The men are returned to their camp, seem exceedingly sorry
for their behavior and promise amendment.[10]

Lukens, perhaps reasonably, placed the burden of the blame
upon the remissness of the officers in enforcing discipline,
and he foresaw that "the men being employed will yet, no
doubt, do honor to their provinces, for this much I can say
for them that upon every alarm it was impossible for men to
behave with more readiness or attend better to their duty: it
is only in the Camp that we cut a poor figure."

Violent sectional prejudices colored the opinion of general and private. In his comprehensive look at the Americans, Benjamin Thompson, now serving the British but himself a New Englander, did not forget it:

Another reason why the army can never be well united
and regulated is the disagreement and jealousies between the
different troops from the different colonies, which must never
fail to create disaffection and uneasiness among them. The
Massachusetts forces already complain very loudly of the
partiality of the General to the Virginians and have even
gone so far as to tax him with taking pleasure in bringing
their officers to court martials and having them cashiered that
he may fill their places with his friends from that quarter. The

gentlemen from the Southern colonies, in their turn, complain of the enormous proportion of New England officers in the army, and particularly of those belonging to the province of Massachusetts Bay and say, as the cause is now become a common one and the expense is general, they ought to have an equal chance for command with their neighbors.[11]

New Yorkers suspected Connecticut men, and Connecticut men suspected New Yorkers. Even cultured Alexander Graydon of Pennsylvania gave way to sectional prejudices, and when he came to the army he thought the "only exception . . . to these miserably constituted bands from New England was the regiment of Glover of Massachusetts." But even in Glover's regiment he found a "number of Negroes, which to persons unaccustomed to such associations had a disagreeable, degrading effect." Jesse Lukens told his friend, John Shaw, that he did not dare write all he could about the truth of the army, for his letter might fall into "the hands of infidels or the Heathen," but he did sigh, "Such sermons, such Negroes, such colonels, such boys, and such great-greatgrandfathers." Washington himself had found them "dirty and nasty," although Benjamin Thompson thought this derived not from their normal habits but from the fact that they had no women to do women's work and the men were too proud to do their own washing. Jesse Lukens commented that "such a cursed set of sharpers cannot be matched"; Washington found them stingy and grasping and peculating, but perhaps he did not sufficiently take into consideration that the bulk of them were common men whose pittance pay was important to the well-being of their families at home.

Nathanael Greene, a New Englander judging his own, made a wise and sympathetic observation:

His Excellency . . . has not had time to make himself acquainted with the genius of this people. They are naturally as brave and spirited as the peasantry of any other country, but you cannot expect veterans of a raw militia of only a few months' service. The common people are exceedingly avaricious; the genius of the people is commercial from their long intercourse with trade. The sentiment of honor, the true characteristic of a soldier, has not yet got the better of interest. His Excellency has been taught to believe the people here a superior race of mortals, and finding them of the same temper and disposition, passions and prejudices, virtues and vices of the common people of other governments, they sink in his esteem.[12]

Greene, a kindly, understanding man who had toiled shoulder to shoulder with the most common of them, proved to know his people. As time passed, the majority of the men remained steadfast and devoted. They stood by their commitment and carried on a war. In time, their aristocratic General came to understand his New Englanders, and the day arrived when he proudly proclaimed them the finest troops in the world. Even the rowdy riflemen redeemed themselves, so that it was with sincerity, the following spring, that Washington told the Congress that they were "a valuable and brave body of men . . . indeed, a very useful corps."

Fortunately, the summer and fall of 1775 gave Washington an almost uninterrupted opportunity to make of the "mixed multitude" before Boston an army he could carry into the field. Military actions were very few and mostly unimportant. Aside from petty skirmishes and frequent, long, harmless bombardments on both sides, the only actions were the snatching of a few British by the riflemen, a reprisal raid by the British, and the occupation by the Americans of Plowed Hill, a low drumlin between Winter Hill and Bunker Hill, commanding the Mystic.

As summer ran into autumn, each day of military stalemate brought Washington nearer his goal: erasure of the "distinction of colonies . . . so that one and the same spirit may animate the whole," the making of good soldiers of them all. "We mend every day," he wrote to General Schuyler in New York, "and I flatter myself that in a little time, we shall work up these raw materials into good stuff."

7

"THEIR RAGGAMUFFINS ALL ROUND US"

The British in Boston

SUMMER-FALL 1775

WHILE WASHINGTON endeavored to make an army out of his untrained and often unruly volunteers, Gage in Boston did very little. He planned no move against his enemy. Although more troops reached Boston after the battle of Bunker Hill, bringing Gage's total force to about six thousand effectives (with some fourteen hundred more in the hospitals sick or wounded), he felt it was unwise to attempt a general offensive. His forces were not strong enough, nor was there any prospect of significant reinforcements before winter. He knew that New York was the proper base from which to re-establish British power in America, but he did not feel that he should move his troops there and abandon the loyalists of Boston. So, for months, he did nothing, except make himself secure in Boston and in Charlestown. This was relatively simple. The Neck was the most vulnerable point. It had been given a double line of defenses, which during the summer were strengthened. Additional flèches were thrown up on the edge of Back Bay. At the wharves, Fort Hill, Copp's Hill, Beacon Hill, and Barton's Point, works were built or strengthened, but they never were made very strong because they already were defended by water.

Although Gage had little to worry about from a military standpoint, life for the redcoats in the besieged town was far from pleasant, and it was much less so for the unfortunate Whigs trapped there, and even for the Tory civilians. Some sixty-five hundred citizens remained, more than two-thirds of them Whigs, who were held almost as hostages for the safety of the town. The soldier population, counting their women—British wives, colonial wives, camp followers, and all the rest—and children, was perhaps nearly double that number. For them, life took on a sobering tenor after Bunker Hill. On the following Monday "the chapel bell tolled almost all day for people that died with their wounds, which was so melancholy that the General has stopped the tolling of bells for funerals."

For weeks the British wounded of Bunker Hill kept their surgeons working. One of them groaned:

I have scarce time sufficient to eat my meals. . . . The Provincials had either exhausted their ball, or they were determined that every wound should prove mortal; their muskets were charged with old nails and angular pieces of iron, and from most of our men being wounded in the legs, we are inclined to believe it was their design, not wishing to kill the men, but leave them as burdens on us.[1]

Frequent street auctions of the effects of dead officers created a lugubrious air, and even the rollicking good nature of Jonathan Sewall, royal Attorney General, gave way to sobering philosophy:

Death has so long stalked among us that he is become much less terrible to me than he once was. Habit has a great influence over that mystical substance, the human mind. Funerals are now so frequent that for a month past you met as many dead folks as live ones in Boston streets, and we pass

them with much less emotion and attention than we used to
pass dead sheep and oxen in days of yore when such sights
were to be seen in our streets. . . .

I sometimes scold, but I oftener laugh; and I assure you I
have never from the beginning felt the least disposition to
cry. Everything I see is laughable, cursable, and damnable;
my pew in the church is converted into a pork tub; my
house into a den of rebels, thieves, and lice; my farm in possession of the very worst of all God's creation; my few debts
all gone to the devil with my debtors. I have just parted
with my coach horses for £24 sterling, which cost me £40
last fall and £20 more in keeping, while the circuit of my
riding ground has been confined to my own yard or little
more. I parted with them because they were starving in the
midst of British armies and British fleets in the most plentiful
country in the world.[2]

Even the nerves of officers grew taut, and in July one of
them admitted that the petty raids of the Americans were
eating away at his optimism:

As far as I can guess from a matter not perfectly known,
we at present are worse off than the rebels. In point of numbers they so far surpass us that we are like a few children in
the midst of a large crowd. Trusting to this superiority, they
grow daily more and more bold, menacing us most insolently;
and we fear when the days shorten, and the dark nights come
on, they'll put some of their threats in execution, unless other
reinforcements and a fleet of war arrive soon. They know our
situation, as well as we do ourselves, from the villains that
are left in town, who acquaint them with all our proceedings,
making signals by night with gunpowder, and at day, out of
church steeples.[3]

In addition to tensions and distress, the annoying old
curses of garrison life persisted in the British encampments
as well as Washington's: laziness, lax discipline, pranks—
sometimes vicious ones—desertions, all infuriated the commander and brought forth a rash of orders and severe punishments. The British troops were observed to be "languid
and tardy" in digging fortifications. Opening of graves had
to be forbidden since "added to the meanness of such practice a pestilence from the Infection of the Putrify'd Bodys
might reach the camp." When the women of Charlestown
brought "spiritous Liquors from Boston to this Camp, contrary to Orders" their permission to pass "from thence,
hither" was stopped for a while. Theft prevailed at all levels
of rank and "some evil minded person did on Monday last
in the Middle of the day Cut[4] off the Tail of a little black

Cow belonging to Brigr. General Pigot." For such crimes and misdemeanors harsh punishments began to appear with greater frequency in British orderly books.

Neither the regulars nor the Tories, however, underwent the hardships of the Whigs. Upon many of them Gage's untrustworthy insubordinates exercised savage ferocity and extorted various forms of tribute. John Leach, a prominent Whig teacher of navigation, was jailed on false charges of spying. Confined in the Stone Gaol, on whose top floor lay the captured American Bunker Hill wounded, he recorded the treatment they received from William Cunningham, Gage's brutal provost marshal:

> The poor sick and wounded prisoners fare very hard, are many days without the comforts of life. Dr. Brown complained to Mr. Lovell and me, that they had no bread all that day and the day before. He spoke to the Provost, as he had the charge of serving the bread; he replied they might "eat the nail heads, and gnaw the planks and be damn'd." The comforts that are sent us by our friends, we are obliged to impart to these poor suffering friends, and fee the soldiers and others with rum to carry it them by stealth, when we are close confined and cannot get to them. They have no wood to burn many days together, to warm their drink, and dying men drink them cold. Some of the limbs which have been taken off, it was said, were in a state of putrefaction, not one survived amputation.[4]

Leach was but one of many Whigs imprisoned as fear and suspicion of the patriots took hold of Gage. "Poor, harmless Shrimpton Hunt, standing by the door at the time of the engagement [Bunker Hill], was overheard saying he hoped our people would get the better of the others, was taken up and confined in gaol. Sam. Gore, for calling over to his sister to come and see a funeral pass, was taken up and confined some time," reported a Whig citizen. The British officer who heard that Whigs were "making signals by night with gunpowder" was unacquainted with the practice of some householders of "blowing up flies," but "Dorrington, his son and maid" were twelve days obtaining release from jail by that explanation. The man said to have been caught swimming over "to the rebels with one of their General's passes in his pocket," evidently had no such document in his possession, but he was "taken by the night Patrole—upon examination he had swam over to Dorchester and back again, was tried here that day and sentence of death passed on him and to be executed the next day,—his coffin brot into the Goal-yard, his halter bought, and he dressed as criminals are before execution. Sentence was respited and a few days after was pardoned." Peter Edes, the printer, was jailed for having in his house a concealed weapon, although the Whigs believed he was arrested for the unconcealed joy with which he watched the decimation of the British at Bunker Hill.

Summer drifted to its close without changing the military situation at Boston. The thousands of balls and shells that the British rained on the American fortifications continued to fall with indifferent effect, amusing stout Henry Knox:

> Last Saturday, let it be remembered to the honor and skill of the British troops, they fired one hundred and four cannon-shot at our works, at not a greater distance than half pointblank shot,—and did what? Why, scratched a man's face with the splinters of a rail fence! I have had the pleasure of dodging these heretofore engines of terror with great success; nor am I afraid they will hit me, unless directed by the hand of providence.[5]

And individuals in the ranks found that individuals in the enemy camp were often copies of themselves. Governor Cooke of Rhode Island observed an incident:

> . . . two or three gentlemen from Putnam's entrenchment last week were down viewing the works, etc., who discovered two or three officers from the [British] encampment on Bunker Hill. Each party edged toward the other, till they got so near as to talk together. Then they laid down their swords and walked up together. The gentlemen that were officers in the regular army seemed to lament much of the unhappy contest and asked the other if there was no way that could be hit upon to settle matters and asked if the Congress was now setting and if they could not find out some means for a cessation of hostilities. They made no doubt, if taxation was all we were contending for, it would be given up.[6]

Such exchanges among the men were not uncommon. Lieutenant Jabez Fitch enjoyed one:

> While I commanded the redoubt . . . I attended four flags of truce, had considerable discourse with the regular officers, who told me of their dogs eating roast beef, chickens, etc. I also see one Mr. Parker, who desired me to acquaint Mrs. Green that he had certain intelligence that Captain Callahan with whom her son David sailed for Great Britain had arrived there in twenty days and landed his passengers all well. He also acquainted me of the welfare of Daniel Hubbard and family with their connections. I could do no less than ask some questions of this kind. I also made a great

deal of enquiry after such regular officers as I had known in the army, was answered to every question in the most free, affable and polite manner, and indeed we held a discourse of near half an hour while some gentlemen were doing business, which appeared agreeable enough on both sides. I proposed to them to erect a coffee house for the convenience of such occasional conferences, upon which we held a considerable banter with good humor on both sides, and we finally parted with great appearance of friendship.[7]

One September day, a remarkable man named Benjamin Church, Junior, threw the American camp, in fact, all America, into an uproar. At the time he was forty-one years old, a graduate in medicine of Harvard and the London Medical College, a writer, poet, and eloquent speaker. Apparently very well-to-do, he resided in an "elegant mansion" outside Boston. As poet, he enjoyed a measure of fame as the author of "The Choice"; as speaker, he had delivered the 1773 oration on the third anniversary of the Boston Massacre; as Whig politician, he had been a confidant of Joseph Warren, Sam Adams, and the others, had served on many committees, was active in the provincial congresses, and a member of the Committee of Safety; as physician, he now served ably as Director General of the Hospitals under Washington. On October 3, Ebenezer Huntington, who had run off from his studies at Yale to join the army two days after Concord, wrote his brother:

> You will be much surprised to hear that our famous Doctor Church, that great pretended patriot, is now under a special guard of a captain and forty men for corresponding with Gage and other of his hellish gang. The plot was discovered by his miss, who is now with child by him and he owns himself the father (for he has dismissed his wife). She was the bearer of some of his letters from this place [Roxbury] to Newport to Captain Wallace who hath the forwarding them to Boston. She left them with a man she supposed friendly to Doctor Church, but was mistaken; he having a curiosity to know the contents opened them, but they were wrote in characters so that he was not able to understand them, but guessing the contents, brought the letters and girl to General Washington, who after an examination and four hours under guard confessed she carried them from Doctor Church. His trial has not been yet, but suppose it will be ere long.[8]

Washington's first action was to summon James Warren. After talking with Church, Warren reported to John Adams that Church "owns the writing and sending the letter, says it was for Flemming [Church's brother-in-law] in answer to

one he wrote to him, and is calculated by magnifying the
numbers of the army, their regularity, their provisions and
ammunition, etc., to do great service to us. He declares his
conduct though indiscreet was not wicked. There are, however, many circumstances, new and old, which time won't
permit me to mention, that are much against him. . . ."

The letter was deciphered. Church insisted that it was a
private bid for peace. Nevertheless, there was nothing to do
but to try him before a court-martial, which found him guilty
of carrying on "a criminal correspondence with the enemy."

Ironically, the court discovered, on studying the Articles
of War, that no adequate punishment had been established
for so serious an offense. Therefore, it could vote only to
confine the prisoner until the Continental Congress should determine his punishment. Church's letter itself made question-
able evidence, but generally his colleagues thought that it and
"collateral evidences" were enough to prove him guilty.

When the news reached Philadelphia the Massachusetts delegates "could hardly conceive it possible." John Adams exclaimed: "I stand astonished. A man of genius, of learning,
of family, of character, a writer of liberty songs and good
ones, too, a speaker of liberty orations . . . Good God! What
shall we say of human nature? What shall we say of American patriots?"

The Congress dismissed Church, appointed a successor, and
ordered "that Dr. Church be close confined in some secure
gaol in the colony of Connecticut, without the use of pen,
ink, and paper." He was incarcerated at Norwich, but in the
spring of 1776 he petitioned for release on the grounds of ill
health and was allowed to return to Boston where for a while
he continued in easier confinement. At last he obtained permission to go to the West Indies. The vessel in which he
sailed disappeared without a trace, and Benjamin Church vanished from history. In him, America had her first traitor.
General Washington would be better prepared to handle the
next one.

On September 26, H.M.S. *Scarborough* dropped her hook in
Boston Harbor. Aboard her were papers which brought to a
close the career in America of General Thomas Gage, sincere,
devoted servant of the King. He had been an able, honorable,
and patient executive. Ironically his mildness and reasonable-
ness, his unwillingness to rush his country into hostilities on
his own responsibility, had contributed to his downfall. His
fatal error was that he had failed to recognize the intent and
abilities of his adversaries. For some time before the march

to Lexington, powerful political enemies had been determined to destroy him. Within three days after the news of Bunker Hill was received in London, a decision to replace him was made. The King insisted the blow to Gage should be lightened as much as possible, and the letter the general received on the twenty-sixth from Lord Dartmouth was not a discharge; it simply instructed him to return home to help plan action for 1776, since nothing more could be done aggressively in America this year. Sir Guy Carleton was to command all British troops in Canada, and William Howe, all troops south of there, until Gage's return.

No one was deceived, least of all stout-hearted Gage. Resigned, he turned over his affairs to Howe, packed his own papers in solid white-pine boxes, and on October 11 set sail for home. The man who stepped into his place was the idol of his troops—"a man almost adored by the army and one with the spirit of a Wolfe who possesses the genius of a Marlborough."

The coming of cold weather worsened conditions in and around Boston. In the American camp Washington worried because wood was depleted and "different regiments were upon the point of cutting each others' throats for a few standing locusts near their encampments, to dress their victuals with." Wood for cooking, wood for warmth, thought Washington. "From fences to forest trees, and from forest trees to fruit trees, is a natural advance to houses, which must next follow." How right he was, General Howe was discovering in town. On December 5, Howe issued a General Order:

The frequent depredations committed by the soldiers in pulling down fences and houses in defiance of repeated orders has induced the Commander-in-Chief to direct the provost to go his rounds attended by the executioner, with orders to hang up, upon the spot, the first man he shall detect in the fact, without waiting further proof by trial. The commanding officers are to take particular care that the soldiers are acquainted with this order.[9]

Toward the end of October, Lord Percy, writing from "the highest summit" of the Boston hill called Mount Whoredom, remarked the exceptionally cold, rainy weather; he found a tent "no very agreeable habitation just now" and feared it would be some time before the British got into warmer quarters. "The rebels," he wrote, "have built barracks for their raggamuffins all round us, so that I suppose they intend to be our neighbours for *this* winter. I don't believe they will be very troublesome ones."

Especially to the officers and men in the British posts outside of town, the winds and snows of the winter brought misery. At Charlestown peninsula only a few of the houses of the formerly flourishing town still stood. In bleak huts and tents the regiments shivered, and even the officers found their duty severe. Francis, Lord Rawdon, captain in the Sixty-third Regiment, was a heroic young man, no complainer, but the New England winter was hard on him.

At our lines [he wrote to his uncle] neither officer or man have the smallest shelter against the inclemency of the weather, but stand to the works all night. Indeed in point of alertness and regularity our officers have great merit. I have not seen either drinking or gaming in this camp. If anything, there is too little society among us. In general, every man goes to his own tent very soon after sunset, where those who can amuse themselves in that manner, read; and the others probably sleep. I usually have a red herring, some onions, and some porter about eight o'clock, of which three or four grave sedate people partake. We chat about different topics and retire to our beds about nine. There is not quite so much enjoyment in this way of life as in what . . . the troops in Boston enjoy. For some days past it has not ceased raining; every tent is thoroughly wet, and every countenance thoroughly dull. A keen wind which has accompanied this rain, makes people talk upon the parade of the comforts of a chimney corner; and we hear with some envy, of several little balls and concerts which our brethren have had in Boston.[10]

In mid-December, Lord Rawdon's detachment moved into Boston. There many were billeted in houses, which were much warmer than the drafty, soaked tents; but fuel and fresh food continued to be scarce. The crowding of more men into town increased disorder. General Orders for January 3, 1776, continued the depressing picture of a cold, miserable city in wartime:

Thomas MacMahan, private soldier in His Majesty's Forty-third Regiment of Foot, and Isabella MacMahan, his wife, tried by . . . court martial for receiving sundry stolen goods, knowing them to be such, are found guilty of the crime laid to their charge, and therefore adjudge the said Thomas MacMahan to receive a thousand lashes on his bare back with a cat-of-nine-tails . . . and the said Isabella MacMahan, to receive a hundred lashes on her bare back, at the cart's tail, in different portions and the most conspicuous parts of the town, and to be imprisoned three months.[11]

A thousand stripes might kill a man, or they might be administered in broken doses to sustain his life but give him body-breaking punishment. This same court was more summary with Thomas Owen and Henry Johnston, found guilty of robbing a store; they were ordered to "suffer death by being hanged by the neck until they are dead."

But for the officers in the beleaguered town, life had its lighter side. "We have plays, assemblys, and balls and live as if we were in a place of plenty. Gen. Robertson is quite the young man, gives balls and routs." These were the "balls and concerts" that Rawdon, shivering in Charlestown, had envied; now transferred to town, he was lucky enough to attend them. And, he told his uncle, "we are to have plays this winter. . . . I am enrolled as an actor. . . . General Burgoyne is our Garrick." A meetinghouse was proposed for use as a theater, but, he confessed, "we feared your censure at home. . . ." And so Faneuil Hall was chosen.

No such regard for the proprieties deterred another group of officers from establishing a riding school in one of the town's fine churches. Brattle Street Church was spared only because its interior pillars, supporting the roof, could not be removed. The Old South, however, proved ideally suited. Timothy Newell lamented, "The pulpit, pews and seats, all cut to pieces and carried off in a most savage manner. . . ." After spreading the floor with tanbark, Lieutenant Colonel Samuel Birch's Seventeenth Dragoons boisterously put their mounts through paces where pious Bostonians formerly had prayed and had scarcely dared to whisper.

Sometimes the rebels on the cold lines in the country added spice to British social activities in town. A double bill one night at Faneuil Hall included a farce called *The Blockade of Boston*. An officer in attendance described the evening:

. . . the play was just ended, and the curtain going to be drawn up for the farce, when the actors heard from without that an attack was made on the heights of Charlestown, upon which one of them came in, dressed in the character of a Yankee sergeant (which character he was to play), desired silence, and then informed the audience that the alarm guns were fired; that the rebels had attacked the town; and that they were at it tooth and nail over at Charlestown. The audience thinking this was the opening of the new piece, clapped prodigiously; but soon finding their mistake, a general scene of confusion ensued, they immediately hurried out of the house to their alarm posts; some skipping over the orchestra, trampling on the fiddles, and, in short, everyone making his most speedy retreat, the actors (who were all officers) calling out for water to get the paint and smut off their faces; women fainting, etc. . . . We expected a general attack that night, but the rebels knew better, and in a few hours everything was quiet.[12]

So the winter promised to pass in the same deadlock that had marked the summer and fall. If the lives of the officers of the besieged city, despite moments of relaxation and well-being, were generally unpleasant, and those of their men and of the civilians, wretched, there was no panic and no terror. The inactivity of both armies led a citizen to write:

. . . both armies kept squibbling at each other, but to little purpose. At one time a horse would be knocked in the head, and at another time a man would be killed or lose a leg or an arm; it seemed to be rather in jest than in earnest: at some times, a shell would play in the air like a sky rocket, rather in diversion, and there burst without damage; and now and then, another would fall in the town, and there burst, to the terror or breaking of a few panes of glass: and during the whole blockade, little else was done but keeping both armies out of the way of idleness, or rather the whole scene was an idle business.[13]

8

"MUTUAL CONGRATULATIONS AND TENDER EMBRACES"

Victory at Boston

WINTER 1775-SPRING 1776

THE COLD, biting winds of November daily reminded Washington that his men were in critical need of blankets and fuel, but his problem was vastly more serious than providing for the comfort of his army: it was how to keep that army in the field.

When the Continental commanders had first arrived in Massachusetts in July, they thought the conflict would be brief. Surely, they thought, Gage would be commanded to come to terms with the Americans, and the war would be over. Independence was not the common object in those days, and the task of accommodation within the Empire seemed possible even after some blood had been let. Washington himself had hoped to be home before the end of the year; as late as August 20, he was urging Lund Washington to complete renovations and remodeling at Mount Vernon "before I return," and not until October had he given up the prospect of returning to "family and friends this winter" and invited Mrs. Washington to come to him.

While Gage remained inactive, the Americans had cause to be sanguine of a short struggle. But as he continued to strengthen his works, and after his recall, his successor also showed no inclination to attack or evacuate, it began to appear that the British had determined to quarter in Boston for the winter, perhaps in the expectation that the long freezing months would scatter the rebels and completely wear out their taste for resistance. If this were Howe's plan, no one knew better than Washington himself how sound it was. As the hammers rang on one hundred and twenty slowly-rising American barracks, George Washington feared the complete dissolution of his own army much more than a cold-weather attack by his enemy.

On December 10, the enlistment of all Connecticut and Rhode Island troops would terminate, and the service-weary men who had been six months from home would be free to return to their hearthsides. On December 31, all the other enlistments in the New England army expired. Unless, before the end of the year, the General could persuade most of the men to re-enlist, his siege lines would empty and overnight his dream of victory would vanish.

Facing the difficulties of securing re-enlistments, Washington turned to Congress for aid in remodeling the army. He pointed out that the soldiers had often refused to sign the Continental Articles of War for fear that doing so would subject them to longer service than they had engaged for under their individual provincial establishments. Now he faced the more serious difficulty of differences in pay: some services under the provincial establishments had advantages; some provinces paid by lunar months, giving their men an advantage of one month's extra pay during a year; most of the men had become accustomed to enlistment bounties, which had prevailed for many years; the pay offered the lower grade of officers was so small that most of them were likely to quit. And, added to all this, Washington wrote, "The military chest is totally exhausted. The paymaster has not a single dollar in hand."

The Congress hurried a committee to Cambridge. With Washington it devised a model for the new army to consist of no less than 20,372 men in regiments of 728 each, including officers, to be paid by the calendar month. The rate of pay was unchanged, field officers were to surrender their companies, and if the required number of men could not be raised out of the army, Washington was to recruit from the colonies and, meantime, to call out the militia.

Before his present army could drift away, Washington twice considered an assault on Boston. His council of officers both times rejected his proposal, although the second time he submitted the idea, he told the council that the Congressional Committee then in camp implied that it desired an attack. In the hope that he eventually would have a sufficient number of heavy guns to bombard the town, he extended his earthworks on his left and took Cobble Hill, which he had marked as an excellent gun position when he had first seen it, the day he entered Cambridge.

While the Congressional Committee was in camp, on October 18, Washington asked the Connecticut officers to ascertain how many of their men would be willing to stay on through December, so that he might know how many men he could count on till the end of the year. Some officers said they thought their men would stay if they were allowed furloughs to go home for warmer clothing, but the poll of the men was discouraging; one company to a man refused to stay.

When the committee departed, Washington immediately called for the names of the officers who intended to remain in the service. From that moment, his troubles began. On the second of November he expected to report in a few days on the prospects for the new army, but on the eighth he admitted to the Congress that he had been overly optimistic:

> I have been in consultation with the generals of this army ever since Thursday last [seven days] endeavoring to establish new corps of officers, but find so many doubts and difficulties to reconcile, I cannot say when they are to end, or what may be the consequences, as there appears to be such an unwillingness in the officers of one government mixing in the same regiment with those of another; and without it, many must be dismissed, who are willing to serve, notwithstanding we are deficient in the whole. I am to have another meeting today upon this business.[1]

On the eleventh, he wrote to the Congress:

> The trouble in the arrangement of the army is really inconceivable. Many of the officers sent in their names to serve in expectation of promotion; others stood aloof to see what advantage they could make for themselves, whilst a number who had declined have again sent in their names to serve. So great has the confusion arising from these and many other

perplexing circumstances been that I found it impossible to fix this very interesting business exactly on the plan resolved on . . . though I have kept up to the spirit as near as the nature and the necessity of the case would admit of.

The difficulty with the soldiers is as great, indeed more so if possible, than with the officers. They will not enlist until they know their colonel, lieutenant colonel, major, captain, etc., so that it was necessary to fix the officers the first thing, which at last is in some manner done, and I have given out enlisting orders.[2]

Enlistment went badly. As of November 19, only 996 men of eleven regiments had agreed to continue service. Nine days later Washington again wrote to the Congress: "The number enlisted since my last are 2,540 men. . . . Our situation is truly alarming and of this General Howe is well apprized. . . . No doubt when he is reinforced he will avail himself of the information."

Joseph Reed, the Philadelphia lawyer, who had served indispensably as an aide since June, had returned home on October 29 to look after cases pending in his law practice. Washington missed him, both as officer and as trustworthy friend. On the same day he wrote facts to the Congress, he poured out his feelings to Reed:

> Such a dearth of public spirit and want of virtue, such stock-jobbing and fertility in all the low arts to obtain advantages of one kind or another in this great change of military arrangement I never saw before, and pray God I may never be witness to again. What will be the ultimate end of these maneuvers is beyond my scan. I tremble at the prospect. . . . The Connecticut troops will not be prevailed upon to stay any longer than their term, saving those who have enlisted for the next campaign and mostly on furlough. And such a dirty mercenary spirit pervades the whole that I should not be at all surprised at any disaster that may happen.
>
> In short, after the last of this month, our lines will be so weakened that the minutemen and militia must be called in for their defense; these being under no kind of government themselves will destroy the little subordination I have been laboring to establish and run me into one evil, whilst I am endeavoring to avoid another, but the lesser must be chosen. Could I have foreseen what I have and am likely to experience, no consideration upon earth should have induced me to accept this command. A regiment or any subordinate department would have been accompanied with ten times the satisfaction and perhaps the honor.[3]

Though the Connecticut enlistments expired on the tenth of December, most of the men believed that they expired on the first, and many of them were determined to march for home that day. To forestall that calamity, Washington called up five thousand militia to report for duty on the tenth. The general officers tried in every way to persuade the Connecticut men to stay until the militia replacements arrived. Simeon Lyman was one of the Connecticut men. On December 1 he wrote in his diary:

We was ordered to parade before the general's door, the whole regiment, and General Lee and General Sullivan came out; and those that would not stay four days longer after their enlistments was out, they was ordered to turn out; and there was about three-quarters turned out and we was ordered to form a hollow square. And General Lee came in and the first words was, "Men, I do not know what to call you, [you] are the worst of all creatures," and flung and cursed and swore at us, and said if we would not stay, he would order us to go on Bunker Hill, and if we would not go he would order the riflemen to fire at us. And they talked they would take our guns and take our names down, and our lieutenants begged of us to stay and we went and joined the rest. And they got about ten of their guns, and the men was marched off. And the general said that they should go to the work house and be confined, and they agreed to stay the four days. And they gave them a dram, and the colonel told us that he would give us another the next morning, and we was dismissed. There was one that was a mind to have one of his mates turn out with him, and the general see him and he catched his gun out of his hands and struck him on the head and ordered him to be put under guard.[4]

High-tempered Charles Lee would not be outdone. The next morning a paper appeared posted on his door, apparently a copy of a notice he had sent to innkeepers along the road to Connecticut, warning them not to feed or lodge the homeward-bound men. But, Simeon Lyman wrote, "the paper was took down as soon as it was dark, and another put up that General Lee was a fool and if he had not come here, we should not know it."

The militia responded nobly in the crisis. On December 11, Washington could report to Congress:

The militia are coming fast. I am much pleased with the alacrity which the good people of this province, as well as those of New Hampshire, have shown upon this occasion; I expect the whole will be in this day and tomorrow, when what remains of the Connecticut gentry who have not enlisted will have liberty to go to their firesides.[5]

Two days later a letter from the camp reported, "things

wear a better complexion here than they have done for some time past. The army is filling up. The barracks go on well. Firewood comes in. The soldiers are made comfortable and easy."

The reaction of the militia and the remaining troops to the departure of the men from Connecticut afforded Lee much satisfaction. He wrote to Benjamin Rush:

> Some of the Connecticutians who were homesick could not be prevailed on to tarry, which means in the New England dialect to serve any longer. They accordingly marched off bag and baggage, but in passing through the lines of other regiments, they were so horribly hissed, groaned at, and pelted that I believe they wished their aunts, grandmothers, and even sweethearts to whom the day before they were so much attached at the devil's own palace.[6]

The departure, which nevertheless threw a damper on the whole army, was coincident with the arrival of Mrs. Washington to spend the winter with her harried soldier-husband. Her tour from Mount Vernon, with a visit en route in Philadelphia, had been full of excitement. The friendly, simple woman was delighted with the attentions she received. In her party were Mrs. Horatio Gates, Washington's adopted son, John Parke Custis, and his wife, and George Lewis. Commenting on the ladies, Joseph Reed remarked they were "not a bad supply, I think, in a country where wood is scarce."

Martha's presence brightened the headquarters residence and perhaps even softened the General's own asperity. At least so thought an orderly sergeant of artillery, Joseph White, who was ordered to deliver a message to the General absolutely in person. White related:

> After a great deal of ceremony, I was admitted into the house. One of his aid-de-camps stood at the bottom of the stairs, the General being up chamber. He said, "Tell me, and I will go up and tell him."
>
> I told him my orders were to see him myself. The General hearing that came to the head of the stairs and said, "Tell the young man to walk up."
>
> I did and told my business.
>
> "Pray, sir, what officer are you?"
>
> I said I was Assistant Adjutant of the Regiment of Artillery.
>
> "Indeed," said he. "You are very young to do that duty."
>
> I told him I was young, but was growing older every day. He turned his face to his wife and both smiled. He gave me my orders and I retired.[7]

Christmas Day could not have been very happy for the General, although the weather was clear, bright, and cold, following yesterday's snow. He wrote long letters to the Congress and to Joseph Reed, and otherwise busied himself with his old problem of building up an army. Officers dropped in during the day to pay their respects to the General and Mrs. Washington. To them he must have confessed the brightest thing about his Christmas was the fact that the militia had come out much stronger and had behaved much better than he had expected. With these newcomers and the numbers who had re-enlisted, he felt confident that now he could "give the enemy a warm reception, if they think proper to come out."

The General was encouraged also by the knowledge that siege guns for softening the enemy and perhaps even bombarding them out of Boston were on the way. In November he had transferred old Colonel Richard Gridley from the artillery to be his Chief of Engineers. In his place, he had appointed big, young Henry Knox, who had impressed him so favorably that hot summer day when he had inspected the works at Roxbury. Without awaiting Congressional confirmation of Knox as Colonel Commandant of Artillery, Washington had sent him off to haul down fifty-odd pieces of heavy ordnance from captured Fort Ticonderoga. It was a job for a giant. The tremendous guns would have to be dismounted by hand, floated in scows and boats the length of Lake George, and then sledded nearly three hundred miles across the snowy Berkshires and Massachusetts; the Hudson would have to be crossed perhaps four times. But two-hundred-fifty-pound Knox was the man for the job. From Fort George he wrote Washington on the seventeenth:

I returned to this place on the fifteenth and brought with me the cannon. . . . It is not easy to conceive the difficulties we have had in getting them over the lake, owing to the advanced season of the year and contrary winds; but this danger is now past.

Three days ago it was very uncertain whether we should have gotten them until next spring, but now, please God, they must go. I have made forty-two exceeding strong sleds and have provided eighty yokes of oxen to draw them as far as Springfield, where I shall get fresh cattle to carry them to camp. . . . I have sent for sleds and teams to come here and expect to begin to move them to Saratoga on Wednesday or Thursday next, trusting that between this and then we shall have a fine fall of snow, which will enable us to proceed further and make the carriage easy. If that shall be the case,

I hope in sixteen or seventeen days' time to present your Excellency a noble train of artillery.[8]

On New Year's Day, Washington raised a new flag "in compliment to the United Colonies": an ensign of thirteen red and white stripes with British colors in the canton. When the strange new flag flying on Prospect Hill was seen by the British in Boston, they at first thought it was a flag of surrender. Three nights later, when Washington heard this from "a person out of Boston," he quipped, "By this time I presume they begin to think it strange that we have not made a formal surrender of our lines."

But the day was marked less by ceremony than by the turnover in the army. General Heath recorded in his journal:

January 1st, 1776, presented a great change in the American army. The officers and men of the new regiments were joining their respective corps; those of the old regiments were going home by hundreds and by thousands. . . . Such a change in the very teeth of the enemy, is a most delicate maneuver; but the British did not attempt to take any advantage of it.[9]

The moment of great confusion passed successfully, much to the General's vast relief. He declared:

Search the vast volumes of history through and I must question whether a case similar to ours is to be found; to wit, to maintain a post against the flower of the British troops for six months together, without [powder] and at the end of them to have one army disbanded and another to raise within the same distance of a reinforced enemy.[10]

It did not work out as well as he had hoped. He expected that by mid-January his new army would be full, but by the tenth he had only 8,212 of an anticipated 10,500, enrolled, and only 5,582 present and fit for duty. The militia which had come in before Christmas now was free to depart, but he prevailed on many to stay another fortnight; and on the eighteenth, after his council at last agreed to an attack on Boston as soon as practicable, he was obliged to beg the New England governments to send him thirteen regiments of militia to serve till April.

Early in the month the General heard that the British were fitting out at Boston a fleet whose object might be New York. By the time five transports sailed on the twentieth, he had already sent General Lee toward New York to put it "into the best posture of defense which the season and circumstances will admit of," using volunteers and whatever troops New Jersey could furnish; Washington could spare none from his lines. And fretfully the General continued to await a propitious moment for attacking Boston. The shortage of small arms gradually lessened. On January 20, Henry Knox with his "noble train of artillery" had come within twenty miles of camp. If the guns could be mounted on the lines—if the lines could be extended to include the Dorchester hills, and if powder enough were available—then said Colonel Moylan, "I do believe Boston would fall into our hands."

Only the lack of sufficient powder held up an attack on the town. Although he could not admit so publicly, Washington realized that his scant supply would never sustain a bombardment long enough to rout the enemy from his works. When news trickling out of Boston continued to forecast an evacuation, the General and his council concluded that the only way to get at Howe, before he should slip away, was to lure him out. And the way to do that was to seize Dorchester Neck. Howe had shown his concern over the high ground there. If Washington were to grab it, Howe might be tempted to sortie. If he were repulsed from a fortified position on the heights, a victory might be bought cheaply.

It was not going to be as easy to fortify Dorchester Heights as it had been Breed's Hill in June. The ground on the heights now was frozen a foot or more deep. Works could not be completed in a single night, or perhaps even made tenable in that short a time, and once they were discovered, they would be sure to draw heavy enemy fire.

Colonel Rufus Putnam suggested that earthworks be built on top of the ground instead of dug into it. Construct them, he said, of fascines, held in place by wooden frames called chandeliers. Haul up bundles of hay. Throw earth over the fascines and the hay and make parapets.

Scores of men were put to work cutting fascines and making chandeliers. Others collected hay and screwed it into great bundles. Details collected wagons and carts from the country. Solid shot and shell were brought up to the guns in easy range of Boston. Boats were assembled in the Charles for use if the occupation of Dorchester Heights should lead to an immediate assault on Boston. Militia was called up from neighboring towns.

As February rushed through its course, Washington spent time clearing his desk of accumulated papers and writing letters. To his wife's brother-in-law, Burwell Bassett, he wrote on the twenty-eighth: "We are preparing to take possession of a post (which I hope to do in a few days, if we can get provided with the means) which will, it is generally thought, bring on a rumpus between us and the enemy."

He ordered for himself a light wagon for the field, equipped to handle a dozen and a half camp stools, a couple of folding tables, plates, dishes, tent and other items. He wrote a polite letter to the young Negro poetess, Phillis Wheatley, to thank her for the heroic poem in his praise he had received from her in December: "If you should ever come to Cambridge, or near headquarters, I shall be happy to see a person so favored by the muses and to whom nature has been so liberal and beneficent in her dispensations." He advertised for nurses, ordered two thousand bandages. He and his officers studied the tides, the weather, the circumstances, and decided that they should take the positions on Dorchester Neck on Monday night, March 4. To divert Howe's attention from Dorchester Heights, a cannonade on Boston was opened on the night of the second. It was a trifling affair; eleven shells and thirteen solid shot, but it was warmly returned though with little damage. It was repeated the next night with similar results. On the night of the fourth, the heaviest American fire of all burst from Cobble Hill, Lechmere's Point, and Lamb's Dam at Roxbury.

At dusk—about 7 P.M.—General Thomas with three thousand men chosen for the night's work started from Roxbury for the hills on Dorchester peninsula. Behind them plodded three hundred teams, hauling fascines, chandeliers, screwed hay, and barrels. The night was clear and mild, the moon full. Like a well-rehearsed stage company, the men ascended the hills, the teams dumped their loads and returned for others, and the shadowy toilers fell to their task of making fortifications.

General Heath described them:

The Americans took possession of Dorchester Heights and nearly completed their works on both the hills by morning. Perhaps there never was so much work done in so short a space of time. The adjoining orchards were cut down to make the abatis, and a very curious and novel mode of defense was added to these works. The hills on which they were erected were steep and clear of trees and bushes. Rows of barrels, filled with earth, were placed round the works. They presented only the appearance of strengthening the works, but the real design was, in case the enemy made an attack, to have rolled them down the hill. They would have descended with such increasing velocity, as must have thrown the assailants into the utmost confusion, and have killed and wounded great numbers. This project was suggested by . . . [a] merchant of Boston to our general, who immediately communicated it to the Commander-in-Chief, who highly approved of it, as did all the other officers.[11]

The long months of the siege had bored young Major John Trumbull, so he found the new action exhilarating:

> Our movement was not discovered by the enemy until the following morning, and we had an uninterrupted day to strengthen the works which had been commenced the night preceding. During this day we saw distinctly the preparations which the enemy were making to dislodge us. The entire water front of Boston lay open to our observation, and we saw the embarkation of troops from the various wharves, on board of ships, which hauled off in succession, and anchored in a line in our front, a little before sunset, prepared to land the troops in the morning.

> We were in high spirits, well prepared to receive the threatened attack. Our position[s], on the summits of two smooth, steep hills, were strong by nature, and well fortified. We had at least twenty pieces of artillery mounted on them, amply supplied with ammunition, and a very considerable force of well-armed infantry. We waited with impatience for the attack, when we meant to emulate, and hoped to eclipse, the glories of Bunker's Hill.

> In the evening the Commander-in-Chief visited us and examined all our points of preparation for defense. Soon after his visit the rain, which had already commenced, increased to a violent storm, and heavy gale of wind, which deranged all the enemy's plan of debarkation, driving the ships foul of each other, and from their anchors in utter confusion, and thus put a stop to the intended operation.[12]

Thus the Americans, by virtue of boldness, energy, and what an Englishman called "a rank storm," occupied the post which was perhaps the most important key to the enemy defenses. The one loss was noted in General Orders of March 9:

> His Excellency the General lost one of his pistols yesterday upon Dorchester Neck. Whoever will bring it to him or leave it with General Thomas shall receive two dollars reward and no questions asked; it is a screwed barreled pistol mounted with silver and a head resembling that of a pug dog at the butt.[13]

The "finger of Providence," upon which Washington had relied before, stayed Howe's attack and gave the Americans time to make their defenses on the heights so strong that they could not be forced. With Washington's guns commanding a large part of the city and the harbor and his positions impregnable, Howe, who had been instructed by Dartmouth months before to abandon Boston, decided at last to evacuate. According to Josiah Quincy, clergyman John Murray dined with Washington on the ninth:

[He] was present at the examination of a deserter, who upon oath says that five or six hundred troops embarked the night before without any order or regularity; the baggage was hurried on board without an inventory; that he himself helped the General's baggage on board, and that two hospital ships were filled with sick soldiers, and the utmost horror and confusion amongst them all. The General received a letter from the selectmen informing him that in the midst of their confusion, they applied to Mr. Howe, who told them that if Mr. Washington would order a cessation of arms, and engage not to molest him in his embarkation, he would leave the town without injuring it; otherwise he would set it on fire. To which the General replied that there was nothing binding on Mr. Howe. He, therefore, could not take any notice of it.

The deserter further says that Mr. Howe went upon a hill in Boston the morning after our people took possession of Dorchester Neck, when he made this exclamation: "Good God! These fellows have done more work in one night than I could have made my army do in three months. What shall I do!"[14]

Washington, at first suspicious of the letter from the selectmen, gradually was convinced, as he saw the wharves grow busy and ships sail down the harbor, that Howe was preparing to leave. Nevertheless, he finished his works on Dorchester Heights and stayed on the alert, while at the same time preparing some of his troops for a fast journey overland to New York, to which he was sure Howe would sail. A few anxious, nervous days passed. Then on the clear Sunday morning of the seventeenth of March, St. Patrick's Day, a newspaperman wrote:

This morning the British army in Boston, under General Howe, consisting of upwards of seven thousand men, after suffering an ignominious blockade for many months past, disgracefully quitted all their strongholds in Boston and Charlestown, fled from before the army of the United Colonies, and took refuge on board their ships. . . .

About nine o'clock, a body of the regulars were seen to march from Bunker's Hill, and, at the same time, a very great number of boats, filled with troops, put off from Boston, and made for the shipping, which lay chiefly below the castle.

On the discovery of these movements, the Continental Army paraded; several regiments embarked in boats and proceeded down the river from Cambridge. About the same time, two men were sent to Bunker's Hill, in order to make discoveries. They proceeded accordingly, and, when arrived, making a signal that the fort was evacuated, a detachment was im-

mediately sent down from the army to take possession of it.
The troops on the river, which were commanded by General Putnam, landed at Sewall's Point, where they received intelligence that all the British troops had left Boston, on
which a detachment was sent to take possession of the town,
while the main body returned up the river. About the same
time, General Ward, attended by about five hundred troops
from Roxbury, under the command of Colonel Ebenezer
Learned, who embarked and opened the gates, entered the
town on that quarter, Ensign Richards carrying the standard. . . .

The joy of our friends in Boston, on seeing the victorious
and gallant troops of their country enter the town almost at
the heels of their barbarous oppressors, was inexpressibly
great. The mutual congratulations and tender embraces which
soon afterwards took place, between those of the nearest
connections in life, for a long time cruelly rent asunder by
the tyranny of our implacable enemies, surpasses description. From such a set of beings, the preservation of property
was not expected. And it was found that a great part of the
evacuated houses had been pillaged, the furniture broken and
destroyed, and many of the buildings greatly damaged. It is
worthy of notice, however, that the buildings belonging to the
honorable John Hancock, Esquire, particularly his elegant
mansion house, are left in good order. All the linen and woollen goods, except some that may be secreted, are carried
off, and all the salt and molasses is destroyed. The regulars
have also destroyed great quantities of effects belonging to
themselves, which they could not carry away, such as gun carriages and other carriages of various kinds, house furniture,
&c., together with a quantity of flour and hay. All their forts,
batteries, redoubts, and breastworks remain entire and complete. They have left many of their heaviest cannon mounted
on carriages, and several of them charged, all of which are
either spiked, or have a trunnion beaten off. They have also
left several of their largest mortars; quantities of cannon shot,
shells, numbers of small arms, and other instruments of war,
have been found, thrown off the wharves, concealed in vaults
or broken in pieces. In the fort on Bunker's Hill, several hundred good blankets were found. It is said about fifteen or
twenty of the king's horses have also been taken up in the
town; and it is thought that about the same number of Tories
remain behind.

We are told that the Tories were thunder-struck when
orders were issued for evacuating the town, after being many
hundred times assured, that such reinforcements would be
sent, as to enable the king's troops to ravage the country at
pleasure. . . . Many of them, it is said, considered themselves
as undone, and seemed, at times, inclined to throw themselves
on the mercy of their offended country, rather than leave it.

One or more of them, it is reported, have been left to end their lives by the unnatural act of suicide.

The British, previous to their going off, scattered great numbers of crow's feet [four-pointed irons which always fell with one point up] on Boston Neck, and in the streets, in order to retard our troops in case of pursuit; and with such silence and precaution did they embark, that a great part of the inhabitants did not know it until after they were gone.

To the wisdom, firmness, intrepidity and military abilities of our amiable and beloved general, his Excellency George Washington, Esquire, to the assiduity, skill, and bravery of the other worthy generals and officers of the army, and to the hardiness and gallantry of the soldiery, is to be ascribed, under God, the glory and success of our arms, in driving from one of the strongest holds in America, so considerable a part of the British army as that which last week occupied Boston.[15]

Washington did not make a triumphal entry into Boston on the day of the evacuation. Instead, at Cambridge, he attended business and went to church and puzzled why the enemy fleet did not sail with favorable winds and tides. On Monday he visited Boston. It had suffered greatly, but was not "in so bad a state" as he had expected to find it.

That day, although the enemy unaccountably tarried in Boston waters, Washington dispatched, under command of General Heath, five regiments of foot and two companies of artillery to follow the rifle battalion already marching for New York. Despite general rumors that Howe would sail for Halifax, Washington never wavered in his conviction that Howe's real destination was New York: "It is the object worthy their attention; and it is the place that we must use every endeavor to keep from them."

If the enemy occupied New York, he would sever communication between the northern and southern colonies, separating the leadership and spirit of New England from the men and supplies of the South and dismembering the rebellion; also, he would command the best of all roads to Canada, the Hudson River. This was precisely what Howe had in mind; he conceived the 1776 campaign as an attack upon New York City, a dash up the Hudson to join forces with the British operating out of Canada, and the capture of Newport. Washington thought it inconceivable that with such a view in mind—and the British made no secret of their plans but rather advertised them—Howe would brook any delay by sailing to Halifax to refresh his forces, provision and supply them, and await a vast reinforcement promised him from England for the spring campaign.

Therefore, as soon as possible after the fleet sailed on the twenty-seventh, Washington started sending his army to New York, with the exception of five regiments under command of Artemas Ward left to defend Boston. He himself prepared to follow.

The twenty-eighth was given to thanksgiving and celebration: a new general, a new army, and a new country had won their first great military victory. No matter how much the British Ministry excused Howe's withdrawal as a strategic one, the public in America and England considered it a defeat. In commemoration of this glorious event, the selectmen of Boston delivered an address to Washington; the Massachusetts Assembly, a testimonial; the Continental Congress voted its thanks and a gold medal; and the academicians— the President and Overseers of Harvard College—not to be outdone, voted the General the honorary degree of Doctor of Laws.

On the fourth of April, George Washington LL.D., Commander-in-Chief of the Continental Army, bade farewell to the scene of his triumph and took the road to New York.

9

"MY HEART SICKENS AT THE RECOLLECTION"

Quebec

JULY-NOVEMBER 1775

IN MARCH the cannon of the siege of Boston had fallen silent and on the fourth of April, when Washington rode quietly out of the city, the roll of their thunder on the Mystic and on the Charles was only a remembered echo. But nearly six hundred miles northward across the frozen Canadian wilderness, where snow lay five feet deep that April day, American and British guns still boomed and crashed with stubborn hatred.

In the summer of 1775, while Washington lay before Boston, the United Colonies had launched an offensive into Canada. From the moment guns were fired at Lexington, that vast wild domain had been a threat and a temptation to America. New Englanders could not forget how the French had used the rivers and lakes from the St. Lawrence to the Hudson as an avenue of war, and they had every reason to suspect the British would use them the same way, severing New England from the Middle Colonies. And forward-looking Americans had a way of regarding Canada as a possible fourteenth colony to join with them in their stand against the King.

For a few weeks after the capture of Ticonderoga and Crown Point by the flamboyant team of Allen and Arnold, the Continental Congress was timorous of further aggression against royal establishment in the North. But when word filtered back to Philadelphia that Sir Guy Carleton, military governor of Canada, was "making preparations to invade these colonies and . . . instigating the Indian nations to take up the hatchet against them," the Congress changed its mind and instructed General Philip Schuyler, "commanding the New York Department," to invade Canada if "it will not be disagreeable to the Canadians."

Carleton was known to have less than eight hundred regulars with which to protect his sprawling colony. If the Americans moved quickly, it was unlikely he would be reinforced in time from England or Boston. They calculated, too, that once they had seized the principal cities and posts, Canadians and Indians would join them.

In assigning the invasion of Canada to Philip Schuyler, however, the Congress made the worst possible choice. A tall, slight, pleasant-looking, brown-eyed man, he appeared hearty, but his jaunty carriage belied chronic ill-health that made him moody, sensitive, and often indecisive.

The task would have been enormous for a robust man of action. For Schuyler it was almost insurmountable. Trouble plagued him from the start and he did not have the force to shoulder through it. Enlistments were incredibly slow. Materiel haphazardly dribbled in from tardy suppliers. He discovered that Ticonderoga, upon which he depended, was in "a perfectly defenseless state," the garrison in wretched condition, undisciplined, and insubordinate. He went there to lend his presence to preparations for the Canadian expedition, but nothing he could do seemed to hurry the carpenters building batteaux or to bring up supplies and troops.

Fortunately Schuyler's second in command was a strong man and a determined one. Brigadier General Richard Montgomery had been one of General Jeffrey Amherst's captains in the French and Indian War. "Tall and slender, well-limbed, of genteel, easy, graceful, manly address," according to a fellow officer, "he had the voluntary esteem of the whole army."

At forty, he was only two years younger than his chief, but he had the vigor of a youth. When he came up from Albany and took charge of details, the expedition began to take shape, but already valuable time had been lost.

Schuyler was ill back in Albany when Montgomery's spies reported Carleton ready to launch two heavily armed vessels at St. John's to defend the Sorel River above Lake Champlain. The brigadier knew he could wait no longer. Once Carleton put armed craft into the water, he would be able to tear apart Montgomery's unprotected troops moving up in open batteaux.

Writing to Schuyler to come and take command, Montgomery shoved off with his whole force for Ile-aux-Noix, twenty miles below St. John's, to boom the Sorel. Although Schuyler overtook him in a whaleboat in time for his landing on the fifth of September, he was forced by a bilious fever to give up and return, leaving the fate of the expedition to his second. Montgomery promptly laid siege to stockaded Fort St. John's.

Except for a sortie the first afternoon, the garrison, feeling secure behind the massive log walls, did not sally from its post. Great trees cleared from the dense forests had been anchored in the earth with their interlaced branches sharpened and pointing outward to make an impenetrable abatis.

The woods were soggy with early fall rain, and on the squelching, morassy ground, within a week, "upwards of six hundred" men, nearly half Montgomery's force, lay too sick to stand duty. The rest shoveled siege lines in the muddy soil. Each day the weather grew colder, and the rains steadied in. "Whenever we attempt to raise batteries, the water follows in the ditch," complained one of the besiegers, and his brigadier sympathized, "We have been like half-drowned rats crawling through a swamp." After the troops had lain for seventeen or eighteen straight days in pelting rain with their bellies growling between meager meals, they grumbled and balked, and as always the New Englanders resented authority. "The privates are all generals," Montgomery snapped, but he was not much better satisfied with his own people: "The sweepings of the York streets," he called them.

The British garrison hung on while the light rebel guns pounded monotonously and ineffectually, and numbing gray week followed gray week. The rebels who had expected "in five days" after sailing to be the "possessors of Montreal" began to abandon hope altogether of ever seeing it.

To add to Montgomery's woes, there came letters from an overly ardent wife, to whom he wrote back from the Canadian woods:

I must entreat the favor of you to write no more of those whining letters. I declare if I receive another in that style, I will lock up the rest without reading them. I don't want anything to lower my spirits. I have abundant use for them all, and at the best of times I have not too much.[1]

When the inexhaustible brigadier managed to raise a gun battery north of the fort on an eminence that commanded the enemy's works, the garrison at last gloomily stacked arms in surrender.

Two days later, under snowy skies, Montgomery's drenched troops, cleanly outfitted from the supplies of a small nearby post taken by a detachment before St. John's capitulated, were tramping along the broken corduroy road to Montreal.

Ethan Allen, by now deposed as commander of the Green Mountain Boys, had joined the expedition and had already gone forward to adventure. Sent ahead to enlist Canadians, with Major John Brown he concerted an independent assault on Montreal. The two agreed to separate their force of three hundred and close in on the city from opposite sides. When Allen found himself alone and unsupported before the fortress walls on the appointed day, September 25, he brazenly advanced alone. The minute the garrison sallied, all but twoscore of his men vanished, and the rest, including the former Green Mountain Boy, ran nearly a mile before they were overtaken and captured. Typically, when Allen told the story, he made himself a hero:

The officer I capitulated with, then directed me and my party to advance towards him. . . . I handed him my sword, and in half a minute after, a savage, part of whose head was shaved, being almost naked and painted . . . came running to me with an incredible swiftness. . . . As he approached near me, his hellish visage was beyond all description. . . . And in less than twelve feet of me [he] presented his firelock.

At the instant of his present, I twitched the officer, to whom I gave my sword, between me and the savage; but he flew round with great fury, trying to single me out to shoot me without killing the officer. But by this time I was nearly as nimble as he, keeping the officer in such a position that his danger was my defense. But in less than half a minute, I was attacked by just such another imp of hell. Then I made the officer fly around with incredible velocity for a few seconds . . . when I perceived a Canadian . . . taking my part against the savages; and in an instant an Irishman came to my assistance with a fixed bayonet and drove away the fiends, swearing by Jasus! he would kill them. . . . The escaping from so awful a death made even imprisonment happy.[2]

Allen's captors led him back to town, "very merry and facetious, and no abuse was offered me till I came to the barrack yard." There he was accosted by General Richard Prescott, Montreal commandant, who asked him if he were the Colonel Allen who took Ticonderoga. Allen replied. "Then he shook his cane over my head, calling many hard names." Allen shook his fist in the general's face and warned him not to use the cane.

"I will not execute you now," Prescott barked. "But you shall grace a halter at Tyburn, God damn you!"

And Prescott endeavored to carry out the threat: he put Allen in chains and subsequently sent him to England for trial.

Allen's impetuous little foray irreparably damaged the American cause in Canada. Its failure heartened the loyal Canadians and discouraged those who might have joined Montgomery. The Indians also as a result turned to the English. Montgomery openly lamented Allen's "imprudence and ambition," and when word reached Washington at Cambridge, the Commander-in-Chief declared to Schuyler:

Colonel Allen's misfortune will, I hope, teach a lesson of prudence and subordination to others who may be too ambitious to outshine their general officers and regardless of order and duty rush into enterprises which have unfavorable effects to the public and are destructive to themselves.[3]

Said the *New England Chronicle* in a pungent appraisal: "Allen is a high flying genius, pursues every scheme on its first impression, without consideration and much less judgment."

When Montgomery's force crossed the St. Lawrence on the blowing cold morning of November 12 and landed north of Montreal, only a hundred and fifty men were in the garrison. Sir Guy Carleton, who was present, and Prescott, the commandant, tried to get the men away by boat, but the Americans took the whole body, except for Carleton himself, who slipped away.

Nothing now lay between the long-legged brigadier and Quebec, last British stronghold of Canada. But Benedict Arnold with another American force was there ahead of him, after an overland trek through the Maine and Canadian wilderness so frightful that it made Montgomery's northward drive, with all its difficulties, seem like a Sunday stroll.

Arnold owed his presence before Quebec to a decision of General Washington in August to send a diversionary expedition to Canada by way of the Kennebec River, with the expectation that it would distract Carleton from Schuyler's advance by way of the lakes. Carleton either would follow the diversionary force and leave Schuyler's way open, or would be forced to allow Quebec to fall into Arnold's hands.

To lead such an expedition a man of stamina, enterprise, ambition, and daring was needed, a leader, not a driver, a man who never doubted himself. Such a man was Benedict Arnold, who, after the ugly controversies about command at Ticonderoga, had come to Watertown to settle his financial accounts with the Provincial Congress. While he stamped about, fuming at the suspicious, miserly attitude of the legislators who tediously studied each item of his claim for more than £1,060 he had spent in the service, he improved his time by getting acquainted at Washington's headquarters and working up a scheme of his own for a Canadian invasion through Maine, which Adjutant General Gates presented to the Commander-in-Chief. Washington talked it over with Arnold and in Arnold's blunt energy and quick intelligence, he recognized a proper mainspring for the expedition.

Washington concluded that a force of about eleven hundred men, the equivalent of a battalion, including three rifle companies, would be required for the expedition. The rifle companies, two from Pennsylvania and one from Virginia, were to be drawn by lot and as units, but the rest of the troops were invited to volunteer. The response was greater than expected; by now the siege of Boston had become a boresome job for most of them.

Speed was the primary requisite; the march must begin before summer slipped away. Washington saw it, and Arnold understood it, in a way in which Schuyler had not. Arnold sped his preparations.

In command of the rifle companies, Arnold placed Daniel Morgan, a giant of a man, big-chested and bull-necked, with a plain, open, friendly face and a mighty temper. He had spent a good part of his thirty-nine years on the rough and tumble Virginia frontier as a wagoner hauling freight between remote settlements. His education was negligible, but he had a fine, strong, understanding mind, and was a natural leader. He had fought in the Indian wars, and his muscled back still bore the scars of 499 stripes, a miscount for five hundred, delivered for striking a British officer at Fort Chiswell, nearly twenty years ago. Recently he had been a farmer in Virginia's beautiful Shenandoah Valley. Big Dan Morgan was his county's unanimous choice to lead its rifle company to Boston in 1775, and he had come to war with a personal grudge to settle with George III.

Many disappointed soldiers were left behind as the force

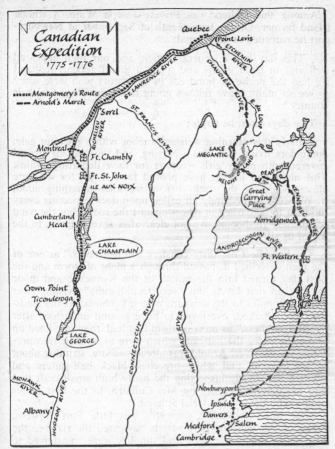

Canadian
Expedition
1775-1776

····· Montgomery's Route
- - - Arnold's March

Quebec
Point Levis
ETCHEMIN RIVER
ST. LAWRENCE RIVER
CHAUDIERE RIVER
R. DU LOUP
Sorel
ST. FRANCIS RIVER
RICHELIEU RIVER
Montreal
Ft. Chambly
Ft. St. John
ILE AUX NOIX
LAKE MEGANTIC
HEIGHT OF LAND
Great Carrying Place
DEAD RIVER
KENNEBEC RIVER
Cumberland Head
Norridgewock
LAKE CHAMPLAIN
ANDROSCOGGIN RIVER
Ft. Western
Crown Point
Ticonderoga
CONNECTICUT RIVER
MERRIMACK RIVER
LAKE GEORGE
MOHAWK RIVER
HUDSON RIVER
Albany
Newburyport
Ipswich
Danvers
Salem
Medford
Cambridge

set out from the Cambridge camp. Rifleman Jesse Lukens, in
the long letter he wrote to his Philadelphia friend on September 13, said he accompanied the departing men on foot
as far as Lynn, nine miles:

Here I took leave of them with a *wet eye*. The drums
beat and away they go as far as Newburyport by land, from
there they go in sloops to Kennebec River, up it in batteaux,
and have a carrying place of about forty miles over which
they must carry on their shoulders their batteaux and baggage, scale the walls [of Quebec] and spend the winter in
joy and festivity among the sweet nuns.[4]

Among the soldiers was Private Joseph Ware, a Rhode Island farmer. On the seventeenth of September at Newburyport he recorded in his journal:

This day had a general review and our men appeared well and in good spirits and made a grand appearance, and we had the praise of hundreds of spectators who were sorry to see so many brave fellows going to be sacrificed for their country.[5]

Two days later, he wrote:

Early this morning weighed anchor with a pleasant gale, our colors flying and fifes a-playing, and the hills all around covered with pretty girls weeping for their departing swains. This night had like to have proved fatal to us, for we were close aboard of the rocks before we knew anything about it. We were immediately all called upon deck expecting every moment to be dashed in pieces against the rocks, but the wind fortunately freshening, we got clear after several tacks, to the joy of us all.[6]

The little fleet of "dirty coasters and fish boats," as one of the men described it, passed through a night of storm and the next day turned into the mouth of the Kennebec and made its way up that lovely but "very troublesome" twisting river forty-nine miles to the shipyard of one Colburn. As the landsmen disembarked, overjoyed to have ground underfoot after "such a sickness," as most of them had had, they saw lined up along the shore the batteaux which were to be their transportation up the river. Arnold was already ashore, strutting about in scarlet coat and white breeches, black half-gaiters and plumed hat, sourly inspecting the badly built small craft that had been flung together by Mr. Colburn, to the best of his ability with the only material at hand.

Nine miles above the shipyards was little Fort Western. Some of the Newburyport vessels navigated the river to the fort; from others the men and supplies were transferred to the batteaux, and for several days at the fort the army organized itself for its plunge into the wilderness to begin the 385-mile trek to Quebec. Two advance parties were sent up the river on the twenty-fifth, and the following day the march began.

Neither rank nor seniority entitled Captain Morgan to lead the vanguard, but he already was being recognized tacitly as second only to Arnold as leader of the expedition. The "large, strong-bodied personage," thought sixteen-year-old Pennsylvania rifleman John Henry, "gave the idea history has left us of Belisarius."

As the divisions moved out, four or five men rode in each

batteau and the rest marched beside the river, taking turns in the boats. When the last of them left Fort Western, Arnold set out in a canoe to gain the head of the column.

As always, different men saw things differently, but they all agreed about the passage of the Kennebec. For a few days they were in inhabited country, but from the first the going was hard. Everything, including the batteaux, had to be carried around a quarter-mile of rapids above the fort with the help of teams and carts from the neighborhood, but it was at Ticonic Falls, about eighteen miles farther, that the men began to learn what a portage was like. Over sixty-five tons of supplies had to be hauled around the falls on aching, raw shoulders; the long pointed batteaux, weighing four hundred pounds apiece, were each carried by four men. Soon came Five Mile Falls, where the river fell thirty-four feet through rapids, "very dangerous and difficult to pass." Frequently the boatmen were forced to leap overboard and drag their clumsy boats through the icy shoals in water to their waists, to their chins, and sometimes they "plunged over the head into deep basins."

Often it rained. On the first of October it poured during the night, and the men's wet clothes were frozen "a pane of glass thick." At Skowhegan Falls getting up the boats seemed impossible. In the face of the rock that split the falls was a crevice up which Indians for centuries had pulled their birch canoes. Now up this "steep, rocky precipice" the men dragged their awkward batteaux, while they cursed at the contractor who made the leaky, cumbersome things. A few miles farther, tall Dr. Isaac Senter, twenty-two-year-old New Hampshire surgeon, recorded at fearsome Norridgewock Falls:

By this time, many of our batteaux were nothing but wrecks, some stove to pieces, etc. The carpenters were employed in repairing them, while the rest of the army were busy in carrying over the provisions, etc. A quantity of dry cod fish by this time was received, as likewise, a number of barrels of dry bread. The fish lying loose in the batteaux and being continually washed with the fresh water running into the batteaux [was spoiled]. The bread casks not being waterproof admitted the water in plenty, swelled the bread, burst the casks, as well as soured the whole bread. The same fate attended a number of fine casks of peas. . . . We were now curtailed of a very valuable and large part of our provisions, ere we had entered the wilderness or left the inhabitants. Our fare was now reduced to salt pork and flour. Beef we had once now and then, when we could purchase a fat creature, but that was seldom. A few barrels of salt beef remained . . . of so indifferent quality as scarce to be eaten.[7]

When the boats were patched and reloaded and the rain let up, the army moved forward. Private James Melvin noted, "We are now to take our leave of houses and settlements of which we saw no more, except one Indian wig-wam, till we came among the French in Canada." And many awful days lay between.

Dr. Senter began to note dysentery and diarrhea, "of which disease Captain Williams . . . came nigh to lose his life." Thirty-two miles north of Norridgewock Falls, "three days march into the wilderness," was the Great Carrying Place from the Kennebec to the brown waters of the Dead River. Here for eight miles the men carried across four portages between a string of lakes. Rough wooded hills of hemlock and birch shining in the rain and quick brooks and ponds wild with winter wind impressed Arnold to write down: "the prospect is very beautiful and noble."

But it was also a malevolent country. When Dr. Senter came up to the mountain that stood in the Kennebec "in the shape of a sugar loaf," where the army left the river, he found most of the men and boats already across the first portage. It was Thursday, the twelfth of October, and it took him a week to reach Dead River. During that week his journal reflected the plight of his comrades as well as his own:

> *Saturday, 14th.* . . . The army was now much fatigued, being obliged to carry all the batteaux, barrels of provisions, warlike stores, etc., over on their backs through a most terrible piece of woods conceivable. Sometimes in the mud knee deep, then over ledgy hills, etc. The distance was three and three-quarters miles. . . .
> *Sunday 15th.* . . . Many of us were now in a sad plight with the diarrhea. Our water was of the worst quality. . . . With this we were obliged not only to do all our cooking, but use it as our constant drink. . . . No sooner had it got down than it was puked up by many of the poor fellows.
> *Monday 16th.* . . . We now found it necessary to erect a building for the reception of our sick.[8]

On the nineteenth, the fourth and worst portage began:

> This carrying place was four miles . . . two and a half of which ascending till we rose to a great height, then a sudden descent into a tedious spruce and cedar swamp, bog mire half knee high, which completed the other mile and half. . . .[9]

When Benedict Arnold reached the Dead River, it was October 16. He had miscalculated. He had figured the distance to Quebec to be 180 miles, which was a little less than half the actual distance. He had figured the march would take twenty days, although he had provided food for forty-five. By October 24, his army had been on the journey seven days longer than he had calculated for the whole march and had come less than half way. Provisions already were almost totally lost or consumed.

Dr. Senter already was on half rations and Colonel Greene's division for supper the night before had eaten candles "by boiling them in water gruel."

Arnold sent the sick back toward the hospital Senter had built and ordered colonels Greene and Enos, who commanded the two rear divisions, to send back as "many of the poorest men of their detachment as would leave fifteen days provision for the remainder." Greene and Enos and the officers of their companies held a council and considered whether the two divisions should go on or turn back. "Here sat a council of grimacers," said Senter, "melancholy aspects who had been preaching to their men the doctrine of impenetrability and non-perseverance. Colonel Enos in the chair." Greene and his men were made of firm stuff and voted to go on, but Enos and his party voted to return.

Captain Henry Dearborn's black dog somehow had managed to survive the ordeal, and now trotted beside him. When his company received "the unhappy news of Colonel Enos and the three companies in his division being so imprudent as to return back . . . ," Dearborn reported that "our men made a general prayer that Colonel Enos and all his men might die by the way or meet with some disaster equal to the cowardly, dastardly, and unfriendly spirit they discovered in returning. . . ." No misfortune befell them, however. Enos was later court-martialed and to the disgust of many of his former comrades was exonerated.

The army was now reduced to fewer than seven hundred and in near danger of starvation. Captain Simeon Thayer was one of Greene's officers who voted to push on, although he must have guessed that three days after the council his men would be "taking up some rawhides that lay for several days in the bottom of their boats, intended for to make them shoes or moccasins of . . . and chopping them to pieces, singeing first the hair, afterwards boiling them and living on the juice or liquid that they soaked from it for a considerable time."

Arnold, meanwhile, had boldly pushed ahead with no stores "except a small quantity of specie, attended with a good pilot in a British canoe [and] hands sufficient to carry everything over the various carrying places." He hoped to find French inhabitants and to obtain food for his weakened and famished men. When word came back that he had been well received, "unspeakable joy" swept the camps of the struggling army.

Provisions were pooled, to determine how much each man could depend upon for the last hundred miles before the army reached the Canadian settlements. Each man was issued five pints of flour and about two ounces of pork, and upon these each man must subsist. Several devoured the whole of their flour "determined . . . to have a full meal, letting the morrow look out for itself." And still more miserable morrows lay ahead.

On November 1, wrote Dr. Senter:

Our greatest luxuries now consisted in a little water, stiffened with flour, an imitation of shoemakers' paste, which was christened with the name of "Lillipu." Instead of the diarrhea, which tried our men most shockingly in the former part of our march, the reverse was now the complaint, which continued for many days. We had now arrived as we thought to almost the zenith of distress. Several had been entirely destitute of either meat or bread for many days. . . . The voracious disposition many of us had now arrived at rendered almost anything admissable. Clean and unclean were forms now little in use. In company was a poor dog [who had] hitherto lived through all the tribulations [and who] became a prey for the sustenance of the assassinators. This poor animal was instantly devoured, without leaving any vestige of the sacrifice. Nor did the shaving soap, pomatum, and even the lip salve, leather of their shoes, cartridge boxes, etc., share any better fate. . . .[10]

The following morning, Private Abner Stocking, twenty-two, wrote:

When we arose this morning many of the company were so weak that they could hardly stand on their legs. When we attempted to march, they reeled about like drunken men, having now been without provisions five days. As I proceeded, I passed many sitting wholly drowned in sorrow, wishfully placing their eyes on everyone who passed by them, hoping for some relief. Such pity-asking countenances I never before beheld. My heart was ready to burst and my eyes to overflow with tears when I witnessed distress which I could not relieve.

The circumstances of a young Dutchman and his wife, who followed him through this fatiguing march, particularly excited my sensibility. They appeared to be much interested in each other's welfare and unwilling to be separated, but the husband, exhausted with fatigue and hunger, fell a victim to the king of terrors. His affectionate wife tarried by him until he died, while the rest of the company proceeded on their way. Having no implements with which she could bury him, she covered him with leaves and then took his gun and other implements and left him with a heavy heart. After traveling twenty miles she came up with us.[11]

The gaunt, half-dead men had fought their way through the Chain of Ponds and up the granite walls of the Height of Land, a four-and-a-quarter-mile portage over the watershed between the streams flowing north to the St. Lawrence and south to the Kennebec. They named the snow-laden hillsides "The Terrible Carrying Place." Nearly all the batteaux were gone, beaten to bits, and finally all but a few were abandoned. Over ridges, ruts, and morasses the men stumbled toward their goal. Private George Morison, another Pennsylvania rifleman, kept a florid, opinionated diary, but his words about the march as the army struggled over the Height of Land and into the marshes of Lake Megantic ring sincerely:

> The universal weakness of body that now prevailed over every man increased hourly on account of the total destitution of food; and the craggy mounds over which we had to pass, together with the snow and the cold penetrating through our death-like frames made our situation completely wretched, and nothing but death was wanting to finish our sufferings. . . .
> It would have excited commiseration in the breast of a savage to have beheld those weak creatures, on coming to the brow of one of those awful hills, making a halt, as if calculating whether their strength was sufficient for the descent; at last he casts his eyes to the adjacent hill and sees his comrades clambering up among the snow and rocks. He is encouraged—he descends—he stumbles . . . and falls headlong down the precipice, his gun flying far from him. . . . His comrade staggers down to his assistance, and in his eagerness falls down himself. At length the wretches raise themselves up and go in search of their guns, which they find buried in the snow. They wade through the mire to the foot of the next steep and gaze up at its summit, contemplating what they must suffer before they reach it. They attempt it, catching at every twig and shrub they can lay hold of, their feet fly from them —they fall down to rise no more. Alas, alas, our eyes were too often assailed with these horrid spectacles—my heart sickens at the recollection.[12]

On November 2, Dr. Senter wrote:

> We were scattered up and down the [Chaudiere] River at the distance of perhaps twenty miles. Not more than eight miles had we marched, when a vision of horned cattle, four-footed beasts, etc. rode and drove by animals resembling Plato's two-footed featherless ones. Upon a nigher approach our vision proved real! Exclamations of joy! Echoes of glad-

ness resounded from front to rear with a *te deum*. Three
horned cattle, two horses, eighteen Canadians, and one
American. A heifer was chosen as victim to our wants, slain
and divided . . . each man was restricted to one pound of
beef. Soon arrived two more Canadians in . . . canoes, ladened
with a coarse kind of meal, mutton, tobacco, etc. Each man
drew likewise a pint of this provender. The mutton was destined for the sick. They proceeded up the river in order to
the rear's partaking of the same benediction. We sat down,
eat our rations, blessed our stars, and thought it luxury.[13]

That night the first of the men reached the habitations of
the first Canadians they had seen. Starvation was past.
Through bitter cold, snowy weather, the army now pressed
for the St. Lawrence. Some of the men, too weakened to recover even upon a good diet, died; three, Captain Dearborn
thought, ate themselves to death, and one recovered enough
to steal the captain's purse and receive a whipping for it when
apprehended. November 8, Private Melvin, his clothes in tatters, no doubt as bearded and "meager" as the rest, wrote in
his journal: "Marched six miles and came to Point Levi, on
the River St. Lawrence, opposite Quebec."

10

"I HAVE NO THOUGHTS OF LEAVING THIS PROUD TOWN"

Quebec

NOVEMBER 1775-JUNE 1776

ON THE nights of November 13 and 14, in commandeered
boats and canoes, Arnold put his army across the St. Lawrence into Wolfe's Cove, and then ascended to the Plains of
Abraham within a mile and a half of the city. "The first day
we came over the river," Private Joseph Ware said, "we passed
close by the walls of the town and gave three cheers without
being molested by the enemy who fired a few shots from their
cannon, but did us no harm."

After escaping from Montreal, where Montgomery nearly

caught him, Carleton had entered Quebec safely and now commanded a force of regulars, British and Canadian militia, marines and seamen from ships in the harbor, probably totaling twelve hundred in all—on the whole an insufficient force to defend long walls. Arnold, however, thought he would need two thousand men "to carry the town"; he was without cannon to breach the walls, short of ammunition, and even of small arms. He retired twenty miles up the river to Pointe aux Trembles to await Montgomery's army.

General Montgomery arrived on the third of December with his vanguard. Two days later, when all his force had arrived, the combined army took up positions before Quebec. Arnold posted his "famine-proof veterans," as they now called themselves, on the northern side in the half-burned suburb of St. Roche, and Montgomery posted his force on the Plains of Abraham between St. Roche and Cape Diamond.

Even before he had left Montreal, Montgomery reluctantly had reached the conclusion that the only way to master Quebec was by storm, regardless of the high loss in lives an attack would cost. A siege would be a long and drawn-out affair of regular approaches and battering guns to breach the wall. Ammunition, food, and money would run out before he could starve Quebec into submission—or else the term of enlistment of Arnold's New Englanders would run out and finish him. In spring when the ice in the St. Lawrence broke, British reinforcements would sail in. Assault he must, despite "the melancholy consequences."

First, then, he must go through the customary formality of summoning the garrison. Arnold had done so, only to have his flag fired upon. Montgomery tried a less formal presentation, which Carleton reported to General Howe:

> The seventh [of December] a woman stole into town with letters addressed to the principal merchants, advising them to an immediate submission and promising great indulgence in the case of their compliance. Enclosed was a letter to me in very extraordinary language and a summons to deliver up the town. The messenger was sent to prison for a few days and drummed out [of town].[1]

To frighten the population, Montgomery also sent copies of his letter into the city in the heads of a flight of arrows, but to no avail. He pushed an artillery battery within one hundred and fifty yards of the city walls on the St. Roche side, and young Dr. Senter, using his recently acquired medical vocabulary, recorded: "Agreeable to prescription, fifty-five more of the fire pills were given . . . last evening. Operated with manifest perturbation . . . bells beating, dogs barking, etc. . . . Forty-five more pills as cathartic last night."

While Montgomery tried to write Carleton into capitulation, his army toiled to erect batteries and make approaches. The fierce Canadian winter had set in early. Already snow was piled up to the second story of many of the houses in town, and on the shelterless heights raw, blistering northeast wind howled over ground frozen too hard to break with pick and shovel. A subsoil of rock forbade mining. The ingenious Yankees, with the aid of Canadian workers, made a vast number of gabions (great baskets of twigs usually filled with earth to serve as the core of works) and filled them with snow; when they were in place, the troops piled on more snow and poured water over them. The snow and water froze almost instantly in the sub-zero weather. Unhappily the ice batteries, no matter how ingenious, could not withstand "the monstrous force of their 32s and 42s" and began to fly to pieces when the guns of Quebec scored hits.

Montgomery advanced the riflemen near the walls to emphasize his summons. They were not very successful: an American said, "We popped away at one another all day without hurt on either side," and a British officer scornfully barked, "Skulking riflemen in St. Roche watching behind walls to kill our sentries—soldiers, indeed!"

The American army now lived in unaccustomed comfort in spite of the fierce weather. Arnold's men especially reveled in warm uniforms from the St. John's garrison and enjoyed good billets in a monastery, a nunnery, and houses of inhabitants of the Quebec suburbs. And Sergeant John Pierce, surveyor and engineer, noted that "a certain officer of the field keeps with the nuns."

When Montgomery's bluster and his guns failed to make any visible impression upon Carleton, he began to prepare the minds of his officers and men for carrying the town by an escalade over unbroken walls. On Christmas night, he ordered a general review of the troops and harangued them "in a handsome manner . . . on the subject of the intended attack." He was answered with a cheer. Two days later, Dr. Senter, quartered at the General Hospital on the St. Charles, half a mile from St. Roche, entered in his journal:

> Preparations were made in a manner as secret as possible for the storming the city in the night. After all things were arranged . . . the weather cleared away serene and bright, which foiled our undertaking. For a mark of distinction each soldier was ordered to procure a fir sprig and fix it in the front of their caps. . . .[2]

The commanding officers awaited another snowy night.

Several diversionary attacks were planned, chief of which was a push by Canadians against the Upper Town from the Plains of Abraham. The main assaults were to be sent against the Lower Town where a cluster of warehouses and residences crowded back from the low beach to the gray precipice up whose steep face Mountain Street climbed to the Upper Town. Montgomery was to descend to Wolfe's Cove and march along the road toward Cape Diamond, while Arnold came round from the north, or St. Charles River, side to meet him. When the columns met in the Lower Town, they were to push up Mountain Street.

On the last day of the year the hoped-for snowstorm began. A "thick small snow" driven by an "outrageous" wind piled drifts upon those already on the ground. As the long night hours passed, the wind howled louder and hail mixed with the snow. The men were ordered to their stations. John Pierce was allowed to remain behind at St. Roche with "cannon fever." At four in the morning he, as well as the British watchers on the walls of Quebec, saw three rockets split through the whirling snow. The rocket signals to the American troops were alarms for the British, and the town burst awake. "I had a fair view of the whole," wrote Pierce. "The bells were all set on ringing, cannon playing, bombs flying, small arms constantly going, drums beating. . . ."

Montgomery made his way along the narrow lane between the cliff of Quebec and the St. Lawrence, leading around Cape Diamond. The guard at the blockhouse south of the Cape fled in confusion and Montgomery hurried forward to go around Cape Diamond. Stocking, who marched with Arnold's corps, later obtained an account of Montgomery's assault. He wrote:

Unfortunately, the difficulties of the route rendered it impossible for Montgomery instantly to avail himself of this first impression. Cape Diamond, around which he was to make his way, presents a precipice, the foot of which is washed by the river, where enormous and rugged masses of ice had been piled on each other, so as to render the way almost impassable.

Along the scanty path leading under the projecting rocks of the precipice, the Americans pressed forward in a narrow file, until they reached the block-house and picket [beyond Cape Diamond on a narrow road leading into the Lower Town]. Montgomery, who was himself in front, assisted with his own hands to cut down or pull up the pickets and open a passage for his troops. But the excessive roughness and difficulty of the way had so lengthened his line of march that he found it absolutely necessary to halt a few minutes in order to collect a force with which he might venture to proceed. Having reassembled about two hundred men, whom he encouraged alike by his voice and his example, he advanced boldly and rapidly at their head to force the barrier.

One or two persons had now ventured to return to the battery; and, seizing a slow-match standing by one of the guns, discharged the piece when the American front was within forty paces of it.

This single accidental fire was a fatal one. The general, with captains [John] McPherson and [Jacob] Cheeseman, two valuable young officers, near his person, the first of whom was his aide, together with his orderly sergeant and a private, were killed on the spot. The loss of their general, in whom their confidence had been so justly placed, discouraged the troops; and Colonel [Donald] Campbell, on whom the command devolved but who did not partake of that spirit of heroism which had animated their departed chief, made no attempt to prosecute the enterprise. The whole division retired precipitately from the action, and left the [British] garrison at leisure, after recovering from the consternation into which they had been thrown, to direct their undivided force against Arnold. . . .[3]

Arnold, meanwhile, personally led his six hundred men around the northern wall of the city through snow "deeper than in the fields." The van passed the Palace Gate unchallenged. The main body—"covering the locks of our guns with the lappets of our coats, holding down our heads"—had safely passed the gate when it received a tremendous fire of musketry from the ramparts above, and ran along the gantlet for a third of a mile seeing nothing "but the blaze from the muzzles of their muskets." Down into the Lower Town drove the warrior Arnold, until he and his advance ran into a narrow street blocked by a barricade mounting two guns. One fired ineffectually, the other flashed. Arnold yelled to his men to come on, and then stumbled with a bullet in his left leg. He struggled to his feet but, he reported later, "the loss of blood rendered me very weak. As soon as the main body came up . . . I returned to the hospital, near a mile, on foot, being obliged to draw one leg after me and a great part of the way under the constant fire of the enemy from the walls. . . ."

Crowding up the little street was the giant Daniel Morgan, who later wrote a friend:

I . . . took his place, for, although there were three field officers present, they would not take the command, alleging that I had seen service and they had not. . . . I ordered the ladder, which was on two men's shoulders, to be placed (every two men carried a ladder). This order was immediately obeyed and for fear the business might not be executed with spirit, I mounted myself and was the first man who leaped into the town among [the British gun captain] McLeod's guard [of fifty men] who were panic struck and after a faint resistance ran into a house that joined the battery and platform.

I lighted on the end of a heavy piece of artillery which hurt me exceedingly and perhaps saved my life, as I fell from the gun upon the platform where the bayonets were not directed.

Colonel Charles Porterfield, who was then a cadet in my company, was the first man who followed me. The rest lost not a moment, but sprang in as fast as they could find room. All this was . . . in a few seconds. I ordered the men to fire into the house and follow up their fire with their pikes (for besides our rifles we were furnished with long espontoons). This was done and the guard was driven into the street.

I went through a sally port at the end of the platform, met them in the street, and ordered them to lay down their arms, if they expected quarter. They took me at my word and every man threw down his gun. We then made a charge upon the battery and took it and everything that opposed us, until we arrived at the barrier-gate [at the intersection of Sault-au-Matelot and Mountain Street] where I was ordered to wait for General Montgomery. And a fatal order it was, as it prevented me from taking the garrison, having already made half the town prisoners. The sally port through the barrier was standing open. The guard left it, and the people came running in seeming platoons and gave themselves up in order to get out of the way of the confusion. . . . I went up to the edge of the Upper Town with an interpreter to observe what was going on, as the firing had ceased. I found no person in arms at all. I returned and called a council of war of what officers I had, for the greater part had missed their way and had not got into the town.

Here I was overruled by hard reasoning: it was stated that if I went on I would break an order, in the first place. In the next . . . I had more prisoners than I had men . . . if I left them, they might break out, retake the battery, and cut off our retreat. . . . General Montgomery was certainly coming down the river St. Lawrence and would join us in a few minutes, so that we were sure of conquest if we acted with caution. To these arguments I sacrificed my own opinion and lost the town.[4]

The indecision of Morgan's advisers in truth lost the day. From beyond the second barrier, the British took grip upon themselves and dashed back to man it and gain houses around the Americans. Suddenly the Americans were targets for converging fire in a narrow confined street. Private George Morison of one of the rifle companies thought the tactics the Americans had used in driving the redcoats from Concord to Boston were now, when adopted by the British, most foul:

> Some cowards fire upon us from the windows of houses which only serves to make us laugh. They point out the muzzles of their guns, screening themselves behind the window frames, and fire at random, the bullets seldom coming within perches of us. Some of us amuse ourselves by emptying our rifles in at these windows.
> We have heard for some time heavy discharges of musketry and artillery in different parts of the town. We are elated . . . and shout, "Quebec is ours." We again invite the enemy to come out from behind their covert and try our rifles, which we offer to them for sale at a low rate. They, however, decline the offer, observing that they shortly expect them for nothing.
> Our main body now appears, having taken a wrong route through narrow and crooked streets. . . . We heartily cheer each other. . . . The ladders are laid to the wall. Our gallant officers are mounting . . . when a furious discharge of musketry is let loose upon us from behind houses. In an instant we are assailed . . . with a deadly fire. We now find it impossible to force the battery. . . . We rush on to every part, rouse the enemy from their coverts . . . some of our riflemen take to houses and do considerable execution. We are now attacked by thrice our number. . . .
> Betwixt every peal the awful voice of Morgan is heard, whose gigantic stature and terrible appearance carries dismay among the foe wherever he comes. . . . We are now attacked in our rear. . . . They call out to us to surrender, but we surrender them our bullets and retreat to the first battery. Here we maintain ourselves until ten o'clock [in the morning], when surrounded . . . many of our officers and men slain, and no hope of escape, we are reluctantly compelled to surrender . . . having fought manfully for more than three hours.[5]

Tears of rage streamed down the bearded cheeks of Captain Morgan, backed against a wall and daring a ring of the enemy to force his sword from his hand. Suddenly in the crowd in the noisy street he spotted a man in clerical garb.

"Are you a priest?" he cried.

"I am."

"Then I give my sword to you. No scoundrel of those cowards shall take it out of my hands."

The fight for Quebec was over. Throughout the town, small units of Americans, lost in the maze of streets and alleys, were surrounded and forced to surrender, while some individuals managed to make their way back to the lines. The

Americans had lost about a hundred killed and wounded and four hundred prisoners.

Back at St. Roche, Arnold's force scarcely had left its camp to march to the attack when the wounded began streaming back to Dr. Senter, and at daylight the colonel himself came limping in. News of both attacking parties had been brought by the wounded, and every moment it became increasingly dismal until someone reported the enemy was advancing toward the hospital. According to Dr. Senter:

> Under these circumstances we entreated Colonel Arnold for his own safety to be carried back into the country . . . but to no purpose. He would neither be removed, nor suffer a man from the hospital to retreat. He ordered his pistols loaded, with a sword on his bed, etc., adding that he was determined to kill as many as possible if they came into the room. We were now all soldiers, even to the wounded in their beds were ordered a gun by their side.[6]

But Carleton did not pursue. The storm still raged, and he was busy seeking out every American in the Lower Town. Those who escaped retired to their lines and began to fire away at the city again. Of the prisoners, a British officer observed:

> You can have no conception what kind of men composed their officers. Of those we took, one major was a blacksmith, another a hatter. Of their captains, there was a butcher . . . a tanner, a shoemaker, a tavern-keeper, etc. Yet they all pretended to be gentlemen.[7]

To Carleton's credit, he treated them so. He sent Major Meigs to the American camp to bring in their baggage, allowed them their own cook, arranged outdoor walks when the weather turned warm, and otherwise tried to make their confinement endurable.

With Montgomery dead, Arnold from his hospital bed assumed command of the army outside Quebec. "I have no thought," he wrote his sister, "of leaving this proud town, until I first enter it in triumph." He pulled the forces together, tried to check the flight of deserters to Montreal, and implored antiquated, alcoholic, lethargic General David Wooster, who now commanded there, to "for God's sake, order as many men down as you can possibly spare, consistent with the safety of Montreal, and all the mortars, howitzers, and shells that you can possibly bring." His reports to Washington and to the Congress produced reinforcements, but they did not begin arriving for two months, while he tenaciously hung on in temperature that dropped as low as twenty-eight degrees below zero. The natives refused to furnish food for his men and smallpox visited his camp. "We labor," he declared, "under almost as many difficulties as the Israelites did of old, obliged to make bricks without straw." Although Wooster was afraid to release many of his men to Quebec, he wrote to Washington, "General Arnold has, to his great honor, kept up the blockade with such a handful of men that the story, when told, will be scarcely credited." It was a dynamic, shining thing to do, but a little ridiculous: Carleton could hold out fairly comfortably until spring thaw, when he surely would be reinforced and drive his besiegers out of Canada. Meanwhile, Arnold's sick and his well suffered for every necessity, "for to tell you the truth," he admitted, "our credit extends no farther than our arms."

Before the thaw came, Wooster arrived to assume command. The old relic of the French and Indian War was the commanding officer who had tried to prevent Arnold's marching his Foot Guard off for Cambridge at the time of Lexington, and the old relic of the French and Indian War and the resourceful younger man could not understand each other any better now than then. Wooster seemed to have plans for taking Quebec, which he pointedly refused to share with Arnold. Arnold, who but a week before had started riding again, bruised his wounded leg in a fall, the day after Wooster's arrival, and was glad enough for an excuse to retire to Montreal on leave until he recovered.

Now the Canadian story ran to a tragic end. Wooster was completely inept before Quebec, but he was succeeded within a month by General John Thomas, who was appointed commander of the Canadian expedition by Congress. Thomas inspected the city, the siege lines, and his forces, and promptly concluded the siege should be raised. While he was preparing to do so, British reinforcements arrived from England; Carleton quickly organized a force of nine hundred, sallied out, and drove the Americans in panic toward the Sorel.

The Congress by now had been aroused to the importance of what was happening in Canada and the end of May saw splendid troops sweeping up Lake Champlain, making, in the words of one of their captains, "a most formidable and beautiful appearance—I presume, something like the Grecian fleet going to the siege of Troy." With them came a new commander, John Sullivan, New Hampshire lawyer, self-made son of Irish indentured servants, who had come to war with an Irishman's hatred of the English and an almost pathetic desire to please. He was overly optimistic, always sure of success, seldom achieving it. Into the growing strength of the Americans he read every harbinger of glory; he scarcely could wait to throw a force against the British at Trois Rivieres.

It was brutally crushed. His mercurial dreams plummeted. He evacuated Sorel and marched southward, joined on June 17 at St. John's by Arnold with the Montreal garrison.

From St. John's, the army struggled back along the way Montgomery had advanced until it lay gasping on Ile-aux-Noix, where the men died epidemically of smallpox, malaria, and dysentery; their bodies were tossed into huge pits in the center of each regimental camp until the survivors could push to Crown Point. Here only the Sixth Pennsylvania was left as an advance guard. The rest of the army of less than three thousand effectives went into quarters at Ticonderoga in early July, and the Canada vision evaporated.

Everything had conspired against its success. The long wildernesses between the St. Lawrence and the supply bases of the rebels put them before the walls of Quebec less well supplied for a siege than was the garrison of the city. The light artillery Montgomery could bring to bear on the great walls was inadequate. Montgomery's fall in the attack and Arnold's wound had fatal effects upon the one assault. The illnesses of the Americans steadily weakened the seige after the first of the year. Their failure initially to enlist the support of the Canadian clergy, and finally their desperate plundering of priests and populace alike, together with their fast-dwindling military chest, turned the inhabitants against them at the last, and they left behind a hostile country.

The Americans probably could not have held Quebec if they had taken it. Their campaign at least delayed a British thrust southward along the lakes-and-Hudson waterway, but at the time it seemed that five thousand men and a fortune in money had been wasted on a campaign cursed by bad management and bad luck.

11

"NEVER DID MEN FIGHT MORE BRAVELY"

Sullivan's Island

JUNE 29, 1776

WHILE A defeated, disillusioned American army stumbled out of the vast, thawing wilderness of Canada, danger of another distant war front suddenly threatened far to the south, in a warm land of palmettos, oaks, and pines, of placid tidal rivers and plantations already a century old.

The Southern colonies had been chosen by the British Ministry as the field for a major effort against the rebels as early as the summer of 1775. The King himself had been led to believe by his royal governors—especially by Josiah Martin, ardently loyal, energetic, overly optimistic chief executive of North Carolina—that the loyalists in the Southern provinces could destroy the sons of sedition with the aid of a few trained British regulars. From Virginia, Lord Dunmore claimed that with only two or three hundred men, he could secure the "obedience" of his colony. Martin was equally confident that at least three thousand of the recently emigrated Scottish Highlanders in the back parts of North Carolina would support the King; around them, he contended, he could build a force of at least twenty thousand loyal fighting men. Governors Lord William Campbell of South Carolina and Sir James Wright of Georgia were similarly sanguine. Through the persuasion of the Earl of Dartmouth, George III was easy to convince.

Opulent Charleston, South Carolina, with its magnificent harbor, vast enough to accommodate all the fleets of the world, and its waterways reaching up into plentiful tidewater and Piedmont country, logically was the initial objective: it would furnish a base for operations that might range from the river James in Virginia to the St. John's in Florida. Governor Martin, however, persuaded the King that if North Carolina first returned to the royal fold, the reduction of the rebels in South Carolina would be much easier, because a route would be opened to the "well affected people" in the back parts of that colony.

In the fall of 1775, the British force for the South had begun to assemble. Seven regiments with two companies of artillery were to sail from Cork under command of Major General Charles, Lord Cornwallis, who had advanced rapidly in the King's service and had requested permission to accompany the expedition. A strong fleet of eleven warships under command of Vice Admiral Sir Peter Parker, an old salt bred to the navy, was to convoy Cornwallis' two thousand troops on thirty-odd transports. Off North Carolina's Cape Fear River, the force was to be met by a detachment under one of the general officers from Boston chosen by Howe to assume full command. Landing at the Cape Fear, the expedition was to unite with the Tories of North Carolina, secure the province, and then choose its further objectives in the South.

Of necessity, the timetable for the expedition was loose. A

winter ocean voyage might vary a number of weeks in duration, and communication between Governor Martin and the Ministry, between the Ministry and General Howe, and between General Howe and Governor Martin also was subject to all the vagaries of long sea carriage. Both Howe and Martin were told that the fleet would sail by the first of December, but it did not get away from Cork until February 13, 1776. Howe chose for the Southern command the moody, withdrawn General Clinton, and when Clinton sailed from Boston in mid-January with three small troop units, was probably relieved to be rid of his unsocial, nervous colleague.

Meanwhile, in North Carolina, Governor Martin, "moved by the pressing and reiterated assurances" given him by the loyalists, did not wait for the expedition from Ireland, but decided that the happy moment "when this country might be delivered from anarchy" was at hand and called upon the loyalists to rendezvous.

North Carolina Whigs quickly gathered, and a thousand threw themselves behind earthworks at a bridge on Moore's Creek, on the road the loyalists must take to reach the coast. The creek was an insignificant, swampy stream flowing into the Black River eighteen miles above Wilmington, but the action the rebels planned there was not a haphazard, impulsive one like that at Concord's North Bridge. North Carolina's Colonel James Moore carefully lured the Highlanders, under an experienced old soldier, to ground of Moore's own choosing, where he had posted rebel forces under Colonel's Richard Caswell and Alexander Lillington. The rebels had withdrawn from earthworks beyond the bridge to a better position behind it. A Whig account of the action there on the twenty-seventh of February was published a few days later in several newspapers:

This morning, the North Carolina minute men and militia . . . had an engagement with the Tories at Widow Moore's Creek bridge. At the break of day an alarm gun was fired, immediately after which, scarcely leaving the Americans a moment to prepare, the Tory army with Captain [Donald] McLeod at their head made their attack on Colonels Caswell and Lillington, posted near the bridge, and finding a small entrenchment vacant concluded that the Americans had abandoned their post. With this supposition, they advanced in a most furious manner over the bridge. Colonel Caswell had very wisely ordered the planks to be taken up, so that in passing they met with many difficulties. On reaching a point within thirty paces of the breastworks they were received with a very heavy fire, which did great execution. Captains

McLeod and [Farquard] Campbell were instantly killed, the former having nine bullets and twenty-four swan shot through and into his body.

The insurgents retreated with the greatest precipitation, leaving behind them some of their wagons, etc. They cut their horses out of the wagons and mounted three upon a horse. Many of them fell into the creek and were drowned. Tom Rutherford ran like a lusty fellow: both he and Felix Keenan were in arms against the Carolinians, and they by this time are prisoners, as is Lieutenant Colonel [James] Cotton, who ran at the first fire.

The battle lasted three minutes. Twenty-eight of the Tories, besides the two captains are killed or mortally wounded, and between twenty and thirty taken prisoners, among whom is his Excellency General Donald MacDonald [the aging commander-in-chief of the Tories, who had remained in the Tory camp too ill to lead the assault]. This, we think, will effectually put a stop to Toryism in North Carolina.[1]

The unknown newspaper correspondent wrote his account before the day was over and did not report that the fleeing loyalist army was overtaken and captured almost to a man: nearly eight hundred and fifty rank and file and thirty officers were made prisoner. When the rebel militia returned triumphantly to their homes, wearing plundered "Scottish clothes," Josiah Martin's scheme came to an end. No matter how earnestly he tried to convince himself that the rebels had given only a "little check" to the loyalists, they would never again, as the *Annual Register* predicted, be raised so readily. In fact, royal government in North Carolina came to its end on the dark, twisting waters of Moore's Creek.

It was May before Sir Peter Parker's whole fleet anchored off the Cape Fear and found Clinton already there wondering what to do. Days passed in indecisive discussion before the admiral broke out canvas and set the course of the expedition for South Carolina.

By this time, South Carolina, with the aid of the Continental Congress, had nearly completed plans for a warm reception. As long ago as New Year's Day, the Continental Congress had recognized that "it appears the British ministry and their agents have meditated and are preparing to make attacks upon Charleston . . . and several places in Virginia and probably in North Carolina" and recommended that the committees of these colonies make a "vigorous defense." The admonition was scarcely necessary for South Carolina. Charleston, which virtually thought, felt, and acted for the colony, had a long Whig tradition, and from the first its leaders recognized its vulnerability. Christopher Gadsden, gaunt and violent favorite of the mechanics and darling of the Liberty Boys, was a choleric Sam Adams, arguing for independence and the defense of his colony. In John Rutledge, the great port town had its Joseph Warren, and in Henry Laurens, staid merchant prince who had been brought reluctantly to "lay his finger upon his nose" at the British, it had a mature, intellectual John Hancock. The town had enjoyed its own tea party, and the Whigs had spirited away public gunpowder and royal arms under cover of night. In June, 1775, the colony had raised two regiments of a thousand men each and a regiment of rangers for the frontier. It had taken possession of a royal fort in the harbor, established a rebel government, and for President had elected John Rutledge, already in his late thirties the brilliant, influential dean of the Charleston bar.

When the Continental Congress succumbed to the pressure of John Rutledge's brother, Edward, and other Southern members, and on the first of March, 1776, named General Charles Lee to command the newly created Southern Department, Charleston already was fortifying. Crumbling batteries on its waterfront were being replaced and rotting gun carriages repaired, and a large fort was building on Sullivan's Island "as this was looked upon," according to a local officer, "as the key of the harbor." With Lee to take command, thought the Congress, Charleston would be safe, for next to the Commander-in-Chief the legislators considered him the most competent general in the army.

Indifferently leaving unpaid personal bills behind him in New York, Lee hurried south and set himself up in the Governor's Palace in Williamsburg, Virginia, to direct the defense of that colony. He concluded that since North Carolina had no strategic center of importance, the British would land their Southern expedition either in Virginia or South Carolina. When he learned from an intercepted British letter that a fleet was bound for the North Carolina coast, he thought himself in "a damned whimsical situation . . . I know not where to turn . . . I am like a dog in a dancing school. . . . I may be in the north when, as Richard the Third says, I should serve my sovereign in the west." As long as Virginia seemed a likely target, Lee remained there. When South Carolina cried to him for help, he sent Brigadier General John Armstrong to Charleston, and finally, when the enemy fleet was sighted off the Cape Fear, he started for Charleston with thirteen hundred Virginia troops, who were joined along the way by seven hundred North Carolinians.

Because of the extended absence from Charleston of Colonel Christopher Gadsden, of the First South Carolina Regiment, attending the Second Continental Congress, the direc-

tion of the city's defense had rested largely in the colonel of
the Second Regiment, William Moultrie. The colonel was
medium tall, stout and florid, a Low Countryman who had
served for years in the militia and fought the Cherokee on
the mountainous Carolina frontier. He was a man of bold,
clean features and a direct gaze, heavy-jawed, his hair thin
and parted to the right, so that a curling lock swept down
over his left eye. He was amiable enough and slow and deliberate: in some ways, his manner was reminiscent of Artemas
Ward, whom Lee had said was better suited to be a church
warden than a general. But Moultrie had some capability and
he did not hesitate to speak his mind and call a man, in person or in print, "a stupid, ignorant blockhead," if that were
his opinion. His military knowledge and comprehension were
limited, but he was valorous, open-minded, and rigorously
honest. In him were Israel Putnam's fiery personal courage
and love of a fight, and like Putnam he possessed the at-
tributes of a good regimental or field officer but few of a
general officer.

The city he had been called upon to defend was on the tip
of the peninsula formed by the confluence of the Ashley and
Cooper rivers. Down a long harbor, the peninsula pointed
like a stern index finger, some eight miles to the sea. Two
islands faced each other across the harbor mouth, Sullivan's
on the east and James on the west. Sullivan's Island lay northeast and southwest, its western end curving in like a cupped
hand toward Charleston. Here the fort was being built, across
from Fort Johnson on the marshy shore of James Island. The
sharp hooked end of Sullivan's Island formed a cove a little over a mile across between the site of the fort and the
mainland. Northeast of Sullivan's Island along the outward
slanting Atlantic coast lay Long Island, separated from it by
an inlet called the "Breach." While some defenses were being thrown up in Charleston, it was the fort on Sullivan's
Island that the South Carolinians were relying on to halt the
enemy fleet before it could reach the town and land its troops.
Colonel Moultrie had been in command of the construction
and defense of the fort since the first of the year.

On May 31, expresses pounded into Charleston to tell President Rutledge that a large fleet of British vessels had been
sighted twenty miles north. The next day, wrote Colonal
Moultrie in his memoirs, fifty of them swarmed into view off
the Charleston bar:

The sight of these vessels alarmed us very much. All
was hurry and confusion: the President with his council
busy in sending expresses to every part of the country to has-

ten down the militia, men running about the town looking for horses and carriages and boats to send their families into the country; and as they were going out through the town gates to go into the country, they met the militia from the country marching into town. Traverses were made in the principal streets, fléches thrown up at every place where troops could land, military works going on everywhere, the lead taken from the windows of the churches and dwelling houses to cast into musket balls and every preparation to receive an attack which was expected in a few days.

June [sixth], General Lee arrived from the northward and took the command of the troops. His presence gave us great spirits, as he was known to be an able, brave, and experienced officer, though hasty and rough in his manners, which the officers could not reconcile themselves to at first. It was thought by many that his coming among us was equal to a reinforcement of a thousand men, and I believe it was, because he taught us to think lightly of the enemy and gave a spur to all our actions.[2]

Lee, trailed as always by his dogs, poked into every street, path and alley of scented, semitropical Charleston, now, in June, aflame with oleanders, roses, and the blooming pomegranates. Nothing about the defenses of the gracious, flourishing city suited him. Its genteel, easy-going leaders had been ignorant and remiss in their task of fortifying the town and its harbor. Too little had been done in leveling warehouses and dwellings near the wharves and waterfronts to provide a field for gunfire and to deprive landing parties of cover. All too few of the pleasant, shaded streets had been slashed with earthworks and barricades. Too much reliance was being placed upon the harbor to defend the town. A personal reconnaissance convinced Lee that the peculiar situation of the place had lulled its defenders into a false sense of security.

When Lee crossed the cove to the rolling sand dunes and myrtle bushes of Sullivan's Island, he told Moultrie in unmistakable terms what he thought of the unfinished fort. Moultrie had not been exactly energetic in its construction, and now with the enemy fleet sounding the bar and seeking a way into the harbor, only two sides of the ponderous square structure were completed—the eastern and the southern, which faced the ship channel. Lee told Moultrie that he did "not like that post at all," and then, according to Moultrie, he elaborated:

He said there was no way to retreat, that the garrison would be sacrificed, nay, he called it a "slaughter pen" and wished to withdraw the garrison and give up the post. But President Rutledge insisted that it should not be given up.

Then General Lee said it was "absolutely necessary to have a bridge of boats for a retreat." But boats enough could not be had, the distance over being at least a mile. . . . For my part, I never was uneasy on not having a retreat because I never imagined that the enemy could force me to that necessity.[3]

Moultrie's confidence derived from his conviction that the fleet could do little damage to his fort and that he was prepared quite adequately to handle a landing force. Logically, a hostile force would come ashore on Long Island, and then when ready, would attempt to cross the Breach to the northeastern end of Sullivan's. Therefore, facing the Breach, Moultrie had stationed behind earthworks some eight hundred men, about half of them riflemen, and a small battery of two pieces. He doubted that the enemy could force a landing, but if he succeeded, the riflemen would gall his flanks for three miles and then throw themselves into the fort ahead of the redcoats. Furthermore, fifteen hundred men stood ready to cross the cove from Haddrell's Point to reinforce him. "I therefore felt myself perfectly easy," he said, "because I never calculated Sir Henry Clinton's numbers to be more than three thousand men."

Whatever the colonel lacked in perception he made up in valor. A former master of a man-of-war came to the fort one day and walked along the gun platforms with him, peering out of the embrasures at the fleet. To Moultrie he said, "Colonel, what do you think of it now?" Moultrie said he would "beat them."

"Sir," the seaman said, "when those ships . . . come to lay alongside of your fort, they will knock it down in half an hour. . . ."

"Then," said Moultrie, "we will lay behind the ruins and prevent their men from landing."

That was not the way that Charles Lee saw it. He had little faith in Moultrie's fort and none in the whole strategic concept that fathered its construction. He was sure that the enemy would sail past the fort and bombard it to ruins from the west. He was so annoyed by Moultrie's stubborn insistence that he could maintain it and his paradoxical lassitude in working on the structure that he seriously considered removing the colonel from command. Only the swift rush of events saved Moultrie's position.

What worried Lee even more than Sullivan's Island was the inadequacy of preparations on the mainland for meeting the British. He thought surely they would land their army on Long Island or perhaps Sullivan's Island, cross to the mainland, and fall upon Charleston while the warships supported

them by hammering the city from the water. What he did not
figure in his calculations was a sea marsh almost two miles
wide that lay between the islands and the main, through
which Clinton could not possibly move his troops. So Lee's
emphasis went upon strengthening the city from the Ashley,
around the point and up to Gadsden's great wharf on the
Cooper, although he did not neglect Haddrell's Point opposite
the islands or James Island facing the harbor. Perhaps only
the elements saved the city, for unfavorable winds prevented
the fleet from conquering the bar for several days, and squalls
and tempestuous weather made its anchorage uneasy.

For eight days Clinton landed troops on Long Island, until
on June 15, almost his whole force was there, but the fleet
was not yet ready to act. These tense days gave the Americans an opportunity to strengthen their positions, especially
on the island. When the month had almost run its course,
the eastern and southern curtains and bastions were complete
and inside them a brick-supported platform mounted twenty-
five French and English cannon of various weights. Cavaliers
to the right and left boasted another six guns. The northern and western sides of the fort, however, were logged up
only seven feet high.

For days neither the British land forces nor the fleet
showed their intentions while the Americans kept a constant
guard. The night of June 27 passed, hot and quiet but for
the night noises of the insects and the rippling surf on the
beach. Toward morning it grew cooler. Moultrie, aching with
gout, spent a restless night and soon after dawn rode out of
the fort to visit his advance guard facing Long Island:

While I was there I saw a number of the enemy's boats
in motion at the back of Long Island, as if they intended a
descent upon our advanced post. At the same time I saw the
men-of-war loose their topsails. I hurried back to the fort as
fast as possible. When I got there the ships were already
under sail.

I immediately ordered the long roll to beat and officers and
men to their posts. We had scarcely manned our guns when
the . . . ships of war came sailing up as if in confidence of
victory. As soon as they came within the reach of our guns,
we began to fire. They were soon abreast of the fort, let go
their anchors with springs upon their cables and begun their
attack most furiously about ten o'clock. . . .[4]

The first vessel to find her place before the fort was the
bomb-ketch, *Thunder*. Covered closely by a twenty-two-gun
frigate, the *Friendship*, she opened on the salient angle of
the southeastern bastion. Said Moultrie:

The *Thunder* . . . had the beds of her mortars soon disabled [as a result of deliberate overcharges of powder to give their projectiles distance]. She threw her shells in a very good direction. Most of them fell within the fort, but we had a morass in the middle that swallowed them up instantly and those that fell in the sand in and about the fort were immediately buried, so that very few of them bursted amongst us.[5].

The *Thunder's* solo bombardment continued while the rest of the fleet found their positions. The *Active*, twenty-eight-gun frigate, ignoring the American fire that tore through her rigging, came up "less than half-musket shot from the fort" and swung broadside, springs on her cables. Close behind were the *Bristol*, the commodore's fifty-gun ship, and the *Experiment*, fifty guns, and the *Solebay*, twenty-eight guns. At one time, Moultrie wrote:

During the action, General Lee paid us a visit through a heavy line of fire [across the cove] and pointed two or three guns himself, then said to me, "Colonel, I see you are doing very well here. You have no occasion for me. I will go up to town again," and then left us.[6]

Lee, who was no stranger to the roar of battle, was appalled by the awesome crash of the fleet's cannonade: "the most furious fire I ever heard or saw." Three enemy vessels peeled off the fleet and sailed westward to gain stations from which to shield the rest of the fleet against attack by Continental vessels that might be hovering in the rivers and to enfilade the southern platform. They fouled each other and went aground. Only one cleared without damage and then not until it was too late to accomplish their mission. Had they succeeded, thought Moultrie, they would have driven his crews from their guns.

Through the day, said Moultrie:

Never did men fight more bravely and never were men more cool. Several of the officers as well as myself were smoking our pipes and giving orders . . . but we laid them down when General Lee came into the fort.[7]

Lack of sufficient powder, the Achilles' heel of every rebel action, was again their "only distress." At the opening of action, the fort possessed only enough for twenty-eight rounds each for twenty-six guns and for twenty rounds of musketry. Soon after noon, two hundred pounds were brought in from a schooner lying in the cove, and late in the afternoon, five hundred pounds from Haddrell's Point. But often during the day, to conserve powder, Moultrie ordered the men to slow

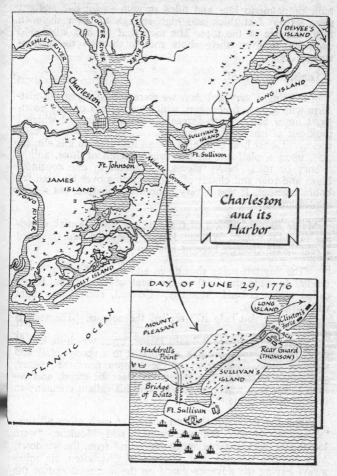

Charleston and its Harbor

DAY OF JUNE 29, 1776

and for a while to cease altogether their fire. He was convinced:

There cannot be a doubt but that if we had had as much powder as we could have expended in the time, that the men-of-war must have struck their colors, or they would certainly have been sunk, because they could not retreat, as the wind and tide were against them, and if they had proceeded up to town they would have been in a much worse situation. They could not make any impression on our fort built of palmetto logs and filled in with earth; our merlons were sixteen feet thick and high enough to cover the men from the fire of the tops. The men that we had killed and wounded received their shots mostly through the embrasures. . . .[8]

Later, he observed:

It being a very hot day, we were served along the platform with grog in firebuckets, which we partook of very heartily. I never had a more agreeable draught than that which I took out of one of those buckets. . . . It may be very easily conceived what heat and thirst a man must feel in this climate . . . upon a platform on the twenty-eighth of June, amidst twenty or thirty heavy pieces of cannon in one continual blaze and roar and clouds of smoke curling over his head for hours together. It was a very honorable situation, but a very unpleasant one.[9]

Major Barnard Elliott of the Artillery saw a genial, drawling sergeant named William Jasper, whom he had recruited a year ago in Georgia become a hero:

The flagstaff being shot down and the staff falling to the ground [outside the fort] in the heat of the action, Jasper called to his colonel, Moultrie, "Colonel, don't let us fight without our color."

"How can you help it?" replied the colonel. "The staff is gone."

"Then I will replace it," said Jasper, upon which he leaped over the wall, took the flag and tied it to a sponge staff and stuck it upon the merlon of the bastion near the enemy, gave three huzzas in the dangerous place he stood, and retired to his gun, where he fought with his gallant company to the end of the battle.[10]

While the fleet and the fort roared at each other all day, "thousands of our fellow citizens," said Moultrie, "were looking on with anxious hopes and fears" from the windows, high piazzas, steeples, and wharves of Charleston, six miles away. Facing the advance guard on the northeast end of the island, Clinton was unable to get at the rebels. To his "great mortification" he had discovered that the Breach which had been reported to him to be eighteen inches deep at low tide was, in reality, seven feet deep and could not be forded. During the morning he made one effort to push a few boats across in the face of the fire of Moultrie's fieldpieces, but was turned back and passed a miserable day of frustrated inactivity. Defeat of the rebels depended then entirely upon the fleet which, badly mauled, never slackened its fire.

Through the weary, close twilight of the sultry evening and into the smothering darkness, the flash of the big guns blossomed over the harbor. At last, at nearly nine-thirty, silence settled over the water, and Moultrie hurried a courier to General Lee to report that the fleet had not knocked the fort down around his ears; on the contrary, he thought he had just about finished the fleet. Without the usual piping of orders and cry of anchor chains, the enemy vessels silently slipped their cables, and the watch on the fort saw their lights move off about eleven o'clock toward their old anchorage three miles away.

Morning of the twenty-ninth revealed the full extent of the battering the fort had received: its embrasures were ragged, some guns awry, timbers were torn, and the parade was pocked with holes and scattered with debris. But only ten men were killed and twenty-four wounded of the three hundred and eighty officers and rank and file who had served in the fort on the twenty-eighth.

Nearly a mile away, the *Actaeon* heeled over on the Middle Ground; the enemy had failed to float her, and soon smoke was seen curling from her. Her own crew had set her afire. During the morning she exploded. Farther away, the fleet and the transports lay quiet. Through their glasses, officers at the fort could see the damage they had done the ships.

In the days that followed, while work continued on the fort, Lee and President Rutledge visited the island. The President gave the regiment a hogshead of rum, and at a review of troops unbuckled his own dress sword and handed it to the abashed but proud Sergeant Jasper. Lee thanked the troops for their gallant conduct and stood by while Mrs. Barnard Elliott, wife of the artillery regiment's major, presented the Second Regiment with "a most Elegant pr of Colours Embrodered."

Five deserters from the fleet brought details of the suffering of the fleet that were very satisfying to the defenders of Charleston. The ships' carpenters, they said, were "all hard at work, and that we need not expect another visit from them at present." Clinton's troops lingered for days on Long Island, entirely inactive, plagued by mosquitoes and lack of fresh provisions and water. Lee sent the British general a present of fresh food, in return for which Clinton sent ashore porter and cheese. At length, the British troops boarded their transports and sailed for New York, followed by their fighting ships.

Lee was probably sound in his judgment on the fort. Only the accident that befell the three ships on the Middle Ground prevented their reaching a station from which they certainly would have blasted the garrison from its fort. But Rutledge, who had insisted on defending Fort Sullivan, General Moultrie, and General Lee shared credit for shattering the King's hope of Southern conquest. Their success was celebrated in a ballad expressing Sir Peter's version of the affray and making ribald allusion to the fact that those of his damaged parts he thought "not worth mentioning" included his "posteriors." The deserters had reported that "the commodore had his breeches tore off, his backside laid bare," and the song ran:

> . . . With much labour and toil
> Unto Sullivan's Isle
> I came fierce as Falstaff or Pistol,
> But the Yankees ('od rot 'em)
> I could not get at 'em:
> Most terribly maul'd my poor Bristol.

> Bold Clinton by Land
> Did quietly stand
> While I made a thundering clatter;
> But the channel was deep,
> So he could only peep
> And not venture over the water.

> De'el take 'em; their shot
> Came so swift and so hot,
> And the cowardly dogs stood so stiff, sirs,
> That I put the ship about,
> And was glad to get out,
> Or they would not have left me a skiff, sirs!

> Now bold as a Turk
> I proceed to New York,
> Where with Clinton and Howe you may find me.
> I've the wind in my tail,
> And am hoisting my sail,
> To leave Sullivan's Island behind me.

> But, my lords, do no fear
> For before the next year,
> (Altho' a small island could fret us,)
> The Continent whole
> We shall take, by my soul,
> If the cowardly Yankees will let us.[11]

"GEORGE REJECTED AND LIBERTY PROTECTED"

New York

APRIL-AUGUST 1776

THE CANADIAN expedition already was sealed, and the British stroke against Charleston had been launched, when in March Howe evacuated Boston. Although Washington's thoughts were upon both these distant fronts, his first consideration was the immediate defense of New York, which he was sure Howe would endeavor to capture. From Boston he rode there without delay, and in the forenoon of April 13, he was on Manhattan Island.

In contrast to siege-worn Boston, a city nearly dead, New York, with a swelling population of nearly twenty-five thousand, was all bustle and elegance in spite of the curbs put upon its normal life by the tensions and shortages of war. The town covered an area less than a mile square at the southern tip of the island that lay between the East and Harlem rivers on the east and the Hudson on the west. Its streets were wider and more regular than those of Boston, and its main thoroughfare, Broadway, running northward a mile from the ancient stone fort at the Battery, was shaded by rows of trees and lined with fine residences, churches, and public buildings. Beyond the limits of the city, country roads meandered through the wooded hills and marshes and farmlands that stretched some twelve miles to little wooden King's Bridge that crossed Spuyten Duyvil to the mainland. The whole length of the long island tilted eastward like a listing ship, so that the craggy, bold banks of the Hudson sloped brokenly down to a level shoreline on the East River and the Harlem. Near the northern end, the banks of the Harlem also were lofty, wilderness cliffs. In this "Out Ward" lay the baronial country seats of the DeLanceys, the Hogelands, the Murrays, and others; beyond the city wall were little settlements at places called the Bowery, Bloomingdale, and Harlem. There great mansions at the end of tree-lined drives were as imposing as the splendid town houses; but it was the city and not

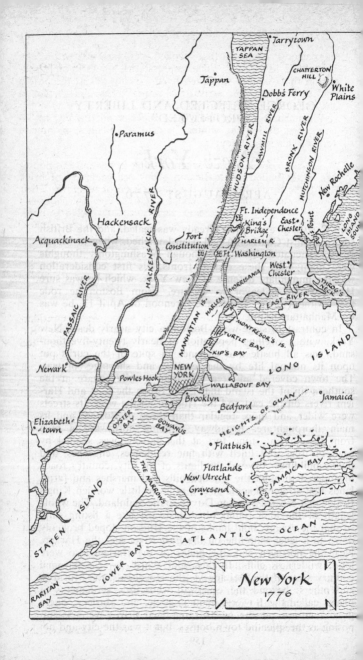

New York
1776

its pastoral environs that evoked comparisons with "any metropolis in Europe." The impression it made upon Washington that April is suggested by his giving out as the parole for the day after his arrival the words "New York," and as the countersign "Prosperity."

When Henry Knox had visited the city on the way to Ticonderoga during the winter, he had described it in precise terms to his wife, Lucy:

> New York is a place where I think in general the houses are better built than in Boston. They are generally of brick and three stories high with the largest kind of windows. Their churches are grand; their college, workhouse, and hospitals most excellently situated and also exceedingly commodious, their principal streets much wider than ours. The people— why, the people are magnificent: in their equipages which are numerous, in their house furniture which is fine, in their pride and conceit which are inimitable, in their profaneness which is intolerable, in the want of principle which is prevalent, in their Toryism which is insufferable, and for which they must repent in dust and ashes.[1]

The face and the spirit of the city had changed considerably in the five months since Henry Knox's November visit, although "inimical persons," said Washington, were "too many." The mayor was a virulent Tory, and even the Committee of Safety humored the royal governor, who lay off New York in a British vessel—too timid to remain in the city, too stubborn to sail away. During the winter, many hundreds of fearful families had moved out of the city, which they knew inevitably would become a battleground. When General Charles Lee had arrived in February it had seemed deserted. Houses were empty, doors locked, shutters drawn; but it had come quickly to life as regiments from neighboring colonies marched in. "Troops are daily coming in," wrote a New Yorker on February 23. "They break open and quarter themselves in any houses they find shut up."

Lee had recognized that Manhattan, surrounded by navigable water, would be next to impossible to hold against a combined land and naval force, but like another Bunker Hill a high price could be exacted for the taking of it. So he planned traverses and barricades on the streets, and redoubts on three hills just north of the city; in fact, he told Congress, "the whole island is to be redoubted . . . quite to King's Bridge," which must also be fortified to preserve communication with Connecticut and New England. He reasoned that secure possession of Long Island, east of Manhattan, was of greater importance than that of New York, for if the enemy should batter down the defenses of New York they would find it almost impossible to subsist in the city cut off from supplies by Long Island. Furthermore, crossfire between the island and New York, Lee thought, could close the East River to the British.

With characteristic disregard of polite by-your-leave, Lee put every one of the seventeen hundred soldiers he could muster to work digging trenches, cutting down trees, and throwing up works, until the streets, when the Continentals from Boston arrived, were chopped up everywhere with earthworks and barricades.

Lee, so recently from Boston, was more than ordinarily aware of the Columbia heights, which rose a hundred feet above the East River on Long Island and commanded New York much as Dorchester Heights had commanded Boston. Out of sight beyond the wooded bluff was the little cluster of houses of Brooklyn village; here he hoped to place the center of a projected encampment of three thousand men behind a series of strong defensive works from Wallabout Bay on the northeast to Gowanus Cove on the southwest, about a mile and a half apart. Thus he could protect the heights. For the present, however, he could spare only a few hundred men for Long Island, and the work had to wait.

Lee was not destined to see completed all the plans he had made for the defense of New York. Early in March he had departed for the South, and had left the New York command to a brand-new brigadier, William Alexander, Earl of Stirling, who had come there as colonel of New Jersey Continentals a few weeks earlier.

In his own way, Lord Stirling was as odd a character as Lee. First of all, Lord Stirling was not an earl. He was a ruddy-faced, handsome, hard-drinking, fifty-year-old American, whose claim to an extinct title, through his father, a prominent and wealthy lawyer, had been denied by the House of Lords but had been pleasantly accepted by his neighbors and associates in the hills of northern Somerset County, New Jersey, where he lived as a genuine nobleman. Although skilled in mathematics and astronomy and the possessor of an extensive library, he was a man of no especial brilliance or attainments. He either lived blindly beyond his means, or was ridiculously incapable of managing money; his pretentious estate and his extravagant belongings were mortgaged to the hilt, and in 1775 he tottered on the verge of bankruptcy. For years he had stood with the conservatives. No one could explain why he had embraced the Whig cause, though his detractors claimed that he made the "desperate push" of joining the rebel Americans "to get rid of the inconvenience of his legal obligations." His associates often ridiculed his pretensions, and one of them, who thought him "graceful . . . pleasing and interesting," was not above repeating a story of his jealousy of his title: "Being present at the execution of a soldier for desertion, the criminal at the gallows repeatedly cried out, 'The Lord have mercy on me!' His Lordship with warmth exclaimed, 'I won't, you rascal, I won't have mercy on you!' "

But for all his weaknesses, Lord Stirling, who had served in the French and Indian War, was respected by his superior officers. Though afflicted with severe rheumatism, he was agreeable and considerate. And when there was fighting to be done, he was in the thick of it, sober and as courageous as a lion.

Stirling no sooner had taken command in New York with a force of 2,422 Continentals and about sixteen hundred militia when he heard from Washington that Howe appeared ready to evacuate Boston and advance on New York. In every direction he sent urgent appeals for more men, and redoubled efforts to complete the city's defensive works. His command at New York was shorter than Lee's, less than a month, but he was efficient and energetic; he turned out every citizen to work in shifts on fortifications. On April 4, Putnam arrived and took over command; he added to the fortifications Governor's Island and Red Hook, opposite it on Long Island. To these, Washington, a few weeks later, added still others, Forts Washington and Independence, on the northern stretches of Manhattan Island, and Constitution, soon to be named Fort Lee, across on the Jersey shore. Between Forts Washington and Constitution he stretched ship obstructions across the river. He also fortified Powle's Hook, on the Jersey side opposite the city.

When the last of the Continentals arrived from Boston, Washington had a force all too small, and unhappily he was forced to surrender four badly needed regiments under General William Thompson to the Canadian expedition, to be followed a few days later by six more under General John Sullivan. On April 23, Washington had only eighty-three hundred men fit for duty, which he brigaded, sending Nathanael Greene's to Long Island and scattering the others appropriately on Manhattan. He appealed to both New York and New Jersey for more men, meanwhile setting to work those he had on the one great urgent task, fortifying to meet Howe's attack.

The presence of the Continentals in the restless, divided city emboldened the Whigs immensely. Soon Peter Elting reported with glee:

We had some grand Tory rides in this city this week.
. . . Several of them were handled very roughly, being carried through the streets on rails, their clothes tore from their
backs and their bodies pretty well mingled with the dust. . . .
There is hardly a Tory face to be seen this morning.
Our [New York] Congress published a Resolve on the occasion, expressing their disapprobation, though it might have
proceeded from a proper zeal for the liberties of American
freedom, and desire that it may cease and that a mode for
punishing such offenders will soon be adopted for this colony.[2]

Problems of discipline among the troops became much
more difficult than they had been at Boston. The city, full
of women, offered temptations that had not existed in the
villages and camps of New England. A certain neighborhood,
an old-time church property, and still called "the holy
ground," now supported quite unchurchly activity. Colonel
Baldwin wrote an unvarnished letter about it to his wife:

The whores (by information) continue their employ,
which is become very lucrative. Their unparalleled conduct
is a sufficient antidote against any desires that a person can
have that has one spark of modesty or virtue left in him. . . .
Perhaps you will call me censorious and exclaim too much
upon bare reports when I say that I was never within the
doors of nor exchanged a word with any of them except in
the execution of my duty as officer of the day in going the
grand round with my guard of escort, have broke up the
knots of men and women fighting, pulling caps, swearing,
crying, "Murder!" etc., hurried them off to the Provost Dungeon by half dozens, there let them lay mixed till next day.
Then some are punished and some get off clear—Hell's
work. . . .[3]

Another man recorded that "Several limbs and heads of
men were found at the holy ground which was supposed to
be killed by the whores. . . . No man is suffered to be there
after nine o'clock at night."
Liquor, bane of every army, brought from Washington one
of the first "Off Limits" designations in American military history:

The gin shops and other houses where liquors have been
heretofore retailed within or near the lines (except the house
at the Two Ferries) are strictly forbidden to sell any for the
future to any soldier in the army and the inhabitants of said
houses near the lines are immediately to move out of them;
they are to be appropriated to the use of the troops.
If any soldier of the army shall be found disguised with
liquor, as has been too much the practice heretofore, the Gen-

eral is determined to have him punished with the utmost severity, as no soldier in such situation can be either fit for defense or attack. The General orders that no sutler in the army
shall sell to any soldier more than one half pint of spirit per
day.[4]

Even on rural Long Island, Nathanael Greene had his dis-
ciplinary troubles as the weather turned warmer. He issued
a General Order:

Complaint having been made by the inhabitants situated
near the Mill Pond that some of the soldiers come there to go
into swimming in the open view of the women and that they
come out of the water and run to the houses naked with a
design to insult and wound the modesty of female decency,
'tis with concern that the general finds himself under the disagreeable necessity of expressing his disapprobation of such a
beastly conduct. Whoever has been so void of shame as to
act such an infamous part, let them veil their past disgrace
by their future good behavior, for they may depend upon it,
any new instances of such scandalous conduct will be punished with the utmost severity.[5]

The army had been two months at New York when the
"discovery of the greatest and vilest attempt ever made
against our country" provided exciting mess gossip for the
troops. It evoked a shocked letter from a Continental surgeon
who retailed some truth and every exaggerated rumor that
swept the army:

The Mayor (David Matthews) of [New] York with a
number of villians who were possessed of fortunes, and who
formerly ranked with gentlemen, had impiously dared an undertaking, big with fatal consequences to the virtuous army
in York, and which in all probability would have given the
enemy possession of the city with little loss. Their design was,
upon the first engagement which took place, to have murdered (with trembling I say it) the best man on earth: General Washington was to have been the first subject of their
unheard of SACRICIDE. Our magazines . . . were to have been
blown up; every general officer and every other who was active in serving his country in the field was to have been as-
sassinated; our cannon were to be spiked up; and in short,
every the most accursed scheme was laid to give us into the
hands of the enemy and to ruin us. . . .
Their design was deep, long concerted, and wicked to a
great degree. But happily for us, it has pleased God to discover it to us in season, and I think we are making a right
improvement of it (as the good folks say). We are hanging
them as fast as we find them out. I have just now returned
from the execution of one of the General's Guard, [Thomas

Hickey]. He was the first that has been tried. Yesterday at 11 o'clock he received sentence; today at eleven he was hung in the presence of the whole army.[6]

In reality the "Hickey plot" was neither so wide nor so deep as the gossip of the army had it. Headquarters probably thought that former Royal Governor Tryon was behind the affair, though no conclusive evidence against him ever was produced. At the least, the plot appeared to have as its objectives the destruction of King's Bridge, the seizing of a battery, the encouragement of the Tories to rise when the British fleet came, and the persuasion of a number of men to desert to the enemy's forces. At the most, some of the rabid parties to it might have entertained certain of the schemes peddled by rumor-mongers, but in all likelihood this was not the case.

Though Thomas Hickey's execution provided the chief topic of tavern talk the night of June 28, by the next morning it was surely forgotten. About nine o'clock, officers, looking to the high grounds on Staten Island, where three flagpoles stood, saw in their glasses long-expected signals flying—the British fleet was in sight. Rifleman Daniel McCurtin "was upstairs in an out-house and spied as I peeped out the bay something resembling a wood of pine trees trimmed. . . . I could not believe my eyes . . . when in about ten minutes, the whole bay was full of shipping as ever it could be. I declare that I thought all London was afloat." By afternoon almost one hundred vessels were anchored in the Hook.

On the first of July many vessels raised sail, came closer, and anchored off Gravesend, Long Island; hurriedly Washington sent five hundred men to strengthen Greene's small force there. Next day some of the men-of-war were close to Long Island, and before dark about fifty-five of them had anchored hard by Staten Island. Washington was sure that Howe's whole fleet was off New York. His fear that the British general intended to quickly surround the city was heightened by an enormous enemy landing of over nine thousand men on Staten Island on the third. A couple of days later, when they began to throw up works, Washington's apprehension eased momentarily. Spies and deserters reported that the enemy might be planning a simultaneous advance into Jersey and attack on New York, and probably was waiting for another vast fleet and tremendous reinforcement under General William Howe's brother, Admiral Viscount Howe, newly appointed to command of the North American station.

There was no doubt about it: a great battle, perhaps a long campaign—the first test of the Continentals and their commanders in the field—was near, though no one knew when or exactly where the British would deliver their first blow.

To add to the gravity of the situation, word came at this moment, while the enemy was assembling, that the Congress had at last renounced every allegiance to the King. The rebels, if they failed now to win their independence on the field of war, no longer could hope for mercy as misguided subjects. Henceforth, if defeated, they could expect the treatment according a subjugated foe. A British observer expressed a general Tory view:

> The Congress have at length thought it convenient to throw off the mask. Their Declaration . . . while it avows their right to independence, is founded upon such reasons only, as prove *that* Independence to have been their object from the beginning. A more impudent, false, and atrocious Proclamation was never fabricated by the hands of man.[7]

Actually that "impudent" proclamation had come about through troubled argument, endless debate, and the final resolution of bitter differences between those equally well-meaning Americans who opposed and those who supported separation from the mother country. As late as March, 1775, Benjamin Franklin swore that he had never heard an American "drunk or sober" express a desire for permanent separation from England. Not even Lexington and Concord had produced an immediate demand for independence. Two months afterward, Thomas Jefferson of Virginia had written to John Randolph, "I am sincerely one of those . . . who would rather be in dependence on Great Britain, properly limited, than on any other nation on earth, or than on no nation. But I am one of those, too, who, rather than submit to the rights of legislating for us, assumed by the British Parliament, and which late experience had shown they will so cruelly exercise, would lend my hand to sink the whole island in the ocean." And so a war had come and continued for month on month, while Congress had vacillated and refused to take a stand.

The passage by Parliament of the Prohibitory Acts at the end of 1775, notifying all nations that a state of war existed, delighted the more radical Whigs; by thus declaring war, England voluntarily gave the colonies the legal status of a foreign nation—and therefore an independent one. By removing his protection, they reasoned, the King forfeited the colonies' allegiance. Hundreds of Americans were relieved of the disagreeable decision for independence. In a sense, it was thrust upon them, and talk of independence, previously upon the tongues of the radicals only, became common.

An instrument almost as effective as the Prohibitory Acts in bringing about the decision for independence was an anonymous pamphlet called *Common Sense*, which appeared in January, 1776, and flooded the country. It actually was the work of an English immigrant stay-maker, minor tax official, and political writer named Thomas Paine. John Adams reviewed it for his wife, Abigail:

> You ask what is thought of *Common Sense*. Sensible men think there are some whims, some sophisms, some artful addresses to superstitious notion, some keen attempt upon the passions, in the pamphlet. But all agree, there is a great deal of good sense delivered in clear, simple, concise, and nervous style. His sentiments of the abilities of America and of the difficulty of a reconciliation with Great Britain are generally approved. But his notions and plans of continental government are not much applauded. Indeed, this writer has a better hand in pulling down than building.
>
> It has been very generally propagated through the continent that I wrote this pamphlet. But although I could not have written anything in so manly and striking a style, I flatter myself I should have made a more respectable figure as an architect, if I had undertaken such a work. This writer seems to have very inadequate ideas of what is proper and necessary to be done in order to form constitutions for single colonies, as well as a great model of union for the whole.[8]

Adams, always an advocate of independence, admitted that that part of *Common Sense* dealing with the question of independence was "clearly written, and contained a tolerable summary of the arguments which I had been repeating again and again in Congress for nine months."

Over one hundred thousand copies of *Common Sense* were soon in circulation; it was read by cobblers in their shops, bakers by their ovens, teachers in their schools, and by officers in the army to their standing ranks. Its influence was clear. "*Common Sense* has made independents of the majority of the country," observed a South Carolinian in March, 1776. In April, Washington was writing: ". . . by private letters . . . from Virginia, I find *Common Sense* is working a powerful change there in the minds of many men."

On the seventh of June, in accordance with instructions from the legislature of Virginia, Richard Henry Lee submitted the resolution "that these United Colonies are, and of right ought to be, free and independent states, that they are absolved from all allegiance to the British Crown, and that all political connection between them and the State of Great Britain is, and ought to be, totally dissolved. That it is expedient forthwith to take the most effectual measures for forming foreign alliances. That a plan of confederation be prepared and transmitted to the respective colonies for their consideration and approbation." The resolution was moved and seconded.

A committee of Thomas Jefferson, Benjamin Franklin, John Adams, Roger Sherman, and Robert R. Livingston was appointed June 11 to draw up a document of independence; the same day another committee was created to construct a plan of confederation.

Thirty-three-year-old Jefferson, with "a reputation for literature, science, and a happy talent for composition," according to John Adams, thought the honor of writing a declaration of independence should go to the old statesman Franklin, but Franklin insisted that Jefferson should be the author, for Jefferson wrote better than he. Canny Ben Franklin also remarked to a friend that "I have made it a rule . . . whenever in my power, to avoid becoming the draftsman of papers to be reviewed by a public body."

A half-century later, Jefferson recalled those busy Philadelphia days:

> At the time of writing that instrument, I lodged in the house of a Mr. Graaf, a new brick house, three stories high, of which I rented the second floor, consisting of a parlor and bedroom, ready furnished. In that parlor I wrote habitually, and . . . this paper particularly. . . .
>
> The proprietor . . . was a young man, son of a German, and then newly married. I think he was a bricklayer and that his house was on the south side of Market Street, probably between Seventh and Eighth streets and if not the only house on that part of the street, I am sure there were few others near it. I have some idea that it was a corner house. . . .[9]

In Graaf's upstairs parlor, on a folding writing-box, the tall, lean, red-headed, freckled man of a thousand interests labored over the declaration far into the warm June nights. The writing did not come easy, though he had fresh in mind the thoughts and phrases he had fashioned a few weeks before in the preamble to a draft of a constitution for his native state of Virginia; the preamble consisted of charges against the King, and was the foundation of the longest section of the document he now composed. He consulted "neither book nor pamphlet." As he deleted a word here, changed one there, he kept before him a purpose which he stated frankly in after years:

> . . . Not to find out new principles, or new arguments, never before thought of, not merely to say things which had

never been said before; but to place before mankind the common sense of the subject, in terms so plain and firm as to command their assent, and to justify ourselves in the independent stand we are compelled to take. Neither aiming at originality of principle or sentiment, nor yet copied from any particular and previous writing, it was intended to be an expression of the American mind, and to give to that expression the proper tone and spirit called for by the occasion.[10]

Both John Adams and Benjamin Franklin read Jefferson's draft of a declaration and made minor changes in it. The committee made a few more and then reported the document to the Congress on June 28.

On the first of July, the Congress resolved itself into a committee to consider Richard Henry Lee's "resolution respecting independency." Lee had returned to Virginia to attend an ailing wife, and in his absence John Adams argued the cause of the affirmative in a powerful speech, which was answered with equal vigor by conservative John Dickinson of Pennsylvania, who attacked Lee's resolution on the basis of logic, asserting that it would be foolish to declare independence before establishing an American government. But the next day, the motion for independence was carried by a vote of nine colonies, though adoption of the written declaration was deferred for further study of the document. John Adams wrote jubilantly to Abigail:

The second day of July, 1776, will be the most memorable epocha in the history of America. I am apt to believe that it will be celebrated by succeeding generations as the great anniversary festival. It ought to be commemorated as the day of deliverance, by solemn acts of devotion to God Almighty. It ought to be solemnized with pomp and parade, with shows, games, sports, guns, bells, bonfires, and illuminations, from one end of this continent to the other, from this time forward forevermore.

You will think me transported with enthusiasm, but I am not. I am well aware of the toil and blood and treasure that it will cost us to maintain this Declaration and support and defend these states. Yet, through all the gloom, I can see the rays of ravishing light and glory. I can see that the end is more than worth all the means. And that posterity will triumph in that day's transaction, even although we should rue it, which I trust in God we shall not.[11]

It was not until July 4 that Jefferson's Declaration of Independence was adopted by all the colonies; Caesar Rodney of Delaware rode all night through a violent thunderstorm to cast his vote for the Declaration—still in "boots and spurs"

—to break the tie of a divided Delaware delegation. The actual signing of the document did not take place until sometime later, when a proper parchment copy was made; years afterward, John Adams, recalling the struggle to get the document approved, erroneously referred to the adoption of the Declaration on the fourth as the signing of it, but cast interesting light upon the spirit of the day:

They who were then members, all signed it, and, as I could not see their hearts, it would be hard for me to say that they did not approve it; but, as far as I could penetrate the intricate, internal foldings of their souls, I then believed, and have not since altered my opinion, that there were several who signed with regret, and several others, with many doubts and much lukewarmness. The measure had been upon the carpet for months, and obstinately opposed from day to day. Majorities were constantly against it. For many days the majority depended upon Mr. Hewes of North Carolina. While a member, one day, was speaking, and reading documents from all the colonies, to prove that the public opinion, the general sense of all, was in favor of the measure, when he came to North Carolina, and produced letters and public proceedings which demonstrated that the majority of that colony were in favor of it, Mr. Hewes, who had hitherto constantly voted against it, started suddenly upright, and lifting up both his hands to Heaven, as if he had been in a trance, cried out, "It is done! and I will abide by it." I would give more for a perfect painting of the terror and horror upon the faces of the old majority, at that critical moment, than for the best piece of Raphael. The question, however, was eluded by an immediate motion for adjournment.

The struggle in Congress was long known abroad. Some members, who foresaw that the point would be carried, left the house and went home, to avoid voting in the affirmative or negative. Pennsylvania and New Jersey recalled all their delegates who had voted against independence, and sent new ones expressly to vote for it. The last debate but one was the most copious and the most animated; but the question was now evaded by a motion to postpone it to another day; some members, however, declaring that, if the question should be now demanded, they should vote for it, but they wished for a day or two more to consider of it. When that day arrived, some of the new members desired to hear the arguments for and against the measure. When these were summarily recapitulated, the question was put and carried. There were no yeas and nays in those times. A committee was appointed to draw up a declaration; when reported, it underwent abundance of criticism and alteration; but, when finally accepted, all those members who had voted against independence, now declared they would sign and support it.[12]

The parties to the Declaration did not deceive themselves about the seriousness of the step they were taking; few ignored the shadow of the gallows that fell across their action that day. But even in this grave moment they were able to make jests, however grisly. An anecdote went around the country:

Mr. Harrison, a delegate from Virginia, is a large portly man. Mr. Gerry, of Massachusetts, is slender and spare. A little time after the solemn transaction of signing the instrument, Mr. Harrison said smilingly to Mr. Gerry, "When the hanging scene comes to be exhibited, I shall have the advantage over you on account of my size. All will be over with me in a moment, but you will be kicking in the air half an hour after I am gone."[13]

The Declaration of Independence was first proclaimed in the State House yard in Philadelphia on July 8, where the reading was greeted by "3 repeated huzzas." Throughout the day bells tolled, people paraded, and in the evening bonfires blazed. Despite the critical shortage of gunpowder, salutes were fired.

The next day the Declaration was read to the assembled troops at New York at six P.M., and Washington remarked, "The General hopes that this important event will serve as a fresh incentive to every officer and soldier to act with fidelity and courage, knowing that now the peace and safety of his country depend, under God, solely on the success of our arms, and that he is now in the service of a State possessed of sufficient power to reward his merit, and advance him to the highest honors of a free country."

Washington's Continentals roared three cheers. Almost forgotten was the great fleet in the harbor—the gathering danger. Dismissed, many of the soldiers made their way toward the street called Broadway. On the iron-fenced Bowling Green near the Battery stood a gilt equestrian statue of George III. The sculptor, Wilton of London, had neglected to put stirrups on the horse, which had given rise to a saying among the soldiers: "The tyrant ought to ride a hard trotting horse without stirrups." Around this figure of the King milled the excited soldiers in company with a crowd of excited civilians. Lieutenant Isaac Bangs of the Massachusetts militia went along to watch the proceedings.

Last night the statue on the Bowling Green representing George Ghwelps alias George Rex was pulled down by the populace. In it were four thousand pounds of lead and a man undertook to take ten ounces of gold from the superfices, as both man and horse were covered with gold leaf; the lead we hear is to be run up into musket balls for the use of the Yankees, when it is hoped that the emanations from the leaden George will make . . . deep impressions in the bodies of some of his red-coated and Tory subjects. . . .[14]

Everyone in New York had probably become acquainted with the Declaration as soon as it was read to the soldiers, but it was not published officially until the eighteenth. As news of it spread through the colonies, demonstrations marked each public reading. That of Worcester, Massachusetts, was typical:

On Monday last [July 22] a number of patriotic gentlemen of this town, animated with a love of their country, and to show their approbation of the measures lately taken by the Grand Council of America, assembled on the green near the liberty pole, where after having displayed the colors of the Thirteen Confederate Colonies of America, the bells were set a ringing and the drums a beating: after which, the Declaration of Independency of the United States was read to a large and respectable body (among whom the Selectmen and Committee of Correspondence) assembled on the occasion, who testified their approbation by repeated huzzas, firing of musketry and cannon, bonfires, and other demonstrations of joy, —when the arms of that tyrant in Britain, George the III of execrable memory, which in former reigns decorated, but of late disgraced the courthouse in this town, were committed to the flames and consumed to ashes; after which a select company of the Sons of Freedom repaired to the tavern, lately known by the sign of the King's Arms, which odious signature of despotism was taken down by order of the people, which was cheerfully complied with by the innkeeper, where the following toasts were drank—and the evening spent with joy, on the commencement of the happy era.

Prosperity and perpetuity to the United States of America
The President of the Grand Council of America
The Grand Council of America
His Excellency General Washington
All the generals in the American Army
Commodore [Esek] Hopkins
The officers and soldiers in the American Army
The officers and seamen in the American Navy
The patriots of America
Every friend of America
George rejected and Liberty protected
Success to the American arms

Sore eyes to all Tories and a chestnut burr for an eye stone

Perpetual itching without the benefit of scratching to the enemies of America

The Council and Representatives of the State of Massachusetts Bay

The officers and soldiers in the Massachusetts service

The memory of the brave General Warren

The memory of the magnanimous General Montgomery

Speedy redemption to all the officers and soldiers who are now prisoners of war among our enemies

The State of Massachusetts Bay

The town of Boston

The Selectmen and Committee of Correspondence for the town of Worcester

May the enemies of America be laid at her feet

May the freedom and independency of America endure till the sun grows dim with age, and this earth returns to chaos

The greatest decency and good order was observed and at a suitable time each man returned to his respective home.[15]

Despite the downing of gallons of rum and pipes of wine in countless toasts, the useless waste of gunpowder in hundreds of salutes, and the continuous tolling of bells and burning of bonfires, acceptance of the Declaration of Independence was not by any means unanimous, even among the soldiery. Lieutenant Alexander Graydon voiced himself to a friend:

The Declaration of Independency is variously relished here, some approving, others condemning it—for my own part, I have not the least objection did I know my rulers and the form of government. Innovations are always dangerous particularly here, where the populace have so great an ascendancy, and popular governments I could never approve of. However, I acquiesce in the measure as it becomes daily more necessary, although I am of opinion that delaying it awhile longer could have had no bad tendency. On the contrary, it would still have kept the door open for a reconciliation, convinced the world of our reluctance to embrace it, and increased our friends on t'other side of the water—but the greatest danger is that subtle, designing knaves, or weak insignificant blockheads may take the lead in public affairs. . . . However, the matter is now settled and our salvation depends upon supporting the measure.[16]

News of the Declaration reached England in late August. Historian Edward Gibbon remarked, "They have now crossed the Rubicon, and rendered the word of a treaty infinitely more difficult. You will perhaps say, so much the better; but

I do assure you that the *thinking* friends of Government are by no means so sanguine."

Profligate but courageous John Wilkes, champion of the individual, defended Jefferson's document on the floor of the House of Commons, declaring that the Ministry "drove the Americans into their present state of independency. . . ." When the Declaration was criticized by one of the King's supporters as "a wretched composition, very ill written, drawn up with a view to captivate the people," Wilkes pointed out that "beautiful diction" captivates the American people very little, "but manly nervous sense they relish."

And so the independence that Sam Adams and Joseph Warren dreamed about in Boston—ages ago, it seemed now—came a great stride closer to reality.

On July 12 Admiral Howe's flagship appeared, foretelling the imminent arrival of 150 ships with a reported 15,000 reinforcements aboard for General Howe. With a light and confident pen, Ambrose Serle, civilian secretary to Admiral Howe, described his emotions on completion of a three-months' voyage from England:

This morning, the sun shining bright, we had a beautiful prospect of the coast of New Jersey at about five or six miles distance. The land was cleared in many places, and the woods were interspersed with houses, which being covered with white shingles appeared very plainly all along the shore. We passed Sandy Hook in the afternoon, and about six o'clock arrived safe off the east side of Staten Island. The country on both sides was highly picturesque and agreeable. Nothing could exceed the joy that appeared throughout the fleet and army upon our arrival. We were saluted by all the ships of war in the harbor, by the cheers of the sailors all along the ships and by those of the soldiers on the shore. . . .

What added to their pleasure was that this very day about noon the *Phoenix* of forty guns and the *Rose* of twenty, with three tenders, forced their passage up the river in defiance of all their vaunted batteries, and got safe above the town, which will much intercept the provisions of the rebels.[17]

The British ships caused great consternation as they sailed up the Hudson past the shore batteries which were supposed to be impassable. Although "a number of our shots hulled them," a broadside from them threw the town into lamentable confusion. Washington deplored the presence of women and children and the infirm, who were subjected to this British display of strength and would, if not removed, be victims of much worse violence in the future:

When the men-of-war passed up the river, the shrieks and cries of these poor creatures, running every way with their children, was truly distressing, and I fear will have an unhappy effect on the ears and minds of our young and inexperienced soldiery.[18]

Even more objectionable to Washington was the spectacle of his soldiers:

The General was sorry to observe . . . many of the officers and a number of men instead of attending to their duty at the beat of the drum, continued along the banks of the North [Hudson] River, gazing at the ships; such unsoldierly conduct must grieve every good officer, and give the enemy a *mean* opinion of the army as nothing shows the brave and good soldier more than in case of alarms, coolly and calmly repairing to his post and there waiting his orders, whereas a weak curiosity at such a time makes a man look mean and contemptible.[19]

So eager were the artillerymen to watch the race up the river, that not half of them even went to their guns. Some who did were killed and wounded because they carelessly failed to sponge their guns while watching the ships. Others were absent, said a disgusted comrade, "at their cups or whoring."

Richard, Lord Howe, unlike his pleasure-loving brother, was an earnest, meticulous man, although generous and liberal. "Black Dick" was a Whig, who hoped that he could induce the Americans to see the folly of their ways; he arrived in American waters empowered to offer certain peace terms to the colonies. His first step was to send to Joseph Reed, who had returned to the army in New York as Adjutant General, a letter from Reed's brother-in-law, who expressed the hope that Reed would not be inhospitably disposed toward the Viscount. To this Reed did not reply; instead, he forwarded the letter to the Congress. Then, two days after his arrival, Viscount Howe decided to arrange an interview with the American Commander-in-Chief himself. The comedy of manners that followed was related with relish by Henry Knox to his wife:

Lord Howe . . . sent a flag of truce up to the city. They came within about four miles of the city, and were met by some of Colonel Tupper's people, who detained them until his Excellency's pleasure should be known. Accordingly, Colonel Reed and myself went down in the barge to receive the message. When we came to them, the officer, who was, I believe, captain of the *Eagle*, man-of-war, rose up and bowed, keeping his hat off.

"I have a letter, sir, from Lord Howe to Mr. Washington."

"Sir," says Colonel Reed, "we have no person in our army with that address."

"Sir," says the officer, "will you look at the address?" He took out of his pocket a letter which was thus addressed:

GEORGE WASHINGTON, ESQ.,

NEW YORK

HOWE

"No, sir," says Colonel Reed, "I cannot receive that letter."

"I am very sorry," says the officer, "and so will be Lord Howe, that any error in the superscription should prevent the letter being received by General Washington."

"Why, sir," says Colonel Reed, "I must obey orders."

"Oh, yes, sir, you must obey orders, to be sure."

Then, after giving him a letter from Colonel Campbell to General Howe, and some letters from prisoners to their friends, we stood off, having saluted and bowed to each other. After we had got a little way, the officer put about his barge and stood for us and asked by what particular he chose to be addressed.

Colonel Reed said, "You are sensible, sir, of the rank of General Washington in our army?"

"Yes, sir, we are. I am sure my Lord Howe will lament exceedingly this affair, as the letter is quite of a civil nature, and not a military one. He laments exceedingly that he was not here a little sooner."

Which we suppose to allude to the Declaration of Independence, upon which we bowed and parted in the most genteel terms imaginable.[20]

But Lord Howe was a persistent man. On July 20 the Continentals received "a capital flag of truce, no less than the adjutant general of General Howe's army." Henry Knox reported to Lucy:

> He had an interview with General Washington at our house. The purport of his message was in very elegant, polite strains, to endeavor to persuade General Washington to receive a letter directed to George Washington, Esq., etc. etc. In the course of his talk every other word was, "May it please your Excellency," "If your Excellency so please." In short, no person could pay more respect than the said adjutant general, whose name is Colonel Paterson, a person we do not know. He said the "etc. etc." implied everything.

"It does so," said the General, "and anything."

He said, Lord and General Howe lamented exceedingly that any errors in the direction should interrupt that frequent intercourse between the two armies which might be necessary in the course of the service, that Lord Howe had come out with great powers.

The General said, he had heard that Lord Howe had come out with very great powers to pardon, but he had come to the wrong place; the Americans had not offended, therefore they needed no pardon.

This confused him. After a considerable deal of talk about the good disposition of Lord and General Howe, he asked, "Has your Excellency no particular commands with which you would please to honor me to Lord and General Howe?"

"Nothing, sir, but my particular compliments to both"—a good answer.[21]

Washington had no faith whatsoever in any peace negotiations that might be conducted with the Howe brothers, and with the departure of Colonel Paterson considered the matter closed.

To add to Washington's worries, while sails came into the harbor thick as the wings of birds of prey, sickness decimated his ranks. To oppose an enemy force that was mushrooming to an expected strength of over thirty thousand, Washington now had but 10,514 men in the posts around New York; and about 3,700 of his forces were sick and unfit for duty.

Nevertheless, those fit were ready. "So far as I can judge from the professions and apparent disposition of my troops, I shall have their support," reported Washington to Congress. "The superiority of the enemy and the expected attack do not seem to have depressed their spirits." And as the weeks passed, "a noble spirit" seemed to him to pervade his army.

The day following the visit of Howe's emissary, Washington received cheering news from Congress of the signal success of American arms at Charleston, South Carolina, and read it to his troops. Charles Lee and the South Carolinians had beaten off General Henry Clinton's attack. By now enemy ships were "popping in"; the General thought they were part of Howe's expected forces, which had been scattered at sea. Daily the bay grew thicker with sails and masts.

On August 1, some forty ships arrived. Washington guessed they brought the German mercenaries he had heard Britain had hired to fight him. Six days later, he was appalled to discover from two deserters that they were not part of Howe's fleet, but were from South Carolina with probably three thousand troops aboard. This was a totally unexpected reinforcement, not in his calculations; the addition of their strength to the enemy was "just alarming," thought the General. But while Washington viewed the battered ships with apprehension for the strength they represented, an Englishman took a melancholy, contrary view of the arrival of the *Bristol,* Sir Peter Parker's flagship: "The arrival of a crippled ship and a defeated officer, at *this time,* was very unwelcome; for it infused *fresh spirits* into the rebels, and showed them that ships were sometimes obliged to retreat from batteries."

By mid-August, perplexed at the enemy's failure to attack, Washington deemed it wise to box his headquarters papers and send them to Congress at Philadelphia for safekeeping until the issues of the campaign were decided. Bad, rainy weather was postponing the attack, he supposed, or else the enemy was awaiting still more forces, including the Hessians.

The weeks of waiting ground sharp on the nerves of the enemy troops, also. But like all resourceful soldiers, they availed themselves of the daily amusements offered by Staten Island, a land of Tories. Their recreational activities evoked a long letter from Captain Francis Rawdon to his uncle, the Earl of Huntingdon:

The fair nymphs of this isle are in wonderful tribulation, as the fresh meat our men have got here has made them as riotous as satyrs. A girl cannot step into the bushes to pluck a rose without running the most imminent risk of being ravished, and they are so little accustomed to these vigorous methods that they don't bear them with the proper resignation, and of consequence we have most entertaining courts-martial every day. To the southward they behaved much better in these cases, if I may judge from a woman who having been forced by seven of our men made a complaint to me "not of their usage," she said—"No, thank God, she despised that"—but of their having taken an old prayer book for which she had a particular affection.

A girl of this island made a complaint the other day to Lord Percy of her being deflowered, as she said, by some grenadiers. Lord Percy asked her how she knew them to be grenadiers, as it happened in the dark.

"Oh, good God," cried she, "they could be nothing else, and if your Lordship will examine I am sure you will find it so."

All the English troops are encamped, or in cantonment, upon this island, as healthy and spirited a body of men as ever took the field. . . .

Some of the Hessians are arrived and long much to have a brush with the rebels, of whom they have a most despicable opinion. They are good troops, but in point of men nothing equal to ours. Some of the Guards are arrived, but not yet landed. Everybody seems to have formed a most favorable opinion of them. . . . I imagine that we shall very soon come to action, and I do not doubt but the consequence will be fatal to the rebels. An army composed as theirs is cannot bear the frown of adversity.[22]

For Washington these suspenseful days were relieved somewhat by the fact that his forces had risen to a total of twenty-three thousand, although many of the number were militia whose terms varied and whose service was likely to be unsteady. Pleasing also was the retreat of the *Phoenix* and the *Rose,* which ran back down the Hudson River and joined the fleet, after being attacked by American built fire-rafts.

Less cheering was a note from General Nathanael Greene that on August 15 he was confined to bed with a raging fever; the next day his aide wrote he was unimproved: it developed he had little chance of quick recovery. Washington had come to rely upon the competent Rhode Islander, who had developed into a superb officer. With "six broken regiments" he had built an imposing series of works at Brooklyn, stretching a mile and a half across the peninsula there, which was to be the main defensive ground of Long Island. Washington could not risk an enemy attack on Brooklyn without an officer in Greene's place, so he chose John Sullivan, who had returned disgruntled from the Canadian front late in July. He was a good and capable officer, but Washington's confidence in him was not complete. It was the General's opinion that he "has his wants, and he has his foibles . . . a little tincture of vanity and . . . an overdesire of being popular, which now and then leads him into some embarrassments." On the twentieth, Sullivan went to Long Island. He had little or no acquaintance with the place that Greene knew so well, but he recognized its importance as a potential battleground.

Not an attack, but a most remarkable storm struck the city and battered it the next day, while the enemy lay outside. On the night of August 21, at sundown, the sky suddenly blackened. Lightning raced wildly through a mushrooming, roiling cloud. Thunder rolled and crashed and shook the earth underfoot. Torrents of rain fell, and there came "a crash louder than a thousand cannon discharged at once." Lightning fell in "masses and sheets of fire to the earth." The great cloud "appeared to stand still and swing round and round like a horizontal wheel" over the city. For three terrifying hours, the strange display continued unabated.

Morning dawned mild and peaceful, but devastation and death lay in the wake of the storm. Said a witness:

There was no end of the accounts of almost miraculous escapes of the inmates of houses that were struck. In others the inhabitants were more or less injured. A soldier, passing through one of the streets, without receiving apparently any external injury was struck deaf, dumb, and blind. A captain and two lieutenants belonging to [Alexander] McDougall's regiment were killed by one thunderbolt; the points of their swords melted off, and the coin melted in their pockets. Their bodies appeared as if they had been roasted, so black and crisped was the skin. Ten men encamped outside the fort near the river, . . . were killed by a single flash. . . . They belonged to one of the Connecticut regiments and were buried in one grave. . . . Familiar as we become with death in the midst of of war, it somehow affects us very differently when sent, apparently, direct from the hand of God.[23]

13

". . . WE HAVE GIVEN THE REBELS A D——D CRUSH"

Long Island

AUGUST 22-29, 1776

THE STORM, which the natives called a tornado and Washington "a most violent gust," was over. Dawn, the twenty-second, was fresh and clear. Puddles in the streets of New York and the lanes of Long Island reflected a pale, promising sky.

Before the sun burst from the ocean, six British men-of-war weighed anchor and lay close over against Long Island. On Staten Island shore, scores of flatboats, batteaux, and two galleys swarmed around the transports. At eight o'clock "the admiral hoisted the red flag." Four thousand redcoats climbed into the small craft, were rowed across the Narrows, and landed near Gravesend on Long Island. The small boats returned for more men. The transports crossed. They met no opposition; only Colonel Hand's light guard of two hundred Pennsylvania riflemen had been posted at that end of the island, and it withdrew, burning supplies and crops that might be useful to the enemy and taking only a few random shots at the redcoats.

At last Howe's movement against New York was under way.

A Hessian officer was surprised at the lack of opposition and considered it the second mistake the Americans had made since he arrived with the fleet; the first was "when we disembarked on Staten Island, for they might then have destroyed a good many of our people with two six-pounders, and now they might have made it very nasty for us."

Lieutenant General Charles, Lord Cornwallis, who had been with the rebuffed Britons at Charleston less than sixty days before, now commanded Howe's reserves and the Hessians under Colonel Carl von Donop, who pushed ahead with six fieldpieces to the village of Flatbush, about four and a half miles from the landing place. The advancing troops cleared the woods and lanes of Hand's riflemen and encamped before dark. According to a Hessian officer, they "slept quietly all night."

So far Howe's operation was working smoothly: his forces occupied a broad plain extending northward from Gravesend Bay four to six miles and eastward a farther distance. It was prosperous farm country, in which lay the four hamlets of Gravesend, New Utrecht, Flatbush, and Flatlands. North of the British encampments lay the Heights of Guan, a ridge of hills reaching northeasterly from Gowanus Bay nearly all the way across the island, making an imposing barrier between them and the defenses of Brooklyn. In height, the ridge varied from one hundred to one hundred and fifty feet, rising abruptly from the plain forty to eighty feet and on the north or far side falling more gradually to low ground beyond. It was covered with dense woods and thickets, forming a huge natural abatis, difficult for foot-soldiers and impassable to artillery except at four points where roads penetrated it.

The roads across the ridge passed through its natural depressions. The first, on the left of the British, started at Gravesend, ran westerly through New Utrecht to a point near the Narrows, turned north along Gowanus Bay bent around the westerly end of the ridge to Brooklyn. It was called the Gowanus Road, and before it cleared the end of the ridge, it was joined by an auxiliary road from New Utrecht called Martense Lane.

The second road ran from Flatbush almost due north, through Flatbush Pass to Brooklyn; beyond the pass a branch called Port Road split to the left.

The third road split off from the second before it reached Flatbush Pass, swung eastward, then northward, running through Bedford Pass to the village of Bedford.

The fourth road ran northeasterly from Flatlands to Ja-

maica Pass, three miles east of Bedford Pass. These four roads
were the possible avenues through the barrier to Brooklyn.

The first report of the landing led Washington to believe
that Howe intended to strike Sullivan's Brooklyn lines by
making a forced march, whereupon he quickly threw six regiments across the East River to reinforce the post. He assumed that Howe would make a feint on Long Island and direct a main attack on New York, for his faulty intelligence
told that only eight or nine thousand redcoats had been
landed at Gravesend. Even after the enemy halted at Flatbush, Washington feared a two-pronged attack. On the morning of the twenty-third he waited apprehensively for the flood
tide, which would begin to make about eleven o'clock, when
the fleet might move up against the city. But that day, the
British merely extended their lines around Flatbush. In doing so, they encountered some sharp skirmishing, and the
Hessian officer who had slept so quietly the previous night
was surprised at the aggressiveness of the rebels:

> The rebels approached twice, fired howitzers and used
> grape and ball, so that all our artillery had to come up. At
> noon I slept a little while, and was waked by two cannon-balls
> which covered me with earth. The rebels have some very good
> marksmen, but some of them have wretched guns, and most
> of them shoot crooked. But they are clever at hunters' wiles.
> They climb trees, they crawl forward on their bellies for one
> hundred and fifty paces, shoot, and go as quickly back again.
> They make themselves shelters of boughs, etc. But today they
> are much put out by our green-coats (jägers), for we don't
> let our fellows fire unless they can get good aim at a man, so
> that they dare not undertake anything more against us.[1]

Washington himself went over to the island to observe the
ground; he returned to New York and made a second change
in command. On the twenty-fourth, Putnam crossed to
Brooklyn to supersede Sullivan. Washington gave no reason
for replacing Sullivan, who continued as second in command,
but a headquarters officer suspected that the General was
displeased with some of the minor actions of the twenty-
third and, anyhow, considered Putnam the more capable officer.

Another reinforcement came over on the twenty-fourth to
strengthen Putnam: Lord Stirling, half of whose brigade was
now on the island, joined his forces there. Washington had
expected hostilities to open immediately after the British were
settled on the island, but Howe's plans did not call for haste.
Although skirmishing was continual from the twenty-fourth to
the twenty-sixth, the enemy did not move in force. Instead,
on the afternoon of the twenty-sixth, Cornwallis, leaving the

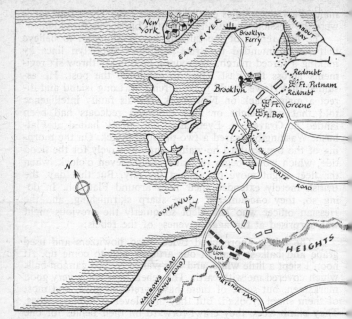

Forty-second Highlanders and the Hessians at Flatbush under gnarled old General Philip von Heister, who had landed the day before with two brigades, drew back most of his troops to Flatlands. Washington was on the island again that day and realized from the enemy strength there that Howe's main attack would be against Brooklyn. He ordered over more troops, while Putnam made his final dispositions for battle.

The line of parapets and string of forts over a mile long that had been constructed to protect Brooklyn were now complete; they extended from the marshes of Wallabout Bay to Gowanus Creek, which was believed impassable. The Heights of Guan, the five-mile ridge about a mile and a half advanced from the works, formed the natural outwork of the line. Putnam decided to guard the main defensive line in person and to delegate to Sullivan the battle on the heights.

Sullivan followed traditional seniority in placing his forces. Lord Stirling commanded the right. The center, astride the Flatbush and Bedford roads, he himself commanded. His extreme left he entrusted to Colonel Samuel Miles's Pennsylvania Regiment of Stirling's brigade. This wing was in the air, because the Jamaica Pass, three miles east of the Bedford road, was not guarded; it was patrolled by only a horse guard

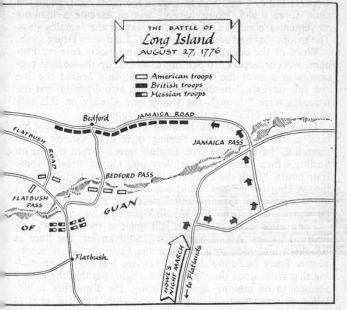

THE BATTLE OF
Long Island
AUGUST 27, 1776

☐ American troops
■ British troops
▦ Hessian troops

FLATBUSH ROAD
Bedford   JAMAICA ROAD
JAMAICA PASS
BEDFORD PASS
FLATBUSH PASS
GUAN
OF
Flatbush
HOWE'S NIGHT MARCH
to Flatlands

of five young officers, who were to report any enemy movements. About twenty-eight hundred men in all were to hold these outworks, a line oblique to the man-made inner line, six miles long with wide unguarded intervals between units on it. Below on the plains lay the enemy, nearly ten times their number, about twenty-one thousand men. In all, the American forces on the island totaled about seven thousand.

Washington spent almost all of the twenty-sixth on the island, convinced now that against it Howe would make his "grand push." During the day, additional American regiments came over. After sundown, the weather became unseasonably cold. As the hours wore on, it was as if a bone-chilling autumn night were at hand.

On the American right, a heavy picket guard shivered in the darkness near the Red Lion Inn at the junction of Martense Lane and the road from the Narrows. About one o'clock the sentries described troop movement in the hilly woods. A sharp volleying, and the guard retreated. The enemy was on the move!

In the night Howe had mounted a three-pronged assault. The Hessians and Highlanders under General von Heister at Flatbush were to hold the attention of the rebel center.

General James Grant was to engage the rebel right, while the main force under Howe himself was to execute a flanking movement around the rebel left, by way of the Jamaica Pass. The troops that had come up to the Red Lion were Grant's van.

Word of the activity at the Red Lion quickly reached Putnam, who ordered Lord Stirling to snatch up the nearest regiments and meet the enemy. When Stirling neared the inn "by fair daylight," he discovered to his astonishment that the redcoats were "through the woods and already on this side of the main hills" on the road to Brooklyn.

Drawing up his sixteen hundred troops in formal order behind a creek and marsh, Stirling offered to Grant's seven thousand "battle in the true English taste." Grant played on Stirling's firm troops with artillery and mortar fire for some four hours. "Both the balls and shells flew very fast, now and then taking off a head," said one of them. But the redcoats did not advance. Grant wanted merely to amuse them, until he was signaled from the British right to advance.

Long after daylight all was still quiet at the Flatbush and Bedford passes. About eight-thirty, Sullivan left the lines at Brooklyn and rode to a hill near the Flatbush line to reconnoiter. There he found that the Hessians had been cannonading that front since shortly before daylight, but that the enemy seemed to be moving against Stirling. He dispatched a battalion to strengthen Stirling and held eight hundred men at the Flatbush Pass.

About this time, Washington arrived from New York, but found that as yet there was nothing he could do. He took command of the Brooklyn line in Sullivan's rear. An enlisted man recalled in later years that the General used much the same words he had used in his General Orders of the twenty-third:

I saw him walk along the lines and give his orders in person to the colonels of each regiment. . . . I also heard Washington say, "If I see any man turn his back today, I will shoot him through. I have two pistols loaded, but I will not ask any man to go further than I do. I will fight so long as I have a leg or an arm." . . . He said the time had come when Americans must be freemen or slaves. Quit yourselves like men [he told us], like soldiers, for all that is worth living for is at stake.[2]

Yet undiscovered by the Americans, Howe's main column had had a busy and successful night. Captain Rawdon marched with that force about ten thousand strong, when it moved from Flatlands about nine P.M., the twenty-sixth. To his uncle in England he wrote:

General Howe . . . marched with the greatest silence towards a pass some miles to the right of Flatbush, which being but little known we thought would be but weakly guarded. The advanced guard under General Clinton consisted of light dragoons, light infantry, grenadiers, and six battalions with some light guns. We got through the pass at daybreak without any opposition, and then turned to the left towards Bedford. When we were within a mile of that town, we heard firing in that part of the mountain where General Grant was expected. We fired two pieces of cannon to let him know we were at hand.[3]

To get around the American left, Howe, guided by three Tories, had crossed fields, come in behind and swallowed up the five-man picket, and advanced to the Jamaica Road just southeast of the pass.

The signal guns fired to tell Grant that Howe was around the left end of the American lines were heard by Sullivan, who realized that the enemy was in his rear. Retreat to the lines was his only chance. He turned his force to face Howe, leaving advanced pickets to fall back before the Hessians who were sure to force the pass. He found himself confronted by light infantry and dragoons dashing down from Bedford. His front was overwhelmed. He recoiled, and turned about, only to meet the Hessians flooding through the pass. These seasoned foemen did not fire a shot, but pressed forward, bayonets at the ready, until they fell upon Sullivan's men, whose rifles were good for only a few shots before the Hessians went to work. One of them, Colonel von Heeringen, commented:

The enemy was covered by almost impenetrable brushwood, lines, abatis, and redoubts. The greater part of the riflemen were pierced with the bayonet to the trees. These dreadful people ought rather to be pitied than feared; they always require a quarter of an hour's time to load a rifle, and in the meantime they feel the effects of our balls and bayonets.[4]

The Americans could not defend themselves against the bayonet. A few reversed their muskets and rifles and used them as clubs, but these made poor defense against the blade. Trapped between Howe's and Heister's forces, Sullivan's troops broke, leaving in the hands of the enemy their red damask flag inscribed "Liberty." The Hessians had been briefed to give no quarter, and a British officer gleefully related their efficacy:

Rejoice, my friend, that we have given the Rebels a d——d crush. . . . The Hessians and our brave Highlanders gave no quarter, and it was a fine sight to see with what alacrity they dispatched the Rebels with their bayonets after we had surrounded them so that they could not resist. . . . It was a glorious achievement, my friend, and will immortalize us and crush the rebel colonies. Our loss was nothing. We took care to tell the Hessians that the rebels had resolved to give no quarter to them in particular, which made them fight desperately, and put all to death that fell into their hands.[5]

Nonetheless, many Americans fought their way back into the lines, although General Sullivan shared the fate of hundreds of his troops. An American soldier wrote home:

General Sullivan I believe is taken prisoner; the last I heard of him, he was in a corn field close by our lines with a pistol in each hand, and the enemy had formed a line each side of him, and he was going directly between them. I like to have been taken prisoner myself; crossing from the lower road to the Bedford, I came close upon the advanced party of the enemy. I very luckily got within the lines time enough to give the alarm or I believe they would have been in upon us in surprise, for we had not at that time above two thousand men in our lines.[6]

By eleven o'clock the British had swept the ridge clear of all but Stirling's two regiments, the Marylands and the Delawares, facing Grant on the American right. Stirling had news of the collapse of the center and the left about ten o'clock, when he had complied with an order to send off a battalion to succor Sullivan. Grant had heard the signal guns, but did not move until he got a fresh supply of ammunition and a reinforcement of two thousand marines. Then he opened seriously against Lord Stirling's front, while the enemy force from Flatbush shouldered through the woods to hit his left, and Cornwallis, with the Seventy-first Regiment and the Second Grenadiers, took position on the Gowanus Road at the Cortelyou house, blocking Stirling's rear. Here developed the hottest fighting of the day.

When Grant pressed forward, Stirling faced an impossible situation with courage and resolution. At his right rear was Gowanus Creek and its marshes, usually considered impassable at high tide, and the tide was flowing in. He ordered his forces to retreat across the creek, while with Major Mordecai Gist he personally turned two hundred and fifty of Smallwood's Marylands and marched against Cornwallis in his rear, determined to cut his way through or to cover the retreat of his main body. Five times the Marylands advanced in their forlorn hope, and five times deadly fire drove them back. On the fifth try, it looked as though they might break through, but Cornwallis, who had been reinforced, drove them back in confusion, though Stirling "fought like a wolf."

The exhausted officers and men knew that further resistance would be the "height of rashness and imprudence"; breaking into little groups, they plunged into the woods and attempted to escape to the Brooklyn lines. Only Major Gist and nine of his men were successful. Stirling was missing. Two hundred and fifty-six of the Marylands were killed or surrendered to Heister.

A rifleman who had stood up to Grant early in the morning finished his account of the day's adventure:

. . . the main body of British, by a route we never dreamed of, had surrounded us, and driven within the lines or scattered in the woods, all our men except the Delaware and Maryland battalions, who were standing at bay with double their number. Thus situated, we were ordered to attempt a retreat by fighting our way through the enemy, who had posted themselves and nearly filled every road and field between us and our lines. We had not retreated a quarter of a mile, before we were fired on by an advanced party of the enemy, and those in the rear playing their artillery on us. Our men fought with more than Roman valor. We forced the advanced party which first attacked us to give way, through which opening we got a passage down to the side of a marsh, seldom before waded over, which we passed, and then swam a narrow river, all the while exposed to the enemy's fire. . . . The whole of the right wing of our battalion, thinking it impossible to march through the marsh, attempted to force their way through the woods, where they, almost to a man, were killed or taken. . . .

Most of our generals on a high hill in the lines, viewed us with glasses, as we were retreating, and saw the enemy we had to pass through, though we could not. Many thought we would surrender in a body without firing. When we began the attack, General Washington wrung his hands, and cried out, "Good God! what brave fellows I must this day lose!"[7]

During the morning, reinforcements had been ordered out of New York City. Among them was Private Joseph Plumb Martin, a Massachusetts lad who would not be sixteen until November. He had enlisted in June as a "new levy" for six months because he "wished only to take a priming before I took upon me the whole coat of paint for a soldier." As soon as he heard that the British were in force on Long Island he knew that his time had come to "snuff a little gunpowder." He was uneasy enough about his baptism of fire, but he resolved to do his best and reported to the regimental parade. Every detail of the day stayed fresh in his memory for years:

. . . as soon as the regiment was formed, we were marched off for the ferry. At the lower end of the street were placed several casks of sea-bread, made, I believe, of canel and peas-meal, nearly hard enough for musket flints; the casks were unheaded and each man was allowed to take as many as he could, as he marched by. As my good luck would have it, there was a momentary halt made. I improved the opportunity thus offered me, as every good soldier should upon all important occasions, to get as many of the biscuit as I possibly could. No one said anything to me, and I filled my bosom and took as many as I could hold in my hand, a dozen or more in all, and when we arrived at the ferry-stairs, I stowed them away in my knapsack.

We quickly embarked on board the boats. As each boat started, three cheers were given by those on board, which was returned by the numerous spectators who thronged the wharves. They all wished us good luck, apparently, although it was with most of them, perhaps, nothing more than ceremony.

We soon landed at Brooklyn upon the Island, marched up the ascent from the ferry to the plain. We now began to meet the wounded men, another sight I was unacquainted with, some with broken arms, some with broken legs, and some with broken heads. The sight of these a little daunted me, and made me think of home, but the sight and thought vanished together. We marched a short distance, when we halted to refresh ourselves. Whether we had any other victuals besides the hard bread I do not remember, but I remember my gnawing at them; they were hard enough to break the teeth of a rat. . . .

While resting here, which was not more than twenty minutes or half an hour, the Americans and British were warmly engaged within sight of us. . . .

The officers of the new levies wore cockades of different colors to distinguish them from the standing forces, as they were called. The field officers wore red, the captains white, and the subaltern officers green. While we were resting here, our lieutenant colonel and major (our colonel not being with us) took their cockades from their hats. Being asked the reason, the lieutenant colonel replied that he was willing to risk his life in the cause of his country, but he was unwilling to stand a particular mark for the enemy to fire at. He was a fine officer and a brave soldier.

We were soon called upon to fall in and proceed. . . . Our officers . . . pressed forward towards a creek, where a large party of Americans and British were engaged.

By the time we arrived, the enemy had driven our men into the creek, or rather mill-pond (the tide being up), where such as could swim got across; those that could not swim and could not procure anything to buoy them up, sunk.

The British having several fieldpieces stationed by a brick house were pouring the canister and grape upon the Americans like a shower of hail; they would doubtless have done them much more damage than they did but for the twelve pounder mentioned above, the men having gotten it within sufficient distance to reach them, and opening a fire upon them, soon obliged them to shift their quarters.

There was in this action a regiment of Maryland troops (volunteers), all young gentlemen. When they came out of the water and mud to us, looking like water rats, it was a truly pitiful sight. Many of them were killed in the pond and more were drowned. Some of us went into the water after the fall of the tide, and took out a number of corpses and a great many arms that were sunk in the pond and creek.[8]

By early afternoon, most of the Continentals who had escaped the fury of the enemy had found safety in the Brooklyn defenses. Washington's loss in killed, wounded, and missing was high. Stirling was still missing. Sullivan last had been seen surrounded by the enemy. Good officers were known to have fallen and others to have been taken prisoner.

Tensely, during that afternoon, the Americans waited for Howe to storm the lines; instead, he drew back and halted. Night came. As the hours dragged by, no night attack developed, and the morning brought no movement from Howe, In the afternoon of the twenty-eighth, a cold northeast rain fell; into the night it pelted the hungry, unhappy men, tentless and lightly clothed. The next morning in the gray rain, the British could be seen at work on regular approaches. Although the northeaster added to the misery of the men who stood ankle-deep in water, it prevented Howe's fleet from beating up into the East River and cutting Washington off from New York. Shivering and weary and wet, young Major Benjamin Tallmadge, adjutant of Colonel John Chester's Connecticut Regiment, thought it "most wonderful" that Howe did not attempt to storm the Brooklyn works, since they were so weak:

General Washington was so fully aware of the perilous situation of this division of his army, that he immediately convened a council of war, at which the propriety of retiring to New York was decided on. After sustaining incessant fatigue and constant watchfulness for two days and nights, attended by heavy rain, exposed every moment to an attack by a vastly superior force in front, and to be cut off from the possibility of retreat to New York by the fleet which might enter the East River, on the night of the twenty-ninth

. . . Washington commenced recrossing his troops from Brooklyn to New York.

To move so large a body of troops with all their necessary appendages across a river full a mile wide, with a rapid current, in face of a victorious, well-disciplined army nearly three times as numerous as his own and a fleet capable of stopping the navigation so that not one boat could have passed over, seemed to present most formidable obstacles. But in face of these difficulties, the Commander-in-Chief so arranged his business that on the evening of the twenty-ninth by ten o'clock, the troops began to retire from the lines in such a manner that no chasm was made in the lines, but as one regiment left their station on guard, the remaining troops moved to the right and left and filled up the vacancies, while General Washington took his station at the ferry and superintended the embarkation of the troops.

It was one of the most anxious, busy nights that I ever recollect; and being the third in which hardly any of us had closed our eyes in sleep, we were all greatly fatigued.[9]

The success of this great withdrawal hinged upon its being screened from the eyes of the enemy, and this depended largely upon the troops occupying their post right up to the moment of withdrawal. They were brought off slowly and in order. General Thomas Mifflin, promoted to brigadier in May and in command of two Pennsylvania battalions, was honored with command of the rear. Under him served Colonel Hand. Catastrophe nearly overwhelmed the operation, when the covering party received confused orders about two in the morning. Alexander Scammell was acting aide to Washington and came hurrying from the far left of the lines in the night, asking for General Mifflin. Hand was with the general, and according to Hand:

Scammell told him that the boats were waiting, and the Commander-in-Chief anxious for the arrival of the troops at the ferry. General Mifflin said he thought he must be mistaken, that he did not imagine the General could mean the troops he immediately commanded. Scammell replied he was not mistaken, adding that he came from the extreme left, had ordered all the troops he had met to march; that in consequence they were then in motion, and that he would go on and give the same orders. General Mifflin then ordered me to call my advance pickets and sentinels, to collect and form my regiment, and to march as soon as possible, and quitted me.

I obeyed, but had not gone far before I perceived the front had halted, and, hastening to inquire the cause, I met the Commander-in-Chief, who . . . said, "Is not that Colonel Hand?" . . .

His Excellency said he was surprised at me in particular, that he did not expect I would have abandoned my post. I answered that I had not abandoned it, and I had marched by order of my immediate commanding officer. He said it was impossible. I told him, I hoped, if I could satisfy him I had the orders of General Mifflin, he would not think me particularly to blame. He said he undoubtedly would not.

General Mifflin just then coming up, and asking what the matter was, His Excellency said: "Good God! General Mifflin, I am afraid you have ruined us by so unseasonably withdrawing the troops from the lines."

General Mifflin replied with some warmth: "I did it by your order."

His Excellency declared it could not be.

General Mifflin swore: "By God, I did," and asked: "Did Scammell act as an aide-de-camp for the day, or did he not?"

His Excellency acknowledged he did.

"Then," said Mifflin, "I had orders through him."

The General replied it was a dreadful mistake, and informed him that matters were in much confusion at the ferry, and unless we could resume our posts before the enemy discovered we had left them, in all probability the most disagreeable consequences would follow. We immediately returned, and had the good fortune to recover our former stations, and keep them for some hours longer, without the enemy perceiving what was going forward.[10]

Major Tallmadge continued at his post with the covering troops.

As the dawn of the next day approached, [he wrote later,] those of us who remained in the trenches became very anxious for our own safety, and when the dawn appeared there were several regiments still on duty. At this time a very dense fog began to rise and it seemed to settle in a peculiar manner over both encampments. I recollect this peculiar providential occurrence perfectly well, and so very dense was the atmosphere that I could scarcely discern a man at six yards distance.

When the sun rose, we had just received orders to leave the lines, but before we reached the ferry, the Commander-in-Chief sent one of his aides to order the regiment to repair again to their former station on the line. Colonel Chester immediately faced to the right about and returned, where we tarried until the sun had risen, but the fog remained as dense as ever.

Finally, the second order arrived for the regiment to retire, and we very joyfully bid those trenches a long adieu. When we reached Brooklyn ferry, the boats had not returned from their last trip, but they very soon appeared and took the whole regiment over to New York, and I think I saw General Washington on the ferry stairs when I stepped into one of the last boats that received the troops. I left my horse tied to a post at the ferry.

The troops having now all safely reached New York, and the fog continuing as thick as ever, I began to think of my favorite horse and requested leave to return and bring him off. Having obtained permission, I called for a crew of volunteers to go with me, and guiding the boat myself, I obtained my horse and got off some distance into the river before the enemy appeared in Brooklyn.

As soon as they reached the ferry, we were saluted merrily from their musketry and finally by their fieldpieces, but we returned in safety. In the history of warfare, I do not recollect a more fortunate retreat. After all, the providential appearance of the fog saved a part of our army from being captured, and certainly myself among others who formed the rear guard.[11]

It was a miserable, beaten army that came back to New York. Brother Shewkirk, pastor of the Moravian congregation, observed the bedraggled, crestfallen troops:

Friday 30th: In the morning, unexpectedly and to the surprise of the city, it was found that all that could come back was come back; and that they had abandoned Long Island, when many had thought to surround the King's troops and make them prisoners with little trouble. The language was now otherwise. It was a surprising change: the merry tones on drums and fifes had ceased, and they were hardly heard for a couple of days. It seemed a general damp had spread, and the sight of the scattered people up and down the streets was indeed moving.

Many looked sickly, emaciated, cast down, etc.; the wet clothes, tents—as many as they had brought away—and other things were lying about before the houses and in the streets to dry. In general everything seemed to be in confusion. . . .[12]

Bad as it was, Washington had managed to snatch ninety-five hundred men, and all their baggage, field guns, horses, equipment, stores, and provisions from under Howe's mighty paw and get them safely to New York.

Even Washington's enemy recognized the brilliance of this feat. Charles Stedman, once a student at William and Mary College in Virginia, now an officer in the British army, commented: "Driven to the corner of an island, hemmed in within a narrow space of two square miles, in their front . . . near twenty thousand men, in their rear, an arm of the sea a mile wide . . . they secured a retreat without the loss of a man."

This master stroke, accomplished by the tall commander, sleepless for forty-eight hours before, riding his big gray charger everywhere that night, saved from utter ruin an army and the hopes of a country.

Most of the officers and men of Howe's army felt that Howe had missed the opportunity of a lifetime in failing to crush the rebels and end the rebellion. In spite of the fact that his report, when it reached London on October 10, filled the Royal Court with "an extravagance of joy," and won for the victor the Order of the Bath, Sir George Collier, in his cabin aboard the *Rainbow* off New York, sarcastically recorded his own bitterness in his journal:

> The having to deal with a generous, merciful, *forebearing* enemy, who would take no unfair *advantages*, must surely have been highly satisfactory to General Washington, and he was certainly very deficient in not expressing his gratitude to General Howe for his *kind* behavior towards him. Far from taking the rash resolution of *hastily passing* over the East River . . . and *crushing at once* a frightened, trembling enemy, he generously gave them time to recover from their panic,—to throw up *fresh works*,—to make new arrangements,—and to recover from the torpid state the rebellion appeared in from its late shock.

For *many succeeding* days did our brave veterans, consisting of twenty-two thousand men, stand on the banks of the East River, like Moses on Mount Pisgah, looking at their promised land, little more than half a mile distant. The rebel's standards waved insolently in the air from many diffent quarters of New York. The British troops could scarcely contain their indignation at the sight and at their own *inactivity*; the officers were *displeased and amazed*, not being able to account for the strange delay.[13]

"A CHOICE OF DIFFICULTIES"

New York and Harlem Heights

AUGUST-SEPTEMBER 1776

AUGUST 30 must have been for General Washington a day of mingled emotions. In responding to a communication from the New York Legislature, he pointedly reminded the gentlemen that he was "not a little fatigued."

He had successfully brought off his army from Long Island, but what to do with it now and what to do about New York were baffling problems demanding prompt solutions. Tempering any pride he might have felt in the sound and economical retreat from the island were the hard realities that he had been outthought and outfought by the English general. The dispositions of troops made on Long Island at his orders or with his concurrence were inexcusable. Equally so was his failure to change them when he personally had viewed the ground. Back in July, he had dismissed a regiment of mounted volunteers from Connecticut because he could see no advantage in its use, yet cavalry patrolling between the passes in the ridge before Brooklyn very likely would have thwarted Howe's flanking movement by feeling it out and giving the American command a chance to withdraw its troops. The division of his army between New York and Brooklyn had been a grave error. Altogether, he had erred in almost every particular. As a commander he had failed, and as soldiers his men had failed him.

Some of his officers expressed a veiled desire to see someone else in command, and Colonel John Haslet, whose Delawares had fought so stoutly under Stirling, wrote to Caesar Rodney:

The General I revere; his character for disinterestedness, patience and fortitude will be had in everlasting remembrances, but the vast burden appears much too much his own. Beardless youth and inexperience regimentated are too much about him. The original scheme for the disposition of the army appears to have been on too narrow a scale, and everything almost sacrificed, or endangered for the preservation of

New York and its environs, all which deserve from every honest American [political] damnation. We have alarm upon alarm. Orders now issue, and the next moment reversed. Would to Heaven General Lee were here, is the language of officers and men.[1]

But it was richly to Washington's credit that, after dark fell on the night of August 27, he had reasoned courageously and well: had he attempted to flee Long Island that night, he probably would have met disaster. He took the risk of remaining until he could leave without heavy loss, reasoning that Howe would not press his victory, but would undertake regular approaches. Did he perhaps wonder if Howe's memory of Bunker Hill would discourage him from flinging himself and his men upgrade through the woods against entrenched Americans? In any event, Washington's judgment saved his army and salved the pride of the country.

Even the most successful evacuations, however, do not win wars. Now back in New York, Washington again faced a crisis so absorbing that he had no time for retrospection upon Long Island. Leave to the men in the barracks and the officers in the taverns the earnest arguments about the reasons for what happened. The General must reorganize his commands and dispose his army for the next move of his powerful enemy.

His army was quartered in houses in town, because the tents were too wet to be occupied and the weather too miserable. The men were as troublesome as they had ever been. Washington published that "the General is sorry to see soldiers, defending their country in time of imminent danger, rioting and attempting to do themselves justice." They took it upon themselves to redress annoyances by violent abuse of officers; they plundered the citizens mercilessly. Not even the house of captured Lord Stirling was spared the busy fingers of the soldiery, who were ordered to return to the Quartermaster General what they had taken.

The General deemed it wise to explain to his army that the retreat was a strategic one and not undertaken "from any doubts of the spirit of the troops." He expressed perfect confidence in the ultimate success of his arms, but he cautioned regimental officers to keep their men constantly furnished with two days' supply of prepared bread and pork rations, marching fare, so that they would not be caught short if they were called upon to make a sudden movement from New York. He brigaded the regiments and then arranged them in "three Grand Divisions" to better dispose them for the defense of Manhattan. Putnam, who had apparently suf-

fered none in Washington's eyes for his inactivity on Long Island, was given command of one division of five brigades that
was posted in the city of New York, facing the East River.
Spencer was given temporary command of the division to become Greene's when Greene recovered from his illness, and
was stationed with six brigades on a line from Putnam's north
to Harlem Heights. The third division of two brigades was
given to Heath, who was to take post where he could watch
King's Bridge and the Westchester shore.

Washington, for more than twenty-four hours after his
return from Long Island, continued so weary as to be "entirely unfit to take a pen in hand." Not until the morning of the
thirtieth did he feel able to "write or dictate" a report to
Congress. Complete returns of the losses on Long Island were
not in, but he guessed that he had lost from seven hundred to
a thousand men killed and taken. He told the Congress that
in spite of all he could do to persuade the troops that their
defeat need not be a fatal one, "The check our detachment
sustained . . . has dispirited too great a proportion of our
troops and filled their minds with apprehension and despair.
The militia, instead of calling forth their utmost efforts . . .
in order to repair our losses, are dismayed, intractable, and
impatient to return. Great numbers of them have gone off,
in some instances almost by whole Regiments, by half ones,
and by companies at a time." Their behavior, injurious enough
in itself in front of a superior enemy, was the more appalling
because their example "infected" the rest of the army, who
either walked home or utterly disregarded "that order and
subordination necessary to the well-being of an army." Rapacious Hessian plundering on Long Island, which was disgust-
ing even the British themselves, was scarcely more ruthless
than that in which Washington's own men now engaged. The
cowardly, trifling majority was described angrily by the loyal
few. Lewis Morris, Jr., wrote to his father, General Morris
(of Morrisania, across the Harlem River in Westchester,
but at the time in Philadelphia, at the Continental Congress):

As for the militia of Connecticut, Brigadier [Oliver]
Wolcott and his whole brigade have got the cannon fever and
very prudently skulked home. Such people are only a nuisance
and had better be in the chimney corner than in the field of
Mars. We have men enough without them who will fight and
whose glory is the defense of their country—Colonel Hand's
regiment plunder everybody in Westchester County indiscriminately, even yourself has not escaped. Montresor's island
they plundered and committed the most unwarrantable destruction upon it, fifty dozens of bottles were broke in the
cellar, the paper tore from the rooms and every pane of glass

broke to pieces. His furniture and clothes were brought over
to Morrisania and sold at public auction. Jimmy DeLancey,
Oliver, and John, after giving their parole, are gone off to the
enemy and their house is plundered. Mrs. Wilkins is upon
Long Island with her husband and her house is plundered,
and hers and Mrs. Moncrief's clothes were sold at vendue.
Seabury has likewise eloped, and Mrs. Wilkins has very industriously propagated that you had fled to France. Such
brimstones will certainly meet their desert.[2]

All the time that Washington was trying to hold together
his diminishing, rapacious, riotous men, he was endeavoring
to guess Howe's plans. More than likely the enemy would
attempt a landing about King's Bridge to "hem in our army
and cut off the communication with the country." This prospect seemed probable when, on the night of September 3, the
Rose, convoying thirty boats, passed up the East River and
anchored close into Wallabout Bay.

Washington called a council of officers on September 7 to
decide what to do. A majority, over the protests of Greene
who had returned to duty on the fifth, recommended that an
effort be made to save the city. Five thousand men should
be stationed in the city, nine thousand at King's Bridge to be
ready if the enemy should attempt to land from Long Island,
and the rest between the town and the bridge, part of them
at Fort Washington, to support either of the other bodies of
troops.

Ever since the arrival of the first of Howe's fleet, Washington, without a single heavy vessel at his command, had been
at the mercy of the British, so far as point of attack was concerned. True, he had a motley little "fleet" of armed schoon-
ers, sloops, row galleys, and whaleboats, all commanded by
a land officer, Lieutenant Colonel Benjamin Tupper of Ward's
Massachusetts Regiment. But beyond scouring the waters
along the Jersey and Long Island coasts to prevent communication between Tories and the enemy fleet and watching the
movements of that fleet, Tupper's flotilla was useless.

Washington and many others interested in the defense of
America had long recognized that the mighty ships of the
enemy constituted a menace against which the colonies as
yet had no defense. From the first days of the war, inventive
men had offered to Congress schemes for destroying the British shipping. David Bushnell, of Connecticut, fresh from the
college at New Haven, actually constructed a manually pow-
ered, one-man submarine and brought it to New York. Because the inventor was too frail to operate the machine, he
had trained his brother to do so. After Washington granted
permission for a trial effort against the enemy ships, the

brother fell ill. One Sergeant Ezra Lee volunteered to go
down in Bushnell's *American Turtle*. Lee, naturally interested in every detail of the craft, described it minutely:

Its shape was most like a round clam but longer and set
up on its square side. It was high enough to stand in or sit,
as you had occasion, with a composition head [metal door
plate] hanging on hinges. It had six glasses inserted in the
head and made water tight, each the size of a half-dollar piece
to admit light. In a clear day a person might see to read in
three fathoms of water. The machine was steered by a rud-
der, having a crooked tiller which led in by your side through
a water joint. Then sitting on the seat, the navigator rows
with one hand and steers with the other. It had two oars of
about twelve inches in length and four or five in width, shaped
like the arms of a windmill, which led . . . inside . . . in
front of the person steering and were worked by means of a
winch (or crank); and with hard labor the machine might be
impelled at the rate of three knots an hour for a short time.
Seven hundred pounds of lead were fixed on the bottom
for ballast, and two hundred . . . so contrived as to let . . .
go in case the pumps choked, so that you could rise at the surface . . . It was sunk by letting in water by a spring near the
bottom, by placing your foot against . . . but if you had sunk
too far, pump out water until you got the necessary depth.
These pumps forced the water out of the bottom, one . . .
on each side of you. . . . A pocket compass was fixed in the
side, with a piece of light wood on the north side . . . to
steer by while under water.
Three round doors were cut in the head . . . to let in fresh
air until you wished to sink, and then they were shut down
and fastened. There was also a glass tube, twelve inches long
and one inch diameter with a cork in it with a piece of light
wood fixed to it, and another piece at the bottom of the tube,
to tell the depth of descent. One inch rise in the cork in the
tube gave about one fathom water.
It had a screw . . . through the top of the machine . . .
which was so very sharp that it would enter wood with very
little force, and this was turned with a winch or crank, and
when entered fast in the bottom of the ship the screw is then
left, and the machine is disengaged by unscrewing another
one inside that held the other. From the screw now fixed on
the bottom of the ship a line let to and fastened to the magazine to prevent its escape. . . . The magazine of powder was
. . . freed from you by unscrewing a screw inside. Inside the
magazine was a clock machinery, which immediately sets
a-going after it is disengaged, and a gun lock is fixed to strike
fire to the powder at the set time after the clock should run
down. The clock might be set to go longer or shorter; twenty

or thirty minutes was the usual time to let the navigator escape.[3]

Sergeant Lee practiced with the submarine several times and then awaited proper circumstances.

The first night after we got down to New York with it that was favorable (for the time for a trial must be when it is slack water and calm, as it is unmanageable in a swell or a strong tide), the British fleet lay a little above Staten Island. We set off from the city. The whaleboats towed me as nigh the ships as they dared to go, and then cast me off. I soon found that it was too early in the tide, as it carried me down by the ships. I, however, hove about and rowed for five glasses by the ships' bells before the tide slacked, so that I could get alongside of the man-of-war, [the *Asia*], which lay above the transports.

The moon was about two hours high, and the daylight about one. When I rowed under the stern of the ship, I could see the men on deck and hear them talk. I then shut down all the doors, sunk down, and came under the bottom of the ship. Up with the screw against the bottom, but found that it would not enter [the coppered hull]. I pulled along to try another place, but deviated a little one side and immediately rose with great velocity and came above the surface two or three feet between the ship and the daylight, then sunk again like a porpoise.

I hove about to try again, but on further thought I gave out, knowing that as soon as it was light, the ship's boats would be rowing in all directions, and I thought the best generalship was to retreat as fast as I could, as I had four miles to go before passing Governor's Island. . . . When I was abreast of the fort on the island, three or four hundred men got upon the parapet to observe me. At length, a number came down to the shore, shoved off a twelve-oared barge with five or six sitters and pulled for me.

I eyed them, and when they had got within fifty or sixty yards of me, I let loose the magazine in hopes that if they should take me, they would likewise pick up the magazine and then we should all be blown up together. But as kind Providence would have it, they took fright and returned to the island, to my infinite joy. I then weathered the island, and our people seeing me, came off with a whaleboat and towed me in. The magazine, after getting a little past the island, went off with a tremendous explosion, throwing up large bodies of water to an immense height.[4]

But the *American Turtle* never succeeded, and Howe's fleet continued to threaten Washington with a landing in either or both rivers.

The foreboding movements of Howe's fleet, the massing of his troops on the west side of Long Island, and intelligence reports all convinced Washington that his position actually was hopeless. On the eighth of September, weighing his problems carefully, he wrote a long letter to Congress to tell that body what it might expect.

The General acknowledged that the defense of New York had "occasioned an expense of labor which now seems useless and is regretted by those who form a judgment from afterknowledge," but he justified it by pointing out that Howe's "point of attack could not be known" and preparations for it had to be made at several places. He trusted that men of discernment would recognize that he had succeeded in delaying Howe's campaign until it was too late for him to make a "capital incursion into the country" and he had drawn Howe's forces to a point, so that he could make his own future plans with some certainty. He wrote:

It is now extremely obvious . . . that having landed their whole army on Long Island (except about four thousand on Staten Island) they mean to enclose us on the island of New York by taking post in our rear, while the shipping effectually secure the front and thus . . . oblige us to fight them on their own terms, or surrender at discretion, or by a brilliant stroke endeavor to cut this army in pieces. . . .
Having therefore their system unfolded to us, it became an important consideration how it could be most successfully opposed. On every side there is a choice of difficulties, and every measure on our part (however painful the reflection is from experience) to be formed with some apprehension that all our troops will not do their duty.[5]

The problem was yet unsolved, Washington informed the legislators, and he reported on yesterday's council at which the general officers, although agreed that the town was indefensible if Howe was resolved to take it, had determined to divide their forces in an effort to hold it as long as possible, "suspecting that Congress wished it to be maintained at every hazard." But the General thought the Congress should know that inevitably it must be abandoned.

It seemed perfectly clear to Washington that the grand strategy of the war already was determined. On deliberating the question of evacuation and retreat, he wrote:

. . . it was impossible to forget that History, our own experience, the advice of our ablest friends in Europe, the fears of the enemy, and even the declarations of Congress demonstrate that on our side the war should be defensive. It has even been called a war of posts: that we should on all occasions avoid a general action or put anything to the risk, unless compelled by a necessity, into which we ought never to be drawn.[6]

Four days later, as the enemy shifted his vessels in the rivers under a harmless American bombardment, Nathanael Greene, who had argued on the seventh for immediate evacuation, urged that another council be assembled. Now on the twelfth, the officers voted to evacuate all the island, except Fort Washington, where eight thousand men should remain. Washington was confident it could be maintained and, supported by Fort Constitution on the opposite Jersey shore "with the assistance of the obstructions already made and which may be improved in the water," could secure the passage of the Hudson River. If Fort Washington were too heavily pressed, its garrison could be removed northward or rowed across to Jersey.

Washington was doubtless cheered at this juncture by the arrival of the Third Virginia Continentals, under Colonel George Weedon, a German-American tavern keeper Washington had known in Fredericksburg. He was followed into camp by the Ninth Virginia, under Colonel Isaac Read.

Now it was a race to remove the excess stores and the sick from town before Howe, whose troops were massing, could strike. Washington wrote to Congress on the fourteenth, "I fear we shall not effect the whole before we shall meet with some interruption." He was right. Although all horses and wagons in the city were impressed and boats, heavily-laden, sailed up the Hudson, the "interruption" Washington feared already was afoot.

The enemy's first movement was noted by Private Joseph Plumb Martin. Colonel William Douglas' Connecticut militia, which the colonel admitted to his wife, "give me much fatigue and trouble," boasted no more casual young soldier than Private Martin. He had had a baptismal fire on Long Island and learned almost to his own surprise that he could act the veteran. Now he was stationed in the center of the East River line, in breastworks more than a mile long between Kip's Bay, a cove opposite Newtown Creek on Long Island, and Turtle Bay, a little higher up the river on the Manhattan side. Downstream to the right lay the rest of the brigade, five regiments of Connecticut militia, supported by Brigadier General John Fellows' small brigade of Massachusetts militia and Brigadier General Samuel Parsons' brigade of Connecticut Continentals and Brigadier General John Scott's New York militia. Of Kip's Bay on the evening of the thirteenth, Private Martin wrote:

We heard a heavy cannonade at the city, and before dark saw four of the enemy's ships that had passed the town and were coming up the East River; they anchored just below us. . . .

Half of our regiment was sent off under the command of our Major, to man something that were called "lines," although they were nothing more than a ditch dug along on the bank of the river, with the dirt thrown out towards the water. They stayed in these lines during the night, and returned to the camp in the morning unmolested. The other half of the regiment went the next night [the fourteenth], under the command of the Lieutenant Colonel, upon the like errand.

We arrived at the lines about dark. . . . We "manned the lines" and lay quite . . . unmolested the whole night. We had a chain of sentinels quite up the river for four or five miles. . . . Every half-hour, they passed the watchword to each other, "All is well."

I heard the British on board their shipping answer, "We will alter your tune before tomorrow night,"—and they were as good as their word for once!

It was quite a dark night and at daybreak the first thing that saluted our eyes was all the four ships at anchor, with springs upon their cables, and within musket shot of us. The *Phoenix*, lying a little quartering and her stern towards me, I could read her name as distinctly as though I had been directly under her stern. . . . As soon as it was fairly light, we saw their boats coming out of a creek or cove on the Long Island side of the water, filled with British soldiers.

When they came to the edge of the tide, they formed their boats in line. They continued to augment their forces from the island until they appeared like a large clover field in full bloom. . . . We lay very quiet in our ditch, waiting their motions, till the sun was an hour or two high. We heard a cannonade at the city, but our attention was drawn toward our own guests. . . .

All of a sudden, there came such a peal of thunder from the British shipping that I thought my head would go with the sound. . . .

We kept the lines till they were almost leveled upon us, when our officers, seeing we could make no resistance, and no orders coming from any superior officer and that we must soon be entirely exposed to the rake of their guns, gave the order to leave the lines.

In retreating we had to cross a level, clear spot of ground, forty or fifty rods wide, exposed to the whole of the enemy's fire. And they gave it to us in prime order. The grapeshot and langrage flew merrily, which served to quicken our motions. . . .

We had not gone far [in the highway] before we saw a party of men, apparently hurrying on in the same direction with ourselves. We endeavored hard to overtake them, but on approaching them we found . . . they were Hessians. We immediately altered our course and took the main road leading to King's Bridge.

We had not long been on this road before we saw another party, just ahead of us, whom we knew to be Americans. Just as we overtook these, they were fired upon by a party of British from a cornfield, and all was immediately in confusion again. I believe the enemy's party was small, but our people were all militia, and the demons of fear and disorder seemed to take full possession of all and everything on that day. When I came to the spot where the militia were fired upon, the ground was literally covered with arms, knapsacks, staves, coats, hats. . . . [7]

The militia, overtaken in flight by Martin's regiment, were some of the troops from Douglas' right who also had broken. Howe's first division under General Clinton had begun landing from eighty-four boats under the guns of the men-of-war just left of Douglas' position, and had struck towards the estate of Robert Murray on the Post Road, which ran the length of the island to King's Bridge. Douglas' troops tried to gain the road ahead of the enemy. Below Douglas' position, the rest of Wadsworth's brigade had fled the shore and was making up the Post Road.

Washington had recently moved his headquarters to Roger Morris' house on Harlem Heights, to be nearer King's Bridge. When the British cannonade had opened, he had mounted and ridden at a gallop toward the point of attack. When he arrived in the vicinity of Murray's, he found the troops streaming north up the Post Road and west on the crossroad to Bloomingdale Road, which paralleled the Post Road on the west side of Manhattan. Flinging himself into the mass of frightened men, the General desperately attempted to halt their flight and rally them.

"Take the walls!" he shouted, hoping the men would form behind Murray's fences.

"Take the cornfield!" he called, trying to get them out of the choked road.

Up near King's Bridge, Colonel George Weedon was stationed with his newly arrived Virginia regiment, and he was appalled by the eyewitness accounts he received of the action lower down on the island. To John Page, President of the Virginia Council of State, he wrote:

. . . though General Washington was himself present . . .

all he, his aide-de-camps, and other general officers could do, they were not to be rallied, till they had got some miles. The General was so exasperated that he struck several officers in their flight, three times dashed his hat on the ground, and at last exclaimed, "Good God! Have I got such troops as those?"

It was with difficulty his friends could get him to quit the field, so great was his emotions. He however got off safe. . . .[8]

The Americans, in spite of their haste, did not get off unscathed. Seventeen officers and three hundred and fifty men were lost, most of them captured. The Hessians especially, who had earned a bloodthirsty reputation on Long Island, zealously cut the rebels down.

Washington was forced to give ground and ordered Harlem Heights to be secured. New York was doomed. General Thomas Mifflin hurried to Harlem with a heavy force from his post across the Harlem River at Morrisania. The routed Americans did not rally until they were beyond McGowan's Pass, several miles north at the entrance to Harlem Plains.

Washington's army was saved only by the failure of Howe's landing craft to bring all of his force over promptly. Howe's plan was first to take possession of Murray's Hill, where his first division of four thousand was to await a second. Then the whole force was to strike across the waist of the island, cutting off the Americans south of Kip's Bay. With his vanguard, Howe arrived at Murray's Hill about two o'clock; there he halted to await his reinforcements, which did not land until about five.

Meanwhile, Israel Putnam was making up for any inactivity he had shown on Long Island. As soon as he saw that no stand could be made against the advancing enemy at Murray's Hill, he galloped south through the retreating throngs to attempt to rescue Colonel Gold S. Silliman's Connecticut Brigade, some of Knox's artillery detachments, and other troops of his division still in New York City. When Private Hezekiah Munsell reached the Post Road, he saw Putnam "making his way towards New York when all were going from it." Colonel David Humphreys, a volunteer serving Old Put as adjutant, frequently saw him that day, "for the purpose of issuing orders and encouraging the troops, flying on his horse, covered with foam, wherever his presence was necessary."

Howe's halt at Murray's Hill gave birth to a legend that created one of the first heroines of the war, a middle-aged Quaker mother of twelve children, who was credited by her contemporaries with saving Putnam. Surgeon's Mate James

Thacher, a young man of Barnstable with a small, sharp Yankee face, thin mouth, straight hair, and hooked nose, had joined the medical corps at Cambridge in the summer of 1775. He was an omnivorous gatherer of facts and gossip and kept a rich journal. In August, 1776, he was at Ticonderoga, but he read every published account and listened to every story of activities at New York, and he set down the story of Mrs Murray:

. . . Putnam at the head of three thousand, five hundred Continental troops was in the rear and the last that left the city. In order to avoid any of the enemy that might be advancing in the direct road to the city, he made choice of a road parallel with and contiguous to the North River [Hudson], till he could arrive at a certain angle whence another road would conduct him in such a direction as that he might form a junction with our army.

It so happened that a body of . . . British and Hessians were at the same moment advancing on the road, which would have brought them in immediate contact with General Putnam before he could have reached the turn into the other road.

Most fortunately the British generals, seeing no prospect of engaging our troops, halted their own and repaired to the house of Mr. Robert Murray, a Quaker and a friend of our cause. Mrs. Murray treated them with cake and wine, and they were induced to tarry two hours or more, Governor Tryon frequently joking her about her American friends. By this happy incident, General Putnam by continuing his march, escaped an encounter with a greatly superior force which must have proved fatal. . . . Ten minutes, it is said, would have been sufficient for the enemy to have secured the road at the turn and entirely cut off General Putnam's retreat. It has since become almost a common saying among our officers that Mrs. Murray saved this part of the American army.[9]

Late that broiling afternoon, Howe's forces lay across the island. One of his brigades marched down to the city, while he with the rest of his force marched up the Post Road parallel to Putnam's sweating men and encamped for the night at McGowan's Pass.

Admiral Howe's secretary, Serle, had watched from shipboard the entry of the British troops into the city of New York.

The King's forces took possession of the place, [he recorded,] incredible as it may seem, without the loss of a man. Nothing could equal the expressions of joy shown by the inhabitants upon the arrival of the King's officers among them. They even carried some of them upon their shoulders about the streets and behaved in all respects, women as well as men, like overjoyed Bedlamites. One thing is worth remarking: a woman pulled down the rebel standard upon the fort, and a woman hoisted up in its stead His Majesty's flag after trampling the other under foot with the most contemptuous indignation.[10]

In camp on Harlem Heights, Washington spent an uneasy night. The rocky heights were a strong defensive position, but only if his troops would be steadfast. The morning after the disaster at New York, the General sent out reconnoitering parties to see what the British were doing, and sat down to express his doubts to Congress:

We are now encamped with the main body of the army on the Heights of Harlem, where I should hope the enemy would meet with a defeat in case of an attack, if the generality of our troops would behave with tolerable resolution. But experience, to my extreme affliction, has convinced me that this is rather to be wished for than expected.[11]

The British were busy in New York. They inspected the rebel "works (which are innumerable) [and] appear calculated more to amuse than for use," and they placed "a broad R on every door in New York that is disaffected to government," in order to make examples of their inhabitants. But Howe was also busy on another front. Washington's adjutant general, Joseph Reed, wrote his wife that at headquarters, just as he was sealing a letter:

. . . an account came that the enemy were advancing upon us in three large columns. We have so many false reports that I desired the General to permit me to go and discover what truth there was in the account. I accordingly went down to our most advanced guard and while I was talking with the officer, the enemy's advanced guard fired upon us at a small distance. Our men behaved well, stood and returned the fire, till overpowered by numbers they were obliged to retreat. The enemy advanced upon us very fast. I had not quitted a house five minutes before they were in possession of it.[12]

Washington, meanwhile, had set out soon after Reed and arrived at the American advance post about two and a half miles south. Here he was informed that the firing had been between one hundred and fifty of Lieutenant Colonel Thomas Knowlton's Connecticut Rangers and a British party of three hundred.

Finding how things were going, [Reed continued,] I

went over to the General to get some support for the brave fellows, who had behaved so well. By the time I got to him, the enemy appeared in open view, and in the most insulting manner sounded their bugle horns as is usual after a fox chase. I never felt such a sensation before. It seemed to crown our disgrace.[13]

Washington, upon being told that the British force was three hundred strong and hidden behind a hill, resolved to throw a force to their rear and surprise them while making a demonstration directly in their front. He chose for the encircling movement three companies of Weedon's Virginia Regiment, under command of Major Andrew Leitch, and Knowlton's Connecticut Rangers. Among the party making the frontal demonstration was Captain John Chilton, a tobacco planter from Fauquier County in Virginia, a beautiful land of rolling hills and endless vistas in the shadow of the Blue Ridge. He wrote to his friends at home:

We discovered the enemy peeping from their heights over the fencings and rocks and running backwards and forwards. We did not alter our position. I believe they expected we should have ascended the hill to them, but finding us still, they imputed it to fear and came down skipping towards us in small parties. At the distance of about two hundred and fifty or three hundred yards they began their fire. Our orders were not to fire till they came near, but a young officer (of whom we have too many) on the right fired and it was taken [up] from right to left. We made about four fires. I had fired twice and loaded again, determined to keep for a better chance, but Colonel Weedon calling to keep up our fire (he meant for us to reserve it, but we misunderstood him), I fired once more.

We then all wiped and loaded and sat down in our ranks and let the enemy fire on us near an hour. Our men observed the best order, not quitting their ranks, though exposed to a constant and warm fire. I can't say enough in their praise; they behaved like soldiers who fought from principle alone.

During this, three companies of riflemen from our regiment . . . with other companies of riflemen were flanking the enemy and had began a brisk fire on the right of them.[14]

Washington's aide-de-camp, Tench Tilghman, Philadelphia merchant serving without rank or pay, described to his father what happened to the companies making for the enemy rear:

Unluckily Colonel Knowlton and Major Leitch began

their attack too soon; it was rather in flank than in rear. The action now grew warm. Major Leitch was wounded early in the engagement and Colonel Knowlton soon after, the latter mortally. He was one of the bravest and best officers in the army. Their men, notwithstanding, persisted with the greatest bravery.

The General, finding they wanted support, ordered over part of Colonel Griffith's and part of Colonel Richardson's Maryland regiments. These troops, though young, charged with as much bravery as I can conceive; they gave two fires and then rushed right forward, which drove the enemy from the wood into a buckwheat field, from whence they retreated. The General, fearing (as we afterwards found) that a large body was coming up to support them, sent me over to bring our men off. They gave a "huzza" and left the field in good order. . . . The prisoners we took told us, they expected our men would run away as they did the day before, but that they were never more surprised than to see us advancing to attack them. The Virginia and Maryland troops bear the palm. They are well-officered and behave with as much regularity as possible. . . .[15]

Washington was satisfied with the "brisk little skirmish." It demonstrated that his army still had some spirit. Less cautious men were tremendously excited that Americans for the first time had worsted redcoats in a stand-up fight. It had never happened before. Joseph Reed wrote to his wife: "You can hardly conceive the change it has made in our army. The men have recovered their spirits and feel a confidence which before they had quite lost."

In the late afternoon all the troops withdrew to the lines which had been thrown up hastily during the day from the Hudson River to the Harlem River, about a half mile north of the Hollow Way on Harlem Heights.

"... MAD, VEXED, SICK, AND SORRY"

White Plains and the Hudson River Forts

AUGUST-NOVEMBER 1776

THE NEXT day, the seventeenth of September, was quiet. On a hillslope near the King's Bridge road, the Americans buried Colonel Knowlton with "every honor . . . the situation of things would admit of," and details roamed yesterday's ground, the buckwheat fields, the woods, and the great dark boulders, interring rebels and redcoats alike, where they had fallen.

A British deserter brought word that more of the enemy had been engaged than Washington had guessed; he told that Howe had encamped "a considerable body of men" from river to river between two and three miles south of the American position. "The general officers," said William Heath, "were divided in opinion" about Howe's next move. Some expected that he would endeavor to master the island, and therefore would make the reduction of Fort Washington a first object. Others thought he would make a landing from Long Island Sound behind Washington's position.

Whichever he did, Washington reasoned, he would do during the few remaining weeks of good weather, so Washington prepared for either move by strengthening Harlem Heights in depth with three lines of redoubts and entrenchments, spread a mile apart northward, and by dividing his force between the lines and two other positions. He ordered ten thousand men for the lines; ten thousand under Heath to hold the King's Bridge sector, posted in Westchester and tied to the forces on Manhattan by a floating bridge; and five thousand under Greene to take post at or near Fort Constitution across the Hudson River. Actually these were only paper figures. No more than sixteen thousand men in all were present and fit for duty. Many of these were militia which continued to disappear in unbelievable numbers.

While Washington prepared to meet Howe's next move and worried about holding his men together, the British lost much of their recent prize. On Friday night, the twentieth, Lieutenant Frederick Mackenzie was bedded down for the night in New York. About ten o'clock a sentry called him out and said the town was on fire. Mackenzie, in his diary, wrote:

On going to the window I observed an immense column of fire and smoke and went and called General Smith, who said he would follow me into town as soon as possible.

I dressed myself immediately and ran into town, a distance of two miles, but when I got there the fire had got to such a head, there seemed to be no hopes of stopping it, and those who were present did little more than look on and lament the misfortune. As soon as buckets and water could be got, the seamen and the troops, assisted by some of the inhabitants, did what they could to arrest its progress, but the fresh wind and the combustible nature of the materials of which all the houses were built rendered all their efforts vain.

From a variety of circumstances which occurred, it is beyond a doubt that the town was designedly set on fire, either by some of those fellows who concealed themselves in it since the 15th . . . or by some villains left behind for the purpose. Some of them were caught by the soldiers in the very act of setting fire to the inside of empty houses at a distance from the fire. Many were detected with matches and combustibles under their clothes, and combustibles were found in several houses. One villain who abused and cut a woman who was employed in bringing water to the engines and who was found cutting the handles of the fire buckets, was hung up by the heels on the spot by the seamen.

One or two others who were found in houses with firebrands in their hands were put to death by the enraged soldiery and thrown into the flames. There is no doubt, however, that the flames were communicated to several houses by means of the burning flakes of the shingles . . . carried by the wind. . . .

No assistance could be sent from the army 'til after daybreak, as the general was apprehensive the rebels had some design of attacking the army.

It is almost impossible to conceive a scene of more horror and distress. . . . The sick, the aged, women, and children, half naked were seen going they knew not where, and taking refuge in houses which were at a distance from the fire, but from whence in several instances driven a second and even a third time by the devouring element, and at last in a state of despair, laying themselves down on the Common.

The terror was increased by the horrid noise of the burning and falling houses, the pulling down of such wooden buildings as served to conduct the fire (in which the soldiers and seamen were particularly active and useful), the rattling of above one hundred wagons sent in from the army . . . constantly employed in conveying to the Common such goods and effects as could be saved; the confused voices of so many men; the shrieks and cries of the women and children; and seeing the fire break out unexpectedly in places at a distance, which manifested a design of totally destroying the city. . . .

The appearance of the Trinity Church, when completely in flames, was a very grand sight, for the spire being entirely framed of wood and covered with shingles, a lofty pyramid of fire appeared, and as soon as the shingles were burnt away, the frame appeared with every separate piece of timber burning until the principal timbers were burnt through when the whole fell with a great noise.[1]

The burning of New York was not an official piece of American sabotage, although Washington admitted to his brother Lund, "Providence, or some good honest fellow, has done more for us than we were disposed to do for ourselves." But he had to add that "enough remains to answer" the purpose of the British.

It was, perhaps, the fury of the British, convinced of an American plot to destroy the city, that led to the summary execution of a young captain before the ashes were cold. Mackenzie noticed the event in his journal:

A person named Nathaniel Hales [*sic*], a lieutenant in the rebel army and a native of Connecticut, was apprehended as a spy last night [September 21] upon Long Island. And having this day made a full and free confession to the Commander-in-Chief of his being employed by Mr. Washington in that capacity, he was hanged at eleven o'clock in front of the park of artillery. He was about twenty-four years of age and had been educated at the College of New Haven in Connecticut. He behaved with great composure and resolution, saying he thought it the duty of every good officer to obey any orders given him by his Commander-in-Chief, and desired the spectators to be at all times prepared to meet death in whatever shape it might appear.[2]

Washington himself apparently knew little or nothing of Nathan Hale's mission, until he learned of Hale's death from Howe's aide, Captain John Montresor, who came into his lines under flag of truce to arrange a prisoner exchange on the evening of the twenty-second. Evidently Captain Hale had volunteered when Colonel Knowlton asked for a man to enter

New York on behalf of headquarters to try to determine Howe's activities and possible plans. Knowlton had fallen at the head of his troops in the buckwheat fields of Harlem, and his gentle schoolmaster turned soldier died as valiantly in the enemy's city.

Howe left Washington undistrbed on Harlem Heights for nearly a month after the New York fire, although Washington expected an attack every day. They were heartbreaking weeks for the General. His army seemed to be falling apart. Straggling, plundering, malingering, desertion, and a dozen other offenses forced him to issue successive General Orders that somehow seemed futile. He and his generals considered the incompetent corps of officers largely responsible for the poor discipline that prevailed. Washington begged the states to seek out good officer material, and he wrote imploringly to the Congress to provide inducements to "gentlemen of abilities to engage to serve during the war." At the same time he exhorted the Congress to hurry plans for a standing army.

The medical corps also needed an overhauling. Many of the regimental surgeons he thought were "very great rascals, countenancing the men in sham complaints to exempt them from duties and often receiving bribes to certify indispositions with a view to procure discharges or furloughs."

Even Washington's friend and loyal assistant, Joseph Reed, was pessimistic, and wondering if he should not ask to be replaced. Colonel Moylan, during these weeks, manfully confessed that he did not think he was equal to the task of Quartermaster General and resigned, to be replaced by General Mifflin. Washington, to his own family, declared his weariness and unhappiness. To his brother John he wrote, ". . . it is not in the power of words to describe the task I have to act. Fifty thousand pounds should not induce me again to undergo what I have done." And to Lund he wrote a few days later:

. . . Such is my situation that if I were to wish the bitterest curse to an enemy on this side of the grave, I should put him in my stead with my feelings; and yet I do not know what plan of conduct to pursue. I see the impossibility of serving with reputation, or doing any essential service to the cause by continuing in command, and yet I am told that if I quit the command, inevitable ruin will follow from the distraction that will ensue.

In confidence I tell you that I never was in such an unhappy, divided state since I was born. To lose all comfort and happiness on the one hand, whilst I am fully persuaded that under such a system of management as has been adopted, I cannot have the least chance for reputation, nor those allowances made which the nature of the case requires; and to be told, on the other, that if I leave the service all will be lost, is, at the same time that I am bereft of every peaceful moment, distressing to a degree.[3]

But the hard-fibered man added that "if the men will stand by me (which, by the by, I despair of), I am resolved not to be forced from this ground while I have life."

Days wore on into weeks, and officers and men had little news to write home. Captain John Chilton wrote to his friends in Fauquier on October 4:

Since the skirmish of the sixteenth September, the enemy have been peaceable but seem vastly busy, and we expect something every hour. We are on our guard and our men seem resolutely bent to give them a warm reception at the meeting. The Yankees who were timorous when we first came have plucked up a heart and I hope will fight lustily. . . .

The brave Major Leitch who died of the wounds received the sixteenth was interred yesterday. . . . Our men have been sickly with fevers and agues but are mending. We have plenty of good beef, but no variety of other food and though we are between two rivers we get no fish and very few oysters or clams or cockles. . . . We sometimes get pork and pease, rum, brandy, etc. . . .[4]

The forces continued close to each other, and the men in the ranks lost much of their personal hatred for the foe. Heath's division kept a force of four hundred and fifty men at Morrisania with a chain of sentinels down to the beach facing Montresor's Island, at the mouth of the Harlem River between Morrisania and Manhattan Island, which the British had occupied since September 10. At first there was some firing back and forth between pickets, but after the commanding officers on both sides came to an understanding, "there was no firing between the sentinels at that place any more." In fact, reported Heath, the rebels and the redcoats became downright friendly:

. . . and they were so civil to each other, on their posts, that one day, at a part of the creek where it was practicable, the British sentinel asked the American, who was nearly opposite to him, if he could give him a chew of tobacco: the latter, having in his pocket a piece of a thick twisted roll, sent it across the creek, to the British sentinel, who after taking off his bite, sent the remainder back again.[5]

At last, on October 12, the cautious Howe moved. Embarking the greater part of his force on eighty boats of all sorts, he passed up the East River under cover of a warm, heavy fog and about 9 A.M. landed an advance force of four thousand on Throg's, sometimes called by the natives "Frog's," Neck. The Neck was considered to be a peninsula jutting two miles into Long Island Sound to the rear and left of Washington's lines. From the Neck a road ran directly to King's Bridge. Actually, the Neck became an island at high tide, separated from the mainland by a creek with marshy borders. There were two approaches to the main, both guarded—a causeway and wooden bridge over a milldam at the lower end, and a ford at the upper.

The military importance of the bridge over the milldam at Westchester village had been recognized by General Heath several days earlier when he reconnoitered the neighborhood. An enormous pile of cordwood lay on the west side of the creek; behind it he placed a small guard of riflemen. Another detail watched the fording place.

His men lay at these crossings on the twelfth. He reported:

The troops landed at Frog's Neck and their advance pushed towards the causeway and the bridge at Westchester Mill. Colonel [Edward] Hand's [thirty] riflemen took up the planks of the bridge as had been directed and commenced a firing with their rifles.

The British moved towards the head of the creek, but found here also the Americans in possession of the pass. Our General [Heath] immediately (as he had assured Colonel Hand he would do) ordered up Colonel [William] Prescott, the hero of Bunker Hill, with his regiment and Captain Lieutenant [David] Bryant of the Artillery with a three-pounder to reinforce the riflemen at Westchester causeway, and Colonel [John] Graham of the New York Line with his regiment and Lieutenant [Daniel] Jackson of the Artillery with a six-pounder to reinforce at the head of the creek—all of which was promptly done to the check and disappointment of the enemy.

The British encamped on the Neck. The riflemen and [Hessian] jägers kept up a scattering popping at each other across the marsh, and the Americans on their side and the British on the other threw up a work at the end of the causeway. Captain Bryant, now and then, when there was an object, saluted the British with a fieldpiece.

In the afternoon, forty or fifty sail of vessels passed up

and came to anchor off Frog's Point. The same evening General [Alexander] McDougall's Brigade joined our General's [Heath's] division.[6]

When Washington received word of the landing, he perceived that Howe intended to work around to the rear of his whole position, but the enemy's halt on Throg's Neck was inexplicable. Thirty riflemen, behind a pile of wood, for several hours held up the advance of four thousand British troops with fieldpieces, and probably did a great deal to save Washington's whole army. If Howe had pushed across the creek, he would have cut off Washington's only road of retreat and smashed the Americans between two strong forces. The distance from Westchester Creek to King's Bridge was about four miles, and Washington's army was about the same distance from King's Bridge. Even if Washington had hurried across the Harlem River, he probably could not have defended himself against a flank attack by Howe and an attack on his rear by the British troops Howe left in New York. Howe also might have bypassed the small American guards, if he mistakenly over-estimated their strength, by crossing over to Pell's Point, three miles north, crossing the Bronx River and cutting Washington off west of it. Yet he tarried for six days, his excuse later being that he was obliged to await supplies from New York and three battalions of Hessians from Staten Island.

When Howe made his landing, Washington at first believed the ground he held between King's Bridge and Throg's Neck was defensible. Personal reconnaissances confirmed his belief, and he reassigned his troops so that the stronger ones would meet the brunt of Howe's move. General Charles Lee returned from South Carolina on the fourteenth, just in time to be given command of the troops north of King's Bridge—the key position—and on the sixteenth Washington brought Lee and his other generals together for a strategy council. The council decided that Manhattan Island could be held no longer, for it now seemed certain Howe meant to encircle the Americans. He repeatedly had run his warships up the Hudson past Fort Washington, two miles south of King's Bridge, proving that he could land troops in Washington's rear while his main body advanced westward from Throg's Neck and turned the American flank. The time had come to move or to be cut off, either to starve or to fight on ground of the enemy's choosing. Nevertheless, the council agreed that Fort Washington should be held as long as possible. The Congress desired it, and General Greene, who commanded on the Jersey side of the river at Fort Constitution, believed that the two forts were powerful enough to stop enemy ships in spite of the previous success of British vessels in running past them.

As Howe continued to lie at Throg's Neck, it appeared that he would either proceed up the shore of Connecticut, scorching the earth as he went, or move northward to turn Washington's left. His advance probably would be to White Plains, little more than twenty miles north. Washington determined to be the first to take the strong position at White Plains.

While Washington and his officers studied their position and that of the enemy, the General sent to Pell's Point Colonel John Glover, the Marblehead fisherman whose skill had enabled him to bring off his troops from Long Island. With Glover went a mixed little "brigade" of eleven hundred men —a regiment of his fishermen, together with parts of three other Massachusetts regiments—and three fieldpieces. They were to protect the road from Pell's Point to the rear of Washington's position.

There the stocky little redhead kept a sharp eye toward Howe's position on Throg's Neck. Early on the morning of the eighteenth, he mounted a hilltop near Eastchester to look down the Sound with his spyglass. What he saw galvanized him into action: "a number of ships in the Sound under way. In a very short time saw the boats, upwards of two hundred sail, all manned and formed in four grand divisions." Quickly the colonel marched about 750 of his men with his three fieldpieces to oppose the landing enemy. When he deployed in echelon, he confessed, "I would have given a thousand worlds to have had General [Charles] Lee or some other experienced officer present to direct or at least to approve of what I had done." He "looked around," but "could see none," so he led his troops forward. A savage little action developed. Although Glover pulled back to more favorable ground, even after the enemy main body came up with seven fieldpieces, he clung to his position all day with negligible loss. He disputed the ground so ferociously, in fact, that Howe delayed his advance three more days and lost another opportunity to put his army across the American route of retreat.

It was valuable time gained, for Washington, on the morning of the eighteenth, moved his army across the Harlem River and along the west bank of the little Bronx River toward the village of White Plains. The way was toilsome, and he was hampered by lack of teams and wagons and horses for the guns. The long column of thirteen thousand men moved their wagons forward, dumped their loads, and returned to load again, spending four days on a journey which normally should have taken one. Washington's top-command personnel was strengthened for the coming ordeal, however, by the return to the army of his generals Sullivan and Stirling, who had been exchanged.

To secure White Plains before Howe could reach it, Washington, on the night of the twentieth, sent an order to Lord Stirling to hurry forward with his brigade. Stirling got the message at two o'clock in the morning of the twenty-first, and his Delawares arrived on the ground by nine. Washington himself followed that day with Heath's division.

Headquarters were opened at White Plains on October 23. At this place, Washington chose to defend a position on a series of hills, north and east of town, overlooking the so-called "plains." His men busily threw up shallow fortifications extending from the Bronx River on his right to a swamp on his left. His right and left were drawn back at right angles. Two factors endangered his position: the lines were three miles long, and in advance of the right was a high hill, known as Chatterton's Hill. It was separated from the main position by the upper waters of the Bronx, and although it somewhat dominated the American front and enfiladed the approaches from the south, it had been garrisoned with only a small force of militia and was not yet fortified when the General arrived.

Howe had missed an opportunity to destroy the greater part of Washington's army when he allowed it to retreat northward unmolested. But the British general was busy with the movement of his own troops. The all-day check he had received from Glover led him to encamp on a short line from Eastchester to New Rochelle. There he lay until the twenty-first, when he moved his right and center up two miles north of New Rochelle. Here he encamped for a few more days, moving on the twenty-fifth up to within four miles of White Plains, where now most of Washington's army was gathered and more troops were arriving. The two armies watched each other. The British seemed to be a little more impressed by the soldierliness of the rebels. Colonel Stephen Kemble, Deputy Adjutant General of the British Army, heard from a fellow officer:

The rebels in our front supposed not to be above two thousand, their sentries and ours very near, and no firing from our side or theirs. An officer observed that they marched off with great composure the last evening and in much better order than he had ever seen them when he first came to the ground, and behaved more like soldiers than he had ever known them to do before.[7]

On the twenty-sixth, General Charles Lee and his division arrived in the camp. Lee was among the officers who considered the heights to the rear of Washington's lines as the best ultimate position, a fact of which Washington was not unaware. Washington suggested first a reconnaissance of Chatterton's Hill. On the morning of the twenty-seventh, according to General Heath, who had arrived with his division at four in the morning of the twenty-second after an all-night march:

> The Commander-in-Chief ordered the general officers who were off duty to attend him to reconnoiter this ground. . . . When arrived at the ground, although very commanding, it did not appear so much so as other grounds to the north, and almost parallel with the left of the army, as it was then formed.
> "Yonder," says Major General Lee, pointing to the grounds just mentioned, "is the ground we ought to occupy."
> "Let us go and view it," replied the Commander-in-Chief.
> When on the way, a light horseman came up in full gallop, his horse almost out of breath, and addressed General Washington.
> "The British are on the camp, sir!"
> The General observed, "Gentlemen, we have now other business than reconnoitering," putting his horse in full gallop for the camp and followed by the other officers.
> When arrived at headquarters, the Adjutant General Reed who had remained at camp informed the Commander-in-Chief that the guards had been all beat in, and the whole American army were now at their respective posts, in order of battle.
> The Commander-in-Chief turned round to the officers and only said, "Gentlemen, you will repair to your respective posts and do the best you can."[8]

But the British did not pursue the advance guard and fell back to their own positions.

Before dawn the next day, according to Benjamin Tallmadge, brigade major, "we learned that the enemy was in full march directly in front of us." Tallmadge was with an advance corps under General Spencer which was out to meet the enemy advance.

General Spencer . . . immediately made the necessary disposition to receive the enemy, having the river Bronx on our right and between us and the troops on Chatterton's Hill. At the dawn of day, the Hessian column advanced within musket shot of our troops, when a full discharge of musketry warned them of their danger. At first they fell back, but rallied again immediately, and the column of British troops having advanced on our left made it necessary to retire.

As stone walls were frequent, our troops occasionally formed behind them and poured a destructive fire into the Hessian ranks. It, however, became necessary to retreat wholly before such an overwhelming force.

To gain Chatterton's Hill, it became necessary to cross the Bronx, which was fordable at that place. The troops immediately entered the river and ascended the hill, while I being in the rear and mounted on horseback endeavored to hasten the last of our troops, the Hessians being then within a musket shot. . . . By the time I reached the opposite bank of the river, the Hessian troops were about to enter it and considered me as their prisoner. As we ascended the hill, I filed off to the right, expecting our troops on the hill would soon give them a volley.[9]

The volley Tallmadge hoped for came and he escaped. The fire which covered him came from the forces of General Alexander McDougall. Early that morning, Washington had decided that Chatterton's Hill must be fortified if he expected to hold his main position. Colonel Reed ordered Haslet's Delawares to the hill to support the militia already there, and also sent General McDougall's brigade to throw up earthworks. Back upon these troops, between nine and nine-thirty, fell the advanced parties. The redcoats and Hessians pressed forward and splashed against the hill and then withdrew, seemingly to await their fieldpieces and main body. Colonel Haslet, now atop Chatterton's Hill with his Delawares, perceived them "stop in the wheatfields a considerable time. I saw their general officers on horseback assemble in council, and soon their whole body face about, and in one continued column march to the hill opposite to our right."

Howe and his officers had decided that Chatterton's Hill must be taken and that it should be enfiladed from another eminence a half mile away. Thence Howe marched eight regiments and a dozen fieldpieces.

Amid artillery fire from the hill south of Chatterton's, Howe moved against the American position. According to Heath, while much of the British army were spectators:

A part of the left column, composed of British and Hessians, forded the river and marched along under the cover of the hill, until they had gained sufficient ground to the left of the Americans, when, by facing to the left, their column became a line, parallel with the Americans. When they briskly ascended the hill, the first column resumed a quick march. As the troops which were advancing to the attack ascended the hill, the cannonade on the side of the British ceased, as their own men became exposed to their fire if continued. The fire of small arms was now very heavy and without any distinction of sounds. This led some American officers, who were looking on, to observe that the British were worsted, as their cannon had ceased firing, but a few minutes evinced that the Americans were giving way. They moved off the hill in a great body, neither running, nor observing the best order. The British ascended the hill very slowly, and when arrived at its summit, formed and dressed their line without the least attempt to pursue the Americans.[10]

With the loss of the hill, Washington lost the day. His right was no longer tenable and he withdrew his lines. Howe did not press him. "After cannonading for a short time," a Continental said, "they became very still and quiet." Washington drew in his right and moved his sick, wounded, and baggage to the high ground of North Castle that evening and the next day. The British army dug in on Chatterton's Hill.

For several days, "the two armies lay looking at each other and within long cannon shot." Each was busy throwing up fortifications in anticipation of attack by the other. The Americans uprooted cornstalks in nearby fields and bound them into fascines to protect their works.

On the night of November 4, American sentinels reported that they could hear the rumble of the wheels of British gun carriages. Washington ordered his troops to lie on their arms, but it soon developed that Howe was pulling his forces back to Dobb's Ferry and New York with the evident intention of invading New Jersey. On the morning of the tenth, Washington marched out of White Plains. Below Stony Point he ferried across the Hudson River that portion of his troops with which he intended to oppose an enemy advance in the Jerseys. To guard the New York Highlands, he left Heath at Peekskill, about eighteen miles from White Plains on the Hudson, with about four thousand men. Charles Lee with some seven thousand remained at North Castle, and with only about two thousand men he himself turned to Fort Constitution, now called Fort Lee. Here Greene commanded about thirty-five hundred men, about twelve hundred of them across the river at and near Fort Washington. It was a desperate dispersion of force by a general who was exhausted and perplexed, whose every day was made a nightmare by the departure of shoals of militia and the imminent expiration of the terms of many Continentals. Then suddenly it was clear that Fort Washington would be Howe's first objective. A Hessian officer said of it:

The enemy had erected a fort on a high rocky elevation, which seemed fortified by nature itself, which they called Fort Washington. Human skill had also been employed to make it very strong. Without possession of this fort, we could not keep up communication with New York, nor could we think of advancing any farther, much less get quiet winter-quarters.[11]

And this was the post which Washington left garrisoned in the country of the enemy. The fort itself was an earthwork with a surrounding abatis covering about four acres of ground; it had no casemates, bombproofs, barracks, or buildings of any kind except a "wooden magazine and some offices." It was without interior water supply and, in case of siege, would be forced to get its water from the Hudson River, two hundred and thirty feet below the rocky heights on which the fort crouched. That any one believed the fort could withstand siege or attack by Howe's whole army of twenty thousand men in command of sea and land seems incredible, but Israel Putnam was confident it could be held. Colonel Robert Magaw, its commandant, declared he could hold it "till the end of December," and then, if forced to do so, could safely carry off its garrison and stores to the Jersey shore. Nathanael Greene, in command of both forts, Lee and Washington, agreed with Magaw. Washington, however, now had his doubts, but he was willing to leave a final decision to Greene, who knew the forts and was one of his most reliable general officers.

As soon as it was certain Howe meant to attack the fort, American reinforcements from New Jersey were thrown across the Hudson River, until the total of men under Magaw was nearly twenty-nine hundred. Magaw disposed them in a way in which he thought they might hold all of the ground between Harlem Heights and King's Bridge, an utterly hopeless scheme. It was an area about four miles long and three-quarters of a mile wide. At this upper end of Manhattan, the banks of both the Hudson and the Harlem were precipitous cliffs with a valley running between them. On the Hudson side, Fort Washington stood on a mile-long, especially high hill called Mount Washington; east on the Harlem reared Laurel Hill.

Magaw stationed Colonel Moses Rawlings with a regiment of riflemen in a small work about a half mile north of Fort Washington. Colonel Baxter with two hundred Pennsylvania militia occupied flèches on Laurel Hill. Two miles south, near the Harlem River, about eight hundred men under Lieutenant Colonel Lambert Cadwalader occupied the front line of the old entrenchments on Harlem Heights. The detachments were about a mile from each other.

Howe planned to attack all of Magaw's points simultaneously. Lord Percy was to drive from the south against Cadwalader on Harlem Heights. Generals Matthews and Cornwallis were to lead an assault from the east against Laurel Hill. General Wilhelm von Knyphausen, who had arrived from Europe with forty-seven hundred Hessians while Howe was at New Rochelle, was given the honor of commanding the frontal attack from the north on Fort Washington itself. The Highlanders were to advance from the southeast as a feint. A total of eight thousand men were committed to the assault.

Unknown to Washington, the plan of the fort and its defenses was in Howe's hands. On November 2, William Demont, a Pennsylvanian, adjutant of Magaw's battalion, had deserted to the enemy with sketches of the works and other information. British Lieutenant Mackenzie noted:

He says the rebels remaining on this island [of New York, on November 2] amount to about two thousand men, who, if they are obliged to abandon their advanced works, are to retire into Fort Washington and defend it to the last extremity, having therein two months provisions, many cannon, and plenty of ammunition.

He says there are great dissensions in the rebel army, everybody finding fault with the mode of proceeding, and the inferior officers, even ensigns, insisting that, in such a cause, every man has a right to assist in council and to give his opinion. They are much distressed for clothing. The people from the Southern colonies declare they will not go into New England, and the others that they will not march to the Southward. If this account is true in any degree, they must soon go to pieces.[12]

The first stage of the battle for Fort Washington commenced November 14. Lieutenant Colonel Paterson, Howe's adjutant general, accompanied by a drummer beating a parley, approached the fort with a white flag and called upon Magaw to surrender or suffer death by the sword. Magaw answered that "he did not expect inhumanity from Englishmen, and that he would defend the place to the last extremity." His refusal to surrender signaled the launching of the attack, which opened the next morning with a cannonade from British batteries on the east side of the Harlem and from the *Pearl*, a frigate anchored in the Hudson River.

Robert Auchmuty, a loyalist of Boston, exiled in London, forwarded a "particular account" he had received from America to the Earl of Huntingdon:

> . . . the attack was begun at daybreak. . . . A detachment of Hessians with cannon marched round from General Howe's army by King's Bridge along the clear road (which . . . is a kind of causeway) through a hollow way, commanded on both sides by very steep, craggy hills on which the rebels had redoubts which enfiladed the whole length of the valley. The Hessians with great firmness marched through this way, until they came to the north end of the steep mountain on the Harlem River, on the left side, which they began to clamber up, notwithstanding the heavy fire from the rebels on the top of the hills, and after very great difficulties and labors gained the summit, which as soon as the rebels saw they ran away towards the fort with great precipitation.[13]

That Hessian column making the main assault split into two columns, the right under Colonel Rall and the left under Knyphausen himself. Rall's column moved along the western ridge, and the general's along the eastern ridge and part of the ravine between. The columns joined before the north front of the fort.

While the Hessians were driving against Magaw's forces north of the fort, Lord Percy attacked with British and other Hessians from the south.

Howe's effort east of Cadwalader was the landing about noon of Matthews and Cornwallis with about three thousand men north of the fort. They came ashore about two miles above Cadwalader, against the positon held by Baxter's militia. The militia fled to Fort Washington when Baxter fell, and Cornwallis took quick advantage of his easy victory by turning the proposed feint by Lieutenant Colonel Thomas Sterling with the Forty-second Highlanders, at a point between Cadwalader and the fort, into a much more important maneuver. The Highlanders, with two battalions of the Second Brigade, struck across the Harlem to squeeze Cadwalader between themselves and Percy. This forced Cadwalader's retreat into the fort, with a loss of one hundred and seventy men captured.

The strike across the Harlem freed Knyphausen to push forward. Hessian Captain Andreas Wiederhold described the advance:

> At this moment, the real attack was begun near us, and we stood facing their crack troops and their riflemen all on this almost inaccessible rock which lay before us, surrounded by swamps and three earthworks, one above the other.
>
> In spite of this, every obstacle was swept aside, the earthworks broken through, the swamps waded, the precipitous rocks scaled, and the riflemen were driven out of their breastworks, from where they had been seconded by their artillery, and we gained this terrible height, pursued the enemy, who were retreating behind the lines and batteries; routed them there also, took the batteries, one of which lay on the very top of the rock, and we followed the fleeing enemy to the fort proper. There we seated ourselves at the side of the precipitous mountain to protect ourselves from the cannonade from the fort. But only our regiment [Wutgenau] and that of Rall were here.[14]

With the Hessian regiments halted behind a large storehouse, Colonel Rall ordered Captain Hohenstein to tie a white cloth on the end of a musket barrel, advance upon the fort, and call on it to surrender. The captain might have had his doubts about the respect a white flag would be shown by the angry rebel rifles, but he had been long disciplined.

> I did this at once, [he related later,] but they kept firing at me and the drummer, until we came to the glacis, where the rebels led us off with our eyes bound. They sent me to a colonel [John Cadwalader], who was second in command, to whom I made the following proposal:
>
> He should immediately march out of the fort with the garrison, and they should lay down their arms before General von Knyphausen. All ammunition, provisions, and whatever belonged to Congress should be faithfully made known. On the other hand, I gave him my word that all, from the comanding officer down, should retain their private property. Finally, a white flag should be immediately hoisted to put a stop to all hostilities.
>
> The commander asked for four hours time to consider, which, however, I refused, and allowed him only half an hour to speak with his officers. When the half-hour was past, the commander came himself, and his fate seemed hard to him. Thereupon he said, "The Hessians make impossibilities

possible." I then said to him, "General von Knyphausen is a hundred paces off. Come with me, on my safe-conduct, and see if he will give you better terms." He was contented with this and went with me.[15]

Knyphausen was not disposed to give better terms, and Magaw was forced to surrender, on the Hessians' conditions, two hundred and thirty officers, twenty-six hundred men, and a considerable supply of stores and articles of war. Loyalist Colonel Stephen Kemble reported:

To our shame, though they capitulated for the safety of their baggage, they were stripped of their wearing apparel as they marched out by Hessians, till a stop was put to it by making them take a different route.

They were so thronged in the fort that they could not have subsisted there above three days.[16]

Lieutenant Mackenzie described the cold, tattered Americans:

The rebel prisoners were in general but very indifferently clothed. Few of them appeared to have a second shirt, nor did they appear to have washed themselves during the campaign. A great many of them were lads under fifteen and old men, and few had the appearance of soldiers. Their odd figures frequently excited the laughter of our soldiers.[17]

There was no laughter across the Hudson River at Fort Lee. During the day, Washington had sent a messenger to Magaw to tell him that if he could hold out till dark, some way would be found to bring his men off to the New Jersey side. The messenger had returned with news that Magaw had been forced to capitulate—thus spelling Washington's greatest defeat. Nathanael Greene, whose star had been in the ascendant, was miserable. To his friend, Henry Knox, still at White Plains, Greene wrote feelingly on the next day:

I feel mad, vexed, sick, and sorry. Never did I need the consoling voice of a friend more than now. Happy should I be to see you. This is a most terrible event; its consequences are justly to be dreaded. Pray what is said upon the occasion? A line from you will be very acceptable.[18]

Even Joseph Reed, Washington's adjutant general and personal friend of Greene, condemned without hesitation both his General and his friend in a letter to Charles Lee:

> They hold us very cheap in consequence of the late affair at Mount Washington, where both the plan of defense and execution were contemptible. If a real defense of the lines was intended, the number was too few; if the fort only, the garrison was too numerous by half. General Washington's own judgment seconded by representations from us would, I believe, have saved the men and their arms, but unluckily, General Greene's judgment was contrary. This kept the General's mind in a state of suspense till the stroke was struck. Oh! General—an indecisive mind is one of the greatest misfortunes that can befall an army. How often have I lamented it this campaign.[19]

Reed's charge was not without justification. Greene and Magaw should have been overruled firmly when Washington himself doubted that the post could be held. It was the General's indecision that evoked Charles Lee's wail: "Oh, General, why would you be overpersuaded by men of inferior judgment to your own? It was a cursed affair."

With the fall of Fort Washington, the Americans lost their last foothold in New York. They faced a well-supplied, healthy, reinforced enemy, vastly superior in numbers, while their own force, ragged, ill-accoutered, and restless, was quickly becoming but a shadow of the throng that had turned out eighteen months before.

". . . OUR PEACH-BRANDY FELLOWS CAN NEVER BE BEAT"

The New Jersey Campaign

NOVEMBER 1776-JANUARY 1777

ALTHOUGH WASHINGTON had momentary hopes that Fort Lee could be held in spite of the collapse of Fort Washington, three days after Fort Washington was lost he came to the conclusion that Fort Lee had been important only "in conjunction with that on the other side of the river," and proposed to evacuate it and remove its stores. Except for the removal of gunpowder, he was too late.

About daylight on the twentieth of November, an American officer riding patrol five or six miles north of the fort ran into an enemy advanced column. During the rainy, cold night, Howe had landed four thousand men under the command of Lord Cornwallis between the western terminus of Dobb's Ferry and the fort to pen Greene and his garrison of two to three thousand men between the Hudson and the Hackensack rivers. The American patrol, on running into Cornwallis' van, wheeled and galloped down to the fort, shook Greene out of bed, and reported the enemy. Greene hurriedly put his men under arms. Leaving tents standing and breakfast kettles bubbling, they set out in flight across the Hackensack to join Washington, who was gathering his forces at the village of Hackensack.

So close was Cornwallis upon Greene's heels that several Americans were killed and one hundred and five captured, although the captives, Greene declared, were but "a set of rascals that skulked out of the way for fear of fighting," and were flushed from the woods by the enemy.

At the fort the British found many cannon, three hundred precious tents, hundreds of muskets, thousands of shot, shell, and cartridges, and over a thousand barrels of flour. Washington considered it a serious loss, but at least one Britisher was no more impressed by the booty than by the rebels:

On the appearance of our troops, the rebels fled like scared rabbits, and in a few moments after we reached the hill near their entrenchments, not a rascal of them could be seen. They have left some poor pork, a few greasy proclamations, and some of that scoundrel Common Sense man's letters, which we can read at our leisure, now that we have got one of the "impregnable redoubts" of Mr. Washington's to quarter in. . . . We intend to push on after the long-faces in a few days.[1]

No longer was there any doubt in Washington's mind about Howe's intentions: he would throw large forces into New Jersey and shift the war to the right of the Hudson River. Already Cornwallis was there. There was nothing to prevent Howe, holding control of the river, from following with thirty thousand more men.

Once again Washington found himself between two rivers, this time the Hackensack and the Passaic. There, in command of an army of "not above three thousand men . . . much broken and dispirited," he could not hope to face the British. Nor did the country offer any of the natural strongholds to which he had become accustomed. It was, so he said, "almost a dead flat." Without the picks and shovels lost at the Hudson River forts, his men could not even dig entrenchments. There was nothing for it but further retreat and, if possible, consolidation of his scattered forces. Even the good, clear weather turned off to gloomy, freezing, winter rain terrible on men so poorly clothed that an enemy officer remarked on the attire of the dead found near Fort Washington: ". . . many were without shoes or stockings and several were observed to have only linen drawers on, with a rifle or hunting shirt without any proper shirt or waistcoat. They are also in great want of blankets."

Reluctantly, and with heavy heart, on the morning of November 21, Washington left a "very fine country" to the ravages of the enemy and marched on miry, broken roads to Aquackinack Bridge, crossed the Passaic, and pushed on to Newark.

While appealing frantically to New Jersey for militia and to Congress for aid of all sorts, Washington urged Charles Lee, who stubbornly continued to hold the area around White Plains, to come near him with his thirty-five hundred Continentals, leaving behind two brigades to guard stores until their time was out, when Washington expected they would go home. To Congress he sent smooth-tongued General Mifflin, an accomplished politician, to report his circumstances in language politicians could understand.

Lee argued against his chief's decision to move his forces, and tarried. Washington found Newark untenable and was forced to retreat to New Brunswick; his rear guard was leaving Newark on the twenty-eighth as Cornwallis' vanguard entered the opposite side of town.

At Brunswick on the seventeenth, there had arrived the only other American force yet across the river, Lord Stirling's thousand men, "broken down and fatigued—some without shoes, some had no shirts." A picturesque malady affected many of them. According to one of their lieutenants:

> Here our soldiers drank freely of spiritous liquors. They have chiefly got a disorder which at camp is called the "Barrel Fever," which differs in its effects from any other fever —its concomitants are black eyes and bloody noses.[2]

Washington was running to save his remnant of army, and Cornwallis pursued with a puzzling leisure. One British officer observed:

> As we go forward into the country, the rebels fly before us, and when we come back, they always follow us; 'tis almost impossible to catch them. They will neither fight, nor totally run away. But they keep at such a distance that we are always above a day's march from them. We seem to be playing at Bo-Peep.[3]

Washington was not thinking of children's games. The story circulated around his camp that he asked Colonel Reed, "Should we retreat to the back parts of Pennsylvania, will the Pennsylvanians support us?" Reed answered, "If the lower [eastern] counties are subdued and give up, the back counties will do the same." Washington passed his hand over his throat and said, "My neck does not feel as though it was made for a halter. We must retire to Augusta County, in Virginia, . . . and, if overpowered, we must pass the Allegheny Mountains."

But if Washington was momentarily depressed, he was not yet finished. The Maryland and the New Jersey militia brigades left him in the very face of the enemy, the day after he reached Brunswick; yet he declared, "I will not despair."

The next morning, scouts reported the enemy within ten miles. After noon, Washington wrote to Congress, "The enemy are fast approaching, some of 'em in sight now." While his gunners played a smart cannonade on the redcoats across the Raritan, he put his army in motion once more. At Princeton, he paused only long enough to write Congress that Lee had not yet joined him, to post Stirling with two brigades to slow Cornwallis' advance, and to afford his men a moment of laughter at the expense of a Tory. Solomon Clift wrote in his diary that second of December at Princeton:

> . . . we arrived early this morning. We are in a terrible situation, with the enemy close upon us and whole regiments

Paramus

Pompton

HACKENSACK RIVER

HUDSON RIVER

PASSAIC RIVER

Acquackanack

Orange

Newark

Morristown

Springfield

Connecticut Farms

NEW YORK BAY

Chester

Basking Ridge

Elizabeth-town

Scotch Plains

STATEN ISLAND

Pluckemin

Perth Amboy

Middle Brook

Bound Brook

Quibble Town

RARITAN RIVER

RARITAN BAY

Somerset Court House

New Brunswick

MILLSTONE CREEK

Middletown

NEW JERSEY

English Town

CORYELL'S FERRY

Princeton

Cranberry

Monmouth

Pennington

Maidenhead

ASSUNPINK CREEK

N

McKONKEY'S FERRY

Allentown

YARDLEY'S FERRY

Trenton

Newtown

Crosswicks

PENNSYLVANIA

Bordentown

Bristol

Burlington

DUNK'S FERRY

DELAWARE RIVER

New Jersey
FALL 1776

. . . leaving us. Tomorrow, we go to Trenton, where the General is determined to make a stand. . . . A Tory . . . was brought in here today by a party of the Pennsylvania boys. He mistook them for the regulars and came quite into camp without perceiving his mistake. This afternoon, after taking off his breeches and giving him an absolution by setting him on the ice (to cool off his loyalty), they set him to work bringing in faggots. He seems pleased with his new office, knowing that he got off easy. Notwithstanding General Stirling deprecates severity to the infernal Tories we catch, they get absolution often.[4]

On Washington marched, the same day, to Trenton, to get his baggage and stores across the Delaware to safety. Then, with a small, unstable, but disencumbered "army," he would make whatever move the enemy's course suggested. For some inexplicable reason, Cornwallis stopped at Brunswick, giving Washington time to cross his baggage, stores, sick, and wounded, and also to collect or destroy every boat on the river for seventy miles above Philadelphia, so that he controlled passage to the Pennsylvania side.

Then Washington started back on the seventh for Princeton, where he thought he might be in a better position to meet the enemy, now reinforced and under Howe's personal command. But en route he heard that Stirling had pulled his brigades out of Princeton and was falling back on the main force at Trenton. Washington quickly reversed his march. He joined Haslet's Delawares in the rear guard on the retreat. To captain Enoch Anderson of the Delawares he set an example for any wavering Continental:

We continued on our retreat—our regiment in the rear, and I, with thirty men, in rear of the regiment, and General Washington in my rear with pioneers—tearing up bridges and cutting down trees to impede the march of the enemy. I was to go no faster than General Washington and his pioneers. It was dusk before we got to Trenton.[5]

On the cold Sunday afternoon of December 8, Cornwallis, again close on the Americans with Howe's vanguard, came into Trenton in time to see the last of his quarry pushing off for the Pennsylvania shore.

The next morning, Washington posted the brigades of Generals Stirling, Mercer, Stephen, and Roche de Fermoy—about two thousand men in all—in detachments at different landing places from Yardley's up to Coryell's Ferry, "to prevent them from stealing a march upon us from above." General Ewing with some 550 men was posted along the river south of the ferry to Bordentown. Beyond him a sensible, aggressive Pennsylvanian, Brigadier General John Cadwalader, with one thousand men, mostly recently arrived militia, guarded the river to Dunk's Ferry with headquarters at Bristol.

The drive of the British toward Philadelphia panicked the city. Washington sent Israel Putnam to fortify it and put it under martial law, and Mifflin to take charge of stores and to raise militia.

To a "false and malicious report . . . by the enemies of America" that it was about to disperse, the Congress responded by resolving that Washington should scotch the rumor and by declaring that it had too much faith in the army and the people to decamp. The next day, however, it adjourned to reconvene a little over a week later in the comparative security of Baltimore, after resolving that "General Washington be possessed of full power to order and direct all things relative to the department [of the army] and to the operation of the war."

There was no question about it: everything now depended upon the arrival of Lee. Only with the addition of his battle-proved troops could Washington dare hope to halt the British advance, or to so discourage them as to force them into winter quarters beyond the Delaware. On the other hand, Howe was so confident that he dispersed part of his force in another operation entirely. He sent Clinton from New York with six thousand men to take Rhode Island. Clinton accomplished this without opposition on December 8, and settled around Newport, where the British remained for three years.

Lee's strange, infuriating behavior frustrated Washington's every attempt to hasten his march. Finally, on December 8, the General was reduced to the humiliation of entreating his subordinate to join him. "Do come on," he begged. "Your arrival may be happy, and if it can be effected without delay, may be the means of preserving a city, whose loss must prove of the most fatal consequences to the cause of America."

Lee actually had crossed the Hudson River on December 4 and proceeded via Pompton to Morristown. By the twelfth, he had come a few miles southwest of Morristown. That night he decided to sleep at a tavern kept by a widow at Basking Ridge, three miles from his camp. He was accompanied by his guard and some of his military family.

Next morning, while his army marched off, he remained at the tavern in dressing gown and slippers, to write some dispatches. Earlier he had boasted, "I am going into the Jerseys for the salvation of America." He not only had entered into correspondence with Joseph Reed criticizing Washington, but also had castigated Congress, complaining that they "seem to stumble at every step. I do not mean one or two of the cattle, but the whole stable." Now he sat in his bedroom writing a letter to his friend, General Horatio Gates, to send by the courier who had come to him from Gates the evening before. Again he took the opportunity to flail the Commander-in-Chief and to stress his own value to the cause:

> The ingenious maneuver of Fort Washington has unhinged the goodly fabric we had been building. There never was so damned a stroke. *Entre nous,* a certain great man is most damnably deficient. He has thrown me into a situation where I have my choice of difficulties: if I stay in this province I risk myself and army, and if I do not stay, the province is lost forever. . . . In short, unless something which I do not expect turns up, we are lost.[6]

Lee's aide-de-camp, William Bradford, Jr., related to Ezra Stiles:

> The general had sent forward . . . the Division about eight o'clock . . . tarrying himself to finish dispatches to General Gates. Which having just done, dressed and sent for his horses, was ready to mount and would have been gone in five or ten minutes, when about ten o'clock, they were surprised with about fifty horse, which came on the house from the wood and orchard at once and surrounding, fired upon it.
> . . . General Lee looked out of the window to see how the guards behaved and saw the enemy twice with his hanger cut off the arm of one of the guards crying for quarter. The guard behaved well, fired at first, but were rushed upon and subdued. The general saw then that they must submit, and after walking the chamber perhaps ten or fifteen minutes, told his aide-de-camp to go down and tell them General Lee submitted.[7]

Lieutenant Colonel William Harcourt, who had served under Lee in Portugal, commanded the party that now took him. Writing to his brother, he claimed he had taken the "most active and most enterprising of the enemy's generals." His exploit, he declared, was so advantageous to the British that "it seems to be the universal opinion the rebels will no longer refuse treating upon the terms which have been offered them." Sir William Howe was thought to hold the same opinion. A contemporary Whig newspaper rebutted:

> The enemy showed an ungenerous, nay, boyish triumph after they had got him secure at Brunswick, by making his horse drunk, while they toasted their king till they were in the same condition. A band or two of music played all night to proclaim their joy for this important acquisition. They say we cannot now stand another campaign. Mistaken fools!

to think the fate of America depended on one man. They will find ere long that it has no other effect than to urge us on to a noble revenge.[8]

Some Americans whose opinion of Lee was not exalted, perhaps thought he chose this way to go over to the enemy. "Oh! what a damned sneaking way of being kidnaped," cried William Shippen, Jr. "I can't bear to think of it." Most of them, however, including Washington, considered his loss to the cause a disaster. Exasperated as he was by Lee's recent conduct and the unfriendly criticism the waspish officer was screeching into any sympathetic ear, Washington received the news as "melancholy intelligence." "Our cause," he wrote to Congress, "has . . . received a severe blow."

It is barely possible that Lee's capture was one of the reasons Howe decided he could now safely consider the campaign of 1776 at a close and go into winter quarters. Whatever his reasons, he considered the conquest of East Jersey a sufficient accomplishment for the year and on December 14 issued a general order closing the campaign.

He distributed some fourteen thousand troops in a long chain of posts stretching from Staten Island to Princeton, and along the Delaware at Pennington, Trenton, Bordentown, and, for a short while, at Burlington. The southern end of this chain, which he himself admitted was "rather too extensive" but necessarily so, was in command of Colonel von Donop with about three thousand troops, Hessians and Highlanders, half of whom were stationed at Trenton and half at Bordentown, six miles south. In his General Order, Howe cautioned:

> The Commander-in-Chief calls upon the commanding officers of corps to exert themselves in preserving the greatest regularity and strictest discipline in their respective quarters, particularly attending to the protection of the inhabitants and their property in their several districts.[9]

With a string of posts covering his conquered territory, Howe now could look forward to a comfortable winter in New York in the arms of the wife of his commissary of prisoners, Joshua Loring. Drawing rooms had begun to titter and guffaw over his romantic attachment to the blue-eyed "flashing blond" and a pretty piece of doggerel was popular:

> Awake, arouse, Sir Billy,
> There's forage in the plain.
> Ah, leave your little Filly,
> And open the campaign.
> Heed not a woman's prattle

Which tickles in the ear,
But give the word for battle
And grasp the warlike spear.[10]

If the verse ever came to Sir Billy's ears, it gave him no concern. After granting leave to Cornwallis to return to England for a visit with his ailing wife, the British commander-in-chief, on December 13, returned to New York.

Almost before his back was turned, his army began to disregard his admonition to protect the inhabitants of the Jerseys. Not only the Hessians, who considered plundering one of the prerogatives of victory, but also the British themselves embarked upon a career of terror until now unmatched in the war. Stories of rapine in the Jerseys were not fanciful creations of American propagandists. The loyalist Charles Stedman deplored the practictices of his own army, with their inevitable repercussions:

. . . No sooner had the army entered the Jerseys than the business (we say business for it was a perfect trade) of plunder began. The friend and the foe . . . shared alike. The people's property was taken without being paid for or even a receipt given. . . . The British army foraged indiscriminately, procuring considerable supplies of hay, oats, Indian corn, cattle, and horses, which were never or but very seldom paid for. . . . The people of the Jerseys were well effected to his Majesty's government . . . but when the people found that the promised protection was not afforded them, that their property was seized and most wantonly destroyed, that in many instances their families were insulted, stripped of their beds with other furniture—nay, even of their very wearing apparel —they then determined to try the other side, trusting that they would at least, at one period or other, receive compensation for the supplies taken from them for the use of the American army.

And it is but justice to say that the Americans never took anything from their friends but in cases of necessity, in which cases they uniformly gave receipts for what they did take, always living as long as they could upon their enemies and never suffering their troops to plunder their friends with impunity. But at the same time, it is to be noticed that the American troops were suffered to plunder the loyalists and to exercise with impunity every act of barbarity on that unfortunate class of people, frequently inflicting on them scourges and stripes.[11]

The loss of General Lee, the successful British suppression of occupied territory, the vast number of Americans eagerly grasping Howe's pardons, seemed to herald the end of the

American cause. In the field, Washington's army had been beaten pitifully from Long Island and White Plains to the Delaware; in camp, it had been reduced frightfully by disease and desertion. His tattered ranks still were dazed by their harrowing flight through the Jersey's in freezing weather, wretchedly clothed and poorly fed, with seldom an issue of rum to warm the belly and ease the spirit. To Congress he pleaded for clothing; his men's distresses, he urged, "are extremely great, many of 'em being entirely naked and most so thinly clad as to be unfit for service." His anguished appeals to Jersey and Pennsylvania for troops—any kind of men—went unheeded, except for some Philadelphia city militia who barely offset the loss of the two brigades that left him at Brunswick the first of the month. Daily Washington awoke to the possibility that Howe would cross the river, rout him, and drive to Philadelphia. It was a question whether he would bring boats from New York, or make them of lumber Washington knew was stacked plentifully in Trenton, or simply wait for heavy ice in the river on which to cross.

In the long retreat across the Jerseys, there had marched, as a volunteer, the same Thomas Paine whose *Common Sense* had opened the year on the political front. His new pamphlet, *The American Crisis*, now appeared in the Philadelphia streets. Instantly it was seized upon. Everyone quoted it, for its words seemed to spring from the very soul of Washington's army and of the leader himself:

These are the times that try men's souls: The summer soldier and the sunshine patriot will, in this crisis, shrink from the service of his country; but he that stands it NOW deserves the love and thanks of man and woman. Tyranny, like Hell, is not easily conquered. Yet we have this consolation with us, that the harder the conflict, the more glorious the triumph.[12]

General Sullivan arrived in camp on December 20 with the forces of captured Charles Lee, amounting not to the anticipated five thousand, but to only two thousand. Horatio Gates arrived from Ticonderoga the same day with six hundred men—all that remained of seven regiments. Counting all the militia that had joined Washington since he had crossed the Hudson River, it looked as though he would have, by late December, an effective force of seventy-six hundred. But was it not an illusion? The General remembered that on December 31 the enlistments of so many would expire that, if they all left, no more than fourteen hundred would remain to oppose the enemy. As in the camp before Boston at the close of the year before, this was the most chilling prospect of all: his little army would dissolve almost entirely in two or three weeks.

Yet with his miserably supplied men, unsupported by the very people whose territory they endeavored to protect, the dogged Washington dreamed of a stroke against the enemy posts than even now, in his darkest hour, might bring a change of fortune. Despite defeat and retreat, a confidence persisted also among those tough-fibred stalwarts who loyally remained at his side. On December 16 one young brigade major wrote:

> . . . You ask me our situation. It has been the Devil, but is to appearance better. About two thousand of us have been obliged to run damned hard before about ten thousand of the enemy. Never was finer lads at a retreat than we are. . . . No fun for us that I can see. However, I cannot but think we shall drub the dogs. . . . Never mind, all will come right one of these days.[13]

And this Washington believed. Meanwhile, he gave the Hessians across the river little quiet.

Over at Trenton, Commandant Colonel Johann Rall did not allow himself to be disturbed by the presence of the ragged little army of Americans—"country clowns," he is said to have called them—and he ignored Donop's instructions to build redoubts. Instead, he ornamentally placed two of his six fieldpieces in front of his headquarters, marched his bandsmen about on a snowy morning like figures in a German comic opera, and warmed his frosty bones with good liquor.

Washington knew that if he were to accomplish any attack, he must make it now, while he had the boats with which to cross the river and before it froze to permit an enemy crossing. He decided to cross the river on Christmas night and attack Trenton before daylight. If successful there, he would push on for Princeton. It was not a sudden resolution, but its success depended upon secrecy. Washington had mulled it over for some days, but not until the evening of the twenty-fourth did he hold a council of war and detail his plan. To Dr. William Shippen, at the army hospital at Bethlehem, he sent word to come at the earliest possible moment with surgeons, as it was expected their services would be needed. Dr. Benjamin Rush of Philadelphia thought it was evident that the awful weight of his venture settled heavily upon him.

On the [23] of December, I visited General Washington . . . at the General's quarters about ten miles above

Bristol and four from the Delaware. I spent a night at a farmhouse near to him, and the next morning passed near an hour with him in private. He appeared much depressed and lamented the ragged and dissolving state of his army in affecting terms. I gave him assurance of the disposition of Congress to support him under his present difficulties and distresses.

While I was talking to him, I observed him to play with his pen and ink upon several small pieces of paper. One of them by accident fell upon the floor near my feet. I was struck with the inscription upon it. It was, "Victory or Death." . . . I . . . believe he had been meditating upon his attack upon the Hessians . . . for I found that the countersign of his troops at the surprise of Trenton was, "Victory or Death."[14]

Although none of the men knew of the impending attack, it was apparent to many of them that the high command had something afoot. One of Washington's aides, probably young Irish Colonel John Fitzgerald, was certain that Washington intended "to make some movement soon. He keeps his own counsel, but is very much determined." Then he recorded:

Dec. 23—Orders have been issued to cook rations for three days. Washington has just given the countersign, "Victory or Death." He has written a letter to General Cadwalader at Bristol, which he has entrusted to me to copy. He intends to cross the river, make a ten-mile march to Trenton, and attack Rall just before daybreak. Ewing is to cross and seize the bridge crossing the Assunpink [on the road leading south to Bordentown]. Putnam and Cadwalader are to cross and make a feint of attacking Donop [at Bordentown] so that he cannot hasten to Rall's assistance.

Dec. 24—A scout just in says that the Hessians have a picket on the Pennington road half a mile out from Trenton, and another at Dickenson's house on the river road.

Dec. 25—Christmas morning. They make a great deal of Christmas in Germany, and no doubt the Hessians will drink a great deal of beer and have a dance tonight. They will be sleepy tomorrow morning. Washington will set the tune for them about daybreak. The rations are cooked. New flints and ammunition have been distributed. Colonel Glover's fishermen from Marblehead, Massachusetts, are to manage the boats just as they did in the retreat from Long Island.

Christmas, 6 P.M.—The regiments have had their evening parade, but instead of returning to their quarters are marching toward the ferry. It is fearfully cold and raw and a snowstorm setting in. The wind is northeast and beats in the faces of the men. It will be a terrible night for the soldiers who have no shoes. Some of them have tied old rags around their feet; others are barefoot, but I have not heard a man complain. They are ready to suffer any hardship and die rather than give up their liberty. I have just copied the order for marching. Both divisions are to go from the ferry to Bear Tavern, two miles. They will separate there; Washington will accompany Greene's division with a part of the artillery down the Pennington road. Sullivan and the rest of the artillery will take the river road.

Dec. 26, 3 A.M.—I am writing in the ferry house. The troops are all over, and the boats have gone back for the artillery. We are three hours behind the set time. Glover's men have had a hard time to force the boats through the floating ice with the snow drifting in their faces. I never have seen Washington so determined as he is now. He stands on the bank of the river, wrapped in his cloak, superintending the landing of his troops. He is calm and collected, but very determined. The storm is changing to sleet and cuts like a knife. The last cannon is being landed, and we are ready to mount our horses.

Dec. 26, noon—It was nearly four o'clock when we started. The two divisions divided at Bear Tavern. At Birmingham, three and a half miles south of the tavern, a man came with a message from General Sullivan that the storm was wetting the muskets and rendering them unfit for service.

"Tell General Sullivan," said Washington, "to use the bayonet. I am resolved to take Trenton."

It was broad daylight when we came to a house where a man was chopping wood. He was very much surprised when he saw us.

"Can you tell me where the Hessian picket is?" Washington asked.

The man hesitated, but I said, "You need not be frightened, it is General Washington who asks the question."

His face brightened, and he pointed toward the house of Mr. Howell.

It was just eight o'clock. Looking down the road I saw a Hessian running out from the house. He yelled in Dutch and swung his arms. Three or four others came out with their guns. Two of them fired at us, but the bullets whistled over our heads. Some of General Stephen's men rushed forward and captured two. The others took to their heels, running toward Mr. Calhoun's house, where the picket guard was stationed, about twenty men under Captain Altenbrockum. They came running out of the house. The captain flourished his sword and tried to form his men. Some of them fired at us, others ran toward the village.

The next moment we heard drums beat and a bugle sound, and then from the west came the boom of a cannon. General Washington's face lighted up instantly, for he knew that it was one of Sullivan's guns.

We could see a great commotion down toward the meeting-house, men running here and there, officers swinging their swords, artillerymen harnessing their horses. Captain Forrest unlimbered his guns. Washington gave the order to advance, and we rushed on to the junction of King and Queen streets. Forrest wheeled six of his cannon into position to sweep both streets. The riflemen under Colonel Hand and Scott's and Lawson's battalions went upon the run through the fields on the left to gain possession of the Princeton Road. The Hessians were just ready to open fire with two of their cannon when Captain [William] Washington and Lieutenant [James] Monroe with their men rushed forward and captured them.

We saw Rall coming riding up the street from his headquarters, which were at Stacy Potts' house. We could hear him shouting in Dutch, "My brave soldiers, advance!"

His men were frightened and confused, for our men were firing upon them from fences and houses and they were falling fast. Instead of advancing they ran into an apple orchard. The officers tried to rally them, but our men kept advancing and picking off the officers. It was not long before Rall tumbled from his horse and his soldiers threw down their guns and gave themselves up as prisoners.

While this was taking place on the Pennington road, Colonel John Stark from New Hampshire, in the advance on the river road, was driving Knyphausen's men pell-mell through the town. Sullivan sent a portion of his troops under St. Clair to seize the bridge and cut off the retreat of the Hessians toward Bordentown. Sullivan's men shot the artillery horses and captured two cannon attached to Knyphausen's regiment.

Dec. 26, 3 p.m.—I have been talking with Rall's adjutant, Lieutenant Piel. He says that Rall sat down to a grand dinner at the Trenton Tavern Christmas Day, that he drank a great deal of wine and sat up nearly all night playing cards. He had been in bed but a short time when the battle began and was sound asleep. Piel shook him, but found it hard work to wake him up. Supposing he was wide awake, Piel went out to help rally the men, but Rall not appearing, he went back and found him in his nightshirt.

"What's the matter?" Rall asked.

Piel informed him that a battle was going on. That seemed to bring him to his senses. He dressed himself, rushed out, and mounted his horse to be mortally wounded a few minutes later.

We have taken nearly one thousand prisoners, six cannon, more than one thousand muskets, twelve drums, and four colors. About forty Hessians were killed or wounded. Our loss is only two killed and three wounded. Two of the latter are Captain [William] Washington and Lieutenant [James] Monroe, who rushed forward very bravely to seize the cannon.

I have just been with General Washington and Greene to see Rall. He will not live through the night. He asked that his men might be kindly treated. Washington promised that he would see they were well cared for.

Dec. 27, 1776—Here we are back in our camp with the prisoners and trophies. Washington is keeping his promise; the soldiers are in the Newtown Meeting House and other buildings. He has just given directions for tomorrow's dinner. All the captured Hessian officers are to dine with him. He bears the Hessians no malice, but says they have been sold by their Grand Duke to King George and sent to America, when if they could have their own way, they would be peaceably living in their own country.

It is a glorious victory. It will rejoice the hearts of our friends everywhere and give new life to our hitherto waning fortunes. Washington has baffled the enemy in his retreat from New York. He has pounced upon the Hessians like an eagle upon a hen and is safe once more on this side the river. If he does nothing more, he will live in history as a great military commander.[15]

Back at his headquarters near Newtown, Washington hurried off to the President of Congress a proud dispatch, relating the success of his enterprise against Trenton. The behavior of his men, he wrote enthusiastically, "reflects the highest honor upon them. The difficulty of passing the river in a very severe night and then marching through a violent storm of snow and hail did not in the least abate their ardor. But when they came to the charge, each seemed to vie with the other in pressing forward. . . ."

If only Cadwalader and Ewing had not allowed the severity of the night to turn them back, he reflected, some four hundred of the enemy would not have escaped to Donop at Bordentown, and to General Alexander Leslie's lines at Princeton. In fact, he was confident that with their support he would have been able to drive the enemy from all his posts below Trenton.

Nevertheless, the victory at Trenton revived the disheartened Quaker City. "This affair has given such amazing spirit to our people," John Nicholson wrote to Baltimore the next day, "that you might do anything or go anywhere with them. We have vast numbers of fine militia coming in momently." Washington had no intention of losing his advantage; as soon as his troops were fed and refreshed he planned to recross the river and strike again as "our situation will justify."

Meanwhile Cadwalader, who had failed on the twenty-fifth, crossed on the twenty-seventh to discover to his surprise that the General was no longer there. Encouraged by the news of Washington's success, Mifflin was able to gather some eighteen hundred militia and also cross the river. These forces awaited Washington, and he called in Heath from Peekskill, urged Generals Maxwell and McDougall at Morristown to annoy the enemy flanks, and prepared to cross the Delaware again.

The General again did not divulge details of his plans, the specific movements or strategy, to his officers. Howe's forces were strung out in a long line of posts across New Jersey, from Amboy through Brunswick to Princeton and would extend to Trenton if and when he recovered it. The main road to Philadelphia ran through these towns, and he had to hold that road to keep his positions safe. Washington probably thought of cutting this line. While Trenton, at the end of the string, was not important, Brunswick was, for its possession by the Americans would isolate Princeton, and also because it was Howe's principal storehouse; reoccupation of Trenton, then, would be the first step on Washington's way to Brunswick.

On the twenty-eighth, a young private in Washington's camp noted in his diary, "This Day we have been washing Our things." Two days later, in fresh rags, the men were again pushing through the icy waters of the Delaware to the landing at Trenton.

Among them was a sergeant, who was not looking forward to further service. His enlistment was nearly up and already he was thinking of home:

At this time our troops were in a destitute and deplorable condition. The horses attached to our cannon were without shoes, and when passing over the ice, they would slide in every direction and could advance only by the assistance of the soldiers. Our men, too, were without shoes or other comfortable clothing; and as traces of our march towards Princeton, the ground was literally marked with the blood of the soldiers' feet. Though my own feet did not bleed, they were so sore that their condition was little better.[16]

These footsore soldiers now made for Washington the heartbreaking problem he had anticipated before Christmas. Once more the end of a year had come. Enlistments were up. Could the men be cajoled into staying only a few weeks more, or would they, on the very threshold of complete victory, exercise their right and seek the warmth, the food, and the love that awaited them at home? Only so short a time ago as Christmas Eve, the General had written to Congress that on the first day of the new year, he would have perhaps no more than fourteen or fifteen hundred effective men. To Robert

Morris he admitted that even tough little John Glover's fine fishermen wanted water service and might leave him. In the face of this gloomy prospect, he had dauntlessly driven across the Delaware for the brilliant stroke at Trenton, and now, not sure how many might remain with him for further service, he again had carried them into the enemy's country.

While we were at Trenton [the same sergeant reported], on the last of December, 1776, the time for which I and most of my regiment had enlisted expired. At this trying time, General Washington, having now but a handful of men and many of them new recruits in which he could place but little confidence, ordered our regiment to be paraded and personally addressed us, urging that we should stay a month longer.

He alluded to our recent victory at Trenton, told us that our services were greatly needed, and that we could now do more for our country than we ever could at any future period, and in the most affectionate manner entreated us to stay. The drums beat for volunteers, but not a man turned out. The soldiers, worn down with fatigue and privations, had their hearts fixed on home and the comforts of the domestic circle, and it was hard to forego the anticipated pleasures of the society of our dearest friends.

The General wheeled his horse about, rode in front of the regiment, and addressing us again said, "My brave fellows, you have done all I asked you to do and more than could be reasonably expected. But your country is at stake, your wives, your houses, and all that you hold dear.

"You have worn yourselves out with fatigues and hardships, but we know not how to spare you. If you will consent to stay only one month longer, you will render that service to the cause of liberty and to your country which you probably never can do under any other circumstances. The present is emphatically the crisis which is to decide our destiny."

The drums beat the second time. The soldiers felt the force of the appeal. One said to another, "I will remain if you will."

Others remarked, "We cannot go home under such circumstances."

A few stepped forth, and their example was immediately followed by nearly all who were fit for duty in the regiment, amounting to about two hundred volunteers.

An officer inquired of the General if these men should be enrolled. He replied, "No! Men who will volunteer in such a case as this need no enrollment to keep them to their duty."[17]

So on December 30, the General was able to write to the commander at Morristown, "I have the pleasure to acquaint you that the Continental Regiments from the Eastern Governments have, to a man, agreed to stay six weeks beyond their term of enlistment, which was to have expired the last day of this month; for this extraordinary mark of their attachment to their country, I have agreed to give them a bounty of ten dollars per man besides their pay."

At Trenton, Washington's intelligence was meager, but it was obvious that his Christmas expedition had panicked the enemy. Gambling on the chance that Howe now would drive to Philadelphia via Princeton and Trenton, Washington called in Cadwalader and Mifflin on the thirty-first; the roads were still deep in mud, and it would be many hours before the militia would strengthen him at Trenton. Therefore, he posted a large body of tried troops on the line of the enemy's most probable advance, the road from Princeton.

The anticipated enemy advance was not long in coming. On New Year's Day, General Grant, leaving at Brunswick only six hundred men to guard his stores and a military chest containing £70,000, moved with one thousand men to Princeton to strengthen Leslie. That day, Cornwallis, whose trip to England had been canceled by the grim news from the Jersey front, rode a frigid fifty miles from New York to take command at Princeton. Counting the men Cornwallis brought with him, British troops at Princeton on the second totaled eight thousand and possessed considerable artillery. Washington's total force brought to a point at Trenton was fifty-one hundred, and he set them to fortifying the east bank of the Assunpink, where he awaited his Lordship.

Before daylight of the second, Cornwallis was on the march to Trenton. A heavy rain had fallen during the night. Along the road and in the fields, his columns marched three abreast, the men sinking deep in mud. At ten in the morning they reached Maidenhead, where they met their first American fire from the cover of a thick wood.

Rebel riflemen the rest of the day stubbornly contested every foot of the British march. Washington urged his skirmishers to delay the enemy as long as possible, to use up the daylight hours, so that Cornwallis could not assault the position beyond the Assunpink, and it was four in the afternoon before the redcoat advance entered Trenton. The Continentals withdrew calmly, firing from behind houses, until at last they crowded over the humpbacked stone bridge spanning the creek. Henry Knox, newly made brigadier general in command of all artillery, described the scene at the Assunpink—"another tussle"—to his wife, Lucy:

Their retreat over the bridge was thoroughly secured by the artillery. After they had retired over the bridge, the enemy advanced within reach of our cannon, who saluted them with great vociferation and some execution. This continued till dark, when, of course, it ceased, except a few shells we now and then chucked into town to prevent their enjoying their new quarters securely. . . .

[Now] the creek was in our front, our left on the Delaware, our right in a wood, parallel to the creek. The situation was strong, to be sure, but hazardous on this account, that had our right wing been defeated, the defeat of the left would almost have been an inevitable consequence, and the whole thrown into confusion or pushed into the Delaware, as it was impassable by boats.[18]

Washington now was in a tight spot, and he knew it. But he was as ingenious as he was daring. He reported to the Congress:

Having by this time discovered that the enemy were greatly superior in numbers and that their drift was to surround us, I ordered all our baggage to be removed silently to Burlington soon after dark, and at twelve o'clock (after renewing our fires and leaving guards at the bridge in Trenton and other passes on the same stream above) marched by a roundabout road to Princeton, where I knew they could not have much force left and might have stores. One thing I was sure of, that it would avoid the appearance of a retreat (which was of consequence) or to run the hazard of the whole army's being cut off was unavoidable, whilst we might by a fortunate stroke withdraw General Howe from Trenton, give some reputation to our arms.[19]

Midnight found the baggage already on the road. The wind had shifted to the north. The roads quickly froze hard, giving purchase to the wheels of the cannon, muffled in rags, and to the aching feet of the resolute men. George Weedon reported that Washington "filed off in so private a manner that the rear guard and many of his own sentinels never missed him."

"We moved so slow," one of the men remembered, "on account of the artillery, frequently coming to a halt, or stand still, and when ordered forward again, one, two, or three men in each platoon would stand, with their arms supported, fast asleep; a platoon next in the rear advancing on them, they, in walking or attempting to move, would strike a stub and fall."

The sergeant who had re-enlisted at Trenton was in the vanguard, commanded by General Hugh Mercer; he welcomed the bright, cold sun, sparkling on the hoar frost "which bespangled every object."

About sunrise . . . reaching the summit of a hill near Princeton, [said he,] we observed a light-horseman looking towards us as we view an object when the sun shines directly in our faces.

General Mercer, observing him, gave orders to the riflemen who were posted on the right to pick him off. Several made ready, but at that instant, he wheeled about and was out of their reach.

Soon after this, as we were descending a hill through an orchard, a party of the enemy who were entrenched behind a bank and fence, rose and fired upon us. . . .

We formed, advanced, and fired upon the enemy. They retreated eight rods to their packs, which were laid in a line. I advanced to the fence on the opposite side of the ditch which the enemy had just left, fell on one knee, and loaded my musket with ball and buckshot. Our fire was most destructive. Their ranks grew thin and the victory seemed nearly complete, when the British were reinforced. Many of our brave men had fallen, and we were unable to withstand such superior numbers of fresh troops. I soon heard General Mercer command in a tone of distress, "Retreat!" He was mortally wounded and died shortly after.

I looked about for the main body of the army, which I could not discover, discharged my musket at part of the enemy, and ran for a piece of wood at a distance where I thought I might shelter.

At this moment, Washington appeared in front of the American army, riding towards those of us who were retreating, and exclaimed, "Parade with us, my brave fellows, there is but a handful of the enemy, and we will have them directly." I immediately joined the main body and marched over the ground again. . . .

The British were unable to resist this attack and retreated into the College, where they thought themselves safe. Our army was there in an instant, and cannon were planted before the door, and after two or three discharges, a white flag appeared at the window and the British surrendered. They were a haughty, crabbed set of men, as they fully exhibited while prisoners on their march to the country.

In this battle, my pack, which was made fast by leather strings, was shot from my back and with it went what little clothing I had. It was, however, soon replaced by one which had belonged to a British officer and was well furnished. It was not mine long, for it was stolen shortly afterwards. . . .[20]

The battle at Princeton lasted less than an hour, but it was among the most savage of the war. Washington had been in the thick of it. At one moment, thirty yards from the enemy, he sat astride his white horse at the head of his troops, such a vulnerable target that young John Fitzgerald, his aide, covered his face, because he could not bear to see the General fall. But, enveloped in smoke, the General escaped harm. When the enemy broke and ran across an open field, the old hunter could not restrain himself. Leaving his officers to secure the town, he spurred after the redcoats, shouting, "It is a fine fox chase, my boys!"

A young naval officer from Pennsylvania who had been granted leave to serve as a volunteer in the Jersey campaign wrote to his wife: "O, my Susan! it was a glorious day, and I would not have been absent from it for all the money I ever expect to be worth." Washington's greatness, the young man said, was "far beyond my description . . . I shall never forget what I felt at Princeton on his account . . . when I saw him brave all the dangers of the field and his important life hanging as it were by a single hair with a thousand deaths flying around him. Believe me, I thought not of myself."

The troops Washington had routed were the British Seventeenth, Fortieth, and part of the Fifty-fifth regiments under Colonel Charles Mawhood, who had been leading the Seventeenth and Fifty-fifth toward Trenton when the forces met. The Fortieth had remained in Princeton. In this spirited stand the British had lost heavily, nearly four hundred killed, wounded, or taken prisoner, including a hundred dead on the field. All during the morning the completely demoralized remnants of Mawhood's troops fled toward Trenton and Brunswick.

On his side, Washington lost only about forty-four men, but in officers he suffered grievously. Five were killed in the action of the day. Especially felt was the loss of Hugh Mercer, cut down by enemy bayonets, and of handsome, athletic Colonel John Haslet of the Delawares, who died with a bullet in his brain. In his pocket, he carried an order detaching him on recruiting service, but he had said nothing about it, lest it keep him out of the fighting.

Washington's troops, without rest, rum, or provisions for two nights and a day, were unequal to his original plan. When he set out from Trenton, he had hoped to go on to Brunswick, but now the men were too exhausted to march seventeen miles farther. Later, the General ruefully reflected that with only six or eight hundred fresh troops he would have been able to march on and destroy all the enemy's stores and magazines, taken their fat military chest, and "put an end to the war."

Instead, Washington paused at Princeton, figuring perhaps how he might seize some smaller British post like Somerset Court House. Less than two hours after the engagement with

Mawhood, he heard that troops were advancing from the direction of Trenton. They were the enemy force under Cornwallis, who had swung back quickly for Princeton when he discovered at dawn at Trenton that Washington had duped him. Washington could not hazard a general action against him, and fell away eastward before his advance, breaking the bridge over the Millstone to halt pursuit, and then northward to Somerset. Here the exhausted Americans bivouacked, pleased to hear that behind them the enemy had arrived at Princeton "in a most infernal sweat—running, puffing and blowing and swearing at being so outwitted."

The next day, while Cornwallis, who had pushed on all night, was reaching Brunswick to protect that post, Washington moved about fourteen miles to Pluckemin, with Morristown as his ultimate destination.

This lovely village of some fifty houses lay on a high triangular plateau backed against Thimble Mountain, some forty-four miles northeast by north of the recent field of battle. It was a superb defensive position, where the General thought he could safely restore his men, rendezvous others, and "watch the motions of the enemy and avail myself of every favorable circumstance."

It was a difficult position for an enemy to attack. Directly eastward, on either side of the main road approach, large swamps guarded the town. Farther east, almost halfway between Morristown and the Jersey coast, lay the protecting barriers of Long Hill and the First and Second Watchung Mountains, like great natural earthworks shielding the village. From the security of Morristown, Washington could watch British movements in New York, guard the roads connecting New England with Philadelphia, and move to any threatened point. His army arrived on Monday, January 6, "at five P.M. and encamped in the woods, the snow covering the ground." The General made his headquarters at Jacob Arnold's Tavern on the north side of the village green.

Worn, half-naked, and cold, the troops were further jeopardized by the scourge of smallpox. But, as one of Howe's officers admitted, the British had "been boxed about in Jersey as if we had no feelings." In ten brilliant, hard days the rebels had snatched victory from despair; the redcoats had been driven into a few square miles of Jersey at Amboy and Brunswick. The ragged soldiers warming themselves around their fires in the shadow of Thimble Mountain had swept Jersey clear of the enemy. They could with some spirit bellow a ribald song:

> Come on, my brave fellows, a fig for our lives,
> We'll fight for our country, our children and wives.

Determin'd we are to live happy and free;
Then join, honest fellows, in chorus with me.
    Derry down, down, *etc.*

We'll drink our own liquor, our brandy from peaches,
A fig for the English, they may kiss all our breeches.
Those blood-sucking, beer-drinking puppies retreat;
But our peach-brandy fellows can never be beat.
    Derry down, down, *etc.*

A fig for the English, and Hessians to boot,
Who are sick half the time with eating of crout.
But bacon and greens, and Indian corn-bread,
Make a buck-skin jump up, tho' he seem to be dead.
    Derry down, down, *etc.*[21]

17

"O! BRITAIN, HOW THY LAURELS TARNISH . . ."

The Second New Jersey Campaign

JANUARY-JUNE 1777

AN ARMY which had mauled Howe's outposts so severely had cause for pride, even though it had not unseated Sir William from his base at New York or loosened his grip on New Jersey. Before the third of January, redcoats again were walking the streets of Princeton unmolested. Anguished cries once more sounded from American farmhouses and villages as Britons and Hessians took their pleasure with rebel women and filled their knapsacks with plunder. However, the disdain with which these foemen had looked upon the rebel soldier showed signs of giving way. Lieutenant Colonel William Harcourt, captor of Charles Lee, wrote to his father:

    . . . though they seem to be ignorant of the precision, order, and even of the principles, by which large bodies are moved, yet they possess some of the requisites for making good troops, such as extreme cunning, great industry in mov-

ing ground and felling of wood, activity and a spirit of enterprise upon any advantage. Having said thus much, I have no
occasion to add that, though it was once the fashion of this
army to treat them in the most contemptible light, they are
now become a formidable enemy.[1]

Had Howe suspected, however, that his "formidable
enemy" had shrunk to only a thousand Continentals just after
the first of the year, he probably would have left his warm
quarters long enough to wipe them out. But militia detachments gave Washington the semblance of an army at Morristown, and he managed to conceal his weakness and to
create an impression of power by an activity which evoked
the comment of an ememy officer:

The rebels were scattered about the country and took up
their quarters in the different towns our troops had withdrawn
from. They were frequently very troublesome to us, and every
foraging party that went out was pretty certain to have a
skirmish with them.
Besides which, they made a practice of waylaying single
persons or very small bodies on the road and killing them
from behind trees or other cover in a most savagelike manner. Large detachments were often sent out to surprise them
and sometimes succeeded, but, in general, their fears kept
them so alert that when we showed in any force, they disappeared.[2]

That disillusioned loyalist Justice Thomas Jones of New
York blamed the success of these little rebel enterprises as
much upon Howe as upon rebel wit and daring:

Their [British] numbers were sufficient to have driven
Washington out of Jersey with the greatest ease. But orders
were wanting. Cornwallis commanded at Brunswick, Vaughn
at Amboy, both generals of spirit. Nothing could be done
without the directions of the Commander-in-Chief [Howe],
who was diverting himself in New York in feasting, gunning,
banqueting, and in the arms of Mrs. Loring. Not a stick of
wood, a spear of grass, or a kernel of corn could the troops
in New Jersey procure without fighting for it, unless sent
from New York. Every foraging party was attacked. . . . The
losses upon these occasions were nearly equal, they could be
called nothing more than mere skirmishes, but hundreds of
them happened in the course of the winter. The British, however, lost men who were not easily replaced; the rebel loss
was soon repaired by drafts from the militia. It was of further service to the rebels; it taught them the art of war. It in-
ured them to hardships, and it emboldened them to look a

British or a Hessian soldier in the face, whose very phiz would make a hundred of them run after the battle of Brooklyn and prior to the affair of Trenton.[3]

Washington hoped to draw the enemy's attention from these militia attacks on detachments, supply trains, and depots by threatening Howe close to New York. He gave Heath command of thirty-four hundred New York and Connecticut militia for an attack on Fort Independence near King's Bridge, now held by about two thousand British and Hessians. After giving the garrison twenty minutes to surrender or abide the consequences, Heath waited ten days for his answer! When the enemy sallied, his army panicked—and soon afterward Washington was happy, on the resignation of Artemas Ward, to transfer Heath to Boston, which promised to be an inactive post, for the remainder of the war.

Howe was not altogether idle. In March and April his detachments raided Peekskill, up the Hudson, and Danbury, in Connecticut, burning a number of dwellings, warehouses, and barns, and great quantities of food, clothing, and tents. In general, however, both forces followed the time-honored custom of hibernating for the winter.

At Morristown, Washington spent another winter season of anguish and apprehension, inundated with administrative detail and again recruiting a new army in the face of the enemy. Lack of money hampered procurement of food, clothing, and equipment, and Congress did not make the General's life happy when it favored an early spring offensive without furnishing the wherewithal to pay for it. Every advantage seemed to be offset by a fresh disadvantage. Congress at last had agreed to long-term enlistments, but the recruiting situation in Philadelphia as described by Robert Morris was repeated everywhere:

It was not until conviction of the absolute necessity of it stared every man in the face that the wholesome measure of enlisting for three years or during the war could be carried in Congress; and since it was carried there, it meets with insuperable obstacles, raised by the former practice; for the bounties, high wages, and short service have vitiated the minds of all that class of people, and they are grown the most mercenary beings that exist.

I do not confine this observation to the soldiery merely, but extend it to those who get their livings by feeding and entertaining them. These are the harpies that injure us much at this time. They keep the fellows drunk while the money holds out; when it is gone, they encourage them to enlist for the sake of bounty, then to drinking again. That bounty gone, and more money still wanted, they must enlist again with some other officer, receive a fresh bounty, and get more drink, etc. This scene is actually carrying on here daily, and does immense injury to the recruiting service. But still I hope our new army will be got together before long, at least so many as will enable you to put a good face toward your enemies.[4]

To add to Washington's cares and to the plight of his men, smallpox was spreading alarmingly through the Morristown encampment. The General ordered inoculation of the whole army, at Morristown and in other garrisons. Dread of the disease was universal, for pitifully few survived it and they were marked for life. Inoculation was feared almost as much as the disease itself. Those who were fortunate enough to be treated by such surgeons as Benjamin Rush and Edward Archer were spared at least some pain and stood a better chance of successful treatment. These physicians had adopted the method of the English doctor Daniel Sutton, whose simplified procedure employed a small puncture instead of the deep gash formerly required. But regardless of technique, the men were afraid; they complained bitterly and some argued that the General was taking liberties with their lives and health, although the opinion of such men as Sergeant William Young, who saw him riding by, remained unchanged: "May God long preserve his valuable life."

The General was not to be deterred in his resolution; his power was now virtually dictatorial and had been so since December 27, 1776, when Congress, in answer to a letter stating that "desperate diseases require desperate remedies," had granted him extraordinary powers. Armed with this authority, he was soon lodging convalescents in the houses of town over the squalls of the inhabitants. Had General Howe chosen this time to attack, there is no doubt that he could have destroyed the American army.

But with spring came a rebirth. The first of some eight thousand Continentals began to arrive at Morristown. The General recovered from a brief illness likely induced by strains and worry. Optimism displaced fear. Social amenities revived sickened spirits. Lieutenant James McMichael had noticed promptly on his arrival at Morristown in January that "the young ladies here are very fond of the soldiers, but much more so of the officers." Now to add to the feminine charms of the town and camp came many wives of officers, among them Martha Washington, to preside over the social life of headquarters.

Martha Dangerfield Bland came, too, the twenty-five-year-

old, twice-married wife of tall, grave, handsome Colonel
Theodorick Bland of Virginia. She had been inoculated with
smallpox in Philadelphia, "was for four weeks very ill," and
her face was marked by the pocks. "I shall be pitied with
them," she said. "However, every face almost keeps me in
countenance. Here are few smooth faces and no beauties, so
that one does very well to pass."

To her sister-in-law, Fanny Randolph, in Virginia, Martha
Bland wrote gay letters about her sojourn:

I left Philadelphia last month [April 1] and came to
Morristown, where General Washington keeps headquarters.
Mrs. Washington had arrived three weeks before me, so that
I could with a good face make a visit to camp. . . .
I found Morris a very clever little village . . . in a most
beautiful valley at the foot of five mountains. It has three
houses with steeples which give it a consequential look. . . .
It has two families, refugees from New York, in it, otherwise it is inhabited by the errantist rustics you ever beheld.
. . . There are some exceeding pretty girls, but they appear
to have souls formed for the distaff, rather than the tender
passions, and really I never met with such pleasant-looking
creatures. And the most inhospitable mortals breathing. You
can get nothing from them but, "dreadful good water," as
they term everything that is good. Desperate and dreadful
are their favorite words. You'd laugh to hear them talk. . . .
Now let me speak of our noble and agreeable commander
(for he commands both sexes, one by his excellent skill in
military matters, the other by his ability, politeness, and attention). We visit them twice or three times a week by particular invitation. Every day frequently from inclination. He
is generally busy in the forenoon, but from dinner till night
he is free for all company. His worthy lady seems to be in
perfect felicity, while she is by the side of her "Old Man," as
she calls him. We often make parties on horseback, the General, his Lady, Miss Livingston, and his aides-de-camp,
who are Colonel [John] Fitzgerald, an agreeable broad-
shouldered Irishman; Colonel [George] Johnston . . . who is
exceedingly witty at everybody's expense, but can't allow
other people to be so at his own, though they often take the
liberty; Colonel [Alexander] Hamilton, a sensible, genteel,
polite, young fellow, a West Indian; Colonel [Richard Kid-
der] Meade; Colonel [Tench] Tilghman, a modest, worthy
man who from his attachment to the General voluntarily
lives in his family and acts in any capacity that is uppermost
without fee or reward; Colonel [Robert Hanson] Harrison,
brother of Billy Harrison that kept store in Petersburg and
as much like him as possible, a worthy man; Captain [Caleb]
Gibbs of the General's Guard, a good-natured Yankee who

makes a thousand blunders in the Yankee style and keeps the dinner table in constant laugh. These are the General's family, all polite, sociable gentlemen, who make the day pass with a great deal of satisfaction to the visitors. But I had forgot my subject almost, this is our riding party, generally at which time General Washington throws off the hero and takes on the chatty agreeable companion. He can be downright impudent sometimes, such impudence, Fanny, as you and I like, and really, I have wished for you often.[5]

Even the coming of warm weather did not bring Howe from New York. He evidently preferred the contests of Eros to those of Mars, and although he thought indecisively about another campaign against the rebels, he waged with resolution one against the resistance of the fair sex. His paramour, Mrs. Elizabeth Loring, became notorious, but suffered much less condemnation than her avaricious husband, Joshua, whose career in greed had commenced in Boston during the siege. There he had attached himself to Howe's army, and since then he had become Commissary of Prisoners. Justice Jones neatly summed up the business relationship between Mr. Loring and Howe: "Joshua had a handsome wife. The General . . . was fond of her. Joshua made no objection. He fingered the cash, the General enjoyed Madam." Elizabeth Loring's contribution to the American cause by entertaining its enemy defies measure, but it was not overlooked by the loyalists, who could see everything they possessed being threatened while the general indulged himself at the theater, the faro table, and in the boudoir. In March, when Howe was awarded the Order of the Bath, Justice Jones lashed out:

This month was remarkable for the investiture of General Howe with the Order of the Bath, a reward for *evacuating* Boston, for *lying indolent* upon Staten Island for near two months, for suffering the whole rebel army to escape him upon Long Island and again at the White Plains, for *not putting an end to rebellion* in 1776 when so often in his power, for making such *injudicious cantonments* of his troops in Jersey as he did, and for *suffering* ten thousand veterans under experienced generals to be cooped up in Brunswick and Amboy for nearly six months by about six thousand militia under the command of an inexperienced general.[6]

New York's social life was enlivened by the company of Howe's prize catch, Charles Lee, who was a most congenial prisoner, and a talkative one. Colonel John Maxwell dined with him and gossiped to Ambrose Serle:

Lee being rather gay with liquor said that when our

army went to West Chester, if we had either landed at first in the right place where we should have met with no considerable obstructions, or if afterwards at White Plains one of our brigades (which were the Hessians) had pushed up briskly and turned their left flank, we had cut off their retreat and finished the whole business of the controversy at once.[7]

Lee, the perpetual busybody and meddler, continued to regard the war as a "controversy" and himself as capable of resolving it in either the field of war or of diplomacy. Probably to ingratiate himself with the Howes, he worked up a plan by which Philadelphia could be taken by sea, Annapolis and Alexandria occupied, and the colonies divided, North from South. Although his scheme, dated March 29, 1777, was delivered to Sir Henry Strachey, who was serving as secretary to Admiral Lord Howe, there is no evidence that it actually reached the general, except perhaps the dubious evidence that Howe, on April 2, changed plans he had made to march on Philadelphia. He wrote to Germain:

From the difficulties and delay that would attend the passage of the river Delaware by a march through Jersey, I propose to invade Pennsylvania by sea, and from this arrangement must probably abandon the Jersies, which by the former plan would not have been the case.[8]

But months more of inactivity passed before Howe did anything.

Meanwhile, his distinguished prisoner continued to be the subject of exchange negotiations, although Washington was at a distinct disadvantage because he did not hold an officer of equal rank to exchange. Then, on July 10, with some daring, a Rhode Island militia officer brought equity to the dickering. Major General Richard Prescott, British commander of forces in Rhode Island, was reported to have left his headquarters for a Mr. Overing's house, near Newport, "to lodge there that night with some of his whores."

The general's romp made a good news story:

Thursday evening last a party of thirty-eight men [plus seven volunteers] . . . under the command of Lieutenant Colonel William Barton . . . went in five boats from Warwick Neck with a view to take Major General Prescott . . . whose headquarters were then at a house about four miles from Newport. The Colonel and his party . . . about twelve at night . . . got to Prescott's quarters undiscovered. A sentinel at the door hailed, but was immediately secured and the party instantly breaking the doors and entered the house took the general in bed. His aide-de-camp leaped from a window in his shirt and attempted to escape, but was taken a few rods from the house. The party soon after returned to their boats with the prisoners. . . .[9]

Even the London press chuckled:

> *On General Prescot being carried off naked,*
> *"unanointed, unanealed"*
>
> What various lures there are to ruin man;
> Woman, the first and foremost all bewitches!
> A nymph thus spoil'd a General's mighty plan,
> And gave him to the foe—without his breeches.[10]

Capture was becoming an old story to Prescott. He had been taken by the Americans in Canada in 1775 and the next year exchanged for John Sullivan. Although Ambrose Serle considered "He is not much regretted," Washington now had trading bait for Lee. Prescott was not allowed parole, because Washington heard that Lee was being allowed no privileges, and when Ethan Allen, the Green Mountain catamount, taken prisoner in Canada, was carried to England in chains, Prescott was thrown into a jail for felons. It was not until the following spring, April, 1778, that a final exchange of Lee and Prescott was effected.

And so winter and spring passed, while the English chieftain formulated three different plans for the next campaign, and the American general saw his army through smallpox, encouraged continual militia raiding, wrote voluminously on a welter of matters, recruited a new army, and covered the nakedness of the one he had.

By the middle of May, Washington had almost nine thousand men—not nearly enough, but an impressive number when compared to the skeleton army of the winter. Desertions still ran high—the enemy boasted that three thousand rebels joined them the first five months of the year; discipline was all too easy. The quality of officers was poor, and the militia, while often energetic against the enemy, continued to be undependable. Nonetheless, optimism prevailed among most of the experienced officers, and Washington himself was never more resolute than in the balmy spring days that followed a harsh winter.

Howe manifestly was certain to move soon, but whither Washington could not guess. Evidently the fleet and transports at New York would be used, for Washington's intelligence reported that they were being readied. He decided to move closer to Brunswick into a strong position whence he could follow quickly any enemy advance toward the Eastern states or toward Philadelphia. He broke up winter quarters and marched, beginning May 28, twenty miles south to Middlebrook, on the left bank of the Raritan, seven miles north-west of Brunswick, to be nearer Howe's probable line of march. Here he was in the first range of the Watchung Mountains behind some heights from which the country between Amboy and Brunswick and the road to Philadelphia could be watched. At Princeton, he stationed Smallwood's Maryland and Delaware brigade and Hazen's regiment under Sullivan.

It was not until the middle of June that Howe made his first move of the new campaign. On the night of the thirteenth he marched his force of eighteen thousand from Amboy to Brunswick. At Brunswick he split his advance into two columns, one pointed toward Somerset and the other toward Middlebush. By cutting off Sullivan at Princeton from the main Continental army and appearing to drive for the Delaware, he hoped to entice his adversary down from Middlebrook onto the plains, where he could be attacked at better advantage. Washington, however, saw through his ruse, extricated Sullivan, and sat tight.

Checkmated, Howe tried a second maneuver. Precipitately he retreated toward Brunswick, hoping to draw Washington out. He nearly succeeded. After two watchful days, Washington sent Greene with a substantial force to gnaw at the British rear. Although Greene pulled back when he got as far as Piscataway, Washington on the twenty-fourth did come down from the hills to Quibbletown, where he was nearer his enemy. He posted Lord Stirling off his left flank near Metuchen.

Howe, quick to take advantage of Washington's shift of position, made his third move. On the morning of the twenty-sixth he suddenly turned about and moved in two columns toward Woodbridge and Bohamton. He planned to encircle Stirling and to seize the passes back to Middlebrook, cutting Washington off from the heights in his rear. At last, he thought, he would bring the rebel general into the open. In brutal heat, under an unsparing sun, the columns joined and came to Stirling, who stood angrily and then managed to make off. The sound of firing near Woodbridge warned Washington of his danger, and he quickly drew back to the heights behind Middlebrook.

In three attempts, Howe had failed to lure his canny foe into an unfavorable position. He gave up at last and marched back to Amboy, whence he transported his whole army to Staten Island.

For the first time in eight grinding months, New Jersey was completely empty of redcoats. Though the citizens might jubilate, Howe's departure simply raised another question for

Washington: where would the enemy next move, northward to join Burgoyne, or southward toward Philadelphia?

The ineffectiveness of the British campaign galled many of Howe's officers, as well as English statesmen and observers. But even the unquestionably loyal British traveler in America, Nicholas Cresswell, who before the war had visited "the happy pair" of Washingtons at Mount Vernon, felt constrained to admit:

> Washington is certainly a most surprising man, one of Nature's geniuses, a Heaven-born general, if there is any of that sort. That a Negro-driver should with a ragged banditti of undisciplined people, the scum and refuse of all nations on earth, so long keep a British general at bay, nay, even oblige him, with as fine an army of veteran soldiers as ever England had on the American continent, to retreat, it is astonishing. . . .
> General Howe, a man brought up to war from his youth, to be puzzled and plagued for two years together with a Virginia tobacco-planter. O! Britain, how thy laurels tarnish in the hands of such a lubber! . . .
> He certainly deserves some merit as a general that he . . . can keep General Howe dancing from one town to another . . . with such an army as he has. . . . Washington, my enemy as he is, I should be sorry if he should be brought to an ignominious death.[11]

18

"A MOST INFERNAL FIRE OF CANNON AND MUSQUETRY"

Brandywine

SEPTEMBER 11, 1777

AFTER HOWE withdrew his troops to Staten Island on the first of July, Washington's situation, as he himself admitted, was "truly delicate and perplexing." Now it was he who danced from place to place, as he had obliged Howe to do in the winter just gone. If then the Virginia tobacco-planter had called the tune, Howe was dancing-master now! Which way would he move? By land or by sea? Although Washington had spies on Staten Island itself, he could not deduce Howe's designs.

And a new element had entered into the question of Howe's next move. General John Burgoyne, recently arrived in Canada, intended, as everyone in the world seemed to know, to drive southward by way of Lake Champlain and the Hudson to Albany in a plan to sever New England from the rest of the colonies. Logic suggested that Howe would push up the Hudson to form a junction with Burgoyne. But it also was possible that he would leave splitting of the colonies to Burgoyne and himself dash south to take Philadelphia.

On July 3, after noting "a great stir among their shipping" in New York Harbor and hearing that Burgoyne was advancing rapidly from Canada, Washington marched his army back to Morristown, whence he could move in either direction. Then he heard that the fleet was preparing for a voyage obviously longer than up the Hudson, and he warned the Eastern states that Howe might descend upon them. He feared for even the distant South.

A few days later, Howe began embarking between fifteen and eighteen thousand men. His loyalist chronicler, Thomas Jones, watched him spend the next "fortnight in dalliance with Mrs. Loring, while the troops were lying on board the transports crowded together in the sultry heat of summer."

While the fleet lay in the harbor, mystifying Washington, he received word that Fort Ticonderoga had been evacuated and its garrison, perhaps, captured. Although he could scarcely believe the incredible report, he felt compelled now to move northward in the direction he was sure Howe would move. He marched for Pompton Plains, eighteen miles east, where rainy weather delayed him two days, and then he drove forward to Smith's Clove in the Highlands near West Point. By the time he reached the Clove, he knew certainly that Ticonderoga was lost. And now began a dizzy shifting back and forth that lasted for weeks.

Howe's conduct, Washington thought, was "puzzling and embarrassing beyond measure," and so "are the informations which I get." Finally, on the twenty-fourth, the General heard with some reliability that Howe had sailed from the Hook. He ordered heavy detachments to Philadelphia and started his army in that direction, sure that Howe was bound for the capital via the Delaware. By the time Washington reached that river, he began to have doubts; although the enemy fleet had been at sea six days, it was not in sight at Delaware Bay. So he held his forces on the west side of the river and stopped detachments at Morristown and Trenton.

On the thirty-first he heard that the fleet was off the capes of Delaware Bay. Ordering the army to Philadelphia, he started forward for the city with his staff. But the next day, while at Chester seeking a campsite for the army, he heard that the fleet had moved off. Hastily he dispatched letters to his officers. "This surprising event gives me the greatest anxiety," he declared to Putnam. To Sullivan he said, "it appears General Howe has been practicing a deep feint, merely to draw our attention and whole force to this point." "This unexpected event makes it necessary to reverse our disposition," he declared to Greene, and he ordered his "eastern" divisions en route from Peekskill to countermarch at once. But only two days later he halted the detachments, "as it is terrible to march and countermarch the troops at this season," and settled his main force for a while at a position near Germantown to await the next turn of affairs.

It was hot and humid, and racing back and forth had fatigued the troops, but young Lieutenant James McMichael, of the Thirteenth Pennsylvania, who had the stuff of a professional soldier, allowed neither weather nor weariness to dampen his spirits, especially when the ladies of the neighborhood decided to cheer the boys:

August 3—The largest collection of young ladies I almost ever beheld came to camp. They marched in three columns. The field officers paraded the rest of the officers and detached scouting parties to prevent being surrounded by them. For my part, being sent on scout, I at last sighted the ladies and gave them to know that they must repair to headquarters, upon which they accompanied me as prisoners. But on parading them at the Colonel's marquee, they were dismissed, after we had treated them with a double bowl of Sangaree.[1]

The annoying weather the lieutenant dismissed in verse:

> Since we came here for to encamp,
> Our mornings have been very damp.
> But at noonday excessive warm,
> And like to do us all great harm.[2]

When several days passed without clarifying the mystery of Howe's whereabouts, Washington started back toward Coryell's Ferry. On the march, a dispatch rider brought word that the enemy fleet was seen off Maryland, headed south. Washington halted again and went into camp in the meadows bordering Neshaminy River, some twenty miles north of Philadelphia. For eleven days he lay there, until he learned that

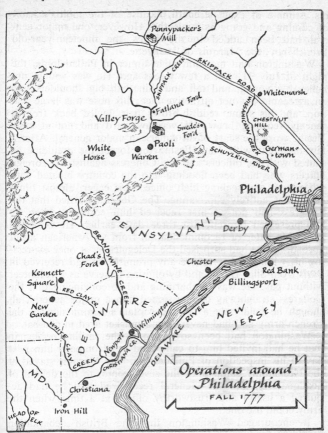

Operations around
Philadelphia
FALL 1777

the British fleet was standing into Chesapeake Bay, and a day later, that the fleet was well into that water.

Evidently the British general, instead of attacking Philadelphia by an overland march from the north or by forcing the defenses in the Delaware River, would land at the head of Chesapeake Bay and march fifty-five miles to the capital. At last, the exhausting weeks of suspense and perplexity for Washington were over. Now to interpose his army between Howe and the British goal!

The American force gradually had been strengthened by new detachments until, counting militia, it numbered about sixteen thousand, although Washington never was confident in his estimate of exact strength because of the militia's habit of coming and going as it pleased. However, one major general had been added to the army, the nineteen-year-old French boy, the Marquis de Lafayette.

Washington had met him at a dinner in Philadelphia, the night of July 31, just a few weeks ago. He was young, unbelievably young, and tall and thin with big shoulders and an agreeable but not attractive face: his nose was large and thin, and his scant, reddish-brown hair flowed back from a sharply receding brow. He was awkward and not at ease. Yet he wore the scarf of an American major general. After a few moments with him, Washington forgot the prejudice he shared with his officers and the Congress against the foreign officers who had been flooding into the country bloated with self-esteem and seeking high office. This eager, almost timid youth was entirely captivating. The General learned that the Congress had not at first received him cordially when he had presented himself, just three days earlier. He bore the inevitable letter of recommendation from an American agent abroad, but he had surprised the Delegates by at once expressing his willingness to ignore any promises he had received in Paris from Silas Deane and by offering to serve as a volunteer without pay. He was so charming and so convincing that the Congress straightway commissioned him a major general, although he held only a reserve captain's commission in the French army and had never seen a musket fired in combat.

Washington had been so drawn to the smiling nobleman that he had invited him to camp and to accompany him next day in his inspection of Philadelphia. The Marquis stayed at the Neshaminy camp until the seventeenth, to the delight of headquarters, and the General recognized that he had acquired a useful and trustworthy officer at a time when the army could use one.

It encouraged Washington that the British debarkation would be far enough from Philadelphia to give him a chance to place himself between Howe and the city. Fine news from the Hampshire Grants gave a further lift to his spirits: a strong detachment from Burgoyne's army on a raid to Bennington had been routed by American militia on the sixteenth with an enormous loss.

Washington's officers easily persuaded him to parade his confident army, buoyed by the victory at Bennington, through the streets of Philadelphia on the way to meet Howe. Clothes were washed, arms burnished, and to offset the shabbiness of his uniform, each man was ordered to wear in his hat a "green sprig, emblem of hope." General Orders insisted that all men "carry their arms well," and that none should

leave ranks on the march. . . . Drums and fifes were to play
a quick step, "but with such moderation that the men may
step to it with ease and without *dancing* along, or totally disregarding the music." The Commander-in-Chief already, on
the fourth of August, had issued an order planned to spare
the respectable citizens of Philadelphia embarrassment: that
day he "earnestly" had recommended the officers "use every
reasonable method in their power to get rid of all such as
are not absolutely necessary" of "the multitude of women in
particular, especially those who are pregnant and have children."

The march to the city began at three in the morning of
Sunday, the twenty-fourth; the parade through the city itself
began about seven o'clock. John Adams, who early in the day
had noted, "it is overcast and rains very hard, which will
spoil our show and wet the army," happily reported to Abigail, at home in Braintree:

> The rain ceased, and the army marched through the
> town between seven and ten o'clock. The wagons went an-
> other road. Four regiments of light horse, Bland's, Baylor's,
> Sheldon's and Moylan's. Four grand divisions of the army and
> the artillery . . . marched twelve deep and yet took up above
> two hours in passing by. General Washington and the other
> general officers with their aides on horseback. The colonels
> and other field officers on horseback.
> We have now an army well appointed between us and Mr.
> Howe, and this army will be immediately joined by ten thou-
> sand militia, so that I feel as secure as if I were at Braintree,
> but not so happy. My happiness is nowhere to be found but
> there. . . .
> The army . . . I find to be extremely well armed, pretty
> well clothed, and tolerably disciplined. . . . There is such a
> mixture of the sublime and the beautiful, together with the
> useful, in military discipline that I wonder every officer we
> have is not charmed with it. Much remains to be done. Our
> soldiers have not yet quite the air of soldiers. They don't step
> exactly in time. They don't hold up their heads quite erect,
> nor turn out their toes so exactly as they ought. They don't
> all of them cock their hats; and such as do, don't all wear
> them the same way.[3]

But out of step and shabby—and not half so well-armed as
civilian Adams supposed—the army, nonetheless, made a
good show for the uneasy townspeople.

Down Front Street, up Chestnut, turning to the Common,
and then over Middle Ferry to the heights of Derby, it
marched. The next morning, two divisions moved toward
Wilmington, and the horse was ordered there. Washington

rode ahead and at Wilmington learned that the enemy had begun landing that morning six miles below the Head of Elk. The next day, after breakfast, Washington, accompanied by Greene and Lafayette and his aides, personally reconnoitered the country within two miles of Howe's camp. On their return that night, a heavy rain forced them to take refuge "in a disaffected house at the Head of Elk," wrote the General, "but I was equally guarded against friend and foe," which prevented the Tory householder from notifying the enemy.

As the American army gathered at Wilmington, Washington was in the saddle constantly, personally reconnoitering toward White Clay Creek, where his advance parties lay and occasionally skirmished with enemy patrols. Advance American pickets were out as far as Christina Bridge, and on the seventh the whole army moved up to the village of Newport, eight to ten miles from Iron Hill, to which Howe had advanced seven miles since landing.

At three A.M. on the eighth, the general alarm sounded; tents were struck, and the regiments paraded and kept under arms until nine. A line of battle was then established on the east of Red Clay Creek, and Washington waited all day for an enemy attack he felt sure would come. In the evening, the enemy halted two miles from the American position. Washington scouted them warily and supposed that their real intention was to amuse him in front, while turning his right flank and getting between him and Philadelphia. To prevent this, he set his army in motion at two in the morning of the ninth, put Brandywine Creek between his men and Howe's, and took a position on the high grounds behind one of the principal crossings, Chad's Ford.

At and below the forks of the Brandywine, which were about seven or eight miles northwest of Wilmington, were a scattering of fords through which an army marching toward Philadelphia from the southwest might pass. The most likely crossing place was Chad's, and it was a good position from which to maneuver to cover the other fords or to manage a withdrawal if necessary.

At Chad's Ford, Washington established his center under command of Greene. The General himself assumed direction of the defense there. He posted Wayne's Pennsylvanians on the brow of a hill near Chad's house, a little above the ford, and Weedon's and Muhlenberg's Virginians directly east of the ford. Maxwell's eight hundred light troops of Lincoln's division he placed across the Brandywine on the southern bank nearest the enemy.

The right wing was composed of three divisions on the east

bank of the stream, spread from Brinton's Ford, next above Chad's, to Painter's Ford. Stirling held the extreme right, Stephen the one below him, and Sullivan, in command of the wing, the near position at Brinton's Ford. The left wing was posted on the steep, rough heights at Pyle's Ford, where there was little apprehension of a crossing; this wing was composed of a thousand Pennsylvania militia under Armstrong. To guard the fords above the right, Sullivan detached light forces to three of them and threw picket guards across the upper part of the stream.

Here on the Brandywine, Washington would face his foe. Every effort was made to prepare the minds of the men, as well as their military positions, for battle. On the tenth, the Reverend Mr. Joab Trout preached to the troops—his text: "All they that take the sword shall perish with the sword." And, of course, he said, the Almighty was on the right side:

. . . the doom of the British is near! Think me not vain when I tell you that beyond the cloud that now enshrouds us, I see gathering thick and fast the darker frown and a blacker storm of Divine indignation.[4]

That night Howe lay at Kennett Square, six miles away. Scouting Washington, he planned to rely on the strategy that had won at Brooklyn. Hessian General von Knyphausen was to advance to Chad's Ford and make a feint of attacking there, while the main force under command of Cornwallis was to march up the Brandywine, cross the stream above its fork, turn Washington's flank, and fall on his rear. Howe was to accompany Cornwallis.

At half past eight the next morning, as the fog burned away and the sun began to bear down hot and sultry, General George Weedon on the heights above Chad's Ford saw the British—green ranks of loyalist rangers and riflemen—come to Maxwell on the south bank and engage. "With great firmness" Maxwell twice repulsed them before they obliged him to withdraw in good order, about ten o'clock, across the ford. He re-formed on the near bank, and occasionally advanced across the ford during the rest of the morning to skirmish with their vanguard. To Washington he sent a report that he had killed or wounded three hundred of the enemy with a loss of not over fifty casualties. Although his figure for the enemy loss was high, they suffered severely, admitted Stephen Jarvis of their vanguard, when he confessed the ignominy of his own injury: ". . . my pantaloons received a wound, and I don't hesitate to say that I should have been very well pleased to have seen a little blood also."

More and more British troops concentrated on the sheltered ground opposite the ford. Artillery began dueling. "Our battery was on an eminence which commanded the ford," remembered Weedon, "and in the cannonading made the enemy retire several times; it was better served than theirs."

As the forenoon passed, Washington and his officers began to suspect that Howe was amusing them at the ford while he crossed elsewhere. A little after eleven o'clock Washington began to receive reports that the enemy was attempting to flank him, but he would not accept this intelligence until he could confirm it. He wrote to Colonel Theodorick Bland, who was patrolling with the Light Horse on the far right, to send out an officer to reconnoiter and ascertain the truth. About an hour later, Charles Cotesworth Pinckney, of the First South Carolina Continentals, was with the General near Colonel Proctor's battery on the height above the ford. He reported that the General was impatient:

> I heard him bitterly lament that Colonel Bland had not sent him any information at all and that the accounts he had received from others were of a very contradictory nature.

About one o'clock, intelligence was brought that the enemy's left wing were marching in the Valley Road and were about crossing the Brandywine above its forks. At length, Colonel Bland sent intelligence that he had seen two of the enemy's brigades marching in that road. . . . [Stephen's] and Lord Stirling's divisions were ordered to march up the Brandywine and attack them in case they should cross, and some Light Horse were dispatched above the forks . . . to see if they actually had crossed. And they . . . brought information that there was no appearance of the enemy in that quarter, which induced the General to suppose that the movement of the enemy was a feint and that they were returning to reinforce Knyphausen at Chad's Ford.[5]

This latest report prompted Washington to halt the two divisions on their way up the Brandywine, and until the situation clarified, to hold back the attack across the ford that he himself might have launched. Further confusion was added by the appearance of a swarthy, thickset farmer, who trotted up on a little mare demanding to see the General. The stranger announced himself vociferously as Squire Cheney of the neighborhood. His clothes were carelessly flung on, for, said he, when he had heard the firing in the morning, he swung himself hurriedly into the saddle and rode up to the hills around Birmingham Meeting House to take a look around. The stone meetinghouse, prettily situated on the brow of a hill some three and a half miles north of Chad's Ford, had been commandeered from the Quakers for an American hospital. It not only commanded the road over

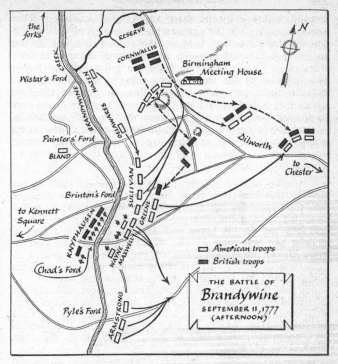

the forks

RESERVE

CORNWALLIS

Birmingham
Meeting House

Wistar's Ford

BRANDYWINE CREEK

HAZEN

DELAWARES

Painters' Ford

BLAND

SULLIVAN

Dilworth

Brinton's Ford

to Kennett
Square

KNYPHAUSEN

GREENE

to Chester

Chad's Ford

WAYNE MAXWELL

☐ American troops
■ British troops

THE BATTLE OF
Brandywine
SEPTEMBER 11, 1777
(AFTERNOON)

Pyle's Ford

ARMSTRONG

which the British would be most apt to advance from the
forks, but afforded the most distant views in the vicinity.
From it Cheney had seen the enemy marching up the west
side of the river. He knew where they could be halted in a
defile on this side by as few as two hundred men, he said.
To his howling dismay, Washington brushed aside his story,
because his own intelligence had not confirmed the enemy's
flanking movement.

Soon, however—Charles Pinckney recalled the time as between three and four o'clock, though it probably was earlier
—"authentic intelligence was brought" that the enemy was
across the Brandywine and in the rear of Sullivan's right.
Washington hurried orders to Sullivan to march to meet the
column in his rear, and instructed Stephen and Stirling again
to proceed "in a trot" to gain the hills around the meetinghouse ahead of the enemy. He decided to remain with
Greene at Chad's Ford.

At length, around four-thirty, the ominous growling of

cannon, followed by the sharp volleying of muskets and the crack of rifles from the extreme right, announced to Washington that indeed he had been outflanked and that Sullivan was in heavy action. Meanwhile, a thunderous cannonade commenced at Chad's. Soon he began to guess that more than two brigades of the enemy were engaged with Sullivan and that he ought personally to join him. He ordered Lincoln's division to hold Chad's Ford and Greene to move to the right to support Sullivan, while he assembled his staff and headed toward the firing. To guide him on the shortest course to the point of action, he snatched up a neighborhood farmer, Joseph Brown. Brown's brief adventure at the battle was recorded by a friend:

Brown was an elderly man and extremely loath to undertake that duty. He made many excuses but the occasion was too urgent for ceremony. One of Washington's suite dismounted from a fine charger and told Brown if he did not instantly get on his horse and conduct the General by the nearest and best route . . . he would run him through on the spot. Brown thereupon mounted and steered his course directly towards Birmingham Meeting House with all speed, the General and his attendants being close at his heels.

He said the horse leapt all the fences without difficulty and was followed in like manner by the others. The head of General Washington's horse, he said, was constantly at the flank of the one on which he was mounted, and the General was continually repeating to him, "Push along, old man. Push along, old man."[6]

As Washington rode off, the sounds of Howe's attack late in the afternoon were the signal for Knyphausen's column at Chad's Ford to advance. Stephen Jarvis, with the Queen's Rangers who had opened against Maxwell early that morning, strode into battle:

The Fourth Regiment led the column and the Queen's Rangers followed, the [American] battery playing upon us with grapeshot which did much execution. The water took us up to our breasts and was much stained with blood before the battery was carried and the guns turned upon the enemy.

Immediately after our regiment had crossed, two companies (the Grenadiers and Captain McKay's) was ordered to move to the left and take possession of a hill which the enemy was retiring from and wait there until further orders. From the eminence we had a most extensive view of the American army, and we saw our brave comrades cutting them up in great style.[7]

So at the ford, Wayne and Maxwell's valiant troops were forced to retreat, losing their guns, while the militia downstream made an easy withdrawal.

On the principal field of action, up near the meeting-house, General Weedon's brigade had arrived with Greene's division. Howe's main body—Weedon estimated it at six thousand—now faced the Americans frantically forming for battle. Weedon, witness to Maxwell's gallantry early that morning, was himself engaged. Our troops, he wrote John Page, formed in an "agreeable" manner:

> General [William] Woodford's brigade [of Stephen's Division] being to the right, he detached Colonel [Thomas] Marshall with his regiment (only 170 men) to a fine wood on the right to cover his fieldpieces and right flank. Thus prepared, they discovered General Sullivan's Division marching up, and the brigadiers rode to him . . . to receive orders, when he directed them to move all to the *right* to make room for his division on the *left*.

In making this alteration, unfavorable ground made it necessary for Woodford to move his Brigade two hundred paces back of the line, and threw Marshall's wood in his front. The enemy came on rapidly. Scott, who was next to Woodford, was removed to bad ground, and from his Brigade to the left of the whole line appeared in some confusion.

Woodford's Brigade stood firm and in good order. Marshall had orders to hold the wood as long as it was tenable and then retreat to the right of the brigade. He received the enemy with a firmness which will do honor to him and his little corps as long as the eleventh of September is remembered. He continued there three quarters of an hour and must have done amazing execution. He was called off for fear of being surrounded and retreated in good order.

The action became general. Woodford was wounded and retired to be dressed. The left wing gave way, and the right followed. . . .[8]

Although the Commander-in-Chief came on the field at the moment the left was beginning to break, he merely observed the action and did not assume personal command. Instead, he left the fight to Sullivan; he and his aides and Lafayette rode among the fugitives, attempting to rally them. About six o'clock, Weedon's Virginians spread to the right, opened to allow the broken American regiments to pass to the rear, and then closed again to hold off the enemy.

Greene's Division made possible a retreat instead of a rout; as it was, Washington did not succeed in getting his forces into order around Chester, to which he ordered withdrawal, until nearly midnight. The retreat was not entirely an orderly movement, even if Sergeant Major John Hawkins of Congress' Own Regiment felt that "no troops behaved better, nor any troops left the field in greater order," for subsequently he noted in his diary:

> . . . I lost my knapsack, which contained the following articles, viz: 1 uniform coat, brown faced with white; 1 shirt; 1 pair stockings; 1 sergeant's sash; 1 pair knee buckles; ½ lb. soap; 1 orderly book; 1 memo book of journal and state of my company; 1 quire paper; 2 vials ink; 1 brass inkhorn; 40 morning returns, printed blanks; 1 tin gill cup; a letter, and a book . . . I likewise lost my hat, but recovered it again.

The weather was very warm and though my knapsack was very light, was very cumbersome, as it swung about when walking or running and in crossing fences was in the way, so I cast it away from me, and had I not done so would have been grabbed by one of the ill-looking Highlanders, a number of whom were firing and advancing very brisk towards our rear. The smoke was so very thick that about the close of the day, I lost sight of our regiment and just at dark I fell in with the North Carolina troops and about two o'clock in the morning arrived at Chester. . . .[9]

A British officer found the affair just as confusing as Hawkins, and his expressed reactions are spiced with the wittiness of relief:

> What excessive fatigue. A rapid march from four o'clock in the morning till four in the eve, when we engaged. Till dark we fought. Describe the battle. 'Twas not like those of Covent Garden or Drury Lane. Thou hast seen Le Brun's paintings and the tapestry perhaps at Blenheim. Are these natural resemblances? Pshaw! quoth the captain, *en un mot*. There was a most infernal fire of cannon and musquetry. Most incessant shouting, "Incline to the right! Incline to the left! Halt! Charge!" etc. The balls plowing up the ground. The trees cracking over one's head. The branches riven by the artillery. The leaves falling as in autumn by the grapeshot. . . .

> The misters on both sides showed conduct. The action was brilliant. Mr. Washington retreated (i.e., ran away), and Mr. Howe remained master of the field. . . . I took a high cap lined with fur, which I find very comfortable in the now "not summer evenings in my tent." A ball glanced about my ankle and contused it. For some days I was lifted on horseback in men's arms.[10]

It was estimated that Washington lost during the day between twelve and thirteen hundred men—killed, wounded, and missing. Howe's loss, the American officers thought, was greater than their own, although it actually amounted to only 89 killed, 488 wounded, and 6 missing. When the day was nearly over, Joseph Townsend, a peripatetic young

Quaker of the neighborhood who had watched the day's fighting from behind the British lines, proposed to his companions that they go over the field "and take a view of the dead and wounded, as we might never have such another opportunity." Some consented and "others with reluctance" yielded:

> . . . awful was the scene to behold—such a number of fellow beings lying together severely wounded and some mortally—a few dead but a small proportion of them, considering the immense quantity of powder and ball that had been discharged. It was now time for the surgeons to exert themselves. . . . Some of the doors of the meetinghouse were torn off and the wounded carried thereon into the house to be occupied for an hospital. . . .
> The wounded officers were first attended to. . . . After assisting in carrying two of them into the house I was disposed to see an operation performed by one of the surgeons, who was preparing to amputate a limb by having a brass clamp or screw fitted there on a little above the knee joint. He had his knife in his hand, the blade of which was . . . circular . . . and was about to make the incision, when he recollected that it might be necessary for the wounded man to take something to support him during the operation. He mentioned to some of his attendants to give him a little wine or brandy . . . to which he replied, "No, doctor, it is not necessary, my spirits are up enough without it."
> He then observed "that he had heard some of them say there was some water in the house, and if there was he would like a little to wet his mouth." As I was listening . . . one of my companions . . . mentioned that it was necessary to go . . . as they were fixing the picket guards and if we did not get away . . . we should have to remain within the lines . . . during the night. I instantly complied. . . .[11]

Lafayette, late in the day, had taken a wound in the leg. But with an improvised bandage around it, he set up a guard at Chester Creek to help bring order out of the confusion of the night flight. Though beaten, the army was not despondent. Captain Enoch Anderson of the Delawares, who had fought on the right, remembered that he saw that night "not a despairing look nor did I hear a despairing word. We had our solacing words always ready for each other, 'Come boys, we shall do better another time,' sounded throughout our little army." Even Weedon, who had covered the retreat, thought at the time that "such another victory would establish the rights of America, and I wish them the honor of the field again tomorrow on the same terms."

The defeat at Brandywine, oddly enough, did not evoke severe criticism of Washington, although the General certainly failed to procure the fullest intelligence both before and during the day, failed to employ his Light Horse adequately, and failed to analyze correctly the information he did receive. Sullivan was charged with incompetence, but his valor and control on the field were everywhere recognized. Some critics tried in vain to procure the dismissal of Maxwell. It was hinted that "Scotch Willie" was drunk on the day of the action and Lieutenant Colonel William Heth—himself not without blemish—charged that never did Maxwell avail himself of the opportunity to do what was expected of his command of the light troops: "He is, to be sure, a damned bitch of a general." But the Congress voted thirty hogsheads of rum to the army, "in compliment . . . for their gallant behavior," and neither the General nor his men were blamed for failure.

Nevertheless, the defeat called for a deep withdrawal. On the morning of the twelfth, Washington marched from Chester, cross the Schuylkill, and encamped on the edge of Germantown, placing himself between the enemy and Philadelphia. He guessed that Howe would endeavor again to turn his right flank, cut off a retreat to the west, and force him into a pocket between the Schuylkill and the Delaware. To prevent this, he took the offensive again on the morning of the fifteenth, broke camp, crossed the Schuylkill, and took a position in the neighborhood of the Admiral Warren and the White Horse taverns on the Lancaster Road. He thus imposed himself between Howe and Swedes Ford, by which he expected the British to cross the Schuylkill.

On the sixteenth, as Howe advanced toward him, Washington prepared to give battle; the two armies faced each other, when suddenly a storm that had been several days brewing struck with terrifying violence. Since the day of Brandywine, a hard northwest, then a northeast, wind had blown colder and colder. The sky had remained overcast until now it broke into furious rain. "It came down so hard," a Hessian officer recorded, "that in a few minutes we were drenched and sank in mud up to our calves." Guns and ammunition on both sides were soaked and useless; Washington's men lost forty rounds of ammunition apiece—"a most terrible stroke," moaned Knox. The wind and driving rain united with a quagmire underfoot to discourage reliance on even the bayonet. In rain, driven by howling wind, the shivering Americans moved off and trudged through the mud that evening and night to Yellow Springs, eleven miles away. The next day they moved farther to Warwick. Opposite Washing-

ton's columns Howe maneuvered as if to envelop both the
American flanks, so that on the nineteenth Washington recrossed the Schuylkill at Parker's Ford.

Behind him on the nineteeth, Washington had detached
Anthony Wayne's division, fifteen hundred men and four
fieldpieces, to lie near and harass the enemy's rear, especially
if Howe should attempt to cross the river. Wayne posted his
men in a forest clearing in the neighborhood of the Paoli
Tavern, not far from his own home, and three miles from
the enemy. Howe quickly learned of the presence of the rebel
force. About midnight of the twentieth, Major General
Sir Charles Grey with three battalions fell upon the unsuspecting, sleeping Continentals. To make surprise more certain, Grey had instructed his men "on no account to fire," but
to rely on cold steel: no nervous, premature firing, no flashes
to give away their positions in the dark. The redcoats had
perfect targets as the rebels struggled to their feet in the glow
of their campfires. They cut down more than fifty, wounded
and took prisoner a hundred, and sent the rest plunging for
safety into the rainy woods. Wayne got them off at last during
the night to Chester.

The danger to Philadelphia had compelled the removal
of stores to less exposed towns. A principal depot was at
Reading Furnace. Now by a feint in that direction, Howe induced Washington to march north to protect it, whereupon
the British reversed their march, slipped down the river in
the night, and crossed at Fatland and Gordon's fords. On
the twenty-sixth, Howe, who once more had easily outwitted
Washington, walked into Philadelphia unopposed.

Congress already had fled, after renewing for a period of
sixty days substantially the same dictatorial powers voted
Washington the year before. Robert Morton, a teen-age
Tory, had witnessed its departure:

> *Sept. 19th.* This morning, about one o'clock, an express
> arrived to Congress, giving an account of the British Army
> having got to the Swedes Ford on the other side of the
> Schuylkill, which so much alarmed the Gentlemen of the
> Congress, the military officers, and other friends to the gen-
> eral cause of American freedom and independence, that they
> decamped with the utmost precipitation, and in the greatest
> confusion, insomuch that one of the delegates, by name
> [Nathaniel] Fulsom [of New Hampshire] was obliged in a
> very *fulsom* manner to ride off without a saddle.[12]

Actually, the flight of the Congress had not been so confused. The papers of the guiding body of the country had
been sent for safekeeping to Bristol, and as early as the four-

teenth of September its members had resolved to depart, when necessary, to reconvene in Lancaster, whence they moved immediately to York. For several days members had been leaving, the more timid first, then even the stubborn, until at last some few dashed away unceremoniously.

Robert Morton was among the thousands who crowded the streets, windows, and roofs to watch the British march in:

> About eleven o'clock A.M., Lord Cornwallis with his division of the British and auxiliary troops, amounting to about three thousand, marched into this city, accompanied by Enoch Story, Joseph Galloway, Andrew Allen, William Allen, and others, inhabitants of this city, to the great relief of the inhabitants who have too long suffered the yoke of arbitrary power, and who testified their approbation of the arrival of the troops by the loudest acclamations of joy.
>
> Went with Charles Logan to headquarters to see his Excellency General Sir William Howe, but he being gone out, we had some conversation with the officers, who appeared well disposed towards the peaceable inhabitants, but most bitter against and determined to pursue to the last extremity the army of the United States.
>
> The British army in this city are quartered at the Bettering House, State House, and other places, and already begin to show the great destruction of the fences and other things, the dreadful consequences of an army, however friendly. The army have fortified below the town to prevent the armed vessels in our river coming to this city, likewise have erected a battery at the Point.
>
> This day has put a period to the existence of Continental money in this city. "Esto Perpetua."[13]

A victorious, self-confident Howe encamped his main army at Germantown, five miles northwest of town, to hold off Washington, but did not order his forces to fortify, because to do so might be considered an admission of weakness. Three thousand of his best troops he stationed in Philadelphia, and about three thousand more across the river in Jersey.

Curiously, the fall of Philadelphia was not universally dispiriting. Only the autumn before, Washington had thought its loss "must prove of the most fatal consequences to the cause of America." But now its importance had diminished. It had been emptied of stores, Congress was gone, it was not a source of supply. If Washington could hold the water approaches, Howe would be hard put to feed his army. Besides, the Americans were resting and their army was growing.

Howe had captured Philadelphia? "No," said sage old Franklin when he heard the news in Paris, "Philadelphia has captured Howe!"

"TROPHIES LAY AT OUR FEET"

Germantown

OCTOBER 4, 1777

WASHINGTON, OFTEN accused of unwarranted caution, was anything but Fabian after Brandywine. Eagerly he sought another chance at Howe. As soon as he learned, on the twenty-third of September, that his foe had eluded him, he called a council of war to weigh the advisability of attacking before the British could reach the Quaker City. In spite of the weakness of his force, without its detachments and expected reinforcements, he was ready to rush at Howe. His council voted against an attack. Nevertheless, he moved nearer to Philadelphia, and at Pennypacker's Mill received intelligence that Howe's main body lay near Germantown, with only a smaller force billeted in Philadelphia. In all, Howe's army did not exceed eight thousand men.

When, on the twenty-eighth, Washington called another council to debate whether to attack Howe, nine hundred men under McDougall had arrived from Peekskill, and eleven hundred Maryland militia, under William Smallwood, and six hundred New Jersey militia, under David Forman, were expected. Although his force was now eleven thousand strong, again his council advised him to wait. Again he moved closer to the enemy, to the point where Skippack Creek crossed Skippack Road. When he learned from two intercepted enemy letters that a substantial detachment of the enemy was off trying to open the Delaware, his officers at last agreed upon an attack. He moved up to within fifteen or sixteen miles of Germantown, and made careful plans for a complex surprise attack against Howe's lines in the early morning of October 4.

The plan called for an approach in four thrusts. The divisions of Sullivan and Wayne, with General Thomas Conway in the van, were to make the frontal attack on the enemy camp along the Chestnut Hill Road. Greene's and Stephen's divisions, with McDougall's brigade in front, were to advance by the Lime Kiln Road against the enemy right. Smallwood's Maryland militia and Forman's New Jersey militia were to march along the Old York Road, farther to Greene's left, to

fall on the rear of the enemy right. Against the river, John
Armstrong with his militia was to advance down the Mana-
tawny Road to reach the rear of the enemy left. Under Stirling, the brigades of Francis Nash and William Maxwell were
to form the *corps de réserve.*

The plan was too intricate. The four approach roads were
separated from each other over a space of seven miles, and
not even the best efforts of the Light Horse to keep the columns in communication was likely to succeed on a sixteen-
mile march at night in strange, uneven country. The troops
were to march at seven o'clock on the evening of the third
and to halt at 2 A.M. within two miles of the enemy pickets;
at 4 A.M. they were to make final dispositions; at 5 A.M. they
were to take out the pickets with "charged bayonets without
firing," and to move to the attack as soon as possible. To distinguish friend from foe in the dark of the morning, every
man was to "have a piece of white paper in their hat."

For several nights prior to the march, American patrols
had kept British nerves on edge by assaulting and driving in
their pickets. About midnight of the third, a British officer
guessed that the firing "this night all round the sentries" indicated that the Americans were trying to feel their situation.
British patrols reported the presence of American troops at
three in the morning of the fourth, and Howe put his whole
force under arms. But for some reason, a proud, intelligent
British officer on outpost duty at Biggenstown was unaware
of Washington's movement until the first attack struck:

General Wayne commanded the advance and fully expected to be revenged for the surprise we had given him
[at Paoli]. When the first shots were fired at our pickets,
so much had we all Wayne's affair in remembrance that the
battalion was out and under arms in a minute.

At this time, the day had just broke, but it was a very
foggy morning and so dark we could not see a hundred yards
before us. Just as the battalion had formed, the pickets came
in and said the enemy were advancing in force. They had
hardly joined the battalion when we heard a loud cry of,
"Have at the bloodhounds! Revenge Wayne's affair!" And
they immediately fired a volley.

We gave them one in return, cheered, and charged. As
it was near the end of the campaign, it was very weak: it did
not consist of more than three hundred men and we had no
support nearer than Germantown, a mile in our rear. On
our charging, they gave way on all sides but again and again
renewed the attack with fresh troops and greater force. We
charged them twice, till the battalion was so reduced by
killed and wounded that the bugle was sounded to retreat. In-

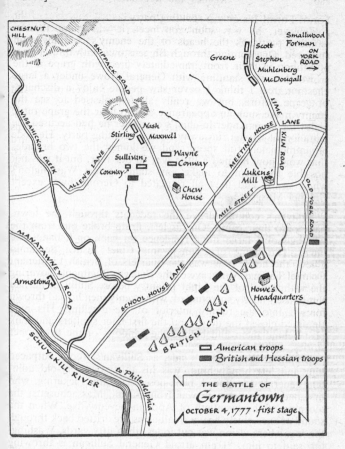

CHESTNUT
HILL

SKIPPACK ROAD

WISSAHICKON CREEK

ALLEN'S LANE

Nash
Stirling   Maxwell

Sullivan
Conway   Wayne
              Conway

              Chew
              House

MANATAWNEY ROAD

Armstrong

SCHOOL HOUSE LANE

SCHUYLKILL RIVER

to Philadelphia

Scott
Greene   Stephen
          Muhlenberg
          McDougall

Smallwood
Forman
ON
YORK
ROAD

LIME HOUSE LANE

MEETING HOUSE LANE

KILN ROAD

OLD YORK ROAD

MILL STREET

Lukens'
Mill

Howe's
Headquarters

BRITISH CAMP

□ *American troops*
■ *British and Hessian troops*

THE BATTLE OF
Germantown
OCTOBER 4, 1777 · *first stage*

deed had we not retreated at the very time we did, we should
all have been taken or killed, as two columns of the enemy
had nearly got round our flank. But this was the first time we
had retreated from the Americans, and it was with great difficulty we could get our men to obey our orders.

The enemy were kept so long in check that . . . two brigades [the Second Battalion of Light Infantry and the Fortieth Regiment] had advanced to the entrance of Biggenstown, when they met our battalion retreating. By this time
General Howe had come up and seeing the battalion retreating, all broken, he got into a passion and exclaimed,
"For shame, Light Infantry. I never saw you retreat before.

Form! Form! It's only a scouting party."

However, he was soon convinced it was more than a scouting party, as the heads of the enemy's columns soon appeared. One coming through Biggenstown with three pieces of cannon in their front immediately fired with grape at the crowd that was standing with General Howe under a large chestnut tree. I think I never saw people enjoy a discharge of grape before, but we really all felt pleased to see the enemy make such an appearance and to hear the grape rattle about the commander-in-chief's ears after he had accused the battalion of having run away from a scouting party. He rode off immediately full speed, and we joined the two brigades that were now formed a little way in our rear, but it was not possible for them to make any stand against Washington's whole army, and they all retreated to Germantown, except Colonel Musgrave. . . .[1]

Sullivan's column drove the redcoats through the town, back onto their camp. On his left, firing broke out from the windows of a large stone residence set back on a handsome lawn. The home of Pennsylvania Chief Justice Benjamin Chew, the house now was the quarters of British Lieutenant Colonel Thomas Musgrave of the Fortieth Regiment. Covering the withdrawal of the Light Infantry before Sullivan, he had felt himself nearly surrounded; with twenty men he had thrown himself into the roomy interior of the dwelling. His men slammed closed the doors and the first-floor shutters and took post behind them and behind the windows of the two upper stories.

Riding at Washington's side, as Sullivan's troops outpaced him and left him behind, was his thirty-two-year-old adjutant general, dour-faced, beak-nosed Timothy Pickering, who first had come down to war from Salem, Massachusetts, the morning of the twentieth of April in 'seventy-five. When the sound of excessively heavy small-arms fire drifted back through the fog, where vision was cut to less than fifty yards, Washington said to him, "I am afraid General Sullivan is throwing away his ammunition. Ride forward and tell him to preserve it."

Pickering spurred ahead and delivered the General's message to Sullivan, three or four hundred yards beyond Chew's house. Said he:

At this time I had never heard of Chew's house and had no idea that an enemy was in my rear. The first notice I received of it was from the whizzing of musket balls across the road, before, behind, and above me, as I was returning after delivering the orders to Sullivan.

Instantly turning my eye to the right I saw the blaze of

the muskets, whose shot were still aimed at me from . . .
Chew's. . . . Passing on I came to some of our artillery who
were firing very obliquely on the front of the house. I remarked to them that in that position their fire would be un-
availing and that the only chance of their shot making any
impression on the house would be by moving down and firing directly on its front. Then . . . passing on I rejoined
General Washington, who, with General Knox and other officers, was in front of a stone house (nearly all the houses
. . . were of stone), next northward of the open field in which
Chew's house stood.

I found they were discussing in Washington's presence . . .
whether the whole of our troops then behind [the reserves
under Maxwell and Nash] should . . . advance, regardless
of the enemy in Chew's house, or first summon them to surrender.

General Knox strenuously urged the sending of a summons. Among other things he said, "It would be unmilitary
to leave a castle in our rear."

I answered, "Doubtless that is a correct general maxim,
but it does not apply in this case. We know the extent of this
castle . . . and to guard against the danger from the enemy's
sallying and falling on the rear of our troops, a small regiment may be posted here to watch them. . . . But," I added,
"to summon them to surrender will be useless. We are now
in the midst of the battle and its issue is unknown. In this
state of uncertainty and so well secured as the enemy find
themselves, they will not regard a summons. They will fire at
your flag."

However, a flag was sent with a summons. Lieutenant
[Colonel Matthew] Smith of Virginia, my assistant in the
Office of Adjutant General, volunteered his service to carry
it. As he was advancing, a shot from the house gave him a
wound of which he died. . . .[2]

The shot that brought down Lieutenant Colonel Smith fired
the Americans with fierce determination to tear Musgrave
from his stronghold. Their three-pounders knocked open the
doors, and then they fired away at the upper windows with
round and grape while infantrymen tried to force their way
in. But in spite of the hammering of the field guns and the intrepidity of the men who fired and clubbed their way into
doors and windows, the redcoats held out. After losing a
half-hour in futile struggle, Washington ordered his Continentals to stay out of range of the house and by-pass it.

It was a day of "the most horrid fog" General Weedon ever
had seen, and soon it turned into a day of mounting mistakes
and frenzied confusion. Greene arrived at his position on the
enemy right a half-hour late; his march was four miles longer

than the others and his guide had been led astray. When he did meet the enemy's advance at Lukens' Mill he drove through almost to the center of the enemy line with great success. However, without Greene's orders, Adam Stephen, drunk at sunup and hearing the cannon and musket fire around Chew's house, had swung his division to the right and marched for the scene, thus departing from the attack plan and weakening it. Wayne, pushing up the opposite side of the main road from Sullivan, also hearing the fire around the Chew house, guessed Sullivan was in trouble, and turned back to succor him. He met Stephen's division coming down to the main battle. Stephen's men mistook Wayne's for the enemy and volleyed. Wayne fired back smartly. Both groups broke and fled, and the seed of panic was planted.

Something happened which no officer on the field ever was able to explain: What appeared to be an American victory swiftly turned into a rout. Reported General Weedon:

> Our men behaved with the greatest intrepidity for three hours, driving them from their camps, fieldpieces, stone walls, houses, &c. Trophies lay at our feet, but so certain were we of making a general defeat of it that we pass them by in the pursuit and by that means lost the chief part of them again, for when the unlucky idea struck our men to fall back, the utmost exertions to rally them again was in vain, and a few minutes evinced the absolute necessity of drawing them off in the best manner we could. . . .[3]

Some blamed the fog and smoke which made co-operation almost impossible; some thought it started with the collision of Wayne's and Stephen's men; some blamed Greene for his late arrival; some, including Washington, thought the delay at the Chew house contributed; some suspected that by bringing up fresh troops on the right, Howe turned the tide. Private Joseph Martin knew, at least, why many of his comrades turned tail:

> The enemy were retreating before us until the first division that was engaged had expended their ammunition. Some of the men, unadvisedly calling out that their ammunition was spent, the enemy were so near that they overheard them, when they first made a stand and then returned upon our people, who, for want of ammunition and reinforcements, were obliged to retreat which ultimately resulted in the rout of the whole army.[4]

Citizen Thomas Paine, now serving as Secretary to the Foreign Committee of the Congress, had been with the army as an observer, residing at Greene's quarters. At five in the morning, he rode toward Germantown to see the action. At first he heard the enemy had broken; then five or six miles from Germantown, he "met several of the wounded in wagons, horseback and on foot." To Benjamin Franklin he wrote:

I passed General [Francis] Nash on a litter made of poles but did not know him. I felt unwilling to ask questions, lest the information should not be agreeable, and kept on. About two miles after, I passed a promiscuous crowd of wounded and otherwise, who were halted at a house. Colonel [Clement] Biddle, D.Q.M.G., was among them, who called after me that if I went further on that road I would be taken, for the firing which I heard ahead was the enemy's.

I never could, and cannot now [six months later] learn, and I believe no man can inform truly the cause of that day's miscarriage. The retreat was as extraordinary. Nobody hurried themselves. Everyone marched at his own pace.[5]

And for very good reasons, thought Private Martin. The least any man had marched the previous night was fourteen miles—and he himself had marched many more since last he had slept.

They had fought fatigued, and now Washington led them all the way back to Pennypacker's Mill to encamp, some twenty-four miles. Most of the men were twenty-four hours without food, and like Private Martin, "tormented with thirst all the morning, fighting being warm work."

Washington's total loss, including prisoners, was about eleven hundred men and Howe's about half that many, but the American army was, as after Brandywine, optimistic. No one questioned the impossible intricacy of the General's plan; the troops were infinitely superior to what they had been a year before, and the officers were beginning to understand each other. General Weedon thought that "though the enterprise miscarried, it was worth the undertaking," and the General himself regarded it "rather more unfortunate than injurious."

Although Howe was now in undisputed possession of Philadelphia, he could not occupy it comfortably without clearing the Delaware of the rebels and opening it as an avenue of communication and supply from the sea. Bringing in supplies across the Jerseys from New York or from the Head of Elk would be extremely hazardous, because Washington could play havoc with cumbersome supply trains.

The Delaware defenses consisted of three forts and lines of *chevaux-de-frise* across the river. The *chevaux-de-frise* were iron-pointed wooden beams embedded in enormous cratelike structures loaded with stones and sunk in the river; the points sloped up within a few feet of the surface and pointed down-stream to impale or rip the bottoms of advancing vessels. A *cheval-de-frise* lay across the channel of the river at Billings-port on the Jersey side, and a fort stood at the same place. Five miles above at Red Bank was Fort Mercer, protecting, with Fort Mifflin on Port Island near the opposite bank, an-other double row of *chevaux-de-frise*. Above these lay the twoscore light vessels of assorted character that constituted the American fleet.

Howe had begun a move against the river forts two days before Brandywine, when he sent two and a half regiments against the unfinished redoubt at Billingsport. The rebel gar-rison spiked its guns, fired the half-completed barracks, and retreated. The British opened passage in the *cheval-de-frise* and passed through six ships. But Howe, as usual, did not press his advantage, and waited two weeks before moving against Fort Mercer, garrisoned by four hundred men under Colonel Christopher Greene of Rhode Island and mounting fourteen guns. On the twenty-second of October he sent an assaulting column of about two thousand Hessians under Colonel von Donop against it. The attack was a humiliating failure, which cost the Hessians nearly four hundred casual-ties, including Donop, who suffered a mortal wound. The Americans lost only fourteen killed and twenty-three wounded.

Failing to knock out Fort Mercer, Howe turned his atten-tion to Fort Mifflin on Port Island, described by a Contin-ental soldier as "a burlesque upon the art of fortification." Washington reinforced it at the last minute, and when Howe opened shore batteries, on the tenth of November, to bom-bard the "mud flat in the Delaware," Private Joseph Martin said, "the grape shot would come down like a shower of hail." On November 15, after the fort had been hammered steadily for five days and nights, six men-of-war and several floating batteries under Admiral Howe worked within range and, said Martin, "the enemy's shot ate us up."

After nightfall, with more than half the garrison of four hundred and fifty dead or wounded, the survivors slipped across the river to Fort Mercer. But with the fall of Fort Mif-flin, Fort Mercer was doomed. Cornwallis led two thousand men across the river and attacked it. On the night of the twentieth, Colonel Greene abandoned the place, and the Del-aware became a British river.

"... UNTIL WE SHOOT A GENERAL"

Gentleman Johnny Burgoyne
Opens His Campaign

SUMMER 1777

ON THE sixth of May, Lieutenant General John Burgoyne, handsome soldier, litterateur, and man-about-London, fresh from an English winter, strode off H.M.S. *Apollo* at Quebec. His epaulets blinked furiously in the warm sunshine that flooded the green St. Lawrence, and he was thoroughly happy for the first time since the American rebellion had begun. Ever since he had first landed in Boston two years ago, as one of the now-famous trio of Burgoyne, Clinton, and Howe, he had longed and schemed for an independent command, and at last he had achieved it. He had wintered in England both years of the war. Although he was rumored to share the King's disfavor with Carleton, who had failed on the lakes in 1776, he had been seen riding, the January just past, with the King in Hyde Park. In February he had presented to His Majesty a paper he called *Thoughts for Conducting the War from the Side of Canada*. In March, with the King's recommendation, it had been accepted by the Ministry as the war plan for the year, and Burgoyne had been chosen to command the field force that was to carry it out.

It was a sound plan, but hardly an original one. Only insignificantly did it differ from earlier ones suggested by Lord Dartmouth, General Howe, and Sir Guy Carleton. Its principal elements were an advance from Montreal through Lake Champlain and the Hudson to Albany, a drive by a smaller force down the Mohawk Valley from Oswego, and an advance up the Hudson by a column from Howe's army. Converging at Albany, the three would come down on the rebels—front, flank, and rear. Even if Washington, by not risking his army in an attempt to meet the offensive, should thus escape immediate destruction, the operation would wound the rebellion mortally. By occupying the line of the Hudson, the British would sever New England from the rest of the colonies;

the flow of men and supplies from the heartland of the rebellion would be cut off. And then with the Hudson line established, Howe would be free to destroy Washington's army in good time wherever it might be.

After six weeks in Quebec, with the unstinting co-operation of Carleton, who had been shelved for his less able but glibber junior in rank, "Gentleman Johnny" was ready to mount his offensive. Sir Guy had handed him an army of over 8,300, including 600 artillerymen for a train of 138 guns, 650 Canadian and Tory auxiliaries, 400 Indians of the Six Nations, and a main force of 3,700 smartly-trained regulars and 3,000 Germans, almost all of the latter Brunswickers. The Germans were commanded by the officer who would second Burgoyne, thirty-nine-year-old Baron Friedrich Adolph von Riedesel. Though considerably younger than Burgoyne, the stocky, blue-eyed German was as thoroughly experienced, an intelligent, aggressive soldier and a ferocious disciplinarian. With the familial sentimentality of the Germans, the Baron had allowed his petite, gay baroness to follow him from Europe with their three small daughters and two maids, and he had ordered made for a large calash in which to trail the army through the American wilderness.

On the sparkling morning of the twentieth of June, from its assembly point at Cumberland Head, north of Valcour Island, Burgoyne's expedition set sail in a mile-long flotilla up the shimmering blue waters to Crown Point. There, about eight miles north of Ticonderoga, the general tarried to establish magazines and hospitals, repair batteaux, issue ammunition. Then on the last day of June, after giving out a bombastic General Order that "This Army Must Not Retreat," George III's new favorite moved up to within four miles of the rebel stronghold.

Carleton had informed Burgoyne that the fort was weakly guarded by a sickly, poorly supplied garrison. But he did not know that it was the outpost of a Department weakened almost to death by intersectional discord between officers and men and by the quarrel of the rival Continental Generals Philip Schuyler and Horatio Gates, who fought for its command like dogs for a bone.

Almost from the beginning, Schuyler, first commander of the Northern Department of the Continental Army, though well regarded by his Commander-in-Chief, had been extremely unpopular with his army and with a strong segment of the Continental Congress. A large proportion of the fighting men who had gone to Canada in 1775 had been New Englanders, the same ones who had infuriated Montgomery. They did not take to Schuyler's autocratic views of discipline. One

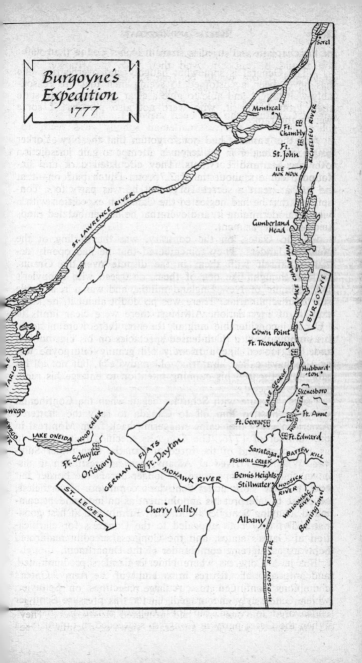

Burgoyne's
Expedition
1777

Sorel

Montreal

Ft. Chambly

St. John

ILE AUX NOIX

RICHELIEU RIVER

ST. LAWRENCE RIVER

Cumberland Head

LAKE CHAMPLAIN

BURGOYNE

Crown Point
Ft. Ticonderoga

Hubbardton

Skenesboro

LAKE GEORGE

WOOD CREEK

Ft. Anne

Ft. George

Ft. Edward

Saratoga

BATTEN KILL

FISHKILL CREEK

Bemis Heights
Stillwater

HOOSICK RIVER

WALLOOMSAC RIVER

Bennington

LAKE ONTARIO

Oswego

LAKE ONEIDA

WOOD CREEK

Ft. Schuyler

Oriskany

GERMAN FLATS

Ft. Dayton

MOHAWK RIVER

ST. LEGER

Cherry Valley

Albany

HUDSON RIVER

of his chaplains had tried to explain to his Connecticut wife:

> The General is somewhat haughty and overbearing. He has never been accustomed to seeing men that are reasonably well taught and able to give a clear opinion and to state their grounds for it, who were not also persons of some wealth and rank.[1]

And the Yankees had not forgotten that the New Yorker had been a leader in his colony's attempt to gain jurisdiction over the Hampshire Grants. They circulated dark and unfounded rumors about the frail, proud Dutch patroon—that he was at heart a secret Tory, that he was party to a conspiracy, that he had neglected the Canadian expedition with a view to undermining it, and even that he had embezzled funds sent to his Department.

Horatio Gates, on the contrary, was the darling of the New Englanders. They remembered that he had openly declared himself with them in the dispute over the Grants, that he thought like one of them, disagreed with Schuyler's low estimate of New England militia, and was a reasonable sort of disciplinarian. There was no doubt about it, he knew the art of ingratiation. Although there were clear limits to his not inconsiderable military talents, there were none to his ambition. With thick-lensed spectacles on his big, hooked nose, he looked like a friendly old granny (Burgoyne was said to have called him "that old midwife"), but not all his affability obscured his cunning intention to enlarge his reputation at any cost.

Gates's dispute with Schuyler began when the Continental Congress hustled him off to Canada to rally the shattered American army that came staggering back from Montreal in the summer of 1776. The Congress specified that he should assume command of the force in Canada, then under Sullivan. When he arrived at Albany, he was crestfallen to discover that the troops were no longer across the border but back in New York under Schuyler's command. Nevertheless, he chose to interpret his appointment as an independent command, denying Schuyler's authority. Firmly and at first good-naturedly, they both appealed to the Congress for clarification of Gates's status, and the Congress speedily reaffirmed Schuyler as supreme commander of the Department.

But in a Congress where New Englanders predominated, and among public figures in and out of the Army, Gates's champions continued to circulate reflections on Schuyler, which Gates slyly encouraged. Under this pressure Schuyler endeavored to resign, but the Congress would not have it. When the Gates party in Congress succeeded in organizing a

committee to investigate the Northern Department, directing
it to confer not with Schuyler but with Gates, then at Ticonderoga, Schuyler obtained permission to go to Philadelphia to discuss his situation, but he never went because
pressure of military affairs held him at Albany.

Gates, however, upon orders from Washington, conducted
the New Jersey and Pennsylvania troops from the North to
the main army defending Philadelphia that December. After
delivering his troops, he pleaded ill health and retired from
the field, only to rush to Congress and argue his cause. Schuyler must have suspected his fine hand behind a belittling
reprimand he received from Congress in March for the sharp
tone of one of his recent letters. And ten days later, Gates
was appointed to command at Ticonderoga with such authority as virtually if not officially made him chief of the Department. This time Schuyler did throw up his command and
journeyed to the Congress for vindication. To his surprise,
the Delegates, on the twenty-second of May, withdrew their
earlier resolution of censure and made clear that he was to
command Fort Ticonderoga and all the rest of the Northern
Department.

By the time the general, once more reinstated, reached Albany, it was the eighth of June. Burgoyne's forces already
were assembling for his stab at the outer defenses of the
Hudson. Schuyler discovered to his dismay that Gates in his
absence had established himself at Albany, instead of going
on to Ticonderoga, and although he had written copiously in
all directions for men, supplies, and stores, actually he had
done "nothing, comparatively speaking" to strengthen Ticonderoga; he had also failed utterly to furnish food stores upon
which its defense would depend. Although Gates had urged
the commandant, General Arthur St. Clair, to "call lustily
for aid of all kinds," the force at the fort was inadequate and
sickly—many "actually barefooted and most of them ragged."
There were 2,300 of them, survivors of an icy winter of sickness and death under choleric Colonel Anthony Wayne, who
called the post "the last place in the world that God made
. . . finished in the dark . . . the ancient Golgotha or place of
skulls." St. Clair admitted they were "ill armed, naked, and
unaccoutered." As late as the twenty-fifth of June, he confessed he saw not "the least prospect of our being able to
defend the post unless the militia come in," and time
was running out and he could provide for only a limited
number of militia if they came in. Gates seemed to have
accomplished little more than the consumption of two
months' provisions and the furthering of his epistolary campaign against Schuyler.

With the Congress' reappointment of Schuyler, it was Gates's turn to bellow. Instantly he resigned his command and headed for Philadelphia. He arrived in the Quaker City "discomposed, chagrined, and angry," leaving behind him a Department for whose defenseless condition he must share responsibility with Schuyler. He obtained an audience at the Congress, seated himself before the Delegates "in a very easy, cavalier posture in an elbow chair and began to open his budget." The hubbub that ensued as he lashed out at his enemies brought from William Duer, New York Delegate, the observation:

It is impossible . . . to give . . . an idea of the unhappy figure which G. G. made. . . . His manner was ungraciously and totally void of all dignity, his delivery incoherent and interrupted with frequent chasms in which he was peering over his scattered notes, and the tenor of his discourse a compound of vanity, folly, and rudeness . . . notwithstanding his conduct has been such as to have eradicated from my mind every sentiment of respect and esteem for him, I felt for him as a man and for the honor of human nature wished him to withdraw before he had plunged himself into utter contempt. . . .[2]

While Schuyler tried too late to patch up his defenses and Gates harangued the Congress in yet another effort to unseat his rival, the enemy closed in on the American outpost for whose tottering weakness both men were responsible. The works at battle-scarred old Fort Ti spread over both sides of the lake. Under the shadow of forested Sugar Hill on the west frowned the principal stupendous bluestone fortress, its walls and bastions rising above its star-shaped trench and defiant abatis. A mile west, a new outwork lay on Mount Hope. Across the lake, about a quarter-mile away, crouched strong works on the headland called Mount Independence. A floating bridge joined Ti with Mount Independence. Ten thousand men were needed to defend all the works, but St. Clair's fit were not a fifth that number.

On the first of July, Burgoyne came ashore with the British regulars on the west and Riedesel's Germans waded out of their boats in the marshes on the east. St. Clair quickly learned of the landing, but he had no idea of the strength of the enemy force. His little blockhouse on Mount Hope was abandoned, outposts banged away briefly, and for the next three or four days a strangling scarlet and green and blue cord of British and German troops looped about his works. On the fifth of July, an enemy cannon boomed from the summit of Sugar Hill and he realized that the enemy had hacked a road through the maples and evergreens to a position where their siege guns overlooked him, and his position was hopeless.

During the clear moonlit night, St. Clair drew his troops across to Mount Independence. After midnight he loaded his invalids with stores into batteaux and set them sail south for Skenesborough, at the head of the lake. With his main force, he started southeast along the new, rutted wagon road that led through the hilly country to Hubbardton: there he would skirt Lake Bomoseen and march west to rendezvous with the party at Skenesborough. Thence he would continue southward until he could meet Schuyler, to whom he wrote he was retreating, and they could decide their next move.

Toward daylight on the sixth, when British General Simon Fraser's scouts discovered the Americans' escape, Burgoyne ordered his tough Scots friend to cross the floating bridge, join the Germans, and pursue St. Clair. He himself set out in his boats to chase the other fugitives up the lake.

Fraser overtook St. Clair's rear guard of several hundred at Hubbardton, twenty-four miles away, early the next morning, had a brush with them, and scattered them, but St. Clair got away. Burgoyne fared little better in overtaking Colonel Pierce Long, commanding the rebels' waterborne contingent. He nearly came up with Long at Skenesborough, but the American colonel had sent his invalids and part of his force up Wood Creek, and with 150 men set out in a lope southward, just as Burgoyne's vessels swung ashore at the log-walled fort of Skenesborough. The Ninth Regiment drove through the woods in pursuit and came on the fugitives at crumbling Fort Anne about dark on the seventh. Next morning the rebels sallied, roughed up the veteran regulars, and safely made off toward Fort Edward. Upon word from Long, St. Clair swung his retreat eastward toward Rutland, thence to work his way around to meet him at Fort Edward.

Philip Schuyler first heard of the evacuation of Ticonderoga on the seventh from an officer he met while on the road between Saratoga and Fort Edward with a small detachment. His informant had no details. St. Clair's fate and present whereabouts were mysteries. The steady, dependable Scotsman had vanished into the night of the fifth. But Schuyler, sending a courier out to find him and direct him to Fort Edward, marched on with a "handful of men," hoping somehow to hold up Burgoyne's advance.

Schuyler sent a prompt report to Washington, who was shocked by "an event of chagrin and surprise, not apprehended, nor within the compass of my reasoning." Upon his return east, Gates had expressed confidence the place could be held, and although before the evacuation St. Clair had written Schuyler in bald, realistic terms, the last letter St. Clair wrote Washington on July 3, with the enemy before him, was, the General observed, "seemingly in good spirits and without the least apprehension."

The letters that now tumbled upon the Commander-in-Chief from his hard-pressed general in the Northern Department rang with despair: "My prospect of preventing them from penetrating is not much," Schuyler said on the seventh. "They have an army flushed with victory, plentifully provided with provisions, cannon, and every warlike store. Our army, if it should once more collect, is weak in numbers, dispirited, naked, in a manner destitute of provisions, without camp equipage, with little ammunition, and not a single cannon." He begged for all sorts of supplies, as well as men, and reiterated his needs two days later when he still did not know "what is become of St. Clair." "The country," he said, is "in the deepest consternation."

To succor the north, Washington sent forward troops under Glover and John Nixon; and he sent Benedict Arnold and Benjamin Lincoln to inspire the New Englanders, and finally the riflemen under the command of Colonel Daniel Morgan, who had been exchanged after refusing a general's commission from the enemy at Quebec.

Despite Schuyler's anguished cry, "What could induce General St. Clair and the general officers with him to evacuate Ticonderoga, God only knows," the New Englanders especially were willing to believe that Schuyler was the evil genius behind the collapse of the northern defenses. Surgeon James Thacher, accompanying American wounded back to Albany, recorded in his journal the current rumor:

. . . It has been industriously reported that Generals Schuyler and St. Clair acted the parts of traitors to their country and that they were paid for their treason by the enemy in *silver balls* shot from Burgoyne's guns into our camp and that they were collected by order of General St. Clair and divided between him and General Schuyler.[3]

Even men of intelligence swallowed the story. New Englander William Gordon, a minister and historian who should have known better, wrote to Washington, six months later, that he had been told by a friend who had been told by a captured British officer "of rank and character," that "the *silver* bullets flew plentifully at Ticonderoga," and that the officer "declared upon his honor that there was bribery and treachery."

While the scandalmongers were digging Schuyler's grave,

he himself, in frantic letters to Washington, the substance of which was reported to Congress, hastened his own removal. His army was melting away, and though he was begging for reinforcements to turn out in New York and New England, he admitted, "I doubt much if any will come up, especially from the Eastern States, where the spirit of malevolence knows no bounds and I am considered a traitor." Before this final confession could reach Philadelphia, the Congress resolved, on the first of August, that an inquiry should be made into the conduct of both Schuyler and St. Clair, and Washington was requested to appoint a successor to Schuyler. Washington, friend both of Gates, whom Congress obviously wished him to name, and of Schuyler, whom he was unwilling to condemn offhand, asked to be excused from making the appointment, whereupon Congress elected Horatio Gates to replace the disgraced general.

Certainly among the New Englanders Schuyler was without a friend. Samuel Adams wrote to Roger Sherman:

Schuyler has written a series of weak and contemptible *things* in a style of despondency which alone, I think, is sufficient for the removal of him . . . for if his pen expresses the true feelings of his heart, it cannot be expected that the bravest veterans would fight under such a general, admitting they had no suspicion of treachery. In a letter dated the fourth instant at Stillwater, he writes in a tone of perfect despair. He seems to have no confidence in his troops, nor the states from whence reinforcements are to be drawn. A third of his Continental troops, he tells us, consists "of boys, Negroes, and aged men not fit for the field or any other service." "A very great part of the army naked, without blankets, ill armed, and very deficient in accouterments, without a prospect of relief." "Many, too many of the officers would be a disgrace to the most contemptible troops that ever was collected." The exertions of others of them of a different character "counteracted by the worthless." "General Burgoyne is bending his course this way. He will probably be here in eight days, and unless we are well reinforced" (which he does not expect,) "as much farther as he pleases to go." Was ever any poor general more mortified? But he has by this time received his quietus. Gates takes the command there, agreeably to what you tell me is the wish of the people, and I trust our affairs in that quarter will soon wear a more promising aspect.[4]

But John Adams, who always unburdened his mind to Abigail, was advocating truly drastic measures in the north when he wrote:

In the northern department they begin to fight. . . . I presume Gates will be so supported that Burgoyne will be obliged to retreat. He will stop at Ticonderoga, I suppose, for they can maintain posts although we cannot. I think we shall never defend a post until we shoot a general. After that, we shall defend posts, and this event, in my opinion, is not far off. No other fort will ever be evacuated without an inquiry, nor any officer come off without a court-martial. We must trifle no more.[5]

Gates was given powers which were almost dictatorial in range and in some respects rivaled those of Washington, but he seemed in little hurry to execute them, despite the gravity of the situation. After his appointment on August 4, he dawdled so long on the trip between Philadelphia and Albany that by the time he reached Albany on August 19, the tide of war in the north had begun to turn, thanks in part to the efforts of his rival, Schuyler.

21

"A GATHERING STORM UPON MY LEFT"

Bennington

AUGUST 16, 1777

As THE American survivors of Hubbardton and Fort Anne plunged southward to join St. Clair, their exultant pursuer regrouped his forces about Skenesborough for the next stage of his drive to the Hudson. Here in the yellow fieldstone house of Tory Philip Skene, Gentleman Johnny Burgoyne lived up to his name, dining choicely, grumbling genially over the paucity of good madeira and port, and radiating charm for his new mistress, the wife of one of his commissaries. The rest of his campaign appeared easy. The fleeing rebels were falling apart; their shipping on Lake Champlain and their sorely needed stores were taken or destroyed. Soon Colonel Barry St. Leger with his supporting column would be driving down the Mohawk, and Howe moving up the Hudson. Nothing remained for Gentleman Johnny but to traverse the twenty-three miles from the heart of Mr. Skene's great wilderness empire to Fort Edward on the upper Hudson.

1777]   *Bennington*   295

When Burgoyne had originally drawn up his plan, he had insisted that the "most expeditious and most commodious" way to reach Albany was to transport boats overland from Ticonderoga to the foot of Lake George, sail to its head, and march overland a little more than ten miles to Fort Edward. He had warned that an army going by way of Skenesborough to the Hudson, traveling Wood Creek to Fort Anne, and thence sixteen miles on the wagon road to Fort Edward, would encounter "considerable difficulties." The narrow parts of the creek could be easily choked up by an enemy, and the rutted wagon trail passed through swamps, bogs, and "great gutters," where causeways and log bridges had to be built or replaced. Nevertheless, he now chose the inferior route, justifying himself by saying that a return march to Ticonderoga to gain the better route would appear to be a retrograde movement and might "abate the panic of the enemy." He sent large labor parties into the hot, close, mosquito-infested forests to put the road in shape for the army and its vehicles while he sat at Skenesborough, waiting for his baggage and supplies to come up.

The toil of Burgoyne's artificers was made immeasurably greater by Philip Schuyler. Although his letters to his Commander-in-Chief trembled with anxiety and his days of command were numbered, he neither fled nor stood idle before the invading enemy. For long days and nights the redcoats heard the thud of his axes up ahead in the virgin wilderness; across the road they were rebuilding, Schuyler's men felled giant pines, so that the branches interlaced and made abatis that could not be dragged away but had to be hewn apart. In Wood Creek they made crude dams of trees and mountainous boulders around which the rain-fattened waters spread, filling existing swamps and creating vast new bogs.

Burgoyne, instead of thrusting out a flying column to destroy the rebels obstructing the road ahead, ordered his axmen to redouble their efforts, and complained:

The troops had not only layers of these [trees] to remove, in places where it was impossible to take any other direction, but also they had above forty bridges to construct and others to repair, one of which was of log-work over a morass two miles in extent.[1]

For sixteen days his fatigue parties hacked away. Not until the twenty-fourth did he advance to Fort Anne, four days later to within two miles of Fort Edward, and on the twenty-ninth to the Hudson.

Schuyler withdrew as Burgoyne moved up. His patrols ranged far and wide warning the inhabitants to scatter their

cattle, burn their standing crops, and hide their food from
the enemy. "It seems a maxim with General Schuyler," an
American observed, "to leave no support to the enemy as he
retires. All is devastation and waste when he leaves. By this
means the enemy will not be able to pursue as fast as they
could wish."

It was not only Schuyler's scorched earth that held Burgoyne at the dilapidated river fort, but also a delay in the
arrival of "provisions, batteaux, and artillery." Gentleman
Johnny should have been striking the rebels, but he loafed
while thirty carts rattled into camp with his own baggage
and belongings, dozens more followed with the possessions
of favored officers, and a ponderous train of superfluous
artillery slowly assembled. No one could understand why
Burgoyne tied himself to such impedimenta when, surely,
not a single strong fort stood in his path.

All the while Burgoyne was inactive his Indians were not.
In the judgment of a Hessian officer, "Our Indians . . . behaved like hogs. When it comes to plundering, they are on
hand every time."

One warm day an Indian appeared in the British camp
waving a freshly taken scalp of long, lustrous hair, which another captive recognized as that of her neighbor, Jane Mc-
Crea, fiancée of a loyalist militiaman, Lieutenant David
Jones. Quickly speculation spread through the army as to the
manner in which the twenty-three-year-old beauty had met
her fate. It was rumored that Lieutenant Jones had promised
a reward to two Indians to give his sweetheart safe convoy
from her home near Fort Edward to the army. Lieutenant
Thomas Anburey, serving in his first campaign as a gentleman volunteer in the Twenty-ninth Regiment, later recorded
his belief:

> Some Indians who were out on scout by chance met
> with her in the woods; they at first treated her with every
> mark of civility . . . and were conducting her into camp, when
> within a mile of it, a dispute arose between the two . . . whose
> prisoner she was; and words growing very high, one of them,
> . . . fearful of losing the reward for bringing her safe into
> camp, most inhumanly struck his tomahawk into her skull
> and she instantly expired.[2]

At the beginning of the campaign, Burgoyne had "positive-
ly forbid" his Indians to shed blood "when you are not opposed in arms" or to scalp indiscriminately. He had not always succeeded in enforcing his injunction, which was
ridiculed bitterly by Parliamentary Whigs who abhorred his
employment of savages. A rebel paymaster with Schuyler's

army told a relative, "It is believed the Tories have sculp'd many of their countrymen, as there is a premium from Burgoyne for sculps. . . . One hundred Indians in the woods do as much harm than a thousand British troops. They have been the death of many brave fellows."

The story of the death of Jane McCrea with its romantic circumstances winged over New York and New England, giving credence to the rumors that Burgoyne offered a scalp bounty. Hundreds of men, imagining a similar fate for their families in spite of Burgoyne's disavowals, picked up their muskets to join Schuyler. Lieutenant Jones, Jane's fiancée, was the forgotten man of the tragedy. Years later, his grandniece told a sequel:

He was so crushed by the terrible blow and disgusted with the apathy of Burgoyne in refusing to punish the miscreant . . . that he and his brother . . . asked for a discharge and were refused, when they deserted—he having first rescued the precious relic of his beloved from the savages— and retired to this Canadian wilderness, which he had never been known to leave, except upon one mysterious occasion many years before.[3]

But the effect of Jane McCrea's death, which ultimately inspired many Whigs to storm forth with a new battle cry on their lips, was not instantaneous. Schuyler, although he had been joined now by St. Clair and by John Glover's brigade, fell farther back on Saratoga and finally to Stillwater with what a captain called "this retreating, ragged, starved, lousy, thievish, pockey army." Here he wrote Washington he would fortify his camp in hopes that reinforcements would enable him to keep his ground. But, he confessed, he was at a loss to know where they were coming from, and his Continentals were daily decreasing in number and the militia preparing to desert him in a week when its time was up. His only hope lay with Major General Benjamin Lincoln.

General Lincoln, an enormously obese Massachusetts militia officer, had served much to Washington's satisfaction in the hard winter days of last year. He was fatuous-looking and far from brilliant, but to the Commander-in-Chief he had "proved himself on all occasions, an active, spirited, and sensible man," and Washington had got for him a Continental commission. In the present crisis, Washington sent him north to take command of the New England militia, "over whom I am informed you have influence and who place confidence in you." Militia was said to be assembling in the Hampshire Grants, and Lincoln was there.

The Grants, whence Schuyler hoped to draw fresh troops, also claimed the attention of John Burgoyne. He needed provisions and draft animals. No army had marched through the Grants, which recently had declared themselves the independent state of Vermont, and a plethora of horses and oxen and bulging rebel supply depots invited a heavy foraging expedition. Furthermore, Mr. Skene assured the general that countless Tories there were merely waiting for the appearance of Burgoyne's troops to pour into his ranks.

To lead a raid into the Grants, Burgoyne selected Lieutenant Colonel Fredrick Baume, a stout blond officer of experience in Europe, who could not "utter one word of English," and gave him a mixed company of some six hundred men, a squad of artillerymen, and two little three-pounders.

Burgoyne and Riedesel, who first had suggested the foray, assumed that its only opposition would be Seth Warner's rebel militia force at Manchester, and Burgoyne thought it "highly probable" Warner would retreat before Baume. If not, Baume was to decide whether to attack him, remembering not to hazard his valuable corps.

But the British were not aware of the activities of a tall, blue-eyed, thin-faced, weathered man, named John Stark. He was a farmer on the Merrimack, and although only in his forties, a famed old fighter who had marched with Major Robert Rogers' Rangers in the French and Indian War. From Bunker Hill to Trenton he had served with distinction, but when he was passed over for promotion, he had left the service and returned home. When Vermont called upon neighboring states for protection, the New Hampshire legislature voted, on July 18, to raise a brigade to meet the enemy, and found its leader in Brigadier General John Stark. In one week's time he recruited fifteen hundred men for two months' duty, the fastest turnout of New Englanders since the nineteenth of April, 1775. But upon accepting command, Stark made one firm proviso: that he and his men be independent of Congress and the Continental Army. He had had enough of both of them. The New Hampshire General Court, willing both to express its dislike of New York and to put its local interests before those of the united cause, gave Stark *carte blanche* to operate against Burgoyne's force when, where, and how he pleased. With the legislature's commission in his pocket, he ordered his men forward to Manchester, and followed them a week later.

At Manchester, the men came under command of General Lincoln, who was assuming command of all the militia raised in the East. A farmer from Lyndeboro in the Grants, reported to his wife on the sixth of August:

We have made us tents with boards, but this moment we have had orders to march for Bennington and leave them and from thence we are to march for Albany to join the Continental Army and try to stop Burgoyne in his career. . . . P.S. August 7th. A few minutes after I finished my letter, there was a considerable turn in affairs, by reason of General Stark arriving in town. The orders we had for marching was given by General Lincoln. What passed between Lincoln and Stark is not known, but by what we can gather . . . Stark chooses to command himself. I expect we shall march for Bennington next Sabbath, and where we shall go to from there I cannot tell.[4]

What had happened between the generals was that Stark promptly let Lincoln know he "considered himself adequate to the command of his own men," and waved his commission before the astonished commander's long nose. He said he had no intention of joining the Continental Army until the Continental Congress gave him a proper commission, and that was that. Instead, he intended to harass the enemy's left rear. Very prudently, Lincoln agreed and said he would endeavor to persuade Schuyler to support Stark's move, although he reported to the Continental Congress what he considered Stark's insubordination in refusing to act under the authority of the Continental Army. Lincoln rode off to confer with Schuyler, and Stark set out for Bennington, twenty miles south, halfway to Schuyler's headquarters at Stillwater, to await Lincoln's return.

By posting himself at Bennington, Stark protected an important depot of provisions and horses, and also made communication with Lincoln easier. Burgoyne had not known of the Bennington depot when he drew up orders for Baume's expedition. Just as Baume was moving from his camp at Fort Miller, eight miles from Fort Edward, on the eleventh of August, Burgoyne himself rode up and ordered him to change his march directly for Bennington, where he had heard that only a light force of three or four hundred militia guarded a rich magazine of supplies. Baume set out confidently for Bennington, leaving Burgoyne's advance corps under General Fraser at Fort Miller to support the expedition. His march was slow, for the country was rugged and the roads primitive, and at best the heavily clothed, excessively equipped Germans were notoriously lethargic movers. He mounted the great notch of the watershed between the Battenkill and the Hoosick River and moved toward Cambridge, Vermont, some fifteen miles. On the morning of the fourteenth, he reached Van Schaick's Mill on the Walloomsac near the Hoosick. At nine o'clock, after a brisk but almost bloodless skirmish with a detachment of Stark's force from Bennington, he hurriedly wrote to Burgoyne, using the head of a barrel for a desk:

> By five prisoners taken here, they agreed that fifteen hundred to eighteen hundred men are in Bennington, but are supposed to leave it on our approach. I will proceed so far to-day as to fall on the enemy tomorrow early, and make such disposition as I think necessary from the intelligence I may receive. People are flocking in hourly, but want to be armed. The savages cannot be controlled; they ruin and take everything they please.[5]

When Stark heard that a large enemy force was approaching, he rallied at Bennington every man he could find, hastened a summons to Seth Warner to join him, and marched to rescue his detachment at the mill. About five miles west of Bennington he met it in retreat, closely pursued. Quickly he deployed for battle, but when the enemy came in sight, he reported, "they halted on a very advantageous hill or piece of ground." Here, behind the Walloomsac, Baume took a position, and Stark withdrew about a mile toward Bennington.

The morning of the fifteenth came in with heavy rains and "a perfect hurricane of wind." Soon after "early parade" there was commotion at Baume's outposts, petty skirmishing that died in the heavy downpour. Baume recognized that the Americans did not intend to flee before him and started fortifying his position. Here he planned to await supplies and a reinforcement he expected coming up from Battenkill. An "absolute torrent" fell all day, washing down the earth as quickly as the men threw it up and flooding their ditches. They passed the night, said Baume's Lieutenant Glich "not very comfortably . . . and . . . impressed with a powerful sense of impending danger." After a long, anxious night, Glich welcomed a red eastern sky.

> All was perfectly quiet at the outposts . . . for several hours previous to sunrise. So peaceable . . . that our leaders felt warmly disposed to resume the offensive, without waiting the arrival of the additional corps . . . and orders were already issued for the men to eat their breakfasts, preparatory to more active operations. But the arms were scarcely piled, and the haversacks unslung, when . . . our people were recalled to their ranks in all haste. . . . From more than one quarter, scouts came in to report that columns of armed men were approaching, though whether with friendly or hostile intention, neither their appearance nor actions enabled our informants to ascertain.
>
> . . . During the last day's march our little corps was joined by many of the country people, most of whom demanded

and obtained arms, as persons friendly to the royal cause. How Colonel Baume became so completely duped as to place reliance on these men, I know not, but having listened with complacency to their previous assurances, that in Bennington a large majority of the populace were our friends, he was somehow or other persuaded to believe that the armed bands, of whose approach he was warned, were loyalists on their way to make tender of their services to the leader of the king's troops. Filled with this idea, he dispatched positive orders to the outposts that no molestations should be offered to the advancing columns, but that the pickets retiring before them should join the main body, where every disposition was made to receive either friend or foe. Unfortunately for us, these orders were but too faithfully obeyed.

About half past nine o'clock, I, who was not in the secret, beheld, to my utter amazement, our advanced parties withdraw without firing a shot, from thickets which might have been maintained for hours against any superiority of numbers, and these same thickets occupied by men whose whole demeanor, as well as their dress and style of equipment, plainly and incontestably pointed them out as Americans.

I cannot pretend to describe the state of excitation and alarm into which our little band was now thrown. With the solitary exception of our leader, there was not a man among us who appeared otherwise than satisfied that those to whom he had listened were traitors. . . .

We . . . stood about half an hour under arms, watching the proceedings of a column of four or five hundred men, who, after dislodging the pickets, had halted just at the edge of the open country, when a sudden trampling of feet in the forest on our right, followed by the report of several muskets, attracted our attention. A patrol was instantly sent in the direction of the sound, but before . . . it had proceeded many yards from the lines, a loud shout, followed by a rapid though straggling fire of musketry, warned us to prepare for a meeting the reverse of friendly. Instantly the Indians came pouring in, carrying dismay and confusion in their countenances and gestures. We were surrounded on all sides: columns were advancing everywhere against us, and those whom we had hitherto trusted as friends had only waited till the arrival of their support . . . in advancing. . . .

If Colonel Baume had permitted himself to be duped into a great error, it is no more than justice to confess that he exerted himself manfully to . . . avert its consequences. Our little band, which had hitherto remained in column, was instantly ordered to extend, and the troops lining the breastworks replied to the fire of the Americans with extreme celerity and considerable effect. So close and destructive . . . was our first volley that the assailants recoiled . . . and would have retreated, in all probability, . . . but ere we could take advantage of the confusion produced, fresh attacks developed themselves, and we were warmly engaged on every side. . . .

It was at this moment, when the heads of columns began to show themselves in rear of our right and left, that the Indians, who had hitherto acted with spirit and something like order, lost all confidence and fled. . . .

The vacancy, which the retreat of the savages occasioned, was promptly filled up by one of our two fieldpieces, whilst the other poured destruction among the enemy in front, as often as they showed themselves in the open country, or threatened to advance. In this state . . . we continued upwards of three quarters of an hour. Though repeatedly assailed in front, flank, and rear, we maintained ourselves with so much obstinacy, as to inspire a hope that the enemy might even yet be kept at bay till the arrival of Breymann's corps, now momentarily expected, when an accident occurred, which at once put an end to this expectation and exposed us, almost defenceless, to our fate.

The solitary tumbril, which contained the whole of our spare ammunition, became ignited and blew up with a violence which . . . caused a momentary cessation in firing, both on our side and that of the enemy. But the cessation was only for a moment. The American officers, guessing the extent of our calamity, cheered their men to fresh exertions. They rushed up the ascent . . . in spite of the heavy volley which we poured in to check them, and finding our guns silent, they sprang over the parapet and dashed within our works.

For a few seconds, the scene which ensued defies all power of language to describe. The bayonet, the butt of the rifle, the saber, the pike were in full play; and men fell, as they rarely fall in modern war, under the direct blows of their enemies. But such a struggle could not . . . be of long continuance. Outnumbered, broken, . . . our people wavered and fell back, or fought singly and unconnectedly, till they were either cut down at their posts . . . or compelled to surrender.[6]

While Stark's shirt-sleeved farmers were hacking to pieces Baume's burdened, booted-and-spurred dragoons, his scarlet regulars, and his Tories, a British supporting force was approaching. Upon receiving Baume's letter of the fourteenth, Burgoyne had ordered to his aid five hundred and fifty bluecoated "pig-tailed, leather-breeched" Brunswick Grenadiers with two fieldpieces, under command of lean, dark Lieutenant Colonel Heinrich von Breymann, between whom and Baume lay "an old picque."

Breymann had started forward slowly from his camp in

advance of the army the rainy morning of the fifteenth and had crept forward on the boggy road at a pace of half mile an hour. When he bivouacked that night, after covering only about eight miles, he dispatched a message to Baume that he was on his way, and Baume was encouraged to hold his entrenched position.

It was half past four the next afternoon before the relief column, still sodden from the rains, came to Van Schaick's Mill about six miles from the field of battle, and advanced, unaware that Baume had already been defeated.

Stark had heard of Breymann's approach. The victorious Americans were scattered, some pursuing the fugitives, others, remembering Stark's promise that the spoils should belong to the men, plundering. A party of them ran into Breymann about a mile from the mill and were driven back in a running fight that tumbled toward the battlefield. Stark's men probably would have suffered a bad turn had not Warner's troops from Manchester now arrived, fresh and full of fight, giving new spirit to the weary New Hampshiremen. An American captain later stated that "after the first action, General Stark ordered a hogshead of rum for the refreshment of the militia, but so eager were they to attack the enemy upon their being reinforced that they tarried not to taste of it, but rushed on the enemy with an ardor perhaps unparalleled."

Breymann, who stood with supreme personal courage, reported to Burgoyne:

> The troops did their duty, and I know of no one who doubts this fact. After our ammunition was all expended, and the artillery in consequence ceased firing, nothing was more natural than to suppose that the enemy would be encouraged to renew his attack. . . . In order, therefore, not to risk anything (as I was unable to return the enemy's fire, my ammunition being exhausted), I retreated on the approach of darkness, destroyed the bridge, had as many of the wounded as possible brought thither that they might not be captured, and, after a lapse of half an hour . . . pursued my march and reached Cambridge toward twelve o'clock at night. Here, after taking precautionary measures, I remained during that night, and marched thence at daybreak of the seventeenth of August to the camp.[7]

The clumsy Germans who lumbered away, panicked in the dark, had fought as manfully as Baume's force, but both had been outnumbered and outfought. American losses, according to Stark's report of the affair, were only thirty killed and forty wounded. He claimed 207 Germans found dead, a large number wounded, and 700 prisoners. Although the Germans put their losses lower, they admitted the loss of 596 men, exclusive of the losses of the British units.

In the country of the Hampshire Grants, Stark's brilliant victory over Burgoyne's professional mercenaries was celebrated with parades and ceremonies. A week later, the farmer from Lyndeboro was writing:

> We do not know how many we have killed. Our scouts daily find them dead in the woods. One of our scouts found, the beginning of this week, twenty-six of the enemy lying dead in the woods. They stank so they could not bury them. . . . The wounded Hessians die three or four in a day. They are all in Bennington Meeting House, which smells so it is enough to kill anyone to be in it.[8]

Stark, who by his flat refusal to join Schuyler, might have exposed the army to defeat, had instead won a startling victory and become a hero by accidentally being in Baume's way and making the most of his opportunities. He not only cost Burgoyne some eight hundred casualties, but he also heightened discord between the redcoats and their German comrades, discouraged the Indians, forced the conquering army to continue to subsist on salt meat and flour from Canada, and slowed its progress southward. The Continental Congress, to whom Lincoln had appealed about Stark, did not censure him; instead, in October, it made him a Continental brigadier. A month after the battle, however, he was raging over one of the losses of the day of the sixteenth. Some "sly, artful, designing" villain had entered the field while his comrades were in action and pilfered Stark's little brown mare, his doeskin saddle, and bridle. Nearly a month later he still was advertising for her, offering twenty dollars reward. And he was once again standing aloof from the Continental Army, stubbornly refusing to co-operate.

General Burgoyne, who by now had taken a position about the mouth of the Battenkill, could not understand how his mismanaged expedition had failed. In a private letter to Lord George Germain, he tried to vindicate himself to the King "and to the world." He said he had, in principle, recognized the hazard but thought the advantages to be expected from success were superior to the evils that might attend failure. He admitted that the troops he sent were those whose loss would least weaken his army and he pointed out with restrained sarcasm that "could Mr. Breymann have marched at the rate of two miles an hour any given twelve hours out of the two and thirty, success would have probably ensued; misfortune would certainly have been avoided." At least, he now was no longer blind to the abilities and loyalties of the rebels.

The great bulk of the country is undoubtedly with the Congress, in principle and in zeal; and their measures are executed with a secrecy and dispatch that are not to be equaled. Wherever the King's forces point, militia to the amount of three or four thousand assemble in twenty-four hours; they bring with them their subsistence, etc., and the alarm over, they return to their farms. The Hampshire Grants in particular, . . . abounds in the most active and most rebellious race of the continent, and hangs like a gathering storm upon my left.[9]

Although the defeat of his detachment at Bennington was a staggering blow to Burgoyne, he could comfort himself that he held a trump in reserve, Lieutenant Colonel Barry St. Leger's expedition down the Mohawk. As far as he knew, St. Leger was sweeping eastward to come in on Schuyler's flank. Surely victory would be theirs. In fact, however, St. Leger was also running into trouble.

Holding temporary rank as a brigadier, St. Leger with some four hundred British, German, and Tory troops arrived at Oswego from Montreal on the twenty-fifth of July, the day after Burgoyne moved south from Skenesborough. At Oswego he was met by a force of about a thousand Iroquois under a very remarkable Indian, Thayendanegea, called Joseph Brant, who had lived intimately with the white man's world. He had been entertained by James Boswell and painted by Romney and served as secretary to Colonel Guy Johnson, British Superintendent of Indian Affairs. St. Leger, confident of the success of his march through the fertile but thinly settled valley, had sent his baggage from Canada with Burgoyne's army and in one day after landing at Oswego was on the march.

Barring the way to the Hudson was Fort Schuyler at the Great Carrying Place, the portage between Wood Creek, emptying into Lake Oneida, and the Mohawk. It had been built during the French and Indian War and with peace had been allowed to decay. When its present commandant, towering Colonel Peter Gansevoort, and his Third New York Regiment had reoccupied it in April, it had been refurbished and named for General Schuyler.

As soon as Colonel Gansevoort heard from friendly Oneida Indians of St. Leger's approach, he evacuated the women, children, and invalids, and prepared to defend the star-shaped post with 750 men against more than double that number. His second-in-command was Lieutenant Colonel Marinus Willett, nine years older than his twenty-eight-year-old chief, but considered "quite a lad" and a "bold enterprising fellow." Willett wrote for newspapers an account of the enemy's

appearance before the fort on Sunday, the third of August—
four days after Burgoyne, far to the east, had reached the
Hudson at Fort Edward:

> . . . The enemy appeared in the edge of the woods,
> about a mile below the fort, where they took post, in order
> to invest it on that quarter and to cut off the communica-
> tion with the country. . . . They sent in a flag, who told us of
> their great power, strength, and determination, in such a
> manner as gave us reason to suppose they were not pos-
> sessed of great strength sufficient to take the fort. Our answer
> was a determination to support it.
> All day on Monday we were much annoyed by a sharp
> fire of musketry from the Indians and German riflemen,
> which, as our men were obliged to be exposed on the works,
> killed one and wounded seven. The day after, the firing
> was not so heavy, and our men under better cover, all the
> damage was, one man killed by a rifle ball. . . .
> Wednesday morning there was an unusual silence. We dis-
> covered some of the enemy marching along the edge of the
> woods downwards. About eleven o'clock three men got into
> the fort, who brought a letter from General Harkaman,
> [commander] of the Tryon County Militia, advising us that
> he was at Oriska (eight miles from the fort) with part of his
> militia, and proposed to force his way to the fort for our re-
> lief.[10]

This "Harkaman" was a middle-aged, square-built Dutchman with raven hair and dancing eyes, whose name was Nicholas Herkimer. He was the son of an immigrant named Erg-
heimer, and had acquired extensive land in the village of
Danube. There he had built a fabulous brick mansion, much
envied and admired. Before St. Leger came to the Valley,
Herkimer had issued a brief, stirring proclamation, calling
upon all able-bodied men between sixteen and sixty to be
prepared to mobilize for the defense of their homes. Now he
had assembled eight hundred volunteers at Fort Dayton and
marched to the relief of Fort Schuyler, about thirty miles up-
river.

From Oriskany Creek, Herkimer sent runners to the fort
to arrange for the firing of three guns as a signal that they
had arrived and so that the fort could co-operate with him
against the encircling enemy. As he awaited the sound of the
guns, on the morning of the sixth, his officers grew impatient
and insisted on pushing ahead. Herkimer hesitated. The officers boldly accused him of timidity and hinted that perhaps
he was a Tory like his brother, who was with St. Leger. Herkimer yielded. Behind sixty Oneida scouts, he led his six hundred militia forward in a column of twos. Behind them rocked

four hundred shrieking oxcarts of baggage and supplies, and a rear guard of two hundred followed. The column was nearly a mile long and St. Leger's scouts reported it as soon as it was under way.

Opinions of the dashing St. Leger differed. Some men called him a brutal drunkard and others a slack disciplinarian, but none of them questioned his courage. Instead of pulling back in the face of the overwhelming numbers building up to repel him, he sent four hundred Indians and a Tory detachment to ambush "old Honikol." They laid a trap at a place called Oriskany, about six miles east of the fort. Here Herkimer's road dipped through a deep, ragged defile with a corduroy road across its marshy bottom.

About ten o'clock Herkimer reached the ravine. His Oneidas failed to detect the enemy in the woods fringing the cut, and suddenly St. Leger's people were upon him, whooping and firing on his rear. The general turned back his great white horse and started toward the firing. Hardly had he turned when his van was fired on, and he and his mount fell toward the brook running in the bottom of the ravine, a bloody wound in the Dutchman's leg.

The stout-hearted militia did not panic; the officers formed the men in a circle on a knob of rising ground west of the ravine, and Herkimer ordered them to set him astride his saddle at the foot of a beech within the circle. He lit his pipe and sat puffing it "with his sword drawn, animating his men." After several hours the attackers weakened and then withdrew. Herkimer had lost between a hundred and fifty and two hundred killed and many prisoners. His force was in no condition to continue to Fort Schuyler, so his men retraced their march to Fort Dayton, bearing him in a litter.

At Fort Schuyler a sortie planned to divert attention from Herkimer was postponed by rain, but was successfully executed in the afternoon. From prisoners taken, Willett learned of the ambush of Herkimer. Two nights later, recognizing that St. Leger had cut off relief, Willett and "a good woodsman" struck out for help through the wilderness to German Flats, fifty miles east. When they arrived, they discovered that a relief force was on its way to Fort Schuyler under General Benedict Arnold, who had been hurried north to help Schuyler after St. Clair evacuated Ticonderoga. General Schuyler, at Stillwater, over the protests of his officers and insinuations of cowardice and even treachery, had resolved to drain off part of his little army of forty-five hundred to save the Mohawk Valley. Burgoyne with seven thousand victorious troops lay only twenty-four miles away, a single day's forced march, but to save the Mohawk, Schuyler took risks on the

Hudson. Only the fireater, Arnold, supported him, and joyfully accepted orders to march at once for Fort Schuyler.

Nine hundred and fifty Massachusetts Continentals eagerly followed the flamboyant general. Possibly because they were New Englanders, Arnold felt constrained, on the thirteenth of August, to publish a letter denying any intention on the part of New England to protect New York and then later reconquer and divide the state.

By the time Arnold reached Fort Dayton on the twenty-first, he had been reinforced by a hundred of the Tryon militia, no longer led by "old Honikol." Herkimer's leg had been amputated by an inexperienced surgeon who could not stop the flow of blood. On the day that Stark's men were fighting to the eastward at Bennington, the militia general, ever weakening, with the end in sight, took up his German Bible and read aloud the Thirty-eighth Psalm. "My wounds stink," wrote the Psalmist, "and are corrupt because of my foolishness." Wearily, Herkimer shut the book and closed his eyes in death.

At Fort Dayton, Arnold learned that St. Leger had some seventeen hundred effectives, but Arnold, from the beginning of his march, had had no illusions about the difficulty of relieving the fort. At German Flats he issued a ferocious proclamation threatening his enemy with "no mercy" if they did not lay down their arms within ten days. Overriding the reluctance of his officers to move before receiving reinforcements, he dashed forward, upon hearing that St. Leger was squeezing the fort tightly in his siege lines, while—so it was rumored—he devised a ruse to help disperse the enemy. Among some prisoners recently taken for planning a Tory uprising in Tryon County and condemned to death, one was John Joost Schuyler, a nephew of Herkimer. "Hon-Yost" was a half-wit, but perhaps not so crazy as his neighbors thought. When his parents came to beg for his life, Arnold agreed to a deal. Some years later, Timothy Dwight heard the story in his travels in the neighborhood and set it down:

Arnold . . . proposed to him a scheme for alarming the enemy, particularly the savages, by announcing to them that a formidable army was in full march to destroy them, and assured him of his life and estate if he would . . . faithfully execute a mission of this nature. [Hon-Yost] Schuyler, who was shrewd, resolute, versed in the language and manners of the Indians . . . and therefore perfectly qualified for this business, readily engaged in the enterprise. His father and brother were, in the meantime, kept as hostages . . . and were both to be hung without mercy if he proved unfaithful. One of the Sachems of the Six Nations, a friend of

the Americans and of Schuyler also, was let into the secret
and cheerfully embarked in the design. . . .

Colonel St. Leger had pushed the siege . . . and advanced
his works within one hundred and fifty yards of the fort.
Upon [Hon-Yost] Schuyler's arrival he told [St. Leger's In-
dians] . . . of his being taken by Arnold, his escape [from]
hanging, and . . . flight. He . . . declared . . . that a formidable army of Americans was marching with full speed to attack the British. The Americans, he observed, had no hostility toward the Indians and wished not to injure them, but
added that if the Indians continued with the British they
must unquestionably take their share of whatever calamities
might befall their allies.

The Indians being thus thoroughly alarmed, the chief,
who was in the secret, arrived, as if by mere accident, and
. . . began to insinuate to his countrymen that a bird had
brought him intelligence of great moment . . . concerning warriors in great numbers, marching with the utmost rapidity
and already far advanced. In the meantime he had dispatched
two or three young warriors in the search of intelligence.
These scouts, who had now received their cue, returned, as
they had been directed, at different times and confirmed, as
if by mere accident also, all that had been said by Schuyler
and the Sachem. The Indians, already disgusted with the
service, which they found a mere contrast to the promises
of the British commanders and their own expectations, and
sore with the loss which they had sustained in the battle
with General Herkimer, were now so completely alarmed
that they determined upon an immediate retreat.

St. Leger, who had unwisely boasted, at first, of his own
strength and his future exploits against the Americans and
spoken contemptuously of their weakness and cowardice,
who had predicted in magnificent terms the certainty of
their flight and the ease and safety with which the Indians
would reach Albany, had disgusted these people thoroughly
by failing altogether of the fulfillment of his promises. In
vain, therefore, did he exert all his address . . . to dissuade
them from their purpose. . . . They reproached him with
having violated all his former promises and pronounced him
undeserving of any further confidence. He attempted to get
them drunk, but they refused to drink. When he found all
his efforts fruitless and saw they were determined to go,
he urged them to move in the rear of his army, but they
charged him with a design to sacrifice them for his own
safety.

In a mixture of rage and despair, he broke up his encampment with such haste that he left his tents, cannon, and
stores to the besieged. The flight of his army (for it could not
be called a retreat) . . . through a deep forest . . . was . . .

not a little embarrassed and distressing.

The Sachem, who had been partner with Schuyler in the plot, accompanied the flying army. Naturally a wag . . . he engaged several of his young men to repeat, at proper intervals, the cry "they are coming." This unwelcome sound . . . quickened the march of the fugitives whenever it was heard. The soldiers threw away their packs, and the commanders took care not to be in the rear. Mortified beyond measure . . . these gentlemen began to speedily accuse each other of folly and misconduct . . . during the enterprise. Accusation begat accusation, and reproach, until they at length drew their swords upon each other. Several of the Sachems now interfered and . . . persuaded them to a reconciliation. After much fatigue . . . they finally reached the Oneida lake; and there, probably, felt themselves for the first time secure from the pursuit of their enemies.[11]

Arnold, who had vowed he would raise the siege or "be no more," forced a march twenty-two miles to the fort on the twenty-fourth, and when he found the enemy gone, threw a pursuit party after them. The pursuit died out, but not before a few persistent Americans arrived at Oneida Lake in time to see the last of the British going off in boats.

Thus storms had broken on both Burgoyne's right and left. His dream of a triumphant march through the wilderness vanished; in less than sixty days he had come from victory to the possibility of a starving army. Unless Howe drove up the Hudson to save him, he might be forced to make a terrible reverse march to Canada.

But already Howe had made it clear that no help could be expected from him. Since August 3 John Burgoyne must have guessed that his fate was sealed. That day a winded messenger had delivered a letter from Howe, who congratulated Burgoyne on the capture of Ticonderoga and then announced, "My intention is for Philadelphia, where I expect to meet Washington, but if he does go to the northward contrary to my expectations, and you can keep him at bay, be assured I shall soon be after him to relieve you. After your arrival at Albany, the movements of the enemy will guide yours. . . ." From that moment, Burgoyne had known that something strange had happened to his plan since he had left London. Obviously, Howe had no intention of co-operating with him, unless Washington moved toward him—an unlikely possibility.

Burgoyne probably consoled himself with the thought that Howe's remark that Clinton would continue in New York and act "as occurrences may direct" could mean that Clinton would come North when reinforcements arrived from

England. But the distressing fact remained that it was very likely the task of John Burgoyne to get through to Albany alone. He had no other choice—his orders had been explicit, to force his way to Albany. He thought "the peremptory tenor of my orders and the season of the year admitted no alternative." Perhaps it warmed the man, but it scarcely gratified the soldier, that the only conquest he could claim for these two months was that of Ticonderoga, unless one counted also that of the lady who now shared his headquarters. Upon this latter victory, Madame von Riedesel, who had bundled up her three tiny daughters, crossed the ocean, and valiantly followed her soldier-husband through the wilderness, commented, "It is very true that General Burgoyne liked to make himself easy and that he spent half his nights in singing and drinking and diverting himself with . . . his mistress . . . who was as fond of champagne as himself."

22

"LIKE MEN FIGHTING FOR THEIR ALL"

Saratoga

SEPTEMBER-OCTOBER 1777

ON AUGUST the nineteenth, when General Horatio Gates rode into Albany with orders to supersede General Schuyler as supreme commander of the entire Northern Department, the question of authority in the North was at last settled.

Philip Schuyler had toiled manfully there since the evacuation of Ticonderoga. Both General Gates and his country were much in his debt, though neither felt inclined to acknowledge the obligation. The Hudson Valley aristocrat, for all his despondent letters to his Commander-in-Chief, had courageously stood up to Burgoyne's menacing behemoth, and his steady, calculated retreat had been as wise as it had been valorous. He had measured his enemy correctly when he risked splitting his little army to send Arnold to the relief of Fort Schuyler. In short, Burgoyne's present dilemma was due in great measure to Schuyler's stiff determination.

But when Gates, upon reaching Albany, summoned a council of war to which he invited all the Continental officers in the Department and even the brigadier of Albany County militia, he pointedly omitted Schuyler. Gouverneur Morris of the New York Provincial Congress, a man usually without malice, commented: "The new commander-in-chief . . . may, if he please, neglect to ask or disdain to receive advice. But those who know him will, I am sure, be convinced that he needs it." However, Gates did welcome Arnold back from the Mohawk, apparently disregarding the fact that Arnold was his rival's friend. To him he assigned command of the left wing of the growing army, including the newly arrived riflemen of Daniel Morgan. And his attitude toward militia was displayed in his efforts to placate General Stark and bring him in to the main American force about the mouth of the Mohawk, facing Burgoyne at Fort Miller.

As affairs now stood, Gates thought he should move northward. Burgoyne would soon either fall back on Ticonderoga or advance; in either event, to harass his retreat, or upon favorable ground to contest his advance, Gates wanted to be closer to him. On the eighth of September, he marched about sixteen miles north to a place near Stillwater, on a high plateau above the Hudson, called Bemis Heights after the man who kept a tavern on the road below. Here, six thousand strong, he ordered his talented young Polish engineer, Colonel Thaddeus Kosciuszko, to lay out lines. Kosciuszko, who was considered "a beautiful limner" as well as a superbly trained military engineer, went to work industriously to devise a strong, secure system of defense.

Burgoyne was up against it. His mind was fixed tenaciously upon his sovereign's orders: "to force his way to Albany." But how to do it? The rebels now equaled if they did not outnumber him. Hubbardton and Bennington had cost him casualties he could not replace, while the rebels were growing angrier and stronger. The Tories he had been led to believe would flock to him had not come. Instead, his Indians had lost interest and slipped away by scores; his Germans were wandering off into the woods never to return; frantically he offered rewards not only for deserters apprehended, court-martialed and shot, but also for the scalps of any killed while being chased. To compound his trouble, his supply line already was much too long, and it was proving impossible to feed his army in enemy country. His communications were in constant danger of being severed. Yet he must go forward.

The route of march presented still another problem to the troubled invader. His destination lay on the west side of the mighty Hudson, and he was on the east. If he were to march down the east side and cross opposite Albany he would find the river hazardous there and the Americans sure to have moved down to face him. If he were to cross where he was, he reasoned that the rebel army, whose whereabouts he guessed vaguely, would stand in his path. But he could not winter where he was. He chose finally to take the western road and fight his way past the rebels, wherever they might be.

So on September 13, Burgoyne crossed the Hudson about three-quarters of a mile above the mouth of the Battenkill on a bridge of boats which he dismantled behind him. Cautiously he advanced along the road that flanked the river under continuous wooded heights. Blindly he crept forward past river farms and forests beginning to turn the scarlet and gold of autumn, feeling for his enemy. His Indian scouts were gone; none of his advance parties picked up the enemy until, on the sixteenth of October, his camp heard the unreal tap of morning drums drifting through the lightening forests. He halted to reconnoiter; next morning he moved slowly forward, and took a position four miles from that of Gates; not until one of his foraging parties, digging in an abandoned potato field, was cut up by an American patrol did he discover how near the rebels really were.

Gates felt perfectly secure in his fortifications on Bemis Heights. Here the Hudson rolled between mountainous, irregular banks; the plateau was two or three hundred feet high, covered with broken heights separated by deep ravines through which agile creeks leaped and turned. One of them, Mill Creek, ran northwesterly across the position Kosciuszko chose to defend. Another, the Great Ravine, was farther north. The whole area was thickly wooded, save for a few small farm clearings and the wagon tracks crisscrossing Bemis Heights and dipping down to the river plain and river road to the east. Beginning at the Hudson's bank, American works straddled the river road and then turned, followed the course of the river northeasterly, then turned and turned again to make three sides of a square a little over three-quarters of a mile long on each side. The rear was left open, protected somewhat by a ravine. In the middle of each line a small redoubt mounting artillery was built, and near the northwest corner of the lines a log house and barn were stockaded.

Gates himself commanded his right wing, composed of Continentals under General John Glover, General John Paterson, and Colonel John Nixon, on the high ground near the river and the narrow level plain below. Massachusetts regiments under General Ebenezer Learned and New Yorkers under Colonel James Livingston held the center. Benedict Arnold commanded the left with New Hampshire regulars, New Yorkers, Connecticut militia, Daniel Morgan's riflemen, and Lieutenant Colonel Henry Dearborn's Light Infantry.

General Burgoyne, having found his foe, prepared to attack. But, instead of advancing in force along the river road, covered by grenadiers and light infantry on the bluff, until he met resistance, he divided his forces. Along the river road, a column of Germans under Riedesel, with guns under command of General Phillips, was to strike the American right. Burgoyne himself planned to accompany four regiments led by Brigadier General Hamilton against the rebel center. The strongest force, under General Fraser, assisted by Breymann, would be aimed at Gates's left in the hope that it could push his flank and rear and drive him against the river.

Gentleman Johnny's battle plan was as blind as his advance had been. Without knowing where the enemy would stand, or whether he would come out to fight, three columns were to advance out of sight of each other until approximately abreast, communicating by signal guns and messengers in broken country, and then lunge forward. Evidently Gentleman Johnny was not yet convinced that the rebels were to be feared.

When the British army moved from its camp on the bright morning of the nineteenth of September, it was closely watched by American scouts high in the trees; for three hours it advanced, before separating and working toward its chosen positions.

Gates had resolved to stand behind his works and let the enemy shatter himself against them. To Benedict Arnold, a fighter by instinct, this seemed suicidal, for the redcoats would emerge from the forests and work their artillery and fire their volleys in open meadows. If they stormed the lines and the American troops broke, the rebels would have no rallying point. He pleaded with Gates to carry the battle to the attackers, so that the Americans could fight from cover; Gates agreed to commit Morgan's riflemen and Dearborn's Light Infantry on the left to bring on the fight, but ordered Arnold to hold his main force in reserve.

Through dense woods beyond Mill Creek, gigantic Dan Morgan's riflemen spread and poked toward a ten- or twelve-acre clearing around an abandoned cabin that constituted the farm of a man named Freeman. About a quarter to one, a strong picket in faded scarlet tumbled out of the trees and brush from the north; they were the advance elements of Burgoyne's center. And as they took open order in the weeds near Freeman's log dwelling, the rifles of Morgan's "shirtmen" under the trees on the south crackled: every officer and many men of the picket fell; the survivors stumbled back, while the fierce rebels in hunting shirts sprinted after them. Suddenly, the rebel riflemen faced Burgoyne's main body coming out of the woods.

Colonel James Wilkinson, Gates's adjutant, had been sent forward to the field to find out what was happening. Later he recalled:

> I crossed the angle of the field, leaped the fence, and just before me on a ridge discovered Lieutenant Colonel Butler with three men, all *treed*. From him I learned that they had "caught a Scotch prize," that having forced the picket they had closed with the British line, had been instantly routed, and from the suddenness of the shock and the nature of the ground, were broken and scattered in all directions. . . .
> I then turned about to regain the camp and report . . . when my ears were saluted by an uncommon noise which I approached and perceived Colonel Morgan, attended by two men only, who with a *turkey call* was collecting his dispersed troops.[1]

Regrouped, supported by New Hampshire Continentals who had hurried up to his left, and extended beyond the enemy's right, Morgan hoped to turn that flank. An obstinate struggle developed with Freeman's farm the field of contest, as first one and then another of the valiant enemies drove across the bloody clearing. As the obstinate British forced forward and then gave ground, one of them thought the equally obstinate rebels "were in general drunk, a piece of policy of their general to make them fight."

Arnold ordered up the rest of his division and, said some witnesses, himself dashed onto the field, probing for a weak spot between Fraser's column, which had taken the high ground on the American left, and Burgoyne's center, which converged on the farm.

Detractors were to quibble over Arnold's presence on the field, but whether he sent or led the troops that fought for four ghastly hours in the sulphurous smoke and fierce din of Freeman's place, General John Glover proudly declared:

> Both armies seemed determined to conquer or die. One continual blaze without any intermission till dark, when by consent of both parties it ceased. During which time we several times drove them, took the ground, passing over great numbers of their dead and wounded. Took one field-piece, but the woods and bush was so thick, and being close pushed by another party of the enemy coming up, was obliged to give up our prize. The enemy in their turn sometimes drove us. They were bold, intrepid, and fought like heroes,

and I do assure you, sirs, our men were equally bold and courageous and fought like men fighting for their all.[2]

Gates's command post was in "a small hovel" near the rear of the western side of his fortifications. When it appeared that the British were breaking toward their center, Arnold sent to him for reinforcements, but the general refused to weaken his lines by drawing off further units.

On the enemy left near the river, Generals von Riedesel and Phillips guessed that Gates would not advance toward them, so Phillips hastened through the woods more than a mile and a half toward the British center with four pieces of artillery; later in the afternoon Riedesel received orders from Burgoyne to draw off as many of his column as he did not need to guard the left and support the action at the farm. Riedesel, who was fat and forty but an active man, outstripped his own men in his dash to the front. It was these reinforcements from the British left that saved their center from complete collapse and turned the tide of battle.

Toward the end of the day, Gates had sent in Learned's brigade, but he had refused to allow Arnold to direct its movements, and it had gone astray. It blundered too far left into Fraser's outposts, banged away ineffectually, and achieved nothing.

Lieutenant William Digby of the British army never had dreamed of such "an explosion of fire" as he heard that day —". . . the heavy artillery, joining in concert like great peals of thunder, assisted by the echoes of the woods, almost deafened us with the noise." He wrote:

. . . This crash of cannon and musketry never ceased till darkness parted us, when they retired to their camp, leaving us masters of the field; but it was a dear bought victory if I can give it that name, as we lost many brave men. . . . During the night we remained in our ranks, and tho' we heard the groans of our wounded and dying at a small distance, yet could not assist them till morning, not knowing the position of the enemy, and expecting the action would be renewed at daybreak. Sleep was a stranger to us, but we were all in good spirits and ready to obey with cheerfulness any orders the general might issue before morning dawned.[3]

One of Burgoyne's Germans thought no more had been accomplished that day than to bring fame to "the house of a poor farmer . . . for it has given to this day's engagement the name of the Battle of Freeman's House." But Burgoyne, although he had lost six hundred men, twice Gates's casualties, was sanguine of ultimate victory now. To the commander of the garrison he had left at Ticonderoga, he wrote: "We have

had a smart and very honorable action, and are now encamped in front of the field, which must demonstrate our victory beyond the power of even an American newswriter to
explain away."

After a freezing night, during which neither army slept
soundly, the twentieth dawned quiet, except for a couple of
light picket skirmishes. In the dripping fog, both sides gathered up their wounded. British Lieutenant Anburey was assigned that grimmest of duties, burial detail. Fifteen, sixteen,
or twenty men were "buried in one hole," but, Anburey remembered in later years:

> I . . . observed a little more decency than some parties
> had done, who left heads, legs, and arms above ground.
> No other distinction is paid to officer or soldier than that the
> officers are put in a hole by themselves. Our army
> abounded with young officers, in the subaltern line, and in
> the course of this unpleasant duty, three of the Twentieth
> Regiment were interred together, the age of the eldest not
> exceeding seventeen.

This friendly office to the dead, though it greatly affects
the feelings, was nothing to the scene in bringing in the
wounded. . . . They had remained out all night, and from the
loss of blood and want of nourishment, were upon the point
of expiring with faintness: some of them begged they might
lay and die, others again were insensible, some upon the
least movement were put in the most horrid tortures, and all
had near a mile to be conveyed to the hospitals. . . .[4]

That morning the thick fog that rolled over the ground
completely cloaked the enemies from each other. Briefly, Burgoyne entertained the idea of renewing battle, but decided
not to attack. The engagement of the previous day had been
a series of lost opportunities on both sides, but this decision
was the greatest lost opportunity of all, for quite possibly
Burgoyne could have finished his opponent. American ammunition was nearly exhausted; the left wing failed to draw
rounds to replace what it had expended; and the camp was
confused. On Sunday, the twenty-first, however, news came
to both armies that destroyed the propitious moment forever.

Before dawn a messenger arrived in Burgoyne's camp with
a brief note from Sir Henry Clinton at New York; it was
the first communication Burgoyne had received from southward since early August, when Howe's note had come saying
that he was going away from Burgoyne toward Philadelphia
instead of up the Hudson. Sir Henry's note was dated the
twelfth of September and told Burgoyne that he would make
a "push at [Fort] Montgomery in about ten days," in an

effort to bring him about two thousand men, provided the rebels did not move on Clinton's flanks and force him to draw the attack back to New York. Those brief words were like manna: Burgoyne knew that Sir Henry had been expecting reinforcements from England and guessed they would be large when they came; he pictured Clinton closing in on Albany from the south, as he had hoped Howe would do. Perhaps by now, the twenty-first, Sir Henry already had attacked the rebel fort, some forty miles north of New York on the Hudson.

Burgoyne sent off a message urging Sir Henry to hurry, saying he considered his communications with Canada already severed, but could hold out until October 12 before being obliged to fall back on Ticonderoga to feed and supply his army. Meanwhile, he resolved to entrench and await the day that Gates began to feel the pressure of Clinton behind him. With pickax, shovel, spade, the British made lines two miles long, slightly nearer the river, but approximately on the ground they had taken.

So the armies sat deadlocked, while Burgoyne grew weaker from sickness and desertions, and his supplies and provisions dwindled, and Gates grew stronger, and materiel and food came in.

Later Burgoyne was to remember:

> . . . the armies were so near that not a night passed without firing and sometimes concerted attacks on our advanced pickets. No foraging party could be made without great detachments to cover it. It was the plan of the enemy to harass the army by constant alarms and their superiority of numbers enabled them to attempt it without fatigue to themselves. . . . I do not believe either officer or soldier ever slept during that interval without his clothes, or that any general officer or commander of a regiment passed a single night without being upon his legs occasionally at different hours and constantly an hour before daylight.[5]

Gentleman Johnny's hope was in Sir Henry Clinton. He had appealed to the commander at New York to hurry. Later he sent other messengers to say he must have succor. But his messengers did not get through. The first of them, sent off on the night of the twenty-first of September, was given a message capsuled in a silver ball he was to swallow if captured; or, at least, that was the story Sergeant Roger Lamb heard. The courier's experiences probably paralleled those of Captain Scott of the Fifty-third Regiment, another courier: keeping to the woods in the day, occasionally borrowing a horse from "a friend of government" for a night ride, bribing a farmer to carry him concealed in a canoe across a water. But finally the first messenger arrived near Fort Montgomery, according to a captain of the Connecticut line:

> . . . he fell in with a small scouting party of ours under the command of a sergeant of Webb's regiment, who with his men were dressed in British uniform which had been captured in a transport ship. Their speech and appearance being the same, and our sergeant managing with the utmost address, proposed themselves to General Clinton, who, our sergeant said, was out from the fort and not far off.

On seeing the American general [George] Clinton, he instantly discovered that he was deceived and swallowed something hastily, which being noticed, the general ordered the regimental surgeon to administer a strong emetic, which in its powerful operation occasioned his throwing up a silver ball of the size of a pistol bullet, which on being cleansed and opened was found to contain the note. He was tried the next day and the proof being full and complete was condemned and executed as a spy.[6]

Unhappiness spread in the British camp. On the twenty-fourth, Burgoyne announced the failure of St. Leger's expedition on the Mohawk. Three days later news was given out of the capture of the messenger to Clinton and another messenger was dispatched. On October 2, the story of the rebel action against Ticonderoga was confirmed. "At no time," a German soldier declared, "did the Jews await the coming of the Messiah with greater expectancy than we awaited the coming of General Clinton." But Burgoyne's savior never came.

The salt pork and flour that constituted the whole British ration began to run out. Horses died of starvation. Uniforms and footgear were worn to tatters. On October 3, when no more had been heard from Clinton, Burgoyne reduced rations by a third. And on the fourth, he called a council of war and proposed action: to leave eight hundred men to guard his supplies and with the rest of his army, about four thousand strong, to fall upon Gates's left flank and rear. The scheme was rash in the extreme. Every effort he had made to ascertain the exact American position had been thwarted by the dense woods, his reconnaissance parties still had gained only the sketchiest notion of his enemy's line; his officers protested it might take three or four days to work through the wilderness to Gates's rear, while the position Burgoyne hoped to defend with eight hundred men was certain to be rushed successfully by the Americans and his supplies and stores utterly destroyed. His main force then would be cut off from retreat and food and left to die of starvation. The officers argued fruitlessly for a retreat to the mouth of the Battenkill, across the Hudson, to await Clinton. Burgoyne agreed to modify his plan to a reconnaissance in force by a party of auxiliaries and fifteen hundred regulars, whose object he never made very clear, although he seemed determined to concentrate on a height he said lay on the American left which he would make an artillery post. If he could seize it, he felt he could turn Gates's left, but he did not know that it had been strengthened since the nineteenth. With his officers he agreed to a retreat if the American left turned out to be strong.

By now Gates's force had grown to about eleven thousand, well-fed, confident, and determined; he considered that he had all but halted the invasion of the enemy and that Burgoyne soon would make a decision. To New York's Governor George Clinton he wrote, ". . . perhaps his despair may dictate to him to risk all upon one throw: he is an Old Gamester and in his time has seen many chances."

These days, when Gates looked forward to a last struggle with his great adversary, were days of misery for Benedict Arnold: that high-strung fighter was out of a command. Gates had relieved him. Bad blood, developing between them for trivial reasons, was roiled by James Wilkinson's interference with Arnold's authority, further worsened by disputes about command on the field of September 19, and brought to eruption by Gates's failure even to mention Arnold's name in his report to Congress of the Battle of Freeman's Farm. Colonel Wilkinson, who loved to pit men in controversy much as other men pitted cocks, wrote purringly to General St. Clair, whose promotion over him Arnold could scarcely bear: "General Arnold was not out of camp during the whole action [of the nineteenth]. . . . General Gates despises a certain pompous little fellow as much as you can. . . ." Wilkinson did not bother to mention that Gates himself had not been out of the camp that day and that Arnold actually commanded the troops who brought on the action.

When Gates directed Colonel Morgan, whose troops nominally belonged to Arnold's division, to report directly to him, Arnold could stand no more. He stormed into Gates's headquarters and demanded to know why his division had not received full credit for its work of the nineteenth, why arrangements for Morgan's regiment had been tampered with. Arnold roared and Gates ridiculed and "high words and gross language ensued." Gates told Arnold he would be happy to give him a pass out of camp. Only the insistence of other officers kept Arnold from riding away to join Washington. Instead, he remained, stripped of command and excluded from headquarters. Gates gave Lincoln the right wing of his army and took over Arnold's division himself. Neither man was entirely at fault, but the trouble was deep-rooted and at the same time simple: Arnold was Schuyler's friend.

Between ten and eleven o'clock on the morning of October 7, Burgoyne's fifteen hundred, accompanied by Fraser, Phillips, Riedesel, and Burgoyne himself, with ten fieldpieces, moved out. James Wilkinson in his memoirs told of the first American notice of the movement:

On the afternoon of the 7th October, the advanced guard of the center beat to arms. . . . On reaching the guard where the beat commenced, I could obtain no other satisfaction, but that some person had reported the enemy to be advancing against our left.

I proceeded over open ground, and ascending a gentle acclivity in front of the guard, I perceived about half a mile from the line of our encampment several columns of the enemy, sixty or seventy rods from me, entering a wheat field which had not been cut and was separated from me by a small rivulet; and without my glass I could distinctly mark their every movement. After entering the field they displayed, formed the line, and sat down in double ranks with their arms between their legs. Foragers then proceeded to cut the wheat or standing straw, and I soon after observed several officers mounted on the top of a cabin, from whence with their glasses they were endeavoring to reconnoiter our left, which was concealed from their view by intervening woods.

Having satisfied myself . . . that no attack was meditated, I returned and reported to the general, who asked me what appeared to be the intentions of the enemy.

"They are foraging, and endeavoring to reconnoiter your left and I think, sir, they offer you battle."

"What is the nature of the ground, and what your opinion?"

"Their front is open, and their flanks rest on woods, under cover of which they may be attacked; their right is skirted by a lofty height. I would indulge them."

"Well, then, order on Morgan to begin the game."

I waited on the colonel, whose corps was formed in front of our center, and delivered the order. He knew the ground and inquired the position of the enemy.

They were formed across a newly cultivated field, their grenadiers [under "plain, rough" Major John Dyke Acland] with several fieldpieces on the left, bordering on a wood and a small ravine formed by the rivulet before alluded to; their light infantry [under General Simon Fraser] on the right, covered by a worm fence at the foot of the hill before mentioned, thickly covered with wood; their center composed of

British and German battalions [under youthful Major the Earl of Balcarres]. Colonel Morgan with his usual sagacity proposed to make a circuit with his corps by our left, and under cover of the wood to gain the height on the right of the enemy and from thence commence the attack, so soon as our fire should be opened against their left. . . .

This proposition was approved by the general, and it was concerted that time should be allowed the colonel to make the proposed circuit and gain his station on the enemy's right before the attack should be made on their left. Poor's brigade was ordered for this service, and the attack was commenced in due season on the flank and front of the British grenadiers, by the New Hampshire and New York troops. True to his purpose, Morgan at this critical moment poured down like a torrent from the hill and attacked the right of the enemy in front and flank. Dearborn, at the moment when the enemy's light infantry were attempting to change front, pressed forward with ardor and delivered a close fire, then leaped the fence, shouted, charged, and gallantly forced them to retire in disorder; yet, headed by that intrepid soldier, the Earl of Balcarres, they were immediately rallied, and reformed behind a fence in rear of their first position. . . .[7]

Colonel John Brooks, of Massachusetts, recalled that Arnold was among several officers dining with Gates at headquarters that afternoon:

I was among the company and well remember that one of the dishes was an ox's heart. While at table, we heard a firing from the advanced picket. The armies were about two miles from each other. The firing increasing, we all rose from the table; and General Arnold, addressing General Gates, said, "Shall I go out and see what is the matter?"

General Gates made no reply, but upon being pressed, said, "I am afraid to trust you, Arnold." To which Arnold answered, "Pray let me go. I will be careful, and if our advance does not need support, I will promise not to commit you."

Gates then told him he might go and see what the firing meant.[8]

Arnold flung himself upon a borrowed "Spanish horse" and galloped to the front. Samuel Woodruff of Windsor, Connecticut, found himself at the general's side: "He behaved, as I then thought, more like a madman than a cool and discreet officer." The Earl of Balcarres was unable to hold his force behind the second fence in the face of Dearborn's fierce pressure, and his troops fell back in disorder toward the shelter of their lines. General Fraser, prominent on a big iron-gray horse as Arnold came up, was shifting to form a second line to cover their retreat. Arnold shouted to Morgan that

the Scot was a fair target for a sharpshooter and one of them
—tradition finally named Tim Murphy—brought him down
with a mortal wound. Burgoyne, who had exposed himself
valiantly during the hot fighting, pulled his battered force
back into its works.

There was no stopping Arnold now, although Gates had
sent an aide, Major John Armstrong, to bring him back. Arnold gathered up Paterson's and Glover's brigades and crashed
against the enemy center, driving through the abatis, but the
works were too strong, and he was pushed back. Suddenly he
sighted Learned's brigade on the left, marching toward the
enemy's extreme right. He charged across the line of fire (Wilkinson called it "a mad prank") and took command of
Learned's men and swept away a force of irregulars holding
two stockaded cabins between Balcarres and German Colonel von Breymann's redoubt on Burgoyne's extreme right.
Morgan's riflemen and two other regiments had made a circuit of the enemy right; Arnold snatched them up with Colonel Brooks's regiment and pointed his sword toward Breymann's redoubt. Breymann took a mortal wound, and his men
abandoned the position, but Arnold, charging through the
sally port, was hit in the same leg that had been wounded at
Quebec. As he was carried off on a litter through the thick
dusk of the field, the fighting began to die down. The British
lines were exposed in right and rear by the capture of Breymann's redoubt. But the American troops were tired and disordered, darkness was coming in with the swiftness of an
autumn night, and the advantage was not pressed.

Burgoyne's loss had been appalling: about six hundred
killed, wounded, and missing of the fifteen hundred he had
led into action. The American loss was only some hundred
and fifty. As usual, the British suffered heavily in officers,
among them General Simon Fraser. Petite, blue-eyed, bubbling Madame von Riedesel had expected him with other officers for dinner that day. In her graceful, human memoirs
she wrote:

> About three o'clock in the afternoon . . . they brought in
> to me upon a litter poor General Fraser. . . . Our dining
> table which was already spread was taken away and in its
> place they fixed up a bed for the general. . . .
> The general said to the surgeon, "Do not conceal anything
> from me. Must I die?"
> The ball had gone through his bowels. . . . Unfortunately,
> however, the general had eaten a hearty breakfast, by reason
> of which the intestines were distended and the ball, so the
> surgeon said, had not gone . . . between the intestines but
> through them. I heard him often amidst his groans exclaim,

"Oh, fatal ambition! Poor General Burgoyne! My poor wife!"

Prayers were read to him. He then sent a message to General Burgoyne begging that he would have him buried the following day at six o'clock in the evening on the top of a hill which was a sort of redoubt.[9]

Fraser died the next morning at eight o'clock.

Desultory cannonading and skirmishing between outposts filled the day. At sundown on a calm and beautiful evening, Fraser was buried, while American cannoneers, ignorant of the purpose of the gathering on the enemy lines, fired steadily on the party. After dark, leaving many tents standing and fires kindled to deceive Gates, Burgoyne began a full retreat.

In retreat, Burgoyne was as slow as in advance. In a night and a day his dismal troops moved only six or seven miles, burdened with the now useless guns to which the general clung with an almost mad perversity and with the baggage carts and paced by the slow crawl upstream of batteaux carrying provisions. After a miserable night, during which Burgoyne himself rested in Philip Schuyler's house, Baroness von Riedesel prepared to move:

On the tenth at seven o'clock in the morning, I drank some tea . . . and we now hoped from one moment to another that at last we would again get under way. General Burgoyne in order to cover our retreat caused the beautiful houses and mills . . . belonging to General Schuyler to be burned. . . . Thereupon we set out . . . but only as far as another place not far from where we had started. The greatest misery and the utmost disorder prevailed in the army. The commissaries had forgotten to distribute provisions. . . . There were cattle enough but not one had been killed. More than thirty officers came to me who could endure hunger no longer. I had coffee and tea made . . . and divided among them all the provisions with which my carriage was constantly filled, for we had a cook who, although an arrant knave, was fruitful in all expedients, and often in the night crossed small rivers . . . to steal from the country people sheep, poultry, and pigs. He would then charge us a high price for them, a circumstance, however, that we only learned a long time afterward. . . .

The whole army clamored for a retreat and my husband promised to make it possible, provided only that no time was lost. But General Burgoyne, to whom an order had been promised if he brought about a junction with the army of General Howe, could not determine upon this course and lost everything by his loitering. About two o'clock in the afternoon, the firing of cannon and small arms was again heard, and all was alarm and confusion.[10]

The firing the baroness heard on the afternoon of the tenth of October was the first death rattle of Burgoyne's ambitions. Even before the action of the seventh, Gates had begun posting detachments of militia in Burgoyne's rear. Stark had captured Burgoyne's guards at Fort Edward and thrown up an entrenched camp north of the fort to hold the road from there to Fort George. Brigadier General John Fellows with thirteen hundred Massachusetts militia was entrenched at Saratoga. Upon Burgoyne's advance, Fellows led his troops splashing across a ford of the Hudson to a high bluff on the opposite shore. Meanwhile, Burgoyne had sent a corps north some twelve miles toward Fort Edward, there to bridge the river and prepare for the army's passage. To cover them, he entrenched in a strong position north of the Fishkill. And after a slow start, Gates's army appeared in pursuit on the afternoon of the tenth, and to the alarm of the baroness and the army, fired on the work parties busily strengthening Burgoyne's position.

The next day, Gates, basing his plan upon inaccurate intelligence, almost committed his army to an assault on Burgoyne, but he was saved in time by the lifting of the morning fog that revealed in full the strength of the enemy. The day was thick with cannonading and petty firing, as the Americans steadily threw a net around their quarry.

Madame von Riedesel took refuge in a house behind Burgoyne's lines, as soon as Gates's army appeared on the tenth.

On the following morning the cannonade again began, but from a different side. I advised all to go out of the cellar for a little while, during which time I would have it cleaned, as otherwise we would all be sick. They followed my suggestion, and I at once set many hands to work, which was in the highest degree necessary; for the women and children being afraid to venture forth had soiled the whole cellar. . . .

I had just given the cellars a good sweeping and had fumigated them by sprinkling vinegar on burning coals and each one had found his place prepared for him, when a fresh and terrible cannonade threw us all once more into alarm. Many persons, who had no right to come in, threw themselves against the door. My children were already under the cellar steps and we would all have been crushed if God had not given me strength to place myself before the door and with extended arms prevent all from coming in. . . .

Eleven cannon balls went through the house and we could plainly hear them rolling over our heads. . . .[11]

The baroness, spirited, attractive, and young, spent six dreadful days in her shelter, which the refugees managed to divide into chambers by hanging curtains. She nursed the wounded, comforted the dying, cheered other anxious wives, and cared for her own children.

[Finally she wrote] they spoke of capitulating, as by temporizing for so long . . . our retreat had been cut off. A cessation of hostilities took place, and my husband, who was thoroughly worn out, was able for the first time in a long while to lie down upon a bed.[12]

On the morning of the fourteenth of October, Major Kingston, Burgoyne's adjutant general, by prearrangement with Gates in an exchange of notes, was met between the lines by Colonel Wilkinson and conducted blindfolded to Gates's headquarters. It was the custom of war for the vanquished to propose terms of honor on which he would surrender. These the victor might modify or reject. To Kingston's amazement, no sooner had he handed Gates a letter from Burgoyne asking for a cessation of arms long enough to enable Burgoyne to state his terms, than Gates reached into his pocket, pulled out, and gave him the terms to which he insisted the British must consent. This unusual behavior gave Burgoyne the opportunity of offering counterterms equally as impossible, hoping for a compromise. Gates, to the consternation of his own officers and to the astonishment of the enemy, accepted Burgoyne's terms almost without modification.

Burgoyne particularly prided himself upon the agreement that the capitulation be called a "convention" and provide that his troops should march to Boston and embark for England, on the condition they would not serve again in America during the war. The alacrity with which Gates accepted the strange terms aroused Burgoyne's suspicions that Gates had heard of the approach of Clinton. He tried then to drag out negotiations and even considered breaking the convention, but Gates pushed him for his signature.

On the seventeenth, the American army was drawn up in two lines, flags flying and fifes and drums shrilling "Yankee Doodle," while the enemy entered the meadow north of the Fishkill, reeking with the stench of dead British horses, to lay down their arms. Lieutenant Digby recalled:

About 10 o'clock, we marched out, according to treaty, with drums beating and the honors of war, but the drums seemed to have lost their former inspiring sounds, and though we beat the Grenadiers March, which not long before was so animating, yet then it seemed by its last feeble effort, as if almost ashamed to be heard on such an occasion.

As to my own feelings, I cannot express them. . . . I never shall forget the appearance of their troops on our marching past them; a dead silence universally reigned through their numerous columns, and even then, they seemed struck with our situation and dare scarce lift up their eyes to view British troops in such a situation. I must say their decent behavior during the time (to us so greatly fallen) merited the utmost approbation and praise.[13]

Wilkinson told how he had personally escorted Burgoyne:

Early on the morning of the seventeenth, I visited General Burgoyne in his camp, and accompanied him to the ground, where his army was to lay down their arms, from whence we rode to the bank of the Hudson's river, which he surveyed with attention, and asked me whether it was not fordable.

"Certainly, sir; but do you observe the people on the opposite shore?"

"Yes," replied he, "I have seen them too long."

He then proposed to be introduced to General Gates, and we crossed the Fishkill, and proceeded to his headquarters, General Burgoyne in front, with his adjutant general Kingston, and his aides-de-camp, Captain Lord Petersham, and Lieutenant Wilford, behind him. Then followed Major General Phillips, the Baron Riedesel, and the other general officers, and their suites, according to rank.

General Gates, advised of Burgoyne's approach, met him at the head of his camp, Burgoyne in a rich royal uniform, and Gates in a plain blue frock. When they had approached nearly within sword's length, they reined up, and halted. I then named the gentleman, and General Burgoyne, raising his hat most gracefully, said, "The fortune of war, General Gates, has made me your prisoner," to which the conqueror, returning a courtly salute, promptly replied, "I shall always be ready to bear testimony, that it has not been through any fault of your excellency." Major General Phillips then advanced, and he and General Gates saluted, and shook hands with the familiarity of old acquaintances. The Baron Riedesel and the other officers were introduced in their turn.[14]

As Burgoyne's files passed toward the meadow, he and Gates stepped out and stood side by side in view of the armies: big, resplendent Burgoyne and gray-haired, bespectacled Gates in a plain blue coat. The two turned and faced each other. Without a word, Burgoyne drew his sword and handed it to Gates, who received it with a bow and returned it to its owner. They turned and re-entered the tent.

After this formality, a newspaper reported a more jovial atmosphere within the tent:

General Gates invited General Burgoyne and the other principal officers to dine with him. The table was only two planks laid across two empty beef barrels. There were only four plates for the whole company. There was no cloth, and the dinner consisted of a ham, a goose, some beef, and some boiled mutton. The liquor was New England rum, mixed with water, without sugar; and only two glasses, which were for the two Commanders-in-Chief; the rest of the company drank out of basins. The officer remarks, "The men that can live thus, may be brought to beat all the world."

After dinner, General Gates called upon General Burgoyne for his toast, which embarrassed General Burgoyne a good deal; at length, he gave *General Washington*; General Gates, in return, gave *the King*.[15]

Soon the British army set out for Boston.

Clinton had failed Burgoyne, but not by far. Sir Henry had waited until the third of October to make the promised diversion up the Hudson. Although he had received one of Burgoyne's messengers two days later, he had first taken Forts Montgomery and Clinton before sending Burgoyne a note: "*Nous y voici* and nothing now between us but Gates; I sincerely hope this little success of ours may facilitate your operations." But that messenger, too, had been taken by the Americans and forced to vomit up the silver capsule containing the message. When another of Burgoyne's calls for help got through, it was too late.

It was news of Clinton's victories on the Hudson and the fear that he would drive through to Albany that influenced Gates to accept Burgoyne's terms, and prompted Burgoyne to procrastinate in making final surrender. Clinton had garrisoned the forts, sent Vaughn to burn Esopus, and returned to New York. His contribution to his country's welfare in helping Burgoyne get easy terms might have become important, however, were it not for a well-founded suspicion on the part of the rebels that the British might attempt to violate those terms, so that Burgoyne's troops were not returned home during the war, but moved from one American prison cantonment to another.

For the Americans the victory was stupendous. Not only had they taken seven generals and over three hundred more officers, and over five thousand others of all ranks, and great quantities of materiel. But also, coming close after Washington's defeats at Brandywine and Germantown, the defeat of Burgoyne quickly restored wavering American confidence.

Ticonderoga and Crown Point were evacuated by the enemy.
Clinton relinquished his hold on the Highlands and returned
to New York. Rhode Island and Philadelphia were the only
other places where the redcoats remained. The most momentous consequence of the Saratoga victory, however, was its
decisive influence in bringing France openly to the aid of the
United States.

On a more intimate, human level, Hannah Winthrop at
Cambridge wrote one November day to Mercy Warren, her
old friend and steady correspondent, about Gentleman Johnny
and his army:

Last Thursday, which was a very stormy day, a large
number of British troops came softly through the town via
Watertown to Prospect Hill. On Friday we heard the Hessians
were to make a procession in the same route. We thought we
should have nothing to do with them, but view them as they
passed. To be sure, the sight was truly astonishing. I never
had the least idea that the Creation produced such a sordid set
of creatures in human figure—poor, dirty, emaciated men,
great numbers of women, who seemed to be the beasts of burden, having a bushel basket on their back, by which they
were bent double; the contents seemed to be pots and kettles,
various sorts of furniture, children peeping through gridirons
and other utensils, some very young infants who were born
on the road, the women bare feet, clothed in dirty rags; such
effluvia filled the air while they were passing, had not they
been smoking all the time, I should have been apprehensive of
being contaminated by them.

After a noble looking advanced guard, General J[ohnny]
B[urgoyne] headed this terrible group on horseback. The
other G[enerals] also, clothed in blue cloaks. Hessians, Anspachers, Brunswickers, etc., etc., etc., followed on. The Hessian G[eneral] gave us a polite bow as they passed. Not so
the British. Their baggage wagons [were] drawn by poor, half-
starved horses. But to bring up the rear, another fine, noble-
looking guard of American, brawny, victorious yeomanry, who
assisted in bringing these sons of slavery to terms; some of
our wagons drawn by fat oxen, driven by joyous-looking Yankees closed the calvacade.

The generals and other officers went to Bradishs, where they
quarter at present. The privates trudged through thick and thin
to the hills, where we thought they were to be confined, but
what was our surprise when in the morning we beheld an
inundation of those disagreeable objects filling our streets!
How mortifying is it? They in a manner demanding our
houses and colleges for their genteel accommodation. Did the
brave G[eneral] Gates ever mean this? Did our legislature

ever intend the military should prevail above the civil? Is there not a degree of unkindness in loading poor Cambridge, almost ruined before this great army seem[ed] to be let loose upon us, and what will be the consequence time will discover.

Some polite ones say, we ought not to look on them as prisoners. They are persons of distinguished rank. Perhaps, too, we must not view them in the light of enemies. I fear this distinction will be soon lost. Surprising that our g[eneral] or any of our c[olonels] should insist on the first university in America being disbanded for their more genteel accommodation, and we poor, oppressed people seek an asylum in the woods against a piercing winter.

. . . G[eneral] B[urgoyne] dined a Saturday in Boston with G[eneral] H[eath]. He rode through the town, properly attended down Court Street and through the Main Street, and on his return walked on foot to Charlestown Ferry, followed by a great number of spectators as ever attended a pope and generously observed to an officer with him the decent and modest behavior of the inhabitants as he passed, saying if he had been conducting prisoners through the city of London, not all the Guards of Majesty could have prevented insults. He likewise acknowledges Lincoln and Arnold to be great generals.

It is said we shall have not less than seven thousand persons to feed in Cambridge and its environs, more than its inhabitants. Two hundred and fifty cord of wood will not serve them a week. Think then how we must be distressed. Wood is risen to £5.10 pr. cord, and but little to be purchased. I never thought I could lie down to sleep surrounded by these enemies. But we strangely become enured to those things which appear difficult when distant.[16]

23

"FIRE CAKE AND WATER, SIR"

Valley Forge and the Conway Cabal

WINTER 1777-1778

THE DEFEAT of the enemy in the North found Washington's main army still near Philadelphia. For a month after Germantown he shifted his encampment from place to place in the vicinity of Skippack Creek, roughly twenty miles from Philadelphia. The weather was turning cold, and much of the General's time was devoted to pressing for blankets, shoes, and clothing; he instructed his procurers to buy if possible—if not, to take.

The dreary task of outfitting and feeding his army in lean country was brightened momentarily by news, late on October 14, of Gates's victory over Burgoyne at Bemis Heights, followed three days later by a dispatch from Putnam informing the Commander-in-Chief that Burgoyne had surrendered his army. The "important and glorious" triumph, as Washington called it, was celebrated in camp by a thirteen-cannon salute, a *feu-de-joie* by the army drawn up in two lines, and short discourses by the chaplains.

Next day came word that Howe had withdrawn his forces from Germantown into Philadelphia. Although this maneuver would enable him to send forces against the Delaware River defenses, it also promised his settling down to winter quarters in the snug Quaker City. Washington promptly moved in closer, and soon was settled around White Marsh, about twelve miles north-northwest of Philadelphia.

A foray by Howe, leading to a small skirmish at White Marsh, seemed to put a close to his campaign for 1777.

It was getting cold. Snow had fallen, though it did not stay. It was time to plan for winter for the Continentals. The distance that Washington cantoned from Philadelphia would govern the extent of the area open to the British, and sharp argument arose over the selection of winter quarters. When the officers could not agree, Washington chose the place.

On the eleventh of December, the army broke up from White Marsh to move west of the Schuylkill. In the Connecticut ranks was a man with the droll name of Albigence Waldo, surgeon, wit, amateur musician and artist, orator and faithful diarist. Dr. Waldo was twenty-seven; his health was poor, but he had served in New England the first year of the war and around Peekskill with the First Connecticut Infantry until it was ordered to Pennsylvania in September. Though sickly, he complained only to his diary:

December 12. A bridge of wagons made across the Schuylkill last night, consisting of thirty-six wagons with a bridge of rails between each. Some skirmishing over the river. Militia and dragoons brought into camp several prisoners. Sun set. We were ordered to march over the river. It snows. I'm sick. Eat nothing. No whisky. No forage. Lord, Lord, Lord. The Army were till sunrise crossing the river, some at the wagon bridge and some at the raft bridge below. Cold and uncomfortable.[1]

Beyond the river three miles, the army halted and pitched its ragged tents at a place locally known as "the Gulph" on Gulf Creek, "on account of a remarkable chasm in the hills." At the Gulph, Private Joseph Martin said, "we encamped some time and here we had liked to encamp forever, for starvation here *rioted* in its glory." Dr. Waldo commented: "this Gulph seems well adapted by its situation to keep us from the pleasures and enjoyments of this world, or being conversant with anybody in it. It is an excellent place to raise the ideas of a philosopher beyond the glutted thoughts and reflections of an epicurean."

Waldo had difficulty, however, raising his own thoughts beyond those of an epicurean:

I am sick, discontented, and out of humor. Poor food. Hard lodging. Cold weather. Fatigue. Nasty clothes. Nasty cookery. Vomit half my time. Smoked out of my senses. The Devils in it, I can't endure it. Why are we sent here to starve and freeze? What sweet felicities have I left at home, a charming wife, pretty children, good beds, good food, good cookery. . . . Here all confusion, smoke and cold, hunger and filthiness. A pox on my bad luck.

There comes a bowl of beef soup, full of burnt leaves and dirt, sickish enough to make a Hector spew. Away with it, boys. I'll live like the chameleon upon air.[2]

But Dr. Waldo ate persimmons, which acted as a purgative, and soon was feeling better in body and spirit. Private Joseph Martin also was being sustained at the Gulph by a soldier's philosophy:

While we lay here, there was a Continental Thanksgiving ordered by Congress, and, as the Army had all the cause in the world to be particularly thankful, if not for being well off, at least that it was no worse, we were ordered to participate in it. We had nothing to eat for two or three days previous except what the trees of the fields and forests afforded us. But we must now have what Congress said: a sumptuous Thanksgiving to close the year of high living we had now nearly seen brought to a close.

Well, to add something extraordinary to our present stock of provisions, our country, ever mindful of its suffering army, opened her sympathizing heart so wide upon this occasion as to give us something to make the world stare. . . . You cannot guess, be you as much of a Yankee as you will. I will tell you: it gave each and every man *half a gill of rice* and a *tablespoon full of vinegar!*

After we had made sure of this extraordinary superabundant donation, we were ordered out to attend a meeting and hear a sermon delivered upon the happy ocasion. We accordingly went, for we could not help it.

I heard a sermon, a "Thanksgiving" sermon, what sort of one I do not know now, nor did I at the time I heard it. . . . I remembered the text, like an attentive lad at church. . . . "And the soldiers said unto him. And what shall we do? And he said unto them, Do violence to no man, nor accuse anyone falsely." The preacher ought to have added the remainder of the sentence to have made it complete, "And be content with your wages." But that would not do; it would be too apropos. However, he heard it as soon as the service was over; it was shouted from a hundred tongues. . . .[3]

At the Gulph, on December the seventeenth, Washington issued a General Order, in which, after thanking his troops for "the fortitude and patience with which they have sustained the fatigues of the campaign," he said:

The General ardently wishes it were now in his power to conduct the troops into the best winter quarters. But where are these to be found? Should we retire to the interior parts of the state, we should find them crowded with virtuous citizens, who, sacrificing their all have left Philadelphia and fled thither for protection. To their distresses humanity forbids us to add. That is not all; we should leave a vast extent of fertile country to be despoiled and ravaged by the enemy from which they would draw vast supplies and where many of our firm friends would be exposed to all the miseries of the most insulting and wanton depredation. A train of evils might be enumerated but these will suffice.

These considerations make it indispensably necessary for the army to take such a position as will enable it most effectually to prevent distress and to give the most extensive security, and in that position we must make ourselves the best shelter in our power. With activity and diligence huts may be erected that will be warm and dry. In these the troops will be compact, more secure against surprises than if in a divided state and at hand to protect the country. These cogent reasons have determined the General to take post in the neighborhood of this camp. And influenced by them, he persuades himself that the officers and soldiers with one heart and one mind will resolve to surmount every difficulty with a fortitude and patience becoming their profession and the sacred cause in which they are engaged. He himself will share in the hardship and partake of every inconvenience.[4]

To Dr. Waldo, Private Martin, and their desolate companions, these words—"take post in the neighborhood of this camp"—must have sounded bleak and unpromising! The whole area had been stripped of food and supplies by the enemy in September. All that the chosen site offered was timberland to furnish wood for huts and a natural defensive area so strong that any enemy could be defied, unless he was so powerful he could command every road leading to it and literally could starve it out.

The place was called Valley Forge, and lay a few miles northwest of the Gulph. The village was insignificant, a scattering of a few houses at the junction of Valley Creek and the Schuylkill, and the ruins of a forge the enemy had destroyed in September. The campsite was a densely wooded slope about two miles long, rising from the curving bank of the river to a ridge, which terminated in an eminence called Mount Joy; beyond Mount Joy lay Valley Creek, providing a natural protection for the right flank. The long, concave sweep of the river covered the rear and left. Here, on the windswept, gray hillside, on December 18, the weary, hungry men pitched camp.

Fitful, green-wood fires, tattered shreds of blanket, and worn, drafty tents did little to dispel the cold that swept the barren camp, while the axemen brought in logs to be made into cabins. Dr. Waldo was no more pleased with his lot at Valley Forge than he had been at the Gulph:

December 21. Preparations made for huts. Provisions scarce. . . . Sent a letter to my wife. Heartily wish myself at home. My skin and eyes are almost spoiled with continual smoke. A general cry through the camp this evening among the soldiers, "No meat! No meat!" The distant vales echoed back the melancholy sound, "No meat! No meat!" . . .

"What have you for your dinners, boys?"

"Nothing but fire cake and water, sir."

At night, "Gentlemen, the supper is ready."

"What is your supper, lads?"

"Fire cake and water, sir."

Very poor beef has been drawn in our camp the greater part of this season. A butcher, bringing a quarter of this kind of beef into camp one day, had white buttons on the knees of his breeches. A soldier cries out, "There, there, Tom, is some more of your fat beef. By my soul, I can see the butcher's breeches buttons through it."

December 22. Lay excessive cold and uncomfortable last night. My eyes are started out from their orbits like a rabbit's eyes, occasioned by a great cold and smoke.

"What have you got for breakfast, lads?"

"Fire cake and water, sir."

The Lord send that our Commissary of Purchases may live on fire cake and water till their glutted guts are turned to pasteboard.[5]

And, still, as in every army, there were enduring souls whose love of beauty led them to cling, however tenuously, to a touch of home and a richer time. One evening Waldo heard from the next tent "an excellent player on the violin in that soft kind of music which is so finely adapted to stir up the tender passions." Soggy fire-cake, that bread baked on a fire without an oven, carrion beef, and smoky fire—all were forgotten; the music called up in Albigence Waldo "all the endearing expressions, the tender sentiments, the sympathetic friendship that has given so much satisfaction and sensible pleasure to me from the first time I gained the heart and affections of the tenderest of the fair. . . . I wished to have the music cease and yet dreaded its ceasing lest I should lose sight of these dear ideas which gave me pain and pleasure at the same instant."

Christmas Day was but another day. Washington spent it in preparing never-to-be-used "Orders for a Move That Was Intended Against Philadelphia by Way of Surprise." Dr. Waldo also kept himself busy:

December 25, Christmas. We are still in tents when we ought to be in huts. The poor sick suffer much in tents this cold weather. But we now treat them differently from what they used to be at home under the inspection of old women and Dr. Bolus Linctus. We give them mutton and grog and a capital medicine once in a while to start the disease from its foundation at once. We avoid Piddling Pills, Powders, Bolus's Linctus's Cordials and all such insignificant matters whose powers are only rendered important by causing the patient to vomit up his money instead of his disease. But very few of the sick men die.[6]

In Lancaster, Pennsylvania, apothecary Christopher Marshall, voluntary exile from Philadelphia, also kept a journal. Like many civilians, he had seen or heard enough about the mercenary self-interest of his fellow citizens, the activities of the enemy, and Washington's army to plunge him into despair. He was almost ludicrously misinformed about the ragged troops at Valley Forge, but there was an unhappy content of truth in much of what he had heard about his fellow citizens. On the twenty-eighth of December, while Dr. Waldo recorded laconically in his diary only this, "Building our huts," Mr. Marshall wrote bitterly in his:

Our affairs wear a very gloomy aspect. Great part of our army gone into winter quarters, . . . wanting breeches, shoes, stockings, [and] blankets, and . . . in want of flour, yet being in the land of plenty, our farmers having their barns and barracks full of grain, hundreds of barrels of flour lying on the banks of the Susquehannah perishing for want of care in securing it from the weather and from the danger of being carried away if a freshet should happen in the river; fifty wagon loads of cloths and ready-made clothes for the soldiery in the Clothier General's store in Lancaster . . . our enemies reveling in balls, attended with every degree of luxury and excess in the City, rioting and wantoning, using our houses, utensils, and furniture; all this [and] a numberless number of other abuses we endure from that handful of banditti, to the amount of six or seven thousand men, headed by that monster of rapine, General Howe. Add to this their frequent excursions round about for twenty miles together, destroying and burning what they please, pillaging, plundering men and women, stealing boys above ten years old, deflowering virgins, driving into the City for their use droves of cattle, sheep, [and] hogs; poultry, butter, meal, meat, cider, furniture and clothing of all kinds, loaded upon our horses.

All this is done in the view of our generals and our army who are careless of us, but carefully consulting where they shall go to spend the winter in jollity, gaming, and carousing. . . . O, Americans, where is now your virtue? O, Washington, where is your courage?[7]

Few thinking soldiers were unaware of the rising tide of impatience with the army and its Commander-in-Chief. But most of them also knew something closer to the truth and shared the opinion of Dr. Waldo:

December 26 . . . The enemy have been some days [on] the west [of the] Schuylkill, from opposite the city to Derby. Their intentions not yet known. The city is at present pretty clear of them. Why don't his Excellency rush in and retake the city . . .? Because he knows better than to leave his post and be catched like a d———d fool cooped up in the city. He has always acted wisely hitherto. His conduct when closely scrutinized is uncensurable. Were his inferior generals as skillful as himself, we should have the grandest choir of officers ever God made.

Many country gentlemen in the interior parts of the states who get wrong information of the affairs and state of our camp are very much surprised at General Washington's delay to drive off the enemy, being falsely informed that his army consists of double the number of the enemy's. Such wrong information serves not to keep up the spirit of the people, as they must be by-and-by undeceived to their no small disappointment. It brings blame on his Excellency, who is deserving of the greatest encomiums. It brings disgrace on the Continental troops who have never evidenced the least backwardness in doing their duty, but on the contrary have cheerfully endured a long and very fatiguing campaign. . . . Impartial truth in future history will clear up these points and reflect lasting honor on the wisdom and prudence of General Washington. . . .[8]

Washington himself, however, could not be so sure that winter of the final judgment of history. Toward him, during the fall, a tide of cynicism had taken rise, mounting alarmingly after Gates's smashing triumph at Saratoga. The effulgence of Gates's victory blinded the common eye to the insurmountable handicaps that hamstrung the Commander-in-Chief. The manifoldness of his daily tasks, so much more complex than those of any field commander, was forgotten when his failure was compared to Gates's success. Even John Adams, who in 1775, had been first to support Washington for Commander-in-Chief, had written his wife upon the occasion of Burgoyne's defeat:

Congress will appoint a thanksgiving, and one cause of it ought to be that the glory of turning the tide of arms is not immediately due to the Commander-in-Chief nor to the southern troops. If it had been, idolatry and adulation would have been unbounded, so excessive as to endanger our liberties. . . . Now we can allow a certain citizen to be wise, virtuous, and good, without thinking him a deity or a savior.[9]

Adams' principal worry was that deification of the General might lead to a military dictatorship; although he questioned Washington's military actions, he conceded that perhaps the General "is right." No such charity softened the animus of other critics after Washington's failures at Brandywine and Germantown; many of them charged his failures to plain inability, lost opportunities, or an indecision that led him to harken to counsel from advisors even less competent than he. Thomas Mifflin particularly accused Nathanael Greene and Henry Knox of excessive influence at headquarters. Early in October, James Lovell, one of Washington's most consistent enemies, had predicted to Horatio Gates that "by the winter the . . . army will be divided into Greenites and Mifflineans, if things do not take a great turn from their present situation." Things did not turn, because Mifflin continued to gabble freely about Washington's favorites, until he had built a wall between himself and the Commander-in-Chief, as well as between himself and Greene.

Not only enemies but also admirers, such as Henry Laurens and fiercely loyal Anthony Wayne, made similar accusations. More vicious critics, such as Jonathan D. Sergeant, Attorney General of Pennsylvania, exclaimed:

Thousands of lives and millions of property are yearly sacrificed to the insufficiency of our Commander-in-Chief. Two battles he has lost for us by two such blunders as might have disgraced a soldier of three months' standing, and yet we are so attached to this man that I fear we shall rather sink with him than throw him off our shoulders.[10]

Lovel agreed to the extent that he wrote Gates, "This army will be totally lost unless you come down and collect the virtuous band who wish to fight under your banner and with their aid save the Southern hemisphere."

For all anyone about Washington knew, until the evening of the eighth of November at White Marsh, he never suspected the new hostility of former admirers and friends, or that a number of officers and politicians were even hinting about replacing him. That night a courier arrived with a letter from conscientious Lord Stirling, concerning a number of small matters, but closing with the remark: "The enclosed was communicated by Colonel [James] Wilkinson to Major McWilliams; such duplicity of conduct I shall always think it my duty to detect." The enclosure read: "In a letter from General Conway to General Gates, he says, 'Heaven has been determined to save your country; or a weak General and bad counsellors would have ruined it.' "

It was not the first time that the General had tangled with noisome Thomas Conway. Washington first had met the man at Morristown in May, when he had arrived at headquarters, lately from France, with a letter from Silas Deane promising him a high commission. Though Irish-born, he had been educated in France and had served for some years in the French Army. Washington at first had been impressed by him as a "man of candor," and wrote a pleasant note of introduction for him to the President of Congress. When he had returned from Philadelphia a brigadier and taken a brigade in Sullivan's division, he had acquitted himself well enough to win general admiration. Sullivan thought him far exceeding in military knowledge "any officer we have." But when the Congress, in September, had promoted Baron de Kalb, Conway had written arrogantly demanding a major-generalship. Visiting York, where Congress sat, he spread generous accounts of his accomplishments and threw out sharp hints that he would resign if he were not upgraded. His champions included disgruntled Thomas Mifflin and mercuric Surgeon General Dr. Benjamin Rush, who cried to John Adams, "For God's sake, do not suffer him to resign!" He possessed, Rush thought, all of Charles Lee's amazing knowledge and none of Lee's oddities or vices. "He is, moreover, the idol of the whole army . . . entitled to most of the glory our arms acquired" at Germantown. Although, declared the doctor, "some people blame him [for] calling some of our generals fools, cowards, and drunkards in public company . . . these things are proof of his integrity and should raise him in the opinion of every friend to America."

Washington, however, no longer had any illusions about Conway. On the seventeenth of October he had written Richard Henry Lee:

> General Conway's merit . . . as an officer and his importance in this army exists more in his own imagination than in reality, for it is a maxim with him to leave no service of his own untold, nor to want anything which is to be obtained by importunity.[11]

In short, Washington had insisted, nothing about this man, who had turned out to be an impossible braggart, merited his advancement over all twenty-three of the army's older brigadiers, who surely would resign if he were promoted over them. Lee had replied that he was surprised by rumors that Conway might be promoted to major general, and doubted that he would be. However, it was likely that he would be elected adjutant general to succeed Timothy Pickering, whom Congress probably would appoint to the reorganized Board of War.

For two weeks, the idea of the presence of the impudent, strutting Conway in his headquarters family had rankled Washington. Now came Stirling's note, which suggested just how much of a conniver the Frenchman was.

The eighth of November had been a busy, tiring day for the General. He had written to the President of Delaware, explaining that he was sending an officer to procure clothing for Delaware troops; to Governor William Livingston of New Jersey asking for a reinforcement for Red Bank; to the President of Congress with news and a request for more money; to others about the defense of Forts Mifflin and Mercer; to Colonel Theodorick Bland, who wanted to quit the service; to Brigadier General Thomas Nelson. On top of a day of paper work, he had held a council of war about the Delaware forts and the advisability of attacking General Howe if he should strike at the forts. So Washington considered Lord Stirling's communication overnight. Next day he wrote tersely to Conway:

> Sir: A letter which I received last night contained the following paragraph:
> In a letter from General Conway to General Gates, he says:
> "Heaven has been determined to save your country, or a weak

General and bad counsellors would have ruined it."

> I am, Sir, Yr. Hble Servt.[12]

Washington had been almost the last to hear Conway's contemptuous remark. By the eighth of November, it was a favorite taproom *bon mot,* for James Wilkinson had had many opportunities to repeat it and, evidently, missed none of them. Granted by General Gates the privilege of conveying to Congress official news of the Saratoga victory, Wilkinson had traveled southward in his own good time spreading the story as he went. At Reading, on the twenty-seventh of October, he had repeated it to Stirling's aide, McWilliams. Dr. Rush, however, had written about it to John Adams six days earlier than that.

If Washington thought of doing anything more than informing Conway that he had heard the remark, he did not mention it. His energies were taken up with more urgent concerns than petty controversy with an under officer.

But Conway replied to Washington's letter at once. He explained that on the ninth or tenth of October he had sent his congratulations to the victor of Saratoga:

> I spoke my mind freely [he continued] and found fault with several measures pursued in this army, but I will venture to say that in my whole letter the paragraph of which you . . . send me a copy cannot be found. My opinion of you, sir, without flattery or envy, is . . . you are a brave man, an honest man, a patriot, and a man of great sense. Your modesty is such that although your advice in council is commonly sound and proper, you have often been influenced by men who were not equal to you in . . . experience, knowledge, or judgment. . . . I believe I can assert that the expression, *weak general,* has not slipped from my pen. . . . In order that the least suspicion should not remain . . . about my way of thinking, I am willing that my original letter to General Gates should be handed to you.[13]

Washington wrote no reply. John Laurens probably spoke for the headquarters staff when he snapped, "The perplexity of his style and evident insincerity of his compliments betray his real sentiments and expose his guilt."

If Washington sighed with relief upon learning that on the fourteenth of November Conway had submitted his resignation to Congress, his relief was short-lived. While the army lay at the Gulph, the Congress made Conway a major general to fill the newly created post of Inspector General; at the same time, in deference to the wish of Horatio Gates, Wilkinson was made a brigadier by brevet as reward for carrying Gates's victory dispatch. General Jedidiah Huntington growled that the appointments gave "universal umbrage" to the general officers of the army.

Nine brigadiers remonstrated to Congress. General Greene wrote an individual protest. Actually, Conway's promotion was "on the staff," not "in the line," so that he would have no command over old brigadiers. Upon Wilkinson's elevation, they agreed with John Laurens that "there is a degradation of rank and an injustice to senior and more distinguished officers when a man is so extraordinarily advanced for riding post with good news. Let Congress reward him with a good horse for his speed, but consecrate rank to merit of another kind!"

In December, Inspector General Conway twice called at Washington's Valley Forge headquarters in Mrs. Deborah Hewes's neat little fieldstone house. Both times he was received with icy courtesy such, Conway later said, "as I never met with before from any general during the course of thirty years in a very respectable army." He protested in writing to Washington, who replied coolly. Conway again wrote, a letter combining flattery and sarcasm, closing with the avowal that perceiving he was "not agreeable" to Washington he could not expect the support of the Commander-in-Chief in carrying out his duties and stood ready to return to France.

Washington furiously resolved that Congress should see all the correspondence that had passed between them and the Delegates should know exactly what he thought of their Inspector General!

To the President on January 2, he dispatched the correspondence with the comment:

> If General Conway means by cool receptions . . . that I did not receive him in the language of a warm and cordial friend, I readily confess the charge. I did not, nor shall I ever, till I am capable of the arts of dissimulation. These I despise and my feelings will not permit me to make professions of friendship to the man I deem my enemy and whose system of conduct forbids it. At the same time, Truth authorizes me to say that he was received and treated with proper respect to his official character and that he has had no cause to justify the assertion that he could not expect any support for fulfilling the duties of his appointment.[14]

This, Washington hoped, would close the matter.

But before Washington's letter reached Congress, he received an excited communication from Horatio Gates, who until now had not involved himself directly. From Thomas Mifflin, Gates had learned that the extract from Conway's letter—Mifflin called it "a collection of just sentiments"—

had been sent to headquarters. Now, as the soughing winds of a wretched New Year snarled through the forlorn forests there by the Schuylkill, Washington read Gates's nervous plea that the Commander-in-Chief aid him in apprehending the wretch who "stealingly copied" from his letters, "which of them, when, and by whom" he did not know. Hysterically, Gates wrote that the crime was one that might "capitally injure the very operations under your immediate directions" and deeply affect the safety of the country. No time, he cried, must be lost in "tracing out the author of the infidelity," and since he did not know whether the extract had come to Washington from an officer or a member of Congress, he was sending a copy of his letter to the President of Congress.

Gates's letter at once raised new doubts and forebodings. Gates mentioned "letters" from Conway. Did this mean that a number of letters had passed between these two? Gates suggested that a member of the Congress might have reported Conway's remark to Washington. Did this mean that criticism of the Commander-in-Chief was circulating between the Army and the Delegates? Gates did not deny Conway had made the quoted statement. What infuriated Washington most was the implication that he had acquired his knowledge by some dishonorable means. He wondered, too, why Gates chose to expose the matter to Congress; why had he revealed a staff dispute involving custody of records and personal relationships? But if these were the rules by which Gates planned to play the matter, he would abide by them. When he replied to Gates, he sent a copy of his letter to Congress. On the fourth of January he wrote Gates an account of how the extract had come into his hands and explained that he wrote to Conway "to show that gentleman that I was not unapprised of his intriguing disposition."

Then Washington pointed out:

. . . till Lord Stirling's letter came to my hands, I never knew that General Conway (who I viewed in the light of a stranger to you) was a correspondent of yours, much less did I suspect that I was the subject of your confidential letters. Pardon me then for adding that so far from conceiving that the safety of the states can be affected or in the smallest degree injured by a discovery of this kind or that I should be called upon in such solemn terms to point out the author, that I considered the information as coming from yourself and given with a friendly view to forewarn and consequently to forearm me against a secret enemy. Or, in other words, a dangerous incendiary, in which character sooner or later this country will know General Conway. But in this, as in other matters of late, I have found myself mistaken.[15]

If Gates was puzzled by the General's strange reasoning that the quotation of Conway's remarks had come so deviously to him at the instance of Gates himself, it was not surprising. Perhaps, it was Washington's way of saying that he did not suspect Gates of sharing Conway's sentiments.

It would take time for the letter to Gates to make its way to Albany and for a reply, if any, to return. Meanwhile, many letter writers had gotten busy. By now, the rumor of a diabolical "cabal" to depose Washington had spread cancerously. Mifflin's open admiration for Gates, and his alienation from Washington, as well as his rift with Greene, made him suspect as a ringleader, although no one was ever to prove that he worked actively for the ouster of the Commander-in-Chief. Gates was everywhere considered the only logical successor to Washington. He himself was much too adroit to suggest by any subtlety that possibility, but at the same time, aware of the wild talk going about, he did nothing to quiet it or to support the Commander-in-Chief; his was the waiting game. New England Delegates were considered parties to the intrigue and even Richard Henry Lee was suspected of being "at the bottom of it."

A week after Washington replied to Gates, Dr. Rush wrote an unsigned letter to Governor Patrick Henry of Virginia, again quoting the now-famous Conway quip and urging a "Gates, a Lee, or a Conway" for command of the army. He quixotically suggested that if the name of the author of the letter were "found out by the handwriting," which Rush surely knew was familiar to many of the figures in the controversy, it should not be mentioned and the letter must be thrown in the fire. "But some of its contents ought to be made public . . .," he hastened to add, "to awaken, enlighten, and alarm our country." Rush failed to judge his man: Henry forwarded the letter to Washington who instantly recognized Rush's handwriting. The General sent Rush a stinging rebuke. Rush's military career ended soon after, over disputes about his department, but the seeds of a long, long period of bitterness between him and Washington were sown.

At about the time Rush's letter was on the road south to Patrick Henry, another was en route north to Washington from his intimate old friend, Dr. James Craik, warning Washington that "a strong faction was forming" against him in the Board of War and the Congress. Richard Henry Lee, Doctor Craik reported, was said to be at the bottom of it, and General Mifflin "a very active person." Their technique would be to throw obstacles and difficulties in Washington's way through the new Board of War, the doctor had been told, which would force the General to resign.

Mid-January saw the mysterious appearance "on the stairs of Congress Hall" of a paper handed to Laurens, called "The Thoughts of a Freeman." It consisted of forty-five statements which either reflected directly upon Washington's conduct or insinuated that it deserved Congressional investigation. Without showing the paper to anyone else, Laurens sent it to Washington in the spirit of a friend.

Perhaps at an earlier time no one would have thought the Congress likely to be persuaded to vote a change in command. But the wintertime Congress of 1777 was not the Congress that had so enthusiastically elected Washington in 1775. Nearly all the members who had voted for him then had died, terminated their service, or were on leave, with or without the consent of their colleagues. Only six men who had voted for the Commander-in-Chief remained. Of these, one was departing and the three from Massachusetts were preparing to do so, leaving only two who knew Washington in a body now shrunken to twenty-one or twenty-two members. Of the quality of Congress at the time, a French observer remembered it was "not . . . the illustrious body whose eloquence and wisdom, whose stern virtues and unflinching patriotism had astonished the world. . . . All but a few of the men of superior minds had disappeared from it. Their measures were feeble and vacillating, and their party feuds seemed to forbode some impending calamity." This body of inexperienced legislators was all too likely to sway with the sectional and popular feeling that Gates was the man of the hour.

Throughout these days of attack, secret and open, Washington was struggling almost hopelessly to feed his famishing army and to hold the weary, sick, shivering, discouraged phantom regiments together. If it were not enough that he had to keep men alive in the snow-locked, leafless forest of Valley Forge, where the fierce wind sang mournfully over the silent, lonely huts and the only signs of life were wisps of feeble smoke at the chimneys, the Commander-in-Chief was obliged to hold down mutiny on the one hand and to work out proposals for organizational and administrative reforms of the Army on the other.

Through it all, as Washington told his admirer, Henry Laurens: "My enemies take an ungenerous advantage of me. They know the delicacy of my situation and that motives of policy deprive me of the defense I might otherwise make against their insidious attacks. They know I cannot combat their insinuations, however injurious, without disclosing secrets it is of the utmost moment to conceal." Well the General knew that his enemies expected of his army only what a much stronger one could accomplish, but he had contended, "Next to being strong, it is best to be thought so by the enemy," and he dared not show his hand to political or factional enemies for fear of revealing it to the nation's enemy. "But," he said philosophically to Henry Laurens, "why should I expect to be exempt from censure, the unfailing lot of an elevated station? Merits and talents with which I can have no pretensions of rivalship have ever been subject to it. My heart tells me it has been my unremitted aim to do the best circumstances would permit. Yet I may have been very often mistaken in my judgment of the means and may, in many instances, deserve the imputation of error."

Washington's exchange with Gates dragged on, for on the twenty-third of January Gates wrote a long letter in which he dodged and feinted trying to explain his incoherent first letter. Just as Washington's account of the affair had relieved him of "unspeakable uneasiness," he knew Washington would be pleased to learn that the controversial paragraph was "spurious." It simply was not contained in Conway's letter. When he first learned of Washington's initial note to Conway, his real fear, he said, was that the letter "stealingly copied" had been altered, and that malicious forgery would reflect upon innocent men; he also feared that the thief might obtain and betray secrets of the army. Wilkinson, Gates reported, had endeavored to place blame for the leak upon Alexander Hamilton, but Gates would "not listen to this insinuation against your aide-de-camp and mine." He had, he said, returned Conway's original letter to its author because, although it was an innocuous letter, some things said in it might embarrass a number of other officers.

About this time Conway also wrote to say that the alleged statement was not contained in the letter, which Gates delivered to him in York, and that he had been dissuaded from publishing it only by Henry Laurens and others who thought it would reveal to the world groundless dissensions within the army. Neither Gates nor Conway quoted the letter or offered a copy of it to Washington.

Washington ignored Conway's communication, but to Gates on the ninth of February, he addressed a scathing epistle, in which he explained some of the difficulty he encountered in attempting to reconcile "the spirit and import of your different letters and sometimes of the different parts of the same letter with each other." And why, he wished to know, if the letter from Conway was so harmless, was it not made public? Upon Conway he commented bitingly:

> It is . . . greatly to be lamented that this adept in military science did not employ his abilities in the progress of the campaign. . . . The United States have lost much from that unseasonable diffidence which prevented his embracing the numerous opportunities he had in council of displaying those rich treasures of knowledge and experience he has since so freely laid open to you.[16]

The General was angry; with a few more strokes of his pen he disposed of Thomas Conway as a man "capable of all the malignity of detraction and all the meannesses of intrigue to gratify the absurd resentment of disappointed vanity, or to answer the purposes of personal aggrandizement."

At last Conway, subject of the discord, was passing from spheres of influence. Congress appointed him second-in-command to Lafayette on a proposed "iruption" into Canada, a scheme of the new Board of War. Lafayette, once on friendly terms with Conway, who Lafayette insisted was an "Irishman," had repudiated him and declared that if Conway were forced on him, he would return to France. De Kalb was appointed in Conway's place, but when Lafayette arrived in Albany, he found Conway there attempting to organize the expedition. The whole project soon was abandoned. Conway was sent to General McDougall at Peekskill, and Lafayette and De Kalb returned to Valley Forge.

Gates, intent upon clearing himself, endeavored in a privately circulated letter to cast the blame for the whole dreary business upon Wilkinson. Then he wrote in mid-February to Washington, declaring that Conway "must . . . be responsible," that he himself was "only accidentally concerned." He protested that he was "of no faction," and hoped "no more of that time so precious to the public may be lost upon the subject of General Conway's letter."

Washington himself now was ready to believe that if Gates had been involved in a plot to seize command he probably was the instrument of more dangerous men and that the moment was past. Alexander Hamilton was saying to George Clinton that since last seeing Clinton, when they had talked of "a certain faction," he had "discovered such convincing traits of the monster" that he could not "doubt its reality in the most extensive sense." But he added, "I believe it unmasked its batteries too soon and begins to hide its head; but as I imagine it will only change the storm to a sap, all the true and sensible friends to their country and, of course, to a certain great man ought to be upon the watch to counterplot the secret machinations of his enemies." Like Hamilton, the Commander-in-Chief was willing to close the affair. On the twenty-fourth of February he wrote Gates:

I am as averse to controversy as any man and had I not been forced into it, you never would have had occasion to impute to me even the shadow of a disposition towards it. Your repeatedly and solemnly disclaiming any offensive views in those matters which have been the subject of our past correspondence makes me willing to close with the desire you express of burying them hereafter in silence and, as far as future events will permit, oblivion.

My temper leads me to peace and harmony with all men. And it is particularly my wish to avoid any personal feuds or dissentions with those who are embarked in the same great national interest with myself, as every difference of this kind must in its consequences be very injurious.[17]

But the snarled human relations between a number of proud, ambitious, and sometimes selfish men were not untangled by the mere strokes of the General's quill. Gates shifted such a heavy burden of blame upon Wilkinson, whose role never became clear, that the burly young aide challenged his chief to a duel, which Gates avoided. Nevertheless, Gates, in his private correspondence, continued to belittle the General. The enmity of Mifflin and Greene lay bare before public view, and never healed. The relationship between Washington and Mifflin remained frigid. And for several years Washington considered Gates a "doubtful friend."

Conway fell into almost complete disrepute, except for the support of the men accused of plotting with him. In April he again threatened to resign because he was not being promoted as he supposed he should, and to his surprise the Congress quickly accepted his resignation. Gates wrote to the President of the Congress that Conway "seems much chagrined at the sudden and unexpected acceptance of his resignation with no marks of respect or approbation paid to his services," and urged that Conway be returned to France with the "gratitude, honor, and dignity of the United States of America."

Without command, Conway did not return at once, but wagged his rapier tongue freely, until in July he challenged General John Cadwalader, probably as a result of more argument upon the same manner. Cadwalader's ball struck Conway in the mouth. On what the Frenchman thought was his death-bed, he wrote to Washington:

I find myself just able to hold the pen during a few min-

utes, and take this opportunity of expressing my sincere grief
for having done, written, or said anything disagreeable to
your Excellency. My career will soon be over. Therefore, justice and truth prompt me to declare my last sentiments. You
are in my eyes the great and good man. May you long enjoy
the love, veneration, and esteem of these states whose liberties
you have asserted by your virtues.[18]

It was less extravagant than an earlier letter Conway had
written during the heat of the controversy, comparing Washington with Frederick the Great, and perhaps now Conway
wished that he had not thrown away an American career in
contentious, arrogant correspondence and speech. He did
not die. After his recovery he sailed for France, to a further
military career of some merit.

Perhaps there was a cabal that miserable winter of Valley
Forge. Very likely there was no such organized movement
against the Commander-in-Chief. Many men, in and out of
the army, in and out of Congress, had lost faith in Washington, or had seen in others virtues lacking in him. Gates was
ambitious and probably would have assumed the sword of
Commander-in-Chief with more confidence than competence,
but it is not likely that he, hostile though he had become to
Washington, worked actively to oust the General. Washington thought a cabal did exist, originating with "three men
who wanted to aggrandize themselves," but who finding no
support "professed themselves my warmest admirers." He
would not say any members of Congress "were privy to this
scheme and inclined to aid and abet it, . . . but am well informed that no whisper of the kind was ever heard in Congress." If there were a cabal, it quickly died in the spring as
the Congress filled up. Gates was assigned to command of
the Hudson River forts, directly under Washington. The
Board of War fell into disrepute, and Washington emerged
the gonfalon of American resistance to tyranny. Indeed Congress' prestige steadily declined while that of Washington
steadily increased.

In dealing with his enemies, real or fancied, George Washington had not always been judicious, fair, or gentlemanly:
he had been ruthless and, it might be suspected, perhaps a
little disingenuous, but he resolved, when the whisperings
rose to a clamor, to silence them, and this he did without a
shadow of a doubt.

"... SWEAR FOR ME IN ENGLISH"

Training at Valley Forge

SPRING 1778

WHILE WASHINGTON'S veterans wintered at Valley Forge like animals in burrows, the tide of war fell to its lowest ebb. Not only did cabals, real or fancied, split the army and the Congress, but also many civilians began to give up the cause for lost. Paper money, that barometer of public faith, issued by both the Congress and the states, was practically worthless. Businessmen insisted ruthlessly on "hard money" for every commodity and every army supply. Ironically, even the counterfeiters who were rife were making better money than was the Congress. In February, 1778, newspapers published a warning against counterfeit thirty-dollar bills. They were "easily discovered," the public was informed, because they were printed on better paper and the engraving was of finer quality than that of legal tender. The easiest way to spot one of the bogus bills, however, was to note that on it Philadelphia was spelled correctly, while on the genuine note it read, "Philadelpkia."

Although Pennsylvania farmers in the country surrounding the encampment had plenty of provisions, very little found its way to the starving army. Producers discovered that the British in Philadelphia would pay more for food, and in good, solid English pounds. As a consequence, the enemy lived well enough, while twenty miles distant, the American army at Valley Forge dwindled away through death, desertion, and disgust. "The love of country and public virtues are annihilated," William Ellery growled angrily. "If Diogenes were alive and were to search America with candles, would he find an honest man?" A New York colonel wrote bitterly to Governor George Clinton requesting supplies from the state store for his men:

> I have upwards of seventy men unfit for duty only for the want . . . of clothing, twenty of which have no breeches at all, so that they are obliged to take their blankets to cover their nakedness and as many without a single shirt, stocking,

or shoe, about thirty fit for duty, the rest sick or lame, and, God knows, it won't be long before they will all be laid up, as the poor fellows are obliged to fetch wood and water on their backs half a mile with bare legs in snow or mud.[1]

The colonel had tried vainly before to obtain clothing and had received only thirteen pairs of breeches and a few shoes:

This was all I got. . . . Notwithstanding, was informed that several hundred pair of leather breeches, etc., was delivered to the two Northern regiments, who are in great want, it seems to keep their thighs from scorching this winter in their warm barracks.[2]

Brigadier General James M. Varnum wrote his fellow Rhode Islander, General Greene, that "The horses are dying for want of forage. The country in the vicinity of the camp is exhausted."

Well aware that Valley Forge was "a dreary kind of place and uncomfortably provided," Washington besought officials and citizens of the eastern states to save the army there. To Governor Clinton of New York he wrote of "the present dreadful situation of the army for want of provisions, and the miserable prospects before us with respect to futurity." He said firmly:

It is more alarming than you will probably conceive, for to form a just idea it were necessary to be on the spot. For some days past, there has been little less than a famine in camp. A part of the army has been a week without any kind of flesh, and the rest three or four days.

Naked and starving as they are, we cannot enough admire the incomparable patience and fidelity of the soldiery that they have not been ere this excited by their sufferings to a general mutiny and dispersion.[3]

Washington warned the governor that so "shocking a catastrophe" could be averted only by "the most active efforts everywhere," but in his heart the valiant commander believed in his veterans. "Impressed with this idea, I am on my part putting every engine to work. . . . I am calling upon all those whose station and influence enable them to contribute their aid." Somehow, he begged enough to keep them alive. His faithful officers turned to and worked at every task in order to keep the suffering army together. "The Brigadiers are become soap boilers, oilmen, armorers, tanners, shoemakers, and the Lord knows what," wrote a colonel.

With stern discipline, Washington unrelentingly bore down on officers and men alike, for though their bodies were becoming scarecrows, he would not have them forget that their character should be that of soldiers. One Lieutenant William Williams of the Thirteenth Virginia was charged with behavior unbecoming an officer and gentleman: he bought a pair of shoes from a Continental soldier, "thereby rendering the soldier unfit for service," and he messed and frequently slept with the soldiers, "taking their bread and not returning it, by which the soldiers suffered with hunger." A general court-martial acquitted the lieutenant of the charge of taking soldiers' bread, but he was found guilty of fraternization and of buying the shoes, and forthwith was discharged from the service.

Another officer was accused of absenting himself from camp, associating with a soldier, and stealing; he was "unanimously sentenced to have his sword broke over his head on the grand parade . . . that he be discharged [from] the Regiment and rendered incapable of serving any more as an officer and that it be esteemed a crime of the blackest dye in an officer or even soldier to associate with him after the execution of this just, though mild punishment."

A number of men were apprehended trying to send precious provisions to the enemy: John Williamson was "sentenced to receive two hundred and fifty lashes on his bare back well laid on." (A surgeon was assigned to attend whippings to "see that the criminals do not receive more lashes than their strength will bear.") Even civilians who were caught driving cattle to the enemy felt Washington's iron discipline. Exercising the full powers Congress had granted him, he took them up, confined them to jail, and fined them heavily, using the fines collected to reward their captors and for the sick in the hospitals.

Next only to discipline, Washington deemed most important in the soldier proficiency in manual exercise and maneuver. Until now there had been no one in his army to provide that kind of training, the task of an inspector general. Conway had worked out so badly that he never had come to grips with this basic Continental Army deficiency, and training, which never had been more than primary and haphazard, had continued to languish. The Continentals on the drill field or going into combat, though unified by a common cause, were yet little more skilled than the rustics of the village green: they handled their weapons in their own way; usually they were baffled by the simplest evolutions; and marching in files, they often came up to action late. Almost providentially, while Washington and Conway stood at a personal impasse, there arrived at Valley Forge a man with the knowledge and experience required to mold the regiments into a professional army.

From the Lancaster Road to headquarters on a late February day came riding a party of foreigners, who introduced themselves as Frederick William Augustus Henry Ferdinand, Baron von Steuben, and his retinue. The stout, balding, big-nosed baron, resplendent in a new, blue uniform upon whose breast flashed, as large as a saucer, the dazzling, jeweled Star of the Order of Fidelity of Baden, spoke not a word of English. His translator was a seventeen-year-old secretary, Pierre Duponceau; others of his party were two aides and a German servant. A great, lithe Italian greyhound trotting at the baron's heels must have reminded Washington at least momentarily of another eccentric given to canine companionship. But the baron had not come unannounced and already he had given the Commander-in-Chief reason to be well predisposed toward him. On the eighth of January, Washington had received a letter from him, written at Portsmouth, New Hampshire. The baron enclosed a copy of a letter of introduction from Benjamin Franklin and Silas Deane, describing him as "Lieut. Genl. in the king of Prussia's service . . . recommended to us by two of the best judges of military merit" in France. Not even mention of such elavated rank in the service of Frederick the Great, model general of the world, kept this introduction from sounding like those that had brought Conway to the army, or the even more troublesome Philippe Charles Tronson du Coudray, whose embarrassing expectation of becoming major general in supreme command of artillery and engineers would have led to immeasurable difficulty had he not drowned when his horse bolted off the Schuylkill Ferry. But Steuben's own covering communication had struck a new note. He had written that the introduction of the American Commissioners would inform Washington of his desire to enlist in the Continental Army and he wished only to add:

> . . . that the object of my greatest ambition is to render your country all the services in my power and to deserve the title of a citizen of America by fighting for the cause of your liberty.
>
> If the distinguished ranks in which I have served in Europe should be an obstacle, I had rather serve under your Excellency as a volunteer than to be a subject of discontent to such deserving officers as have already distinguished themselves amongst you.[4]

It was gracious and refreshing, but Washington in the midst of his troubles with Conway had been cautious when he penned a brief reply inviting the baron to Valley Forge, and reminded him that it "lay solely with Congress to make a suitable provision" for him in the American Army.

Washington, talking through dapper John Laurens, his own aide, received the amiable stranger cordially, while appraising him carefully. After four days, he wrote John Lauren's father—Henry Laurens, President of Congress—that the baron "appears to be much of a gentleman and, as far as I have had an opportunity of judging, a man of military knowledge and acquainted with the world." Young John, who had seen a little of the world himself, was charmed by the rotund visitor and shrewdly decided that he was the "properest man" for the neglected post of Inspector General.

The baron was also a jovial liar. He never had been a lieutenant general. He had not served, as he claimed, twenty-two years under the King of Prussia. Benjamin Franklin, when he introduced the baron, probably knew that he was an unemployed, penniless captain, who had been dropped from Frederick's army fourteen years before, and since had been employed as chamberlain at a minor European court. He was, however, the well-schooled, widely read, army-trained son of an accomplished Prussian officer; before his discharge he had been selected by Frederick himself as one of thirteen officers to whom the sovereign chose to give personal instruction in general-staff duties. His exceptional military abilities and their value for Washington's army were genuine enough.

To Washington, who believed so devoutly in the intervention of Providence, Steuben's arrival must have seemed Heaven-sent. But because Conway still nominally held the office of Inspector General, Washington was obliged to move slowly. While the baron, to whom Washington assigned as aides and guides John Laurens and Alexander Hamilton, rode throughout the sprawling encampment, observing the pitiful soldiers in their gloomy huts, talking with every officer, sizing up the potential of the ragged patriots, Washington decided to try him by assigning him the duties of Acting Inspector General, without rank, to drill and train the army.

It was a discouraging assignment. There was not even a set of Continental Army regulations. Steuben wrote his own in French, modifying the Prussian system; they were translated by Duponceau, and put into proper military form by Laurens and Hamilton. They were copied into regimental orderly books from which company copies for all fourteen brigades were transcribed. While this laborious duplication was in process, the baron tried to commit the commands to memory in English in the hope of breaking the language barrier

that loomed between him and his pupils. The individuality of
the state units presented another obstacle: each state, as its
officers saw fit, had taken from the English, the French, or
the Prussian systems what little drill it had adopted. Later the
baron wrote gleefully to a Prussian friend:

My good republicans wanted everything in the English
style; our great and good allies everything according to the
French *mode,* and when I presented a plate of *sauerkraut*
dressed in the Prussian style, they all wanted to throw it out of
the window. Nevertheless, by the force of proving by *"God-
dams"* that my cookery was the best, I overcame the prejudices
of the former; but the second liked me as little in the forests
of America as they did on the plains of Rossbach. Do not,
therefore, be astonished if I am not painted in very bright
colors in Parisian circles.[5]

To another old companion-in-arms he explained:

In the first place, the genius of this nation is not in the
least to be compared with that of the Prussians, Austrians, or
French. You say to your soldier, "Do this," and he doeth it,
but I am obliged to say, "This is the reason why you ought to
do that," and then he does it.[6]

When Steuben came to Valley Forge, the English tradition
that drill instruction was beneath the dignity of the commissioned officer was firmly fixed in America, but experience
had not produced a corps of trained sergeants such as were
the pride of the British army. Steuben calmly assumed the
chore of drillmaster and trainer of drillmasters. Shortly,
Colonel Alexander Scammell was writing:

To see a gentleman dignified with a lieutenant general's
commission from the great Prussian monarch condescend with
a grace peculiar to himself to take under his direction a squad
of ten or twelve men in the capacity of a drill sergeant, commands the admiration of both officers and men.[7]

Of one hundred chosen men, Steuben made a model company; he himself became the model drillmaster. On the
muddy fields of Valley Forge, from six in the morning until
six at night, his guttural voice was familiar above the shuf-
fling of marching feet. At six in the evenings, the adjutants
attended a meeting for instructions in theoretic maneuvering and "the emphasis to be used in giving the word of command."

At first, the work went slowly. For some time the baron's
English was limited to a few phrases and often was confused.
His secretary, Duponceau, was too inexperienced in military
affairs to translate his commands properly to his raw trainees.

But almost the first day, Captain Benjamin Walker of New York came to the rescue of the exasperated, bellowing Prussian. The baron was so pleased with Walker that he promptly appointed him one of his aides. Duponceau later recalled that the baron's "fits of passion were comical and rather amused than offended the soldiers." He wrote:

> When some movement or maneuver was not performed to his mind he began to swear in German, then in French, and then in both languages together. When he had exhausted his artillery of foreign oaths, he would call to his aides, "My dear Walker and my dear Duponceau, come and swear for me in English. These fellows won't do what I bid them." A good-natured smile then went through the ranks and at last the maneuver or the movement was properly performed.[8]

Steuben taught first "the position of the soldier," then the facings, the steps, file marching, wheeling, all the other motions of the individual, the company, the regiment, the brigade. He related:

> My enterprise succeeded better than I had dared to expect and I had the satisfaction, in a month's time, to see not only a regular step introduced into the army, but I also made maneuvers with ten and twelve battalions with as much precision as the evolution of a single company.[9]

And on the twenty-fourth of March, the whole army was at drill. With a vigor John Laurens thought "hardly to be expected of his years," the baron galloped from parade to parade to superintend in their work the brigade inspectors he had created. Four days later, the Commander-in-Chief appointed him officially Inspector General of the Army "till the pleasure of Congress shall be known," and when Washington heard, the last day of April, that Conway had resigned, he wrote Congress strongly on the baron's behalf.

In spite of cold and hunger, sickness and death, it was at Valley Forge that new spirit entered the army. There the army mastered for the first time the manual of the musket, and charged an imaginary enemy by platoons, firing and advancing and rushing with bayonets; no longer was that weapon merely a tool for cooking or an encumbrance to throw away. A man like George Ewing, second lieutenant of the Third New Jersey, expressed his personal satisfaction when on the seventh of April he noted in his diary:

> This forenoon the Brigade went through the maneuvers under the direction of Baron Steuben. The step is about halfway betwixt slow and quick time, an easy and natural step, and I think much better than the former. The Manual also is

altered by his direction. There are but ten words of command, which are as follows:

1. Poise Firelock
2. Shoulder Firelock
3. Present Arms
4. Fix Bayonet
5. Unfix Bayonet
6. Load Firelock
7. Make Ready
8. Present
9. Fire
10. Order Firelock[10]

Since each command involved a number of studied motions—twenty-one usually were judged necessary to "load firelock," three to "make ready," nineteen to "fire," and so on—the simplification that reduced the manual from many to only ten commands not only greatly pleased the befuddled soldier trying to learn an exercise as precise as a ballet, but often was the only thing that made his mastery of it at all possible.

The army learned to march in column and to deploy from column into line. At last, it marched in compact masses. The columns of files gave way to marching in double rank and in columns of four. No longer would it string out so long on the roads that discipline broke, scores straggled, and precious minutes were lost forming to the front to meet the enemy; each battalion learned to occupy on the road no more space than it would in line of battle. Quite properly John Laurens could exult to his father:

It would enchant you to see the enlivened scene on our Campus Martius. If Mr. Howe opens the campaign with his usual deliberation, and our recruits or drafts come in tolerably well, we shall be infinitely better prepared to meet him than ever we have been.[11]

Far from his sociable native Charleston, Laurens shared the baron's leisure hours as well as his long hours of toil. Duponceau described their life in quarters:

We who lived in good quarters did not feel the misery of the times so much as the common soldiers and the subaltern officers, yet we had more than once to share our rations with the sentry at our door.

We put the best face we could upon the matter. Once with the Baron's permission, his aides invited a number of young officers to dine at our quarters, on condition that none should be admitted that had on a whole pair of breeches. This was understood of course as *pars pro toto*, but torn clothes were an indispensable requisite for admission and in this the guests were very sure not to fail.

The dinner took place. The guests clubbed their rations, and we feasted sumptuously on tough beefsteaks and potatoes with hickory nuts for our dessert. In lieu of wine, we had some kind of spirits with which we made *Salamanders,* that is to say, after filling our glasses we set the liquor on fire and drank it up flame and all. Such a set of ragged and at the same time merry fellows were never before brought together. The Baron loved to speak of that dinner and of his *sans culottes,* as he called us. Thus the denomination was first invented in America and applied to the brave officers and soldiers of our revolutionary army. . . .[12]

Duponceau consoled himself that "in the midst of all our distresses, there were some bright sides to the picture" at Valley Forge. He recalled:

Mrs. Washington had the courage to follow her husband to that dismal abode. Other ladies also graced the scene. Among them was the lady of General Greene, a handsome, elegant, and accomplished woman. Her dwelling was the resort of the foreign officers, because she understood and spoke . . . French . . . and was well versed in French literature. There were also Lady Stirling . . ., her daughter Lady Kitty Alexander . . . and her companion, Miss Nancy Brown, then a distinguished belle. There was Mrs. Biddle, the wife of Colonel Clement Biddle, who was at the head of the forage department, and some other ladies, whose names I do not . . . recollect. They often met at each other's quarters and sometimes at General Washington's, where the evening was spent in conversation over a dish of tea or coffee. There were no levees, or formal soirees: no dancing, card-playing, or amusements of any kind, except singing. Every gentleman or lady who could sing was called upon in turn for a song.[13]

If charm reigned at the snug, crowded little house of Widow Hewes or at Isaac Walker's, where Greene resided, it still was not so in the huts on the hillsides. Dr. Waldo, as surgeon, had an opportunity to observe most of the women in camp, wives who could not bear separation from their husbands, washerwomen who followed the army and labored over tubs for subsistence and a little pay, and a vast number of women who plied an older profession. Of them, Waldo wrote one day:

What! though there are in rags, in crape,
Some beings here in female shape,
In whom may still be found some traces,
Of former beauty in their faces,

> Yet now so far from being nice,
> They boast of ev'ry barefaced vice.
> Shame to their sex! 'Tis not in these
> One e'er beholds those charms that please.[14]

On another day Waldo said:

> I was called to relieve a soldier thought to be dying. He
> expired before I reached the hut. He was an Indian, an ex-
> cellent soldier, and an obedient, good-natured fellow. He en-
> gaged for money, doubtless, as others do, but he has served
> his country faithfully. He has fought for those very people
> who disinherited his forefathers. . . .[15]

Waldo's Indian patient was but one of a number of redmen who served the army on many fields and in many encampments. One morning before breakfast, Pierre Duponceau
was walking in the woods at Valley Forge. From a distance,
he heard a "most powerful voice . . . yet melodious" singing
a fashionable French opera song. "I thought myself for a moment at the Comedie Italienne and was lost in astonishment,
when suddenly I saw . . . before me a tall Indian . . . In
American regimentals and two large epaulets on his shoulders."

Steuben's secretary introduced himself, and the officers
struck up a conversation. When Duponceau asked the Indian
how he had become familiar with French opera, he explained
that he was a Canadian Abenaki, who was a Catholic convert. He first had joined the Americans when Montgomery
had invaded Canada; returning to the states on the retreat, he
had been commissioned a Continental colonel.

Among things observed by the Congressional Committee
at Valley Forge early in the year was the shocking condition
of both the Quartermaster and the Commissary departments
of the army. The negligence and wastage in the Quartermaster Department in recent months, under the maladministration
of Mifflin, who had resigned, was appalling: ". . . the property
of the continent dispersed over the whole country; not an
encampment, route of the Army, or considerable road but
abounds with wagons, left to the mercy of the weather and the
will of the inhabitants. . . . Not less than three thousand
spades and shovels and a like number of tomahawks have
been lately discovered and collected in the vicinity of the
camp. . . . In the same way a quantity of tents and tent-cloth,
after having laid a whole summer in a farmer's barn . . . was
lately discovered and brought to the camp by a special order
from the General. . . ."

Mifflin's mismanagement deprived the men of food for their

aching bellies and sometimes it robbed them of life itself. The men slept on the frozen ground, and the Congressional Committee reported that sick soldiers died in their huts for lack of straw to lie on: straw was available, but there were no wagons to fetch it. "Almost every species of camp transportation," said the Committee, "is now performed by men, who without a murmur, patiently yoke themselves to little carriages of their own making, or load their wood and provisions on their backs."

To the post of Quartermaster General now went able, ambitious Nathanael Greene, protesting later his sentiments, "Whoever read of a quartermaster in history . . ." but accepting the post out of a sense of duty to the General and the army. He insisted upon appointing his own assistants and keeping command of his division in the field. His conscientiousness and methods were responsible for a steady improvement in supply, so that the General was optimistic that the army would be able to take the field in the spring adequately furnished.

To the Commissary Department, vacated by ailing Joseph Trumbull, who months before had gone home to New England, and since his departure miserably managed by incompetent officers, went tall, good-humored Jeremiah Wadsworth —one of "the solid men of Connecticut." Wadsworth proved capable and efficient, but not even he could furnish a steady flow of wholesome victuals in a famished, stripped country.

The only military activity during these gray days was an occasional action at the outposts. One morning in January a young, up-and-coming Virginian, Captain Henry Lee of Bland's Light Dragoons, set the camp to talking by a dashing exploit. With a small party he was lying at Scott's farm, six miles down the slope from Mount Joy, when an enemy patrol of two hundred surrounded his billet. He and his seven men held them off by firing from windows until the redcoat patrol worked its way along the flank of the house toward the stable to snatch Lee's horses. From the windows, he bellowed "Fire away, my good fellows! Here comes the infantry! We will have them all, God damn them!"

This maneuver, chortled General Weedon, "sent them scampering. . . . Too many pretty things cannot be said of this gallant little officer." Soon Washington, a friend of the captain's father, offered the boy a place on his staff, but Lee preferred to stay with the horse and instead happily accepted a majority and command of an independent partisan corps.

At last spring came to Valley Forge. There had not been much snow during the winter but plenty of cold rain and icy wind. Now the ground dried and the air was filled with the particular fragrance of green things. Under their new officers, the Quartermaster Department and Commissary Department were furnishing the army's requirements with surprising regularity.

Washington decided to put his winter-trained troops to test by organizing a sham battle between two full divisions. General Steuben, whose training was to be tried, commanded one of them. Duponceau, his earnest, absentminded, and near-sighted aide, recounted that he himself played an important role:

I was sent to reconnoiter with orders to return immediately at full gallop as soon as the enemy should be in sight. I rode on . . . about a quarter of a mile when I was struck with the sight of what I was since informed to be some red petticoats hanging on a fence to dry, which I took for a body of British soldiers. I had forgotten, it seems, the contending parties were all Americans and none of them clothed in scarlet regimentals. Full of my hallucination, I returned in haste to the camp with the news that the enemy were marching upon us.

Our division took the road I had indicated, and, behold! the sight of the red petticoats was all the result of their movement. It excited, of course, a great deal of merriment to my utter confusion and dismay.

The adventure was related the same day at Headquarters to General Washington in my presence, but such was the conduct of that excellent man that I retired comforted. . . . I cannot recollect the particulars of that scene, my mind being so confused . . . All I remember is a huge bowl of punch . . . handed round to the company . . . of which I took my share.[16]

During these spring days one absence continued to haunt the officers' circle at Valley Forge. According to Elias Boudinot, Commissary of Prisoners, Washington turned to him to fill it:

General Washington called me into his room and in the most earnest manner entreated of me, if I wished to gratify him, that I would obtain the exchange of General Lee, for he was never more wanted by him than at the present moment and desired I would not suffer trifles to prevent it. . . .[17]

In exchange for Charles Lee, Boudinot was able to offer General Richard Prescott, who had been taken at Newport. On hearing that Lee would leave the enemy lines on Sunday morning, April 5, under parole, Washington sent a party of horse under his aide, Colonel Meade, to escort him to camp. Boudinot had arranged for Lee's release, but he detested everything about the conceited, conniving man whose return he recorded in his journal:

> When the day arrived, the greatest preparations were made for his reception. All the principal officers of the army were drawn up in two lines, advanced of the camp about two miles towards the enemy. Then the troops with their inferior officers formed a line quite to Headquarters. All the music of the army attended. The General, with a great number of the principal officers and their suites, rode about four miles on the road towards Philadelphia and waited until General Lee appeared. General Washington dismounted and received General Lee as if he had been his brother. He passed through the lines of officers and the army who all paid him the highest military honors to Headquarters, where Mrs. Washington was and there he was entertained with an elegant dinner, and the music playing the whole time. A room was assigned to him back of Mrs. Washington's sitting room and all his baggage was stowed in it. The next morning he lay very late and breakfast was detained for him. When he came out, he looked dirty, as if he had been in the street all night. Soon after I discovered that he had brought a miserable dirty hussy with him from Philadelphia (a British sergeant's wife) and had actually taken her into his room by a back door, and she had slept with him that night.[18]

Lee remained only briefly at Valley Forge. Still on parole, he could not go back to active military duty. Soon he set out for York, where he visited Congress to discuss various matters, including the manner in which the 1778 campaign should be conducted; thence he went home to Virginia for a rest. His exchange became effective on the twenty-first of April. Before he set out on his journey, he happened to meet Boudinot and did not fail to tell him that "he had found the army in a worse situation than he expected, and that General Washington was not fit to command a sergeant's guard."

April was drawing to a close. Genial, tough Steuben had wrought a martial miracle in transforming despondent men into orderly soldiers. Clothing was still scanty, but the worst cases had been accommodated and food was sufficient and beginning to be plentiful. Morale stiffened daily; the troops began to feel the optimism of triumph over adversity and the gaiety of springtime; the new spirit was in Waldo's verses:

> The day serene—joy sparkles round
> Camp, hills and dales with mirth resound,
> All with clean clothes and powder'd hair
> For sport or duty now appear,
> Here squads in martial exercise

> There whole brigades in order rise,
> With cautious steps they march and wheel.
> Double—form ranks—platoons—at will.
> Columns on columns justly roll,
> Advance, retreat, or form one whole. . . .
>
> Then diff'rent companies are found
> Gathered on various plats of ground
> Where'er the elastic ball will hop,
> Or on clean, even places drop,
> When the strong butt's propelling force
> Mounts it in air, an oblique course,
> One Choix at Fives are earnest here,
> Another furious at cricket there. . . .
>
> A third at bat contend alike
> Who best can catch, or best can strike.
> A fourth at bowling rack their skill
> Who best can toss the bowl at will,
> Who its rotations can confine,
> That one fair bowling lay the nine.[19]

On the warm, pleasant days, the Commander-in-Chief pitched ball with his officers, or as George Ewing noted, "did us the honor to play at wicket with us." And Dr. Waldo commemorated in rhyme the unchanging pattern of the soldier's night in camp:

> Now Phoebus plunges in the sea
> And the gray ev'ning shuts the day,
> All parties to prepare for musings
> Repair to huts and drink the loosings.
> There loud talking soon begins
> Of who plays best and who most wins.
> Of politics, or frothy matter
> That sudden raises gen'ral clatter.
> Then of cowards, fools, rascals, rattles,
> Of duels, heroes, wars, and battles,
> Of fornicators, witches, scolds,
> Fatigues and hardships, heats and colds,
> Of beauty, women, wine, and love,
> Of thundering armies and of Jove.
> *Huzza!* the chorus loudly cry,
> Responsive vales *Huzza!* reply.
> Toasts for the Cause, for sweethearts, wives,
> Long peace, long health, and happy lives.[20]

For Washington, whose winter labors had been ceaseless, spring meant that another campaign now lay ahead. On the

twenty-first of April, when he sat down to write a long letter
to John Banister, Virginia Delegate to Congress, his quiet
pride in the way his men had endured shone lustrously:

> . . . without arrogance or the smallest deviation from
> truth it may be said that no history, now extant, can furnish
> an instance of an Army's suffering such uncommon hardships
> as ours have done and bearing them with the same patience
> and fortitude. To see men without clothes to cover their naked-
> ness, without blankets to lay on, without shoes, by which their
> marches might be traced by the blood from their feet, and
> almost as often without provisions as with; marching through
> frost and snow, and at Christmas taking up their winter quar-
> ters within a day's march of the enemy, without a house or hut
> to cover them till they could be built, and submitting to it
> without a murmur, is a mark of patience and obedience
> which in my opinion can scarce be paralleled.[21]

On the bright morning of May 1, while the troops wearing
dogwood wreaths in their hats paraded to fife and drum past
regimental Maypoles, joyous news came: France had recognized the United States. "I believe no event was ever received
with more heartfelt joy," Washington exclaimed.

Clandestine French aid in arms, artillery, ammunition,
clothing, shoes, and other supplies had been flowing into
American ports since the summer of 1776, set in motion by
the Baron de Beaumarchais, courtier, playwright, intriguer,
watchmaker, and wit. An open treaty with the Bourbons long
had been an American hope. Both France and Spain thirsted
to revenge the losses they had suffered from British arms,
especially in the Seven Years' War. Even before Lexington
and Concord, the French ministry had supposed that an independent America would cripple Great Britain commercially
while expanding the French trade, and the Count de Vergennes, Secretary of Foreign Affairs and leader of the interven-
tionists in the French government, did everything in his power
to persuade his monarch, young Louis XVI, to support the
American rebels. But Louis preferred neutrality. He insisted
that the Americans eventually would achieve their independence alone and then France could reap the benefits without paying the price of assistance.

Through Vergennes' steady pressure, France finally was
poised to declare war on Great Britain, with the aid of Spain,
when news reached Paris of Washington's rout at Long Island. France withdrew and watched until July, 1777, when
Vergennes tried again to organize a Franco-Spanish-Ameri-
can alliance, but now Spain refused to join. With the great
American victory at Saratoga, it became obvious that the
rebels would fight on. For more than a year, the fabulous

Franklin and his colleagues, Arthur Lee and Silas Deane, had labored in France to achieve a treaty. The Saratoga triumph placed a capstone upon their efforts. The French minister must have heard or suspected that England now was ready to offer the Americans generous peace terms, and by February 6, 1778, treaties between the United States and France were signed in keeping with the promise Vergennes had made on December 17, 1777, that France would formally recognize the United States.

The terms of the treaty provided that France would help the United States win independence; if a war between France and Great Britain should result, the United States would support her ally; and neither party would make a truce or peace without consent of the other.

Washington was free to inform the army officially on May 5 and to plan a celebration for the next morning.

The sixth was a day of "Universal Happiness & the strictest Propriety." It opened with booming of cannon to assemble the brigades for a reading of the news and a discourse by their chaplains. It was all very impressive, and one of the men recorded the events of the day:

After the chaplains had finished their discourses and the second cannon was fired, the troops began their march to the lines in the following order: each major general conducted the first brigade of his command to the ground; the other brigades were conducted by their commanding officers in separate columns. Major General Lord Stirling commanded on the right; the Marquis de Lafayette on the left; and Baron de Kalb the second line. But this arrangement can convey no adequate idea of their movements to their several posts, of the appearance of his Excellency during his circuit round the lines, of the air of our soldiers, the cleanliness of their dress, the brilliancy and good order of their arms, and the remarkable animation with which they performed the necessary salute as the General passed along. Indeed, during the whole of the review, the utmost military decorum was preserved, while at the same time one might observe the hearts of the soldiery struggling to express their feelings in a way more agreeable to nature.

The Commander-in-Chief, his suite, the Marquis de Lafayette, his train, Lord Stirling, General Greene, and the other principal officers who had joined his Excellency having finished the review, retired to the center of the encampment, to a kind of amphitheater, which had been formed to entertain the officers of the army, who were invited to partake of a collation with his Excellency, after the *feu de joye*.

On firing of the third signal gun, the *feu de joye* commenced. It was conducted with great judgment and regularity. The gradual progression of the sound from the discharge of

the cannon and musketry, swelling and rebounding from the
neighboring hills and gently sweeping along the Schuylkill,
with the intermingled huzzas to "Long Live the King of
France," "Long live the friendly European Powers," and
"Long live the American States," composed a military music
more agreeable to a soldier's ear than the most finished pieces
of your favorite Handel.

The *feu de joye* being over and the troops marched back to
their different quarters, the officers came forward to the entertainment provided by his Excellency. . . .[22]

A fillip was given the reception when Washington, just before the "cold collation" and the toasts, presented to the
guests, under act of Congress of the preceding day, Major
General Baron von Steuben, Inspector General of the United
States.

At six o'clock it was over. The General stood to take his
leave; an officer wrote:

> There was a universal clap, with loud huzzas, which con-
> tinued till he had proceeded a quarter of a mile, during which
> time there were a thousand hats tossed in the air. His Ex-
> cellency turned round with his retinue and huzzaed several
> times.[23]

But spring brings action to armies. To the men of the ranks
driving Howe from Philadelphia seemed but a matter of time.
Lieutenant McMichael wrote in his diary: "To us who had
built ourselves a city on the banks of the Schuylkill, the return of spring brought thoughts of happiness, which we
should have enjoyed more fully, were Philadelphia again in
our possession. We rely on the prudence and military skill of
our worthy General to accomplish this."

Six weeks later the lieutenant thought wise to send part of
his superfluous baggage and some of his books to Jersey before the campaign opened. Among them was his journal and
in a last burst of mawkish verse he penned:

> Farewell my Journal, we must part
> Which contains some nature but no art—
> The companion of my sore fatigues
> Throughout the war, but not intrigues;
> Therefore adieu my ambiguous book,
> May you be pleasing to those who in you look.[24]

"SIR WILLIAM, HE, AS SNUG AS FLEA"

The British in Philadelphia

WINTER 1777-SPRING 1778

WITH THE budding of the mulberries and poplars along the brick walks of Philadelphia, most of the inhabitants of the Quaker City could look back upon a winter that contrasted sharply with the one endured by the American army, only a few miles away. The winter at Philadelphia, for all its petty alarms and minor shortages, afforded a snug rest and not a little frivolity for the officers and men of the occupation force and to a great many citizens. Some few Whigs who stayed on, in and around the city, suffered, and starving American prisoners were seen pulling up grass in their prison yard in order to eat the roots. But the majority even of Americans made their peace with the conquerors, and many of the ladies joined with the loyalists in taking full advantage of the social opportunities offered by the presence of the British army.

Dark, statuesque Rebecca Franks, a sharp-tongued loyalist, described the pleasures of the city to Mrs. William Paca, exiled to the country as a Congressman's wife:

> You can have no idea of the life of continued amusement I live in. I can scarce have a moment to myself . . . and most elegantly am I dressed for a ball this evening at Smith's where we have one every Thursday. . . . No loss for partners, even I am engaged to seven different gentlemen, for you must know 'tis a fixed rule never to dance but two dances at a time with the same person. Oh, how I wish Mr. P. would let you come in for a week or two. . . . I know you are as fond of a gay life as myself. You'd have an opportunity of raking as much as you choose, either at plays, balls, concerts, or assemblies. I've been but three evenings alone since we moved to town.[1]

Little Polly Redman was just as violent a rebel as Miss Franks was a loyalist and refused to compromise her political principles for the sake of amusement. Continually she irritated British officers by singing in their presence popular patriotic songs, such as "War and Washington" and "Burgoyne's Defeat," her eyes twinkling with merry malice as she emphasized a line which ran, "Cooped up in a town."

Still another young lady who professed to be a true rebel, did not carry her scruples so far. To Mrs. Theodorick Bland, Jr., she wrote:

> I . . . suppose you anxious for an account of our last winter. You have, no doubt, heard that 'twas a gay one, as likewise the censure thrown on many of the poor girls for not scorning the pleasures that courted them. You, my friend, I am certain, have liberality of sentiment, and can make proper allowances for young people in the bloom of life and spirits, after being so long deprived of the gaities and amusements of life which their ages and spirits called for; how hard a task must it then be to resist temptation of that nature!
>
> Plays, concerts, balls, assemblies in rotation courted their presence. Politics were never introduced. The known Whig ladies were treated with equal politeness and attention with the Tory ladies. I, myself, though a noted one, was at last prevailed on to partake of some of the amusements, though nothing could have made me believe at the beginning of the winter that such a thing was possible.[2]

A diversion, unscheduled by the British, was furnished in January by David Bushnell, who had startled the redcoats in New York with his *American Turtle*. His Philadelphia appearance was reported in a letter published in a Boston newspaper:

> This city has lately been entertained with a most astonishing instance of the activity, bravery, and military skill of the royal navy of Great Britain. . . .
>
> Some time last week two boys observed a keg of a singular construction floating in the river opposite to the city. They got into a small boat, and attempting to take up the keg, it burst with a great explosion and blew up the unfortunate boys.
>
> On Monday last several kegs of a like construction made their appearance. An alarm was immediately spread through the city. Various reports prevailed, filling the city and the royal troops with unspeakable consternation. Some reported that these kegs were filled with armed rebels, who were to issue forth in the dead of night, as the Grecians did of old from their wooden horse at the siege of Troy, and take the city by surprise, asserting that they had seen the points of their bayonets through the bung holes of the kegs. Others said they were charged with the most inveterate combustibles to be kindled by secret machinery and setting the whole Delaware in flames were to consume all the shipping in the harbor; whilst others asserted that they were constructed by art magic, would of

themselves ascend the wharves in the night time and roll all flaming through the streets of the city, destroying everything in their way.

Be this as it may, certain it is that the shipping in the harbor and all the wharves of the city were fully manned. The battle begun, and it was surprising to behold the incessant blaze that was kept up against the enemy, the kegs.

Both officers and men exhibited the most unparalleled skill and bravery on the occasion, whilst the citizens stood gazing as solemn witnesses of their prowess. From the *Roebuck* and other ships of war whole broadsides were poured into the Delaware. In short, not a wandering chip, stick, or drift log but felt the vigor of British arms.

The action begun about sunrise and would have been completed with great success by noon had not an old market woman, coming down the river with provisions, unfortunately let a small keg of butter fall overboard, which (as it was then ebb) floated down to the scene of action. At the sight of this unexpected reinforcement of the enemy, the battle was renewed with fresh fury; the firing was incessant till the evening closed the affair.

The kegs were either totally demolished or obliged to fly, as none of them have shown their *heads* since. It is said his Excellency Lord Howe has dispatched a swift sailing packet with an account of this victory to the court of London. In a word, Monday, the fifth of January, 1778, must ever be distinguished in history for the memorable BATTLE OF THE KEGS.[3]

Bushnell's crude mines, designed to explode among the British ships, failed in their nocturnal mission because of a miscalculation of tides, but they furnished New Jersey Congressman Francis Hopkinson material for a doggerel song that swept the colonies. Four lines particularly were sung with taproom gusto:

> Sir William, he, as snug as flea
> Lay all this time a-snoring;
> Nor dreamed of harm, as he lay warm
> In bed with Mrs. Loring.[4]

Though many of Howe's own officers grumbled about the bitter truth in the patriot jibe, his army was unhappy when it learned that he would not lead it in the next campaign. Shortly after occupying Philadelphia, he had written to Lord Germain requesting to be relieved of "this very painful service," a command "wherein I have not the good fortune to enjoy the necessary confidence and support of my superiors." Germain, who foresaw the collapse of his plan of campaign in America, was delighted to seize upon Howe's desire as a chance to place the blame for failure on the general. On March 27, Howe received word that his resignation had been accepted and that he was to be succeeded by Sir Henry Clinton.

The British in Philadelphia and their sympathizers took a view different from that prevailing in London, where excoriation of Howe was unmitigating. Sir William's soldiers seemed to sense that the morbidly sensitive, colorless, reserved Clinton was not an officer under whose leadership they could gain new glories. In spite of Howe's shortcomings, they felt a genuine affection for their genial, hearty, indulgent commander, who, after all, had won a half-dozen pitched battles and occupied the enemy's capital. No sooner had gossip of his impending departure reached the mess tables than twenty of his younger, wealthy field officers resolved to give him, as a farewell, the most elaborate festival ever seen in the New World.

All the arrangements were entrusted to General Charles Grey's boyish, debonair aide, witty Captain John André. The captain had been exchanged after his capture at St. John's in '75 and since had served icy-eyed, war-scarred Charles Grey at Brandywine, Paoli, and Germantown. At Philadelphia, where he resided with his general, John André was not only the charmer of bevies of young ladies to whom he wrote love verses as dextrously as he sketched their likenesses, but he also was a clever artist and designer, whose talents had contributed greatly to the success of "Howe's Thespians" and their winter theater.

To commemorate General Howe's departure, Captain André conceived an affair he called the Mischianza, an Italian word signifying a medley. The rebel lady who wrote to Mrs. Bland continued her long letter with a description of Captain André's spectacle. After a detailed description of the ornate tickets, she wrote of the cruise in decorated boats, barges, and galleys from Knight's Wharf on the Schuylkill to the scene of festivities:

At length, we reached the place of destination . . . which was a seat belonging [to] the Wharton family, about half a mile below the town. The house stands about three hundred yards from the river. Here we landed, and in a lane formed by grenadiers and guards we proceeded about halfway to the house where we were stopped. Here a large triumphant arch in honor of Lord Howe engaged our attention. Neptune with his trident was engraved thereon and two sisters guarded it with drawn swords; they were placed in little niches formed for that purpose. On each side of this arch were seats for the ladies; steps, one above another and carpets thrown over the whole. . . .

[At] the particular request of the managers, fourteen young ladies were dressed alike: white Poland dresses of Mantua with long sleeves, a gauze turban spangled, and sashes around the waists. Seven of them wore pink sashes with silver spangles, and the others, white with gold spangles; handkerchiefs of gauze spangled in the same manner. Those of the pink and white were called the Ladies of the Blended Rose, the white and gold were of the Burning Mountain. These ladies, with all the others, were seated on these steps, when a herald from the Blended Rose made his appearance. His dress was quite in the Arabian Nights' style: a white satin waistcoat; small clothes of the same, monstrously large, in the Spanish fashion, trimmed with broad stripes of pink satin, adorned with silver, thrown in a loose manner down them; and the jacket—you have no doubt seen such dresses exactly, on the stage, the Spanish dons generally wear them—white leather boots, and little round beavers. . . . This herald declared the Ladies of the Blended Rose to be fairer than those of the Burning Mountain and dared in the name of his knights anyone to deny it.

The herald of the Burning Mountain appeared . . . his dress being [orange] color and black . . . and he in the name of his knights denied the assertion and declared the Ladies of the Burning Mountain to be fairer than any ladies in the world.

The knights then made their appearance, attended by their squires, whose dress was as fantastical, though in another model, having the short cloak thrown over the one shoulder. These preceded their respective knights, bearing the shield and spear. . . .[5]

Among the Knights of the Blended Rose, resplendent on great gray chargers, was Captain André. André wrote to a lady friend a vivid account of the joust that followed the challenge by his knights. The Black Knights of the Burning Mountain, after circling the lists and making their bows to the ladies, drew up fronting the White Knights of the Blended Rose. The chief of the Knights of the Burning Mountain directed his squire to take up the gauntlet thrown down by the chief of the Knights of the Blended Rose. Saluting each other, the rivals rode off and returned at a gallop to shiver their spears. They rode the field again, discharging pistols, and then engaged with swords. When the two chiefs clashed in single combat, the marshal of the field declared the ladies satisfied. The knights thereupon desisted from further "combat," and rode to the pavilion to salute their ladies.

The knights assembled at the triumphal arch, toward which the ladies in Turkish regalia advanced in procession. The knights saluted, dismounted and joined their partners, and led the whole assemblage through a second ornate arch into a garden in front of the mansion. From the garden they ascended carpeted stairs "into a spacious hall . . . painted in imitation of Sienna marble, enclosing portions of white marble." In the hall and the enormous rooms leading off it, the company drank "cooling liquors" while the knights on bended knee received their ladies' compliments. Then, wrote André, came the ball:

The ball was opened by the knights and their ladies, and the dances continued till ten o'clock, when the windows were thrown open, and a magnificent bouquet of rockets began the fireworks. These were planned by Captain Montresor, the chief engineer, and consisted of twenty different exhibitions. . . .

Toward the conclusion, the interior part of the triumphal arch was illuminated amid an uninterrupted flight of rockets and bursting balloons. The military trophies on each side assumed a variety of transparent colors. The shell and flaming heart on the wings sent forth Chinese fountains succeeded by fireworks. . . .

At twelve supper was announced, and large folding doors, hitherto artfully concealed, being suddenly thrown open, discovered a magnificent saloon of two hundred and ten feet by forty, and twenty-two in height, with three alcoves on each side, which served for sideboards. . . . Fifty-six large pier-glasses, ornamented with green silk, artificial flowers, and ribbons; a hundred branches with three lights in each, trimmed in the same manner as the mirrors; eighteen lusters, each with twenty-four lights, suspended from the ceiling and ornamented as the branches; three hundred wax tapers disposed along the supper tables; four hundred and thirty covers; twelve hundred dishes; twenty-four black slaves in Oriental dresses with silver collars and bracelets, ranged in two lines and bending to the ground as the general and admiral approached the saloon—all these, forming together the most brilliant assemblage of gay objects and appearing at once, as we entered by an easy ascent, exhibited a *coup d'oeil* beyond description magnificent.

Toward the end of the supper, the Herald of the Blended Rose, . . . attended by his trumpeteers, entered the saloon and proclaimed the King's health, the Queen and royal family, the army and navy, with their respective commanders, the knights and their ladies, and the ladies in general. Each of these toasts were followed by a flourish of music. After supper, we returned to the ballroom and continued to dance until four o'clock.[6]

No expense had been spared to make it the greatest pageant imaginable. A Hessian observer commented, "The great English shop of Coffin and Anderson took in £12,000 sterling for silk goods and other fine materials, which shows how much money was lavished on this affair, and how elegantly the ladies were dressed." Much more outraged was Mrs. Henry Drinker, whose husband had been punished for loyalism. "This day," she said, "may be remembered by many for the scenes of folly and vanity. . . . How insensible do these people appear, while our land is so greatly desolated, and death and sore destruction has overtaken and impends over so many." Even Ambrose Serle, whose employer, Admiral Lord Howe was the general's brother, was appalled at the "folly and extravagance of it." One grizzled old artillery major snorted, "The Knights of the Burning Mountain are tomfools and the Knights of the Blended Rose are damned fools! I know of no other distinction between them." But one of the girls thought "we never had, and perhaps never shall have so elegant an entertainment in America again," and André and his fellows were immensely satisfied that their idol was properly saluted.

26

"MY DARLING LIBERTEY"

Valley Forge to Monmouth

MAY-JUNE 1778

WHEN LIEUTENANT McMichael sent off his excess baggage from the "city on the banks of the Schuylkill" and the time for campaigning was at hand, Washington faced three alternatives: an offensive against Philadelphia, an assault on the British in New York, or a continued defensive. His main army at Valley Forge now numbered 11,800 men. About fourteen hundred more were at Wilmington and eighteen hundred in the Highlands. With expected reinforcements he would have some twenty thousand troops, plus three or four thousand militia from the Middle and Southern states. In Philadelphia, the enemy had ten thousand men; in New York, four thousand; in Rhode Island, probably two thousand.

By the twenty-third of April, Washington had heard that Sir Henry Clinton was replacing Howe. What he did not know was the tremendous extent to which the news of Saratoga, reaching London on December 2, 1777, and espionage reports of subsequent Franco-American negotiations had shaken British officials and affected England's plan for prosecuting the war in 1778. The King and the North Ministry, recognizing the difficulty if not the impossibility of conducting a successful land war against the American rebels while fighting France and probably Spain, had framed concessions to offer to the Americans that they thought might lead to a peace and allow England to withdraw her forces from America for commitment to the global war elsewhere.

However, an American peace hinged on one condition only —that Britain recognize the independence of the colonies— and this was the one condition which the King and his government would not consider. Therefore, the ministers had no choice but to make the proposals to America while planning to continue the war, though on a reduced scale. Hoping that the peace proposals, now being conveyed across the Atlantic by a commission, might by chance prove acceptable, the Ministry also had devised a new strategy in the event of their rejection. This provided for a continuance of the American war, with France expected to be an ally of the rebels.

The idea of a land war in the Northern colonies was rejected, and St. Lucia, the French naval base in the West Indies, became a primary objective in a naval war. The British army was to be used to guard naval bases and to help in coastal raids. Clinton was ordered to embark five thousand men immediately for St. Lucia and three thousand for Florida to protect that flank of the British position. Philadelphia was to be evacuated by sea and New York held, pending the outcome of the peace overtures. If these were rejected and Washington should threaten to "drive the troops into the sea," Clinton was to evacuate New York also, but it was hoped that Rhode Island could be retained as a naval base. If not, the army was to withdraw to Quebec, after establishing a base at Halifax. In the fall of the year, when the French would have to leave the Northern theater to care for their fleet at West Indian bases, the Southern colonies would become the theater of effort for the British in America.

Unaware of the new English strategy, Washington and his officers, when they met in May, decided to stay longer at Valley Forge to strengthen the army, increase the mounted arm, and await the first enemy move at Philadelphia. Officers and men now found their hut city tolerable, and in May they were whiling away their time pleasantly enough, taking in rumors, and growing a little impatient. One of them wrote to his sister:

The camp could now afford you some entertainment. The maneuvering of the Army is in itself a sight that would charm you. Besides these, the theater is opened. Last Monday *Cato* was performed before a very numerous and splendid audience. His Excellency and Lady, Lord Stirling, the Countess and Lady Kitty, and Mr. Greene were part of the assembly. The scenery was in taste and the performance admirable. Colonel George did his part to admiration. He made an excellent *die,* as they say. Pray heaven, he don't die in earnest, for yesterday he was seized with the pleurisy and lies extremely ill.

If the enemy does not retire from Philadelphia soon, our theatrical amusements will continue. *The Fair Penitent* with *The Padlock* will soon be acted. The Recruiting Officer is also on foot.

I hope, however, we shall be disappointed in all these by the more agreeable entertainment of taking possession of Philadelphia. There are strong rumors that the English are meditating a retreat. Heaven send it, for I fear we shall not be able to force them to go these two months.[1]

In mid-May "strong rumors" of an impending British evacuation of Philadelphia led Washington to order out almost a third of his effective troops east of the Schuylkill to cover the country and have a close look at the enemy's "motions and designs." On the eighteenth, the Marquis de Lafayette, commanding the expedition, struck out for a position only two or three miles from the British outposts at Chestnut Hill. Two mornings later the ambitious young nobleman almost got trapped by an enemy encircling movement, but he adroitly slipped out of the net like an old veteran, and returned to camp. His escape was so narrow that Washington did not again attempt to set up an observation corps so close. Instead he sent Maxwell's Brigade to Mount Holly in New Jersey, six miles east of Burlington, whence he could report promptly any move toward New York. He stationed at Chad's Ford part of Smallwood's command, which had wintered at Wilmington, in case the British should leave Philadelphia as they had come by way of the Head of Elk.

Clinton was having his troubles. It seemed a simple matter to put his army and its equipment and stores on shipboard and sail back to New York; but the nearest place he could embark his troops was New Castle, forty miles away. Then if unfavorable winds or other accident of nature should delay him, Washington might easily attack New York before a sea-borne force could get there. Moreover, Sir Henry was burdened with several thousand loyalists, who could not be abandoned without a blot upon English honor; they insisted on dismantling their homes and taking their possessions into exile with the army. Clinton had little choice but to allow them to put their families and goods upon his transports. He also embarked two Hessian regiments which on a march might have deserted, and prepared his army for a retreat by land. By the eighteenth of June, the last red-coated detachment had left town, destroying the bridges over which they marched.

The next day, chunky, dark General Benedict Arnold, recently recovered from that second leg wound taken at the head of his troops at Bemis Heights, swaggered into the capital to establish American military government. With "drawn swords in their hands" the American Light Horse galloped triumphantly in, frightening many by their appearance. Lucy Knox considered sojourning for a while in Philadelphia, after her Henry had marched from Valley Forge. The Knoxes went into the city "but it stunk so abominably that it was impossible to stay there. . . ."

A returning civilian recorded his first experiences in the reoccupied capital:

The face of the suburbs on the North side is so much altered that people who were born here and have lived here all their lives are much at a loss to find out the situation of particular houses. The houses themselves are destroyed and redoubts built in the neighborhood of the spots where some of them formerly stood. The timber has been all cut down and . . . the fine fertile fields are all laid waste. In short, the whole is one promiscuous scene of ruin. . . .

Advancing near to the city, you come to an abatis (chiefly if not entirely made of fruit trees) which extends from Delaware to Schuylkill. Redoubts are built at proper distances in this line. . . .

Upon getting *into the city,* I was surprised to find that it had suffered so little; I question whether it would have fared better had our own troops had possession of it; that is, as to *the buildings,* but the morals of the inhabitants have suffered vastly.

The enemy introduced new fashions and made old vices more common; the former are the most absurd, ridiculous, and preposterous you can conceive. I can give no description which will convey an adequate idea of them. So far as they concern the gentlemen, they appear to be principally confined to the *hat,* which is now amazingly broad-brimmed and cocked very sharp. Were they flapped after the manner of the people called the Quakers, these brims would be useful in this hot weather, because they would afford an agreeable shade to the face, but in the present mode they serve only as an encumbrance to the blocks they cover.

The females who stayed in the city while it was in possession of the enemy cut a curious figure. Their hats, which are of the flat, round kind, are of the size of a large, japanned tea-waiter. Their caps exceed any of the sarcastic prints you have seen, and their hair is dressed with the assistance of wool, etc., in such a manner as to appear too heavy to be supported by their necks. If the caps would not blow off, a northwester would certainly throw these belles off their center as Yorick did the milliner—by accident.

I cannot yet learn whether the *cork rumps* have been introduced here, but some artificial rumps or other are necessary to counterbalance the extraordinary natural weight which some of the ladies carry before them. You will probably be surprised at this, but you may rely on it as a fact: indeed many people do not hesitate in supposing that the most of the young ladies who were in the city with the enemy and wear the present fashionable dresses have purchased them at the expense of their virtue. It is agreed on all hands that the British officers played the devil with the girls. The privates, I suppose, were satisfied with the *common* prostitutes.

Last Saturday an imitation of the *Mischenza* . . . was humbly attempted. A noted strumpet was paraded through the streets with her head dressed in the modern *British* taste, to the no small amusement of a vast crowd. . . . She acted her part well; to complete the farce, there ought to have been another lady of the same character (as General Howe had two), and somebody ought to represent a British officer.[2]

Soon thereafter, Congress returned to town—to the "College Hall," because the enemy had left the State House, said New Hampshire Delegate Josiah Bartlett, "in a most filthy and sordid situation, as were many of the public and private buildings in the city." Some of the houses had been used for stables, and holes cut in the parlor floors to clean them out.

Poring over the well-worn map made for him by his cartographer, Washington could not guess which road Clinton would take, and that very morning his own officers had advised him against trying to strike the retreating army, but the General could not bear to see Clinton go unmolested to New York. His own first move must be to cross into Jersey and harass and watch Clinton's march. As soon as he learned of the evacuation, shortly before noon on the eighteenth, he started six brigades under Lee and ·Wayne toward Coryell's

Ferry on the Delaware; Lafayette, De Kalb, and Stirling with
their divisions were to follow at five the next morning.

During the night of the twentieth the advance brigades
crossed the river. Washington halted to bivouac for the night
in the rain ten miles from the ferry. The enemy was reported
near Mount Holly, moving slowly.

Drenching rains, alternating with broiling muggy sunshine, impeded Washington's progress. The sandy roads, dry
or wet, gave little purchase to the grinding wheels of artillery and wagons or weary feet. Two more days brought
the army only to Hopewell, a village twelve miles northwest
of Princeton, where Washington established headquarters on
the twenty-third.

The enemy struggled against even greater difficulties: the
heat that soared to a hundred degrees in the merciless sun
smothered the redcoats and the Hessians, the latter wearing
even heavier clothing and bowed under packs and equipment
weighing nearly a hundred pounds. Whole squads of blank-
faced men reeled to the side of the road and fell flushed
with sunstroke or shivering with heat prostration. American
militia and Continental detachments relentlessly snapped at
their flanks and rear and frequently delayed their tortuous
march by wrecking bridges, felling trees across the road, and
choking wells with earth. Clinton's progress dropped to a
snail's pace. His train of fifteen hundred wagons, carriages,
and carts, creaking under tons of loot and winter baggage,
strung out twelve miles long. Hundreds of the suffering Hessians who had not been sent to New York by water deserted
and made their way to the Americans. In a week Clinton
moved less than forty miles.

At four in the morning of the twenty-fourth, Washington
was roused by a report from Major General Philemon Dickinson, commanding officer of the New Jersey militia, watching the enemy: Clinton seemed to be trying to bring on a
general action. At first, Washington doubted it, but shortly
he called a council of officers, which Alexander Hamilton
attended and described:

> The General unluckily called a council . . . the result of
> which would have done honor to the most honorable society
> of midwives and to them only.

The purport was that we should keep at a comfortable distance from the enemy and keep up a vain parade of annoying them by detachment. . . . A detachment of fifteen hundred
men was sent off under General [Charles] Scott [of Vir-
ginia] to join the other troops near the enemy's lines. General Lee was the *primum nobile* of this sage plan and was

even opposed to sending so considerable a force.

The General, on mature reconsideration . . . determined to pursue a different line of conduct at all hazards. With this view, he marched the army next morning towards Kingston, and there made another detachment of one thousand men under General Wayne, and formed all the detached troops into an advanced corps under the command of . . . Lafayette. The project was that this advanced corps should take the first opportunity to attack the enemy's rear on the march, to be supported or covered as circumstances should require by the whole army.

General Lee's conduct with respect to the command of this corps was truly childish. According to the incorrect notions of our army, his seniority would have entitled him to the command of the advanced corps, but he in the first instance declined it in favor of the Marquis. Some of his friends having blamed him for doing it and Lord Stirling having shown a disposition to interpose his claim, General Lee very inconsistently reasserted his pretentions. The matter was a second time accommodated; General Lee and Lord Stirling agreed to let the Marquis command. General Lee, a little time after, recanted again and became very importunate. The General, who had all along observed the greatest candor in the matter, grew tired of such fickle behavior and ordered the Marquis to proceed.

The enemy in marching from Allentown had changed their disposition and thrown all their best troops in the rear. This made it necessary . . . to reinforce the advanced corps. Two brigades were detached for this purpose, and the General, willing to accommodate General Lee, sent him with them to take the command of the whole advanced corps, which rendezvoused the forenoon of the twenty-seventh at Englishtown, consisting of at least five thousand rank and file, most of them select troops. General Lee's orders were, the moment he received intelligence of the enemy's march, to pursue them and to attack their rear.

This intelligence was received about five o'clock the morning of the twenty-eighth, and General Lee put his troops in motion accordingly. The main body did the same. The advanced corps came up with the enemy's. rear a mile or two beyond the [Monmouth] Court House. I saw the enemy drawn up and am persuaded there were not a thousand men —their front from different accounts was then ten miles off. However favorable this situation may seem for an attack, it was not made, but after changing their position two or three times by retrograde movements, our advanced corps got into a general confused retreat and even rout would hardly be too strong an expression. Not a word of all this was officially communicated to the General. . . .[3]

Washington indeed knew little of what was happening to the advanced corps. When he sent to Lee to find out why he did not press an attack, Lee told his aide, "Tell the General I am doing well enough." Now riding forward in the terrible midday heat, Washington came upon a few soldiers coming back. They said the whole force in front was retreating. The General trotted on to a wooded ridge and saw the road before him filled with men moving toward him. He sent forward his aides, Harrison and Fitzgerald, to see "the situation of things." Soon Fitzgerald was back, saying he could not find the reason for the retreat. Washington spurred ahead to see what he could do.

Private Joseph Martin had been in the rear of the advanced corps when the order had come to retreat. Said he:

Grating as this order was to our feelings, we were obliged to comply. We had not retreated far before we came to a defile, a muddy, sloughy brook. While the artillery were passing this place, we sat down by the roadside. In a few minutes, the Commander-in-Chief and suite crossed the road just where we were sitting. I heard him ask our officers, "by whose order the troops were retreating," and being answered, "By General Lee's," he said something, but as he was moving forward all the time . . . he was too far off for me to hear it distinctly. Those that were nearer to him said that his words were, "D—n him."

Whether he did thus express himself or not, I do not know. It was certainly very unlike him, but he seemed at the instant to be in a great passion. His looks, if not his words, seemed to indicate as much.

After passing us, he rode on to the plain field and took an observation of the advancing enemy. He remained there some time on his old English charger, while the shot from the British artillery were rending up the earth all around him. After he had taken a view of the enemy, he returned and ordered the two Connecticut brigades to make a stand at a fence, in order to keep the enemy in check while the artillery and other troops crossed the before mentioned defile. . . .

When we had secured our retreat, the artillery formed a line of pieces upon a long piece of elevated ground. Our detachment formed directly in front of the artillery, as a covering party, so far below the declivity of the hill that the pieces could play over our heads. And here we waited the approach of the enemy, should he see fit to attack us.[4]

Having disposed part of his retreating troops, Washington galloped up to find General Lee. Tench Tilghman, the General's modest, even-tempered aide, was at his side and remembered:

. . . General Washington rode up to him with some degree of astonishment and asked him, what was the meaning of this?

General Lee answered . . ."Sir, sir."

I took it that General Lee did not hear the question distinctly. Upon General Washington's repeating the question, General Lee answered, that from a variety of contradictory intelligence, and that from his orders not being obeyed, matters were thrown into confusion, and that he did not choose to beard the British army with troops in such a situation. He said that, besides, the thing was against his own opinion.

General Washington answered, whatever his opinion might have been, he expected his orders would have been obeyed, and then rode on to the rear of the retreating troops. . . .[5]

It was a tense moment. The tempers of both Washington and Lee were no less heated than the incredible weather itself, and Lee thought that Washington's brusque, harsh remarks implied more than met the ear, that they impugned both his bravery and his ability. Stories of that fateful, hurried meeting on a confused field of battle burgeoned until even such a sound man as Lieutenant Thomas Washington later recalled, not cold austerity, but hot temper, on the part of General Washington. Thomas Washington rode that day with Colonel William Grayson, a near neighbor of the General in Virginia and commanding officer of the regiment in the vanguard of Lee's column. The lieutenant asserted that Lee's answer to Washington was, "Sir, these troops are not able to meet British Grenadiers."

"Sir," said General Washington, greatly wrought, "they are able, and by God, they shall do it!" And he gave orders to countermarch the column.

General Charles Scott of Virginia claimed the words of Washington were even more colorful. Scott, a connoisseur of profanity, was always quick to display his own and to admire invention in that of others. Asked later if the General ever swore, Scott made a ready reply:

Yes, once. It was at Monmouth and on a day that would have made any man swear. Yes, sir, he swore on that day till the leaves shook on the trees, charming, delightful. Never have I enjoyed such swearing before or since. Sir, on that ever-memorable day, he swore like an angel from Heaven.[6]

Scott never bothered to inform his listeners how he came to be present and was not at that instant with his command, where he belonged.

Magnificently, Washington stemmed the retreat. Lafayette was charmed by the way in which he rode "all along the lines amid the shouts of the soldiers, cheering them by his voice and example and restoring to our standard the fortunes of the fight. I thought . . . that never had I beheld so superb a man."

Upon the New Englanders, whom Washington had placed at the fence, fell the brunt of the British assault. Joseph Martin, who had not been under fire since Germantown, was becoming a seasoned soldier; he and his comrades now reaped the benefits of Steuben's training:

> . . . a sharp conflict ensued; these troops maintained their ground until the whole force of the enemy that could be brought to bear had charged upon them through the fence, and after being overpowered . . . and the platoon officers had given orders . . . to leave the fence, they had to force them to retreat, so eager were they to be revenged. . . .

As soon as the troops had left this ground, the British planted their cannon upon this place and began a violent attack upon the artillery and our detachment, but neither could be routed. The cannonade continued for some time without intermission, when the British pieces being mostly disabled, they reluctantly crawled back from the height which they occupied and hid themselves from our sight.

Before the cannonade had commenced, a part of the right wing of the British army had advanced across a low meadow and brook and occupied an orchard on our left. . . .

After the British artillery had fallen back . . . we were immediately ordered from our old detachment and joined another, the whole composing a corps of about five hundred men. We . . . marched toward the enemy's right wing, which was in the orchard, and kept concealed from them as long as possible by keeping behind the bushes.

When we could no longer keep ourselves concealed, we marched into the open fields and formed our line. The British immediately formed and began to retreat to the main body of their army. Colonel [Joseph] Cilly, finding that we were not likely to overtake the enemy before they reached the main body of the army, on account of fences and other obstructions, ordered three or four platoons from the right of our corps to pursue and attack them and thus keep them in play till the rest of the detachment could come up.

I was in this party. We pursued without order. As I passed through the orchard, I saw a number of the enemy lying under the trees killed by our fieldpiece. . . . We overtook the enemy just as they were entering . . . the meadow which was rather bushy. . . . They were retreating in line, though in some disorder. I singled out a man and took my aim directly between his shoulders (they were divested of their packs); he was a good mark, being a broad-shouldered fellow, but what became of him I know not; the fire and smoke hid him from my sight. One thing I know . . . I took as deliberate aim at him as ever I did at any game in my life. . . .

By this time our whole party had arrived, and the British had obtained a position that suited them . . . for they returned our fire in good earnest, and we played the second part of the same tune.

They occupied a much higher piece of ground than we did and had a small piece of artillery, which the soldiers called a "grasshopper." We had no artillery with us. The first shot they gave us from this piece cut off the thigh bone of a captain, just above the knee, and the whole heel of a private in the rear of him.

We gave it to poor Sawney (for they were Scotch troops) so hot that he was forced to fall back and leave the ground they occupied. When our commander saw them retreating and nearly joined with their main body, he shouted, "Come, my boys, reload your pieces and we will give them a setoff!" We did so, and gave them the parting salute and the firing on both sides ceased.

We then laid ourselves under the fences and bushes to take breath, for we had need of it. . . . Fighting is hot work in cool weather, much more so in such weather as it was on the twenty-eighth of June, 1778. . . .

As soon as our party had ceased firing, it began in the center and then upon the right, but as I was not in that part of the army, I had no "adventure" in it, but the firing was continued in one part or the other of the field the whole afternoon.[7]

The firing Martin heard was on the wings, where fresh British attacks were pressing. After failing to dislodge the reformed center, where Martin fought, Clinton pressed first to turn the left of the main army, which had come up under Stirling, who held; then he struck the right under Greene, where firing was not concentrated. James McHenry was on the field and reported the end of the day. Wayne gave the British a warm reception. Then:

General Greene, at the same critical moment, had taken possession of a piece of ground on their left with a brigade under the immediate command of General Woodford, where he formed a battery of cannon which severely enfiladed the enemy, and co-operating with the gallant opposition given them in front by General Wayne, obliged them to retire with great loss. Here General [Lieutenant Colonel Henry] Monckton of their Grenadiers and several of their officers fell. . . . After this, we had several contentions, all terminating in our favor, in each of which we forced the enemy. . . . Night now coming on prevented our pursuing any further the advantages we had gained. The troops that were ordered to gain the enemy's right and left flank did not reach their ground till night came on. The attack was, therefore, delayed until morning. But the enemy . . . retreated about midnight, leaving behind them all the marks of disgrace and precipitancy. . . .

I do not think that in any one instance the Commander-in-Chief ever unfolded greater abilities or that were attended with happier effects. I am confident that by his presence, exertions, and superior conduct the glory of the day was regained. He, through the whole series of actions, at all times appeared in as much danger as any soldier in the field. But it required it, . . . to recover what we had lost by our morning's misadventure. The enemy, who were advancing rapidly, elated by our retreat, were to be checked; the most advantageous ground to be seized; the main body of the army to be formed; the enemy's intentions and dispositions to be discovered; and a new plan of attack to be concerted; and all this in the smallest interval of time. But it is in those moments of a battle that the genius of a general is displayed, when a very inconsiderable weight determines whether it shall be a victory or a defeat.

General Greene and Lord Stirling gave the most evident and unequivocal marks of great military worth. . . . Lafayette was sadly disappointed. He had flattered himself, from his advanced situation under General Lee, with the first laurels of the day. . . . He was ordered by General Washington to form in the rear of our army, to support us in case of a retreat. . . .

I am told General Lee claims great praise in what he terms a retrograde maneuver. I confess I am no proper judge of its merit, nor ever heard that it was a preconcerted or communicated scheme until after the engagement. . . .

Although the victory was not so *extensive* as we could wish, yet it has every substantial and unequivocal proof of its being one. We gained the field of battle before evening.[8]

From the reddish soil of Monmouth Court House sprang that day some heroes, and a heroine. She appeared in the cannonade and Joseph Martin observed her:

A woman whose husband belonged to the artillery . . . attended with her husband at the piece the whole time. While in the act of reaching a cartridge and having one of her feet as far before the other as she could step, a cannon shot from the enemy passed directly between her legs, without doing any other damage than carrying away all the lower part of her petticoat. Looking at it with apparent unconcern, she observed that it was lucky it did not pass a little higher, for in that case it might have carried away something else, and continued her occupation.[9]

This bawdy hoyden, noticed by several others, was Mary Ludwig Hayes, wife of a private whom she followed to war and who was that day assigned to a gun battery. A woman of no education whatsoever, who smoked, chewed tobacco, and "swore like a trooper," she was as bold a veteran as the field produced. Carrying water for the cannoneers and the wounded won for her a nickname that survived: "Molly Pitcher."

Washington slept on the field, that close Sabbath night, wrapped in his cloak, fully expecting a renewal of conflict in the morning. At dawn he found the enemy gone. Judging no advantage to be gained by pursuit, he rested his men, tended the wounded, buried the dead, and soon discovered himself in a very strange correspondence.

On the hot, still morning of the thirtieth he received a letter from Charles Lee which began astoundingly:

> Sir: From the knowledge I have of your Excellency's character, I must conclude that nothing but the misinformation of some very stupid, or misrepresentation of some very wicked person could have occasioned your making use of such very singular expressions as you did on my coming up to the ground where you had taken post: they implied that I was guilty either of disobedience of orders, of want of conduct, or want of courage. Your Excellency will, therefore, infinitely oblige me by letting me know on which of these three articles you ground your charge, that I may prepare for my justification, which I have the happiness to be confident I can do, to the Army, to the Congress, to America, and to the world in general.[10]

Frigidly, Lee went on to say that neither Washington nor his advisers, none of whom were on the spot, could be "in the least judges of the merits or demerits of our maneuvers," to which he claimed "the success of the day was entirely owing." He accused the General of being "guilty of an act of cruel injustice towards a man who certainly has some pretensions to the regard of every servant of this country." He declared, "I have a right to demand some reparation." He could not believe that Washington's remarks were a "motion of your own breast, but instigated by some of those dirty earwigs who will forever insinuate themselves near persons in high office."

That same day, Wayne and General Charles Scott, who had been with Lee's advanced forces and hardly could be considered "dirty earwigs," felt constrained to pour out to Washington a description of the events of the forenoon of the twenty-eighth. Their purpose was "to convince the world that our retreat from the Court House was not occasioned by the want of numbers, position, or wishes of both officers and men to maintain that post," and they charged that Lee had failed them utterly in not sending them orders, either for attack or retreat.

Furiously, Washington dashed off a note to Lee to be carried personally by Colonel Fitzgerald:

> Sir: I received your letter (dated through mistake the 1st of July), expressed as I conceive, in terms highly improper. I am not conscious of having made use of any very singular expressions at the time of my meeting you, as you intimate. What I recollect to have said was dictated by duty and warranted by the occasion. As soon as circumstances will permit, you shall have an opportunity, either of justifying yourself to the army, to Congress, to America, and to the world in general, or of convincing them that you were guilty of a breach of orders and of misbehavior before the enemy on the 28th instant, in not attacking them as you had been directed and in making an unnecessary, disorderly and shameful retreat. I am, etc.[11]

Shrilly, Lee, who virtually had asked for a court of inquiry and had been given it, retorted:

> You cannot afford me greater pleasure than in giving me the opportunity of showing to America the sufficiency of her respective servants. I trust that the temporary power of office and the tinsel dignity attending it will not be able, by all the mists they can raise, to obfuscate the bright rays of truth. In the meantime your Excellency can have no objection to my retiring from the army.[12]

Not content, Lee brooded a little longer and sent his third letter of the day, expressing the wish that a court of inquiry should be ordered—preferably, on second thought, he said, a court-martial, for it would be quicker, and its decision would be clear-cut and final.

The Commander-in-Chief shot back a note by Adjutant General Scammell, putting Lee under arrest and delivering the charges under which he would be tried: disobedience of orders in not attacking the enemy, misbehavior before the enemy, disrespect in his letters to the Commander-in-Chief.

The court sat during some days as the army resumed its march. Nothing, not even the Conway Cabal, so excited the army. Washington's young staff officers were particularly vehement in condemnation of Lee; John Laurens was perhaps the bitterest, while Alexander Hamilton questioned Lee's mental stability on the day of battle, only to have the brilliant Lee turn the sword and remind Hamilton of silly heroics the young man himself had expressed under fire.

Even more ludicrously, unfavorable testimony was accepted of a battlefield conversation between the French volunteer Pierre L'Enfant and Lee though the Frenchman spoke no English and Lee's French was no longer conversationally fluent.

Lee's own aides appeared ardently in his behalf, supported more objectively to some extent in their accounts of his field behavior by such artillerymen as Eleazer Oswald, Samuel Shaw, and Henry Knox. The case against him proved weak at best; nonetheless, when the trial ended, he was found guilty of all three counts, although the second was softened. He was suspended from any command for twelve months.

Trailed by his ever-faithful dogs, the spindly, homely man whose paranoic ravings coursed from egomania to persecution, departed the army forever. From the scene passed an experienced, promising officer, but withal, as one man said, an odd sort of genius, who continued to fight a verbal rear-guard action in the press and in copious correspondence, violently assailing his detractors and leaving forever in doubt the reason for his indifferent behavior at Monmouth.

With little reason, the Americans claimed an overwhelming victory at Monmouth, but it was Clinton who got off his army and baggage in good condition. Wayne wrote to Richard Peters one of his recklessly poetic effusions:

> The victory of that day turns out to be much more considerable than at first expected . . . by the most moderate computation their killed and wounded must be full fifteen hundred men of the flower of their army. Among them are numbers of the richest blood of England. Tell the Philadelphia ladies that the heavenly, sweet, pretty redcoats, the accomplished gentlemen of the Guards and Grenadiers have humbled themselves on the plains of Monmouth. "The Knights of the Blended Rose" and "Burning Mount" have resigned their laurels to *rebel* officers who will lay them at the feet of those virtuous daughters of America who cheerfully gave up ease and affluence in a city for Liberty and peace of mind in a cottage. . . .[13]

Actually Sir Henry's army was far from mauled; he made his way with no serious opposition to Sandy Hook, where Admiral Howe's fleet embarked his forces. By the fifth of July he was secure in New York, while Washington's men had to make an "inconceivably distressing march," as the General called it, twenty miles to Brunswick through deep, hot, sandy, red and yellow dust, almost without a drop of water. There the exhausted army rested a week.

The almost unendurable heat wave did not lessen in any

way the enthusiastic celebration of the second anniversary of the Declaration of Independence. Private Elijah Fisher, an old soldier but a relative newcomer to the Commander-in-Chief's guard, recorded the event in his journal:

> We Selebrated the Independence of Amarica. the howl army parraded . . . the artilery Discharged thirteen Cannon. we gave three Chears &c. At Night his Excelency and the gentlemen and Ladys had a Bawl at Head Quarters with grate Pompe.[14]

It was a celebration of Monmouth as well as of Independence, and Elijah and his comrades-in-arms all had a double allowance of rum for the day. Philadelphia and other cities extravagantly burned powder in salutes and fireworks. Many a man rededicated himself to the cause of freedom. Probably under just such a spell, a man in Charleston, South Carolina, enthusiastic if not learned, proclaimed, "I would Willingley renounse all my Most Neair and Deair Connections on Earth for my Darling libertey."

27

"A FLOCK OF DUCKS IN CROSS-BELTS"

Newport

SUMMER 1778

FROM NEW BRUNSWICK, Washington's refreshed army moved northward toward Paramus, a small Dutch settlement in the rugged Jersey country north of Passaic. On the leisurely march the General took time to enjoy a view of the falls of the Passaic. Under a giant oak, in sight of the smoking falls that plunged seventy or eighty feet down the craggy walls of the river, Washington and his staff paused for a light repast. "The traveling canteens were immediately emptied," noted James McHenry in his diary, and cold ham, tongue, and "excellent bisquit" served. "With the assistance of a little spirit, we composed some grog over which we chatted away a very cheerful hour. . . ."

Even the rank and file seemed to enjoy the northward journey. "We marched by what was called 'easy marches'," one of them remembered, "that is, we struck our tents at three o'clock in the morning, marched ten miles, and then encamped, which would be about one or two o'clock in the afternoon. Every third day we rested all day."

At Paramus the Commander-in-Chief accepted the owner's invitation and established headquarters in "The Hermitage," seat of Mrs. Theodosia Prevost, whose husband had recently died in the British service in the West Indies. If James McHenry noticed that diminutive, rakish Lieutenant Colonel Aaron Burr was paying court to the much older mistress of the red-stone Gothic mansion, he passed it over, confiding only to his journal:

> At our new quarters, we found some fair refugees from New York on a visit. . . . Here we talked and walked and laughed and frolicked and gallanted away four days and four nights and would have gallanted and frolicked and laughed and walked and talked I believe forever, had not the General given orders for our departure.[1]

The General's orders for departure were dictated by his discovery that the long-awaited French fleet had arrived off Sandy Hook, while the enemy "reposed" on Long Island, Staten Island, and New York. At once he sent his aides, Laurens and Hamilton, to the flagship of the expedition commander, Vice Admiral Charles Hector, Count d'Estaing, to arrange for signals, to furnish pilots, and to acquaint the French of the situation ashore.

With Estaing's arrival two possibilities presented themselves: an assault upon the enemy at New York or at Newport. Success at New York would depend largely upon the success of an attack by the French on the fleet of Admiral Howe, lying within the Hook. In the event that Estaing should not be able or willing to strike Howe, Washington authorized General John Sullivan, commanding in Connecticut opposite Rhode Island, to call out enough militia to raise his strength to five thousand for a combined land and naval assault on the island. Whether Washington's next objective was to be New York with all his forces, or Rhode Island with part of them, he decided he would be most advantageously placed east of the Hudson River, and he marched his army for its old encampment near White Plains.

Washington and his ally were cruelly disappointed at New York. From his flagship the Admiral wrote to Congress:

> Both officers and crews were kept in spirits, notwithstanding their wants and the fatigues of service, by the desire

of delivering America from the English colors, which we saw waving on the other side of a simple barrier of sand upon so great a crowd of masts. The pilots procured by Colonels Laurens and Hamilton destroyed all illusion. These experienced persons unanimously declared that it was impossible to carry us in. I offered in vain a reward of fifty thousand crowns to anyone who would promise success. All refused, and the particular soundings which I caused to be taken myself too well demonstrated that they were right.[2]

Convinced that his deep-draught vessels could not get in to the lighter ones of the enemy in New York Harbor, Estaing sailed toward Newport, the alternate objective. Washington ordered Lafayette with two crack brigades to march for Providence, and a few days later he sent Nathanael Greene. Sullivan was to command the expedition and was instructed to divide his entire force into two equal divisions, Lafayette to command one, Greene the other.

The New England militia—Washington lifted the limit of five thousand he had imposed—turned out so promptly that within thirty days some seven thousand, under John Hancock, who was making his first appearance as an army officer, joined Sullivan. Sullivan, with an Irishman's ebullience, was supremely confident, although a little cautious. Washington was as anxious as he was confident. Perhaps the Commander-in-Chief could not put out of his mind the knowledge that Sullivan was a difficult man whose restless ambition far exceeded his capacities.

In Rhode Island, the British occupied the island cut off from the mainland by Seaconnet Passage on the east, Narragansett or Middle Passage on the west, and narrow straits on the north. Newport was at the southern end. Two roads ran to the northern end of the island; there travelers ferried east to Tiverton or west to Bristol.

The French fleet arrived off Point Judith, just south of Newport, on the twenty-ninth of July, some days before Sullivan's forces could be concentrated. The enemy withdrew his detachments, while Sullivan and Estaing concerted plans. August 10 was set for a joint attack; but on the eighth Sullivan suddenly occupied the northern end of Rhode Island, when he discovered that the enemy works there were abandoned. The French fleet already had landed some four thousand troops on Conanicut Island to the west, in preparation for the joint assault. The next day, thirty sails were sighted, heading for the anchorage the French had just left. They were the English fleet of "Black Dick" Howe.

Over Sullivan's protests, the French admiral, fearing to be trapped by the British squadron, re-embarked his troops and

sailed out on the tenth to engage Howe's fleet, notifying
Sullivan that he would return to complete the conquest of
the island.

While Estaing was at sea, Sullivan decided not to delay his
operations, and advanced his ten thousand men to within
two miles of British General Robert Pigot's lines, north of
Newport. He opened siege lines, and his artillery dueled
harmlessly with that of the sixty-six hundred defenders. Two
of the militia officers with Sullivan's forces were Lieutenant
Colonel Paul Revere and his son Captain Paul. For the past
three years, the elder Revere, disappointed by not being
awarded a Continental commission, had contented himself
with a command in Colonel Thomas Craft's State Regiment
of Artillery of Massachusetts, defending his home town of
Boston. Optimistically, he wrote from Rhode Island to his
"Dear Girl" on North Square:

> I am in high health and spirits and so is our army. The
> enemy dare not show their heads. . . . It is very irksome to
> be separated from *her* whom I so tenderly love, and from my
> little lambs, but were I at home I should want to be here. It
> seems as if half Boston was here. I hope the affair will soon
> be settled. . . . I trust that All-wise being who has protected
> me will still protect me and send me safely to the arms of her
> whom it is my greatest happiness to call my own. Paul is
> well, sends duty and love to all.[3]

For twenty-four hours after Estaing sailed on the tenth,
the fleets maneuvered for the weather gauge, until a gale of
hurricane fury burst over them, scattering and severely dam-
aging the vessels of both. Howe put back to New York for
repairs. Estaing limped back to Narragansett Bay on the
twentieth and announced, to the dismay of his American allies, that he would sail for Boston for refitting and repairs.

Frantically, Greene and Lafayette, aboard the admiral's
ship, beseeched him first to land his troops and attack the
British. Then he could repair his squadron, either at Newport or at Boston. Estaing was adamant. Greene wrung his
hands and cried, ". . . the devil has got into the fleet; they
are about to desert us." He knew that Estaing's withdrawal
would doom the expedition: "To evacuate the island is
death," he groaned. "To stay may be ruin."

And when the French fleet stubbornly fell down the hori-
zon on the twenty-fourth, ruin began. Five thousand militia
deserted in a few days, while Sullivan's Irish temper began to
warm. Washington, at White Plains, wise in the ways of men
and especially those of John Sullivan, who always felt per-
secuted, foresaw what the commander at Rhode Island

might do. On the twenty-eighth Washington wrote him:

I will just add a hint, which, made use of in time may prove important and answer a very salutary purpose. Should the expedition fail, through the abandonment of the French fleet, the officers concerned will be apt to complain loudly. But prudence dictates that we should put the best face upon the matter and to the world attribute the removal to Boston to necessity.

The reasons are too obvious to need explaining. The principal one is that our British and internal enemies would be glad to improve the least matter of complaint and disgust against and between us and our new allies into a serious rupture.[4]

The reasons were not too obvious to Sullivan, and Washington's warning came too late. Sullivan lashed out at the French in his general orders of the twenty-fourth. Summarizing the status quo after the French departure, he concluded that he "yet hopes the event will prove America is able to procure with her own arms that which her allies refused to assist her in obtaining." Sullivan's "absolute censure," Greene deplored, "opened the mouths of the army in very clamourous strains." An outraged Lafayette and other advisers persuaded Sullivan to issue a retraction, and a begrudging explanation was added.

On the night of the twenty-eighth, after hearing from Washington that Admiral Howe had put to sea again, probably with reinforcements for Rhode Island, Sullivan began a withdrawal. At daylight, Pigot moved after him.

Sullivan's planning was sound and he covered himself well. Pigot drove in his light infantry, advanced about three miles in front of his works, but his first line held. His right took a beating for two unremitting hours, as Pigot's troops and four British vessels drummed it steadily with heavy guns. However, an all-Negro Rhode Island regiment stood against both the artillery and "furious onsets" by Pigot's Hessians, until the attacking enemy broke. "The day was spent in skirmishing," reported an American volunteer aide, and at night with the help of John Glover's amphibious Marbleheaders, who had fought during the day on the American left, Sullivan took off his troops to the mainland "with the stores and baggage," he said proudly. "Not a man was left behind, nor the smallest article lost." American casualties were 30 killed, 137 wounded, and 44 missing, and the British, 38 killed, 210 wounded, and 12 missing.

The very next day a British fleet reinforced the Newport garrison with five thousand men, underscoring Sullivan's good fortune in escaping back to Providence relatively unscathed.

But Sullivan did not let the affair rest with his successful withdrawal. The bitterly disappointed glory-seeker was so enraged by the conduct of the French that he ignored Washington's admonitions and continued to bellow and finger-point at Estaing. The French admiral politely cloaked his resentment of Sullivan's implication that he had run from a fight, but his cultured manners were taxed to an extreme as French popularity plummeted. By the time the broad black hulls of the French fleet sailed into Boston Harbor, the story of the rift that Washington tried so hard to smother was widespread.

An unfortunate incident in Boston on the fifth of September might have effectuated a permanent breach between the allies but for the good sense of American gentlemen and the good will, tact, and modesty of the French. The French set up a bakery to supply their fleet, because flour was impossible to obtain in Boston and bread scarce on the open market. The fragrant ovens drew a crowd. Someone tried to buy bread, but the bakers refused to sell. A row started between Bostonians who spoke no French and Frenchmen who spoke no English. Neither seemed to know what the other wanted. French officers ran up, and in the fighting a high-born French lieutenant was killed.

The Frenchman was buried in the vaults under King's Chapel, while the Massachusetts Assembly acted the very next morning to appropriate money for a statue to his memory. Within a few days, Estaing and his officers were enjoying the celebrated hospitality of John Hancock, and somehow the Americans were adroit enough to make the whole matter of the bakery riot appear to have been instigated by a common enemy! Nathanael Greene wrote from Boston to Washington:

> The late affray . . . between the people of the town and those of the fleet has been found to originate from a parcel of soldiers belonging to the convention troops [parolees of Burgoyne's army] and a party of British sailors which were engaged on board a privateer. The secret enemies of our cause and the British officers in the neighborhood of this place are endeavoring to sow the seeds of discord as much as possible between the inhabitants . . . and the French. . . .
>
> The French officers are well satisfied this is the state of the case and it fills them with double resentment against the British. The Admiral and all the French officers are now upon an exceedingly good footing with the gentlemen of the town. General Hancock takes unwearied pains to promote a good understanding. . . . His house is full from morning till night. . . .

General Hancock made the Admiral a present of your picture. He was going to receive it on board the fleet by firing a royal salute, but General Hancock thought it might furnish a handle for some of the speculative politicians to remark the danger of characters becoming too important. He, therefore, dissuaded the Admiral from carrying the matter into execution.[5]

Not all of the resentment growing out of the Rhode Island debacle was American. The Chevalier de Pontgibaud, aide to Lafayette and loyal to the American cause, commented on John Hancock's army:

Hardly had the [French] troops disembarked before the militia . . .horse and foot arrived. I have never seen a more laughable spectacle. All the tailors and apothecaries in the country must have been called out. . . . One could recognize them by their round wigs. They were mounted on bad nags and looked like a flock of ducks in cross-belts. The infantry was no better than the cavalry and appeared to be cut after the same pattern. I guessed that these warriors were more anxious to eat up our supplies than to make a close acquaintance with the enemy, and I was not mistaken; they soon disappeared.[6]

Washington, himself, corresponded patiently with prominent officers and citizens in New England, urging them to endeavor to keep the differences between the allies quiet and to help heal them as quickly as possible. He reminded Sullivan:

The continent at large is concerned in our cordiality, and it should be kept up by all possible means that are consistent with our honor and policy. First impressions, you know, are generally longest remembered and will serve to fix in a great degree our national character among the French. In our conduct towards them, we should remember that they are a people old in war, very strict in military etiquette and apt to take fire where others scarcely seem warmed. Permit me to recommend in the most particular manner the cultivation of harmony . . . and your endeavors to destroy that ill humor which may have got into the officers.[7]

Both Washington and the Congress deplored the protest made by Sullivan's officers to Estaing against his withdrawal to Boston; finally the admiral was appeased and good will restored.

Newport had its value if only as a lesson in the difficulties of co-operation. Perhaps it even suggested to Washington and to some of the Congress that America's war was now becoming but one part of an international conflict and that their French allies had more to consider than merely aiding colonials to break free of England. Certainly the thought was suggested when the French fleet sailed for Martinique, one of the new scenes of war.

Clinton remained strangely inactive in New York. Washington still did not know that when Sir Henry had taken command in May, it already had been decided in London to abandon further offensive operations in the North. While Washington's army reached its greatest strength—July returns showed 16,782 present and fit for duty—it lay idle, most of its forces near White Plains. Intelligence reports from New York suggested that Clinton might yet, before year's end, strike eastward toward Estaing's fleet and Boston, or perhaps westward toward the Hudson River, that constant object. Should the Hudson River line be lost, Washington would be unable to subsist both his army and the French fleet, because most of his supplies continued to come from West of the river.

Washington's reasons for taking position at White Plains vanished with the failure of the expedition against Newport. He now spread his army in cantonments from the Hudson River to the Connecticut, not too far from each other to be able to shift with the enemy's movements, with some small detachments and corps of observation in New Jersey.

With the settling in of winter—not to mention Clinton's "indecisive and foolish" conduct at New York, as Washington called it—the General decided to establish quarters at Middlebrook, New Jersey. At the end of November the army settled in a vast semicircle from Danbury to Middlebrook, except for the cavalry which Washington was forced to disperse from Durham, Connecticut, to Winchester, Virginia, for forage. Also to Virginia were sent the Convention troops of Burgoyne's army, because of the shortage of flour in the North. On the road from Somerville to Raritan in Jersey, at the house of John Wallace, Washington took up residence.

"FINE SPORT FOR THE SONS OF LIBERTY"

War in the Indian Country

1778-1779

IN THAT year of 1778, an often-forgotten war was being fought far from the battlefields of Jersey or Rhode Island or the other civilized areas east of the rugged barriers of the Appalachian Mountains. In the tamed coastal plain, the war had become a formalized business of strategy and tactics, of cannon, muskets, rifles and swords. West of the dark ranges, it was a different story. There, where lone men peacefully plowed their stumpy clearings, war came on moccasined feet. The war was still young when the redmen found the employ of his Britannic Majesty George III a very profitable one indeed.

As early as September, 1774, General Gage at Boston, fearful of the warheads gathering over New England, had asked Sir Guy Carleton about the advisability of hiring Indian warriors "should matters come to extremities." When civilized Stockbridge Indians joined the rebels before Boston, Gage thought he had his justification, and he wrote Lord Dartmouth in London that "we need not be tender of calling on the savages, as the rebels have shown us the example by bringing as many Indians down against us here as they could collect." In a few weeks Dartmouth replied, "The steps which you say the rebels have taken for calling in the assistance of the Indians leave no room to hesitate upon the propriety of you pursuing the same measures." He enclosed instructions to be forwarded to Guy Johnson, royal superintendent of Indian affairs for the northern tribes, that it "is therefore His Majesty's pleasure that you lose no time in taking such steps as may induce them to take up the hatchet against His Majesty's rebellious subjects. . . ." By "the first ship of war that sails after the *Cerberus*," he said, he would send "a large assortment of goods for presents" for the redmen.

His Majesty's seduction of the aborigines was eminently successful. No distinction was made in the British mind between enlisting redmen into armies and turning them loose

on civilian populations. Although some few Indians early were
enlisted into the Continental Army, it was not until June,
1776, that Washington was authorized by Congress to employ them as he saw fit and to offer a reward for enemy
officers and men taken prisoner on the frontiers and in Indian country. By then the sprawling frontiers from New
York and Pennsylvania to the outposts of Virginia were suffering cruelly at the hands of Tories and the copper warriors
of the Six Nations, while to the far south other red nations
loyal to John Stuart, Guy Johnson's counterpart for the southern tribes, harassed the back settlements.

Virginia, largest of the states, claimant to all the territory
drained by the Ohio and Mississippi rivers, was particularly
alive to its responsibilities in protecting the West. As British
Fort Niagara stood an ominous cloud over western New
York and Pennsylvania, so Fort Detroit shadowed the Ohio
and Illinois country at the back parts of Virginia. There
commanded Colonel Henry Hamilton, who had earned the
soubriquet "Hair Buyer" because, the frontiersmen told, he
promised rewards to his Indians for American scalps. In
June, 1777, he had been instructed by the Ministry to assemble Indians and "employ them in making a diversion and exciting an alarm upon the frontiers of Virginia and Pennsylvania. . . ." To support them he was to recruit loyalists
with promises of postwar bounties of two hundred acres, in
addition to soldier's pay.

On the Virginia frontier, since before the war, had been a
tall, lithe, redhead with "black, penetrating, sparkling eyes,"
named George Rogers Clark. He was young—only twenty-
four in 1777—but he had surveyed hundreds of miles of
western lands and had helped the Kentuckians to organize
a government and secure their recognition as a Virginia
colony. By the time 1777 was well along as "the bloody
year" on the frontier, Clark was an implacable foe of both
Hamilton and his sovereign. Late that fall he set out for
Williamsburg with a plan for the conquest of the British-held
French villages north of the Ohio and ultimately of Detroit itself.

George Clark's idea was not new. Early in the war there
had been talk of an expedition against Detroit, but neither
the Continental Congress nor the states set one in motion. In
the spring of 1777, the Congress had sent Brigadier General
Edward Hand to assume command at Fort Pitt, at the confluence of the Alleghany and the Monongahela rivers, and to
organize a punitive expedition into the Ohio country. But
Hand was surrounded by hostiles and was still at Fort Pitt
when Clark trekked eastward to consult Governor Patrick

Henry. In January, 1778, the Virginia Assembly commissioned Clark a lieutenant colonel of Virginia militia, granting him £1,200 and authority to draw supplies at Pittsburgh. Ostensibly he was to defend Kentucky. Secretly he was empowered to take the British post in the French town of Kaskaskia, near the mouth of the river of the same name, and if possible, Detroit.

The young giant in hunting shirt hurried back to the banks of the Monongahela to recruit. It was not an easy thing, in a region whose whole population totaled only a few hundred souls, to persuade men to leave their homesteads thinly protected to go on a vaguely defined march against the Indians. But at length, on the twenty-fourth of June, 1778, leaving twenty families to defend a blockhouse of supplies on an island at the Falls of the Ohio, Colonel Clark set out for Kaskaskia. His flotilla of flatboats carried 175 frontiersmen.

Four days later, the expedition entered the mouth of the Tennessee River and was floated and rowed to the ruins of the old French fort, Massaic, about ten miles below. Here the men hid their boats. To travel the river farther and proceed by the Mississippi, Clark realized, would be to surrender the advantage of surprise.

Next morning, guided by a party of hunters from Kaskaskia who joined him, Clark began a 120-mile march overland to his goal. Accustomed to forest travel, his men traveled light and fast, and reached the Kaskaskia, a mile from the town, on the evening of the fourth of July. Their provisions were exhausted and they had not eaten for two days. Procuring boats, they ferried across the river in the dark. The only sound in the unsuspecting town of two hundred and fifty houses and a stone fort, they guessed to be "the Negroes at a dance." Dividing his little force, Colonel Clark surrounded the town, "broke into the fort," and took Kaskaskia without firing a shot.

"Nothing could excel the confusion these people seemed to be in," the colonel wrote back to his old friend, George Mason, at Williamsburg, "being taught to expect nothing but savage treatment from the Americans. Giving all for lost . . . they were willing to be slaves to save their families." But when the terrified French townspeople learned that France and America now were official allies and that the fierce-looking Americans would not molest them in their persons, property, or religion if they took an oath of fidelity to the state of Virginia, they "fell into transports of joy" and eagerly embraced the conquerors.

While a detachment of thirty of Clark's men raced on borrowed mounts sixty miles to capture Cahokia, across the

Mississippi from the friendly Spanish post of St. Louis, Father Pierre Gibault of Kaskaskia volunteered to travel to Vincennes and win over the French inhabitants. Two more posts accepted the Americans before Father Gibault returned, on the first of August, reporting complete success. Clark promptly sent Captain Leonard Helm to occupy Vincennes and its stronghold, Fort Sackville, and to assume command of the French militia there. He himself gave the rest of the summer to persuading his men not to return home and to a number of conferences in which he cajoled thousands of red chiefs and warriors into good behavior.

But the Virginian did not remain long unchallenged in the territory he had organized as the county of Illinois in the state of Virginia. In the fall, Colonel Hamilton made a hard, long march south from Detroit with some five hundred men, including about three hundred Indians, and in a swirling snowstorm on December 17, retook Vincennes and captured its American garrison—Captain Helm and three soldiers.

While Clark hastened to prepare Kaskaskia for siege, Francis Vigo returned from Vincennes to inform him that "Mr. Hamilton had weakened himself by sending his Indians against the frontier . . . that he had not more than eighty men in garrison, three pieces of cannon and some swivels mounted, and that he intended to attack this place as soon as the winter opened." Vigo, a bold, liberty-loving Italian fur trader and merchant of St. Louis, upon the arrival of Clark had volunteered his energies and money to the Virginian's expedition. At Clark's request he had traveled northeast across the Wabash to spy out Vincennes. He had been a soldier, and the intelligence he brought—after capture and release by Hamilton—was full and explicit. On the basis of it, Clark decided not to await an attack; he resolved instead to carry war to Vincennes. The enemy, he thought, "could not suppose . . . we should be so mad as to attempt to march eighty leagues through a drowned country in the depth of winter, that they would be off their guard and probably would not think it worth while to keep out spies."

"At this moment I would have bound myself a slave to have had five hundred troops," Clark later confessed, but he was obliged to make do with what he had. He built a large row galley and armed it with six light guns. In February, 1779, he sent it, manned by forty-six men, up the Ohio and Wabash to take station "ten leagues below the post Vincennes and wait until further orders." He anticipated that the Wabash would be overflowed so broadly that the only way he would be able to move his artillery and stores was by boat. Should Hamilton by some chance learn of his approach and try to escape down the Mississippi, the row galley was to capture him.

At the head of only a hundred and seventy men, nearly half French volunteers, he himself set out overland for Vincennes, two hundred and forty long, cold miles away. Although some of the march lay through "the most beautiful country in the world," it was also some of the worst at this season. The four rivers he must cross flooded the prairies, and about Vincennes the water spread five miles wide. "We set out," said the colonel, "on a forlorn hope indeed. For our whole party with the boat's crew consisted of only a little upwards of two hundred. I cannot account for it, but I still had inward assurance of success and never could, when weighing every circumstance, doubt it."

Over endless, muddy prairies and ankle-deep lowlands, Clark led his band as if he were on an outing. In latter-day memoirs, he recalled:

My object now was to keep the men in spirits. I suffered them to shoot game on all occasions and feast on them, like Indians' war dances, each company by turns inviting the other to their feasts, which was the case every night. . . . Myself and principal officers hailing on the woodsmen, shouting now and then, and running as much through the mud and water as any of them.

Thus insensibly without a murmur was those men led on to the banks of the Little Wabash, which we reached the thirteenth, through incredible difficulties far surpassing anything any of us had ever experienced.[1]

Here, twenty miles from their goal, began the drowned lands, country almost entirely inundated. The two branches of the Little Wabash were now one, flowing together in a solid sheet of water five miles broad, broken only by the forest of naked trees awash and rearing from its surface into the icy February air. Clark said later, "he viewed this sheet of water for some time with distrust." But then he overcame his doubts and ordered his men to build a great canoe and a platform above water on the opposite shore. He ferried supplies in the canoe and piled them on the scaffold, then swam the horses across and loaded them. He led his men splashing through three feet of water to the far branch of the river and camped. "A little antic drummer afforded them great diversion," remarked the colonel, "by floating on his drum." By the time they pitched camp, Clark said:

They really began to think themselves superior to other men and that neither the rivers or seasons could stop their progress. Their whole conversation now was what they would

do when they got about the enemy and now [they] began to
view the main Wabash as a creek and made no doubt but
such men as they were could find a way to cross it. They
wound themselves up to such a pitch that they soon took
Vincennes, divided the spoil, and before bedtime, was far advanced on their route to Detroit.[2]

Their exploits and ebullient spirits were the more remarkable because their provisions were spoiled and game had fled
from the drowned lands, and they were beginning to hunger.
Four days later when they reached the banks of the Embarrass River, the weak were stumbling and the strong valiantly
helping them push through the waist-deep water. Then scouts
reported that the overflow of the Embarrass had flooded the
whole country nine more miles to the Wabash, beyond which
lay Vincennes.

Resolutely, the young colonel plunged into the freezing
water, shoulder-deep, and beckoned his men to follow. That
night, at the end of a second day without food, they bivouacked on a mucky ground from which the waters had re-
ceded, and at daylight were "amused for the first time by the
morning gun from the British garrison" at Vincennes. They
crossed the Wabash, managed to kill one deer for a pittance
of meat, and faced seven or eight more miles of submerged
bottoms between them and Vincennes.

When Clark's scouts reported the expanse of the water that
yet remained between the expedition and its goal, the distressed commander felt every eye fixed on him:

> I unfortunately spoke serious to one of the officers. The
> whole was alarmed without knowing what I said. They ran
> from one to another, bewailing their situation. I viewed their
> confusion for about one minute, whispered to those near me
> to [do] as I did, immediately took some water in my hand,
> poured on powder, blacked my face, gave the war whoop,
> marched into the water without saying a word. The party
> gasped and fell in, one after another, without saying a word,
> like a flock of sheep. I ordered those that was near me to
> begin a favorite song of theirs. It soon passed through the
> line and the whole went on cheerfully.[3]

Pushing through water breast-high on the twenty-third of
February, the force emerged from the bottom lands in the
early afternoon and halted on a small knoll in sight of Vincennes. From the hill, Colonel Clark sent a letter to the inhabitants announcing his presence and his intention of taking the post that night, and warning them to stay indoors. In
the evening, after parading his troops round and round behind hillocks to give the impression of a thousand men, Clark

led them in wading through deep water to the rising ground on which the town stood. "With colors flying and drums brassed," they entered the town about eight o'clock and took possession, while a company of fourteen went to fire on the fort. One of Clark's captains noted in his diary: "Smart firing all night on both sides. The cannon played smartly, not one of our men wounded . . . fine sport for the sons of Liberty."

About eight in the morning, Clark sent a flag to Hamilton demanding unconditional surrender, which Hamilton curtly refused. After noon, however, the Englishman asked for a parley at the town church, but the enemies could not agree on terms, and Hamilton returned to the fort. During the afternoon, Hamilton reported later to his superior, a party of Indians returning from a scout were attacked by Clark's men and two killed and one wounded. Hamilton was told:

The rest were surrounded and taken bound to the village where being set in the street opposite the fort gate, they were put to death, notwithstanding a truce at that moment existed. . . . One of them was tomahawked immediately. The rest, sitting on the ground in a ring, bound, seeing by the fate of their comrade what they had to expect, the next on his left sung his death song and was in turn tomahawked. The rest underwent the same. . . . One only was saved by the intercession of a rebel officer who pleaded for him, telling Colonel Clark that the savage's father had formerly saved his life.

The chief of this party, after having the hatchet stuck in his head, took it out himself and delivered it to the inhuman monster who struck him first, who repeated his stroke a second and third time, after which the miserable spectacle was dragged by the rope around his neck to the river, thrown in, and suffered to spend still a few moments of life in fruitless strugglings. . . .

Colonel Clark, yet reeking with the blood of these unhappy victims, came to the esplanade before the fort gate, where I had agreed to meet him and treat of the surrender of the garrison. He spoke with rapture of his late achievement, while he washed the blood from his hand stained in this inhuman sacrifice.[4]

Hamilton's report was not exaggerated. Clark candidly admitted his act, saying it was merely a matter of policy. He hoped that the execution of the redmen before their friends would persuade them that the English could not or would not give them the protection they had been promised and would incense them against the British. Captain Joseph Bowman reported the episode casually: "We . . . brought the Indians back to the main street before the fort gate, there tomahawked them, and threw them into the river."

Colonel Henry Hamilton chose to surrender to an almost certain prison confinement rather than risk the lives of his men, but he insisted on including in the articles of capitulation an article relating his reasons for giving up his post: the remoteness from succor, the state and quantity of provisions, the unanimity of officers and men on its expediency, the honorable terms allowed, and lastly his confidence in a generous enemy. At ten o'clock, the twenty-fifth of February, 1779, the American colors rose above Fort Sackville.

George Rogers Clark, the hardened woodsman who matter-of-factly slew the redman wherever he encountered him, did not wreak vengeance upon Hamilton's garrison. The enlisted men were paroled and the officers marched off for Virginia. There Hamilton was confined. An investigation fairly well established that he had been guilty of offering rewards for scalps but none for prisoners, thus encouraging the Indians to slay their white captives. For a long while, Thomas Jefferson, who had become governor of Virginia, refused to exchange the man known as "the Hair Buyer," for fear of his influence and the evil he might again arouse on the frontier.

Clark took not only Vincennes but also claimed all the surrounding country in the name of the commonwealth he served, and so became conqueror of a territory more than half the size of all the thirteen colonies. He successfully bound the redmen of the Ohio and Mississippi valleys to the American cause, but he never realized his dream of an assault on Detroit, largely because Virginia failed to support him further and instead went crazy with land jobbing and speculation in the West.

While George Rogers Clark's prisoners were traveling the rivers and forests eastward on their 850-mile journey to Williamsburg cells, another much greater Indian expedition was organizing in Pennsylvania under mercurial General John Sullivan and New York's Brigadier General James Clinton.

The campaigns of Clark and Sullivan differed in locale, sponsorship, and concept. Clark had marched a mere handful of enraged frontiersmen on an incredible campaign in behalf of a single, aggrieved state; his prisoners were made to understand that their oath of allegiance was not to the Continental Congress or to the United States, but to the "Republic of Virginia." Sullivan's Expedition, as the affair of 1779 came to be known, was, at last, the punitive expedition that the sufferers of the frontier long had begged of the Continental Congress. In July, 1778, Colonel John Butler with four hundred Tories and five hundred Senecas, the most ferocious men of the Six Nations, had swept down from Fort Niagara on Lake Ontario upon beautiful Wyoming Valley in Pennsylvania. He had gobbled up three little stockaded blockhouses, annihilated a small company of American "regulars" and two or three hundred militia defenders of the valley, and harvested 227 scalps. Burning and plundering a thousand homes, he had left the lovely valley a desolate wasteland. In September, Joseph Brant wiped out German Flats in the Mohawk Valley. After the rebels retaliated upon an Indian town fifty miles southwest, Captain Walter Butler with two hundred of his father's Tory Rangers and Brant with five hundred Indians, on a foggy November morning ravaged Cherry Valley, a pretty village about fifty miles west of Albany.

When the Congress, heeding the anguished cries of this frontier, directed Washington to chastise the savages, the Commander-in-Chief already had made inquiries about the number of men needed for an expedition against the Six Nations and their white allies, about the nature of their country, and the roads leading into it. To General Gates he offered command of an expedition against them, with the understanding that John Sullivan should take it if Gates declined. From the Highlands, Gates replied, "The man who undertakes the Indian service should enjoy youth and strength, requisites I do not possess. It, therefore, grieves me that your Excellency should offer me the only command to which I am entirely unequal." General Sullivan, then in Providence, Rhode Island, was not feeling at thirty-eight the infirmities of Gates's fifty years, and he immediately accepted command.

Washington's instructions to Sullivan were explicit. The country of the Six Nations, he said, was not to be "merely overrun but destroyed." Their country extended from Lake Ontario on the north to the Susquehanna River on the south and from the Catskill Mountains on the east to Lake Erie on the west. It was not a land of fabled wigwams but a region of permanent, settled villages of log cabins and houses of framed timbers and stone, of extensive cultivation and fruitful orchards. In addition to totally ravaging it, Sullivan was to capture "as many prisoners of every age and sex as possible" to be held as hostages for the good behavior of the tribes.

The expedition of nearly four thousand men was formed in two columns, one under Sullivan to move up the Susquehanna from Wyoming, and the other under Clinton to advance up the Mohawk Valley to Canajoharie, where it would veer southwest to unite with Sullivan at Tioga for the march into Indian country. Sullivan tarried an unconscionable time at the rendezvous of his men at Easton and at Wyoming, fussing over supplies. When, at length, he marched toward his junction with Clinton, twelve hundred pack horses carried the baggage of his army, a hundred and twenty boats loaded with artillery and stores made their way along the Susquehanna, twenty horses were reserved for Sullivan's personal possessions, and seven hundred head of cattle were driven along the trails to feed the troops. Terribly encumbered, the column crashed its way through the wilderness along the banks of the river to the beat of drums and an occasional burst of martial air from the band of Proctor's artillery regiment. As one General Edward Braddock of tragic memory had announced his presence to a wilderness enemy, Sullivan recklessly trumpeted his.

When Clinton's troops marched into Sullivan's encampment at Tioga on the twenty-second of August, they were saluted "by thirteen pieces of cannon, which was returned by our two little pieces." One of Sullivan's brigades was drawn up on "a very pretty piece of ground" where the Susquehanna and the Chumung rivers joined, "with a band of music which played beautiful," said one of the newcomers, "as we passed by them."

Sullivan already had destroyed the deserted Indian town of Chemung. On the twenty-sixth, the expedition pulled out of camp with a transportation train that Major Jeremiah Fogg, a seasoned campaigner, said "appears to the army in general as impracticable and absurd as an attempt to level the Alleghany Mountains." Major John Burrows felt that "the sight of carriages in this part of the world is very odd, as there is nothing but a footpath." Sergeant Moses Fellows, however, was explicit about the lumbering advance:

> We marched much impeded by the artillery and ammunition wagons through thick wood and difficult defiles. Such cursing, cutting, and digging; oversetting wagons, cannon, and pack horses into the river, etc., is not to be seen every day. The army obliged to halt seven hours at one place.[5]

Three days later, about nine in the morning, with its scouts far out in front, the army approached the Indian village of Newtown. The flight of several Indians after giving one fire doubly alerted the rifle corps in the van. One of them climbed a tree to reconnoiter and discovered an enemy lying in wait behind shrewdly camouflaged breastworks on a rising ground protected on the right by the river and on the left by a hill.

Sullivan disposed his army for an attack with his artillery in front of the center of his line facing the works. While the riflemen and the light corps "amused them in front," two brigades were to make a circuit through the brush work to gain the enemy's left and attack them in flank and rear. When Sullivan judged that his flankers had reached their station, his artillery opened. Lieutenant Robert Parker of the artillery observed:

> We began the attack by opening upon them two 5½ Irish howitzers and six three-pounders, when a pleasing piece of music ensued. But the Indians, I believe, did not admire the sound so much, nor could they be prevailed upon to listen to its music, although we made use of all the eloquence we were masters of for that purpose. But they were deaf to our entreaties and turned their backs upon us in token of their detestation for us.[6]

One of the men in the flanking column, Nathan Davis, saw the redmen flee from "their slender works as fast as their legs could carry them" to the hill on their left flank. Here they secreted themselves behind trees awaiting the approach of the American flankers. Davis remarked:

> When our front had advanced within a short distance of them, they commenced a fire from behind every tree and at the same time gave the war whoop. Not all the infernals of the prince of darkness, could they have been let loose from the bottomless pit, would have borne any comparison to these demons of the forest.
>
> We were expressly ordered not to fire until we had obtained permission . . . but to form a line of battle as soon as possible and march forward. This we did . . . and at the same time the Indians kept up an incessant fire upon us from behind the trees, firing and retreating back to another tree, loading and firing again, still keeping up the war whoop. They continued this mode of warfare till we had driven them halfway up the hill, when we were ordered to charge bayonets and rush on. No sooner said than done.
>
> We then in our turn gave our war whoop in the American style, which completely silenced the unearthly voice of their stentorian throats. We drove them . . . to the opposite side of the hill, when we were ordered to halt, as the Indians were out of sight and hearing.[7]

The defeated hostiles left their dead, about twelve men, on the ground. Two prisoners were taken, one Negro and one white man. "The white man," said Davis, "was found painted black, lying on his face . . . pretending to be dead. . . . He was stripped and washed and found to be white." Questioning revealed that Sullivan's opponents had been Captain Walter Butler with two battalions of the Rangers; a few British regulars; Sir Guy Johnson's Tories, the Royal Greens; and Joseph Brant with four hundred Indians.

Three American dead were buried and thirty-six wounded sent back to Wyoming. Lieutenant William Barton of the

First New Jersey Regiment at the request of his major sent out a small party to find some of the dead Indians. "Towards noon they found them," the lieutenant noted in his journal, "and skinned two of them from their hips down for boot legs, one pair for the major, the other for myself."

The skirmish at Newtown was the only opposition Sullivan met except for the ambush of a reconnaissance party. The expedition continued and swiftly expanded its program of destruction. Newtown was burned, Catherine's Town, Appletown, Kanadaseagea, Kanagha. More than forty of the Indians' towns were leveled and hundreds of acres of fields and orchards.

On September 13, Lieutenant Thomas Boyd of a small detachment of Morgan's riflemen who accompanied the expedition, was sent to scout a town. While his men were disputing the possession of the scalp of an Indian they had slain, they were ambushed, and twenty-two of them killed. Next day the main army entered the town Boyd had gone to reconnoiter. Lieutenant Erkuries Beatty scratched into his journal:

> On entering the town we found the body of Lieutenant Boyd and another rifleman. . . . They was both stripped naked and their heads cut off, and the flesh of Lieutenant Boyd's head was entirely taken off and his eyes punched out. The other man's head was not there. They was stabbed, I suppose, in forty different places in the body with a spear and great gashes cut in their flesh with knives, and Lieutenant Boyd's privates was nearly cut off and hanging down. His finger and toe nails was bruised off, and the dogs had eat part of their shoulders away. Likewise a knife was sticking in Lieutenant Boyd's body. They was immediately buried with the honor of war.[8]

The rest of Boyd's party was found three days later, "tomahawked, scalped, and butchered." This was frontier warfare, and no one was surprised when some of the men set fire to a house that Colonel Dearborn had left standing for the accommodation of an old squaw and a sick Indian, after locking the Indians inside the pyre.

By the end of the month the expedition was back at Wyoming, ready to march east to rejoin the main army. So ruthlessly had the country of the Six Nations been devastated that the redmen were forced to depend upon scanty British supplies of food from Niagara, and that winter hundreds died of starvation and disease. The Six Nations were broken for all time as an organization, although the next summer their surviving warriors again fell upon the frontier. The expedition did not achieve its most important purpose: it did not bring back the hostages that Washington had hoped to use to restrain the Indians from further ravaging the frontier. Major Jeremiah Fogg reflected in his journal:

> The question will naturally arise, what have you to show for your exploits? Where are your prisoners? To which I reply that the rags and emaciated bodies of our soldiers must speak for our fatigue, and when the querist will point out a mode to tame a partridge or the expediency of hunting wild turkeys with light horse, I will show them our prisoners. The nests are destroyed, but the birds are still on the wing.[9]

29

"A PRETTY LITTLE FRISK"

Winter and Stony Point

WINTER 1778-SUMMER 1779

FOR THE main army in the East, winter quarters this fourth year 1778-1779, meant the same sort of life officers and men had lived in previous years, except that provisions were more abundant and the supply of clothing vastly greater. In October, French shipments of coats, breeches, and shoes had enabled whole divisions to assemble some sort of uniform dress. However, want still chilled some bodies and hunger gripped some bellies, and the army which had reached a peak strength in summer began to shrink alarmingly as the autumn leaves swirled down.

Campfire talk of home and whisky and women, and poor pay in increasingly worthless money, and what the enemy might do, and what a man's hopes were, and his fears, sometimes turned to the Articles of Confederation. Passed by the Congress in the winter of 1777, they were not yet accepted by all the states. The thirteen articles had been a long while in the framing, and by the time a plan of confederation had been agreed upon, advocates of state sovereignty and sectionalism won over those of nationalism, with the result that the states remained sovereign in most essentials.

The principal authority vested in the Congress by the Articles was the power to declare war and make peace, but paradoxically it was not empowered to levy taxes to finance war. Although the Congress could make requisitions upon the states for money, it had no means to coerce them. Everywhere the states were neglecting the needs of the Continental Army in favor of those of their own militia, and the Congress could not force them to fill their army quotas. States maintained their own armies, navies, and boards of war. They competed with each other for materiel and raided each other for manpower. All but one boasted a "naval force," though it usually consisted of such ill assortments of row galleys, barges, sloops, and other small craft that a sensible man would not venture to sail beyond his home creeks and inlets. Each state issued letters of marque and reprisal to privateers. Now, even the Continental Army threatened to become an assemblage of thirteen different armies, for in 1778 the states were directed to provide arms, ammunition, and clothing to their own lines.

In encampment, as in field, the army felt keenly the neglect of the states. Proud officers, such as Nathanael Greene, were each unwilling to admit that *his* state was remiss, but Greene felt the pulse of the nation.

The local policy of all the states [he wrote] is directly opposed to the great national plan; and if they continue to persevere in it, God knows what the consequences will be. There is a terrible falling off in public virtue since the commencement of the present contest. The loss of morals and the want of public spirit leaves us almost like a rope of sand. . . . Luxury and dissipation are very prevalent. These are the common offspring of sudden riches. When I was in Boston last summer, I thought luxury very predominant there; but they were no more to compare with those now prevailing in Philadelphia than an infant babe to a full-grown man. . . .[1]

Washington, himself, was alarmed by financial conditions. To Congressman Gouverneur Morris, he wrote of forestallers, those rascals who with previous knowledge bought up supplies needed by the army and sold them at advanced prices, and he asked:

Can *we* carry on the war much longer? Certainly *no*, unless some measures can be devised and speedily executed to restore the credit of our currency, restrain extortion, and punish forestallers.

Without these can be effected, what funds can stand the present expenses of the Army? And what officer can bear the weight of prices that every necessary article is now got to? A rat, in the shape of a horse, is not to be bought at this time for less than £200, a saddle under thirty or forty, boots twenty, and shoes and other articles in like proportion. How is it possible, therefore, for officers to stand this without an increase in pay? And how is it possible to advance their pay when flour is selling . . . from five to fifteen pounds per Ct., hay from ten to thirty pounds per tun, and beef and other essentials in this proportion.

The true point of light then to place and consider this matter in is not simply whether Great Britain can carry on the war, but whose finances (theirs or ours) is most likely to fail. . . .[2]

In December, the General was called to Philadelphia to consult with Congress about plans for a 1779 campaign. Martha was there waiting for him when he arrived just before Christmas, and they took up residence at Henry Laurens'. On the thirtieth, Washington recorded his reaction to the atmosphere in the nation's capital:

I have seen nothing since I came here . . . to change my opinion of men or measures, but abundant reason to be convinced that our affairs are in a more distressed, ruinous, and deplorable condition than they have been in since the commencement of the war. . . .

If I was to be called upon to draw a picture of the times and of the men, from what I have seen, heard, and in part know, I should in one word say that idleness, dissipation, and extravagance seem to have laid fast hold of most of them. That speculation, peculation, and an insatiable thirst for riches seems to have got the better of every other consideration. . . . That party disputes and personal quarrels are the great business of the day whilst the momentous concerns of an empire, a great and accumulated debt, ruined finances, depreciated money, and want of credit (which in their consequences is the want of everything) are but secondary considerations. . . . I have no resentments, nor do I mean to point at any particular characters; this I can declare upon my honor, for I have every attention paid me by Congress than [*sic*] I can possibly expect and have reason to think that I stand well in their estimation, but in the present situation . . . I cannot help asking: Where is Mason, Wythe, Jefferson, Nicholas, Pendleton, Nelson, and another I could name, and why, if you are sufficiently impressed with your danger, do you not (as New York has done in the case of Mr. Jay) send an extra member or two for at least a certain limited time till the great business of the nation is put upon a more respectable and happy establishment? Your money is now sinking five percent a day in this city, and I shall not be surprised if in the course of a few months a total stop is put to the currency of it. And yet an assembly, a concert, a dinner, or supper (that will cost three or four hundred pounds) will not only take men off from acting in but even from thinking of this business, while a great part of the officers of your army from absolute necessity are quitting the service and the more virtuous few . . . are sinking by sure degrees into beggary and want.[3]

While Washington was crying for men of the first rank on the national scene, John White, merchant of Salem, Massachusetts, thought the local public servants no better. On the last day of 1778, he scribbled in his almanac:

We shall forever have reason (I fear) to lament our gloried Revolution, because I have only changed taskmasters, the later the worse, because they are poor creatures. Our country is too poor to be a separate nation. In 1775, April 19th was the first of our battling with the English troops sent here for to keep us in subjection to their unreasonable demands in taxation, etc. All or chiefly the men of knowledge made no resistance to government, and therefore men of little or no knowledge that took part in the opposition to Britain were preferred to places in our government. Thus come in men, poor, without moral virtue, blockheads, etc. . . . The high sheriff of this country is a tanner; two magistrates, one a tanner, the other a joiner, neither of them could speak or read English. . . . Why I describe our condition in the above manner is because it is impossible such men without education should be equal to the business. I bless God it is no worse with me, but I am too proud easily to submit to such things. I am now above sixty-six years old and am glad and rejoice my trial is almost over.[4]

One thing helped that year: at least the weather favored the army. The winter was mild, easing to some degree extreme demands for blankets and clothing. Little snow, or even frost, covered the ground after the first of the year; vegetation began to appear as far north as New Jersey at the beginning of April; fruit trees budded and quickly burst into bloom.

When Washington returned to Middlebrook in February, he found a gay social life at headquarters, and, in spite of his feeling about Philadelphia dissipation, he encouraged these diversions of his comrades-in-arms. One of the liveliest spots was the Jacobus de Veer house near Pluckemin, where lived rotund Henry Knox and his equally rotund wife. Here Knox and his artillery were hosts at a grand celebration of the French Alliance, where General Washington opened the ball with Lucy Knox as his partner. Happy, friendly Henry was proud:

Everybody allowed it to be the first of the kind ever exhibited in this state at least. We had about seventy ladies, all of the first *ton* in the state, and between three and four hundred gentlemen. We danced all night—an elegant room. The illuminating, fireworks, etc., were more than pretty. . . .[5]

The ranks were faring better, and officers of a happy disposition found it a far from miserable life. Said one of them:

We spend our time very sociably here; are never disturbed by the enemy, have plenty of provisions, and no want of whiskey grog. We sometimes get good spirits, punch, etc., and have Madeira sometimes. We have a variety of amusements. Last evening the tragedy of Cato was performed at Brunswick by officers of the army. Will the Congress be displeased?[6]

The Nathanael Greenes in the two-story Holland-brick farmhouse of old Derrick van Veghten on the banks of the Raritan were not to be outdone by anyone in sociability. Vivacious, dark-eyed Catherine Greene drew admirers in swarms, and the house was always bright with laughter. In March, Greene was writing a friend:

We had a little dance at my quarters a few evenings past. His Excellency and Mrs. Greene danced upwards of three hours without sitting down. Upon the whole, we had a pretty little frisk.[7]

But the lilting music of "tea frolicks" did not drown entirely the angry voices of many officers who were eager to be quit of the service for one reason or another, or who had such legitimate complaints as Major Ebenezer Huntington, when food again became short. His father had written to inform him that one of his financial investments at home was losing money. Never mind, the Major said sarcastically, "my loss shall not give me a moment's uneasiness, as I am in a fair way of making a fortune, if I can only continue in the army two years longer, as I receive eighty dollars in wages and subsistence monthly and . . . have spent it weekly." With evident impatience, he wrote:

We have been without bread or rice more than five days out of seven for these three weeks past, and the prospect remains as fair as it hath been. . . .
This whole part of the country are starving for want of bread. They have been drove to the necessity of grinding flaxseed and oats together for bread. Is it not possible for the state to do something else besides promises? Promises cannot feed or clothe a man always. Performance is sometimes necessary to make a man believe you intend to perform. Let

us await if possible the event of the next session and possibly hatters and wire drawers can effect what wise men cannot.[8]

Discipline, that ever-present problem, constantly challenged the patience of the officers; no doubt, the national indifference increased the number of desertions. Washington had recently asked Congress to authorize an increase in the maximum sentence of one hundred lashes for serious offenses; there existed no median punishment between one hundred lashes, which the General felt insufficient for some crimes, and death, which on the other hand was too severe a penalty. The young Virginia blueblood, Major Henry Lee, suggested to the General an extremity that exceeded the Commander-in-Chief's harshest notions. Washington replied:

> The measure you propose of putting deserters from our Army to immediate death would probably tend to discourage the practice. But it ought to be executed with caution and only when the fact is very clear and unequivocal. I think that that part of your proposal which respects cutting off their heads . . . had better be omitted. Examples however severe ought not to be attended with an appearance of inhumanity otherwise they give disgust and may excite resentment rather than terror.[9]

Lee seldom doubted himself. On the day after Washington wrote to him, Brigadier General William Irvine saw:

> . . . the head of a corporal of the First Regiment who . . . left us . . . stuck up on the gallows. He was taken two nights ago by a party of Major Lee's, who it seems were at first determined to kill all, but on consultation or debate agreed to kill only one out of three. It fell to the corporal's lot, whose head was immediately carried to camp on a pole by the two who escaped instant death. These two villians were of the same regiment and have been tried here this day. Presume they will meet the same fate. I hope in future Death will be the punishment for all such. I plainly see less will not do.[10]

Lee notified Washington of his action. The General promptly wrote sharply that he regretted Lee had been precipitous and emphasized his previous letter; he added very shrewdly: "You will send and have the body buried lest it fall into the enemy's hands."

In spite of—or maybe because of—such savage punishments, Henry Knox was able to say with the coming of summer, 1779: "From the high spirit of our troops, their discipline and equipment, I think that if we come into contact with the enemy, we shall at least do justice to ourselves and country, whatever may be the event."

There had been very little "contact with the enemy" during the long encampment. Except for minor demonstrations in Jersey and Connecticut, Sir Henry Clinton had remained close at New York. Although Washington found it difficult to believe the enemy would not move when the weather broke, the spring days lengthened and still Sir Henry did not stir. But on the thirty-first of May, as Washington wrote final instructions to General Sullivan for the Indian campaign, he heard that the enemy had marched to White Plains. At last the campaign of 1779 had opened.

Washington had apprehended an enemy movement to capture West Point, guardian of the Highlands, and already had ordered St. Clair's division to Springfield and Stirling's and De Kalb's to Pompton. McDougall was in the Highlands with five Continental brigades and two North Carolina regiments. Now Washington shifted his whole army for the protection of the fortress on the Hudson.

A few days later, marching northward, the General learned that the enemy with a force of six thousand had snatched the little fort at Verplanck's Point on the east side of the Hudson and the unfinished works opposite at Stony Point, covering King's Ferry. The ferry was the vital link in his short line of communication and supply between New England and the middle states and its loss meant moving supplies overland through the mountains on a route sixty miles longer. Realistically, the Commander-in-Chief admitted he had not the force to dislodge the redcoats. "All we can do," he confessed to Horatio Gates, "is to lament what we cannot remedy and to prevent a further progress on the river and to make the advantage of what they have now gained as limited as possible." To do so, he quickly imposed his army between them and West Point at Smith's Clove, described by an officer as "a most villainous country, rough, rocky, and a bad climate." He might have added that it also was a superb defensive position.

Although Washington feared Clinton would push forward to West Point, Sir Henry stayed through June at King's Ferry and then pulled his forces back to New York, leaving his garrisons at Verplanck's and Stony Points to fend for themselves.

There was a reason behind Clinton's strange behavior. His instructions for the 1779 campaign had been explicit: "bring Mr. Washington to a general and decisive action at the opening of the campaign," or failing that, force him into the Highlands or the Jerseys to allow the inhabitants of the open country freedom to follow their inclinations, which the London War Office thought would be to return to the Crown. Clinton was told also to employ two corps of four thousand each against the New England seacoast and in Chesapeake Bay. To enable him to implement these schemes, substantial reinforcements were promised him for early spring. Sir Henry had complained bitterly to Germain: "For God's sake, my Lord, if you wish that I should do anything, leave me to myself and let me adapt my efforts to the hourly change of circumstances." With weary sarcasm he said that "to force Washington to an action upon terms tolerably equal has been the object of every campaign during this war," and his force was by no means equal to the task. However, he agreed to try to draw Washington forward "by indirect maneuvers" and strike him while he was in motion.

Therefore he had sent an expedition to the Chesapeake to divert rebel attention and had struck the forts covering King's Ferry. Had his reinforcements arrived on time, he would have pushed toward West Point. When they had not, he had waited through June hoping Washington would risk an action to recover the ferry. By sitting tight, Washington had thwarted that part of his plan. He also had considered moving in behind Washington, cutting him off from his depots at Easton and Trenton, but could not without his reinforcements. So he had drawn back five miles north of King's Bridge. In a final effort to tempt Washington from the strong position he had taken west of the river, he launched an amphibious expedition that ruthlessly pillaged and burned New Haven, Fairfield, Norwalk, and other Connecticut communities. But Washington remained fixed.

For Washington a continued defensive, while the country expected action and his army diminished, was humiliating in the extreme. So on the fifteenth of June he directed Major Henry Lee to collect intelligence on the enemy's strength at Stony Point. For several days Captain Alan McLane's partisans, recently detached from the Delaware Regiment and incorporated into Lee's Legion, reconnoitered. Washington recalled to duty from home leave Brigadier General Anthony Wayne, to take command of the newly formed Light Infantry. When the Pennsylvanian arrived, he also viewed the works at Stony Point. Washington, still not entirely satisfied, made a personal reconnaissance. (Subsequently he filed an expense account of ten dollars to cover the cost of this and a later trip from his New Windsor headquarters to look at Stony Point.) Then he concluded that Stony Point and perhaps Verplanck's Point could be retaken by a sudden night attack. It was a task ideally suited to the talents of the Light Infantry and its heavily handsome commander, a soldier's soldier with a reputation for action and daring. On the tenth of July he sent instructions to Wayne, based on scout reports, Wayne's own observations, and his own.

On the morning of the fifteenth at eleven o'clock Wayne drew up his troops, all picked veterans, all tall, young and muscular and keenly drilled, fully equipped, and rationed for dress parade. After inspection, instead of dismissing the corps, he ordered a march westward from camp. The puzzled regiments skirted bold Bear Mountain on a back road and then bent south on a rough trail. They panted over the crest of Degaffles Rugh and down through more rocky woodland, close and stifling in summer heat. In the afternoon they threaded the deep forest ravines through the Donderberg and came shortly after dark to the farm of Mr. Springsteel, a mile and a half from the enemy.

As his columns came up, Wayne called his colonels into council and told them his plans. The scouts had done their job well. Wayne had a map of the Point. Everything was marked, the abatis, the redoubts, the sally ports. On that great pile of rock, Lieutenant Colonel Henry Johnson of the Seventeenth Regiment commanded a garrison of nearly seven hundred redcoats. Wayne's hazel eyes were afire as he showed his officers what he expected.

The colonels gazed and saw the enormity of the task the general had chosen for this dark night. Stony Point was no ordinary work. The point was a promontory jutting a half-mile into the Hudson. On the three sides around which the river swirled, it rose sheer and wooded a hundred and fifty feet, and on its inland side it fell off raggedly to a marsh over which a causeway led to the Point and the ferry landing on its north side. At high tide the flooded morass made the Point virtually an island. On this side an abatis protected three small flèches on knobs of ground, and higher another abatis covered seven or eight batteries on the summit.

The right or main attacking column Wayne ordered to approach along a sand bar on the south and pulled itself up the steep flank of the Point, while the left column climbed the north face, and Hardy Murfree's North Carolinians came in straight on the causeway, by his rifle fire diverting the enemy from the bayonet attacks on their flanks. When the columns formed for the attack, paper was to be passed out so that each man might "fix a piece . . . in . . . his hat or cap as an insignia to be distinguished from the enemy." Wayne ordered all bayonets fixed and charges drawn, except those of Murfree's men. Then he addressed the corps:

The distinguished honor conferred upon every officer and soldier who has been drafted into this corps by his Excellency, George Washington, the credit of the states they respectively belong to, and their own reputations, will be such powerful motives for each man to distinguish himself that the General cannot have the least doubt of a glorious victory. He hereby engages to reward the first man who enters the works. . . .

But, should there be any soldier so lost to a feeling of honor as to retreat a single foot, or skulk in the face of danger, the officer next to him is immediately to put him to death that he may no longer disgrace the name of soldier, or the corps, or the state to which he belongs.[11]

The Light Infantry munched its rations. Before sitting to a late supper, Wayne wrote to his closest friend, Dr. Sharp Delany. With a typical sense of the dramatic he dated his letter: "Springsteel's, 11 o'clock P.M., 15 July, 1779, near the hour and scene of carnage." These lines, he told Delany, would not meet his eyes until the writer was no more. He committed to his friend papers covering his side of his bitter difference with his despised rival, General St. Clair, who, he feared, might attack his name after death, and he asked Delany to see to the education of his little son and daughter, for "I fear that their mother will not survive this stroke."

Wayne laid aside his quill, calmly ate supper, and went out to give his men the signal to advance.

At midnight, bright moonlight shone on his troops, stepping out into the marsh west of the forbidding fortress. The *New York Journal* later reported the action:

The detachment marched in two divisions, and about one o'clock came up to the enemy's pickets who, by firing their pieces gave the alarm and . . . ran to the fort, from every quarter of which in a short time they made an incessant fire upon our people. They, with fixed bayonets and uncharged pieces, advanced with quick but silent motion through a heavy fire of cannon and musketry till, getting over the abatis and scrambling up the precipices, the enemy called out, "Come on, ye damn'd rebels! Come on!"

Some of our people softly answered, "Don't be in such a hurry, my lads. We will be with you presently."

And accordingly, in a little more than twenty minutes from the time the enemy first began to fire, our troops, overcoming all obstructions and resistance, entered the fort. Spurred on by their resentment of the former cruel bayoneting which many of them and others of our people had experienced and of the more recent and savage barbarity of plundering and burning unguarded towns, murdering old and unarmed men, abusing and forcing defenceless women, and reducing multitudes of innocent people from comfortable livings to the most distressful want of the means of subsistence—deeply affected by these cruel injuries, our people entered the fort with the resolution of putting every man to the sword. But the cry of "Mercy! mercy! Dear Americans, mercy! Quarter! Brave Americans, quarter! Quarter!" disarmed their resentment in an instant, insomuch that even Colonel Johnson, the commandant, freely and candidly acknowledges that not a drop of blood was spilled unnecessarily. Oh, Britain, turn thy eye inward, behold and tremble at thyself.[12]

Inside the second abatis, Wayne had fallen with a scalp wound. "Carry me up to the fort, boys!" he had shouted. "Let's go forward!" Supported by two of them, his forehead bloody, he stumbled victoriously into the fort.

As soon as the fort was secured, Wayne turned its guns on the *Vulture,* an enemy sloop-of-war anchored in the river, and on Verplanck's Point. Although the vessel dropped downstream out of range, the fire on the Point proved so ineffectual that the garrison did not bother to return it.

Returning the tactics of "No-Flint" Grey, Anthony Wayne had evened the score of Paoli: with the bayonet his men had killed 63 redcoats at a loss to themselves of 15 dead and 84 wounded. They had captured 543 men, 3 servants, and 15 guns.

Washington arrived on the seventeenth, accompanied by Greene and Steuben, to inspect the fort at Stony Point and decided that it could not be manned successfully by his army. So the next day it was dismantled completely and the Light Infantry withdrew, carrying off stores worth some $158,640, the value of which was divided as prize money among the victors of Stony Point. The day after the fort was abandoned, the enemy rushed up from below and reoccupied it, and their fatigue parties fell to work building stronger fortifications on both sides of the river.

The capture of Stony Point, as the *New Hampshire Gazette* editorialized, was more an emotional than a military victory: "It demonstrates that the Americans have soldiers equal to any in the world, and that they can attack and vanquish the Britons in their strongest works. No action during the war, performed by the British military, had equalled this *coup de main.*"

Baron von Steuben, who had taught the Continentals the art of the bayonet, was understandably pleased to learn the fort was taken without musketry. It was the baron who coached Captain Henry Archer, volunteer aide to Wayne, on the behavior he should exhibit at Philadelphia when he bore the news of the assault to Congress. Archer wrote back to his commanding officer a little self-consciously:

> I came into the city with colors flying, trumpets sounding, and heart elated, drew crowds to the doors and windows, and made not a little parade, I assure you. These . . . were Baron Steuben's instructions and I pursued them literally, though I could not help thinking it had a little of the appearance of a puppet show.[13]

The effects of Wayne's action were perhaps more far-reaching than the press supposed, more perhaps than judged by Washington himself, who pointed out to the Congress the damage inflicted on the enemy, the trouble they would have rebuilding the works, and the probable reduction in the range and strength of Clinton's operations for the rest of the campaign as a result of his loss of men and supplies at Stony Point. The General considered the attack's greatest advantage to be its good effect on the morale of the people and his troops and a proportionate depression of "the spirits of the enemy." Actually, the assault paralyzed Clinton. When his reinforcements failed to show up, he dared not, after his loss in men in Connecticut and at the Point, make an offensive move; he was so completely discouraged that he endeavored to resign the service and return home. However, he successfully cloaked his condition and plans from Washington in the days that followed.

Washington, for his part, considered another attack on the two posts, but abandoned it in favor of strengthening West Point and awaiting the enemy's next move.

On the night of the eighteenth, in imitation of Wayne, Major Henry Lee led a partially successful raid against the enemy post on Powle's Hook, a sandy spit west of the Hudson River, opposite the lower end of Manhattan Island.

Clinton continued to remain quiet, and with the Powle's Hook affair, active military operations for 1779 came to a close. The campaign that might have ended in a draw, because both sides were hobbled by circumstance, became a moral victory for the rebels through the imagination and resourcefulness of their Commander-in-Chief and the vigor and will of his subordinates. It was not too much to say that Washington had outmaneuvered his enemy: he still held the key to the continent: West Point and the Hudson River line. Under the unrelaxed eye of Steuben, he kept his army trained and spent the fall around West Point, which he fortified stoutly.

"THE POSITION BACK OF MR. KEMBLES"

Morristown

WINTER 1779-1780

WITH BOTH armies in repose, the only other military activities in the North were the cruelly successful war Sullivan and Clinton waged against the Tories and Indians on the frontier and an unfortunate expedition by Massachusetts state troops against a small naval base the enemy had established at Penobscot. As a result of that fiasco, undertaken without the knowledge of Washington, Paul Revere was falsely accused of cowardice and disobedience. He lost his commission and for nearly three years fought for the court-martial which finally cleared his name.

In the lull following Lee's attack on Powle's Hook, Washington coped with the complexity of problems that had become his daily burden. Greene was dissatisfied and wanted to retain both his rank in the line of the army and the emoluments he enjoyed as Quartermaster General. Ill health forced Sullivan to retire from the service. The dependable McDougall was suffering from "some alarming symptoms of the stone" and was considering "laying by for the winter." Putnam had withdrawn, enfeebled by hard service. Gates refused command of the Highlands and went home to Virginia for the winter. Jeremiah Wadsworth, who had been a diligent Commissary General, resigned. Clothing was wearing out, and Congress was not replacing it. Depreciation had continued its headlong course, and officers who stayed in the service were outraged by the decline in the purchasing power of their pay. A drought was making it impossible in several Northern states to grind wheat, and wheat and flour stocks were dangerously low. The three-year enlistments of "a great part of the army" had only four or five months more to run, and every day from now till spring could be expected to reduce Washington's numerical strength. The General was himself "again reduced to the necessity of acting the part of Clothier General." Reports of the success of Sullivan and Clinton were counterbalanced by word of the complete failure in October of a combined attempt by Estaing's forces and Americans under General Benjamin Lincoln to retake Savannah, in Georgia. The French fleet, instead of then returning north for combined action against either New York or Newport, sailed to the West Indies.

Nothing, however, dulled Washington's kindly sense of frivolity when he wrote a long, gossipy letter to Lafayette. The young Marquis had returned to France in January, 1779, for an indefinite leave and to propose to the French court a fanciful scheme for Canadian conquest. He had written the General: "I have a wife who is in love with you," and had proposed that Washington visit France after the war, to which the General responded, writing rapidly in his own round hand:

. . . let me entreat you to be persuaded that to meet you anywhere after the final accomplishment of so glorious an event would contribute to my happiness, and that to visit a country to whose generous aid we stand so much indebted would be an additional pleasure; but remember, my good friend, that I am unacquainted with your language that I am too far advanced in years to acquire a knowledge of it, and that to converse through the medium of an interpreter upon common occasions, especially with the *ladies,* must appear so extremely awkward, insipid, and uncouth, that I can scarce bear it in idea. I will, therefore, hold myself disengaged for the *present* and when I see you in Virginia, we will talk of this matter and fix our plans.[1]

The General brought his friend up to date on military matters, tendered his compliments to the Marchioness, and added teasingly:

Tell her (if you have not made a mistake and offered your *own love,* instead of *hers,* to me) that I have a heart susceptible of the tenderest passion, and that it is already so strongly impressed with the most favorable ideas of her that she must be cautious of putting love's torch to it, as you must be in fanning the flame. But here again, methinks, I hear you say, I am not apprehensive of danger. My wife is young, you are growing old, and the Atlantic is between you. All this is true, but know, my good friend, that no distance can keep *anxious* lovers long asunder and that the Wonders of former ages may be revived in this. But alas! will you not remark that amidst all the wonders recorded in holy writ no instance can be produced where a young woman from *real inclination* has preferred an old man. This is so much against me that I shall not be able, *I fear,* to contest the prize with you, yet under the encouragement you have given me I shall enter the list for so inestimable a jewel.

I will now reverse the scene and inform you that Mrs.

Washington (who set out for Virginia when we took the field in June) often has, in her letters to me, enquired if I had heard from you and will be much pleased at hearing that you are well, and happy.[2]

In October, the British evacuated King's Ferry and moved their cannon, equipment, and supplies down the Hudson. A few nights later, they evacuated Newport without committing any final depredations, although previously they had ravaged the island. Obviously, Clinton was concentrating at New York for the winter, Washington thought, so he hastened to get his own men into winter quarters.

As a campsite for the army, the General fixed upon "the position back of Mr. Kembles," about three miles southwest of Morristown, New Jersey, a somewhat mountainous section known as Jockey Hollow, where Greene chose positions for each brigade. On December 1, 1779, during "a very severe storm of hail and snow all day," Washington himself rode into the hilly little community of Morristown and established headquarters in the big white house of recently widowed Mrs. Theodosia Ford. The Commander-in-Chief's guard arrived four days later, tented six days on the frozen ground, and then moved into huts they had built in a meadow directly southeast of the house. The troops began converging on Morristown the first week of December and promptly set to work felling, skinning, and laying up logs.

The stormy day of the General's arrival was like an evil portent: the weather grew harsher by the day as one howling snowstorm after another raged through the tangled forests of Jockey Hollow. The half-naked men chopping the tough old oak, walnut, and chestnut "suffered much without shoes and stockings and working half leg deep in snow." Wayne's Light Infantry was about to be disbanded and reassigned to their respective units, but when Wayne wrote to General Irvine about them, he spoke for the whole army. Snatching at any small promise, he said that he was "much pleased at the prospect of once more clothing our officers and soldiers," adding sardonically:

I must confess that the latter would make a better apperance had they a sufficiency of *hats,* but as Congress don't seem to think *that* an essential . . . part of uniform, they mean to leave us uniformly bare-headed—as well as bare-footed—and if they find that we can *bare* it tolerably well in the two extremes, perhaps they may try it in the *center.*[3]

Often bare—top, bottom, and center—the men nevertheless, in less than two months, spread a "Log-house city" over the hillsides of Jockey Hollow. The weather was without mercy; never had there been a colder winter. Even the Hudson River froze solid from New York to Powle's Hook, a span of about two thousand yards, so that before long it "was practicable for the heaviest cannon, an event unknown in the memory of man." Staten Island could be supplied by sleigh, and once a cavalry troop rode from there to the Battery. At Morristown, while frozen hundreds huddled in their tents awaiting the completion of huts, more snow fell on the twenty-eighth and still lay heavy when the great storm the second through the fourth of January broke over the encampment with blinding snow and screaming wind. A few days later, Dr. James Thacher recorded it:

> . . . No man could endure its violence many minutes without danger of his life. Several marquees were torn asunder and blown down over the officers' heads in the night, and some of the soldiers were actually covered while in their tents and buried like sheep under the snow. . . .

We are greatly favored in having a supply of straw for bedding. Over this we spread our blankets, and with our clothes and large fires at our feet, while four or five are crowded together, preserve ourselves from freezing. But the sufferings of the poor soldiers can scarcely be described. While on duty they are unavoidably exposed to all the inclemency of storms and severe cold. At night they now have a bed of straw on the ground and a single blanket to each man. They are badly clad and some are destitute of shoes.

We have contrived a kind of stone chimney outside, and an opening at one end of our tents gives us the benefit of the fire within. The snow is now from four to six feet deep, which so obstructs the roads as to prevent our receiving a supply of provisions. For the last ten days we have received but two pounds of meat a man, and we are frequently for six or eight days entirely destitute of meat, and then as long without bread. The consequence is, the soldiers are so enfeebled from hunger and cold as to be almost unable to perform their military duty or labor in constructing their huts. It is well known that General Washington experiences the greatest solicitude for the sufferings of his army and is sensible that they in general conduct [themselves] with heroic patience and fortitude.[4]

Joseph Martin had learned by now to take soldiering with philosophical acceptance, but he never forgot the distresses of Morristown when it was locked in the snows.

> We were absolutely literally starved [he wrote]. I do solemnly declare that I did not put a single morsel of victuals into my mouth for four days and as many nights, except a

little black birch bark, which I knawed off a stick of wood, if that can be called victuals.

I saw several . . . men roast their old shoes and eat them, and I was afterwards informed by one of the officers' waiters that some of the officers killed and ate a favorite little dog that belonged to one of them.[5]

The officers and their men, Washington thought, bore their lot with super-human fortitude, but at last they were brought to "such a dreadful extremity" that nothing could restrain them from foraging anywhere they could. Regardless of the understandable hungers which drove men to desperation, the General would not relax discipline.

Not even the piteous existence of the starving men could be allowed to give them license to fight among themselves, steal, plunder, or try to desert. Ebenezer Huntington, who certainly sympathized with the man in the ranks, was president of one court-martial, when one Jesse Pierce was found guilty of desertion. Less fortunate comrades were sentenced to be shot. Pierce was sentenced to "run the Gauntlope thro' the brigade to which he belongs. . . ." Even facing the gauntlet, Jesse Pierce must have been amused by the rest of his sentence: to be confined in the dungeon for one month on bread and water. His guiltless companions were faring little better. The same court sentenced several others to one hundred lashes on the bare back, to be laid on in the freezing wind and snow. Dr. Thacher in his official capacity attended many of those punishments that winter, and described them in his journal:

The culprit being securely tied to a tree or post receives on his naked back the number of lashes assigned him, by a whip formed of several small knotted cords, which sometimes cut through the skin at every stroke. However strange it may appear, a soldier will often receive the severest stripes without uttering a groan or once shrieking from the lash, even while the blood flows freely from his lacerated wounds. This must be ascribed to stubbornness or pride. They have, however, adopted a method which they say mitigates the anguish in some measure. It is by putting between the teeth a leaden bullet, on which they chew while under the lash, till it is made quite flat and jagged. In some instances of incorrigible villains, it is adjudged by the court that the culprit receive his punishment at several different times, a certain number of stripes repeated at intervals of two or three days, in which case the wounds are in a state of inflammation and the skin rendered more sensibly tender, and the terror of the punishment is greatly aggravated.[6]

Not even these brutal exhibits deterred hungry or greedy men from robbing their fellows or the country people, and more than once soldiers "were brought to the gallows for the crime of robbery."

It was a hard business nevertheless to punish a man who had "nothing to cover him from hips to toes save his blanket," one of those who, according to the General, had to "eat every kind of horse food but hay."

Washington saw "no prospect of relief through the ordinary channels." The only hope for his starving army was an appeal to the magistrates and civilians of New Jersey. Generously, New Jersey responded, saving the army single-handedly from starvation and disbandment.

Two abysmal months dragged past before the furious winds began to abate and it was possible to venture out of doors; then some of the officers tried to make the best of their misery by diverting themselves with visits to kin and friends nearby and with dancing the nights away. The enlisted men had few amusements, save an occasional public celebration, such as St. Patrick's Day, when a Pennsylvania officer managed to buy a hogshead of rum for his men.

Washington, who loved to dance, subscribed with thirty-four officers to form a dancing assembly. Girls who were rugged enough to get through the mountainous snowdrifts were energetic enough to wring from Captain Samuel Shaw a groan: "three nights going till after two o'clock have they made us keep it up." The General, always the gallant at every party, ran into difficulty at one of Colonel Biddle's parties, so rumor said, when Mrs. George Olney told him angrily that "if he did not let go her hand, she would tear out his eyes, or the hair from his head; and that though he was a general, he was but a man."

For all their efforts at diversion, officers and men suffered far more severely at Morristown than they had that memorable winter at Valley Forge. At the end of March, eight inches of snow still lay on the ground, and at the close of each day, the army was seldom certain of a crumb of bread the next.

Coming of spring brought relief, at least, from the cruel weather, and an incident evoked from the Commander-in-Chief a flash of sardonic, ghoulish humor. A Spanish official died on a visit to Morristown and was buried in "splendid full dress" including "diamond shoe and knee buckles, a profusion of diamond rings . . . a superb gold watch set with diamonds, several rich seals." The General thought it wise to place a guard at the grave, until the body could be removed to Philadelphia, lest some shabby Continental "dig for hidden treasure."

On the tenth of May, Washington joyfully welcomed Lafayette, who rode into Morristown after more than a year's
absence. While home, the Marquis had sired a son, whom he
named George Washington Lafayette, but Washington heard
such personal reports only after the ebullient Marquis excitedly delivered unbelievably good news: six French ships of
the line and six thousand troops were en route to Rhode Island with orders to co-operate in a joint operation to take
New York and its defenders. Costly misunderstandings such
as those that had arisen between Estaing and the American
high command last year were not likely this time, he
thought, for the new expedition's commander had been given
specific instructions by Louis XVI to act under the orders of
the American Commander-in-Chief. Washington's hopes for
a summer offensive soared.

But the immediate situation at Morristown did not improve, it grew threateningly worse. Food supplies dwindled.
The men growled alarmingly, and mass desertion or worse
threatened. Not even the willingness of officers to put themselves on bread and water could save enough meat to feed
the army. By the twenty-third of May, all meat was gone and
none was in sight. Even the long-suffering Joseph Martin
had reached the limits of his patience. On the twenty-fifth, a
"pleasant day," he wrote, the men spent most of their time on
the parade "growling like soreheaded dogs." Finally, said
Martin:

. . . At evening roll call they began to show their dissatisfaction by snapping at the officers and acting contrary
to their orders. After their dismissal from the parade, the officers went as usual to their quarters, except the Adjutant
who happened to remain, giving details for next day's duty to
the orderly sergeants, or some other business, when the men
(none of whom had left the parade) began to make him sensible that they had something in train. He said something that
did not altogether accord with the soldiers' ideas of propriety. One of the men retorted. The Adjutant called him a
mutinous rascal or some such epithet and then left the parade.

This man, then stamping the butt of his musket upon the
ground, . . . in a passion, called out, "Who will parade with
me?"

The whole regiment immediately fell in and formed. We
had made no plans for our future operations, but while we
were consulting how to proceed, the Fourth Regiment, which
lay on our left, formed and came and paraded with us. We
now concluded to go in a body to the other two regiments
that belonged to our brigade and induce them to join with

us. . . . We did not wish to have anyone in particular to command, lest he might be singled out for a court-martial to exercise its clemency upon. We, therefore, gave directions to the drummers to give certain signals on the drums. At the first signal we shouldered our arms; at the second, we faced; at the third, we began our march to join with the other two regiments, and went off with music playing.

By this time, our officers had obtained knowledge of our military maneuvering, and some of them had run . . . and informed the officers of those regiments of our approach and supposed intentions.

The officers ordered their men to parade as quick as possible *without* arms. When that was done, they stationed a camp guard, that happened to be near at hand, between the men and their huts, which prevented them from entering and taking their arms, which they were very anxious to do.

Colonel [Return Jonathan] Meigs of the Sixth Regiment exerted himself to prevent his men from obtaining their arms, until he received a severe wound in his side by a bayonet in the scuffle. . . . Colonel Meigs was truly an excellent man and a brave officer. The man, whoever he was, that wounded him, doubtless, had no particular grudge against him. It was dark and the wound was given, it is probable, altogether unintentionally. . . .

When we found the officers had been too crafty for us, we returned with grumbling instead of music, the officers following in the rear growling in concert. One of the men in the rear calling out, "Halt in front," the officers seized upon him like wolves on a sheep and dragged him out of the ranks, intending to make an example of him for being a "mutinous rascal"; but the bayonets of the men pointing at their breasts as thick as hatched teeth compelled them quickly to relinquish their hold of him.

We marched back to our own parade and then formed again. The officers now began to coax us to disperse to our quarters, but that had no more effect upon us than their threats. One of them slipped away into the bushes, and after a short time returned, counterfeiting to have come directly from headquarters. Said he, "There is good news for you, boys. There has just arrived a large drove of cattle for the army." But this piece of finesse would not avail. All the answer he received for his labor was, "Go and butcher them," or some such slight expression.

The lieutenant colonel of the Fourth Regiment now came on to the parade. He could persuade *his* men, he said, to go peaceably to their quarters. After a good deal of palaver, he ordered them to shoulder their arms, but the men taking no notice . . . he fell into a violent passion. . . . After spending a whole quiver of the arrows of his rhetoric, he again ordered them to shoulder their arms, but he met with the same success. . . . He, therefore, gave up the contest as hopeless . . . and walked off to his quarters. . . . The rest of the officers, after they found that they were likely to meet with no better success than the colonel, walked off likewise to their huts.

While we were under arms, the Pennsylvania troops, who lay not far from us, were ordered under arms and marched off their parades, upon, as they were told, a secret expedition. They had surrounded us, unknown to either us or themselves (except the officers); at length, getting an item of what was going forward, they inquired of some of the stragglers what was going on among the Yankees. Being informed that they had mutinied on account of the scarcity of provisions, "Let us join them," said they. "Let us join the Yankees. They are good fellows and have no notion of lying here like fools and starving." Their officers needed no further hinting. The troops were quickly ordered back to their quarters, from fear that they would join in the same song with the Yankees. We knew nothing of all this for some time afterwards.

After our officers had left us to our own option, we dispersed to our huts and laid by our arms of our own accord, but the worm of hunger gnawing so keen kept us from being entirely quiet. We, therefore, still kept upon the parade in groups, venting our spleen at our country and government, then at our officers, and then at ourselves for our imbecility in staying there and starving . . . for an ungrateful people who did not care what became of us. . . .

While we were thus venting our gall against we knew not who, Colonel [Walter] Stewart of the Pennsylvania Line, with two or three other officers of that Line, came to us and questioned us respecting our unsoldierlike conduct, (as he termed it). We told him he needed not to be informed of the cause of our present conduct, but that we had borne till we considered further forebearance pusillanimity, that the times, instead of mending, were growing worse, and finally, that we were determined not to bear or forbear much longer. We were unwilling to desert the cause of our country when in distress, that we knew her cause involved our own, but what signified our perishing in the act of saving her when that very act would inevitably destroy us, and she must finally perish with us.

"Why do you not go to your officers," said he, "and complain in a regular manner?"

We told him we had repeatedly complained to them, but they would not hear us.

"Your officers," said he, "are gentlemen. They *will* attend to you. I know them. They cannot refuse to hear you. But . . . your officers suffer as much as you do. We all suffer. The officers have no money to purchase supplies with, any more than the private men have, and if there is nothing in the public store, we must fare as hard as you. . . .

"Besides," said he, "you know not how much you injure your own characters by such conduct. You Connecticut troops have won immortal honor to yourselves the winter past by your performance, patience, and bravery, and now you are shaking it off at your heels. But I will go and see your officers and talk with them myself."

He went, but what the result was, I never knew. This Colonel Stewart was an excellent officer, much beloved and respected by the troops of the Line he belonged to. He possessed great personal beauty. The Philadelphia ladies styled him the *Irish Beauty*.

Our stir did us some good in the end, for we had provisions directly after. . . .[7]

So in 1780, after five years of enduring, the army had its first real mutiny. It happened not to grow violent, but it had all the ugly feeling of that dread business. And Washington and his officers must have known that an evil seed had fallen on the soil of Jockey Hollow. How long before another rank flower would break ground? A few of the men were arrested later, but Washington finally granted pardons to all, save the most violent who had shouldered their packs and tried to march off, hoping that by leniency and patience another outbreak might be averted.

Lafayette, who had been at Philadelphia, returned to Morristown and wrote back to Joseph Reed:

An Army that is reduced to nothing, that wants provisions, that has not one of the necessary means to make war, such is the situation wherein I found our troops and however prepared I could have been to this unhappy sight by our past distresses, I confess I had no idea of such an extremity.[8]

Wearily but with his usual doggedness, the General wrote that same day to Joseph Jones, Virginia Delegate in Congress:

Certain I am, that unless Congress speaks in a more decisive tone; unless they are vested with powers by the several states competent to the great purposes of war, or assume them as a matter of right; and they and the states respectively act with more energy than they hitherto have done, that our cause is lost.[9]

To add to the dreariness of the General's prospects came intelligence of the capture of Charleston by Clinton, with the loss to America of an army of some two thousand Continentals and nearly as many militia, and of its commanding general, Benjamin Lincoln. The fate of reinforcements on the march to Charleston was in doubt. It was safe to assume that before long some of the force Clinton had withdrawn from New York during the winter to assault Charleston would return, strengthening the force facing Washington.

Now it was June, and surely the British could be expected to move. To meet them, Washington called for seventeen thousand militia to rendezvous by July 15. Before it could gather, General Knyphausen, now commanding in New York in the absence of Clinton, crossed from Staten Island to Connecticut Farms with five thousand men about midnight, June 6, and sacked and burned the village. Jersey militia hastily assembled at nearby Springfield and checked the enemy on the way to that village. Knyphausen fell back to Elizabethtown.

Word of Knyphausen's crossing from Staten Island reached Washington in the early hours of June 7. The two Maryland brigades had marched for the South in April, and the New York Brigade had gone to the Highlands; the six still encamped in Jockey Hollow marched for the Short Hills overlooking Springfield, where that afternoon the General learned that the enemy had withdrawn to Elizabethtown Point. For two weeks, the enemies faced each other immobile.

Then intelligence reports began to reach Washington indicating that Sir Henry Clinton and his forces were sailing into New York from Carolina. When six British ships-of-war moved up the Hudson, Washington feared again for the safety of West Point. Dividing his strength, he left Nathanael Greene with a small force at Springfield and marched slowly toward Pompton, sixteen miles northeast, within three or four good marches from the Hudson River citadel.

Dr. Thacher was with Greene's force, diligently keeping up his journal:

At six o'clock in the morning of the twenty-third, the alarm guns were fired, and the drums throughout our camp beat to arms, announcing the approach of the enemy. The whole army is instantly in motion. . . .

Soon after the alarm, our advanced party, consisting of General Maxwell's Brigade and a few militia, discovered the enemy advancing towards the village of Springfield. A close engagement with the enemy's advance immediately ensued, but being pressed by four times our number, General Maxwell, after an obstinate resistance, was obliged to retreat till a reinforcement could arrive.

Our brigade, commanded by General Stark, soon joined Maxwell on the high ground near the village. . . . Colonel Angell's regiment of Rhode Island, with several small parties, were posted at a bridge over which the enemy were to pass, and their whole force of five or six thousand men was actually held in check by those brave soldiers for more than forty minutes, amidst the severest firing of cannon and musketry.

The enemy, however, with their superior force, advanced into the village and wantonly set fire to the buildings. We had the mortification of beholding the church and twenty or thirty . . . houses and other buildings in a blaze. . . .

Having thus completed their great enterprise and acquired to themselves the honor of burning a village, they made a precipitate retreat to Elizabeth Point, and the ensuing night crossed over to Staten Island.[10]

A few days later, the main army encamped at Preakness to await the state drafts and to prepare for the arrival of the French fleet. As soon as the tents were pitched, Simeon De-Witt wrote proudfully to a college friend:

> Should the enemy have presumption enough to lead them to an attack upon our works in the Highlands, you will hear of bloody noses. They have last Friday experienced the resoluteness of our troops, though only a small detachment sufficient to give them a sample of what they may expect.[11]

But, unknown to DeWitt, and scarcely guessed by anyone, the time for bloody noses in the Highlands, or anywhere else in the North, was almost past. Springfield was the last conflict of any size in that theater. The longest phase of the War for Independence was over.

"TREASON! TREASON! TREASON!
BLACK AS H—LL"

Benedict Arnold

AUTUMN 1780

THE SUMMER that opened at Preakness under skies frequently the color of slate was to be one of frustrated hopes and heartbreaking disappointments for General Washington and his companions-in-arms.

Clinton's transports withdrew toward New York, assuring for the time being the safety of West Point and the Highlands. With a sigh of relief, Washington postponed the rendezvous of the militia: until the intractable Continental levies came in and the French forces arrived, the militia would have nothing to do; the army possessed too little food to expose it to their locust-like appetites. The fact of the matter was, the Continental Army was in little better condition than it had been all winter.

Sam Cogswell, a thoughtful, inspired, and sanguine young man, returned in July from furlough in Massachusetts, and he wrote home to his father:

The most of the army I found destitute of tents and encamped in a wood with no other security from the inclemency of the weather than the boughs of trees, or now and then a bark hut. The evening after my arrival in a camp a rain began which continued almost two days, the most of which time I was wet to my skin, as were all that were with me. . . .
I find all the gentlemen, and indeed all the Lords of the Regiment to which I belong, very destitute of almost every convenience. . . . Besides being very ragged and very dirty (which, by the way, they were unable to prevent for want of a change of clothes), they were supplied with but half allowance of meat, bread, or rum. Whilst I pitied the poor fellows . . . my admiration was drawn forth at . . . the patience with which they bore it. Not a single complaint have I heard made by a soldier since I joined the army. Everyone seems willing to wait for a compensation till his country can grant it to him without injuring herself, which happy time we expect is near at hand. . . .[1]

Lieutenant Colonel Ebenezer Huntington was in rags. During the rain that greeted Sam Cogswell's return to camp, the colonel had lain "on the ground for forty hours . . . and only a junk of fresh beef and that without salt to dine on." He remembered all too keenly that he had not been paid since December. He was an old campaigner now, and he was not as idealistic as Cogswell. He had heard that the French were coming, but he no longer put his faith in promises that were likely to turn out empty. Ever hopeful of arousing his Connecticut kinsmen to send aid to the army, he complained to his brother:

The rascally stupidity which now prevails in the country at large is beyond all descriptions. They patiently see our illustrious Commander at the head of twenty-five hundred or three thousand ragged, though virtuous and good, men and be obliged to put up with what no troops ever did before.

Why don't you reinforce your army, feed them, clothe and pay them? Why do you suffer the enemy to have a foothold on the continent? You can prevent it. Send your men to the field, believe you are Americans, not suffer yourselves to be duped into the thought that the French will relieve you and fight your battles. It is your own superiorness that induced Congress to ask foreign aid. It is a reflection too much for a soldier. You don't deserve to be free men, unless you can believe it yourselves. When they arrive, they will not put up with such treatment as your army have done. They will not serve week after week without meat, without clothing, and paid in filthy rags.

I despise my countrymen. I wish I could say I was not born in America. I once gloried in it, but am now ashamed of it. If you do your duty, though late, you may finish the war this campaign. You must immediately fill your regiments and pay your troops in hard monies. They cannot exist as soldiers otherwise. The insults and neglects which the Army have met with from the country beggars all description. It must go no farther; they can endure it no longer. I have wrote in a passion. Indeed, I am scarce ever free from it . . . and all this for my cowardly countrymen who flinch at the very time when their exertions are wanted and hold their purse strings as though they would damn the world rather than part with a dollar to their Army.[2]

Huntington's angry estimate of a strength of only twenty-five hundred to three thousand ragged men was not entirely exaggerated. When Knyphausen, with a force of about five thousand, had entered Jersey, Washington did not have sufficient strength to engage him. By the twelfth of July, with recruits beginning to join, the total of the army and the garrison at West Point was estimated at nearly 9,000 men, but ten days later, the main force returned only 3,278 fit for duty—that is, shod, clothed, and in health. A month later, of 16,500 troops requested from the states to fill their Continental quotas, only slightly more than 6,000 had come in. From the South news was bad, and Washington, instead of being able to unite with the French his maximum strength and all recruits that might come in, was obliged to send as many as could be spared of the Virginia and Carolina men to reinforce the Southern army. On the other hand, he could count on an enemy strength around New York of at least twenty thousand.

A further trial at this particular time was a contemplated reorganization by Congress of the Quartermaster Department on lines which Greene had made clear he would not accept.

When word finally came of the landing of the French at Newport, the tenth of July, Washington dispatched Lafayette to present to their commander an outline of plans for operations against New York. Before the Marquis was out of sight up the valley from Colonel Dey's house, where Washington headquartered, the General began preparations for co-operation with his allies.

At Newport, General Heath, who had been ordered there to greet the allies, slipped up on his timing, and in a cold and clammy fog the Gallic visitors landed unannounced and unwelcomed. Their commander, the handsome, fifty-five-year-old professional soldier, Jean Baptiste Donatien de Vimeur, Comte de Rochambeau, and his staff found "no one about in the streets; only a few sad and frightened faces in the windows." The general put up at the local inn, but by the next morning managed to talk to "some of the principal citizens." He told them that this was only the vanguard of a much larger force coming to support America, and by evening Newport was displaying illuminations and fireworks and ringing bells.

The spanking white uniforms, lapeled and collared in every hue of the rainbow, and the amusing accents and Gallic chivalry of the allies swept the local girls off their feet, and their commander altogether charmed the Rhode Island Assembly when he returned its polite address.

But immediate co-operation between Washington and the French was doomed. Three days after the arrival of the French, Admiral Thomas Graves appeared off Sandy Hook with a six-vessel reinforcement for the English fleet. The French fleet commander, Admiral the Chevalier de Ternay, did not dare match his inferiority against the enemy and was blockaded in Newport.

When Washington learned that British transports were proceeding eastward through Long Island Sound, evidently bent on attacking the French, he projected a demonstration against New York, although he was badly crippled because Greene had resigned as Quartermaster General, enfeebling that service. Greene's letter of resignation was so sarcastic that Congress was considering ordering his dismissal from the army, but in the present emergency Washington persuaded him to continue temporarily. As Washington marched across the Hudson River toward King's Bridge, Clinton drew back to New York; Washington then countermarched to Jersey. There he was helpless, save to wait for a second division of the French which would shift naval superiority. Fortunately, Greene's resignation was accepted with no bar to his service in the line, so Washington assigned him to command his right wing. Benedict Arnold, to whom Washington offered the left wing, declined it in favor of command of West Point which he was soliciting.

Now there was nothing to do but wait. The only action was an unsuccessful foray by restive Wayne against a blockhouse at Bull's Ferry, near Hoboken. After this Washington's supply services collapsed. Timothy Pickering, new Quartermaster General, failed to report promptly for field orders, and by mid-August, Washington was so desperate that he had to turn back militia coming in to fight with the French, because he could not feed them.

Pouches of mail poured from headquarters as the determined General appealed to Congress and to its individual members not to let slip this greatest opportunity the nation had ever been given. To the President of Congress, Samuel Huntington, he wrote a long, cogent review of his problems and prospects, emphasizing again how short-term enlistment related to the future of the country:

On the whole, if something satisfactory be not done, the Army (already so much reduced in officers by daily resignations as not to have a sufficiency to do the common duties of it) must either cease to exist at the end of the campaign, or it will exhibit an example of more virtue, fortitude, self-denial, and perseverance than has perhaps ever yet been paralleled in the history of human enthusiasm.[3]

Food was so scarce that Washington was forced to move his army to the vicinity of Fort Lee on the Hudson River to impress food in that neighborhood. There, on August 25, he received a crushing dispatch from Rochambeau informing him that the second division of the French fleet was blockaded at Brest by an English squadron; with the best of fortune it could not hope to smash the blockade and make

America before October, too late, probably, for military action that year. With a heavy heart, Washington dismissed the idle militia, ordered the army to return to the vicinity of Hackensack, prepared for a possible enemy attack, and warned Benedict Arnold to draw scattered contingents to West Point for protection of the Highlands.

On top of this cruel disappointment came news that Gates had been routed at Camden, in South Carolina, leaving Virginia open to invasion. There was nothing that Washington could do, but he felt that he must consult the French commanders.

On September 17 he and his staff set out for a rendezvous with the French at Hartford. There, according to an aide of Rochambeau, "the two generals and the admiral [the Chevalier de Ternay] were closeted together all day. The Marquis de Lafayette assisted as interpreter, . . . They separated quite charmed with one another, at least they said so."

Behind those closed doors Washington proposed three possible courses of action, but only one met the favor of Rochambeau: If the second contingent arrived in time and won a naval victory over the British, they would attempt to take New York. If naval superiority should not be obtained until later in the fall, however, a combined expedition would be sent to rout the British from the South. But all of this was a fiction. Said Washington, "We could only combine possible plans on the supposition of possible events and engage mutually to do everything in our powers against the next campaign."

Once again, as so many times before, the disappointed Washington could do nothing. Once again he turned back helplessly to the wretched encampments, where hunger and nakedness, bitterness and discouragement dwelled.

Toward this dismal prospect Washington rode from Hartford on the twenty-third, accompanied by Lafayette, Knox, and his staff. He took the "upper road," because it lay by West Point. To command of that post the forbearing General, ignoring the ugly controversy that swirled about the swarthy "horse jockey" from New Haven, recently had appointed energetic General Benedict Arnold. No matter what misgivings the Pennsylvania Council, the Congress, and many others held about Arnold's honesty, Washington believed in him; but he thought he must see for himself what Arnold was doing to strengthen the defenses upon which the Americans must rely more than ever now while awaiting the French reinforcements.

On the way to West Point, Washington met the French Minister, the Chevalier de la Luzerne, and spent the night with him at Peekskill. On the morning of the twenty-fifth, he sprang into the saddle and pressed on to General Arnold's headquarters, expecting an ordinary, busy day.

The same morning marked for Arnold the climax of schemes that first had taken shape when the greedy soldier had ridden into Philadelphia in June, 1778, as occupation commander. There, a military hero and social nobody, he had established himself in the mansion vacated by Howe and had set about purchasing his place as a social somebody. He had employed a housekeeper, a coachman, a groom, and seven lesser servants. His fine chariot, with its handsome team of four and its liveried attendants, was a frequent sight. His fabulous dinners, for which he afforded wine at a thousand pounds a pipe, were the talk of the town.

To support his court, the completely unscrupulous social climber availed himself of every financial advantage his powerful position opened to him. Other Americans were making profits. Robert Morris was to defend himself from the charge of profiteering. Nathanael Greene had made a secret partnership with Jeremiah Wadsworth and Barnabas Deane which was, at least, strange. But the avaricious Arnold drew no fine moral lines; his peculation was indefensible.

Encouraging his penchant for high living was the eighteen-year-old blonde, gray-eyed, Tory socialite Margaret Shippen. After an intense courtship, strong-willed Peggy became the bride of the thirty-eight-year-old hero of Quebec and Saratoga. Arnold was still supporting a devoted sister and his three boys by a first marriage. He had had an expensive courtship, and now he had an expensive wife.

When the Council of Pennsylvania leveled charges of misconduct against Arnold, no one in Philadelphia was surprised. The charges were referred to a Congressional Committee, which dismissed four of the eight. A court-martial, in the winter of 1780, finally found him guilty of two of the four remaining charges, but recommended as his only punishment that he be reprimanded by the Commander-in-Chief. For a man of Arnold's immense pride, Washington's stern words were a mortification. The General had judged his actions reprehensible, imprudent, and improper, but he never lost confidence in Arnold's basic integrity or ability. When Arnold, only weeks after his trial, urgently asked for the command of West Point, pleading his three-year-old wound as an excuse for turning down a field command, Washington readily gave it to him.

The command embraced not only the fort on the west of the river, but also the forts at Stony Point and Verplanck's

Point, some twelve miles below, the posts east of the river from Fishkill to King's Ferry, and the corps of infantry and cavalry spread as far south as North Castle.

For Arnold the appointment seemed the last step up the ladder of fortune. For over a year, he and his pretty wife had been in correspondence with Clinton to arrange the delivery of West Point to the British for twenty thousand pounds, provided that Arnold could obtain command of it. The intermediary in the correspondence was Major John André, who had flirted with Peggy in Philadelphia during the high-spirited days of British occupation and since had become British Adjutant General and a favorite of Clinton.

Until Peggy Arnold could join him at his new post, Arnold wrote her details of American plans, which she sent on to the enemy, until she and her infant son joined her husband in mid-September. By then Arnold had established a new, direct line of communication with André in New York. He had managed even to inform the enemy when Washington would be at King's Ferry, en route to Hartford, and where he would lodge—an invitation to Clinton to seize the Commander-in-Chief. Clinton made no effort to do so— Arnold's tip may not have reached him in time—and Arnold visited briefly with Washington, Sunday night, September 17, at Peekskill.

On Monday, the eighteenth, Arnold was back at his headquarters in correspondence with the enemy, maturing plans for a secret meeting, at which details of the betrayal of West Point could be agreed upon. Joshua Hett Smith, at whose house Washington had lodged en rouute to Hartford, was to conduct André, traveling as merchant John Anderson, to a meeting, which Arnold desired to be within American lines. Clinton insisted that the meeting ground be in neutral territory and cautioned André not to disguise himself and be confused for a spy. Finally, it was agreed that employees of Arnold should row André, under Arnold's pass, from the British ship *Vulture,* moored at the lower end of Haverstraw Bay, to a rendezvous ashore. Thus about midnight, the twenty-first, André was rowed from the *Vulture* to a fir-crowned bluff on the river about fifteen miles below Beverley Robinson's lonely house opposite West Point, where Arnold made headquarters.

The ambitious, greedy American general and the ambitious, patriotic British youth, who had sought solace from a blighted love affair in the service of his King, talked the night away. Because daylight overtook the conspirators before they could finish their conversation, André was hidden in the nearby house of Joshua Smith. Smith later claimed he was serving Arnold without knowing the nature of the business between the general and the "civilian" Anderson, whose British uniform coat, thought he, was only a disguise to enable him more safely to bring Arnold information valuable to America. On the way to Smith's house André reluctantly rode through American lines, but he resigned his safety to Arnold, who assured him that the pass of the commanding officer of the area would protect him against all harm.

That day an enterprising American officer bombarded the *Vulture* from Teller's Point and forced her to drop down the river, so Arnold decided that André should return by land in disguise. He insisted also that André carry papers to Clinton, and he prepared a pass to conduct him to White Plains or below, traveling east of the river, "on public business at my direction." This would enable André to enter his own lines in safety. Smith was to escort him part of the way.

Smith insisted that the man he knew as John Anderson wear a claret-colored coat instead of his British uniform coat, in which he might not be permitted through American lines, no matter whose pass he carried. In borrowed coat, civilian beaver, and on a horse Arnold provided, André set out with Smith at sundown for White Plains. Around nine o'clock, near Crompond, about eight miles from Verplanck's they were stopped by American militia who told them that night riding would be dangerous below Croton River. They were entering the territory of a gang of loyalist partisans and freebooters, who called themselves "Cowboys" and preyed on both sides. Smith suggested, and André was obliged to agree, that they abide the night with a neighborhood farm family.

The next morning, Saturday the twenty-third, at breakfast, seven miles farther on, Smith said he was now turning back, leaving "John Anderson" to travel alone the last fifteen miles to White Plains. Smith would not hazard meeting Cowboy marauders, and said he thought it unlikely that Anderson would meet American patrols beyond that point. The two parted, André feeling that a few miles away lay safety: he had nothing to fear from loyalist patrols, and he thought that Arnold's pass would take him through any rebels he might encounter.

He rode lightheartedly along the Tarrytown Road, through some of the most savagely contested country in America. In the "Neutral Ground," no stranger was safe. Allegedly patriotic "Skinners" fought as relentlessly as Cowboys for plunder more than for politics, and many of them now roamed the land between the two armies, under a recent New York act which permitted them to claim as prize any property they might find on a captured enemy.

About nine or ten in the morning, André was accosted near Tarrytown by "three bushmen," who ordered him to halt. According to the story he later told Lieutenant Joshua King:

> He says to them, "I hope, gentlemen, you belong to the lower party." [Along the river, British and Tories were referred to as the lower party and the rebels, the upper, probably because of their relative possessions on the river.]
>
> "We do," says one.
>
> "So do I," says he, ". . . I am a British officer on business of importance and must not be detained."
>
> One of them took his watch from him and ordered him to dismount. The moment this was done . . ., he found he was mistaken and he must shift his tone. He says, "I am happy, gentlemen, to find I am mistaken. You belong to the upper party, and so do I. A man must make use of any shift to get along, and to convince you of it, here is General Arnold's pass . . . and I am in his service."
>
> "Damn Arnold's pass," says they. "You said you was a British officer. Where is your money?"
>
> "Gentlemen, I have none about me," he replied.
>
> "You a British officer and no money," says they. "Let's search him."
>
> They did so, but found none. Says one, "He has got his money in his boots," . . . and there they found his papers but no money. They then examined his saddle, but found none. He said he saw they had such a thirst for money, he could put them in a way to get it, if they would be directed by him. He asked them to name their sum for to deliver him at King's Bridge. They answered him . . ., "If we deliver you at King's Bridge, we shall be sent to the Sugar House [prison] and you will save your money."
>
> He says to them, "If you will not trust my honor, two of you may stay with me, and one shall go with a letter which I shall write. Name your sum."
>
> The sum was agreed upon. . . . They held a consultation a considerable time, and finally they told him, if he wrote, a party would be sent out and take them, and then they should all be prisoners. They said they had concluded to take him to the commanding officer on the lines.[4]

John Paulding, David Williams, and Isaac Van Wart, the three militiamen who had halted the stranger on the road to supplement their soldier's pay, took their captive to Lieutenant Colonel John Jameson, of the Second Continental Dragoons, in command of a detachment at North Castle. As a precaution for André and for himself, Arnold had ordered the officers at his advanced posts to look out for a John Anderson; if he came from New York, they were to send him to headquarters. Jameson sent André to Arnold, but sent the papers "of a very dangerous tendency" to Washington, known to be on his way back from Hartford and probably between Danbury and Peekskill.

Later in the day, Major Benjamin Tallmadge, who served the American secret service, returned from a scouting trip and suspected that there was much more to the matter of John Anderson. He persuaded Jameson to send after André, who was brought back to Lower Salem on Sunday morning, the twenty-fourth, and held, pending instructions from Washington. The prisoner was under the care of Lieutenant King, who was not impressed by the man called John Anderson:

> He looked somewhat like a reduced gentleman. His small clothes were nankeen with handsome whitetop boots—in fact his undress military clothes. His coat, purple, with gold lace, worn, somewhat threadbare, with a small-brimmed, tarnished beaver on his head. . . .
> After breakfast, my barber came in to dress me, after which I requested him to undergo the same operation, which he did. When the ribbon was taken from his hair, I observed it full of powder. This circumstance, with others that occurred, induced me to believe I had no ordinary person in charge. . . .
> We were close pent up in a bedroom with a vidette at the door and window. There was a spacious yard before the door, which he desired he might be permitted to walk in with me. I . . . disposed . . . my guard in such a manner as to prevent an escape. While walking together, he observed he must make a confidant of somebody, and he knew not a more proper person than myself, as I had appeared to befriend a stranger in distress. . . . He told me who he was and gave me a short account of himself. . . . He requested a pen and ink and wrote immediately to General Washington, declaring who he was.[5]

On Monday morning, the twenty-fifth, riding toward West Point, Washington sent ahead to Robinson's house Major James McHenry, now an aide to Lafayette, and Captain Samuel Shaw, of Knox's staff, to inform the Arnold household that hungry gentlemen were on the way. The aides arrived in time to breakfast with Arnold, who as yet was ignorant of André's fate. During the meal, Jameson's courier brought Arnold the fateful message that André was taken. Arnold, his face dark, his pale blue eyes working, but his harsh voice controlled, excused himself, saying that he must hurry across the river to West Point and that he would return in an hour to meet his Excellency. No one at the table guessed that instead, seeing the frustration of his plans, he was rushing to his barge to be rowed to refuge on the *Vulture*.

Washington arrived and found a disorganized household. Arnold's aide, Major David Franks, reported that Mrs. Arnold was in her room; Lieutenant Colonel Richard Varick, chief aide, was sick with fever; the general had been called to West Point, but would return. Washington put the disturbed officer at ease. After breakfast, he said, he and his staff would cross to the fort and visit Arnold there.

At West Point, where Washington was shocked by the dangerously neglected condition of the works, he was told Arnold had not been seen that day. In the afternoon he and his suite returned to Robinson's and found that Arnold had not returned there. The General began to be disturbed by his continued absence, but it was explained a few minutes later when Alexander Hamilton handed him the packet of papers found in André's boot and sent on by Colonel Jameson.

The General shuffled the papers, appalled, but not for a moment did he lose his accustomed composure. It was clear that Arnold had fled, probably down the river toward the vessel that had brought André. Quietly Washington ordered Hamilton and McHenry to spur after him and then calmly sat down to dinner without a word to anyone about Arnold's disappearance.

After dinner the General invited Colonel Varick, who during the day had dressed and presided at the table, to go for a walk. As they strolled, he told the news to the colonel, and said that he did not suspect either him or Major Franks, but that they must consider themselves temporarily under arrest. The colonel graciously acquiesced and told Washington all he knew about Arnold's recent activities and the suspicions he and Major Franks entertained about Joshua Hett Smith. Poor, unsuspecting Mrs. Arnold, Colonel Varick said, must have sensed nothing wrong, until her husband had told her he was leaving forever. That morning she had screamed for the colonel from her room and he had run to her to find her in her morning gown, too scantily clothed "to be seen by a gentleman of the family, much less by many strangers" and in a frenzy of inexplicable grief. Artful Peggy, probably distraught by the collapse of all her husband's schemes and hers, sobbed all day, convincing Arnold's military family of her entire innocence.

When Colonel Varick and the General returned to the house that evening, Peggy sent for Washington. She repeated the scene she had played for Colonel Varick in the morning, acting nearly insane and convincing the General, Lafayette, Colonel Varick, and Colonel Hamilton, who had returned from a fruitless chase, that the first she knew of her husband's wicked plan was when he had come to her that morning "to tell her he must banish himself from his country and from her forever."

Washington set about swiftly undoing Arnold's mischief. The traitor evidently had weakened West Point deliberately, scattering work parties and detachments. Working until two in the morning, the General completed instructions for manning the works and their dependencies and called up troops under Greene.

An uncomfortable night passed. The next morning, Alexander Hamilton tried to comfort the inconsolable Peggy, whose cleverness in setting the scene must not have been lost on Betsy Schuyler, Hamilton's fiancée, to whom he wrote:

> She received us in bed with every circumstance that would interest our sympathy, and her sufferings were so eloquent that I wished myself her brother to have a right to become her defender. . . . Could I forgive Arnold for sacrificing his honor, reputation, and duty, I could not forgive him for acting a part that must have forfeited the esteem of so fine a woman.[6]

The General was equally taken in and sent Peggy home to Philadelphia with Major Franks as her attentive escort.

On the morning of the twenty-sixth, Greene's General Orders broke the news to the thunderstruck army:

> *Treason* of the blackest dye was yesterday discovered! General Arnold, who commanded at West Point, lost to every sentiment of honor, of public and private obligation, was about to deliver up that important post into the hands of the enemy. Such an event must have given the American cause a deadly wound, if not a fatal stab. Happily, the treason has been timely discovered to prevent the fatal misfortune. The providential train of circumstances which led to it affords the most convincing proof that the liberties of America are the object of divine protection.
> . . . Great honor is due to the American Army that this is the first instance of treason of the kind when many were to be expected from the nature of the dispute. And nothing is so bright an ornament in the character of the American soldiers as their having been proof against all the arts and seduction of an insidious enemy. . . .
> His Excellency, the Commander-in-Chief, has arrived at West Point . . . and is no doubt taking the proper measures to unravel fully so hellish a plot![7]

Washington temporarily assigned ailing but experienced and dependable General McDougall to command of West Point, until he could be relieved by St. Clair. Then the General proceeded to join the main army at Tappan, where he ordered André escorted for trial. Major Benjamin Tallmadge was with the escort and purposely placed himself next to André on the after seat of the barge which took them down the river toward Tappan. Years later he recalled:

As we progressed on our way to Tappan, before we reached the Clove, where we dined, Major André was very inquisitive to know my opinion . . . as to the light in which he would be viewed by General Washington and a military tribunal, if one should be ordered. I endeavored to evade this question, unwilling to give him a true answer.

When I could no longer evade this importunity, I said to him that I had a much-loved classmate in Yale College by the name of Nathan Hale, who entered the Army with me in the year 1776. After the British troops had entered New York, General Washington wanted information respecting the strength, position, and probable movements of the enemy. Captain Hale tendered his services, went into New York, and was taken just as he was passing the outposts of the enemy. Said I, with emphasis, "Do you remember the sequel of this story?"

"Yes," said André. "He was hanged as a spy, but you surely do not consider his case and mine alike."

I replied, "Precisely similar, and similar will be your fate."

He endeavored to answer my remarks, but it was manifest he was more troubled than I had ever seen him before.[8]

The Board of General Officers which tried André was composed of six major generals, including President Nathanael Greene, and eight brigadiers. A British sergeant asserted:

General Greene was originally a Quaker, a stern republican; and such was the rancor displayed throughout the whole transaction, both by him and the Marquis de La Fayette that they may almost literally be said to have thirsted for the blood of the unfortunate victim whom fate had put in their power.[9]

The assertion was preposterous. Quite to the contrary, the American officers were as genuine in their sympathy for the unfortunate André as they were in their detestation of Arnold. His forthright, courteous answers to the Board of Officers, to whom he confessed espionage, aroused their deepest respect and sympathy. Throughout the army, men convinced of his complicity in treason as well, feared not the bloodthirstiness of the Board that sat in the old Dutch church at Tappan, but rather the probability of its excessive leniency. Almost everyone who had met or observed André or had heard about him from others seemed to share the sentiments of Tallmadge: "I can remember no instance where my affections were so fully absorbed in any man."

On October the first, such doubts were dissolved by Washington. Quoting in his General Orders the brief report of the Board, which concluded that Major André "ought to be considered as a spy . . . to suffer death," Washington added: "The Commander-in-Chief directs the execution of the above sentence in the usual way this afternoon at 5 o'clock precisely."

The prisoner was confined in two rooms of the substantial stone tavern belonging to a Mr. Maybie across the lane from the church. Benjamin Tallmadge was one of two American officers lodged in his quarters night and day, and to him the gallant young British gentleman endeared himself:

> Major André, . . . in truth . . . was a most elegant and accomplished gentleman. After he was informed of his sentence, he showed no signs of perturbed emotions, but wrote a most touching and finished letter to General Washington, requesting that the mode of his death might be adapted to the feelings of a man of honor. The universal usage of nations having affixed to the crime of a spy, *death by the gibbet*, his request could not be granted.[10]

On the afternoon of the first of October an enormous throng trudged into a field on the hill behind Maybie's to witness the execution of Major André. But a last-minute stay saved him. Clinton, in a desperate effort to save his adjutant general and friend, requested a meeting between officers; he hinted that further facts bearing on André's conduct might be revealed. It turned out that Clinton had nothing new to add, though his representative begged eloquently for André's life and offered "any prisoner in their possession" for him. The only man in enemy territory for whom the Americans were hungry enough to exchange André was Arnold himself, and Clinton, of course, could not consider surrendering him. So the execution again was set, for noon the next day. Surgeon James Thacher noted in his journal:

> The principal guard . . . who was constantly in the room with the prisoner, relates that when the hour of his execution was announced to him in the morning, he received it without emotion, and while all present were affected

with silent gloom, he retained a firm countenance, with calmness and composure of mind. Observing his servant enter the room in tears, he exclaimed, "Leave me till you can show yourself more manly."

His breakfast being sent to him from the table of General Washington, which had been done every day of his confinement, he partook of it as usual, and having shaved and dressed himself, he placed his hat on the table and cheerfully said to the guard officers, "I am ready at any moment, gentlemen, to wait on you."

The fatal hour having arrived, a large detachment of troops was paraded, and an immense concourse of people assembled. Almost all our general and field officers, excepting his Excellency and his staff, were present on horseback. Melancholy and gloom pervaded all ranks. . . .

Major André walked from the stone house . . . between two of our subaltern officers, arm in arm. The eyes of the immense multitude were fixed on him. . . . He betrayed no want of fortitude, but retained a complacent smile on his countenance and politely bowed to several gentlemen whom he knew, which was respectfully returned.

It was his earnest desire to be shot, as being the mode of death most conformable to the feelings of a military man, and he had indulged the hope that his request [made the day before to Washington] would be granted. At the moment, therefore, when suddenly he came in view of the gallows, he involuntarily started backward and made a pause.

"Why this emotion, sir?" said an officer by his side.

Instantly recovering . . . he said, "I am reconciled to my death, but I detest the mode."

While waiting and standing near the gallows, I observed some degree of trepidation, placing his foot on a stone and rolling it over and choking his throat as if attempting to swallow.[11]

In the crowd that shifted about the gallows on the bare hilltop was an artificer of Colonel Jeduthan Baldwin's regiment. Every detail impressed itself upon him:

The wagon that contained the coffin was drawn directly under the gallows. In a short time, André stepped into the hind end of the wagon, then on his coffin, took off his hat and laid it down, then placed his hands upon his hips and walked very uprightly back and forth as far as the length of his coffin would permit, at the same time casting his eyes upon . . . the whole scenery by which he was surrounded.

He was dressed in what I should call a complete British uniform. . . . All eyes were upon him, and it was not believed any officer in the British Army placed in his situation would have appeared better than this unfortunate man.[12]

Dr. Thacher, who stood close by, thought André at first shrank from the sight of the tall gibbet, but now he saw him lift his head and heard him say, "It will be but a momentary pang." When the executioner, frightfully disguised with blackened grease, stepped into the wagon and attempted to put the halter around the condemned man's neck, the artificer saw André push him away:

André took off the handkerchief from his neck, unpinned his shirt collar, and deliberately took the end of the halter, put it over his head, and placed the knot directly under his right ear, and drew it very snugly to his neck. He then took from his coat pocket a handkerchief and tied it over his eyes. This done, the officer that commanded . . . said that his arms must be tied. André at once pulled down the handkerchief he had just tied over his eyes and drew from his pocket a second one and gave to the executioner and then replaced his handkerchief. His arms were tied just above the elbows and behind the back.

The rope was then made fast to the pole overhead.

The wagon was very suddenly drawn from under the gallows which, together with the length of rope, gave him a most tremendous swing back and forth, but in a few moments he hung entirely still. . . .

He remained hanging, I should think, from twenty to thirty minutes, and during that time the chambers of death were never stiller than the multitude by which he was surrounded. . . .[13]

The quiet, sobered crowd drifted away.

In the oak-beamed parlor of the little Old World house of Johannes DeWint, Washington had sat all morning at a table before the Dutch-tiled fireplace, involved in correspondence and other detail work. About an hour after his officers reported that the sentence of the Board against Major André had been carried out, a messenger brought him two letters by flag from Benedict Arnold, reviewing André's visit behind the lines and again claiming amnesty for him because he had acted under Arnold's orders. The truculent, arrogant traitor threatened, "if that gentleman shall suffer the severity of the sentence, I shall think myself bound by every tie of duty and honor to retaliate on such unhappy persons of your army as may fall into my power, that the respect due to flags and the law of nations may be better understood and observed."

Clinton, though grieving for the victim of Arnold's perfidy, did bring himself to extend a friendly hand to his new general, promptly commissioned in the British Army, bought at such a high cost. But in New York it was observed:

General Arnold is a very unpopular character in the British army, nor can all the patronage he meets with from the commander-in-chief procure him respectability. . . . The subaltern officers have conceived such an aversion to him, that they unanimously refused to serve under his command. . . .[14]

From that same city, John Griffith wrote home to England of André:

He has died a sacrifice to his country . . . an honor to it and his connections, loved and esteemed by those who knew him and admired by those that did not. . . . When the account arrived at York, the soldiers' lips vibrated, "André! André!" and the streets re-echoed, "Vengeance with the bayonet to the Sons of Rebellion!"[15]

André was dead. A night had passed. Adjutant General Scammell, who had served under Arnold, penned a letter: "Treason! treason! treason! black as h-ll! . . . Heaven and earth! we were all astonishment, each peeping at his next neighbor to see if any treason was hanging about him. Nay, we even descended to a critical examination of ourselves."

Suspicious "peeping" happily revealed no further irregularities; full investigation failed to show that Arnold had involved any other person than Joshua Hett Smith, who was tried but acquitted for lack of evidence.

While the country hanged Arnold in effigy and recovered from the shock of its first great treason—Charles Lee's conduct in the Jersey Campaign was remembered, but no one called up Benjamin Church—Washington closed his "inactive campaign" of 1780.

32

"A RUDE SHOCK TO THE INDEPENDENCE OF AMERICA"

The South

1778-1780

For the Continental Army, the campaign of 1780 had been indeed inactive. But its closing at New Windsor did not mean ease of mind for the General or comfort for his men spread in camps from West Point to Morristown. They were not so naked as they had been the previous winter, but neither were they well clothed. They could be made comfortable, Washington complained, only by collecting "all our remnants, and those of a thousand colors and kinds." Food was still so scarce that only by impressing flour could he keep the army together. The military chest was bare. He was forced to send mail by post, because he could not scrape up money enough to pay an express to ride as far away as Rhode Island. Funds could hardly be expected from Philadelphia, for there the Board of Treasury was threatened with ejectment from its quarters for nonpayment of rent! And the annual task of re-enlisting the army promised to be more difficult than in any previous year. In addition to these sorry prospects at his "dreary station" at New Windsor, Washington was obliged to consider an accumulation of dismaying news from the distant South. There 1780 had been an appalling year for American arms.

That vast plantation world which stretched away from the golden fields of Virginia to the dank jungles of British Florida had been free from tread of armies for more than two years after the repulse of Sir Peter Parker at Charleston in 1776. True, Tory Rangers had swept up from steadfastly loyal Florida to harass the Georgia frontier, and anguished Georgia, officially rebel but a colony where bitter Tory fathers battled equally rabid Whig sons, had raised small forces to stab across the St. Johns River. Once a Continental expedition sent from Charleston against Florida had fallen apart on the scorching Georgia sands, but no substantial British effort had been made to conquer the region and so no strong American army under centralized leadership had developed or had been sent there. Instead a relentless, corrosive, internecine war between wild bands of Whigs and Tories had torn at the vitals of the Carolinas and Georgia. As often as not these irregulars were simply marauders who pillaged and killed their neighbors for gain rather than principle.

The inherent military weakness of these distant, thinly populated states, their remoteness from the North and its protection, and the undispelled illusion of sleeping Tory power in the back country constantly drew the thoughts of the King, like a compass needle, to the possibility of backdoor warfare against Washington's army. Therefore, in the spring of 1778, when George III, who followed minutely every military and naval action, often suggesting their plan, formulated the strategy for the first campaign of Sir Henry Clinton, it had for its final objective in autumn, after "operations on the seacoasts of the northern provinces are con-

WAR IN THE
Southern Department
1776-1782

cluded . . . an attack . . . upon the southern colonies with a view to the conquest . . . of Georgia and South Carolina." Once South Carolina was re-established as a royal colony, it would be relatively simple to tramp northward to the area of the Chesapeake, for North Carolina, the King was assured, was but "the road to Virginia."

On the eighth of March, 1778, Lord George Germain conveyed to Clinton by "most secret" dispatch His Majesty's plan. Two thousand men, the King judged, would be "fully sufficient to take and keep possession of Savannah," Georgia's busy port, sprawled on the great bluff eighteen miles up-river from the sea. When Clinton was ready to strike, he was to order General Augustin Prevost to march with a detachment from the British St. Augustine garrison, with the Florida Rangers and Indians, to attack the southern frontiers of Georgia, from Virginia, the Carolinas, and Georgia while John Stuart, Superintendent of Indian Affairs, brought down a body of redmen toward Augusta. Charleston should be the next objective. Five thousand men were thought adequate for its reduction. Perhaps, His Majesty reasoned, enough loyal inhabitants in Georgia would join the regulars to drive up the center of South Carolina to separate the seacoast from the back settlements and open communication with the loyalists of North Carolina. His Majesty was specific about the invasion route through the creeks and inlets around Charleston. Germain concluded:

Could a small corps be detached at the same time to land at Cape Fear and make an impression on North Carolina, it is not doubted that large numbers of the inhabitants would flock to the King's standard and that His Majesty's Government would be restored in that province also. But your own knowledge of those provinces and the information you can collect from the naval and military officers that have been upon service there, will enable you to give the officer to whom you may entrust the command better instructions than I can pretend to point out to you at this distance. I will therefore only further observe . . . that the conquest of these provinces is considered by the King as an object of great importance in the scale of war, as their possession might be easily maintained and thereby a very valuable branch of commerce would be restored to this country and the rebels deprived of a principal resource for the support of their foreign credit and of paying for the supplies they stand in need of, as the product of these provinces make a considerable part of their remittance to Europe.

While these operations are carrying on, every diversion

should be made in the provinces of Virginia and Maryland that the remaining troops which can be spared for offensive service in conjunction with the fleet will admit of. The great number of deep inlets and navigable rivers in these provinces expose them in a peculiar manner to naval attacks, and must require a large force to be kept on foot for their protection and disable them from giving any assistance to the Carolinas. The seizing or destroying their shipping would also be attended with the important consequence of preventing the Congress from availing themselves . . . of their staple commodity, tobacco, on which, and the rice and indigo of Carolina and Georgia, they entirely depend for making remittances to Europe.

Should the success we may reasonably hope for attend these enterprises, it might not be too much to expect that all America . . . south of the Susquehanna would return to their allegiance and . . . the northern provinces might be left to their own feelings and distress to bring them back to their duty, and the operations against them confined to the cutting off all their supplies and blocking up their ports.

I have thus stated the King's wishes and intentions, but he does not mean you to look upon them as orders, desiring . . . that you use your discretion in planning . . . all operations which shall appear the most likely means of crushing the rebellion.[1]

Complying with his sovereign's desires, Clinton had dispatched in November, 1778, thirty-five hundred men from New York and New Jersey, under Lieutenant Colonel Archibald Campbell, to co-operate with Prevost in an attack on Savannah. To oppose them was Major General Robert Howe of North Carolina, in command of the only American army in the South—about 700 Continentals and 150 militia. It lay about thirty miles south of Savannah, following another of Georgia's abortive attempts against Florida in the summer of 1778. Upon hearing of the arrival of the enemy fleet and the approach of Prevost, Howe left part of his force at Sunbury to check Prevost and marched the rest to a position a half-mile east of Savannah, across the main road from the river landings.

Learning from American deserters how slight a force opposed him, Colonel Campbell, without waiting for Prevost, landed on December 29 and feinted against the left of Howe's thin line, while sending a heavy force guided by an ancient slave through swamps to the rear of Howe's right. The rebels, taken in front and rear, fled through Savannah, leaving behind over five hundred dead, wounded and missing, a toll as heavy as Arnold's at the assault on Quebec. The few survivors trotted willy-nilly along roads into South Carolina. Campbell gobbled up Augusta, and Prevost, coming up from Florida, took Sunbury.

But American attention had been focused on the South. British ambitions there were well known. Congress had requested troops from Virginia and North Carolina for the defense of the other two states, and ponderous but dependable Benjamin Lincoln had been named commander of the Southern Department and had arrived in Charleston on the seventh of December. When he had heard of the enemy threat to Savannah, he had gathered up about fifteen hundred men and started to Georgia. About fifteen miles north of the Savannah River he met Howe's remnants, and for several weeks he lay helpless, so near the British across the river, said General Moultrie, who was there with South Carolina troops, that "we hear their drums beat every morn from our outposts; nay, hear their sentinels cough."

At length, encouraged by two small actions of South Carolinians who parried enemy thrusts toward South Carolina in February and by the eager enlistment of nearly three thousand aroused militia, Lincoln sent three forces probing southward. One met disaster on March 3, 1779, at Briar Creek, where four hundred were lost and six hundred dispersed. Undaunted, seven weeks later, he left a thousand men at Purrysburg and Black Swamp under command of General Moultrie to guard the Savannah and led his main force toward Augusta.

To draw Lincoln back from Georgia, General Prevost shrewdly crossed the river at Purrysburg and feinted toward Charleston. Moultrie fell away before him. Governor John Rutledge exhorted the inhabitants along the invader's route to rise and resist his advance. Heedless, they fled in panic. The way to the Carolina capital fell open, and Prevost decided to turn his feint into an actual drive and take the city. Said General Moultrie in his recollections of those harassed days:

There never was a country in greater confusion and consternation . . . five armies . . . marching through the southern parts of it at the same time, and all for different purposes: myself, retreating as fast as possible to get into town, at first with twelve hundred men, but reduced to six hundred before I got near the town; the British army of three thousand men . . . in pursuit of me; and General Lincoln with the American army of four thousand, marching with hasty strides to come up with the British; Governor Rutledge from Orangeburg [the South Carolina militia rendezvous] with about six hundred militia, hastening to get into town lest he should be shut out, and Colonel Harris [of Georgia] with a detachment of 250 Continentals pushing on with all possible dispatch to reinforce me. . . . In short, it was nothing but a general confusion and alarm.[2]

Had Prevost driven straight to Charleston, he surely would have taken it. Charleston Neck, it was observed, "was almost wholly defenseless." But the redcoats could not pass up the money, jewelry, and silver plate of the plantation houses along their road; while they lost valuable days in systematic looting, the rebels "made the greatest exertions to fortify the town," and American troops from all directions reached the city. It was the eleventh of May before the enemy crossed the Ashley with nine hundred men, descended the Neck, and sat down, facing the freshly turned earthworks and green abatis of the hurriedly fortified metropolis.

Probably hoping to amuse the enemy long enough to allow Lincoln to come down on his rear in the narrow Neck between the Ashley and the Cooper rivers, Governor Rutledge answered Prevost's summons to surrender by proposing to give up the city if the rest of the state and the harbor were considered neutral for the duration of the war. Prevost sharply rejected the proposal and repeated his demand for unconditional surrender. But before he could effect it, he learned from an intercepted letter of Lincoln's near approach; he disappeared back up the Neck and across the Ashley in the night of the twelfth of May. Retiring to the coast, he encamped on John's Island to await water transportation for his troops and threw up three strong redoubts on the mainland at Stono to cover his rear. Here Lincoln on the twentieth of June ineffectually attacked him with a heavy loss to himself, before the redcoats finally sailed southward, gorged with plunder. Although Prevost had failed to take Charleston, he had achieved his purpose: Lincoln was out of Georgia.

The enervating Southern summer—ninety-eight, ninety-nine, a hundred in the shade—drowsed away.

In South Carolina, General Lincoln lay ill at Charleston. What was left of his army, about eight hundred Continentals, encamped ten miles from a post Prevost had established at Beaufort when he had retired along the sea islands. Hundreds of rebel militiamen, their brief terms served, wandered home.

But the destruction of the British base at Savannah remained the supreme American military objective in the South. During the spring, Lincoln, Governor Rutledge, and other South Carolina leaders had appealed to Admiral d'Estaing, of unhappy Newport memory, then operating in the West Indies, to join in a Franco-American effort to dislodge the enemy from Georgia. Suddenly, the third of September, came word that the admiral was off Savannah with four thousand men, but would stay only two weeks, for the hurricane season was at hand.

Lincoln, again on his feet, gathered up every available soldier, and calling on South Carolina and Georgia militia, set out through the pines to Georgia. He joined Estaing on the sixteenth of September at the French camp among the moss-hung oaks three miles below Savannah and was astonished to hear that Estaing that morning had summoned Prevost to surrender to the arms of France, without waiting for the Americans or acknowledging their participation in the enterprise. If the glory-hungry Frenchman had instead stormed the city, before its unfinished works and batteries could be completed or its defenders reinforced, he probably could have taken it. But Prevost took advantage of his blustering and stalled until the British garrison from Beaufort could slide in, making him so strong "and so very saucy," said an English officer, "as to refuse to let *Monsieur* and *Jonathan* in."

Negotiations broke off. Sluicing rains drenched the allies as they lay in their soggy camps near Savannah or tried to move supplies and ships' guns up from Estaing's landing place fourteen miles below. At last they broke ground for a siege on the twenty-third. Not until the night of October the fourth did the allied batteries open on the town, and by then Prevost was ready. Day and night their shells, carcasses, and solid shot rained, until, said a citizen in Savannah, hardly one of the four hundred and fifty dwellings in the town "had not been shot through." Yet, after three days and nights, an American militiaman wrote his wife, "The enemy still continue very obstinate."

Siege operations were too tedious for Estaing, who feared for his ships with heavy weather approaching, and who had fallen to bickering with Lincoln about everything including the fare at the New Englander's table. Rather than abandon the siege, he decided, over Lincoln's angry protest, upon an assault on the British works.

At dawn on the ninth of October, French and American columns flung themselves against Prevost's defenses. In an hour the defenders' ditch "was filled with [allied] dead," and said an Englishman, "many hung dead and wounded on the abatis," and outside the lines "the plain was strewed with mangled bodies." In this war, only at Bunker Hill had a single side sustained such casualties as did the allies that foggy morning before staggering back to their camps. In all they lost some eight hundred killed and wounded to an enemy loss of fifty-seven casualties.

Lincoln argued for continuing the siege, but Estaing had had enough. "No argument," moaned Lincoln, "could dissuade" the count. At sea his crews were dying with fever and scurvy, his ships lay in danger, and ashore his troops had been mauled. On the eighteenth the siege was raised, and the next day the Americans crossed the Savannah, twenty-four hours before the French began to retire. Estaing scattered his fleet, some vessels to France, some to the Indies, some to the Chesapeake for repairs. And the rebels settled down for an uneasy winter at Sheldon, facing the enemy.

The failure of the allies to oust the British from Georgia was nothing short of calamitous for the rebellion. A victory at Savannah would have deprived Clinton of a base from which to invade the rest of the South, and the whole plan of the King for reducing the colonies one by one, working northward, would have gone awry. With the war stalemated in the North, British loss of a foothold in the South would have shortened the war immeasurably. But with the successful defense of the town, the British opened a whole new phase of the conflict, and the South was doomed to "scenes of barbarous warfare of which the details would shock an Arab."

In middle November, as soon as Clinton's suspense about the fate of Georgia was ended and he felt sufficiently secure in New York, he prepared to pursue his campaign against Carolina. The departure of Estaing opened the sea lanes for him, and on the twenty-sixth of December he sailed with a force of seventy-six hundred men for the capture of Charleston. Off the fearful North Carolina capes, wild winter storms scattered ninety transports and fourteen escort vessels, sank a ship loaded with cannon, and necessitated the destruction of the cavalry horses; but on February 11 the fleet dropped anchor off John's Island, thirty miles below Clinton's goal. Then inexplicably the British commander frittered away eight weeks, while, with less than four thousand men, half of them militia, General Lincoln prepared to defend the South Carolina capital.

The South Carolinians, in spite of forewarning, had been more than a little remiss in preparations for defense, but upon the appearance of acres of white enemy tents on the sandy islands to the seaward, the governor impressed six hundred slaves to expedite construction of lines of defense and redoubts from river to river across Charleston Neck and on the waterfronts. In the eyes of Hessian Captain Johann Hinrichs, the American works "like mushrooms . . . sprang from the soil." Soon Clinton himself observed that they were, with their eighty cannon and mortars, "by no means contemptible," and called up fifteen hundred more troops from Savannah and twenty-five hundred from New York. These would bring his total strength to ten thousand, exclusive of five thousand seamen he might muster from the fleet.

On the twenty-ninth and thirtieth of March, the British columns crossed the Ashley and marched through drizzling rain toward Charleston. They were unopposed until about two miles from the American lines; then their advance guard was met by a force of two hundred led by Colonel John Laurens, who had returned from the North to serve in the crisis of his native state. General Lachlan McIntosh, in the city, observed:

> Our officers and men, stimulated in view of both armies and many ladies, vied with each other in acts of firmness and gallantry, particularly regaining an old breastwork the enemy took possession of in the evening, after our people were retreating regularly to the garrison. A mere point of honor without advantage and afterwards left it about dark, retreating . . . into the garrison.[3]

The next night, the thirty-first, Clinton opened his siege lines. Although rebel cannon played constantly on their work parties, General McIntosh admitted, "it does not seem to retard their works." Instead, General Moultrie remarked that it provided a display for some of the citizens: "The women walk out from town to the lines with all the composure imaginable to see us cannonade the enemy, but I fancy when the enemy begin, they will make themselves pretty scarce."

Inside the city Lincoln had been strengthened by the arrival of 700 North Carolina Continentals, and on the seventh of April, two days after the enemy opened fire, 750 Virginians and some North Carolina militia arrived, to the heady delight of the defenders.

But the next day, wrote a member of the Governor's council:

> At half past three o'clock, the British fleet got under weigh. The admiral in the *Roebuck* was the headmost ship and the *Renown* brought up the rear. The *Romulus* with four frigates and two smaller vessels in a line in the center. Each of the ships gave the fort [on Sullivan's Island] a broadside, and one of the frigates had her foretopmast carried away by a shot from the fort, which saluted them in very quick succession, so that in a few minutes both fort and passing ships were enveloped in smoke. No other visible damage done to the enemy, and in about three-quarters of an hour from their weighing they cast anchor again under Fort Johnson, thence extending towards Hog Island. . . .[4]

It was no repetition of June 28, 1775. With "scorn and disdain," said Captain Hinrichs, "the proud Briton" sailed past the harbor defenses and sealed Charleston's fate.

On the tenth, reinforced by the troops from Savannah, Clinton summoned Lincoln to surrender. "General Lincoln," reported an American officer, "immediately and without consulting anyone sent . . . answer that his duty and inclination led him to hold out to the last extremity." To be sure, however, that civil government could carry on in South Carolina if the city were forced to capitulate, he persuaded Governor Rutledge and three of his council to slip through the lines and escape the beleaguered city.

Thus far, Lincoln had preserved an escape route from the city across the Cooper. To maintain this line of retreat and communication, he had stationed General Isaac Huger with about five hundred mounted troops at Monck's Corner near the head of the river, thirty miles north. Against them rose a British dragoon officer named Banastre Tarleton, appearing on the canvas of the war for the first time. He was a short, thick-bodied, muscular youth, high-living and running a little to grossness about the eyes and mouth, but fit and tireless. His Tory legion was his life and his pride, and he led it with a studied kind of daring, moving fast and striking fiercely. He wasted no time on the amenities of civilized warfare: to destroy and kill was his job and he did it well. All his horses had perished on the voyage south, and he had been forced to remount with swamp tackies impressed on the Georgia and South Carolina coasts, and he vowed to put his men on good horseflesh and to make his mark on the Southern rebels.

After cutting up a small body of militia in February, Tarleton had run into the cavalry of Colonel William Washington, of Huger's command, operating on the Ashley, and had been repulsed. A few weeks later he had tried to catch the plump, round-faced cavalryman asleep at a bivouac but had failed. Then he conceived an attack on Huger's whole force at its post at Biggin's Bridge near Monck's Corner. In his own narrative of the campaign in the South, he recalled:

At three o'clock in the morning, the advanced guard of dragoons and mounted infantry, supported by the remainder of the Legion and [Mayor Patrick] Ferguson's corps [of American loyalists] approached the American post. A watch word was immediately communicated to the officers and soldiers which was closely followed by an order to charge the enemy's grand guard on the main road, there being no other avenue open, owing to the swamps upon the flanks, and to pursue them into their camp.

The order was executed with the greatest . . . success. The Americans were completely surprised. Major [Paul] Vernier of Pulaski's Legion and some other officers and men who attempted to defend themselves were killed or wounded. General Huger, Colonels Washington and [John] Jameson with many officers and men fled on foot to the swamps close to their encampment, where being concealed by the darkness, they effected their escape. Four hundred horses belonging to officers and dragoons with their arms and appointments (a valuable acquisition for the British cavalry in their present state) fell into the hands of the Victors. About one hundred officers, dragoons, and hussars, together with fifty wagons loaded with arms, clothing, and ammunition shared the same fate. Without loss of time, Major [Charles] Cochrane was ordered to force the bridge and the meetinghouse with the infantry of the British legion. He charged the militia with fixed bayonets, got possession of the pass, and dispersed everything that opposed him. . . .

The British had one officer and two men wounded. . . .[5]

Happily, the Tory press announced: "Colonel Tarleton took so great a number of exceeding fine horses as enabled him to produce four hundred as well mounted and well appointed cavalry as would do him credit *en revue* at Wimbleton."

Tarleton's success slammed shut Lincoln's back door. By eliminating Huger's mobile corps which had commanded the Cooper, Tarleton "gave the command of the country" to the east to Colonel James Webster, who took post with some fourteen hundred men "near the head of the Wando River, forbidding by land all further access to the town from the Cooper. . . ." When, on the eighteenth, the "considerable" British reinforcement of two thousand under Francis, Lord Rawdon, arrived from New York, Clinton was able to strengthen the corps beyond the Cooper so substantially that little possibility remained of American retreat in that direction.

Steadily and unrelentingly the enemy zigzags wormed toward the American abatis. On the nineteenth Clinton's lines were within two hundred and fifty yards of Lincoln's. Lincoln had allowed himself to be trapped, provisions were growing scarcer, and he could not resist indefinitely the enemy bombardment. Though now only a miracle could effect an evacuation, he held two stormy councils to debate whether he should capitulate or attempt to get the troops out. Civil officials sitting in the first council protested against surrender; they warned that the citizens had observed "the boats collected together to carry off the Continental troops" and that if the attempt should be made, they would open the gates to the enemy and assist them in attacking the army before it could escape. The council resolved to hold out. But next day it was decided to propose a capitulation on terms which would allow Lincoln to withdraw his forces, their arms and baggage east of the Cooper, and take off the American vessels which had run up the river before the enemy fleet. If these terms were unacceptable to Clinton, a retreat would be attempted. On the twenty-first, Clinton curtly refused them and bombarded the town that night "with greater virulence and fury than ever . . . until daylight."

The death spasms of Charleston and its garrison became acute. On the lines, Moultrie noticed, "fatigue . . . was so great that, for want of sleep, many faces were so swelled they could scarcely see out of their eyes." In the dark of the morning of the twenty-fourth a desperate sortie of two hundred men with fixed bayonets— "as monkeys mimic men, we have a sortie," the British ridiculed—struck at a fresh enemy advanced work and killed and took a few with an almost equal loss. On the twenty-fifth, British forces took possession of Mount Pleasant and Haddrell's Point. On the night of the twenty-seventh, the last light post Lincoln maintained east of the Cooper was evacuated. "It was not until this moment," noted Captain William DeBrahm, the engineer, "that Charleston was completely invested, the English having possession [now] of James Island, Wappoo, Charleston Neck, Hobcaw Point, and his fleet anchored in the roadstead before the town." On the last day of April Benjamin Smith wrote his wife:

This will give a rude Shock to the Independence of America, and a Lincolnade will become as common a term as Burgoynade. . . . Nothing prevents Lincoln's surrender but a point of honor of holding out to the last extremity. This is nearly at hand, as our provisions will soon fail, and my plan is to WALK off as soon as I can obtain permission. . . . A mortifying scene must first be encountered. The thirteen stripes will be leveled in the dust and I owe my life to the clemency of a conqueror.[6]

Three days later the enemy's third parallel was nearly complete. By draining the canal Lincoln had dug across the Neck outside his lines, British fatigue parties had a ready-made ditch for their new works. On the seventh of May, the commander of Fort Moultrie, after sending out an insouciant reply to a surrender demand—"Tol, lol, derol, lol, Fort Moultrie will be defended to the last extremity," he said—had to haul down his flag.

By then Lincoln had opened negotiations with Clinton, which came to a deadlock on the ninth. That morning after

Clinton had returned Lincoln's proposals for capitulation as inadmissible, both lines were silent for about an hour, each waiting for the other to resume fire. Said Moultrie:

> At length, we fired the first gun and immediately followed a tremendous cannonade, and the mortars from both sides threw out an immense number of shells. It was a glorious sight to see them like meteors crossing each other and bursting in the air. It appeared as if the stars were tumbling down. The fire was incessant almost the whole night, cannon balls whizzing and shells hissing continually amongst us, ammunition chests and temporary magazines blowing up, great guns bursting, and wounded men groaning along the lines. It was a dreadful night! It was our last great effort, but it availed us nothing. After this, our military ardor was much abated. We began to cool, and we cooled gradually, and on the eleventh of May, we capitulated.[7]

On the twelfth, one onlooker saw "tears coursing down the cheeks of General Moultrie," while a Britisher relished the scene:

> The LINCOLNADE was acted. . . . General [Alexander] Leslie with the Royal English Fusiliers and Hessian Grenadiers and some Artillery took possession of the town and planted the British colors by the gate, on the ramparts, and Lincoln limped out at the head of the most ragged rabble I ever beheld. It, however, pleased me much better than the Meschianza.
> They were indulged with beating a drum and to bring out their colors cased. They laid down their arms between their abatis and surrendered prisoners of war. . . . The militia, poor creatures, could not be prevailed upon to come out. They began to creep out of their holes the next day. . . . By the capitulation they are allowed to go home and plow the ground. There *only* they can be useful.[8]

General Moultrie described his standing by as the Continentals piled arms:

> The British then asked where our second division was. They were told these were all the Continentals we had, except the sick and wounded. They were astonished and said we had made a gallant defense. Captain [George] Rochfort had marched in with a detachment of the artillery to receive the returns of our artillery stores. While we were in the hornwork together, . . . he said, "Sir, you have made a gallant defense, but you had a great many rascals among you" (and mentioned names) "who came out every night and gave us information of what was passing in your garrison."[9]

Some five thousand Americans, Continentals, militia, and armed citizens were lost to the cause of independence when they surrendered to Clinton, and heaps of materiel, sorely needed elsewhere, went into the British stores. The cost to Clinton was about 76 killed and 189 wounded. American casualties were 89 killed and 138 wounded. It was the greatest American surrender of the war, and it was, to say the least, "a rude Shock." John Mathews, South Carolina Delegate at Congress, could not believe as late as June 9 that the news of the fall of Charleston was authentic. To fellow Delegate Thomas Bee, he wrote from Morristown:

> If [it] has fallen or does fall, I fear the whole country goes with it, for having nothing but a few discontented, fluctuating militia to depend on, we shall never be in any condition to check the ravages of a merciless enemy, and I imagine our people have not fortitude enough to see their property destroyed when their submissions can be the means of saving it. . . . For my own part, I shall look on myself (whenever this event happens) as not worth a groat, unless we can retake the county or have it restored by treaty, then the land must remain but nothing else.
>
> As to becoming a British subject again if a restoration of my estate is to depend on these terms, why let them keep it, and the Devil help them with it.[10]

Upon spirits like John Mathews would depend resistance to the crushing might of Britain, at last launched inexorably on her course of conquest from the South. Clinton had made an auspicious beginning. Would there be enough John Mathewses to defeat him?

33

"STRAYED, DESERTED, OR STOLEN"

Camden

AUGUST 16, 1780

SIX DAYS after the "13 Stripes with several White Pendants" fluttered down from the rebel works at Charleston, Sir Henry Clinton dispatched three columns into the interior of South Carolina to guarantee its subjugation. One marched toward

Ninety-Six on the western frontier, another toward Augusta, and the main column, under command of Clinton's forty-two-year-old second, career soldier Charles, Lord Cornwallis, was to destroy a rebel force rumored gathering at Camden and, incidentally, another in the neighborhood of Georgetown on the coast.

On the eighteenth of May, with twenty-five hundred men, horse and foot, and five fieldpieces, Cornwallis moved from his ground at Huger's Bridge on the east branch of the Cooper River northward toward the Santee. While his army waited until boats could be rounded up for crossing the broad river at Lenud's Ferry, Tarleton sped to Georgetown with his legion, swept the little town clean of rebels, collected signatures to an oath of allegiance, and returned.

At Nelson's Ferry, farther up the Santee, Cornwallis discovered that the force he was seeking around Camden was retreating northward ten days ahead of him, and consisted of about three hundred and fifty Virginians under Colonel Abraham Buford, moving with a long train of supplies toward Salisbury, North Carolina. With a force of North Carolina militia, the Virginians had advanced for the relief of Charleston as far as Lenud's Ferry; there, hearing of the fall of the city, the combined corps divided. The North Carolinians had retreated toward the Cape Fear River, but the Virginians had been slowed by their wagons. They now were entirely out of reach of Cornwallis' whole force, so he ordered Tarleton to hurry after them.

In fifty-four hours, Tarleton covered a hundred and five miles, and on the twenty-ninth was within striking distance of his quarry. To delay Buford's march until he could be overtaken, Tarleton sent a summons to surrender, exaggerating his force from two hundred and seventy to seven hundred men. Buford refused the demand. About three in the afternoon of May 29, in the beautiful green land known as the Waxhaws, near the North Carolina line, Tarleton came up to the Virginians as they were passing through an open wood. Buford's first warning that Tarleton was upon him was the cry of the British bugle sounding the attack on his rear guard. Lieutenant Pearson commanded there. Dr. Robert Brownfield, a surgeon with Buford, later recalled:

Not a man escaped. Poor Pearson was inhumanely mangled on the face, as he lay on his back. His nose and lip were bisected . . . several of his teeth were broken out in the upper jaw and the under, completely divided on each side. These wounds were inflicted after he had fallen, with several others on his head, shoulders and arms. . . .

This attack gave Buford the first confirmation of Tarleton's declaration by his flag. Unfortunately, he was then compelled to prepare for action on ground which presented no impediment to the full action of cavalry. Tarleton having arranged his infantry in the center and his cavalry on the wings, advanced to the charge with the horrid yells of infuriated demons. They were received with firmness and completely checked, until the cavalry were gaining the rear. Buford, now perceiving that further resistance was hopeless, ordered a flag to be hoisted and the arms to be grounded, expecting the usual treatment sanctioned by civilized warfare.

This, however, made no part of Tarleton's creed. His ostensible pretext for the relentless barbarity that ensued was that his horse was killed under him, just as the flag was raised. He affected to believe that this was done afterwards and imputed it to treachery on the part of Buford. . . .

Ensign Cruit, who advanced with the flag, was instantly cut down. Viewing this as an earnest of what they were to expect, a resumption of their arms was attempted, to sell their lives as dearly as possible. But before this was fully effected, Tarleton . . . was in the midst of them. . . .

The demand for quarter, seldom refused to a vanquished foe, was at once found to be in vain. Not a man was spared, and it was the concurrent testimony of all the survivors that for fifteen minutes after every man was prostrate, they went over the ground, plunging their bayonets into everyone that exhibited any signs of life, and in some instances, where several had fallen one over the other, these monsters were seen to throw off on the point of the bayonet the uppermost, to come at those beneath.[1]

One hundred and thirteen Americans were killed on the field. One hundred and fifty were maimed so badly that Tarleton was obliged to parole them where they lay. In the summer twilight they were loaded into wagons and carried to the church of the Waxhaws, where the good Irishwomen of the neighborhood dressed their wounds and comforted the dying. Only fifty-three of Buford's men survived Tarleton's bayonets and swords to be taken prisoner. Tarleton's loss was five killed, fourteen wounded.

Two days later Tarleton gave the rebels near Camden another taste of "Tarleton's Quarters," when one of his lieutenants cut down a peaceful Quaker boy in his own front yard. That day, as Cornwallis' army approached, two other boys were accused of firing on the enemy column. One was strung up, the other taken into the army for punishment. By the time Lord Cornwallis reached the small, bustling town of flour, grist, and saw mills in the long-leaf pine, its inhabitants were completely cowed.

Elsewhere in the state resistance died as quickly. To encourage the rebels to return to the Royal fold, Clinton issued proclamations offering them pardons under the law and the promise of eventual self-government, with exemption from taxation except by their own assemblies. Thousands of discouraged rebels, many of them convinced that the Continental Congress meant to abandon the two Southern states to their fate, flocked in to give paroles to remain peaceably at home, and Clinton soon had reason to think it "very possible we may have conquered the two Carolinas in Charleston." In his optimism, he went so far as to declare that if a French or Spanish fleet did not interfere, "I think a few works if properly reinforced will give us all between this and Hudson's River. . . ."

However, the day before sailing away and leaving Lord Cornwallis as military administrator in South Carolina, Clinton, by a stroke of his everbusy quill, sought to amend his previous proclamation, so that the Crown forces might use one part of the population to hold down the others. He voided the paroles he had granted and declared outlaw anyone who did not take "an active part in settling and securing His Majesty's government." This abrupt shift of policy, said he, was "most prudent" because it obliged every man to "evince his principles" and gave the loyalists an opportunity of "chasing from among them . . . dangerous neighbors."

By the twenty-fifth of June, with "everything wearing the face of tranquility and submission," Cornwallis was back in Charleston, proudly pointing to his month's work; in sum, said he, he had "put an end to all resistance in South Carolina." Now he felt that he safely could turn his thoughts toward invasion of North Carolina as soon as the broiling heat of summer softened. Then would come Virginia and the realization of His Majesty's plan for conquest of the entire South.

All this must have sounded very good to Clinton, now back in New York, worrying about Washington and a French fleet said to have sailed from Brest. But Cornwallis had not reckoned with the reaction of hundreds of rebels to Sir Henry's final proclamation. By it they considered their paroles violated and themselves free to resist once again. In the tangled forests and swamps of North and South Carolina they were organizing guerrilla bands under leaders of experience like Thomas Sumter, William Hill, William Bratton, William Davie, Francis Marion, and other officers who for one reason or other were out of service but not ready to cry defeat. Although Cornwallis had sent emissaries among the King's friends in North Carolina, urging them to harvest their crops and "remain quiet" until he personally should come to rally them, some four hundred of them engaged with an equal number of Whigs at Ramsour's Mill, north-west of Charlotte, on the twentieth of June, with heavy slaughter on both sides. On the twelfth of July at William-son's plantation, near the headwaters of Fishing Creek, one of Sumter's lieutenants wiped out a scouting party of Tarle-ton's Legion, over a hundred strong. On the first of August, Sumter, whom Cornwallis called "an active and daring man," attacked the British post at Rocky Mount, and a few days later, struck at Hanging Rock. Other partisan forces ranging in strength from fifty to as many as several hundred men fought British detachments at McDowell's Camp, Thicketty Fort, Flat Rock, and elsewhere. When the British post at Cheraw Hill proved to be dangerously unhealthy and was abandoned, the Tory militia which Major Archibald Mc-Arthur had raised there turned coat, seized their officers, and spirited about a hundred sick into North Carolina. By the sixth of August, Cornwallis was admitting that the situation had undergone a rapid change. "The whole country between Peedee and Santee" had flared into "an absolute state of re-bellion."

The fiery resurgence of hatred in the state, Cornwallis re-ported to Lord George Germain, was inspired by "reports industriously propagated in this province of a large army coming from the northward." The reports were not idle rum-ors. A Continental force was on the march for South Caro-lina, and at its head rode General Horatio Gates, appointed by the Congress, after a winter at home in Virginia, to suc-ceed the unfortunate Benjamin Lincoln.

Gates had received the word of his appointment at his home in Berkeley County, Virginia. Perhaps when he wrote Lincoln, he had in mind the words of his old friend and neighbor, Charles Lee, "Take care lest your Northern laurels turn to Southern willows." To the vanquished Lincoln, Gates wrote sympathetically:

The series of misfortunes you have experienced, since you were doomed to the command of the Southern Depart-ment, has affected me exceedingly. I feel for you most sensi-bly. I feel for myself, who am to succeed to what? To the command of an army without strength—a military chest with-out money, a department apparently deficient in public spirit and a climate that increases despondency instead of animating the soldier's arm. . . .

You will oblige me very much by communicating any hints or information which you think will be useful to me . . . You know that I am not above advice, especially where it comes from a good head and a sincere heart.[2]

Gates was not exaggerating his discouraging prospects. By the time he had reached Hillsboro, North Carolina, he was genuinely alarmed by the "multiplied and increasing wants" of his new Department and by the strength and condition of his "army" as it was described by a courier from southward. It consisted of only the Maryland Division, Delaware Regiment, and some 120 dragoons under the French adventurer, Colonel Charles Armand; in April it had set out from Morristown to "give succor to the Southern states," and Washington had admitted gloomily to its commander, gigantic Johann Kalb (who passed himself off as the Baron de Kalb), "Heaven alone can tell" where he would find "provisions, transportation, etc." Gates learned Heaven had provided very niggardly. Without wagons, carrying their baggage on their backs, the soldiers foraged as they went, "often fasting for several days together and subsisting frequently upon green apples and peaches." When Gates arrived at the army's hungry encampment at Hollinsworths' Farm on Deep River, the twenty-fifth of July, the baron joyfully greeted him with a salute from his eight artillery pieces and turned over command with undisguised relief.

To the amazement of the starting troops, Gates ordered them to hold themselves in readiness to march at once. With a flourish he assured them "plenty will soon succeed the late unavoidable scarcity . . . provisions, rum, salt, and every requisite will flow into camp . . . with a liberal hand be distributed." De Kalb had handed him, among other headquarters papers, a letter from General Thomas Sumter, the South Carolina colonel who had now turned partisan general. Sumter, who had been attacking Tory camps and British detached units with as many as five hundred followers, estimated for De Kalb how many of their 3,482 men the British had placed in each of the twelve posts they had established. He believed that they could not be concentrated in less than two weeks, and suggested how a force of a thousand or fifteen hundred men straddling the Santee River could cut off the retreat of many of them. Probably on the strength of this letter, which set at seven hundred the total enemy strength in "Camden and vicinity," and encouraged by dreams of manna for his men and "shoals of militia" gathering in North Carolina, Gates resolved to attack Camden.

At half past three in the morning of the twenty-seventh, the army struck tents, loaded baggage, cooked breakfast, and began a march by the right down the road to Spink's Farm.

Two roads led from Deep River to Camden. One arched westward through Rowan and Mecklenburg counties, where the Scotch-Irish were predominantly Whig and provisions were relatively plentiful. The other road was shorter by fifty miles, but it ran southwestward through a wilderness of pine barrens, cut by hundreds of little watercourses, a desolate and infertile region, a hostile Tory country. In spite of its obvious disadvantages, Gates proposed to follow the shorter road. De Kalb appealed to rational, persuasive Colonel Otho Williams, Inspector of the Maryland Division, to protest the route chosen for the march; and an unofficial council of officers agreed with him. But Gates ignored their suggestion.

Before the sun rose on the twenty-seventh, the army marched on the road Gates had chosen. Otho Williams, appointed deputy adjutant general on the march to succeed an ill officer, noted:

The distresses of the soldiery daily increased. They were told that the banks of the Pee Dee River were extremely fertile, and so indeed they were; but the preceding crop of corn (the principal article of produce) was exhausted and the new grain, although luxuriant and fine, was unfit for use. Many of the soldiery, urged by necessity, plucked the green ears and boiled them with the lean beef which was collected in the woods, made for themselves a repast, not unpalatable to be sure, but which was attended with painful effects. Green peaches also were substituted for bread and had similar consequences. Some of the officers, aware of the risk of eating such vegetables and in such a state, with poor fresh beef and without salt, restrained themselves from taking anything but the beef itself, boiled or roasted. It occurred to some that the hair powder, which remained in their bags, would thicken soup, and it was actually applied.[3]

On the seventh of August, Gates formed a junction with General Richard Caswell, and to his "grand army" added a left wing of twenty-one hundred North Carolina militia. Colonel Williams was amazed by the tables and chairs and bedsteads and other domestic furnishings which they "scattered before the tent doors in great disorder." That night, as the army lay fifteen or twenty miles from the enemy, he and another officer made a security check of the encampment, and he came away with a further impression of the casual way in which the militia was taking the war. Guards and sentinels in the right wing hailed the visiting rounds, but in the left the officers rode through the sleeping encampment without being challenged once, and, said Williams, "even approached the marquees of some of the general and field officers, one of whom complained of being disturbed and intimated that it was an unseasonable hour for *gentlemen to call*."

At Rugley's Mill, sometimes called Clermont Plantation, on the fourteenth, Gates was joined by seven hundred Virginia militia, and he detached one hundred Marylands, three hundred North Carolina militia, and one of his three companies of artillery to reinforce General Thomas Sumter, who wished to take a British wagon train reported on the 140-mile road between Charleston and Camden.

While Gates was weakening his force, the British were reinforcing theirs. Disturbed by rumors of the approach of an American force estimated to be twice Gates's actual number, Cornwallis had hastened to assume personal command at Camden, ordering in four companies more of light infantry from the post at Ninety-Six. In all, he drew 2,239 men into the Camden garrison. After surveying the situation, and "seeing little to lose by a defeat and much to gain by a victory," he resolved "to take the first good opportunity to attack the rebel army." At ten o'clock the night of the fifteenth of August, he marched his forces out of town toward Gates's position to fall on the rebels at dawn.

In his own camp, by an odd coincidence, Gates also had made up his mind to approach his enemy by a night march that night to a point on Sanders Creek, about seven miles from Camden. He arranged disposition of his baggage and set out in General After Orders the order of march. In presenting the orders to Colonel Williams, Gates showed the deputy adjutant general a rough estimate of his forces, upward of seven thousand men. Williams could not believe it and took it upon himself to call for a field return. When he showed Gates that his strength actually was 3,052 present and fit for duty, Gates murmured, "These are enough for our purpose." According to Colonel Williams:

Although there had been no dissenting voice in the council, [which Gates had called to communicate his orders] the orders were no sooner promulgated than they became the subject of animadversion. Even those who had been dumb in council said that there had been no consultation, that the orders were read to them and all opinion seemed suppressed by the very positive and decisive terms in which they were expressed.

Others could not imagine how it could be conceived that an army, consisting of more than two-thirds militia, and which had never been once exercised in arms together, could

form columns and perform other maneuvers in the night and
in the face of the enemy. . . .

A great deal was said . . . but the time was short, and the
officers and soldiers, generally, not knowing or believing any
more than the general that any considerable body of the
enemy was to be met with out of Camden, acquiesced with
their usual cheerfulness and were ready to march at the
hour appointed.[4]

The march that began promptly at ten o'clock on a moon-
less, sultry night was far from orderly. The customary extra
allowance of "spirits" issued the men at the outset of a forced
march or before an action was not in camp. It was "unluckily conceived," Colonel Williams afterwards wrote, "that
molasses would, for once, be an acceptable substitute." Said
he:

Accordingly, the hospital stores were broached, and one
gill of molasses per man and a full ration of cornmeal and
meat were issued to the army previous to their march. . . .
The troops . . . had frequently felt the bad consequences of
eating bad provisions; but at this time, a hasty meal of quick
baked bread and fresh beef, with a desert of molasses, mixed
with mush or dumplings, operated so cathartically as to disorder very many of the men, who were breaking the ranks
all night and were certainly much debilitated. . . .[5]

After tramping some four hours along the deep sand road
through the pines, Gates's miserable men came upon a thinly
set open growth between two branches of Gum Swamp, a trib-
utary of Sanders Creek. Suddenly, after two in the morning,
Armand's horse in front and Charles Porterfield's Virginians
flanking in the woods on the right slammed into Cornwallis'
mounted advance. A few minutes of stabbing pistol and musket fire and blood-chilling huzzaing by the unseen enemy, and
the forces stumbled apart. Neither wanted to engage in the
dark. From prisoners taken on both sides, each learned the
composition of the enemy force six hundred yards away. Colonel Williams questioned a redcoat and discovered that three
thousand British regulars under Cornwallis himself crouched
out there in the night. The colonel brought Gates his findings:

The general's astonishment could not be concealed. He
ordered the deputy adjutant general to call another council
of war. All the general officers immediately assembled in the
rear of the line. The unwelcome news was communicated to
them. General Gates said, "Gentlemen, what is best to be
done?"

All were mute for a few moments, when the gallant [Gen-
eral Edward] Stevens [of the Virginia militia] exclaimed,

"Gentlemen, is it not too late *now* to do anything but fight?"

No other advise was offered, and the general desired the gentlemen would repair to their respective commands.[6]

The armies had met where the open pine forest was flanked on either side by swamps. Somewhat narrower where the British were, it widened behind the Americans. If the Americans were driven back, their wings would be out of touch with the swamps and open to flank attacks, but their ground was higher than that of the enemy and the way of retreat was clear. Behind the British ran the creek waiting to trap them in defeat.

All night skirmishers fired just enough to keep the armies awake. Gates and his staff had assumed a position about six hundred yards back of the line, except for Otho Williams, who was on the line and recounted:

At dawn . . . the 16th . . . the enemy appeared in front advancing in column. Captain [Anthony] Singleton, who commanded some pieces of artillery, observed to Colonel Williams that he plainly perceived the ground of the British uniform at about two hundred yards in front. The deputy adjutant general immediately ordered Captain Singleton to open his battery, and then rode to the general, who was in the rear of the second line, and informed him of the cause of the firing which he heard. He also observed to the general that the enemy seemed to be displaying their column by the right. The nature of the ground favored this conjecture, for yet nothing was clear.

The general seemed disposed to wait events. He gave no orders. The deputy adjutant general observed that if the enemy, in the act of displaying, were briskly attacked by General Stevens' Brigade which was already in line of battle, the effect might be fortunate, and first impressions were important.

"Sir," said the general, "that's right. Let it be done."

This was the last order that the deputy adjutant general received. He hastened to General Stevens, who instantly advanced with his Brigade, apparently in fine spirits.

The right wing of the enemy was soon discovered *in line*. It was too late to attack them displaying. Nevertheless, the business of the day could no longer be deferred.

The deputy adjutant general requested General Stevens to let him have forty of fifty privates, volunteers, who would run forward of the brigade and commence the attack. They were led forward within forty or fifty yards of the enemy and ordered to take trees and keep up as brisk a fire as possible. The desired effect of this expedient, to extort the enemy's fire at some distance, in order to [make] the rendering it less terrible to the militia, was not gained. General Stevens, observing the enemy to rush on, put his men in mind of their bayonets; but the impetuosity with which they advanced, *firing* and *huzzaing*, threw the whole body of the militia into such a panic that they generally threw down their *loaded* arms and fled in the utmost consternation.

The unworthy example of the Virginians was almost instantly followed by the North Carolinians; only a small part of the brigade commanded by Brigadier General Gregory made a short pause. A part of [Lieutenant Colonel Henry] Dixon's regiment of that brigade, next in line to the Second Maryland Brigade, fired two or three rounds. . . .[7]

The militia, to Gates's astonished horror, "ran like a Torrent and bore all before them." Major Charles Magill, Gates's extra aide-de-camp, was at his side when the general rode about twenty yards to the rear of the line to rally them. It was impossible, Magill wrote his father. They carried their exhorting commander with them:

About half a mile further, General Gates and Caswell made another fruitless attempt, and a third was made at a still greater distance with no better success. General Smallwood on Stevens' advancing to the attack advanced to support him, and on the militia giving way, occupied the ground where the right of Stevens and the left of the North Carolina militia were drawn up. This made a chasm between the two brigades through which the enemy's horse came and charged our rear.[8]

As Gates was carried from the field by his efforts to stem the flight of the militia, the battle raged. Wrote Williams:

Notwithstanding some irregularity, which was created by the militia breaking pell-mell through the second line, order was restored there—time enough to give the enemy a severe check which abated the fury of their assault and obliged them to assume a more deliberate manner of acting.

The Second Maryland Brigade, including the battalion of Delawares, on the right were engaged with the enemy's left, which they opposed with very great firmness . . . when their companions of the First Brigade (which formed the second line) being greatly outflanked and charged by superior numbers, were obliged to give ground. At this critical moment the regimental officers of the latter brigade, reluctant to leave the field without orders, inquired for their commanding officer, Brigadier General Smallwood, who . . . was not to be found; notwithstanding . . . a number of other brave officers . . . rallied the brigade and renewed the contest.

Again they were obliged to give way and were again rallied. The Second Brigade were still warmly engaged. . . .

At this eventful juncture, the deputy adjutant general, anxious that the communications between them should be preserved and wishing that in the almost certain event of a retreat, some order might be sustained by them, hastened from the First to the Second Brigade, which he found precisely in the same circumstances.

He called upon his own regiment (the 6th Maryland) not to fly and was answered by the Lieutenant Colonel [Benjamin] Ford, who said, "They have done all that can be expected of them. We are outnumbered and outflanked. See the enemy charge with bayonets."

The enemy . . . directing their whole force against these two devoted brigades, a tremendous fire . . . was, for some time, kept up on both sides with equal . . . obstinacy, until Lord Cornwallis, perceiving there was no cavalry opposed to him, pushed forward his dragoons—and his infantry charging at the same moment with fixed bayonets put an end to the contest. His victory was complete.[9]

As the American survivors ran from the field in wild disorder, they left several hundred dead and wounded on the ground. Among the dying was gallant old De Kalb, splashed with blood from eleven severe wounds; the enemy plundered him of his gold-braided uniform coat and "stripped him even of his shirt," a fate, Williams noted, "which probably was avoided by other generals only by an opportune retreat."

North of the battlefield men swarmed. "This torrent of unarmed militia," said Williams, "bore away with it General Gates, Caswell, and a number of others" who soon saw that all was lost:

General Gates at first conceived a hope that he might rally at Clermont a sufficient number to cover the retreat of the regulars, but the farther they fled the more they were dispersed, and the generals soon found themselves abandoned by all but their aides. . . .

The militia, the general saw, were in the air, and the regulars, he feared, were no more. The dreadful thunder of artillery and musketry had ceased, and none of his friends appeared. There was no existing corps with which the victorious detachment might unite and the Americans had no post in the rear. He, therefore, sent orders to Sumter to retire in the best manner he could and proceeded himself with General Caswell towards Charlotte, an open village on a plain, about sixty miles from the fatal scene. . . .

The Virginians, who knew nothing of the country . . . involuntarily reversed the route they came and fled, most of them, to Hillsboro. . . . The North Carolina militia fled dif-

ferent ways. . . . Most of them preferring the shortest way
home scattered through the wilderness . . . between Wateree
and Pee Dee rivers, and thence towards Roanoke.[10]

As swift as was the militia, swifter was their general, riding
with only his two aides and his chief engineer, Colonel John
Senf, who noted in his journal:

> He arrived that night at Charlotte but no view was left
> to assemble any forces there, and if it was possible, there
> was no ammunition, no arms, no provisions, and in the
> middle of a disaffected country. The general, therefore,
> thought proper, with the advice of his officers, to get by
> the assistance of the night through that part of the country
> to Hillsboro, where there had been left some detachments and
> artillery, and that most chiefly the militia had directed their
> course that way it was therefore more probable to reassem-
> ble some of the scattered militia in that quarter and draw
> all the detachments together till other measures could be
> taken. General Gates arrived at Hillsboro the nineteenth of
> August.[11]

In three days, astride a charger sired by a famed racer
named *Fearnought,* Gates covered the 180 miles from Camden to Hillsboro. As he passed through the Moravian settlement at Salem, those pious folks noted, "General Gates and
several officers breakfasted with us this morning, but seemed
in haste."

Though Gates flew to Hillsboro, he claimed, for military
expediency, many of his critics angrily cried, as did Alexander Hamilton, "Was there ever such an instance of a general
running away . . . from his whole army? And was there ever
so precipitous a flight? . . . It does admirable credit to the
activity of a man at his time of life."

Gates, suffering "a violent disorder" (a Tory newspaperman
called it "a diarrhoea"), sent a forthright report of his disaster to the Congress. The old champion of the militia evidently
now agreed with General Stevens, who wrote Gates after the
retreat:

> I rejoice to hear of your being safe; but most sincerely
> condole with you for our misfortunes, and more especially as
> they were brought on by ye damned rascally behavior of ye
> militia. My feelings never knew what it was to be hurt before,
> tho' to repine is unmanly and answers no good end; there-
> fore, am determined and am now ready to obey your com-
> mands with double ardor.[12]

Civilians were quick to censure Gates, but few soldiers did;
the harshest criticism leveled at him was not that he lost a

battle but that he fought at all. Not many generals would have placed reliance on militia in the circumstances.

Derision had slaughtered as many reputations as gunpowder; with it, James Rivington in his Tory paper, the New York *Royal Gazette*, helped fashion for the tormented Horatio Gates a crown of Southern willows. He published an advertisement said to have been "stuck up at the public places" in Philadelphia:

Millions!—Millions!—Millions!

REWARD,

STRAYED, DESERTED, OR STOLEN, from the Subscriber, on the 16th of August last, near Camden, in the State of South Carolina, a whole ARMY, consisting of Horse, Foot, and Dragoons, to the amount of near TEN THOUSAND (as has been said) with all their baggage, artillery, wagons, and camp equipage. The subscriber has very strong suspicions, from information received from his Aid de Camp, that a certain CHARLES, Earl CORNWALLIS, was principally concerned in carrying off the said ARMY with their baggage, &c. Any person or persons civil or military, who will give information, either to the Subscriber, or to Charles Thompson, Esq., Scretary to the Continental Congress, where the said ARMY is, so that they may be recovered and rallied again, shall be entitled to demand from the Treasurer of the United States, the sum of THREE MILLIONS OF PAPER DOLLARS as soon as they can be spared from the Public Funds, and ANOTHER MILLION, for apprehending the Person Principally concerned in taking the said ARMY off. Proper passes will be granted by the President of Congress to such persons as incline to go in search of said ARMY. And as further encouragement, no deduction will be made from the above reward on account of any of the Militia (who composed the said ARMY) not being able to be found or heard of, as no dependence can be placed on their services, and nothing but the most speedy flight can ever save their Commander. HORATIO GATES, M. G. *And late Commander in chief of the Southern Army August 30, 1780.*[13]

"FROM TREE TO TREE . . . TO THE SUMMIT"

King's Mountain

OCTOBER 7, 1780

SERGEANT MAJOR William Seymour of the Delawares wrote in his journal:

> We assembled at Salisbury, the few that were left . . . this being the first place we made any halt since the action of the sixteenth of August. From here we marched on the twenty-fourth under the command of General Smallwood . . . for Hillsboro, that being the next place of rendezvous, which we reached with much difficulty on the sixth September, two hundred miles from Camden.[1]

From Hillsboro, Gates, his pride badly wounded, wrote to his Commander-in-Chief. "The victory is far from bloodless on the part of the foe," he reassured Washington, and Cornwallis he thought would not likely "be able to reap any advantage of consequence from his victory." He went on to say:

> Anxious for the public good, I shall continue my unwearied endeavors to stop the progress of the enemy . . . to recommence an offensive war, and recover all our losses in the southern states. But if being unfortunate is solely reason sufficient for removing me from command, I shall most cheerfully submit to the orders of Congress and resign an office few generals would be anxious to possess and where the utmost skill and fortitude are subject to be baffled by the difficulties which must for a time surround the chief in command here.[2]

A few days later, still convinced that the only mistake he had made at Camden was being unfortunate, Gates pointed out to Washington the obvious fact that if he were to render any further "good service to the United States," he must appear to have the support of the Congress and his superior; "other wise," his own cunning led him to suspect "some men may think they please my superiors by blaming me and thus recommend themselves to favor." Perhaps he was thinking of William Smallwood, who challenged him openly for command. "But you, sir," he added, purring ingratiation, "will be too generous to lend an ear to such men, if such there be, and will show your greatness of soul rather by protecting, than slighting, the unfortunate."

Having charted the course for the Commander-in-Chief to follow, Gates devoted himself to reorganizing his broken army. There was little he could do. The militia was gone beyond recall. Remnants only of the Delawares and the Marylands remained, encamped about the pillared brick courthouse in Hillsboro. In mid-September, Colonel Buford arrived with "the mangled remains" of his regiment and some recruits, less than three hundred in all. Fifty militia came, and a body of Delawares retaken from their British captors by partisan Colonel Francis Marion. In all, Gates put together a force of some twelve hundred, all that were left of the three thousand he had confused for seven thousand before Camden.

Earl Cornwallis, meanwhile, was ambitious to be on with his dream of gobbling up Virginia and rolling through Maryland and Pennsylvania. Only the sickness of his army and the savagery of little rebel bands of irregulars in South Carolina held him up. Early in September, instead of going into North Carolina as he had hoped to do, he was forced to move to the Waxhaws, where in the higher, cooler country he thought "the change of air might be useful." "The great sickness of the Army, the intense heat, and the necessity of totally subduing the rebel country between the Santee and Pee Dee have detained me longer than I could have wished," he wrote Germain on September 19.

At length, a few days later, the earl got in motion for Hillsboro by way of Charlotte and Salisbury. His drive into North Carolina was planned as a three-column thrust: his right to move up the coast to secure Wilmington and the Cape Fear River as a supply route; his center, the main army under his personal command, to march directly for Hillsboro; and his left, composed of loyalists under Major Patrick Ferguson, who already was operating in the back country of South Carolina, to strike northward in the shadow of the western mountains and join the main force at Charlotte.

On the outskirts of Charlotte, American militia harassed the march of the main column and resolutely stood in its path. Cornwallis' commissary was astonished: "The whole of the British Army was actually kept at bay for some minutes by a few mounted Americans, not exceeding twenty," and the Whig *New Jersey Gazette* reported:

> Lord Cornwallis's aide in a letter . . . which was intercepted says, "Charlotte is an agreeable village, but in a d—d rebellious country."

Oh, had we a well-supported, well-disciplined, permanent force, what a delightful, back county dance we should have led His Lordship at Charlotte.[3]

Cornwallis' left wing found itself in equally hostile country, threatened by a swarm of wolfish rebel frontiersmen, but its commander did not intimidate easily. Patrick Ferguson was one of the best of British professional soldiers. He had entered the service at fifteen and had fought on the continent and in the West Indies and nearly four years in this war in America. Although he was slight of build, with a long, oval, gentle-looking face, and his disposition was even and affable, his fellow officers called him "Bull Dog." Reputedly he was one of the best marksmen in the army, and he had achieved a degree of notoriety as the inventor of a revolutionary breech-loading "rifle gun." An all-weather firearm, it combined the advantage of fast loading from a prone position with firing speed, range, and accuracy; it was not yet in general use because the military first thought it should be battle tested. To test it, Ferguson had been given permission to arm a special corps with the unique gun. The corps had distinguished itself at Brandywine, but General Howe took a jaundiced view of it because it had been formed without consulting him. So when Ferguson was wounded, Howe took advantage of his disability to reduce the organization and store the rifles. If produced in quantity, they might have given the British a superiority of fire power that alone would have defeated the forest-bred Americans, but Ferguson never was given an opportunity to prove it. He did write a kinsman how his rifles nearly cost the rebels their Commander-in-Chief the day of Brandywine, when his corps was concealed on the outskirts of a wood in front of Knyphausen's division:

> We had not lain long . . . when a rebel officer, remarkable by a hussar dress, passed towards our army within a hundred yards of my right flank, not perceiving us. He was followed by another dressed in dark green or blue, mounted on a bay horse, with a remarkably large cocked hat.
>
> I ordered three good shots to steal near . . . and fire at them, but the idea disgusted me. I recalled the order. The hussar in returning made a circuit, but the other passed again within a hundred yards of us, upon which I advanced from the woods towards him.

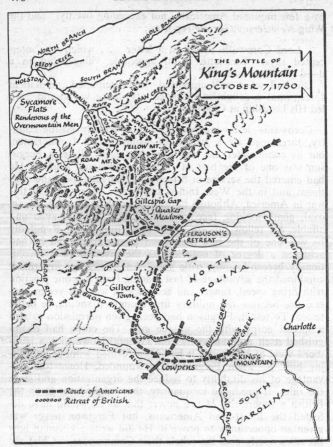

THE BATTLE OF
King's Mountain
OCTOBER 7, 1780

Sycamore
Flats
*Rendezvous of the
Overmountain Men*

NORTH BRANCH
REEDY CREEK
HOLSTON R.
SOUTH BRANCH
MIDDLE BRANCH
WATAUGA RIVER
ROAN CREEK
WATAUGA
YELLOW MT.
ROAN MT.
NOLICHUCKY RIVER
NOLICHUCKY RIVER
Gillespie Gap
Quaker
Meadows
FRENCH BROAD RIVER
CATAWBA RIVER
FERGUSON'S
RETREAT
SILVER CREEK
NORTH
CAROLINA
CATAWBA RIVER
Gilbert
Town
SECOND BROAD R.
BROAD RIVER
FIRST BROAD R.
Charlotte
PACOLET RIVER
BUFFALO CREEK
KINGS CREEK
KING'S
MOUNTAIN
Cowpens
BROAD RIVER
SOUTH
CAROLINA

- - - *Route of Americans*
ooooooo *Retreat of British*

On my calling, he stopped, but after looking at me, proceeded. I again drew his attention and made signs to him to
stop, but he slowly continued his way. As I was within that
distance at which in the quickest firing I could have lodged
half-a-dozen of balls in or about him before he was out of
my reach, I had only to determine. But it was not pleasant to
fire at the back of an unoffending individual, who was ac-
quitting himself very coolly of his duty, so I let him alone.

The day after, I had been telling this story to some wounded
officers who lay in the same room with me, when one of our
surgeons, who had been dressing the wounded rebel officers,
came in and told us they had been informing him that Gen-

eral Washington was all the morning with the light troops
and only attended by a French officer in a hussar dress, he
himself dressed and mounted in every point as above described. I am not sorry that I did not know at the time who it
was. Farther this deponent sayeth not, as his bones were
broke a few moments after![4]

A musket ball had shattered Ferguson's right elbow bone,
leaving the arm stiff and useless. But when he had recovered
from his wound, he accompanied Clinton to Charleston and
was the officer Clinton chose, when he returned to New York,
to "superintend the [loyalist] Militia in the Southern Provinces" as "Inspector of Militia and Major Commandant of the
First Battalion of Militia to be raised. . . ." He retained command of his own corps of a hundred Tory riflemen he had recruited for the Southern expedition and had marched them
into the interior in May, taken a position near Ninety-Six,
and recruited local Tories.

In the elemental back country Ferguson had done well,
despite occasional skirmishes and some pitched engagements
with rebel partisans. He had enlisted seven battalions of
loyalist militia and put a force of about a thousand into the
field.

At the commencement of Cornwallis' northward movement, Ferguson had penetrated as far north as Gilbert Town,
a sprinkling of country houses where roads came together on
Cane Creek, North Carolina; here he hoped to intercept a
rebel force fleeing in that direction after an unsuccessful
attempt on the British post at Augusta. Instead, his spies,
who had been watching the hardy rebel homesteaders on the
Watauga and Holston rivers beyond the craggy peaks of
the Blue Ridge, returned with intelligence that the "overmountain men" were embodying rapidly. Several groups of
them had crossed the range during the summer and fought
him and dispersed. From "the Gap of the Mountains" came
word that they were gathered three thousand strong, almost
triple Ferguson's strength.

At once Ferguson began to fade back toward the protection of Cornwallis' army, marching first south toward Cherokee Ford on the Broad River. On October 1 he issued a dramatic broadside appealing to loyal North Carolinians to "run
to camp" to save themselves from the fury of the "back
water men . . . a set of mongrels." Then he turned his march
on the road that ran north of King's Mountain, intending to
bear east to Charlotte. On the sixth he informed Cornwallis of his retreat and requested reinforcements. "Three
or four hundred good soldiers, part dragoons, would finish

the business. Something must be done soon. . . ." That afternoon he came to King's Mountain, where he decided to encamp and await the rebels.

The mountain was a rocky, wooded outlying spur of the Blue Ridge, rising some sixty feet above the plain around it. A plateau at its summit, about 600 yards long and from about 70 feet wide at one end and 120 at the other, provided an excellent campsite for Ferguson's 1,100 men. The major ordered his sergeants to inspect arms, and the men who did not have bayonets were told to whittle down the handles of their hunting knives, so that they could be fitted into the muzzles of their rifles. Then Ferguson settled down to wait, encouraging his men, it was said, by declaring that "he was on King's Mountain, and that he was king of that mountain and that God Almighty could not drive him from it."

At Sycamore Flats on the Watauga, Ferguson's enemies had begun to gather the day Cornwallis started north. On September 25, Colonel Isaac Shelby arrived with 240 men from Sullivan County, North Carolina; Colonel Charles McDowell with 160 from Burke and Rutherford counties, North Carolina; Colonel John Sevier with 240 from Washington County, North Carolina; and Colonel William Campbell with 400 from Washington County, Virginia. Next day they marched into the mountains, and tramping through snow "shoe mouth deep" in the gap between Roan and Yellow mountains, made their way to Quaker Meadows on the Catawba. Here Colonel Benjamin Cleveland joined them with 350 men from Wilkes and Surry counties.

On the rainy Monday of the second of October they encamped a day's march from Gilbert Town, where they had heard Ferguson lay. Isaac Shelby remembered:

It was now discovered that the American Army thus accidentally collected without a head and was a mere confused mass, incapable of performing any great military achievement. The officers commanding regiments assembled and determined that a commanding officer was expedient, but the senior officer of the army [Colonel Charles McDowell] was unpopular, and as the campaign was a volunteer scheme it was discovered that those who had the right to command [Shelby and Sevier] would not be chosen. It was determined to send for General [Daniel] Morgan or General [William] Davidson to take the command and . . . Charles McDowell proposed to undertake this mission and actually set out. . . .

During their sitting, it was proposed that until General Morgan or General Davidson arrived that the officers composing that board should meet once a day and determine upon the movements of the army; this being agreed to, it was also proposed and agreed . . . that Colonel [William] Campbell should be appointed Officer of the Day to execute the plans adopted by the commandants of the regiments.[5]

The colonels, awaiting a field commander, did not sit idle, according to Shelby:

> On the morning after the appointment of Colonel Campbell, we proceeded towards Gilbert Town, but found that Ferguson, apprised of our approach, had left . . . a few days before. On the next night it was determined . . . to pursue him unremittingly with as many of our troops as could be well armed and well mounted, leaving the weak horses and footmen to follow on as fast as they could.
> We accordingly started about light the next morning with 910 men. . . . We were joined at the Cowpens on the sixth by Colonel John Williams of South Carolina and several field officers with about 400 men. . . . We traveled all that night and the next day through heavy rains.[6]

James Collins, sixteen-year-old lad who had marched to war with his father when the Tories burnt Billy Hill's great iron works, had adjusted himself like an old campaigner as they marched after Ferguson: "Everyone ate what he could get, and slept in his own blanket, sometimes eating raw turnips and often resorting to a little parched corn, which, by the by, I have often thought, if a man would eat a mess of parched corn and swallow two or three spoonfuls of honey, then take a good draught of cold water, he could pass longer without suffering than with any other diet he could use." At least Jimmy wasn't going to starve. "On Saturday morning, October 7th, 1780," he wrote, "the sky was overcast with clouds, and at times a light mist of rain falling." Through the dismal country along bramble paths and by-roads the overmountain men rode slowly, arriving at King's Mountain after noon. They dismounted, fastened their coats and blankets to their saddles, tied their horses, and formed behind their mounted officers.

Collins was with Major William Chronicle's regiment, which got into position on the northeast, the broad end of the mountain, where the ascent was extremely steep:

> Each leader made a short speech in his own way to his men, desiring every coward to be off immediately. Here I confess I would willingly have been excused, for my feelings were not the most pleasant. They may be attributed to my youth, not being quite seventeen . . . but I could not well swallow the appellation of coward. . . .
> We were soon in motion, every man throwing four or five balls in his mouth to prevent thirst, also to be in readiness to

reload quick. The shot of the enemy soon began to pass over us like hail. The first shock was quickly over, and for my own part, I was soon in a profuse sweat. My lot happened to be in the center where the severest part of the battle was fought. We soon attempted to climb the hill, but were fiercely charged upon and forced to fall back to our first position. We tried a second time, but met the same fate. The fight then seemed to become more furious.

Their leader, Ferguson, came in full view within rifle shot, as if to encourage his men, who by this time were falling very fast. He soon disappeared. We took to the hill a third time. The enemy gave way. When we had gotten near the top, some of our leaders roared out, "Hurrah, my brave fellows! Advance! They are crying for quarter!"[7]

The American advance to King's Mountain, through the dripping woods, had caught Ferguson completely unprepared. Captain Alexander Chesney, a South Carolina loyalist officer, had been on reconnaissance:

So rapid was their attack that I was in the act of dismounting to report that all was quiet and the pickets on the alert when we heard their firing [on the pickets] about half a mile off. I immediately paraded the men and posted the officers. . . .

King's Mountain, from its height, would have enabled us to oppose a superior force with advantage, had it not been covered with wood, which sheltered the Americans and enabled them to fight in the favorite manner. In fact, after driving in our pickets, they were able to advance . . . to the crest . . . in perfect safety, until they took post and opened an irregular but destructive fire from behind trees and other cover.[8]

Another sixteen-year-old, Private Thomas Young, had lost his shoes and was barefoot, but he carried his "large old musket" charged with two musket balls. He was on the north side of the mountain:

The orders were at the firing of the first gun for every man to raise a whoop, rush forward, and fight his way as best he could. When our division came up to the . . . mountain, we dismounted and Colonel [Benjamin] Roebuck drew us a little to the left and commenced the attack, I well remember how I behaved.

Ben Hollingsworth and myself took right up the side of the mountain and fought from tree to tree . . . to the summit. I recollect I stood behind one tree and fired until the bark was nearly all knocked off and my eyes pretty well filled with it. One fellow shaved me pretty close, for his bullet took a piece out of my own gun stock. Before I was aware

of it, I found myself apparently between my own regiment
and the enemy, as I judged from seeing the paper which the
Whigs wore in their hats and the pine knots the Tories wore
in theirs, these being the badges of distinction.

On top of the mountain, in the thickest of the fight, I saw
Colonel Williams fall. . . . I had seen him but once before
that day. It was in the beginning of the action, as he charged
by me at full speed around the mountain. Toward the summit, a ball struck his horse under the jaw, when he commenced stamping as if he were in a nest of yellow jackets.
Colonel [Williams] threw his reins over the animal's neck,
sprang to the ground, and dashed onward.

The moment I heard the cry that Colonel Williams was shot,
I ran to his assistance, for I loved him as a father. He had
ever been so kind to me and almost always carried a cake in
his pocket for me and his little son, Joseph. They . . . sprin-
kled some water in his face. He revived, and his first words
were, "For God's sake, boys, don't give up the hill!" . . . I
left him in the arms of his son, Daniel, and returned to the
field to avenge his fate.[9]

Over the vicious snarl of rifles and the yells and the crash-
ing of men through the brush there sounded continually the
piercing shriek of the silver whistle with which Patrick Ferguson maneuvered his men. Cruelly punishing an agile horse,
he was everywhere. Over his uniform he wore a checkered
hunting shirt and with his whistle in his teeth and his dress
sword in his left hand he was an unmistakable target.

Suddenly the whistle blasts were heard no more and the
brilliant shirt disappeared. Ferguson's second-in-command,
the devoted Captain Abraham DePeyster they called "the
Bull Dog's pup," saw his chief go down with several balls in
his body. His foot hung in his stirrup. His men lifted him
down and propped him against a tree, where he died. Hope
deserted his followers, and DePeyster ordered a white flag
shown.

At that moment, Colonel Shelby had just "gained the eastern summit . . . and drove those who had been opposed to us
along the top . . . until they were forced down the western
end about 100 yards, in a crowd, to where the other part of
their line had been contending with Cleveland and Williams."
On spotting the white flag Shelby ordered them "to throw
down their arms, which they did, and surrendered . . . at discretion." He reported:

It was some time before a complete cessation of the firing on our part could be effected. Our men who had been
scattered in the battle were continually coming up and continued to fire, without comprehending in the heat of the mo-

ment what had happened; and some who had heard that at
Buford's defeat, the British had refused quarters . . . were
willing to follow that bad example.

Owing to these causes, the ignorance of some, and the disposition of others to retaliate, it required some time and
some exertion on the part of the officers to put an entire
stop to the firing.

After the surrender of the enemy, our men gave sponta-
neously three loud and long shouts.[10]

Robert Henry heard the lusty shouting and the cry that
Ferguson was dead: "I had a desire to see him," he said,
"and went and found him . . . shot in the face and in the
breast. . . . Samuel Talbot turned him over and got his pocket
pistol."

The battle was over. Ferguson "the great Western Bug-
bear" was dead, wrapped in a raw beef hide and buried on
the field. The "backwater men" he had scorned and then
feared had slain 157 Tories, wounded 163, and taken 698
prisoner. They themselves lost 28 killed and 62 wounded. The
fight had lasted perhaps an hour. Soon the autumn darkness
settled over the gloomy woods, and victors and vanquished
passed the night on the field "amid the dead and the groans
of the dying, who had neither surgical aid nor water to quench
their thirst."

James Collins awoke the next morning, Sunday, to a scene
"really distressing."

The wives and children of the poor Tories came in, in
great numbers. Their husbands, fathers, and brothers lay
dead in heaps, while others lay wounded or dying. . . . We
proceeded to bury the dead, but it was badly done. They
were thrown into convenient piles and covered with old logs,
the bark of old trees and rocks, yet not so as to secure them
from becoming a prey to the beasts of the forests, or the vul-
tures of the air; and the wolves [later] became so plenty,
that it was dangerous for anyone to be out at night for several
miles around. Also the hogs in the neighborhood gathered
into the place to devour the flesh of men, inasmuch as numbers chose to live on little meat rather than eat their hogs,
though they were fat. Half of the dogs in the country were
said to be mad and were put to death. I saw myself in passing the place, a few weeks after, all parts of the human
frame . . . scattered in every direction. . . .
In the evening, there was a distribution . . . of the plunder, and we were dismissed. My father and myself drew two
fine horses, two guns, and some articles of clothing with a
share of powder and lead. Every man repaired to his tent or
home. It seemed like a calm after a heavy storm . . . and for

a short time, every man could visit his home, or his neighbor
without being afraid. . . .[11]

Disposition of the prisoners presented a problem to the
loosely organized patriots. The overmountain men, as well
as a number of Virginians and South Carolinians, wanted to
go home, and like Collins and his father, did go. Others
marched to Gilbert Town and then northward to turn the
captives over to Gates at Hillsboro. Captain Chesney was
one of the hundreds guarded "between double lines of
mounted Americans, the officers in the rear and obliged to
carry two muskets each, which was my fate, although
wounded and stripped of my shoes and silver buckles in an
inclement season without covering or provision until Monday night, when an ear of Indian corn was served to each."

At Gilbert Town, Colonel Campbell was forced in his
general orders to "request the officers of all ranks in the
army to endeavor to restrain the disorderly manner of
slaughtering and disturbing the prisoners." The same furies
that drove many Whigs to continue firing on the defeated
Tories atop the mountain inspired unjustifiable murder of
many prisoners. Bullies beat the captives, some slashed the
helpless Tories with swords, and a committee of colonels
established themselves as a jury to try some of the obnoxious
Tories. Thirty-six were found guilty of "breaking open houses,
killing the men, turning the men and women out of doors,
and burning the houses. The trial," Shelby later recalled,
"was concluded late at night. The execution of the law was
as summary as the trial."

Nine of the convicted were hanged, and according to one
of Ferguson's officers, "died like Romans," but the others
were reprieved. Many prisoners escaped along the way,
and by the time that Colonel Campbell turned them over to
Gates at Hillsboro, they had become such a burden that
Gates appealed to Governor Jefferson to tell him how to dispose of those that remained.

The effect of the defeat of the Tories was instantaneous;
the tide of war no longer flowed hopelessly against the rebels.
Ferguson's appeal to Cornwallis for help reached Charlotte
on the very day of the battle. Cornwallis, on the tenth, ordered Tarleton with the Light Infantry, his Legion, and a
three-pounder to march to Ferguson's assistance. Tarleton,
on his way, heard of the "melancholy fate" of Ferguson,
and when his dispatches back to Charlotte reached Cornwallis, he was recalled hastily. Rumor exaggerated the
strength of the rebels who, Cornwallis feared, would dash to
Camden and Ninety-Six. His own militia was destroyed, and

the loyalists upon whom he depended for support were too dispirited to come out. His plan for the subjugation of North Carolina went glimmering, and on the fourteenth of October, a week after King's Mountain, he began a hurried retreat southward.

The rainy season, which so often introduces the southern winters, had set in; the roads were deep with mud. Wagons were lost, food vanished, and the army lacking tents slept on the wet ground. American militia harassed the march. There was much sickness, and soon Cornwallis himself tossed with fever in one of the hospital wagons. Fifteen days after leaving Charlotte, the British Army encamped at Winnsboro, between Camden and Ninety-Six, with Lord Rawdon temporarily in command, and Cornwallis' plan for the winter campaign smashed.

35

"TARLETON RUN DOON THE ROAD HELTER-SKELTER"

Cowpens

JANUARY 17, 1781

ON THE fifth of October, 1780, while the overmountain men were closing in upon Ferguson on the South Carolina border, the Continental Congress in Philadelphia resolved that General Washington order a court of inquiry into the conduct of General Gates and appoint an officer to command in the Southern Department until the court had acted.

The choice seemed to many to be between William Smallwood and Nathanael Greene, but the Congressional Delegates from the theater concerned very decidedly wanted Greene, this despite the fact that, only sixty days before, his sharp note of resignation as Quartermaster General had thrown the "Congress into a degree of vexatious distress" and led some members to demand his dismissal from the army. Undoubtedly he was Washington's choice as the most resourceful, accomplished officer he could recommend. For years Greene had proved himself, in the words of Henry Lee, "a very highly trusted councellor of the Commander-in-Chief, respected for his sincerity, prized for his disinterestedness, and valued for his wisdom." He was a thoughtful strategist, rather than an inspiring leader. He knew how to make the most of limited resources. He seldom showed brilliance, but he had much of Washington's capacity for enduring.

Greene was at West Point, anticipating a quiet, pleasant winter with his wife, Catherine; after Arnold had fled, Greene asked for the post and Washington gladly assigned it to him on the sixth of October, cautioning him that it might be a temporary assignment. Just nine days later Greene received a letter from the Commander-in-Chief informing him of his appointment to succeed Gates. "I wish your earliest arrival," Washington wrote from Preakness, "that there be no circumstances to retard your proceeding to the southward. . . ."

Greene accepted the appointment with an appreciative note; he regretted that his abilities were "not more competent of the duties required" of him, but he did feel that his "zeal and attention" would compensate for his deficiencies. He asked for a few days at home to settle his "domestic concerns" and to regain his health, "having had a considerable fever upon me for several days."

Then the Rhode Islander wrote another letter:

My dear Angel,
What I have been dreading has come to pass. His Excellency General Washington, by order of Congress, has appointed me to the command of the Southern Army, General Gates being recalled to under[go] an examination into his conduct. . . .
I have been pleasing myself with the agreeable prospect of spending the winter here with you, and the moment I was appointed to the command I sent off Mr. Hubbard to bring you to camp. But, alas, . . . I am ordered away to another quarter. How unfriendly is war to domestic happiness.
I wish it was possible for me to stay until your arrival, but from the pressing manner which the General urges my setting out I am afraid you will come too late to see me.[1]

To Greene's request for a short leave to prepare for the journey, Washington replied within the hour that he received the note: ". . . I wish circumstances could be made to correspond with your wishes . . . but your presence with your command as soon as possible is indispensable. . . ." A British reinforcement had just sailed from New York "in all probability destined to co-operate with Cornwallis," said the General. "I hope to see you without delay."

Greene departed West Point as ordered, again assuring

Caty, "Nothing should have torn me from you but the General's absolute orders to come on and not let anything detain me—not even ill health." Even as he set out upon the road to Preakness, he glanced over his shoulder in the anguished hope that she would catch up with him before he left for the South. She did try, but she failed.

At headquarters, Greene received his orders and the welcome news that he would have Henry Lee's Legion there and Baron von Steuben to assist him in training and regulating his army. Washington, ever the realist, had told the baron that his services in the North would be missed, but in the South "there is an army to be created, the mass of which is at present without any formation at all."

At Philadelphia, Greene spent nine days, endeavoring "to impress those in power with the necessity of sending clothing and supplies of every kind immediately" to his army. He took a dim view of their assurances: "They all promised fair, but I fear will do little: ability is wanting with some and inclination with others. . . ."

Greene and Steuben, traveling with their military families, parted en route while Greene solicited aid from the governors of Delaware and Maryland, but rejoined each other farther on. Stephen Duponceau rode with Steuben and remembered:

On our way, the Baron paid a visit to Mrs. Washington at Mount Vernon. We were most cordially received and invited to dinner. The external appearance of the mansion did not strike the Baron very favorably.

"If," said he, "Washington were not a better general than he was an architect, the affairs of America would be in a very bad condition."[2]

Before the party left early in the morning, Greene wrote the General by candlelight that he thought Mount Vernon was "one of the most pleasant places I ever saw," and either he or the baron indulged in an inoffensive social deceit when he added, "Baron Steuben is delighted with the place. . . ."

At the Virginia capital, Greene learned that the British reinforcements from New York had landed and were established at Portsmouth, but their designs were yet a mystery. With Governor Jefferson, whom he met for the first time, Greene concerted plans for supplying his army and furnishing militia. Leaving Steuben to take command and organize forces and to forward supplies, he hurried on, with two new aides he found out of employ in Richmond.

When Cornwallis had pulled back to Winnsboro after King's Mountain, Gates had moved south to Charlotte, where supplies were said to be more plentiful. There on the cold afternoon of December 2, Greene found his new command busily building huts for the winter. Gate's official family had been dreading the moment of Greene's arrival; perhaps the two generals also had anticipated that moment with anxiety. They were well known to be unfriendly. Now Greene came, not only to take over Gates's lost command, but perhaps also to sit in judgment on his conduct. Colonel Williams witnessed their meeting:

A manly resignation marked the conduct of General Gates on the arrival of his successor, whom he received at headquarters with that liberal and gentlemanly air which was habitual to him.

General Greene observed a plain, candid, respectful manner, neither betraying compassion nor the want of it—nothing like the pride of official consequence even *seemed*. In short, the officers who were present had an elegant lesson of propriety exhibited on a most delicate and interesting occasion.

General Greene was announced to the army as commanding officer by General Gates; and the same day General Greene addressed the army, in which address he paid General Gates the compliment of confirming all his standing orders.[3]

When Gates issued those last orders to his army, for parole he courteously chose "Springfield," scene of Greene's latest battle, and for countersign, "Greene."

The disagreeable duty of calling the court of inquiry was spared Greene, because Steuben, who had been named to head the court, was held in Virginia, and other general officers were not readily available. The court was postponed, and finally was never held. Greene made enough inquiries to satisfy himself that most of the officers who had enough knowledge of the affair at Camden to testify were disposed to favor Gates's action. To Hamilton, he soon wrote:

The battle of Camden here is represented widely different from what it is to the northward . . . The action was short and succeeded by a flight, wherein everybody took care of himself, as well officers as soldiers. . . . The Colonel [Williams] also says that General Gates would have shared little more disgrace than is the common lot of the unfortunate . . . if he had only halted at the Waxhaws or Charlotte. . . . What little incidents either give or destroy reputation.[4]

Gates retired to his home, Traveller's Rest in Virginia, there to become sulky, disgruntled, disillusioned, as no one listened to his pleas for the inquiry to clear his name. At last

Congress passed a resolution dismissing the court, but the general never again saw important service.

At Charlotte, Greene had his own hands full without worrying about Gates's good name. He called for exact returns of the troops and was appalled to discover that he was in command of "but the shadow of an army in the midst of distress." Its paper strength was 90 cavalrymen, 60 artillerymen, and 2,307 infantry, of whom 1,482 were present and fit for duty. Only 949 of his foot soldiers were Continentals; the rest were militia, those irregulars who, in the South even more than in New England, came and went as they pleased, disputed their orders, and plundered the civilian population. "With the militia, everybody is a general," declared Greene, perhaps aware of General Caswell's naive note in one of his letters: "General W——, my aide-de-camp . . ." Fewer than 800 of all ranks were properly clothed and equipped. One entire company of Virginia horsemen was so ill-equipped and ill-clothed that despite his desperate need for men, Greene sent them home, admonishing Governor Jefferson not to send them back until properly supplied.

Part of the difficulty, Greene recognized, lay in Gates's Quartermaster and Commissary departments. The quartermaster was "a very honest, young man, but his views have been confined altogether to the mere camp issues and artificer's concerns." Promptly he replaced him with Lieutenant Colonel Carrington, an artilleryman he had met in Virginia, whose abilities and energies quickly bore out Greene's expectations. Greene was equally shrewd in selecting as commissary general William R. Davie, of North Carolina, to replace Colonel Polk, who had resigned, pleading age.

The troops' addiction to plundering had made them a "terror to the inhabitants" about Charlotte, and the neighborhood had been picked clean. Greene saw that it was necessary to establish "a camp of repose, for the purpose of repairing our wagons, recruiting our horses, and disciplining the troops." Into South Carolina he sent his engineer, Colonel Thaddeus Kosciuszko, to "examine the country from the mouth of Little River, twenty or thirty miles down the Pee Dee and search for a good position for the army."

On the twentieth of December, Greene marched from Charlotte toward the campsite his engineer had chosen. But before leaving the North Carolina village, Greene made a daring decision and split his little army, defying the classic injunction of warfare that to divide an inferior force in the face of a superior army was to invite the enemy to destroy first one and then the other of the parts. But he thought he had compelling reasons. He was not strong enough to meet

Cornwallis; yet he must not appear to retreat. Moving down on the Pee Dee would appear like a retreat, but by sending a wing of his army to the west of the Catawba River, he would be better able to feed both parts, would protect the country, encourage the people, and threaten Cornwallis' flank if he should move northward again.

The command of this wing Greene gave to Daniel Morgan. The giant wagoner had retired from the army in the summer of 1779, disgruntled by Congress' failure to advance him in rank and very uncomfortable in health from an old rheumatic or arthritic condition. For fifteen months he resided at home in Frederick County, Virginia, until called back into service when Gates was ordered south. He had been offended by the way in which Gates had slighted him in reports on Saratoga, but while the two soldiers were both at home in the spring of 1780, Morgan visited his old comrade-in-arms, and the coolness between them began to melt. Almost the first thing Gates did, after being notified of his appointment to command of the Southern Department and the intention of Congress to recall Morgan to service was to write him a note of welcome. Recognizing Morgan's remarkable flair for handling light troops, Gates proposed to give him command of such a corps and endeavored to persuade Congress to promote him to brigadier general. His efforts were in vain, weakened perhaps by Washington's candid, private remarks to Joseph Jones, who solicited the General's opinion, because Morgan had "left the army in disgust under your immediate command." "The gentleman," Washington had written, ". . . is a brave officer and a well meaning man, but his withdrawing from the service at the time he did last year could not be justified on any ground." Washington implied that at the time patriotism should have kept Morgan in service, even if he had had reason for dissatisfaction.

When the promotion did not come, Morgan refused to rejoin the army, but after Gates's rout at Camden, he flung personal pride aside and rushed to Gates's support—in spite of the fact that he was so straitened financially that he was obliged to take along a mare to sell on the way to pay his traveling expenses. Soon after Morgan arrived in Hillsboro, Gates happily delivered him a corps of four regiments of infantry and a company of riflemen under command of Lieutenant Colonel John Eager Howard, and about seventy horse under Lieutenant Colonel William Washington. While Morgan was on detached duty, just before the army had left the "dirty, disagreeable hole" that Hillsboro was to Otho Williams, he received word of his promotion.

Now, on the twentieth of December, as Brigadier General

in command of Light Infantry, Morgan separated from Greene at Charlotte. On the day after Christmas, Greene took a position on the Pee Dee at Hick's Creek. To Morgan he wrote, "Our prospects with regards to provisions are mended, but this is no Egypt." Then Greene applied himself unstintingly to repairing his army; his only offensive operation was a raid, under joint command of Henry Lee and partisan Francis Marion, against the British post at Georgetown.

As Morgan marched toward Ninety-Six, several small militia groups joined him. By Christmas Day he had established himself across the Broad River on the north bank of the Pacolet. Promptly he took into his employ well-recommended Whigs as spies, who reported British and Tory movements.

On the Pacolet, Morgan soon found himself "at a loss how to act." Militia units joined him so fast that it became impossible to provide for his force in the neighborhood. Yet, he feared advancing near the enemy, for he knew that Cornwallis could detach a superior force toward him "with the greatest facility." This would oblige him to retreat, which would discourage the Whigs. He entertained a scheme for a dash into Georgia, if Greene could make a diversion in his favor, but Greene advised against it. British Major General Alexander Leslie with fifteen hundred men was advancing toward Camden, evidently to reinforce Cornwallis, Greene said. Should this combined force, which would amount to four thousand men, move against Greene, he wanted Morgan to return to him at once. Meanwhile, Greene wished him to maintain his position as long as possible, cautioning him to guard carefully against surprise. This Morgan had done, so that by the time a letter reached him from Greene dated the thirteenth of January, Morgan knew what Greene had to tell him: "Colonel Tarleton is said to be on his way to pay you a visit. I doubt not but he will have a decent reception and a proper dismission."

Tarleton's advance on Morgan had been forced upon Cornwallis. At Winnsboro, Cornwallis had recovered from his fever and was laying plans for another invasion of North Carolina. Either he could defeat Greene or force him back across the Roanoke. But then he heard that Morgan was threatening the safety of his important post at Ninety-Six. Therefore, on January 1, 1781, before commencing his major operation, he detached Tarleton with a force of 750 men and two three-pounders across the Broad River to push Morgan "to the utmost," compelling him to fight or flee.

Tarleton discovered that Morgan was not in a position to menace Ninety-Six, so he rested his men, instructed his lieutenant to send up his baggage "but no women," and wrote Cornwallis confidently that he would advance on Morgan, and destroy him or push him toward King's Mountain. When Morgan retreated, he suggested, Cornwallis should move to cut the Virginian off. Cornwallis agreed to this scheme and started north on the seventh, moving slowly to allow Leslie to catch up.

Morgan watched these British movements closely. On the fourteenth he withdrew a few miles to Thicketty Creek, before what he thought was a force of eleven to twelve hundred. As Tarleton drew closer, Morgan pulled farther back until as the cold, raw evening of the sixteenth closed in, he reached a place called Hannah's Cowpens on the Broad River. There he decided to stand and face the foe he knew he could not evade.

When two captured vedettes revealed to Tarleton the position Morgan had taken, the enterprising Englishman was delighted. Morgan lay at the crest of a long, gently sloping ridge, covered with open wood, "certainly as good a place for action as Lieutenant Colonel Tarleton could desire," said Tarleton himself. "America does not produce any more suitable to the nature of the troops under his command." The Broad River at Morgan's back discouraged any hope of retreat. The open, exposed flanks invited encirclement. Though he never admitted it, Morgan probably intended to cross the river and make a stand at Thicketty Mountain, but the river had been swollen by recent hard rains and he could not risk being caught in the middle of a crossing. Years later he offered a defense of the position: had he crossed the river his militia would have fled; he left his wings open for "downright fighting." In short, he wanted his men to be forced to fight.

When Morgan arrived at the Cowpens "about sun-down" and told the men that there they should meet the enemy, Thomas Young was one of the troops who received the news "with great joy." Young was a volunteer with William Washington's cavalry:

We were very anxious for battle, and many a hearty curse had been vented against General Morgan during that day's march for retreating, as we thought, to avoid a fight.

Night came upon us, yet much remained to be done. It was all important to strengthen the cavalry. General Morgan well knew the power of Tarleton's Legion, and he was too

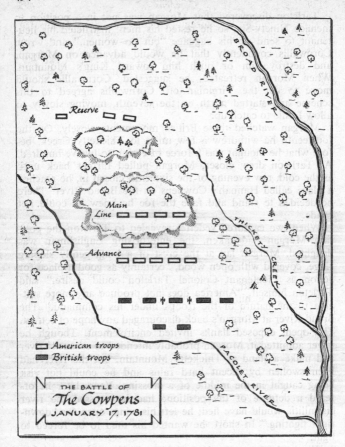

Reserve

BROAD RIVER

Main Line

THICKETY CREEK

Advance

☐ American troops
■ British troops

PACOLET RIVER

THE BATTLE OF
The Cowpens
JANUARY 17. 1781

wily an officer not to prepare himself as well as circumstances would admit. Two companies of volunteers were
called for . . . I attached myself to Major Jolly's company.
We drew swords that night and were informed we had authority to press any horse not belonging to a dragoon or an
officer into our service for the day.

It was upon this occasion I was more perfectly convinced
of General Morgan's qualifications to command militia than
I had ever before been. He went among the volunteers, helped
them fix their swords, joked with them about their sweethearts, told them to keep in good spirits, and the day would
be ours. And long after I laid down, he was going about

among the soldiers encouraging them and telling them that
the old wagoner would crack his whip over Ben [Tarleton]
in the morning, as sure as they lived.

"Just hold up your heads, boys, three fires," he would say,
"and you are free, and then when you return to your homes,
how the old folks will bless you, and the girls kiss you for
your gallant conduct!"

I don't believe he slept a wink that night.[5]

Young's guess was correct. Morgan spent most of the
night moving among his men. His sign and countersign for the
next day, "Fire" and "Sword," would remind them that the
Lord was on their side, but Morgan subscribed to the homily
that He helped those who helped themselves: the old wagoner ordered the militia to prepare twenty-four rounds of
ammunition, and he sent the baggage off. He kept patrols
and scouts close to the enemy and dispatched messages to the
bodies of militia reported on the way to accelerate their pace.
Several small detachments arrived during the night. John
Eager Howard noted, "They were all in good spirits, related
circumstances of Tarleton's cruelty, and expressed the
strongest desire to check his progress."

The next morning, January 17, an hour before daylight,
Morgan's pickets were driven in. They brought word that
Tarleton was within five miles, marching light and fast.
Morgan's thunderous shout, "Boys, get up! Benny is com-
ing," aroused his troops.

The slightly undulating battleground was nearly bare of
undergrowth, which had been cropped by grazing cattle.
The red oak, hickory, and pine was so open that Morgan
could form without difficulty. On the crest of the slope he
placed his main line, the whole under command of John
Eager Howard; Howard's own light infantry, Maryland and
Delaware Continentals, held the center. Virginia and Georgia
militia were placed on the left, and a force of Virginia Continentals on the right. Approximately 150 yards in advance,
Morgan placed North Carolina, South Carolina, and Virginia militia, under command of Andrew Pickens of South
Carolina. About the same distance farther ahead of it, he
deployed 150 skirmishers. To the rear of these lines, as a
reserve, he posted his mounted troops under Colonel William
Washington, and the mounted infantry under Lieutenant
Colonel James McCall.

While his men awaited the enemy in battle order, Morgan
rode the lines, ordering them, "Ease your joints." At eight
o'clock Tarleton's force came in sight, deploying and shed-
ding excess gear as they approached. Their two-pounders

opened a covering fire, as they formed one main battle line
and a short reserve. The vigorous young attacker, impatient
with the sluggishness of his tired troops, ordered them to
advance before his formation was completed.

Thomas Young watched their approach:

> The morning of the 17th . . . was bitterly cold. We were
> formed in order of battle, and the men were slapping their
> hands together to keep warm—an exertion not long neces-
> sary. . . .
> About sunrise, the British line advanced at a sort of trot
> with a loud halloo. It was the most beautiful line I ever saw.
> When they shouted, I heard Morgan say, "They give us the
> British halloo, boys. Give them the Indian halloo, by G——!"
> and he galloped along the lines, cheering the men and telling
> them not to fire until we could see the whites of their eyes.
> Every officer was crying, "Don't fire!" for it was a hard matter
> to keep us from it.
> I should have said the British line advanced under cover
> of their artillery, for it opened so fiercely upon the center
> that Colonel Washington moved his cavalry from the center
> towards the right wing.
> The militia fired first. It was for a time, pop—pop—pop,
> and then a whole volley; but when the regulars fired, it
> seemed like one sheet of flame from right to left. Oh! it
> was beautiful![6]

Hugh McCall was told by veterans:

> The American advanced corps . . . opened their fire and
> supported it with animation under a brisk fire from the Brit-
> ish, until the bayonet was presented, when they retired and
> took their posts in the intervals left for them in the front
> line. . . .
> The British advanced, firing and with loud shouts for ap-
> proaching victory. Pickens received them with a firmness with
> which they were unaccustomed from that description of
> troops, until the British charged them with the bayonet, when
> Pickens ordered a retreat to the post assigned to them on the
> left of the Continental troops. As the militia retreated, they
> were charged by the British light dragoons of the advance, by
> which they were unable to form on the left and they con-
> tinued to retreat toward the reserve under Washington.
> Howard received the British van with firmness. A warm
> fire ensued, and the advance of the enemy was not with such
> a quick step.[7]

James Collins, another militia veteran of King's Mountain, who admitted that he usually became sick at the sight
of blood, had ridden in before the battle to join Morgan. He

had been posted on the right of the dismounted militia. With
it, he had given one fire, and with the flash of bayonets, had
run for his horse. Tarleton's dragoons swept among the militia
who were trying to gain the rear of Howard's right:

"Now," thought I, "my hide is in the loft." Just as we
got to our horses, they overtook us and began to take a few
hacks at some, however, without doing much injury. They,
in their haste, had pretty much scattered, perhaps thinking
they would have another Fishing Creek frolic [where Tarleton had surprised and destroyed Sumter's South Carolina par-
tisans]. But in a few moments, Colonel Washington's cavalry was among them like a whirlwind, and the poor fellows
began to keel from their horses without being able to remount.
The shock was so sudden and violent they could not
stand it, and immediately betook themselves to flight. There
was no time to rally, and they appeared to be as hard to
stop as a drove of wild Choctaw steers going to a Pennsylvania market.
In a few moments, the clashing of swords was out of hearing and quickly out of sight. By this time, both lines of the infantry were warmly engaged and we being relieved from
the pursuit of the enemy began to rally and prepare to re-
deem our credit, when Morgan rode up in front and waving
his sword cried out, "Form, form, my brave fellows! Give
them one more fire, and the day is ours. Old Morgan was
never beaten."[8]

As the British advance was slowed by a "well-directed and
incessant fire," Tarleton brought up his infantry reserve, but
did not yet commit his horse. The British reserve forming on
the ends of Tarleton's line were so extended that they outflanked Morgan's main line. Howard reported:

Seeing my right flank was exposed to the enemy, I attempted to change the front of Wallace's company (Virginia
regulars). In doing this, some confusion ensued, and first a
part and then the whole of the company commenced a retreat. The officers along the line seeing this and supposing
that orders had been given for a retreat, faced their men
about and moved off.
Morgan, who had mostly been with the militia, quickly
rode up to me and expressed apprehensions . . .but I soon
removed his fears by pointing to the line and observing that
men were not beaten who retreated in that order. He then
ordered me to keep with the men until we came to the rising
ground near Washington's horse, and he rode forward to fix
on the most proper place for us to halt and face about.
In a minute we had a perfect line. The enemy were now

very near us. Our men commenced a very destructive fire, which they little expected, and a few rounds occasioned great disorder in their ranks. While [they were] in this confusion, I ordered a charge with the bayonet, which order was obeyed with great alacrity. As the line advanced, I observed their artillery a short distance in front, and called to Captain Ewing who was near me to take it. Captain Anderson, hearing the order, also pushed for the same object; and both being emulous for the prize kept pace until near the first piece, when Anderson, by putting the end of his spontoon forward into the ground, made a long leap which brought him upon the gun and gave him the honor of the prize.[9]

Thomas Young was in the rear of Tarleton's right, "shouting and charging" the broken dragoons, when he heard the call of American bugles and Howard's order, "Charge bayonets!"

"The British broke, and throwing down their guns and cartouche boxes," to Young's entertainment, "made for the wagon road and did the prettiest sort of running!"

Although Tarleton had mistaken Howard's retrograde movement for retreat and charged him, he still did not commit his reserve cavalry. Captain Roderick Mackenzie, who took a wound at Cowpens, later was more than a little critical of Tarleton's field decisions:

. . . the advance of the British fell back and communicated a panic to others, which soon became general: a total rout ensued. Two hundred and fifty horse which had not been engaged, fled through the woods with the utmost precipitation, bearing down such officers as opposed their flight. . . .

Even at this late stage of the defeat, . . . Tarleton with no more than fifty horse, hesitated not to charge the whole of Washington's cavalry, though supported by the Continentals . . . the loss sustained was in proportion to the danger of the enterprise, and the whole body was repulsed.[10]

"After the action," the story was told, "Colonel Howard in conversation with Major McArthur expressed his surprise at the precipitate, desultory manner in which the British troops were brought into action. The gallant Scot observed that nothing better could have been expected when troops were commanded by a rash, foolish boy."

Morgan's victory was complete. Only the enemy's baggage guard and Tarleton himself with a handful of cavalry escaped. A hundred and ten of the British were killed, including ten officers, 702 were taken prisoner. Morgan's booty included the two British three-pounders, eight hundred muskets, one hundred horses, thirty-five wagons of baggage, sixty Negro slaves, a huge quantity of ammunition and "all their music." His loss was twelve killed, sixty wounded. For the enemy it was as costly as the historic Christmas at Trenton, the second day at Freeman's Farm, or the assault on Stony Point, and its effect was perhaps as far-reaching.

Although Morgan had won the field in less than an hour's wild fighting, he knew he could not retain possession of it. Tarleton had vanished across the Pacolet, but Cornwallis surely would now march his whole army to recover the prisoners and revenge the old wagoner's insult to British arms. Morgan paroled the British officers, dispatched word of his victory to Greene, and marched northward to the Catawba with his prisoners.

As the news of Morgan's stunning success spread through the country, rejoicing was universal. In Congress, John Mathews wrote to Greene: "the intelligence received was a most healing cordial to our drooping spirits . . . it was so very unexpected. It seems to have had a very sensible effect on some folks, for this is convincing proof that something is to be done in that department."

Washington, however, feared the Southern states would consider the victory "more decisive . . . than it really is and will relax in their exertions." But William Gordon, already evaluating the battle with a historian's eye, disagreed: "Morgan's success will be more important in its distant consequences than on the day of victory." In England, Horace Walpole gloomily muttered, "America is once more not quite ready to be conquered, although every now and then we fancy it is. Tarleton is defeated, Lord Cornwallis is checked, and Arnold not sure of having betrayed his friends to much purpose."

A grateful Congress voted Morgan a gold medal, and silver ones to Howard and Colonel Washington. Pickens was given a sword. The Virginia House of Delegates voted to award the wagoner a horse "with furniture" and a sword.

And a western Carolina civilian named John Miller considered Cowpens when called upon to pray at a meeting:

Good Lord, our God that art in Heaven, we have great reason to thank thee for the many favors we have received at thy hands, the many battles we have won.
There is the great and glorious battle of King's Mountain, where we kilt the great Gineral Ferguson and took his whole army. And the great battles at Ramsour's and at Williamson's. And the ever-memorable and glorious battle of the Coopens, where we made the proud Gineral Tarleton run doon the road helter-skelter, and, Good Lord, if ye had na

suffered the cruel Tories to burn Billy Hill's Iron Works, we would na have asked any mair favors at thy hands. Amen.[11]

While the country exulted, a tired, arthritic giant named Daniel Morgan led his victorious little army in a retreat along the muddy roads of North Carolina, to Sherrald's Ford beyond the Catawba.

36

"IT'S TIME TO RUN, BOB"

The Race to the Dan

JANUARY-FEBRUARY 1781

ON THE twenty-third of January, Major Edward Giles, Morgan's aide, mud-splashed but smiling, rode into Greene's camp on the Pee Dee with the electrifying news of the victory at the Cowpens. The camp went wild. Joy and rum flowed at headquarters, and as soon as he had a chance, Morgan's good friend, Otho Williams, wrote a warm, excited letter to the victor:

> I am much better pleased that you have plucked the laurels from the brow of the hitherto fortunate Tarleton than if he had fallen by the hands of Lucifer. . . . I am delighted that the accumulated honors of the young partisan should be plundered by my old friend.
> We have had a *feu de joie,* drunk all your healths, swore you were the finest fellows on earth and love you if possible more than ever. The general has, I think, made his compliments in very handsome terms. Enclosed is a copy of his orders. It was written immediately after we received the news and during the operation of some cherry bounce. . . .[1]

Greene's first impulse was to draw Cornwallis' attention from Morgan by moving swiftly against the post the enemy had established in the west at Ninety-Six. But the idea was erased almost instantly when he realized that the enlistment of Stevens' Virginia militia was nearly expired and the men were preparing to march home. The only way to save Morgan and to oppose Cornwallis' new invasion of North Carolina was to unite forces with the old wagoner. To this end, Greene sent orders to the commissaries at Salisbury and Hillsboro to prepare to move their prisoners and stores to Virginia, out of the path of the invaders. He ordered his quartermaster general to assemble boats on the Dan River, on the boundary of North Carolina and Virginia, for use if he were forced to retreat. He placed Brigadier General Isaac Huger of the South Carolina militia in command of his army to march it to Salisbury for a junction with Morgan. Then with an aide, a guide, and a sergeant's guard of dragoons, he himself struck off across Tory-infested country, on the twenty-eighth, to ride a hundred and twenty-five miles to put himself at the head of Morgan's detachment in front of Cornwallis.

On the evening of Cowpens, when several of Tarleton's fugitives brought Cornwallis news of the defeat, the earl, instead of being in Morgan's rear, was twenty-five miles south at Turkey Creek, awaiting his reinforcement under Leslie. At once he determined to destroy Morgan, retake his prisoners, and wipe out the humiliation to British arms. It took him two days to put his army in motion to intercept the retreating wagoner, and when he did start on the nineteenth, he went in the wrong direction, expecting Morgan would have held his ground or moved toward Ninety-Six. By the time he shifted his march, his quarry had eluded him. Floundering through swollen streams and splashing along muddy, icy roads, he reached Ramsour's Mill on the south fork of the Catawba River on the twenty-fifth to discover Morgan had passed there two days before and was two rivers away. To catch the fast-moving rebel, who had traveled a hundred miles in less than five days, he knew he must accelerate his own pace. At the Cowpens he had lost all his light troops; at the mill he boldly stripped his army to convert the whole into a light corps. Except for salt, ammunition, medical stores, and four ambulances, he burned his wagon train, baggage, provisions, and rum, and set an example by burning his personal belongings before his troops. Nevertheless, after thus dangerously risking the future efficiency of his army, by the time he reached the north fork of the Catawba, he found Morgan safely across, the river impassable from the steady downpours, and the fords guarded for forty miles above. For two days he approached various fords to confuse the rebels, while awaiting a fall of the river and planning a passage.

At the Catawba, Morgan had sent his Cowpens prisoners north under escort, and awaited Greene who had sent word he was coming. The giant had requested the general to grant him a leave of absence because he was greatly troubled by his "ceatick," unable to "ride out of a walk." But, though compelled to "lie in a house out of camp" because of the bad weather, he had looked to defense of the river. He had rendered two obscure fords impassable with felled trees and stationed small forces behind them. He had kept unobstructed the principal ford of the region, Beattie's, to accommodate citizens fleeing before the advancing enemy, but he had ordered it held by eight hundred North Carolina militia called out under General William Davidson.

On the afternoon of the thirty-first, about two o'clock, with his army under Colonel Howard already on the march toward Salisbury, Morgan and Colonel Washington rode to Beattie's Ford to inspect the defenses and to meet Greene. According to Major Joseph Graham, who was present, Greene met them ten minutes after they arrived:

They and General Davidson retired with him out of camp, and seating themselves on a log had a conversation of about twenty minutes. They then mounted their horses, General Greene and aide took the road to Salisbury, Morgan and Washington a way that led to the troops marching under Howard.

About the time General Greene had arrived, the British vanguard of about four or five hundred men appeared on the opposite hill beyond the river. . . .

In about an hour after General Greene's departure, General Davidson gave orders to the cavalry and about two hundred and fifty infantry to march down the river to Cowan's Ford, four miles below Beattie's, leaving nearly the same number at that place. . . . On the march he stated to the commanding officer of the cavalry "that though General Greene had never seen the Catawba before, he appeared to know more about it than those who were raised on it," and it was the general's opinion that the enemy were determined to cross the river; and he thought it probable their cavalry would pass over some private ford in the night, and in the morning when the infantry attempted to force a passsage would attack those who resisted it in the rear; and as there was no other cavalry between Beattie's and Tuckasege, he ordered that patrols who were best acquainted with the country should keep passing up and down all night and on discovering any party of the enemy to have gotten over to give immediate information to him. These orders were carried into effect.[2]

Cowan's Ford was a private ford, off the chief routes of travel, and not a particularly good place to cross the river.

The wagon ford lay straight across the stream, but the smoother, more shallow horse ford turned at a forty-five degree angle about midway of the crossing, passed over the corner of a small island, and emerged from the river several hundred yards below the wagon ford. At the "coming-out place" of the wagon ford, Davidson placed a picket guard; at the emergence of the horse ford, where the enemy logically would cross, he posted his infantry. To protect his rear from surprise, he ordered his cavalry, armed with homemade swords and mounted on draught horses, to a position several hundred yards back from the river on a slight hillock.

Robert Henry, recovered from the bayonet thrust he took at King's Mountain, had started to go to school when the news of Cornwallis' advance brought out the local militia. Mr. Beatty, the schoolmaster, dismissed his school, and Robert again shouldered his squirrel rifle and went to fight the British, this time accompanied by his brother Joseph:

When about to start, I gave . . . a hundred-dollar Continental bill for a half pint of whiskey. My brother gave another . . . for half a bushel of potatoes. We dispatched the whiskey. Being thus equipped, we went to the [Cowan] Ford, which was about a mile and a half.

When we arrived, the guard . . . thirty in number, made us welcome. The officer of the guard told us that Cornwallis would certainly attempt to cross that night or early in the morning; that each one of the guard had picked their stands to annoy the British as they crossed, so that when the alarm was given, they would not be crowded, or be in each other's way, and said we must choose our stands. . . . I chose the lowest, next the getting-out place [of the wagon] ford . . . and was well pleased. . . . I could stand it, until the British would come to a place the water was riffling over a rock; then it would be time to run away.

I remember that I looked over the guard to see if there was any person with whom I was acquainted and found none but Joel Jetton, and my lame schoolmaster . . . with my companion, Charles Rutledge. . . .

Shortly after dark, a man across the river hooted like an owl and was answered. A man went to a canoe some distance off and brought word from him that all was silent in the British camp.[3]

However all was not quiet long in the British camp. At one o'clock in the morning of the first of February, Cornwallis awakened his troops and started a march toward the river, intending to force a crossing at dawn. His plan was that which had succeeded so well at Long Island and Brandywine, an outflanking movement. Lieutenant Colonel James Webster, in command of a division including most of the artillery and wagons, was to march to Beattie's Ford. By a vigorous cannonade, he was to create a diversion, while the main body under Cornwallis himself was to march to Cowan's Ford, "then slightly guarded," thought Cornwallis, and make a crossing.

At daybreak the head of Cornwallis' column reached the bank of the Catawba. Through the thick early-morning mist rising from the muddy waters, the redcoats saw the lights of many fires twinkling on the far shore, indicating that the strength of the defenders was greater than they had anticipated. The plan of cannonading the American camp had to be relinquished when it was discovered that the firing match was carried by one of the men who had been left behind in the woods with an overturned gun. But Cornwallis, recognizing that the rain then falling would soon render the river again impassable, thus giving his opponent time to further strengthen his position, ordered his vanguard into the water, while he himself, reported a British sergeant, "according to his usual manner, dashed first into the river, mounted on a very fine spirited horse."

On the opposite shore, said militiaman Robert Henry:

> The guard all lay down with their guns in their arms and all were sound asleep at daybreak, except Joel Jetton, who discovered the noise of horses in deep water. The British pilot, [a Tory named Dick Beal, being deceived by our fires, [instead of turning with the horse ford] had led them into swimming water [in the wagon ford].
>
> Jetton ran to the ford. The sentry being sound asleep, Jetton kicked him into the river; he endeavored to fire his gun, but it was wet. Having discovered the army [he] ran to our fires . . .cried, "The British! The British!" and fired a gun.
>
> Then each man ran to his stand. When I got to my stand, I saw them red, but thought from loss of sleep, my eyes might be mistaken. [I] threw water into them. By the time I was ready to fire, the rest of the guard had fired. I then heard the British splashing and making a noise as if drowning.[4]

The sleep was soon out of Robert Henry's eyes:

> I fired and continued firing, until I saw that one on horseback had passed my rock in the river . . .I ran with all speed up the bank. . . .
> All being silent on both sides, I heard the report of a gun at the water's edge, being the first gun fired on the British

side . . . which I thought Dick Beal had fired at me. That moment [Colonel William] Polk wheeled his horse and cried, "Fire away, boys! There is help at hand."[5]

Down at the emergence of the horse ford, General Davidson had heard the firing of the guard at the wagon ford and hurried his men to the scene of action. This reinforcement did not influence Henry's decision:

> Turning my eye around, designing to run away, I saw my lame schoolmaster, Beatty, loading his gun by a tree. I thought I could stand it as long as he could and commenced loading. Beatty fired, then I fired, the heads and shoulders of the British being just above the bank. They made no return fire. Silence still prevailed. I observed Beatty loading again. I ran down another load. When he fired, he cried, "It's time to run, Bob."
>
> I looked past my tree and saw their guns lowered, and then straightened myself behind my tree. They fired and knocked off some bark from my tree.
>
> In the meantime, Beatty had turned from his tree, and a bullet hit him in the hip. . . . He fell, still hallowing for me to run. I then ran at the top of my speed about one hundred yards, when a thought struck me that the British had no horsemen to follow me. . . .[6]

By the time Davidson's men came up, the redcoats had scrambled up the bank, loaded their muskets, and opened fire. He was withdrawing his men from the river's edge to the cover of the undergrowth when a ball struck him in the breast and he fell dead. The militia then broke and ran so fast that, one of them admitted, they made "straight shirt tails."

Cornwallis marched his dripping troops to join Webster's at Beattie's Ford and sent Tarleton in pursuit of the fleeing rebel militia. Ten miles away he dispersed a number of them at Torrence's Tavern with a small loss.

But Morgan again had escaped. By the time Cornwallis was across the Catawba, the wagoner was thirty miles away on the road to Trading Ford on the Yadkin. Greene had remained behind to bring off the miltia after the British had crossed; he waited vainly at a place of rendezvous, about six miles beyond Torrence's Tavern, until midnight, when a messenger arrived to report that Davidson was dead and the militia hopelessly dispersed. Alone he galloped on to Salisbury, whence he ordered Huger, unless he were across the Yadkin and within twenty-four hours' march from Salisbury, to bend his march toward a junction with Morgan at Guilford Court house, rather than at Salisbury.

Before the enemy had crossed the Catawba, Greene had

written excitedly to Huger that he was "not without hopes of
ruining Cornwallis, if he persists in his mad scheme of pushing through the country." Drive on to a junction, he urged,
and "desire Colonel Lee to force a march to join us. Here is a
fine field and great glory ahead." But now he knew that the
fights at Cowan's Ford and Torrence's Tavern, minor though
they were, would entirely discourage the militia from joining
him, and he would be forced to continue his retreat out of
North Carolina without standing to the enemy. Then, he determined, he would tease Cornwallis along, pull him farther
and farther from his supply bases; eventually an opportune
moment to engage him would arise.

Cornwallis, hoping to overtake Morgan before he could
cross the Yadkin, destroyed more of his baggage, doubled the
teams, and mounted more of his infantry. As he neared the
Yadkin beyond Salisbury, hope of catching his game must
have flared high when his advance units came on Morgan's
rear and took a few wagons. But when he reached the river,
he was chagrined to find his adversary again across the
water. Boats had been awaiting Morgan, through the foresight
of Greene and the energies of his quartermasters; Cornwallis
saw them "secured on the other side."

The ford was impassable for two days, but the hard-driv-
ing Britisher sent scouts in canoes across the river to find
out the direction Morgan was taking. When they reported
that Greene planned a junction of his forces at Guilford,
Cornwallis concluded that Greene, "not having had time to
collect the North Carolina militia and having received no
reinforcement from Virginia . . . would do everything in his
power to avoid an action on the South side of the Dan" on
the Virginia border. "It being my business to force him to
fight," Cornwallis reported to his superior, "I made great expedition to get between Greene and the fords of the Dan."

Greene and Morgan now forced their men, on short rations
and in a steady rain, to Guilford, where they were met by
Huger with the barefoot troops from the Pee Dee. Even to
Sergeant Major Seymour of the Delawares, who himself was
far from well-clad, the newcomers seemed in "a most dismal
condition for the want of clothing, especially shoes," and
perhaps here he learned that in the South, as well as on the
icy roads of Jersey, American foot-soldiers left bloody tracks
on the frozen roads.

At Guilford, Greene was obliged reluctantly to allow General Morgan to leave for home, his sciatic discomfort compli-
cated by such painful hemorrhoids that he could not sit his
horse. With his army reunited, Greene called a council of
war to consider a stand with his two thousand men against

Cornwallis' twenty-five hundred, but his officers unanimously advised him to avoid an action and to continue northward.

To do so presented a new problem: Cornwallis was within twenty-five miles of Guilford and as near as Greene to the shallow crossings of the upper Dan River. But Colonel Carrington assured his commander that he could assemble sufficient boats to cross the army at Boyd's and Irwin's ferries on the lower river. Cornwallis already had been informed that Greene would not be able to collect enough boats on the lower river and was endeavoring to intercept him before he could reach the upper fords. Upon Carrington's information, Greene resumed his march, sending out toward Salem, westward in the path of the enemy, an elite light corps of some seven hundred men, under Colonel Otho Williams, to cover the army's rear and screen its movements in a manner which would convince Cornwallis that its destination indeed was the upper Dan.

The next days, every officer in Greene's army knew, would see a race whose outcome might determine the fate of the South. If Greene were overtaken and defeated, Cornwallis' way would be open to a junction with the British in Virginia. Once that had been achieved, the contest in the South would be at an end.

Greene besought Patrick Henry, ex-governor of Virginia, to use his influence to turn out at least fifteen hundred volunteers to join him in Virginia, and on the ninth sent off his first units toward the Dan.

For five tense days, with his rear guard almost never out of sight of the enemy's van, often drawing up to force him to deploy and then flying once more, Greene raced Cornwallis for the Dan. On the fourteenth, the mud-spattered, exhausted rebels won. When Cornwallis reached the rushing waters of the river every boat was on the farther shore.

Greene's army was safe, but it was a scarecrow army, hungry, ragged, and depleted of strength. The rapidity of British movement had prevented the embodiment of the North Carolina militia, and the militia already with the army had deserted in droves as it made its way to the Dan. Many captains and majors were listed among those absent without leave. By the time the army reached Virginia, only eighty North Carolina militia remained in service. Greene's disgruntled aide, Lewis Morris, Jr., wrote, "The militia . . . gave us no assistance. They were more intent upon saving their property by flight than by embodying to protect it."

Cornwallis had chased Greene out of the Carolinas. From Virginia to Florida, the Southern states belonged to the King.

But in losing the race to the Dan, Cornwallis had lost nearly a month of valuable time. He had extended his line of communication and supply 230 miles from his base. His troops were sorely in need of the supplies and provisions he had burned at Ramsour's Mill and Cowan's Ford, and in too weak condition to enter so powerful a state as Virginia. The depredations of his army had aroused the enmity of the country, and he could never hope to be supplied where he was. Even if he were better equipped and supplied, he had no boats with which to cross the Dan; he could not use the upper fords, for Greene could oppose him, and then, if necessary, fall all the way back to eastern Virginia, join with Steuben and far outnumber him. Cornwallis had allowed himself to be outgeneraled and outmaneuvered in a campaign which even the arrogant Tarleton admitted "was judiciously designed and vigorously executed" by the Rhode Island Quaker, Nathanael Greene. To retreat now would dishearten every Tory in the South.

Said Cornwallis:

My force being ill-suited to enter . . . so powerful a province as Virginia, and North Carolina being in the utmost confusion, after giving the troops a halt of one day I proceeded by easy marches to Hillsboro, where I erected the King's Standard and invited by proclamation all loyal subjects to repair to it and to . . . take an active part in assisting me to restore order and constitutional government.[7]

Greene retreated as far as Halifax Court House in Virginia, where Virginia militia flocked in. Within three days after his passage of the Dan, he was writing Francis Marion, "the people of this country appear to be in earnest. I hope we shall soon be able to push Lord Cornwallis in turn." He also learned that General Andrew Pickens was approaching the Dan with militia from both North and South Carolina, and that now many North Carolinians were marching to join him. On February 18, he sent Lee and his Legion back across the river to co-operate with the South Carolinian in watching Cornwallis, annoying small bodies they might encounter, and serving as a check on the activities of the Tories in the section. While Greene conducted a patisan warfare, Cornwallis' position at Hillsboro became untenable. Various reasons were given for his abandonment of the camp there, but his own commissary, Charles Stedman, thought that the one principal cause was the utter impossibility of supporting the army in the tiny Carolina capital:

There being few cattle to be had in its neighborhood

and those principally draught oxen, Lord Cornwallis had
promised that they should not be slaughtered but in case of
absolute necessity; but that necessity did exist and compelled the author to direct that several of the draught oxen
should be killed. This measure, . . . caused much murmuring
amongst the loyalists, whose property these cattle were. Most
of the cattle in the neighborhood of Hillsboro had been consumed by the Americans who held a post for a very considerable time in that town. . . .

Lord Cornwallis could not have remained as long as he
did at Hillsboro had it not been for a quantity of salt beef,
pork, and some hogs found in the town. Such was the situation of the British army that the author, with a file of men,
was obliged to go from house to house . . . to take provisions
from the inhabitants, many of whom were greatly distressed
by this measure, which could be justified only by extreme
necessity.[8]

The North Carolina Tories upon whom Cornwallis placed
so much dependence failed him. "Our experience," he wrote
Germain, "has shown that their numbers are not so great as
had been represented and that their friendship was only pas-
sive."

On February 23, Cornwallis heard that Greene, heavily reinforced by Virginians, had that day recrossed the Dan into
North Carolina. He recalled Tarleton, and three days later,
marched from Hillsboro across the Haw River to a place
near Alamance Creek, better to protect "the body of our
friends" said to be assembling.

Greene, when he decided to re-enter North Carolina and
take post near Hillsboro to discourage reinforcements from
joining the British, sent Otho Williams, with the same light
troops he had led in the retreat, back across the Dan. Williams was told to keep himself always between the British
and the main American army and to harass Cornwallis if
he should retreat toward Wilmington, a supply base. Cornwallis immediately moved to drive in the light troops and to
attack Greene "if an opportunity offered," before all the militia he knew Greene was expecting should arrive.

At 5:30 in the morning, March 6, Cornwallis moved
toward the American camp on Haw River. The outposts of
Williams' force moved before him toward the ford at Wetzell's Mill on Reedy Fork Creek, while Greene, informed of
Cornwallis' approach, began to march away. As on the retreat to the Dan, Williams frequently deployed at a defile or
a watercourse, slowed the enemy, and then moved on.

For ten or twelve miles the cat-and-mouse game continued,
until Williams came on a ground that suited him for a stand.

Coming up to him, Cornwallis deployed light troops and after a noisy action in which about twenty men fell on each side, Williams resumed his retreat. For another five miles there was a running action, until Cornwallis gave up, and the rebels were safe again.

The activities of Lee and Pickens and the scrap at Wetzell's Mill were no more important than the actions at Cowan's Ford and Torrence's Tavern, but they had an effect on Cornwallis' strength similar to that of the earlier actions upon Greene's. Now the loyalists crept home, and American militia poured into Greene's camp.

Of Cornwallis' quick shift across the Haw, Greene wrote Washington:

> This maneuver occasioned me to retire over the Haw River and move down the North side of it . . . to secure our stores coming to the army and to form a junction with several considerable reinforcements of Carolina and Virginia militia and one regiment of Virginia eighteen-months men on the march from Hillsboro to High Rock. . . . Our militia had been upon such a loose and uncertain footing ever since we crossed the Dan that I could attempt nothing with confidence, though we kept within ten or twelve miles of the enemy for several days.[9]

While Greene moved along the north bank of the river toward a position near High Rock Ford, Cornwallis held to a parallel course on the opposite shore. The earl declared he was "determined to fight the rebel army if it approached," in order to demonstrate to North Carolina loyalists the superiority of British arms. When he came to the Quaker meetinghouse at New Garden in the forks of the Deep River, he encamped until Greene should move.

It was mid-March. In North Carolina the weather had begun to turn warm; at least some days were almost as hot as summer, and the dogwood and the redbud had begun to splash the oak and pine forests with blossoms. The long, dreary winter rains had given way to dashing showers and sunshine. Soon the yellow warbler would return to the woods to join the year-round singers. It was an optimistic season: the blistering heat of summer had not yet enervated the body, nor had drought or rot or bug destroyed the sweet labors of spring.

St. George Tucker, a young Virginian who had risen from private to major of militia, was on his way toward Greene's army with the reinforcements. He and the rest of his comrades-in-arms now began to feel that their spring promised new glory. To his wife he wrote:

The lark is up, the morning gray, and I am seated by a smoky fire to let my dearest Fanny know that her soldier is as blithe as the mockingbird which is at this moment tuning his pipe within a dozen yards of me. If the fatigues of the remainder of the campaign sit as well upon my limbs as those which I have hitherto experienced, you may be assured that I shall return to Cumberland the most portly, genteel fellow that the country will be able to boast of.[10]

37

"THE SWEETS OF LIBERTY AND GRACE"

Guilford Court House

MARCH 15, 1781

THE MILITIA, which had been upon such "loose and uncertain footing," grew rapidly in strength in the few days Greene was north of the Haw. General John Butler, with his North Carolinians, and Colonel Richard Campbell, with a small detachment of eighteen-month men from Virginia, joined the army on the eighth of March. They were followed in a couple of days by more North Carolinians under General Robert Lawson, and four hundred Maryland Continentals.

Greene, however, was not deceived into believing he had a dependable reinforcement. On the tenth he wrote to Governor Jefferson of Virginia:

The militia have flocked in from various quarters, but they come and go in such irregular bodies that I can make no calculations on the strength of my army or direct any future operations that can ensure me success. A force fluctuating in this manner can promise but slender hopes of success against an enemy regulated by discipline and made formidable by the superiority of their numbers. Hitherto I have been obliged to practice that by finesse, which I dare not attempt by force.[1]

This very tendency of the militia to "get tired out with difficulties and go and come," was a principal reason for making an attempt against Cornwallis while the American force was large. "The great advantages which would result from the action if we were victorious," Greene wrote the Commander-in-Chief, "and the little injury if we were otherwise, determined me to bring on an action as soon as possible."

Greene was keenly aware that his enemy was of similar mind and in an even worse situation. Cornwallis had allowed Greene to lure him out of a secure position, and his food problem was as critical as that of the Americans. A move toward the comparative safety of the seacoast would open his rear to harassment, if not to attack. He wanted a contest of arms, but he could not bring it on: with the fords of the Dan to the rear of the American army, there was no way in which he could force the rebels to a stand. But, as Greene said to Washington in great good humor, "When both parties are agreed in a matter, all obstacles are soon removed."

On the thirteenth, Major St. George Tucker, whose militia now had joined the army, again was on the march, and he wrote to his wife:

> We marched yesterday to look for Lord Cornwallis, who probably marched a different route because he did not choose to fight us. We are now strong enough, I hope, to cope with him to advantage. Our army in . . . strength is rather better than I expected, in . . . numbers, less than what is probably represented in your part of the world, for one-half is much too small to allow for lies nowadays. . . . I should conclude that we had about six thousand men, of which, I believe fifteen hundred are regulars. But this is all conjecture, for we little folks walk about with a bandage over our eyes and with wool in our ears.[2]

Greene's force was nearer 4,300—2,600 of them militia, 1,600 Continentals, and 160 cavalrymen of Lee's and William Washington's legions. But with it he was "determined to advance towards the enemy and give them battle upon the first favorable opportunity." So he turned up Troublesome Creek and across country to the tiny village of Guilford Court House. It was thickly settled farm country they traversed, but the Delaware men wondered how the Carolinians could abide such generally unproductive acres. The only things that favorably impressed the Yankees were some fine grain fields and the friendliness of the affable Scotch-Irish natives along the way.

Guilford Court House was the place where the main army had effected its junction with Morgan on the retreat to the Dan. Its advantages as a battlefield for militia had impressed Greene then. He reached the village on the fourteenth, in time to survey the ground and to resolve to meet

Cornwallis on it. He sent Henry Lee and his legion with the militia under Colonel William Campbell along the road toward New Garden meetinghouse to observe the enemy. In the evening, after camp was made, the army's baggage rumbled off to Speedwell Furnace, the iron works on Troublesome Creek, and Greene and his officers sat down to councils that took up much of the clear, cold night.

Cornwallis, meanwhile, had heard during the fourteenth that Greene's reinforcements had brought his strength up to nine or ten thousand and that he had moved to Guilford, some twelve miles northeast from his own camp. He sent off his baggage and marched at daybreak to meet Greene or attack him in his encampment.

A light frost settled in the night, and at Guilford the rebels awoke to a cold but crisp morning. Lee had reported to Greene "a general movement" of the enemy, but it was nearly noon and the columns were deploying for action when the distant rattle of gunfire sounded from the direction Lee had ridden the night before. Ere long a courier galloped in with a report for the general: Lee had met Tarleton in advance of the British army, had driven him in with some loss, and was falling back on the American main body. Cornwallis was four miles away, advancing rapidly. Greene's dispositions were made, and he calmly awaited the eager Briton.

The courthouse stood on the brow of a domesticated hill in the midst of a wilderness. The Great Road from Salisbury to Hillsboro came from the southwest, through a sharp depression whose shoulders were densely wooded, and debouched into undulating forest. Soon it passed through a fenced clearing, turned a little north of east, climbed half a mile of slope into clearings on the right and left in an oak forest. On the left, in a grove, the courthouse sat in a right angle formed by the road to Reedy Fork running off hard from the main road. To the right of the main road, about a quarter of a mile, was a wooded elevation beyond which lay another bearing away east of north.

In disposing his troops for the battle that he sought, Greene had borne in mind a recent letter from Daniel Morgan who was working his way painfully home through Virginia. If the militia fights, the old wagoner said, "you will beat Cornwallis; if not, he will beat you and perhaps cut your regulars to pieces. . . ." A "number of old soldiers" were said to be among the militia. Select them and put them in the ranks with regulars, Morgan had advised. Fight the riflemen on the flanks. Put the militia in the center "with some picked troops in their rear with orders to shoot down the first man that runs. If anything will succeed, a disposition of this kind will."

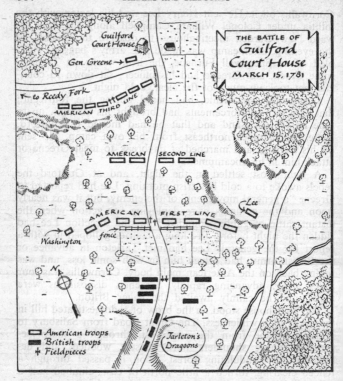

THE BATTLE OF
*Guilford
Court House*
MARCH 15, 1781

Guilford
Court House

Gen. Greene →

← to Reedy Fork

AMERICAN THIRD LINE

AMERICAN   SECOND LINE

Lee

AMERICAN   FIRST LINE

Washington   *fence*

N

◻ *American troops*
◼ *British troops*
✛ *Fieldpieces*

*Tarleton's
Dragoons*

So Greene established his first line, composed of North Carolina militia, across the main road behind the zigzag rail fence on the high side of the clearing that lay five hundred yards from the opening of the defile. The right flank was supported by light infantry of Washington's legion and by Virginia riflemen, formed at an obtuse angle to the ends of the militia line, so that their fire would enfilade the enemy as he came toward the fence. The left flank was supported similarly by Lee's Legion and Campbell's rifles. Many of these were the troops that had met Cornwallis' advance and fallen back on the courthouse. Thus the first line looked downhill over freshly planted corn into an excellent field of fire. On the road, in the center, were two light fieldpieces.

The second line, about three hundred yards behind the first, also was militia, but of hardier experience than the North Carolinians. They were Lawson's and Stevens' Virginians, many of them discharged Continentals with a number of supernumerary Continental officers at their head.

Greene placed his third and principal line—the cream of his forces, his Continentals—in a curve along the brow of the courthouse hill, about five hundred and fifty yards behind the second line. The first two lines straddled the road, this third one lay to the right, out of alignment with the others, following the ground. Formed with a double front behind a slight ravine facing a field, Marylands and Delawares were on the left and Virginians on the right. Two fieldpieces stood in the center. The Continentals, with whom Greene would remain during the battle, were a half-mile back of his first line, and the woods cut both the front and the second line from his view.

After posting his army, the general rode along the militia front line; old men liked later to recall that it was past noon, and some said General Greene held his hat in one hand and mopped his forehead with the other. He called out to the men, showing them the strength of their position. "Three rounds, my boys," he shouted, "and then you may fall back."

It remained for Henry Lee to ease the nervous militia. He "rode along the front line from one end to the other, exhorting them to stand firm and not be afraid of the British, for he swore that he had whipped them three times that morning and could do it again."

Then the leaders were gone, General Greene riding back to his post with the Continentals and Lee to the far left. It was not yet one o'clock, and a restive quiet settled over the men, peering toward the spot where the road opened. Major Richard Harrison, from Granville County, North Carolina, hunched against the rail fence and thought longingly of his Anne; this day she was supposed to give birth to a child. Pulling pencil and paper from his pocket, he began scribbling to her:

> . . . It is scarcely possible to paint the agitations of my mind . . . struggling with two of the greatest events that are in nature at the same time: the fate of my Nancy and my country. Oh, my God, I trust them with thee; do with them for the best!

The day seems nearly at hand that will render North Carolina perfectly happy or completely miserable. Our general is a great and good man, his army numerous and apparently confident of victory. . . . If we succeed against Lord Cornwallis, we expect to be discharged instantly, for by that time the Continental troops will eat all the provisions this country and South Carolina afford.

. . . This is the very day that I hope will be given me a creature capable of enjoying what its father hopes to deserve and earn—the sweets of Liberty and Grace.[3]

It was nearly one-thirty before Cornwallis' troops marched into sight and he made his disposition for the attack. On his right he placed General Leslie's Brigade, on his left Webster's, and in reserve O'Hara's. His artillery, two three-pounders, was advanced up the road, and Tarleton's Legion cavalry held in column on the road to the rear. In all, he had at his disposal about twenty-two hundred men. In Webster's Brigade was Sergeant Roger Lamb, who had escaped from Burgoyne's Convention troops back to the British army and had been sent South. After the brigade was formed, he wrote:

. . . Colonel [Webster] rode on to the front and gave the word, "Charge!" Instantly, the movement was made in excellent order, in a smart run, with arms charged. When arrived within forty yards of the enemy's lines, it was perceived that their whole force had their arms presented and resting on a rail fence . . . They were taking aim with the nicest precision. . . .

At this awful period, a general pause took place. Both parties surveyed each other for the moment with the most anxious suspense. Nothing speaks the general more than seizing on decisive moments: Colonel Webster rode forward in the front of the Twenty-third Regiment and said . . . "Come on, my brave fusiliers." . . . They rushed forward amidst the enemy's fire. Dreadful was the havoc on both sides. . . . At last the Americans gave way and the brigade advanced to the attack of their second line.[4]

When the crimson line swept into the field, muddy from recent rain, Colonel Lee deplored:

To our infinite distress and mortification, the North Carolina militia took to flight, a few only of Eaton's brigade excepted, who clung to the militia under Campbell which, with the Legion, manfully maintained their ground. Every effort was made by . . . the officers of every grade to stop this unaccountable panic, for not a man of the corps had been killed or even wounded. . . .All was vain; so thoroughly confounded were these unhappy men that, throwing away arms, knapsacks, and even canteens, they rushed like a torrent headlong through the woods.[5]

Captain Anthony Singleton wheeled his two six-pounders and rushed them up the road to the left flank of the third American line. Although the militia sprinted away, the

American flank supports stood, and as the huzzaing red-coats pressed over the rail fence and across the field, they met a "most destructive fire" enfilading their line. To advance without staggering losses, Cornwallis was obliged to meet the oblique rebel flankers face to face. Webster with his light infantry and German jägers wheeled to the left, and on the other end of the British line, Leslie's Highlanders and Regiment von Bose swung to the right; his reserve moved into his center. The American right fell back steadily to a position on the flank of the Virginians of the second line; on the left, however, Lee and Campbell with one company of North Carolinians which had not fled drifted all the way to the wooded hill a half-mile beyond the road.

Cornwallis re-formed and moved forward against Greene's second line. "At this place," observed Colonel Tarleton, "the action became more severe." The Virginians stood. "Posted in the woods," said Stedman, "and covering themselves with trees, they kept up for a considerable time a galling fire, which did great execution." Gradually, however, the American right wing swung back like a door until it was at a right angle with the left. Corpulent General Stevens took a ball in the thigh and was carried from the field. Then, Major Tucker wrote home, "we discovered them in our rear." He recounted:

This threw the militia into such confusion that, without attending in the least to their officers who endeavored to halt them and make them face about and engage the enemy, Holcombe's regiment and ours instantly broke off without firing a single gun and dispersed like a flock of sheep frightened by dogs. With infinite labor, Beverley [Tucker] and myself rallied about sixty or seventy . . . and brought them to the charge. Holcombe was not so successful. He could not rally a man, though assisted by John Woodson, who acted very gallantly.

With the few men which we had collected, we at several times sustained an irregular kind of skirmishing with the British and were once successful enough to drive a party for a very small distance.[6]

The Virginians on the left held stubbornly for a time, until Cornwallis himself led the redcoats against them, and they began to fade back through the trees toward the third line. British Sergeant Lamb had paused to replenish his cartridge pouch from that of a slain redcoat. When he looked about, he said:

I saw Lord Cornwallis riding across the clear ground. His Lordship was mounted on a dragoon's horse (his own having been shot). The saddlebags were under the creature's belly, which much retarded his progress, owing to the vast quantity of underwood that was spread over the ground. His Lordship was evidently unconscious of his danger. I immediately laid hold of the bridle of his horse and turned his head. I then mentioned to him that if his Lordship had pursued the same direction, he would in a few moments have been surrounded by the enemy and perhaps cut to pieces or captured. I continued to run alongside of the horse, keeping the bridle in my hand, until his Lordship gained the Twenty-third Regiment, which was at that time drawn up in the skirt of the woods.[7]

According to Colonel Lee:

Persevering in his determination to die or conquer, the British general did not stop to concentrate his force, but pressed forward to break our third line. The action never intermitting on his right was still sternly maintained . . .with the rifle militia and the Legion infantry, so that this portion of the British force could not be brought to bear upon the third line, supported by Colonel Washington at the head of the horse and Kirkwood's Delaware company [which had fallen back from the first line to the right flank of the third].

General Greene was well pleased with the present prospect, and flattering himself with a happy conclusion, passed along the line exhorting his troops to give the finishing blow.

Webster, hastening over the ground occupied by the Virginia militia, sought with zeal the Continental line and presently approached its right wing. Here was posted the First Regiment of Maryland commanded by Colonel [John] Gunby, having under him Lieutenant Colonel [John Eager] Howard. The enemy rushed into close fire. But so firmly was he received by this body of veterans, supported by [Colonel Samuel] Hawes's regiment of Virginia and Kirkwood's company . . . (being weakened in his contest with Stevens' brigade and as yet unsupported, the troops to his right not having advanced from inequality of ground or other impediments) that with equal rapidity he was compelled to recoil from the shock.

Recrossing a ravine to his rear, Webster occupied an advantageous height, waiting for the approach of the rest of the [British] line.[8]

Tarleton considered that "at this period the event of the action was doubtful and victory alternately presided over each army." At this moment, Greene might have thrown his cavalry against the disordered enemy and driven home an attack by the Continentals to match the charge of Morgan's men at Cowpens; the enemy might have been routed. But it was not in Greene's plans to hazard all his army on a single attack; Morgan had been able to gamble a detachment, Greene could not gamble the only army the Americans had in the South. So Webster was allowed to recover. According to Henry Lee:

> Very soon Lieutenant Colonel Stewart, with the first battalion of Guards, appeared in the open field, followed . . . by the remaining corps, all anxious to unite in the last effort. Stewart, discovering [Colonel Benjamin] Ford's regiment of Maryland on the left of the First Regiment [commanded by Gunby] (and a small copse of wood concealing Gunby) pushed forward upon Ford, who was strengthened by Captain [Samuel] Finley with two six-pounders. Colonel [Otho] Williams, commanding the Maryland Line, charmed with the late demeanor of the First Regiment, hastened toward the Second, expecting a similar display and prepared to combine his whole force with all practicable celerity, when, unaccountably, the Second Regiment gave way, abandoning to the enemy the two fieldpieces.[9]

The First Maryland, according to Henry Lee, came to the rescue:

> Gunby, being left free by Webster's recession, wheeled to his left upon Stewart, who was pursuing the flying Second Regiment. Here the action was well fought; each corps manfully struggling for victory, when Lieutenant Colonel Washington, who had upon the discomfiture of the Virginia militia, placed himself upon the flank of the Continentals, . . . pressed forward with his cavalry.
> Stewart beginning to give ground, Washington fell upon him sword in hand, followed by Howard with fixed bayonets, now commanding the regiment in consequence of Gunby being dismounted. This combined operation was irresistible.[10]

When Stewart was struck down, his battalion was driven back. Desperately, the British field guns "opened upon friends as well as foe." This cannonade checked the rebels, who retired "leisurely," as the enemy gained ground on the right and turned Greene's left flank. Greene considered his object won: he had crippled the enemy severely, and he now ordered a retreat.

The last gunfire to fade away was far to the rebel left, where riflemen under Campbell and the infantry of Lee's Legion had fought in the woods around the eminence to which they had withdrawn when the first line had collapsed.

Despite the early spring, this March 15 was a chilly day. As the rebels marched from the field, toward Reedy Fork

Creek, abandoning their fieldpieces because their draught horses were dead, clouds began to gather overhead. For a short distance British units pursued, but were soon recalled. Greene paused beyond the creek to allow his stragglers to catch up, and then marched all night to the iron works on Troublesome. Behind him Cornwallis claimed the field, one made the more awful by the coming of night. Lee described it:

> The night . . . was rainy, dark, and cold. The dead unburied, the wounded unsheltered, the groans of the dying and the shrieks of the living, cast a deeper shade over the gloom of nature. The victorious troops, without tents and without food, participated in sufferings which they could not relieve. The ensuing morning was spent in performing the last offices to the dead and in providing comfort for the wounded. . . . The British general regarded with equal attention friends and foes. As soon as this service was over, he put his army in motion for New Garden, where his rear guard with his baggage met him. All his wounded, incapable of moving (about seventy . . .) he left to the humanity of General Greene.[11]

Day was breaking, wet and gray, when Greene's heavy-legged army trudged into the old encampment at the iron works. The general was as exhausted as any private. For six weeks he had not removed his clothes or slept in a bed. But his fatigue was lessened by a cheerful, gossipy new letter from his vivacious wife and by the regimental reports that began to come into his tent. For a time he feared that although he had inflicted a severe blow on his enemy, his action had been in fine "unsuccessful," that the earl might gather himself up from the battlefield of Guilford and march on him again. So all day long, under the pelting rain, he had his men dig earthworks in the clay soil of the bluffs over Troublesome Creek. As the day passed, however, the general's optimism mounted and with it that of his men. His loss at Guilford, he was led to believe, was "very trifling," as he wrote Thomas Jefferson, "not more than three hundred killed, wounded, and taken," while that of the enemy from the best intelligence he could obtain was at least six hundred, and he had "encumbered them with a number of wounded."

Greene revised his figures when he learned that to his loss must be added a full thousand of the North Carolina and Virginia militia disappeared after the battle—"gone home," Greene snapped, "to kiss their wives and sweethearts." Also he had lost his entire artillery, four brass fieldpieces.

But of the 2,200 Cornwallis had brought to action on the

fifteenth, 11 officers and 88 men were killed, 18 officers and 389 men wounded, and 26 missing. Although he had fought valorously and well against a very superior force, his proportionate loss, particularly at the officer level, was so great that he was paralyzed.

From Troublesome Creek, Greene wrote Sumter before the sixteenth was out that the "army are in the highest spirits and wishing for another opportunity of engaging the enemy." The British "purchase" of the field "was made at so great an expense," he declared, "that   I hope it may yet effect their ruin." Two more days confirmed his opinions. It became apparent that Cornwallis did not have the power to disturb him, and it appeared that the earl must retire as soon as he cared for his wounded. But at the same time, Greene sagely noted that Cornwallis "will not give up this country without being soundly beaten." If only, he thought, the militia had behaved! He expressed his caustic opinion of them so freely that his friend, Joseph Reed, cautioned him that an attitude of superiority on the part of Continental officers would alienate "the bulk of the country." He suggested that Greene look upon the militia as he would upon an unloved wife: "Be to their faults a little blind, And to their virtues very kind."

The rebels lay several days resting and reassembling at Speedwell Iron Works, awaiting the enemy's move, while British energies were consumed in care for the wounded and burial of the dead, and British bellies rumbled for food. From the time of their supper the night before the battle, the redcoats were without sustenance for forty-eight hours; when finally their supply wagons churned through the mud to Guilford on the afternoon of the sixteenth, they brought so little that the daily ration was established at one-quarter pound of flour and the same of beef.

The unknown strength of the rebels, rumored to be greater than it was, and the near impossibility of obtaining food in so "exhausted" a country, led Cornwallis to decide to pull back to the friendly Scottish settlement at Cross Creek, and all the way to his shipping at Wilmington, if necessary, "by easy marches, that we may procure the necessary supplies for further operations and lodge our sick and wounded where proper attention can be paid to them." He had hoped that the loyalists would join him, and he issued a glorious proclamation claiming a "compleat victory" and inviting them to come in. But "many . . ." he said later, "rode into camp, shook me by the hand, said they were glad to see us, and to hear that we had beat Greene, then rode home again." On Sunday, the eighteenth, he began his disheartening march of a hundred miles to Cross Creek. His condition attested the truth of Horace Walpole's observation on the Battle of Guilford Court House: "Lord Cornwallis has conquered his troops out of shoes and provisions and himself out of troops."

Two days later, when Greene learned that the earl was on the march for Bell's Mills, he wrote to Daniel Morgan, "We shall follow him immediately with a determination for another brush." As he decamped, he knew that the enlistment time of many of his men was expiring, and he must back his foe into a fight soon. He sent Lee's Legion ranging ahead of his army to gain intelligence of the enemy's condition and movement and to disturb his flanks. When that vigilant officer reported Cornwallis encamped at Ramsey's Mill on Deep River, to ease the wounded, secure provisions, and build a bridge, Greene ordered him to cross and dispute the enemy's passage of the river until the main army could come up and attack from the rear. But while Greene's ragged army pressed forward on the squelching roads, Cornwallis crossed the Deep uncontested and struck out for Cross Creek.

The course of the fleeing redcoats through the coastal plain of North Carolina was chronicled in detail by a planter named William Dickson, who wrote a cousin in Ireland:

> The whole country was struck with terror; almost every man quit his habitation and fled, leaving his family and property to the mercy of merciless enemies. Horses, cattle, and sheep, and every kind of stock were driven off from every plantation, corn and forage taken for the supply of the army and no compensation given, houses plundered and robbed, chests, trunks, etc., broke; women and children's clothes, etc., as well as men's wearing apparel and every kind of household furniture taken away. The outrages were committed mostly by a train of loyal refugees, as they termed themselves, whose business it was to follow the camps and under the protection of the army enrich themselves on the plunder they took from the distressed inhabitants who were not able to defend it.

> We were also distressed by another swarm of beings (not better than harpies). These were women who followed the army in the character of officers' and soldiers' wives. They were generally considered by the inhabitants to be more insolent than the soldiers. They were generally mounted on the best horses and side saddles, dressed in the finest and best clothes that could be taken from the inhabitants as the army marched through the country.[12]

Ignoring their general's entreaties against "the Shamefull and Dangerous practice of plundering and Distressing the Country," Cornwallis' tatter-demalion redcoats—hungry, shoeless, and annoyed by little Whig gangs—trudged to Cross Creek, found it barren, and pushed on to Wilmington.

"MISCHIEF IS A-BREWING"

Greene in South Carolina

APRIL 1781-DECEMBER 1782

When Nathanael Greene led his men, muddy, famished, and exhausted, into camp at Ramsey's Mill, on the twenty-ninth of March, the day after Cornwallis had left that ground, he gave up pursuit. He had little choice'; the Virginia militia clamored to go home now that its time was up; no recruits were in prospect to bolster his sagging strength; and except for some little left-behind British beef that his men wolfed, offal and all, there was no food to be found in the stripped region around the mill, nor could he hope to feed an army in the wake of the redcoats' course eastward through the pine barrens.

"I am at a loss what is best to be done," the Quaker general confessed to Washington. Nevertheless, in "this critical and distressing situation," he said resolutely:

> I am determined to carry the war immediately into South Carolina. The enemy will be obliged to follow us, or give up their posts in that state. If the former takes place, it will draw the war out of this state and give it an opportunity to raise its proportion of men. If they leave their posts to fall, they must lose more there than they can gain here. If we continue in this state, the enemy will hold their possessions in both.[1]

The principle that dictated Greene's decision, his aide, William Pierce, did not fail to observe, "was the same that actuated Scipio when he led the Carthaginian hero out of Rome to the plains of Zama."

In South Carolina, the British had become discouragingly strong. Charleston still was securely occupied. To protect the great port and to suppress the angry rebelliousness of embattled Whigs in the interior, strong posts had been established at Georgetown, Camden, and Ninety-Six. They were supported by a string of lesser posts—Fort Watson, Fort Motte, and Fort Granby—running northwestward along the Santee and its tributaries. South on a fork of the Edisto was

a garrison at Orangeburg, and on the upper waters of the Savannah, a strong post at Augusta. Thus they covered the country:

In the absence of Cornwallis from South Carolina, Lord Rawdon commanded in the field. He was the agreeable but ugly young officer, now twenty-six, who had distinguished himself from Bunker Hill to Camden as aide to Sir Henry Clinton, as adjutant general of the British army, and as colonel commandant of a loyalist corps, the Volunteers of Ireland. His force in South Carolina and Georgia was slightly in excess of eight thousand men, although only about fifteen hundred of them could be considered a striking force. These he commanded personally at Camden.

To dislodge Rawdon and to master the other enemy posts, Greene could rely upon only about fifteen hundred Continentals. To achieve success he would have to depend further upon the partisans who for months had been harassing the enemy in South Carolina. During the next few days, then,

Greene wrote letters. He begged rum of the governor of North
Carolina: "Without spirits the men cannot support the fatigues of the campaign." He ordered up ammunition and
urged repair of damaged arms. He asked North Carolina militia general Lillington to "keep up the spirits of the people,"
and he sent a courier galloping off to General Sumter with
orders to co-operate and to notify Generals Pickens and
Marion to collect all their men. He desired Sumter to join
him before Camden, Pickens to invest Ninety-Six, and Marion—joined with Colonel Lee—to break down intermediate
posts and sever the communication of Camden with Ninety-
Six and with Charleston. "But the object must be a secret to
all except the generals," he cautioned Sumter—"otherwise
the enemy will take measures to counteract us." If all went
well, before he arrived, "all their small outposts" would fall
to the partisans, supported by the horse and detachments of
light infantry from his army. Sanguinely, he watched his couriers ride off and "Light-Horse Harry" Lee with his Legion depart to join Francis Marion.

Cautiously Greene insured as best he could against Cornwallis' turning into Virginia, where Lafayette had just arrived
to assume Continental command from Steuben, whom
Greene had left there in November. Soon the forces in Virginia would be strengthened by the arrival of Anthony
Wayne's Pennsylvanians. If Cornwallis were to make what
appeared to be a sustained drive northward, Greene planned
to surrender command of the Southern army to General
Isaac Huger and himself rush northward to command the men
opposing Cornwallis. To cover his rear while he marched
south, he ordered out General Jethro Sumner with his North
Carolina militia.

While Lee drifted toward Cheraw Hill in South Carolina to
create for Cornwallis the impression that he still was Greene's
object, Greene broke up from Ramsey's Mill on the sixth of
April and marched for South Carolina. The war of posts
which Greene now developed was a campaign of celerity and
imagination. None of its actions, unless perhaps the culmi-
nating one, was on the grand scale of any of the earlier battles of the war or even of King's Mountain or Cowpens or
Guilford, but coming to the enemy after the staggering jolt of
King's Mountain and the murderousness and attrition of Cowpens and the race for the Dan, it led to Cornwallis' destruction as surely as if Greene himself had held a pistol to his
enemy's heart.

Greene's first objective for his new campaign was to contain Rawdon at Camden while Lee joined his Legion with
Francis Marion's ragged but tough brigade against the post at

Fort Watson, and while Andrew Pickens assaulted Augusta. Greene hoped to come unexpectedly upon Camden and starve it into submission by blockade, because he had no "battering cannon" and not enough men to storm its defenses. But reports of his approach outran him; when he encamped north of the town on the nineteenth of April, he discovered it had been reinforced. Thereupon he took an advantageous position about a mile and a half north, on Hobkirk's Hill, a narrow sandy ridge running east to west, hoping to lure Rawdon out to battle.

The main road from Charlotte to Charleston, called the Great Road, crossed the hill and ran straight into the center of Camden. Thick trees on both sides of the highway, at places ninety feet wide, provided cover for the troops. Because of the forest and the contours of the hill, there was no clear view from the summit toward town.

On the morning of the twenty-fifth, Greene's troops, who had completed morning exercises, were scattered—cooking rations or bathing or washing clothes in a nearby stream. It was about ten o'clock, and Greene was sitting down to a cup of coffee in his tent when he heard the quick, stabbing fire of his pickets. Rawdon had stolen a march on him. By a wide detour from Camden, he had marched toward the hill from the direction of the creek and swamps on the east and approached on a narrow front. Samuel Mathis, a Camden citizen on British parole, that morning was on a relative's farm a few miles away and heard "a very heavy fire of cannon and musketry." He set down what witnesses told him:

Kirkwood's muskets gave the first alarm to the Americans, several of whom . . . had to run a considerable distance before they got to their arms, which were stacked in the very line they had to form. . . .

The Virginia Brigade with General Huger at its head . . . took the right. The Maryland Brigade led by Colonel [Otho] Williams, the left. Thus all the Continentals, consisting of four regiments much reduced in strength, were disposed in one line, with the artillery . . . on the road in the center. The reserve consisted of the cavalry under Colonel Washington . . . and the North Carolina militia. . . .

General Greene . . . directed Colonels Campbell [of the Virginians] and Ford [of the Marylands] to turn the enemy's flanks and ordered the center regiments to advance with fixed bayonets upon him ascending the hill, and detached Colonel Washington's cavalry to gain the rear.

The British when they first attacked . . . pressed directly forward and succeeded in turning our left. Their left had displayed towards our right under cover of thick woods and

could scarcely be seen . . . until they began to rise the hill,
. . . about a hundred and fifty . . . yards from bottom to
top. Their cavalry had reached the Great Road and advanced in close order and slow step up the hill directly in
front of our cannon which . . . opened on them. . . . Can-
nister and grape did great execution and soon cleared the
road. . . . Washington's cavalry . . . completed the rout of
[their horse] . . . took . . . alas! too many prisoners . . .
who hindered their acting when necessary.

Here the battle was equal or rather in our favor and only
one word, a *single word*, and that only because it was spoken
out of season, turned the fate of the day.

Our [extreme] left was somewhat turned or yielding. . . .
The left of the British, at least their cavalry, were routed.
. . . Although our left was giving way, yet General Huger on
our right was gaining ground and was beginning to advance
upon the enemy, and Colonel Gunby's . . . veterans of the
Maryland Line [on the left] . . . were well formed and in
good order.

But too impatient waiting the word of command, some of
them had begun to fire in violation of orders, and seeing
the British infantry coming up the hill in front of them,
Colonel Gunby suffered them to come up within a few paces
and then ordered his men to charge without firing. Those
near him, hearing the word first, rushed forward, whereby the
regiment was moving forward in the form of a bow.

Colonel Gunby ordered a "halt" until the wings should become straight. This turned the fate of the day. Previously
being ordered not to fire and now ordered to "halt," while the
British were coming up with charged bayonets, before the
colonel could be understood and repeat the charge, the enemy
were in among them and made them give way. . . .

The scene was quickly changed. Washington's dragoons
were now attacked by horse and foot, and the very prisoners that they had mounted behind them seized the arms of
their captors and overcame them. General Greene now ordered a retreat and pushed on Washington's cavalry to Sanders Creek, which lay four miles in the rear, to halt the
troops and stop the stragglers, should there be any either
from the militia or regulars attempting to make off.[2]

That night Greene's army bivouacked at Sanders Creek,
scene of Gates's defeat, and two days later moved to Rug-
eley's Mill, where prospects for forage were better.

Officers and men sought the cause of the sudden collapse
of the American army, more than a match for Rawdon's in
strength, and they thought they found it in the conduct of
Colonel Gunby, who asked for a court of inquiry. The court
judged his personal behavior "unexceptionable," but consid-

ered his order to his regiment to halt or retire—to straighten the lines, Sam Mathis was told—"in all probability the only cause why we did not obtain a complete victory." Otho Williams moaned in a letter to his brother:

Many of our officers are mortally mortified at our late inglorious retreat. I say mortally because I cannot doubt but some of us must fall in endeavoring the next opportunity to re-establish our reputation. Dear Reputation! what trouble do you not occasion, what dangers do you not expose us to![3]

But Greene, though chagrined and disappointed, wrote Marion he would invest Camden "in a day or two again," and Steuben that "this repulse, if repulse it may be called, will make no alteration in our general plan of operations."

Elsewhere that plan was working smoothly. On the night of the fourteenth, the rough-and-ready fighters of the swarthy, diminutive militia general, Francis Marion, who had been summoned by Greene's courier from a swampy wilderness hideaway near the meeting of the two Pee Dee rivers, joined Lee's Legion on the banks of the Santee. The next afternoon, a quiet Sunday, the combined corps strode out of the dense pine forest and invested the enemy post, Fort Watson, on the Santee. It was a stockaded work atop an old Indian mound. Without cannon they were unable to reduce it until a country major of Marion's Brigade struck upon a device warring ancients had used, a log tower from which riflemen commanded every part of the fort. Hopeless, 109 officers and men surrendered, and the post was leveled.

Greene was still in front of Camden when Lee and Marion arrived before their next objective, Fort Motte, a depot for convoys from Charleston to Camden, on a ridge near McCord's Ferry on the Congaree River. Motte was the fortified and stockaded brick-and-stone mansion house of the widow Rebecca Motte, who had been evacuated by the enemy to her overseer's house across a little valley to the north. From the sixth of May until the eleventh the besiegers dug siege lines. Then, fearful that Rawdon, rumored to be evacuating Camden, would arrive to relieve the post, Lee and Marion with Mrs. Motte's permission fired the house with pitch balls or fire arrows to smoke out the garrison. The dwelling was saved by the fire-fighting of the attackers, and that night, Harry Lee always remembered, the captured commandant and his officers "accompanied their captors to Mrs. Motte's and partook with them of a sumptuous dinner, soothing in the sweets of social intercourse the ire which the preceding conflict had engendered." The romantic Virginia socialite was enchanted:

The deportment and demeanor of Mrs. Motte gave a zest to the pleasures of the table. She did its honors with that unaffected politeness which ever excites esteem mingled with admiration. Conversing with ease, vivacity, and good sense, she obliterated our recollection of the injury she had received; and though warmly attached to the defenders of her country, the engaging amiability of her manners left it doubtful which set of officers constituted these defenders.[4]

Meanwhile, Rawdon, on the tenth, gave up Camden, and was marching toward Charleston for, he said later, "the unwelcome intelligence" that the "whole interior country had revolted" and that Lee and Marion had taken Fort Watson and were investing Fort Motte revealed the folly of his endeavoring to hold the advance post at Camden.

The partisans upon whom Greene was depending were in full career. Vinegary Thomas Sumter, who steadfastly had refused to join Greene but had gone off on a war of his own in the west, had taken Orangeburg the night before Motte surrendered, and hawk-faced Andrew Pickens was laying siege to Augusta. With the evacuation of Camden, Greene headed his army for Ninety-Six, ordered Lee to take Fort Granby, and Marion to ride Rawdon's flanks as he retreated to see that the shrewd young nobleman did not turn back on Greene's rear. Like a spring tornado, Lee swept thirty miles up the Congaree, took Granby, and on Greene's orders turned south to assist Pickens and Georgia Colonel Elijah Clarke at Augusta. When Marion considered Rawdon "safely" into Monck's Corner, he dashed to Georgetown and drove out its garrison on May 29; then he began patrolling the lower Santee. On the fourth of June, the large garrison of Augusta—over three hundred men commanded by an embittered local Tory—surrendered, and the next day Lee was proceeding "with expedition to join Greene, twenty-five miles away at Ninety-Six."

One after another the enemy posts had flicked out like candles in Greene's whirlwind campaign. At Ninety-Six, however, he struck a snag.

When Lee's Legion arrived in Greene's camp before Ninety-Six, the rebel army had been there eighteen days—days of hot, hard labor for the besiegers, and tough, unshaken resistance by the defenders of that last British stronghold in the interior of the Carolinas and Georgia. Although the post had been left exposed by Rawdon's evacuation of Camden (he had ordered its commandant to abandon it but his messenger had been intercepted), it was strong enough to withstand a long siege. The whole town was surrounded by a rectangular stockade protected by a ditch and abatis. At the easterly corner of the stockade, connected but separate, was a roughly circular redoubt called the Star, and to the west stood a separate fort with two substantial blockhouses to cover the riverlet that ran between it and the the stockade and supplied water for town and garrison.

When Greene, with less than a thousand men, had reached Ninety-Six, his complete inexperience with siege operations or protocol had got him into immediate trouble. Without summoning the garrison, he had ordered his engineer to stake out lines, and Kosciuszko rashly opened ground the first night within eighty yards of the Star. In the morning the garrison sallied, routed the fatigue parties and guards, and leveled the works. The next night Kosciuszko opened a parallel at the much more respectful distance of four hundred yards. The ground "approached very much to soft stone," and it was June 3 before the second parallel was completed and Greene demanded the garrison's surrender. His flag was returned, and when Lee rode in on the eighth, a third parallel was almost finished and a tower like the one used at Fort Watson was rising within thirty-five yards of the enemy's abatis. At Lee's suggestion, Greene also opened ground on the opposite side of town near the outfort.

A few days later came word from Sumter that Rawdon had been reinforced from an English fleet at Charleston and was moving upcountry, probably to relieve Ninety-Six. Greene desperately tried every means to effect a quick capitulation, but though suffering terribly from thirst after the rebels had cut off their water supply, the garrison successfully defended itself from successive efforts to fire the outfort, from fire-arrows shot into the barracks' roofs, from a mine under the Star, from the wooden tower, and finally, on June 18, from a heavy assault on the outfort and the Star. Two days later, after losing 57 killed, 70 wounded, and 20 missing, Greene moved off northeastward to avoid being caught between Rawdon and the 550-man garrison of Ninety-Six. At first, he hoped to draw in enough militia and partisan forces to meet Rawdon on the march, but reluctantly he was forced to admit to Henry Lee, "It is next to impossible to draw the militia of this country from the different parts of the state to which they belong . . . and all I can say . . . is insufficient to induce them to join us."

Rawdon fell back to Orangeburg, however, and Greene learned that Ninety-Six was evacuated on July 3. Rawdon himself, a frail man, gave over command to Lieutenant Colonel Alexander Stewart and returned to Charleston. Once more, though tactically defeated, Greene had achieved his strategic objective. "In hopes to force the enemy at Orangeburg to retire into the lower country," he sent Sumter, Marion, and Lee to raid low down into the country behind Rawdon, while he turned northward to the High Hills of Santee "to refresh the army."

The weary troops sorely needed rest. The whole campaign had been a hungry one. "Rice furnished our substitute for bread," said Henry Lee, "which although tolerably relished by those familiarized to it from infancy was very disagreeable to Marylanders and Virginians who had grown up in the use of corn or wheat bread. Of meat we had literally none. . . ." By the time they reached Orangeburg, he said, nearly half the army was sick and incapable of duty, and Captain Robert Kirkwood of the Delawares carefully computed that the light troops had marched some 771 miles in the cloying heat of the Carolina summer since they had left their ground at Ramsey's Mill and turned back to South Carolina.

The High Hills of Santee began about twenty miles above the meeting of the Congaree and the Wateree rivers. From one to five miles wide, they ran twenty-four miles up the east bank of the Wateree. They were only two hundred feet high, but upon their broad backs, refreshing to the eye, were vast corn and cotton and grain fields, and to rest the gaunt, scorched, hairy bodies of the fatigued rebels were cool, fresh chestnut and oak groves watered by springs and streams.

Balmy airs by day and cool winds by night quickly restored the fever-racked veterans of the cypress swamps and miasmic river bottoms and burning roads of the low country. Here the wonderful days passed, slow and unmeasured, though severely disciplined—filled with morning drill, sunrise until eight—afternoon drill, five until sundown—and roll call four times a day. It was a clean camp, with tents "regularly pitched," necessaries dug properly and used and cleaned, and rubbish burned or buried. Passes were few. And one sundown a Maryland sergeant died before a firing squad for insubordination, and another time deserters were hanged. But withal, it was a time for rest and sport and letter-writing. While the torrential summer rains drummed over the low country, and rivers and streams flooded the lowlands, and all military operations stood still, Greene made an army again of his rabble on the healing, green hills.

On the twenty-third of July, from the High Hills of Santee, William Pierce wrote confidently to a friend:

We are gathering a respectable force together, and perhaps before many weeks shall pass away, we shall again be struggling in some bloody conflict. Mischief is a-brewing by the general, who keeps us in constant hot water, and never fails to make us fight.[5]

Exactly a month later to the day, the army marched from its long camp, good-naturedly bemoaning the end of its summer idyll.

For the six weeks that Greene's exhausted warriors had lolled on the High Hills and recruited their strength up to nearly two thousand, Colonel Stewart with a force of about two thousand was encamped only sixteen miles away, crowflight, on the west side of the Congaree near deserted Fort Motte. It was a short distance, but two great rivers lay between the armies and were so flooded as to seem enormous lakes. It would take a wide circuit to reach the enemy from the High Hills, but by the third week of August, Greene was ready to go for him again.

In the cool of the predawn darkness, on the twenty-third of August, Greene's long, thin line—talkative, jaunty, rested, and confident—filed northward as if away from the enemy, until it crossed the Wateree at Camden. Abruptly, the columns swung southward down the west bank of the river. They marched only in the cooler hours, to escape the midday sun, and on the thirtieth reached Howell's Ferry on the Congaree. Nearly ninety miles they had come around the inundated canebrake, only to learn that their quarry had moved off, down toward Eutaw Springs, forty miles southeast. Resting a few days at Fort Motte, ordering in his detachments, Greene moved after the British force.

On the night of the seventh of September, Greene reached Burdell's Tavern, seven miles from the enemy camp. At Laurens' plantation, during the day, he had picked up Marion's Brigade. His full strength now was about twenty-two hundred, including North and South Carolina militia. He had learned that Stewart's force, all battle-tested and about equal to his own, lay in fancied security at Eutaw Springs, ignorant of his approach. So many of Stewart's men were deserters from American regiments, and so many of Greene's now were deserters from the enemy, that Greene was led to remark that by now "we fought the enemy with British soldiers and they fought us with those of America."

Eutaw Springs was a delightful spot of great rural charm just left of the road from Monck's Corner to Nelson's Ferry, not far from the ferry crossing. Here two springs erupted from a subterranean stream and flowed into Eutaw Creek

that ran between steep, thicketed banks into the Santee at
the ferry. A fine brick house, two stories and an attic, stood
close by the head of the creek, looking upon a large clearing
of about eight acres, which was palisaded and split by the
east-west River Road. Near the house, the road sent off a fork
toward Charleston. Tied to the house, between it and the
creek, was a palisaded garden. Stewart had encamped within
the great clearing. All about were oaks and cypresses, open
like a public forest. But by the creek the blackjack oaks were
an impenetrable tangle.

The night of the seventh was close and hot. The dead calm
prevailed into the early hours of the eighth, and British
pickets found no one stirring. Later Stewart confessed that he
was utterly unaware of the rebels' nearness; despite his "every
exertion . . . to gain intelligence of the enemy's situation,
they rendered it impossible by way-laying the by-paths and
passes through the different swamps, and even detained different flags of truce which I had sent on public business. . . ."

Long before light, the drum, subdued but insistent, dragged
the sleeping rebels from their blankets. By four, breakfast
was over and packs were made, and the silent men had assembled on the Congaree road before the slumbering shape
of the tavern. Sharply at four, the drums tapped the march:
the cavalry trotted out, and the ghostly columns began moving off at a slow step.

The army marched in four columns. Again Lee's Legion
was in the van, followed by South Carolina militia under
Lieutenant Colonel Henderson. When the enemy was met,
these units were to retreat, Lee covering the right flank of
the front line and Henderson the left. The second column
consisted of North and South Carolina militia under Pickens and Marion. The third was made up of three small brigades of Continentals, from North Carolina, Virginia, and
Maryland. The fourth, the reserve, comprised William Washington's cavalry and Kirkwood's Delawares. Two three-
pounders were disposed with the second column and two
six-pounders with the third.

Dawn came, clear and cloudless. The first rays of sun
warned of a hot day. The road lay through somewhat open
woods, and soon the men were welcoming the shade of the
trees. Otho Williams later told a friend:

We . . . moved in order of battle about three miles,
when we halted, and took a little of that liquid which is not
unnecessary to exhilarate the animal spirits upon such occasions. Again we advanced, and soon afterwards our light

troops met the van of the enemy, who were marching out to meet us.

Very serious, very important reflections began to obtrude. But liberty or death, peace and independence, or glory and a grave![6]

The light troops had not, however, met the enemy van as Williams supposed. At first light, Stewart had sent out a "rooting party" to forage for potatoes. About six o'clock when he had discovered from two rebel deserters that Greene was near, Stewart had sent Major John Coffin with a hundred and fifty foot and fifty horse to bring in three hundred and fifty unarmed foragers. It was Coffin's detachment Lee mistook for the enemy van, and he halted to give the main body time to come up. When Coffin, mistaking Lee's points for a small party of rebel militia, pressed them back on the Legion and the South Carolina militia that made up Greene's advance, a sharp skirmish emptied some enemy saddles and Coffin wheeled about for his camp.

Greene also thought Coffin was the enemy van, and as soon as his men had drained the rum casks, he formed them "with coolness and recollection," and came on slowly down the River Road from the west, his first line deployed and moving up through the sun-dappled woods.

Coffin's precipitous return alarmed the British camp. Quickly Stewart drew his men out of camp into the woods in front in a single line, his own Third Regiment on the right resting on the creek. A little advanced of them, to protect their flank, the light infantry and grenadiers took a position in the blackjack under a splendid soldier, Major John Majoribanks of the Nineteenth Foot. Cruger's loyalists, who had so stoutly held Ninety-Six, took the center, and war-long veterans of the Sixty-third and Sixty-fourth regiments formed Stewart's left. Major Coffin, with what was left of his cavalry, covered this wing, which was in the air. A small body of infantry was held in reserve in the rear. The artillery was posted in the line, except for one piece sent forward with a detachment to skirmish with the American front.

It was nearly nine o'clock when Stewart's detachment appeared in Greene's front with its fieldpiece. Lee sent back for artillery. Captain William Gaines of the Virginians, galloping up the road with two three-pounders, unlimbered and dueled with the enemy gun, while Legion infantry and Henderson's militia volleyed with the enemy foot. The artillery exchange was, said Otho Williams, "bloody and obstinate," until the pieces on both sides were dismounted and disabled.

By now Greene's first line was up: South Carolina militia

under Marion on the right and under Pickens on the left, and North Carolina militia in the center. Fire ran from flank to flank. The enemy left wing, instead of holding its position and awaiting the rebel approach—"by an unknown mistake," confessed Stewart—advanced and drove in the right and center of Greene's first line, but not before it had delivered seventeen rounds and wrung from Greene praise for standing with a firmness that "would have graced the veterans of the great King of Prussia."

To fill the first line, Greene advanced North Carolina Continentals, who came handsomely into action from the right of his second line, and maintained the front with Lee's Legion on the right and Henderson's militia on the far left. When the enemy left fell back to its original position, their reserves came in to steady them, and Greene ordered his second line—Maryland and Virginia Continentals—to advance and meet them with bayonets. He ordered Lee to charge Stewart's left flank, and William Washington from his reserves to fall on Majoribanks who was wreaking havoc on Henderson's flank from the security of the blackjack thicket. Washington's cavalry could not penetrate the wooded ground; they were cut up and defeated and he himself, after becoming entangled with his fallen horse, bayoneted and taken.

Lee's Legion, however, poured a raking fire into the British left, and the Virginians and Marylands charged forward shouting. The Virginians, less experienced, returned the enemy fire, but the Marylands, obedient to orders, trotted forward with trailed arms and shattered the enemy left with bayonets. The shock on the British left soon spread to the center; one by one the redcoat regiments gave way and fled through their camp of tents to the cover of the brick house, which a party had occupied just as Musgrave had occupied Chew's house at Germantown. Stewart's own regiment, the Third, held momentarily on his right. Then it, too, was borne down.

Colonel Otho Williams appointed himself unofficial historian of the action, which Greene later wrote Washington was "by far the most obstinate fight I ever saw. Victory was ours," he said, "and had it not been for one of those little incidents which frequently happen in the progress of war, we should have taken the whole British army." Williams related that incident:

The retreat of the British army lay directly through their encampment, where the tents were all standing, and presented many objects to tempt a thirsty, naked and fatigued

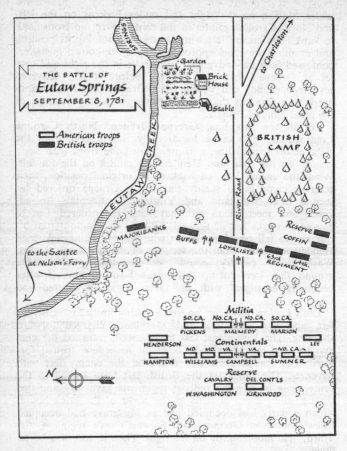

THE BATTLE OF
Eutaw Springs
SEPTEMBER 8, 1781

☐ American troops
■ British troops

to Charleston →

SPRINGS

Garden

Brick House

Stable

EUTAW CREEK

to the Santee at Nelson's Ferry

BRITISH CAMP

River Road

MAJORIBANKS

BUFFS

LOYALISTS

63rd REGIMENT

64th

Reserve COFFIN

Militia

SO.CA.   NO.CA.   NO.CA.   SO.CA.
PICKENS   MALMEDY   MARION

HENDERSON   LEE

Continentals
MD.   MD.   VA.   VA.   NO.CA.
HAMPTON   WILLIAMS   CAMPBELL   SUMNER

Reserve
CAVALRY   DEL.CONT'LS
W.WASHINGTON   KIRKWOOD

N

soldiery. . . . Nor was the concealment afforded by the tents
. . . a trivial consideration, for the fire from the windows of
the house was galling and destructive, and no cover from it
was anywhere to be found except among the tents or behind the building to the left of the front of the house.

Here it was that the American line got into irretrievable
confusion. When their officers had proceeded beyond the encampment, they found themselves nearly abandoned by their
soldiers, and the sole marks for the party who now poured
their fire from the windows of the house.

From the baneful effects of passing through the encampment, only a few corps escaped. Of this number, the Le-

gion infantry appears to have been one. Being far on the
American right, it directed its movements with a view to securing the advantage of being covered by the barn; and the
narrow escape of the British enemy is sufficiently attested by
the fact that this corps was very near entering the house pell-
mell with the fugitives. It was only by closing the door in
the face of some of their own officers and men that it was
prevented; and in retiring from the fire of the house, the
prisoners taken at the door were interposed as a shield to . . .
their captors.

Everything now combined to blast the prospects of the
American commander. The fire from the house showered
down destruction upon the American officers; and the men,
unconscious or unmindful of consequences, perhaps thinking
the victory secure and bent on the immediate fruition of its
advantages, dispersing among the tents, fastened upon the
liquors and refreshments they afforded, and became utterly
unmanageable.

Majoribanks and Coffin, watchful of every advantage, now
made simultaneous movements, the former from his thicket
on the left and the latter from the wood on the right of the
American line. General Greene soon perceived the evil that
threatened him, and not doubting but his infantry, whose
disorderly conduct he was not yet made acquainted with,
would immediately dispose of Majoribanks, dispatched Captain [Nathaniel] Pendleton [his aide] with orders for the
Legion cavalry to fall upon Coffin and repulse him. . . .

In Captain Pendleton's own language: ". . . When I went to
the corps Lee was not there, and the order was delivered to
Major [Joseph] Eggleston, the next in command, who made
the attack without success. The truth is Colonel Lee was very
little, if at all, with his own corps after the enemy fled. He
took some dragoons with him, as I was informed, and rode
about the field, giving orders and directions in a manner the
general did not approve of. General Greene was, apparently,
disappointed when I informed him Colonel Lee was not with
his cavalry and that I delivered the order to Major Eggleston."

By this time General Greene, being made acquainted with
the extent of his misfortune, ordered a retreat.[7]

Back through swirling dust and eddying smoke dove the
rebels, to rally and come to some sort of order in the woods
straddling the road along which they had marched so confidently a little earlier. Greene ordered a strong picket to go
back to the field, and cover parties to bring off the wounded,
except those "too forward under the fire of the house." Dispute the ground, its commanding officer was told. Greene

was convinced that "the enemy could not maintain their
posts but a few hours."

Again Nathanael Greene had stood on the threshold of
triumph. One more push might have won an indisputable
conquest and utterly routed the enemy. But again the Quaker
who had said proudly after his repulse at Camden, "We fight,
get beat, rise, and fight again," could not afford to gamble:
he must save an army for a fall campaign. But his objective
had been accomplished: Stewart was demoralized and certain
to draw back to the coast.

Four long blazing hours Greene's army had lived on that
terrible field, where the fighting had been the most obstinate
the general ever had seen. His powder-blackened, dazed soldiers, sweat-soaked and exhausted, panted for water. The
nearest well was all the way back, seven miles to Burdell's.
There Greene marched them to nuzzle their baked faces in
cool water and to munch ravenously their first meal in twelve
hours. One hundred and thirty-nine of their comrades lay
on the field at Eutaw Springs, 375 had come off wounded, 8
were missing. Their officers had exposed themselves gallantly
and suffered 17 dead, 43 wounded.

Stewart had borne much heavier losses, 866 in all, more
than two-fifths of his force.

Though forced to retire seven miles from the field, Greene
was determined to renew the contest next day. In the morning, he sent Lee and Marion to turn Stewart's left and to
seize the first strong pass on the road to Charleston, to hold
him and to intercept any British reinforcements. A cold
steady rain was falling. The light troops lay in the woods
watching the British camp. Before noon, they saw redcoats
smashing a thousand stand of arms and throwing them into
Eutaw Springs. With considerable pain they watched enemy
details stave in twenty or thirty hogsheads, and pour good
British rum into the inky waters of the creek. Then Stewart's
army formed and struck out along the Nelson's Ferry road.
The Americans followed until the enemy was met by a reinforcement of about four hundred. The rebels nipped at his
heels and took a handful of prisoners and sent word back to
Greene to come get him. But the weather turned hot, and
Greene soon gave up the chase, turned about, and tramped
for the old encampment at the High Hills of Santee.

Both sides claimed victory at Eutaw Springs. Technically,
it was Stewart's: he kept the field. But, as Otho Williams observed, "the best criterion of victory is to be found in consequences, and here the evidence is altogether on the American side." Once again Nathanael Greene had done that which
he seemed to do best: he had fought the enemy, had seen his

chance of total success lost in a blunder, and then had been able to withdraw his army intact and ready to fight another day. Ever since he had come to the Southern Department, his enemies had claimed victory after every engagement, but after each had been forced to draw in their lines. Once more, they did so.

Greene was soon to come down again out of the High Hills of Santee to rattle his sword at the very gates of Charleston, but Eutaw Springs was the last great battle in the deep South. The only places the British Union now flew in the South were Charleston and Savannah. Though Whig and Tory murdered each other with unrelenting bitterness for more than a year longer, and brisk bloody raids took men slashing and shooting through the dank swamplands, and more Continentals came grumbling from the North to do duty in "a country as hot as the antechamber of Hell," the question of ultimate victory was settled. On the day following Eutaw Springs, a French fleet sailed into Chesapeake Bay in Virginia and sealed the fate of the ambitious earl whom Greene had sent into a faraway trap at a village called Yorktown.

At last in South Carolina, in May of the year after Eutaw Springs, a lieutenant of the Pennsylvania Line noted in his journal, "Everybody full of peace," and through that spring and summer and fall loyal Nathanael Greene kept his little army in an arc around Charleston and waited for the day the redcoats would take their leave.

39

"A SUCCESSFUL BATTLE MAY GIVE US AMERICA"

The Virginia Campaign

MAY-AUGUST 1781

IN HIS comfortable headquarters at Wilmington, whence he had come from the Guilford battlefield two weeks ago, Earl Cornwallis bent his wattled face over the letter he was writing to the Secretary of State for the Colonies, Lord George

Germain. He dated it "23 April, 1781." His uneven hand-writing spread across the sheet:

> My Lord, I yesterday received an express . . . informing me . . . that Major General Phillips had been detached into the Chesapeake with a considerable force with instructions to co-operate with this army and to put himself under my orders. This express likewise brought me the disagreeable accounts that the upper posts of South Carolina were in the most imminent danger from an alarming spirit of revolt among many of the people and by a movement of General Greene's army. . . .
>
> The distance from hence to Camden, the want of forage and subsistence on the greatest part of the road, and the difficulty of passing the Pee Dee, when opposed by an enemy, render it utterly impossible for me to give immediate assistance. And I apprehend a possibility of the utmost hazard to this little corps, without the chance of a benefit, in the attempt. For if we are so unlucky as to suffer a severe blow in South Carolina, the spirit of revolt in that province would become very general, and the numerous rebels in this province be encouraged to be more than ever active and violent. This might enable General Greene to hem me in among the great rivers and by cutting off our subsistence render our arms useless. And to remain here for transports to carry us off . . . would lose our cavalry and be otherways . . . ruinous and disgraceful to Britain. . . .
>
> I have, therefore, under so many embarrassing circumstances (but looking upon Charleston as safe from any immediate attack from the rebels) resolved to take advantage of General Greene's having left the back part of Virginia open and march immediately into that province to attempt a junction with General Phillips. . . .[1]

The earl reached for a fresh sheet and began a briefer letter to his commander-in-chief, Sir Henry Clinton, at New York:

> Sir, I have the honor to inclose . . . copies of all my letters to the Secretary of State. As they contain the most exact account of every transaction of the campaign . . . of my great apprehensions from the movement of General Greene . . . and my resolutions in consequence of it, I have nothing to add to it for your Excellency's satisfaction.
>
> Neither my cavalry or infantry are in readiness to move. The former are in want of everything, the latter of every necessary but shoes, of which we have received an ample supply. I must, however, begin my march tomorrow. It is very disagreeable to me to decide upon measures so very important and of such consequence to the general conduct of the war,

without an opportunity of procuring your Excellency's directions or approbation; but the delay and difficulty of conveying letters, and the impossibility of waiting for answers render it indispensably necessary.[2]

As Cornwallis wrote those last words, he knew very well that he was glad to have an excuse for not awaiting his chief's directions; they would be quite contrary to his own desires. Although he had not heard from Sir Henry for months—and deliberately had not written him from January until he had come to Wilmington—he was entirely familiar with Clinton's ideas about war in Virginia. Repeatedly, the commander had made them clear. Clinton saw Virginia as a place in which to establish a naval station, a place from which to launch a northward movement against Pennsylvania or the peninsula between Delaware and Chesapeake bays, a place at which North-South rebel communications could be twisted off by a sea-supported base, a place in which to destroy supplies being stock-piled, or troops being gathered for use of the rebels in the Carolinas. Any or all of these things might be done in the Chesapeake, but repeatedly Clinton had warned that Cornwallis should make no move in that direction until he was sure that Charleston, "a primary object," was secure. Until Clinton could spare sufficient men from New York and rely upon Germain for reinforcements, Clinton insisted, Cornwallis never alone should risk a large operation in Virginia.

Cornwallis could not have disagreed more. From the beginning of the campaign in the South, he was convinced that the conquest of Virginia should be the ambition of His Majesty's forces in America. He even had made the extraordinary suggestion to Clinton that such a strategy was worth the abandonment of New York. He had courted Germain with the idea and had won the approval of the Secretary and of the King. If ever he thought of his insubordination as reprehensible, he made no excuses for it. He had tried for months to force his way into Virginia, and had wrecked his army in the attempt, reducing it from thirty-two hundred effectives in January to a mere seven hundred after Guilford. When Clinton sent diversions on his behalf to the Chesapeake, he considered them forces he might use for conquest. He made no effort to inform Clinton of conditions in the Carolinas, so that his baffled chief, who did not know his whereabouts, was unable to formulate any plans encompassing both the forces under Cornwallis and those he was sending to the Chesapeake.

The first expedition to the Chesapeake, in the fall of 1780,

had accomplished nothing, for Cornwallis had drawn it to
Charleston to strengthen his own force after his wing was
destroyed at King's Mountain. In December, when Clinton
learned that his Chesapeake expedition had been ordered to
Charleston, though he could "ill spare it" he sent another
two thousand strong to Virginia under turncoat Brigadier
General Benedict Arnold. Arnold had raided and destroyed
rebel supply dumps on the James and established a base at
Portsmouth. When he was threatened by a French fleet that
sailed from Newport to trap him, Clinton hastily strengthened him with another detachment from New York. With it,
to supersede Arnold, came Major General William Phillips,
Burgoyne's old gunner who had been exchanged for General
Benjamin Lincoln.

Phillips and Arnold now commanded nearly fifty-five hundred men on the Chesapeake, with very little opposition from
the Virginia militia and the twelve hundred Continentals,
which had been sent from the North under the Marquis de
Lafayette. Virginia, thought Cornwallis, was the place for
him, regardless of Clinton's notions. It was not that he had
a fixed plan in mind. Almost two weeks ago he had written
to Phillips in Virginia:

> Now, my dear friend, what is our plan? Without one,
> we cannot succeed, and I assure you that I am quite tired of
> marching about the country in quest of adventures. If we
> mean an offensive war in America, we must abandon New
> York and bring our whole force into Virginia; we then have a
> stake to fight for and a successful battle may give us Amer-
> ica. If our plan is defensive, mixed with desultory expedi-
> tions, let us quit the Carolinas (which cannot be held de-
> fensively while Virginia can be so easily armed against us)
> and stick to our salt pork at New York, sending now and
> then a detachment to steal tobacco, etc.[3]

The earl had not yet heard from Phillips, who probably
was struck dumb by his proposal. Nevertheless, still without
a plan, Cornwallis was ready by the twenty-third to turn his
broad back on Carolina and carry a war into the Old Dominion. The next day, he strode out of the big white house
that for nearly a month had been his home and led his
army, now up to a strength of 1,435 men, toward Virginia.

Three weeks or so along the way, Cornwallis received the
doleful news that Phillips was dead of a bilious fever and
Arnold awaited him at Petersburg. When, on the twentieth of
May, at the end of 223 miles, he took command of the
Royal forces on the Appomattox, his total strength rose to
seventy-two hundred men. Against him were Lafayette,

twenty-three miles away at Richmond with three thousand
Continentals and militia, and Steuben southeast of Charlottesville training five hundred raw Continentals. Lafayette
expected Wayne with the Pennsylvania Line, but he had not
yet left York. Cornwallis, who was a zealous exponent of
"solid operations" in Virginia, should have seized his chance,
crossed the James above Richmond between Lafayette and
Steuben, and destroyed both. But his base was the sea, and
he did not have the daring to chance Lafayette's getting between him and the shore, and he still feared the arrival of a
French fleet. So he limited his objective and wrote Clinton:

I shall now proceed to dislodge Lafayette from Richmond and with my light troops to destroy any magazines or
stores in the neighborhood. . . . Thence I propose to move to
the Neck at Williamsburg, which is represented as healthy
and where some subsistence may be procured, and keep myself unengaged from operations which might interfere with
your plan for the campaign, until I have the satisfaction of
hearing from you.[4]

It was Lafayette who acted with the celerity that Cornwallis
should have exhibited. When the earl crossed the James,
thirty miles below Richmond, on the twenty-sixth, the grave
young Marquis shied teasingly away from him. Lafayette had
no illusions about his danger. Two days before, he had written to Washington on the Hudson: "Were I to fight a battle,
I should be cut to pieces, the militia dispersed, and the
arms lost. Were I to decline fighting, the country would
think itself given up. I am therefore determined to skirmish,
but not to engage too far." And he remarked sagely, "I am
not strong enough even to get beaten!" He retreated seventy
miles to Ely's Ford on the Rapidan River, where he might
make a safe junction with Wayne. Cornwallis followed only
as far as the North Anna River, about thirty miles, and from
there launched two cavalry raids. He sent Tarleton to break
up a meeting of lame-duck Governor Thomas Jefferson and
his legislature at Charlottesville, and John Graves Simcoe to
break up Steuben's troops. Both missions failed of their objectives: Jefferson, forewarned by a night ride of an innkeeper's son, escaped, and Steuben fled southward without
making a stand. Meanwhile, Wayne had marched briskly from
York and joined Lafayette; Cornwallis retreated through
Richmond to Williamsburg. The combined American corps,
joined by Steuben, followed him.

At Williamsburg, with the rebels hovering but a few miles
away, Cornwallis faced anxious letters from his commander-
in-chief. Clinton enclosed intercepted American dispatches by

which, he told his subordinate, "you will observe I am threatened with a siege in this post." He wished Cornwallis, therefore, to take a defensive post—he suggested Yorktown or Williamsburg—with part of his force and to send two thousand men for the defense of Manhattan.

Arbitrarily, Cornwallis took his chief's order to be a further statement of his opposition to the operations in Virginia. Without completely concealing an impatient irritation, he wrote a restatement of his own concepts. He suggested that a purely defensive post in Virginia scarcely would be worth while, and that he might better serve the cause by returning to South Carolina to replace his ailing lieutenant, Lord Rawdon. Nevertheless, he struck off toward Portsmouth as the best embarkation point for the troops he felt compelled to send to New York.

On the fourth of July, Cornwallis set his troops in motion along the narrow shady road to Jamestown, where he would ferry them across the James. Sending out false word by supposed deserters that his main army would cross on the fifth and sixth, and his rear guard on the seventh, he lured Lafayette to battle. Late on the hot, lazy summer afternoon of the sixth, at Greenspring near Jamestown, Anthony Wayne, leading about five hundred Pennsylvanians, jabbed at Cornwallis' rear, covered by Tarleton's Legion.

Tarleton drew back under sharp fire and faded into a thinset pine forest, where he held. Unknown to Wayne, Cornwallis' whole army was drawn up behind those woods, waiting in the hope that Lafayette would bring on his whole force. Instead, the Marquis sent several hundred more Pennsylvanians to Wayne, who moved forward to pounce upon what he thought was a heavy enemy rear guard. Suddenly Cornwallis threw an army out of the woods. With great presence of mind, Wayne hurled his men forward, bayonets level, and momentarily checked the redcoats until he could come off without confusion. Twenty-eight of the rebels had been killed, ninety-nine wounded, and twelve were missing. Lafayette considered the action another example of the Pennsylvanians' "gallantry and talents," but one of Wayne's men wrote home:

I was brought to bed with a disappointment. Another [Bull's Ferry] blockhouse affair. *Madness!* Mad A——y, by G——, I never knew such a piece of work heard of—about eight hundred troops opposed to five or six thousand veterans upon their own ground.[5]

But Cornwallis did not press his advantage. He continued

to Portsmouth, dispatching Tarleton on a four-hundred-mile raid to destroy supplies across Virginia.

The dog days were woeful for the earl: he was showered with tediously expressed, involved letters from Clinton that were contradictory and confusing. The thinly disguised animosities and jealousies that lay between them came breaking through the veneer of rank and station. From Portsmouth, Cornwallis wrote resentfully his objections to Clinton's pointed criticism of his move from South Carolina and his actions since coming to Virginia. Clinton replied with what he intended to be a mollifying but firm letter. Ere long the men were failing to make themselves understood to each other, either haplessly or willfully.

As Clinton vacillated between drawing off forces from Virginia to defend New York or creating a diversion in Philadelphia to turn Washington's attention there, he instructed Cornwallis not to send troops to New York but to Philadelphia; then he ordered them hurried to New York; then he told his subordinate to go to Yorktown; then he suggested Old Point Comfort for a naval base, supported by works at Yorktown; he asked for reinforcements again, but authorized Cornwallis if necessary to keep his whole force.

It was the twentieth of July before Cornwallis received categorical orders from Clinton to take a post and hold it. The site was left to Cornwallis' discretion, though Old Point Comfort seemed still to be Clinton's preference. But the earl examined the ground there in company with his engineers and decided against it. Instead he chose the village of Yorktown, about eleven miles from the mouth of the York. There the river narrowed to less than a mile between the forty-foot marl bluffs over which some seventy houses spread, mostly on a single street, and Gloucester Point, protruding like an arrowhead into the calm tides. On two sides of Yorktown, nearly impassable swamps guarded its approaches.

Here by the twenty-second of August, Cornwallis had concentrated his forces and started throwing up works. He said he chose Yorktown because an anchorage there could be more easily defended than at Old Point Comfort. What he failed to see was that a fleet commanding the sea could cut off escape by water, while a land army could do the same by straddling the peninsula between the York and the James.

After the clash at Greenspring, Lafayette rested his men at Williamsburg and caught up on neglected correspondence with colleagues and friends. He had not been able to write, he explained, because "when one is twenty-three, has an army to command and Lord Cornwallis to oppose, the time that is left is none too long for sleep."

By slow stages, taking time to wash and to rest, the Americans marched to a high, comfortable, well-watered camp at Malvern Hill, halfway between Richmond and Williamsburg. The Pennsylvanians crossed the James to watch the enemy; some Continental cavalry and riflemen under Daniel Morgan, who had come out of retirement, took a position near Petersburg to intercept Tarleton. Tarleton avoided them, and as he rejoined Cornwallis at Portsmouth, operations fell into what the Marquis called "a state of languor."

It was short-lived. While Cornwallis was still at Portsmouth, a letter came from Washington, hinting great new events. The General had joined forces with those of genial Count de Rochambeau at Newport for a proposed attack on New York. But he said, "I shall shortly have occasion to communicate matters of very great importance to you." Meanwhile, the Commander-in-Chief wished his reliable friend to report every move of Cornwallis. When Cornwallis moved to Yorktown, Lafayette established a new camp on the Pamunkey River, and moved still closer to the redcoats when they began digging in the sandy Yorktown soil. Shortly after the middle of August, and following several veiled allusions to an allied concentration in Virginia, a letter from Washington told him that Count de Grasse had cleared the West Indies for the Chesapeake with twenty-nine warships and three thousand men. A reinforcement from the North would follow. The Commander-in-Chief dared not hazard any more information in a dispatch, but a few days later a confidential officer arrived from Northern headquarters and Lafayette learned that a large contingent of Americans and all the French troops from the North were on their way. All he must do, Washington begged, was not let Cornwallis escape.

Behind the Commander-in-Chief's communications lay the culmination of his dreams. For three years he had endeavored to obtain some tangible military benefit from the French alliance. In 1778 the withered fruit of allied co-operation had been the Newport fiasco, in 1779 it had been Savannah, and in 1780 the French fleet had been bottled up in Newport. In May of this year, Washington had been called by Count de Rochambeau to a conference at Wethersfield, Connecticut, where he had been told that Count de Grasse had sailed from Brest for the West Indies and in July would be off the American coast to break the Newport blockade, making possible an assault on New York. In June the rainbow-hued soldiers of France had marched smartly from Newport through the deep green of the New England countryside; in the Greenburgh hills between White Plains and Dobb's Ferry, they had joined the rebels, who, one of the French officers was surprised to see, were "nearly naked, badly paid, and composed of old men, Negroes, and children."

For several weeks the combined forces peered longingly at New York but were too weak to attack it. On the afternoon of the fourteenth of August, the stalemate was broken when a courier brought Washington word that Grasse was bound for the Chesapeake. On the seventeenth, Washington and Rochambeau wrote the admiral that their armies would march southward to co-operate with him in trapping Cornwallis. If the earl should escape, they suggested an attack on Charleston.

The allied generals in front of New York carefully concealed their new plan from Clinton by misleading him into believing that, at last, they were ready to move against him. It was activity wasted, for he never doubted that his enemy's objective was New York alone. He was confident that Cornwallis was safe. Every adviser, including Admiral Thomas Graves, successor to Arbuthnot, and even Germain himself, assured him that he need have no fear of a blow against Cornwallis or himself from the French fleet in the Indies: Admiral Sir George Rodney could handle it. Instead Clinton was busy with his own plans for an attack on the French fleet that remained at Newport and the now lightly garrisoned naval station there. When the allies began crossing the Hudson on the twentieth, he made no effort to interfere.

A French officer was amazed by Clinton's inactivity. "An enemy, a little bold and able, would have seized the moment of our crossing . . . for an attack. His indifference and lethargy at this moment is an enigma that cannot be solved by me."

The armies fanned out, beginning Saturday morning, the twenty-fifth, over three roads down into Jersey, and the march to the Chesapeake was under way. In the Highlands of the Hudson, Washington left only two thousand men to stand guard under General William Heath.

On the second of September, the Continental Army marched through Philadelphia, the two-mile line raising "a dust like a smothering snow." The next day the French followed. While the allied armies were passing through the city of Quakers, thirty-five hundred men disembarked from Grasse's fleet on Jamestown Island and soon joined the forces of Lafayette.

Rochambeau elected to go from Philadelphia to Chester by water to see the sites of the 1777 campaign. On the fifth of September, Washington, finding "everything in a tolerable train here," bade the Count *au revoir* and hastened to prepare for embarkation of the armies at the Head of Elk. Three miles south of Chester, an express met him with dispatches, announcing the arrival in Virginia of Admiral de Grasse. Joy wreathing his face, the General turned his entourage about and rode back to Chester to await Rochambeau's landing to tell to the Count the glorious tidings.

As the French commander's vessel approached the wharf, "I caught sight of General Washington," said Rochambeau, "waving his hat at me with demonstrative gestures of the greatest joy. When I rode up to him, he explained that he had just received a dispatch . . . informing him that de Grasse had arrived. . . ."

From the Chesapeake, victory beckoned at last! It now remained only to race southward and grasp it.

40

"THE PLAY, SIR, IS OVER"

Yorktown

SEPTEMBER–OCTOBER 1781

SPACIOUS, TREE-LINED Duke of Gloucester Street in Williamsburg was crowded those excessively hot September days. Off-duty soldiers strolled under the Dutch elms; Americans and French, in good fellowship, idled away hours in "a view of the town." Even to the sophisticated eyes of the French, the grand sweep of the tree-trimmed green terminating in the enormous, imposing Governor's Palace was as impressive as any European scene. Riders and carriages, military carts and wagons, an occasional bumping field gun, filled the street with sounds, but some quiet reigned under the stately archways of the Capitol behind its rosy brick walls at the far end of Duke of Gloucester.

The campaigners awaiting the arrival of the armies from the North found equally restful the shady college grounds and, beyond, twisting College Creek, where Lieutenant William Feltman of the Pennsylvania Line occasionally "went a crabbing." They amused themselves at billiard tables in the taverns, sat around their quarters "playing whist," sometimes in the evenings "went to a hop." They were proud of their summer's work.

With their enemy cornered for the moment, twelve miles away, and their own strength growing, they were a confident army. Most of the men thought the end for Lord Cornwallis was merely a matter of time—time for allied might to assemble on the peninsula between the York and the James.

On a very warm September afternoon—the fourteenth—a tremor of excitement swept the camps. Drums pulsed insistently, announcing the eagerly awaited arrival of Washington, Rochambeau, Adjutant General Edward Hand, and a few staff members, who rode into the west end of town, a few days ahead of the approaching armies.

In the French camp, the Commander-in-Chief dismounted and courteously waited to give the French who had already arrived time for any reception they might have planned. Soon Lafayette, roused from a sickbed and accompanied by Governor Thomas Nelson and General Claude St. Simon, head of the troops that had come with Count de Grasse, rode full speed up to Washington's party. The Marquis, his long, thin face alight, swung quickly off his horse and rushed toward his General with arms outstretched. To the amazement of several Americans waiting to be introduced, said St. George Tucker, he "caught the General round his body, hugged him as close as it was possible, and absolutely kissed him from ear to ear once or twice . . . with as much ardor as ever an absent lover kissed his mistress on his return."

"The whole army," St. George Tucker told his wife, "and all the town were presently in motion . . . men, women, and children seemed to vie with each other in demonstrations of joy and eagerness to see their beloved countryman."

Lieutenant Ebenezer Denny's Pennsylvania brigade was paraded to receive the General, and the next day the earnest, twenty-year-old lieutenant wrote in his journal:

Officers all pay their respects to the Commander-in-Chief. Go in a body. Those who are not personally known, their names given by General Hand and General Wayne. He stands in the door, takes every man by the hand. The officers all pass in, receiving his salute and shake. This is the first time I had seen the General. . . .

The presence of so many general officers and the arrival of new corps seem to give additional life to everything. Discipline the order of the day. In all directions, troops seen exercising and maneuvering. Baron Steuben, our great military oracle. The guards attend the grand parade at an early hour, where the Baron is always found, waiting with one or two aides on horseback. These men are exercised and put through various evolutions and military experiments for two hours.

Many officers and spectators present. Excellent school, this.[1]

Washington had expected to consult the Count de Grasse immediately upon arriving in Williamsburg. But the Count, he learned, had been busy at sea. On the fifth, Grasse, lying with his fleet in Chesapeake Bay, was signaled by a sentry ship: strange sails off the Virginia Capes. At first, he thought they were Barras' fleet from Newport, but then they were reported to be English. Quickly Grasse slipped his cables and stood out of the bay for sea room. The strangers were nineteen warships, the fleet of British Admiral Thomas Graves. While Washington and Rochambeau were starting their march through the Jerseys, Count de Barras had sailed from Newport with eight ships-of-the-line, four frigates, and eighteen transports, carrying all the French siege artillery to the Chesapeake, and Graves had sailed to catch him. When he looked into the Chesapeake, however, it was not Barras he discovered, but the twenty-four great ships of Grasse.

On the afternoon of the fifth, until darkness put an end to it, the fleets thundered at each other behind curtains of smoke. The next day they scattered. They drifted southward seeking the weather gauge, until they were off the Outer Banks of North Carolina. Once the French gained the wind, but the British "crowded on sail and turned away. . . ." Count de Grasse at last put about and, on the eleventh, was back at his anchorage in Chesapeake Bay. There he found the squadron of Barras, who had taken advantage of the sea-fight to run into the bay. With thirty-two ships-of-the-line, the combined French fleet was far too strong for Admiral Graves, who sailed for New York.

In response to Washington's request for a meeting, Grasse was able to send up the James a trim, little, captured English vessel, the *Charlotte,* to convey the General, Rochambeau, and their staffs out to his ornate, comfortable flagship—probably the largest warship then afloat. It was a friendly conference. Grasse and St. Simon had said that they could not remain in American waters beyond October 15. The admiral now agreed that the fleet and the troops would stay through October. Washington could feel that, surely then, success was in sight. Adjutant General Hand told a home-town crony:

> If he [Count de Grasse] does not leave us, and we can get provisions, our work is sure. Cornwallis employs his army night and day in fortifying York and Gloucester. He has drawn up his ships to the shore, moored them head and stern, landed their guns, and cut up their sails for tents, and has given orders to bury or sink them on the first attack. The moment our troops are landed, we will invest him closely

with at least double his number of regular troops. At present, our advanced post is seven miles from York.[2]

Washington was over four days returning from the admiral's flagship, because of suddenly cool and squally weather, but while he lay fretfully delayed in the James, he could watch the concentration of craft at last coming in from Head of Elk with his armies and his cannon.

The seventeenth to the twenty-seventh were spent debarking troops and materiel, reorganizing the army, and forming a new order of battle. Joseph Plumb Martin was, at last, a sergeant, by virtue of transfer to the hazardous ranks of sappers and miners. The sergeant kept his private's self-assurance and his saving sense of humor when he considered the prospect before him:

> We prepared to move down and pay our old acquaintance, the British at Yorktown, a visit. I doubt not but their wish was not to have so many of us come at once, as their accomodations were rather scanty. They thought, "The fewer, the better the cheer." We thought, "The more, the merrier." We had come a long way to see them and were unwilling to be put off with excuses. We thought the present time quite as convenient (at least for us) as any future time could be, and we accordingly persisted, hoping, that as they pretended to be a very courtly people, they would have the politeness to come out and meet us, which would greatly shorten the time . . . spent in the visit and save themselves and us much labor and trouble.[3]

Lord Cornwallis, however, had not been sparing himself labor on his "accomodations" and was not the least inclined to come out to meet the allies. His outer line around the town was extensive, but well chosen. His inner one, close about Yorktown, was much less advantageous.

It was still dark at five o'clock in the morning on September 28, but daylight was near and the air was fresh and cool. Already the troops in the camps about Williamsburg had eaten their breakfast. They had made their packs and struck their tents and loaded the wagons and formed at the color line. At five the drums beat the "March," and the first units, the advance rifle corps and cavalry guard, moved off by the right. Then the light infantry of the fighting parson, Peter Muhlenberg, a jingling fieldpiece, the rest of Muhlenberg's Brigade. Then Moses Hazen's Canadians, their brown-and-red rusty and frayed. Two more fieldpieces. Wayne's durable Pennsylvanians, another fieldpiece, the Marylands, others. Then the tremendous host of the French along the sandy road to Yorktown. Because it was heavy forest country, just the kind in which an aggressive enemy might jump a marching column, the artillery was spread through the column and not assigned to its usual position in the rear.

A French officer marched with his men:

> The two armies left Williamsburg in a single column and marched in this order for . . . five miles to a fork. . . . Here the Americans took the road to the right, and we arrived in the evening in two columns in sight of York. The place was immediately invested. Some English dragoons came up to see what was going on, but two companies of Grenadiers and Chasseurs were advanced with two pieces of four, which sent them back immediately.[4]

Inside the town was Captain Samuel Graham of the Seventy-sixth Regiment of Foot, who had come to Virginia with his Highland regiment early in the spring. So far he had enjoyed thoroughly the Virginia campaign. Now that he faced besiegement, his ardor only increased, as did that of his comrades:

> On the twenty-eighth September, information was given by a picket . . . that the enemy were advancing in force by the Williamsburg road. The army immediately took post in the outward position. The French and Americans came on in the most cautious and regular order. Some shots were fired from our fieldpieces. The French also felt the redoubt on our right flank, defended by the Twenty-third and a party of marines, but did not persist. The two armies remained some time in this position observing each other. In ours there was but one wish, that they would advance. While standing with a brother captain . . . we overheard a soliloquy of an old Highland gentleman, a lieutenant, who drawing his sword, said to himself, "Come on Maister Washington, I'm unco glad to see you. I've been offered money for my commission, but I could na think of gangin' hame without a sight of you! Come on!"[5]

But the allies did not gratify the Highland gentleman. They shook down for a siege. St. George Tucker was keeping a diary of the events of this campaign. He was convinced that its close "will probably be more important than any other since the commencement of the American war." He did not accept rumors; he determinedly sought out the truth and reported with meticulous accuracy. For the weekend of the twenty-ninth of September he set down:

Sat. 29. This morning about eight o'clock, the enemy fired a few shot from their advanced redoubts, our right wing having now passed over Munford's Bridge. About nine or ten, the riflemen and jägers exchanged a few shot across Moore's Mill Pond, at the dam of which the British had a redoubt. A few shot were fired at different times in the day and about sunset from the enemy's redoubts. We had five or six men wounded, one mortally and two others by the same ball. The execution was much more than might have been expected from the distance, the dispersed situation of our men, and the few shots fired.

Sunday. 30th. This morning, it being discovered that the enemy had abandoned all their advanced redoubts on the south and east ends of the town, a party of French troops, between seven and eight o'clock, took possession of two redoubts on Penny's Hill or Pigeon Quarter, an eminence which it is said commands the whole town. . . .

It is now conjectured by many that it is Lord Cornwallis' intention to attempt a retreat up York River by West Point, there being no ships yet above the town to prevent such a measure.[6]

Allied occupation of Cornwallis' abandoned works brought them close to his inner lines. For a day or two, little activity marked the trailing hours, although the British maintained a fairly steady cannon fire to discourage the initiation of allied siege works. There was much raillery and braggadocio among the ragged Americans, for October brings a lovely time on the Virginia peninsula. Summer humidity has burned away. The days are balmy, the skies fair blue, the nights brisk and full of close stars. And, as the allies began converting the former British redoubts into works of their own, every man began to think that old 'Wallis was in a bottle and the cork about to be driven in. Four men of James Duncan's regiment were cut down by a single cannon ball while with a covering party on the night of October 2. But their dramatic demise did not dampen other spirits, according to Captain Duncan's diary:

A militia man this day, possessed of more bravery than prudence, stood constantly on the parapet and d——d his soul if he would dodge for the buggers. He had escaped longer than could have been expected, and growing foolhardy, brandished his spade at every ball that was fired till, unfortunately, a ball came and put an end to his capers.[7]

The steady booming of Cornwallis' heavy guns was clearly heard by allied detachments on the far side of the mile-wide shimmer of the York. The earl had fortified Gloucester Point

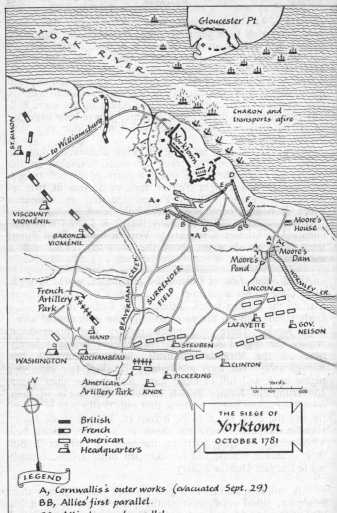

Gloucester Pt.

YORK RIVER

CHARON and
transports afire

Yorktown

St. SIMONS

to Williamsburg

VISCOUNT
VIOMÉNIL

BARON
VIOMÉNIL

Moore's
House

Moore's
Pond

Moore's
Dam

WORMLEY CR.

French
Artillery
Park

BEAVERDAM CREEK

SURRENDER
FIELD

LINCOLN

HAND

LAFAYETTE

GOV.
NELSON

WASHINGTON

ROCHAMBEAU

STEUBEN

CLINTON

N

American
Artillery
Park

KNOX

PICKERING

Yards
100   400   1000

THE SIEGE OF
Yorktown
OCTOBER 1781

British
French
American
Headquarters

LEGEND

A, Cornwallis's outer works (evacuated Sept. 29.)
BB, Allies' first parallel.
CC, Allies' second parallel.
D, Redoubt stormed by Americans, Oct. 14.
E, Redoubt stormed by French, Oct. 14.
F, Battery on extreme right from which Washington fired first sho
G, French battery, first to open fire, Oct. 9.

with a line of entrenchments, four redoubts, and three batteries, mounting nineteen guns. The allies did not attempt to
reduce the Gloucester works by regular approaches. Instead they kept heavy detachments in the country on that side
of the river to discourage British foraging expeditions and to
close it as an escape route. On October 3 after a noisy, brief
collision with British horse while moving nearer the British
works, American militia and French forces closed the point
completely and it ceased to be important in the story of Yorktown.

The next day two deserters fled from Yorktown into the allied lines. They told that Cornwallis' army was "very sickly
to the amount of two thousand men in the hospital and that
the troops had scarce ground to live upon, their shipping in a
very naked state, and their cavalry very scarce of forage."
This was no revelation to Washington and his officers. They
had been able to determine almost as much solely by observation.

Now that the allies had occupied the deserted English positions and reversed the fronts of them, the next step of a
siege operation lay ahead. This was the opening of the first
parallel, in front of the enemy's main defenses, fortified with
artillery batteries.

The ground before Cornwallis' works was studied carefully, Lieutenant Denny observed, at some risk:

> Generals and engineers in viewing and surveying the
> ground are always fired upon and sometimes pursued. Es-
> corts and covering parties stationed at convenient distances
> under cover of woods, rising ground, etc., afford support.
> This business reminds me of a play among the boys, called
> Prison-Base.[8]

Both French and American soldiers busily made fascines
and gabions, and trench depots were established for entrenching tools and materials. After Washington made a personal reconnaissance within three hundred yards of the
enemy on the first of October, he could see no obstacle to
drawing his first parallel, but he reasoned nothing was to be
gained by occupying the ground before all the siege guns were
available. The heavy pieces were being landed on the James
about seven miles from the allied camp. Quartermaster General Timothy Pickering exhausted all his New England in-
genuity procuring horses and ox teams to drag them over
the sandy road to Yorktown.

A dark night was preferred for the secret work of opening
the first parallel, so that the besieged garrison could not see
and attack the workmen. If the work could be kept secret all

night, by morning the trench would be complete enough to protect defenders. However, at Yorktown in early October, when Washington felt ready to open the parallel, the moon was just past full, and he had to chance detection by the garrison unless he was lucky enough to be covered by cloudy weather. By the night of the fifth, enough guns were up and the enterprise was begun. Sergeant Joseph Martin recalled:

One-third part of all the troops were put in requisition to be employed in opening the trenches. A third part of our sappers and miners were ordered out this night to assist the engineers in laying out the works. It was a very dark and rainy night. However, we repaired to the place and began by following the engineers and laying laths of pine wood end to end upon the line marked out by the officers for the trenches.

We had not proceeded far . . . before the engineers ordered us to desist and remain where we were and be sure not to straggle a foot from the spot while they were absent from us. In a few minutes after their departure, there came a man alone to us, having on a surtout, as we conjectured (it being exceedingly dark), and inquired for the engineers. We now began to be a little jealous of our safety, being alone and without arms and within forty rods of the British trenches. The stranger inquired what troops we were, talked familiarly with us a few minutes, when, being informed which way the officers had gone, he went off in the same direction, after strictly charging us, in case we should be taken prisoners, not to discover to the enemy what troops we were. We were obliged to him for his kind advice, but we considered ourselves as standing in no great need of it. For we knew as well as he did that sappers and miners were allowed no quarters, at least are entitled to none, by the laws of warfare, and of course, should take care if taken and the enemy did not find us out, not to betray our own secret.

In a short time, the engineers returned and the aforementioned stranger with them. They discoursed together some time, when by the officers often calling him, "Your Excellency," we discovered that it was General Washington. Had we dared, we might have cautioned him for exposing himself so carelessly to danger at such a time, and doubtless he would have taken it in good part if we had. . . .

It coming on to rain hard, we were ordered back to our tents and nothing more was done that night. The next night . . . the sixth of October, the same men were ordered to the lines that had been there the night before. We . . . completed laying out the works. The troops of the line were there ready with entrenching tools and began to entrench, after General Washington had struck a few blows with a pickaxe, a mere ceremony, that it might be said, "General Washington with his own hands first broke ground at the siege of Yorktown." The ground was sandy and soft, and the men employed that night ate no "idle bread" (and I question if they eat any other), so that by daylight they had covered themselves from danger from the enemy's shot.[9]

The digging was accomplished without molestation largely because the enemy's attention and some fire was diverted to the extreme allied left, next to the river. Here some of General St. Simon's troops threw up a battery to challenge a British one across Yorktown Creek and to disrupt communications between Yorktown and Gloucester.

When daylight came on the seventh, the chagrined redcoats opened an angry fire on the new line without effect. When they brought their mortars into play, recalled Sergeant Martin:

> They had a large bulldog and every time they fired he would follow their shots across our trenches. Our officers wished to catch him and oblige him to carry a message from them into the town to his masters, but he looked too formidable for any of us to encounter.[10]

Fresh laborers devoted the morning to perfecting the trench. The revetments were improved and the ditch dug deeper and wider. A number of guard batteries—field guns— were brought up, while workmen began cutting and fitting wooden platforms for the heavier ordnance.

At noon took place the ceremony that always marked the official opening of a siege. The trenches were to be manned by the divisions of the army alternating on a twenty-four-hour basis. The division commander was to serve in the works as "major general of the trenches" and the division inspector as "major of the trenches." The major of the trenches was to divide the men into fatigue parties and guards. A prescribed decorum, centuries old, demanded that, upon the opening of the trenches, the besiegers march from their camp to the beat of the drum, colors flying, muskets at carry, to the parallel. Entering the parallel, the men shifted their arms to support and marched to their posts, where they planted their flags upon the parapet.

Captain James Duncan, in Colonel Alexander Hamilton's battalion, was among the fifteen hundred troops who relieved General Benjamin Lincoln's division, which had begun the works, and officially opened the trenches. The captain was in for an unexpected thrill, but he found it damnably uncomfortable:

The trenches were this day to be enlivened with drums beating and colors flying, and this honor was conferred on our division of light infantry. And now I must confess, although I was fond of the honor, I had some fear, as I had no notion of a covered way and more especially as I was posted in the center with the colors. We, however, did not lose a man in relieving, although the enemy fired much. The covered way was of infinite service. Immediately upon our arrival the colors were planted on the parapet with this motto: MANUS HAEC INIMICA TYRANNIS.

Our next maneuver was rather extraordinary. We were ordered to mount the bank, front the enemy, and there by word of command go through all the ceremony of soldiery, ordering and grounding our arms. . . . Although the enemy had been firing a little before, they did not now fire us a single shot. I suppose their astonishment at our conduct must have prevented them, for I can assign no other reason. Colonel Hamilton gave these orders, and although I esteem him one of the first officers in the American army must beg leave in this instance to think he wantonly exposed the lives of his men.[11]

Lieutenant William Feltman was on the American lines on the ninth and noted in his diary:

> This morning nine o'clock A.M., a deserter from the enemy's artillery came to us. He left them just as their piece fired. . . . He informed us that Cornwallis had given out orders to them not to be afraid of the Americans, that they had not any heavy pieces of ordnance, except a few pieces of field artillery. He also informed the soldiery and inhabitants that the French fleet was inferior to him and were afraid to attack him, that they came to this place to procure a quantity of tobacco, and if they could not be supplied here that the fleet would set sail in eight or ten days at the farthest and leave the continent. Such are my Lord's addresses to his soldiery, but they have more sense than to believe his weak expressions.[12]

Possibly the British were encouraged to believe something of Cornwallis' estimate of his foe by the curious behavior of persons they could see on the allied lines. Washington's General Orders on the ninth included:

> Persons whose duty does not call them to the trenches and who assemble there merely to indulge curiosity are to walk on the reverse of the trenches, that they may not interrupt the works. The officer superintending the fatigue parties is to be particularly attentive to the execution of this order.[13]

Serving on the British lines was Stephen Popp, a twenty-two-year-old German mercenary from Bayreuth. On the first of August, Popp had noted in his diary that he had reached Yorktown. Only twenty-four hours later he had written that "there are reports that we are in a very bad situation." The ensuing days had given Stephen Popp little rest. He had assumed his role with Teutonic stolidity and would scratch down in his diary such entries as, "Day and night we are at work strengthening our lines. Have hardly time to eat and little food, but we are getting ready to make a stout defense."

That clear, pleasant ninth of October, Popp began his day wondering at "still no firing by the enemy, although we kept discharging our guns at them." Probably the young, untried soldier, inexperienced in siege warfare, did not know that in a siege, batteries did not open fire as they were completed; this would allow the garrison fire to concentrate on a single battery. Besieging batteries remained silent until a sufficient number were ready to return formidable fire, and then the fire was opened ceremoniously.

About three that afternoon, Popp's wonder ceased: the Continental standard was hoisted over the American battery on the right of the allied lines; the white flags of France ran up over the French batteries. "Forty-one mouths of fire were suddenly unmasked." An American officer exclaimed, "Happy day! We return the hostile fire. American and French flags twisted on our batteries." Colonel Philip van Cortlandt, of the Second New York Regiment, later reminisced:

> . . . the first gun which was fired I could distinctly hear pass through the town. . . . I could hear the ball strike from house to house, and I was afterwards informed that it went through the one where many of the officers were at dinner, and over the tables, discomposing the dishes, and either killed or wounded the one at the head of the table. And I also heard that the gun was fired by the Commander-in-Chief, who was designedly present in the battery for the express purpose of putting the first match.[14]

That night, Lieutenant Ebenezer Denny thought:

> The scene viewed from the camp now was grand. . . . A number of shells from the works of both parties passing high in the air and descending in a curve, each with a long train of fire, exhibited a brilliant spectacle.[15]

Not many men watched the fiery tails of the bombs in the air. All night the allies were busy finishing batteries. Early on the tenth, the French Grand Battery opened with ten eighteen- and twenty-four-pounders and four mortars, and the

Americans with four more eighteen-pounders. Stephen Popp finally was impressed by the rebels' vigor:

> The heavy fire forced us to throw our tents in the ditches. The enemy threw bombs, one hundred, one hundred fifty, two hundred pounders; their guns were eighteen, twenty-four and forty-eight pounders. We could find no refuge in or out of the town. The people fled to the waterside and hid in hastily contrived shelters on the banks, but many of them were killed by bursting bombs. More than eighty were thus lost, besides many wounded, and their houses utterly destroyed. Our ships suffered, too, under the heavy fire, for the enemy fired in one day thirty-six hundred shot from their heavy guns and batteries. Soldiers and sailors deserted in great numbers. The Hessian Regiment von Bose lost heavily, although it was in our rear in the second line, but in full range of the enemy's fire. Our two regiments lost very heavily too. The Light Infantry posted at an angle had the worst position and the heaviest loss. Sailors and marines all served in defending our lines on shore.[16]

Captain Graham of the Seventy-sixth Regiment observed that the allied cannonade was so incessant that the British scarcely could fire a gun of their own, their "fascines, stockade platforms, and earth, with guns and gun-carriages, being all pounded together in a mass."

In the afternoon, a flag advanced from the enemy's works, escorting old Thomas Nelson, onetime Secretary of the Virginia Council. His fine house "in the skirt of the town" had been Cornwallis' headquarters and was badly battered. When the earl decided to evacuate for a safer haven, he graciously permitted "Mr. Secretary" Nelson, suffering with gout, to hobble out of town under official protection. The next day, St. George Tucker dined with Mr. Nelson:

> He says our bombardment produced great effects in annoying the enemy and destroying their works. Two officers were killed and one wounded by a bomb the evening we opened. Lord Chewton's cane was struck out of his hand by a cannon ball. Lord Cornwallis has built a kind of grotto at the foot of the Secretary's garden where he lives underground. A Negro of the Secretary's was killed in his house. It seems to be his opinion that the British are a good deal dispirited, although he says they affect to say they have no apprehensions of the garrison's falling.[17]

The crescendo of allied artillery rose as the last of fifty-two pieces of heavy iron was placed on the lines, making, said Adjutant General Hand, "aweful music."

For four days the zigzags had wormed out from the allied parallel toward Cornwallis' works, until on the eleventh they were within 360 yards of the most advanced point of the British defenses. No one knew better than the men digging them that they now were beyond support and the time had arrived for building the second parallel.

At dusk, Steuben's division, furnished with spades, shovels, and grubbing hoes, and carrying fascines, entered the zigzags and at dark began to work on the parallel. Within an hour they had made themselves cover in the soft soil and breathed easier for having it, because, as Captain Duncan observed, "the entire night was an immense roar of bursting shell."

The opening of the second parallel often was the most critical moment of a siege, when the enemy usually sortied. Steuben's guards stood alert through the night, muskets in hand. No one was allowed a shift to sleep or even to sit down. Danger came also from their own lines: the gunners in the first parallel, making overhead fire, cut their fuses too short, and a number of their own shells burst overhead. But morning came without the loss of a single man killed or wounded, and Edward Hand wrote a friend, "As soon as our batteries on the second parallel are completed, I think they will begin to squeak."

On the American right near the river, two advanced British redoubts, called Number Nine and Number Ten, bristling with fraise work above moats and nested in a tangle of abatis, defied the allies to complete their parallel to the shore. All day Sunday, the fourteenth, American batteries concentrated their fire on these strongholds. Early in the evening, American light infantry units prepared to assault Redoubt Number Ten, while French troops stormed Redoubt Number Nine. Lieutenant Colonel, the Count Guillaume de Deux-Ponts, with four hundred men of his own and the Gâtinais regiment—after a tender scene with his brother, the colonel of the Royal Deux-Ponts—awaited darkness and the signal to advance. In reminiscences, he was to write:

The six shells were fired at last, and I advanced in the greatest silence. At a hundred and twenty or thirty paces, we were discovered, and the Hessian soldier . . . on the parapet cried out, "Werda?" to which we did not reply but hastened our steps. The enemy opened fire the instant after the "Werda?"

We lost not a moment in reaching the abatis, which . . . at about twenty-five paces from the redoubt, cost us many men and stopped us for some minutes, but was cleared away with brave determination. We threw ourselves into the ditch at once, and each one sought to break through the fraises and to mount the parapet. We reached there at first in small numbers, and I gave the order to fire. The enemy kept up a sharp fire and charged us at the point of bayonet, but no one was driven back.

The carpenters . . . had made some breaches in the palisades which helped the main body of troops in mounting. The parapet was becoming manned visibly. Our fire was increasing and making terrible havoc among the enemy who had placed themselves behind a kind of entrenchment of barrels, where they were well massed and where all of our shots told. We succeeded at the moment when I wished to give the order to leap into the redoubt and charge upon the enemy with the bayonet; then they laid down their arms and we leaped with more tranquility and less risk. I shouted . . . "Vive le Roi!" which was repeated by all the grenadiers and chasseurs who were in good condition, by all the troops in the trenches, and to which the enemy replied by a general discharge of artillery and musketry.

I never saw a sight more beautiful or more majestic. I did not stop to look at it. I had to give attention to the wounded and directions to be observed towards the prisoners. At the same time, the Baron de Vioménil came to give me orders to be prepared for a vigorous defense, as it would be important for the enemy to retake this work. An active enemy would not have failed, and the Baron . . . judged the English general by himself.[18]

The anticipated counterattack on Redoubt Number Nine never materialized. Meanwhile, to the left, Colonel Alexander Hamilton was attacking Redoubt Number Ten. His forlorn hope, led by a detachment of sappers and miners, under New York Captain James Gilliland, included Sergeant Martin:

We arrived at the trenches a little before sunset. I saw several officers fixing bayonets on long staves. I then concluded we were about to make a general assault upon the enemy's works, but before dark I was informed of the whole plan . . .

The sappers and miners were furnished with axes and were to proceed in front and cut a passage for the troops through the abatis. . . . At dark the detachment . . . advanced beyond the trenches and lay down on the ground to await the signal for . . . the attack, which was to be three shells from a certain battery. . . . All the batteries in our line were silent, and we lay anxiously waiting for the signal. . . . Our watchword was, "Rochambeau." . . . Being pronounced, "Ro-sham-bow," it sounded when pronounced quick like, "Rush on boys."

We had not lain here long before the . . . signal was given for us and the French . . . the three shells with their fiery trains mounting the air in quick succession. The word, "up up" was then reiterated through the detachment. We . . . moved toward the redoubt we were to attack with unloaded muskets.

Just as we arrived at the abatis, the enemy discovered us and . . . opened a sharp fire upon us. We were now at a place where many of our large shells had burst in the ground, making holes sufficient to bury an ox in. The men, having their eyes fixed upon what was transacting before them, were every now and then falling into these holes. I thought the British were killing us off at a great rate. At length, one of the holes happening to pick me up, I found out the mystery of the huge slaughter.

As soon as the firing began, our people began to cry, "The fort's our own!" and it was, "Rush on, boys!" The sappers and miners soon cleared a passage for the infantry who entered it rapidly. Our miners were ordered not to enter the fort, but there was no stopping them. "We will go," said they. "Then go to the d——l," said the commanding officer of our corps, "if you will."

I could not pass at the entrance we had made, it was so crowded. I, therefore, forced a passage at a place where I saw our shot had cut away some of the abatis. Several others entered at the same place. While passing, a man at my side received a ball in his head and fell under my feet, crying out bitterly. While crossing the trench, the enemy threw hand grenades . . . into it. They were so thick that I at first thought them cartridge papers on fire, but was soon undeceived by their cracking.

As I mounted the breastwork, I met an old associate hitching himself down into the trench. I knew him by the light of the enemy's musketry, it was so vivid. The fort was taken and all quiet in a very short time.[19]

Later the skies clouded. All during the night it rained. But allied fatigue parties, going in behind the troops, doggedly labored in the mud. By dawn on the wet and dismal fifteenth, the captured redoubts had been made part of the second parallel, and allied howitzers showed their evil brass mouths within three hundred yards of the enemy works. At New Windsor in June, General Knox had practiced his men in the use of this ricocheting weapon until, said artillery captain William Stevens, they now could drop shells with deadly

REBELS AND REDCOATS

accuracy "just over the enemy's parapet, destroying them where they thought themselves most secure."

Cornwallis, beholding the work of his enemy that morning, was cast into gloom. Only a few days before, he had learned that Clinton, after hemming and hawing, was going to try to save him by sending a rescue fleet from New York. On the fifteenth, using a cipher, the unhappy earl wrote his chief:

My situation now becomes very critical. We dare not show a gun to their old batteries, and I expect that their new ones will open tomorrow morning. Experience has shown that our fresh earthen works do not resist their powerful artillery, so that we shall soon be exposed to an assault in ruined works, in a bad position, and with weakened numbers. The safety of the place is, therefore, so precarious that I cannot recommend that the fleet and army should run great risk in endeavoring to save us.[20]

Although Lord Charles Cornwallis was gray-spirited, tasting the full bitterness of his folly, he was not through. That tough campaigner of the Pennsylvanians, Colonel Richard Butler, recounted:

About twelve o'clock at night [the fifteenth] Major [Robert] Abercrombie of the British with a party of the Light Infantry and Guards made a sally and passing between two small redoubts that were unfinished [where] the line was weak, got possession of the trench. Thence they pushed rapidly to a French battery and spiked the guns and drove out the people, having killed four or five. Thence to the covert way or communication leading from the first to the second parallel, where they halted. They then discovered a battery commanded by Captain Savage of the Americans and challenged, "What troops?" The answer was, "French," on which the order of the British commandant was, "Push on, my brave boys, and skin the b——rs."

This was heard by Count de Noailles, who had the command of a covering party, which he ordered to advance and was guided by the "huzza" of the British. He ordered grenadiers to "Charge bayonet and rush on," which they did with great spirit, crying, "Vive le Roi," and to use the British phrase skivered eight of the Guards and Infantry and took twelve prisoners and drove them quite off. The British spiked Savage's three guns with the points of bayonets, but our smiths and artillerymen soon cleared all the guns and in six hours chastised the enemy for their temerity with the same pieces. Our loss was very trifling, though the British really executed the sortie with secrecy and spirit.[21]

Despite the heavy bombardment that continued next day, General Washington again was forced to issue an order clearing the field of spectators.

In captured Redoubt Number Ten, Alexander Hamilton and Henry Knox were arguing within earshot of a Connecticut soldier, Aeneas Monson, about the soldierliness of trying to dodge enemy missiles. The British had abandoned in the redoubt some "blinds," which Monson said were "hogsheads and pipes filled with sand," behind which the men were to duck whenever shells landed nearby. Usually the fused shells burned several seconds on the ground before exploding, and the blinds could save lives. Monson said:

A general order had been given that when a shell was seen, they might cry out, "A shell," but not . . . "A shot" when a shot was seen. The reason of this distinction was that a shell might be avoided but to cry, "A shot" would only make confusion and do no good. This order was just then discussed, Colonel Hamilton remarking that it seemed to him unsoldierlike to halloo, "A shell," while Knox contended the contrary and that the order was wisely given by General Washington, who cared for the life of the men.

The argument . . . was progressed with a slight degree of warmth when suddenly, *spat! spat!* two shells fell and struck within the redoubt. Instantly the cry broke out on all sides, "A shell! A shell!" and such a scrambling and jumping to reach the blinds and get behind them for defense. Knox and Hamilton were united in action, however differing in word, for both got behind the blinds, and Hamilton to be yet more secure held on behind Knox (Knox being a very large man and Hamilton a small man). Upon this Knox struggled to throw Hamilton off and in the effort himself . . . rolled over and threw Hamilton off towards the shells.

Hamilton, however, scrambled back again behind the blinds. All this was done rapidly, for in two minutes the shells burst and threw their deadly missiles in all directions. It was now safe and soldierlike to stand out.

"Now," says Knox, "now what do you think, Mr. Hamilton, about crying 'shell'? But let me tell you not to make a breastwork of me again!"[22]

The steady pounding of the allied siege guns had uprooted abatis, splintered fraises, breached the enemy lines, and dismounted some of their guns. Replying to Knox's cannon, Cornwallis' artillerymen had consumed most of their own shells.

On the dark, windy night of the sixteenth, the earl decided upon one last desperate effort to save his army. To Tarleton at Gloucester he sent word to concentrate his troops for a breakout and to assemble all wagons and horses for an overland march to New York. Even critical Banastre Tarleton thought the gamble worth taking:

A number of sailors and soldiers were dispatched with boats from Gloucester to assist the troops in passing the river. Earl Cornwallis sent off the first embarkation before eleven o'clock that night . . . and purposed himself to pass with the second, when he had finished a letter to General Washington, calculated to excite the humanity of that officer towards the sick, the wounded, and the detachment that would be left to capitulate.

Much of the small craft had been damaged during the siege; yet it was computed that three trips would be sufficient to convey all the troops that were necessary for the expedition. The whole of the first division arrived before midnight, and part of the second had embarked when a squall, attended with rain, scattered the boats and impeded their return to Gloucester. About two o'clock in the morning the weather began to moderate, when orders were brought to the commanding officers of the corps that had passed to recross the water. As the boats were all on the York side . . . in order to bring over the troops it required some time to row them to Gloucester, to carry back the infantry of the first embarkation. But soon after daybreak they returned under the fire of the enemy's batteries to . . . Yorktown.[23]

The squall blew itself out before morning. The will of the British to resist any longer the relentless pressure of the allies seemed to die with the storm. But to Hessian Johann Döhla, on a firing step on the British lines, it seemed as though the guns never would silence:

Early at the break of day the bombardment began again from the enemy side even more horribly than before. They fired from all redoubts without stopping. Our detachment, which stood in the hornwork, could scarcely avoid the enemy's bombs, howitzer shot, and cannon balls any more. One saw nothing but bombs and balls raining on our whole line.

Early this morning, the English light infantry returned from Gloucester and mounted their post in the hornwork again. They said it would be impossible to break through there . . . nothing at all can pass in and out any more. Also, this morning right after reveille, General Cornwallis came into the hornwork and observed the enemy and his works. As soon as he had gone back to his quarters, he immediately sent a flag of truce with a white standard over to the enemy. The light infantry began to cut their new tents in the hornwork to pieces . . . so one expected an early surrender.[24]

About ten o'clock, Ebenezer Denny wearily was awaiting his relief on the American lines:

> Before relief came [I] had the pleasure of seeing a drummer mount the enemy's parapet and beat a parley, and immediately an officer, holding up a white handkerchief, made his appearance outside their works. The drummer accompanied him, beating. Our batteries ceased. An officer from our lines ran and met the other and tied the handkerchief over his eyes. The drummer [was] sent back, and the British officer conducted to a house in rear of our lines. Firing ceased totally.[25]

The British flag carried a communication from Lord Cornwallis, proposing a cessation of hostilities for twenty-four hours, so that two commissioners from each army might meet at Mr. Augustine Moore's farmhouse in the rear of the first allied parallel to draw up terms of surrender. While the guns again took up their booming, Washington prepared a reply to the earl, which he sent about two o'clock.

"An ardent desire to spare the further effusion of blood," the General wrote, "will readily incline me to listen to such terms for the surrender of your posts and garrisons of York and Gloucester as are admissible." Previous to a meeting of commissioners, he said, he wished to have Cornwallis' proposal in writing, and he granted a cessation of firing for two hours to await it. "Within which time," Washington wrote in his personal journal, "he sent out a letter with such proposals (though some of them were inadmissible) as led me to believe that there would be no great difficulty in fixing the terms. Accordingly, hostilities were suspended for the night, and I proposed my own terms to which, if he agreed, commissioners were to meet to digest them into form."

That morning, when the allies had seen the red-coated drummer on the enemy works and firing had ceased, Ebenezer Denny had thought, "I never heard a drum equal to it —the most delightful music to us all." And now, in the chilly October night, blessed quiet. St. George Tucker wrote happily in his diary:

> A solemn stillness prevailed. The night was remarkably clear, and the sky decorated with ten thousand stars. Numberless meteors gleaming through the atmosphere afforded a pleasing resemblance to the bombs which had exhibited a noble firework the night before, but happily divested of all their horror.

At dawn of day [the eighteenth] the British gave us a serenade with the bagpipe, I believe, and were answered by the French with the band of the Regiment of Deux-Ponts. As soon as the sun rose, one of the most striking pictures of war was displayed. . . . From the Point of Rock battery on one side our lines completely manned and our works crowded with soldiers were exhibited to view. Opposite these at the distance of two hundred yards, you were presented with a sight of the British works, their parapets crowded with officers looking at those who were assembled at the top of our works. The Secretary's [Thomas Nelson's] house with one of the corners broke off and many large holes through the roof and walls, part of which seemed tottering . . . afforded a striking instance of the destruction occasioned by war. Many other houses in the vicinity contributed to accomplish the scene.[26]

Early that morning of the eighteenth, a messenger bore a letter under flag to Cornwallis from Washington, setting forth the terms for surrender. Washington allowed the earl two hours to accept them; otherwise, the bombardment would be renewed.

In his long career as a soldier, George Washington never had had the opportunity of dictating surrender terms, but he was not hampered by lack of experience. He knew what he would require, and he was guided somewhat by the terms the British had allowed the Americans at Charleston. He had only to turn to his elbow for a reminder of that disaster, for Benjamin Lincoln, exchanged, was now second in command before Yorktown. Washington made it clear that his terms might be put into conventional form by the commissioners, but they would not be relaxed.

When a garrison surrendered after a brave defense, when further resistance was impossible, the victor customarily accorded the vanquished certain honors of war. The garrison's exit from its fortress or works was not as a humiliated and conquered force, deprived of all means of self-defense. It was allowed to march forth with flags flying, drums beating, and fully armed and prepared to defend itself against insult. Its drums or band played an air of the conqueror, probably as a gesture in return for the honors of war, demonstrating that the vanquished was not humiliated beyond exchanging compliments with the victor. When General Lincoln surrendered Charleston, he asked for terms permitting his garrison to march out with the honors of war, but Clinton refused them, demanding, "The drummers are not to beat a British march or colors to be uncased." Washington had not forgotten this reflection upon Lincoln's defense and his military character.

Washington named Colonel John Laurens as one of his

commissioners and left the choice of the other to Rochambeau. The Count selected Viscount de Noailles, Lafayette's brother-in-law. The meeting place was to be the one suggested by Cornwallis.

During the day, flags of truce passed frequently between the lines. In the afternoon, the British peace commissioners, Colonel Thomas Dundas and Major Alexander Ross, Cornwallis' aide, came toiling up the bluff from the placid, sparkling river. Awaiting them in a front room of Moore's small white frame house were the American officers. There were introductions, and the articles of capitulation were laid before Major Ross. An American officer described the scene:

That gentleman [Major Ross] observed, "This is a harsh article."

"Which article?" said Colonel Laurens.

"The troops shall march out with colors cased and drums beating a British or a German march."

"Yes, sir," replied Colonel Laurens, "it is a harsh article."

"Then, Colonel Laurens, if that is your opinion, why is it here?"

"Your question, Major Ross, compels an observation which I would have gladly suppressed. You seem to forget, sir, that I was a capitulant at Charleston, where General Lincoln after a brave defense of six weeks [in] open trenches by a very inconsiderable garrison against the British army and fleet . . . and when your lines of approach were within pistol shot of our field works, was refused any other terms for his gallant garrison than marching out with colors cased and drums *not* beating a German or a British march."

"But," rejoined Major Ross, "My Lord Cornwallis did not command at Charleston."

"There, sir," said Colonel Laurens, "you extort another declaration. It is not the individual that is here considered. It is the nation. This remains an article, or I cease to be a commissioner."[27]

The negotiations at Moore's dragged on into the night, and the truce was extended until nine on the morning of the nineteenth. Early that morning, Washington reviewed the terms, granting most, denying a few. "I had [the papers] copied," he wrote in his journal, and sent word to Cornwallis "that I expected to have them signed at eleven o'clock and that the garrison would march out at two o'clock. . . ."

Before noon, the articles subscribed to by Cornwallis and the senior British naval officer in the York arrived from the British lines. Washington and his suite were in the captured Redoubt Number Nine. There the Commander-in-Chief had a line added: "Done in the trenches before Yorktown, in Virginia, October 19, 1781," and he signed, "G. Washington." Rochambeau and Barras signed, and it was done.

At noon, Ebenezer Denny reported:

> All is quiet. Articles of capitulation signed. Detachments of French and Americans take possession of British forts. Major [James] Hamilton commanded a battalion which took possession of a fort immediately opposite our right and on the bank of York River. I carried the standard of our regiment. . . . On entering the fort, Baron Steuben, who accompanied us, took the standard from me and planted it himself.[28]

At last, two o'clock, the appointed hour for formal surrender approached. The victorious armies, who finally had broken the back of British might, marched out to a plain behind Yorktown. From their knapsacks the French had broken out shining, black gaiters to encase their white broadcloth legs. Looking trim and fresh, their bands playing jubilantly, they paraded to the west side of the Hampton Road. Across from them stepped the Americans in their hunting shirts and worn, motley uniforms, much drabber than the blue-and-white Royal Deux-Ponts, or the white piped in violet or black or yellow or rose or crimson or green of the Soissonnais, the Gâtinais, the others. Their music was not so regular, their order was not so perfect. But there stood the men who had fought for six, dreary years to live this glorious moment. The crowd of spectators who had swarmed out from town to see the day's ceremonies could pick out faces that were now famous: Henry Knox, Anthony Wayne, Baron von Steuben, Benjamin Lincoln. And there were many others, fine officers who had been faithful: Brigadier General Moses Hazen, Lieutenant Colonel John Laurens, Chief Engineer Chevalier Louis le Bèque du Portail, Colonel Stephen Moylan, Captain David Bushnell, Brevet Lieutenant Colonel Tench Tilghman, Brigadier General Peter Muhlenberg, Colonel Elias Dayton, Major Caleb Gibbs, Colonel Walter Stewart. There were scores more, and Lieutenant Feltman, Sergeant Martins, Private Monsons, and thousands of nameless ones.

Behind them all lay that winter outside Boston, the plunging defeat of Long Island, the shameless panic at Kip's Bay, the bitterness of Canada, the glory of Trenton, the confusion of Brandywine, the triumph of Saratoga, the disappointment of Monmouth. To the south their brothers, absent this October day, had endured Fort Moultrie, Charleston, Camden, King's Mountain, Cowpens, Guilford, Hobkirk's Hill,

Eutaw Springs. "We have been beating the bush," General Nathanael Greene had written to his friend, Henry Knox, on learning that Washington was pursuing Cornwallis to Virginia, "and the General has come to catch the bird." But in the midst of his operations against the tough English earl, George Washington had sent a message to his Quaker general in South Carolina: "General Washington wishes not only from his personal regard to General Greene, but from principles of generosity and justice to see him crowned with those laurels which from his unparalleled exertions he so richly deserves."

They all had triumphed over neglect, hunger, incompetence, selfishness, half rations or no rations, thirst, cold, no pay or worthless pay, cowards, cheats, speculators—and a tenacious enemy. Now they waited, they and their chieftain and the noble men of France who had made their final victory possible.

The day was warm for October. The sun played among the trees turning yellow and rust-red and fell benignly upon serene Washington on his great, white charger, on boyish Lafayette mounted at the head of his light infantry, and upon old "Papa" Rochambeau, proudly eyeing his smart French legions.

At last, along the road from town, came the scarlet ranks of the defeated, colors cased and their fifes and drums beating a "strain of melancholy." Ebenezer Denny thought the "drums beat as if they did not care how," and Lieutenant William McDowell of the First Pennsylvania thought, "The British prisoners appeared much in liquor."

At their head rode a splendid-looking, ruddy Irishman, Brigadier General Charles O'Hara of the Guards, come to act for Lord Cornwallis, too indisposed to appear. Count Matheiu Dumas was deputized to ride forward to meet the garrison troops and direct them:

I placed myself at General O'Hara's left hand. . . .He asked me where General Rochambeau was. "On our left," I said, "at the head of the French line." The English general urged his horse forward to present his sword to the French general. Guessing his intention, I galloped on to place myself between him and M. de Rochambeau, who at that moment made me a sign, pointing to General Washington who was opposite to him. . . .

"You are mistaken," said I to General O'Hara. "The commander-in-chief of our army is on the right."

I accompanied him, and the moment that he presented

his sword, General Washington, anticipating him said, "Never from such a good hand."[29]

Rochambeau gave as his reason for not accepting O'Hara's blade that "the French army being only an auxiliary on this continent, it devolved on the American general to tender him his orders."

Although Washington would not receive the sword from O'Hara's "good hand," he indicated that O'Hara, Cornwallis' second in command, should present himself to Lincoln, Washington's second. On the right of the road, Lincoln explained to O'Hara, was an open field around which the French hussars had formed a circle. The English should enter the circle, one regiment at a time, and lay down their arms. An officer of the New Jersey Line observed:

> The British officers in general behaved like boys who had been whipped at school. Some bit their lips, some pouted, others cried. Their round, broad-brimmed hats were well adapted to the occasion, hiding those faces they were ashamed to show. The foreign regiments made a more military appearance, and the conduct of their officers was far more becoming men of fortitude.[30]

Captain Graham's spirited Highlanders grieved with their captain:

> Drums were beat, but the colors remained in their cases— an idle retaliation for a very idle slight which had been put by our people on the American garrison of Charleston, and the regiments having formed in columns at quarter distance the men laid down their arms.
> It is a sorry reminiscence, this. Yet the scene made a deep impression at the moment, for the mortification and unfeigned sorrow of the soldiers will never fade from my memory. Some went so far as to shed tears, while one man, a corporal, who stood near me, embraced his firelock and then threw it on the ground, exclaiming, "May you never get so good a master again!"
> Nevertheless, to do them justice, the Americans behaved with great delicacy and forbearance, while the French, by what motive actuated I will not pretend to say, were profuse in their protestations of sympathy. . . .When I visited their lines . . . immediately after our parade had been dismissed, I was overwhelmed with the civility of my late enemies.[31]

That night, an American colonel later recalled, "I noticed that the officers and soldiers could scarcely talk for laughing, and they could scarcely walk for jumping and dancing and singing as they went about."

October 22. The Marquis de Lafayette has written a friend, "The play, sir, is over." Washington has given a dinner for British General O'Hara. So, also, has Rochambeau, and a French officer present has been amazed at the "sang froid and gaity even" of O'Hara and fellow English officers at dinner. The British troops and their mercenaries, except most of the officers who have been granted paroles, have started filing off for Winchester and Fort Frederick, the places assigned for their American captivity. Lieutenant Reuben Sanderson of the Fifth Connecticut, serving with the late Colonel Scammell's corps, has spent two days in Yorktown, the first "Collecting Tents," the second, "Collecting Nigars till 5 o'clock. . . ." Sergeant Joseph Martin also has been securing the pitiful, hungry Negroes turned adrift by Cornwallis, who had lured them to his camp with promises of freedom. The sergeant has earned a reward of twelve hundred dollars in paper money and has squandered the entire sum on a pint of rum. A Mr. Day has come to town, claiming as his master's the fine horse Banastre Tarleton rides. Mr. Day has accosted the cavalryman with a sweet gum stick in hand "as thick as a man's wrist" and the fearless colonel has meekly surrendered the horse, while a street crowd laughed at the show.

This day, the twenty-second, Colonel Richard Butler writes a postscript to a letter to his friend, General William Irvine of Pennsylvania:

Not a principal officer wounded or killed, and but very few men, and I think I may with propriety now congratulate you, my friend, and the country in general with certain Independence and the pleasing approach of Peace.[32]

Just before two that morning in faraway Philadelphia, a panting express rider galloped through the silent streets seeking the President of Congress, Thomas McKean. The express came from Governor Lee of Maryland, bearing a copy of a letter to the governor from Admiral de Grasse. On its cover were the words, "To be forwarded by night and by day with the utmost dispatch—Lord Cornwallis surrendered the garrison of York to General Washington, the 17th October." Newspapers reported:

An honest, old German, a watchman of Philadelphia, having conducted the express rider . . . to the door of his Excellency the President of Congress . . . continued the duties of his office, calling out: "Basht dree o'glock, und Cornwal-lis isht da-ken!"[33]

"HAVING NOW FINISHED THE WORK ASSIGNED ME"

The Last Days

1782-1783

CONGRESS WAS obliged to wait two more anxious days for official confirmation of the news from Yorktown. Washington had chosen Lieutenant Colonel Tench Tilghman, his devoted aide, to carry the "Victory Dispatch" to Congress. Completely fatigued, Tilghman trotted into Philadelphia on October 24, after losing a whole night's run through "the stupidity of the skipper" who had run aground in the Chesapeake. The complete story of the fall of Cornwallis was laid before Congress. At two o'clock the Delegates went in procession to the Dutch Lutheran Church to "return thanks to Almighty God for crowning the allied arms of the United States and France with success. . . ."

But, writing about Tilghman's reception, Elias Boudinot ruefully admitted:

It was necessary to furnish him with hard money for his expenses. There was not a sufficiency in the treasury to do it, and the members of Congress, of which I was one, each paid a dollar to accomplish it.[1]

An utterly bare treasury did not prevent the congress' voting, five days later, to erect "at York, in Virginia, a marble column, adorned with emblems of the alliance between the United States and his Most Christian Majesty, and inscribed with a succinct narrative of the surrender of Lord Cornwallis," nor from ordering the Board of War to present to Colonel Tilghman "a horse properly caparisoned, and an elegant sword."

Neither the cost of "expensive amusements" nor the constant scarcity of gunpowder inhibited the frenzy of celebrations. Artillery in the statehouse yard roared a salute. Ships' cannon in the harbor boomed. The whole city was illuminated. Elsewhere, as the news spread, it was the same. The *New York Packet* reported:

At Fishkill . . . the glorious victory was observed with exuberant joy and festivity. A roasted ox and plenty of liquor formed the repast; a number of toasts were drunk. . . . French and American colors were displayed, cannon fired, and in the evening, illuminations, bonfires, rockets, and squibs gave agreeable amusement. . . .

At Newburgh . . . to enliven the entertainment, they hanged and burnt in effigy the traitor Arnold.[2]

The army in the Hudson Highlands celebrated with the traditional *feu-de-joie,* an officers' dinner at a table spread in the field, and an extra rum ration for the men. General William Heath told in his journal an account he had heard of one of the celebrations:

The company collected had determined to burn General Arnold in effigy. . . . Just as they were going to commit the effigy to the flames, one of the company observed that one of Arnold's legs was wounded when he was fighting bravely for America, that this leg ought not to be burnt, but amputated; in which the whole company agreed, and this leg was taken off and safely laid by.[3]

It was about noon on Sunday, the twenty-fifth of November, before intelligence of the British surrender reached Lord George Germain in London. Promptly from his house in Pall Mall, he traveled to the Downing Street residence of the Prime Minister to give him the news in person. A friend later asked Germain how Lord North took the communication and was told:

As he would have taken a ball in his breast. . . . For, he opened his arms, exclaiming wildly, as he paced up and down the apartment during a few minutes, "Oh, God! It is all over!" Words which he repeated many times, under emotions of the deepest consternation and distress.[4]

Although Yorktown seemed to settle the issue of the war, it did not immediately end it. The King, upon receiving the news, declared that he hoped no one would think that it "makes the smallest alteration in those principles of my conduct which have directed me in past time." Lord North, long sick of the war, was willing to face the granting of independence to the American colonies, but for months he stood almost alone.

The victory at Yorktown did not blind Washington to the reality that although the British lion was wounded sorely, he was far from slain. A week after signing the articles of surrender, the General was writing: "my only apprehension (which I wish may be groundless) is lest the late important success, instead of exciting our exertions, as it ought to do, should produce such a relaxation in the prosecution of the war, as will prolong the calamities of it."

Obviously Washington's next objective should be a concerted allied strike at Charleston, where Greene had cornered another British force, and he urged Admiral de Grasse to undertake a joint attack with him before leaving American waters. But the admiral, already overdue in the West Indies, refused. The Commander-in-Chief then made winter arrangements for the armies: Rochambeau was to remain in the vicinity of Yorktown, the Continentals to proceed, via Head of Elk, to the Hudson and Jersey. To aid Nathanael Greene, Washington sent southward Arthur St. Clair with the Pennsylvania, Maryland, and Virginia forces.

Most of the Continentals started up the Bay on the third of November. On the fifth, after a round of farewell visits, Washington rode northward. Coming south in September, by hurrying ahead of his army, he had stolen a few treasured days at Mount Vernon—his first in six years and four months. Now he passed another week on the Potomac. Then with his military family and Mrs. Washington, the General set out for Philadelphia: he had much to report to Congress.

Fifteen cold winter weeks passed while Washington conferred time and again with Delegates and spent hour upon hour letter-writing at a desk in his quarters in Benjamin Chew's new house on South Third Street; and all winter he labored constantly to formulate plans for 1782, to reorganize the army and to fill it out to the strength authorized in October, 1780, and to arrange to feed and clothe full regiments.

When the General returned to his troops at Newburgh, New York, on the last day of March, 1782, he was confronted with still more problems of the sort he had faced for so many seasons: how to supply his men, to settle disputes between officers, to thwart the greed of contractors, to arouse the states from apathy, to maintain discipline and the will to carry on.

Persistent rumors of impending peace not only dulled the national effort, but also aroused unrest in the army. The inactivity of the enemy, whose main force dozed away the winter at New York and showed no signs of arousing with the spring, strengthened the average soldier's conviction that the British, having lost two whole armies, were ready to quit. News of smashing French victories in the West Indies, the English loss of Minorca, the siege of Gibraltar, revolt in India, was followed by rumors that "the citizens of London and Westminister had petitioned the King in the strongest terms to relinquish the American war."

May came, and with it that fine Irish soldier, Sir Guy Carleton, to take over at New York for Sir Henry Clinton; Clinton, at last recalled home, was full of bitter self-right-eousness, and at once commenced a long and violent public controversy with Lord Cornwallis about who was to blame for the strategy of the Southern campaign and its dismal failure. Sir Guy brought with him further hints of settlement; the newspapers, the halls of Congress, private correspondence, were full of more peace talk. The House of Commons passed a bill authorizing the Crown to negotiate peace. Lord North resigned, and a Whig ministry under the Marquis of Rocking-ham took office, bringing to the administration the men who had been the warmest friends of America.

But Washington remained skeptical, insisting upon his be-lief in "an old and true maxim that to make a good peace, you ought to be well prepared to carry on the war." Those who thought he was a deluded old warrior unwilling to cease shaking the sword were perhaps given some pause when the world-wide war began to flow again in England's favor, but generally Washington's countrymen relaxed.

From Carleton, Washington received a letter on August 4 announcing that a peace conference had opened in Paris, where the English commissioner was authorized to offer America her independence. This note was followed by an-other in which Sir Guy admitted that he had "suspended" all hostilities. Then came word that Lord Rockingham was dead, the ministry changed, and the new Prime Minister was a much less liberal Whig. Washington concluded, "The death of the Marquis of Rockingham has given a shock to the new administration and disordered its whole system. . . . That the King will push the war as long as the nation will find men or money admits not of a doubt in my mind."

But in spite of Washington's stubborn doubt, Carleton set about evacuating the British-held Southern ports. "The evacu-ation," he declared, "is not a matter of choice but of deplor-able necessity in consequence of an unsuccessful war." Sa-vannah was evacuated in July. It was December, however, before Nathanael Greene, whose campaign had proved him the ablest strategist of the war, marched his toughened troops into Charleston on the heels of the departing British.

In late June, meanwhile, Rochambeau's army began a long, hot, leisurely march for the Hudson, and in September the Yorktown allies were reunited at Verplanck. The French regi-ments encamped around Crompond, northeast of Verplanck's, but only for a short while. Rochambeau believed that Carleton would evacuate New York and that he could safely take his troops to Santo Domingo to join the Spanish in accordance with orders from Versailles. But for fear of stirring the enemy to action, he and Washington decided the French forces should appear to be proceeding to New England for the winter. So they broke their camps around Crompond and once more took the road for Boston over the Connecticut hills and valleys, now splashed with the yellow and crimson of autumn.

Frost came early and hard to the "rugged and dreary mountains" around Newburgh. News came in from various quarters. Washington heard that gay, valiant John Laurens had fallen in "a trifling skirmish" in his native South Carolina. The General wrote the gloomy news about "poor Laurens" to Lafayette and mentioned that a soldier they knew of another stripe also had died on the second of October. Postmaster General Ebenezer Hazard wrote Jeremy Belknap to say that, in Philadelphia, at "The Sign of the Conestoga Wagon":

> General [Charles] Lee died . . ., after a few days' illness, in some degree his own physician and but badly attended, except by two faithful dogs, who frequently attempted in vain to awaken their dead master. They laid themselves down by his corpse for a considerable time, so long that it became necessary for new masters to remove them. He lies buried in Christ's Church yard. No stone marks his head. Indeed, those who saw his open grave can scarcely mark the site, as it is continually trodden by persons going into and coming out of church. Behold the honor of the great![5]

Unrelenting to the last, Lee had spoken bitterly to his sister of Washington only a few weeks before he died; he characterized him as a "puffed-up charlatan . . . extremely prodigal of other men's blood and a great economist of his own." He willed that he not be buried "in any church or churchyard, or within a mile of any Presbyterian or Anabaptist meetinghouse. For since I have resided in this country, I have had so much bad company when living that I do not choose to continue it when dead." But they buried him with full military honors in an Anglican churchyard and a large assemblage attended.

That summer of 1782, the Continental Congress had repealed its old order for a court of inquiry into the conduct of Horatio Gates at Camden, and he returned to the Continental Army in the fall as senior Major General. To his friend, Robert Morris, he confided soon after his arrival:

> I am well, and as happy as an old soldier can be, in a tent the latter end of October. We move in a day to winter quarters, when I hope to get warm for once since I arrived

in camp. . . . Upon talking with the General, I have sent for Mrs. Gates to keep me from freezing this winter. . . .[6]

When the winter rolled down from Canada, it was unusually severe. Although Washington thought the army generally "was better organized, disciplined, and clothed" than ever before, serious trouble threatened in the resentment of officers against what they considered the continued neglect of Congress. Washington warned a Delegate at Philadelphia, "The temper of the army is much soured and has become more irritable than at any period since the commencement of the war." Early in the new year of 1783, a committee of officers laid before Congress a memorial requesting payment of arrears in pay, settlement of food and clothing accounts, and assurance of the half-pay for life to the incapacitated and the retired that had been promised in the fall of 1780.

When the Congress failed to assure payment of past-due accounts and rejected the officers' proposed commutation of the pension in exchange for six years' full pay, a meeting of general and field officers was called for the eleventh of March. An anonymous address, rumored to be the work of Major John Armstrong, General Gates's aide, circulated through the surly encampment. It attacked the "coldness and severity" of the Congress toward the officers' financial distress and urged them, should the Congress ignore a "last remonstrance," to desert the country during the war, or in event of peace to refuse to lay down arms until redressed.

Upon reading the anonymous circular, Washington was appalled. This implied a revolt under leadership experienced and intelligent enough to overthrow the government. To forestall "disorderly proceedings," he instantly ordered a meeting of officers for the fifteenth of March to determine "what further measures ought to be adopted as the most rational and best calculated to attain the just and important object in view." Not he, but General Gates was to preside.

Promptly another address passed from hand to hand, expressing the opinion that Washington's call for a meeting "sanctified" the officers' demands, whereupon the General decided that he himself must attend and address the meeting of the fifteenth.

The assembly gathered in the large, wooden building in the camp called the Temple, used for public affairs. Major Samuel Shaw, who was among the officers present when the General walked to the lectern, visibly agitated, to address them, wrote soon afterward:

Every eye was fixed upon the illustrious man and attention to their beloved General held the assembly mute. He opened the meeting by apologizing for his appearance there, which was by no means his intention when he published the order which directed them to assemble. But the diligence used in circulating the anonymous pieces rendered it necessary that he should give his sentiments to the army on the nature and tendency of them. . . . And in order to do it with the greatest perspicuity he had committed his thoughts to writing, which, with the indulgence of his brother officers, he would take the liberty of reading to them.[7]

The anonymous addresses, said Washington, were "drawn with great art," but directed more to the "feelings and passions than to the reason and judgment of the Army," and he bitingly denounced the courses proposed by the papers to the officers. He cited his own long service to the country and to his army as his warrant of loyalty to the army's interests, and then defended the integrity of the Congress and explained why their deliberations were often slow. For himself, the General said, his experience with and affection for the army "will oblige me to declare, in this public and solemn manner that in the attainment of complete justice for all your toils and dangers and in the gratification of every wish, so far as may be done consistently with the great duty I owe my country and those powers we are bound to respect, you may freely command my services to the utmost of my abilities."

"Let me entreat you gentlemen," he continued, "on your part not to take measures which, viewed in the calm light of reason, will lessen the dignity and sully the glory you have hitherto maintained; let me request you to rely on the plighted faith of your country and place a full confidence in the purity of the intentions of Congress. . . ."

By acting thus, the Commander-in-Chief said, "you will by the dignity of your conduct afford occasion for posterity to say, when speaking of the glorious example you have exhibited to mankind, 'had this day been wanting, the world had never seen the last stage of perfection to which human nature is capable of attaining.' "

Major Shaw was stirred deeply by the General's words. But the General was not finished. From his pocket he drew a letter from Joseph Jones, the Virginia Delegate to Congress, and Shaw listened closely as Washington said:

. . . that as a corroborating testimony of the good disposition in Congress towards the army he would communicate to them a letter received from a worthy member of that body and one who on all occasions had ever approved himself their fast friend. This was an exceedingly sensible letter, and while it pointed out the difficulties and embarrassments of Congress, it held up very forcibly the idea that the army should at all events be generously dealt with.

One circumstance in reading this letter must not be omitted. His Excellency, after reading the first paragraph, made a short pause, took out his spectacles, and begged the indulgence of his audience, while he put them on, observing at the same time that he had grown gray in their service and now found himself growing blind. There was something so natural, so unaffected in this appeal as rendered it superior to the most studied oratory. It forced its way into the heart, and you might see sensibility moisten every eye. The General, having finished, took leave of the assembly. . . .[8]

When Washington left the hall, General Gates acted as presiding officer. Washington received a vote of thanks, and the officers expressed their confidence in the Congress, asked the General to act in their behalf, repudiated the proposals of the anonymous addresses and quietly adjourned. Washington, the diplomatist, in the final days of his army had averted a revolt potentially more dangerous than the almost forgotten mutiny of the Connecticut Line or the more successful one of the Pennsylvanians—a revolt which would have robbed the deserving army of much of its hard-won glory.

Almost as if in reward for the army's common sense, the rumors of the signing of a conditional peace treaty in Paris in November were confirmed a few days later. Washington was disappointed to learn that the treaty would not be final until terms had been agreed upon between Great Britain and France. But a courier arrived later in the month with word of the conclusion of peace by France and Spain with Britain. This too was preliminary, but it made operative the November pact between America and Britain. Although the formal close of the war had to wait on the drafting and signing of a definitive treaty, the war was at an end!

On the nineteenth of April, 1783, exactly eight years after General Gage's angry redcoats had fired upon the belligerent rebels on Lexington Green, the "cessation of hostilities between the United States of America and the King of Great Britain" was announced to the army at the door of the building where Washington had spoken at the time of the Newburgh addresses.

Much remained for diplomats to accomplish before a final peace treaty was signed, but for the men, every thought was of home. It was spring—time for planting, for opening the shop, for picking up the rusty implements of half-forgotten professions. They wanted their pay, but the poverty-stricken Congress gave promissory notes and furloughs, until the final treaty was signed. Washington, however, was authorized to discharge them before that date. If the men grumbled at being "turned aside so disgracefully," they were for the most part orderly as they shouldered the muskets voted them as farewell gifts and set out for home "without the settlement of their accounts or a farthing of money in their pockets." Only some men from Lancaster—"Recruits and soldiers of a day," according to Washington, who had "very few hardships to complain of"—mutinied and marched to Philadelphia, joined others, and surrounded the State House. They disbanded, however, before a force from the army that remained could march to arrest them. Only the three-year men were left. The others, with not so much as a last review or the beat of a drum, simply walked off.

Sergeant Joseph Martin faithfully awaited a proper dismissal. For him that last day came on the eleventh of June, 1783:

"The old man," our captain, came into our room . . . and . . . handed us our discharges, or rather furloughs. . . . I confess, after all, that my anticipation of the happiness I should experience upon such a day as this was not realized. . . . We had lived together as a family of brothers for several years (setting aside some little family squabbles, like most other families); had shared with each other the hardships, dangers, and sufferings incident to a soldier's life, had sympathized with each other in trouble and sickness; had assisted in bearing each other's burdens, or strove to make them lighter by council and advice; had endeavored to conceal each other's faults, or make them appear in as good a light as they would bear. In short, the soldiery, each in his particular circle of acquaintance, were as strict a band of brotherhood as Masons, and I believe as faithful to each other. And now we were to be (the greater part of us) parted forever, as unconditionally separated as though the grave lay between us. This, I say, was the case with the most; I will not say all. There were as many genuine misanthropists among the soldiers . . . as of any other class of people whatever, and some in our corps of miners. But we were young men and had warm hearts. I question if there was a corps in the army that parted with more regret than ours did, the New Englanders in particular. Ah! it was a serious time!

Some of the soldiers went off for home the same day that their fetters were knocked off; others stayed and got their final settlement certificates, which they sold to procure decent clothing and money sufficient to enable them to pass with decency through the country, and to appear something like themselves when they arrived among their friends. I was among those. . . . I . . . sold some of them and purchased some decent clothing and then set off. . . .[9]

In August, with the army reduced to a skeleton, Washington moved his headquarters to Rocky Hill, about four miles from Princeton, New Jersey, where Congress had moved after its frightening experience with the Pennsylvania mutineers. At Rocky Hill, he stayed busy with correspondence and committee meetings as well as a vigorous social life. Here he received notice from General Carleton that the British would evacuate New York, their last post in America, in November. By the thirteenth of that month, Washington was back with his remaining forces at West Point. Brevet Lieutenant Colonel Benjamin Tallmadge, the strikingly handsome, daring dragoon officer who had managed Washington's secret service, kept a faithful record of the final days:

The troops now began to be impatient to return to their respective homes, and those that were destined for that purpose, to take possession of the city [of New York]. . . . The twenty-fifth of November, 1783, was appointed for the British troops to evacuate the city and for the American troops to take possession of it. General Knox, at the head of a select corps of American troops, entered the city as the rear of the British troops embarked; soon after which the Commander-in-Chief, accompanied by Governor Clinton and their respective suites, made their public entry . . . on horseback, followed by the Lieutenant Governor and members of the Council. . . .
Governor Clinton gave a public dinner, at which General Washington and the principal officers of the army, citizens, etc., were present. On the Tuesday evening following [the twenty-seventh], there was a most splendid display of fireworks at the lower part of Broadway, near the Bowling Green. . . .
The time now drew near when the Commander-in-Chief intended to leave . . . for his beloved retreat at Mount Vernon. On Tuesday, the fourth of December, it was made known to the officers then in New York that General Washington intended to commence his journey on that day.
At twelve o'clock the officers repaired to Fraunces Tavern in Pearl Street, where General Washington had appointed to meet them and to take his final leave of them. We had been assembled but a few moments when His Excellency entered the room. His emotion, too strong to be concealed, seemed to be reciprocated by every officer present.

After partaking of a slight refreshment, in almost breathless silence, the General filled his glass with wine, and turning to his officers, he said, "With a heart full of love and gratitude, I now take leave of you. I most devoutly wish that your latter days may be as prosperous and happy as your former ones have been glorious and honorable."

After the officers had taken a glass of wine, General Washington said, "I cannot come to each of you, but shall feel obliged if each of you will come and take me by the hand."

General Knox, being nearest to him, turned to the Commander-in-Chief, who, suffused in tears, was incapable of utterance, but grasped his hand, when they embraced each other in silence. In the same affectionate manner, every officer in the room marched up to, kissed, and parted with his General-in-Chief.

Such a scene of sorrow and weeping I had never before witnessed, and hope I may never be called upon to witness again. . . . Not a word was uttered to break the solemn silence . . . or to interrupt the tenderness of the . . . scene. The simple thought that we were then about to part from the man who had conducted us through a long and bloody war, and under whose conduct the glory and independence of our country had been achieved, and that we should see his face no more in this world, seemed to me utterly insupportable.

But the time of separation had come, and waving his hand to his grieving children around him, he left the room, and passing through a corps of light infantry who were paraded to receive him, he walked silently on to Whitehall, where a barge was in waiting. We all followed in mournful silence to the wharf, where a prodigious crowd had assembled to witness the departure of the man who, under God, had been the great agent in establishing the glory and independence of these United States. As soon as he was seated, the barge put off into the river, and when out in the stream, our great and beloved General waved his hat and bid us a silent adieu.[10]

At last, the General was homeward bound. From Powle's Hook, where, four years before, Henry Lee had distinguished himself, Washington spurred southward. At Brunswick and at Trenton, where he had so neatly deceived Cornwallis so many years ago, he was met with the first of many addresses of tribute and good will.

On the eighth, to the pealing of church bells and the roar of cannon, Philadelphia acclaimed its General. In the city of Quakers, Washington totaled up his final accounts, although the Congress to whom he would present them was still absent, meeting at Annapolis. Two settlements of the General's accounts already had been made, but he had numerous later entries, including Martha's expenses in visiting headquarters from 1775 through 1782, which he considered a proper charge. Actual expenses only, he had said in 1776, and these only he charged: equipment, supplies, furnishings, travel, entertainment, all the things he would have purchased if he had lived away from home as a private citizen.

After seven days of business, the General rode out of Philadelphia for Wilmington. Another celebration, a hard ride, and Baltimore on the seventeenth. "Respectable gentlemen" escorted his party into the city, and a citizen said, "a brilliant collection of ladies assembled to entertain him through the evening." A public dinner the next day, and at night General Washington "led and mingled in a joyous dance" until two A.M. His hosts cried for him to linger, but the season was growing late. On the nineteenth, he was in the saddle again for Annapolis, "to make his last bow to Congress," Captain Archibald McAlister wrote his friend, Theodorick Bland, to "unbend his mind from the important charge of public business, receive the applause of the present and succeeding world, and while on earth to be enfolded in the arms of domestic felicity. He stands engaged to dine with Mrs. Washington on Christmas Day. This prevented his longer stay. . . ."

At Annapolis, once more and for the last time, saluting cannon boomed. Old wounds were forgotten: Thomas Mifflin gave the General a dinner on Sunday the twenty-first. Monday brought two addresses. The Congress, though a thin body at the moment, entertained at a ceremonial dinner—"the most extraordinary" James Tilton, Delegate from Delaware, had ever attended. Between two and three hundred gentlemen dined together, Tilton wrote a friend. "The number of cheerful voices with the clangor of knives and forks made a din of a very extraordinary nature and most delightful influence. Every man seemed to be in heaven or so absorbed . . . as to neglect the more sordid appetites, for not a soul got drunk, though there was wine in plenty and the usual number of thirteen toasts drank, besides one given afterwards by the General. . . ." That evening, Washington was at his gayest at a ball given by the governor at the State House. He "danced every set," Tilton noted, "that all the ladies might have the pleasure of dancing with him, or as it since has been handsomely expressed, *get a touch of him*."

Exactly at noon the next day, the General, refreshed and accompanied by two aides, presented himself at the door of the Congressional chamber of the State House for an audience he had requested. Outside in the winter sunshine his horses were waiting to be led to the door, so that, his business completed, he could make an immediate start for Mount Vernon.

Old Charles Thomson, who had been Secretary of Congress when Washington himself was a member, escorted the General to a chair near that of President Thomas Mifflin. At one of Washington's shoulders stood David Humphreys, at the other, aide Benjamin Walker. Only nineteen or twenty members were present, but quickly the gallery and the hall were filled with Maryland's most eminent citizens. A hush fell.

"Sir," said Thomas Miffin, "the United States in Congress assembled are prepared to receive your communications."

The General arose, stood before his chair, bowed to the members. From his pocket he drew a paper which he held before him in a hand that shook noticeably. Solemnly he read:

Mr. President: The great events on which my resignation depended having at length taken place, I have now the honor of offering my sincere congratulations to Congress and of presenting myself before them to surrender into their hands the trust committed to me and to claim the indulgence of retiring from the service of my country.

Happy in the confirmation of our independence and sovereignty and pleased with the opportunity afforded the United States of becoming a respectable nation, I resign with satisfaction the appointment I accepted with diffidence—a diffidence in my abilities to accomplish so arduous a task, which however was superseded by a confidence in the rectitude of our Cause, the support of the supreme power of the Union and the patronage of Heaven. . . .

While I repeat my obligations to the army in general, I should do injustice to my own feelings not to acknowledge in this place the peculiar services and distinguished merits of the gentlemen who have been attached to my person during the war.[11]

Racked as he so often had been these final days with poignant recollections of his officers, the General's emotion mounted, and he grasped his paper with both hands to quiet its trembling. He continued:

It was impossible the choice of confidential officers to compose my family should have been more fortunate. Permit me, sir, to recommend in particular those who have continued in service to the present moment as worthy of the favorable notice and patronage of Congress.

I consider it an indispensable duty to close this last solemn act of my official life by commending the interests of our dearest country to the protection of Almighty God and those who have the superintendence of them to his holy keeping.[12]

The General choked. "His voice faltered and sunk, and the whole house felt his agitation." Spectators like James Mc-Henry, who could remember sitting as in a family with the General by the falls of the Passaic, scarcely could see the tall speaker through their tears. In a moment the General recovered himself and said:

Having now finished the work assigned me, I retire from the great theater of action, and bidding an affectionate farewell to this august body under whose orders I have so long acted, I here offer my commission and take my leave of all the employments of public life.[13]

From inside the breast of his uniform coat, Washington drew his commission. He folded the copy of his address, walked forward, and handed the papers to Thomas Mifflin. The President replied "with much dignity," and Secretary Thomson proffered Washington a copy of Mifflin's remarks. Then the General bowed and withdrew. The spectators were dismissed. Briefly Washington re-entered the room to shake the hand of each Delegate, and then he strode through the door to his waiting horses.

His two former aides, Humphreys and Walker, were going with him. He had his eye upon history: the great trunks of his official papers, carefully packed and painstakingly shipped, would come to Mount Vernon, and as his secretaries, the younger men would put them in order for the hands of the future.

Fifty miles lay ahead, and December days were short.

Gentlemen, mount and ride!

Rivers and towns. South River, Patuxent, Western Branch. Queene Anne, Upper Marlborough. A tavern for the night, up at day. Long familiar miles, and then the ferry across the clear Potomac. The last swift gallop along the lane to Mount Vernon's door. And Martha to welcome him—George Washington, free citizen, home in time for Christmas.

"who have the second sight or see them, to his safe keeping."

The General and staff, His once relaxed and combative whole bearing, his animation of speech as he came for ready, were found trembling, sitting up in a . . . chilly with the General by the fall of his . . . . No one could see the old gentleman through their fingers, the moment the General revealed himself and said:

"Having no written . . . the spoke assured me: Picket from the great theatre of action, and bidding an all desperate farewell to the armed body under whose orders I have to lead abroad, have so far my commission and take my leave of all the important means of a noble life . . . .

From inside the asylum of . . . is Lincoln's coat, Washington gave his commission. He folded the envy of his declined, walked forward and handed the papers to Thomas Mifflin. The President replied with much dignity, and Secretary Thomson proffered Washington a copy of Mifflin's remarks. Then the General bowed and withdrew. The speeches were dismissed. Finally Washington re-entered the room through the hand of each the years and then he shook through the door of his surrounding . . .

His two other aides Humphreys and Walker were going with him. He had the two upon before, the great trunks of the official papers carefully packed, and returned any shipment would come to Mount Vernon, and as his secretary. His valuable men would put them in order for the hands of the future.

Forty miles lay ahead, and December days were short. Through the mellow autumn and frail . . . .

Rivers and towns, South River, Patuxent, Western Branch, Occoquan, the pace faltered on the road for the night, day by day, along familiar miles, and then the ferry across the great Potomac. The last swift gallop along the lane to Mount Vernon's door, and Martha to welcome him — George Washington, free citizen, home in time for Christmas.

Notes

IN THE FOLLOWING NOTES THE EDITION OF THE WRITINGS OF GEORGE
WASHINGTON EDITED BY JOHN C. FITZPATRICK HAS BEEN REFERRED TO
AS *WW-f*; THE EDITION EDITED BY JARED SPARKS AS *WW-s*; THE EDI-
TION EDITED BY WORTHINGTON C. FORD AS *WW-ford*.

CHAPTER 1

1. Mass. Hist. Soc., *Coll.*, V (1798), 106-10.
   There are at least four accounts by Revere of his ride, differing
   only in minor detail. One, addressed to Dr. Jeremy Belknap on
   Jan. 1, 1798, was published in Massachusetts Historical Society
   Collections, V (1798), 106-10. The same manuscript was reprinted
   in the Society's *Proceedings*, XVI (1878), 371-74, with editorial
   notes by Dr. Charles Deane. This version is published also in Goss,
   Life of Colonel Paul Revere, I, 180-212.
   Goss publishes a third, shorter account "evidently written in
   1783," found among Revere's family papers. He reproduces it in
   facsimile and reprints it (I, 213-25). Accompanying this manuscript,
   said Goss, was "the original rough draft, unsigned," which differs
   from the version he published only in minor detail. Goss indicates
   the differences by brackets.
2. Goss, *Revere*, I, 222-23.
3. *Ibid.*, pp. 223-24.
4. *Ibid.*, p. 226.
5. Mass. Hist. Soc., *Coll.*, V (1798), 109.
6. Belknap, "Journal of my Tour to the Camp," Mass. Hist. Soc.,
   Proc., IV (1858-60), 84.
7. Barker, *British in Boston*, pp. 31-32.
8. Deposition of Sylvanus Wood, June 17, 1826, Dawson, *Battles*, I, 22.
9. *Loc. cit.*
10. Deposition of Thomas Willard, April 23, 1775, *American Archives*,
    4th ser., II, 489-90.
11. Deposition of Sylvanus Wood, June 17, 1826, Dawson, *op. cit.*,
    I, 22-23.
12. *Ibid.*, p. 23.

CHAPTER 2

1. Amos Barrett, "Concord and Lexington Battle," in True, *Journal
   and Letters*, pp. 34-35.
2. Barker, *British in Boston*, p. 32.
3. Barrett, *loc. cit.*
4. French, *General Gage's Informers*, p. 95.
5. *Ibid.*, pp. 96-97.
6. Barrett, *loc. cit.*
7. Barker, *op. cit.*, p. 35.
8. Mackenzie, *Diary*, I, 19-22.
9. Unsigned letter, *Wm. and Mary Quart.*, 3rd ser., X (1953), 106.
10. Deposition of Hannah Adams, May 17, 1775, *American Archives*,
    4th ser., II, 674.
11. Deposition of Benjamin and Rachel Cooper, May 19, 1775, *Amer-
    ican Archives, loc. cit.*

CHAPTER 3

1. Timothy Pickering to ———, June 26, 1807, MS letter, Mass. Hist.
   Soc., as quoted in French, *First Year of the American Revolution*,
   p. 26.
2. Hannah Winthrop to Mercy Warren [April or May, 1775], Mass.
   Hist. Soc., *Warren-Adams Letters*, II, 410.

3. Hugh Percy to Edward Harvey, April 20, 1775, Northumberland, *Letters*, pp. 52-53.
4. "Extract of a Letter Received in New York, dated London, June 1, 1775," *American Archives*, 4th ser., II, 871.
5. *Gazetteer and New Daily Advertiser* (London), June 1, 1775, as quoted in French, *op. cit.*, p. 315. The two missing Americans had been taken prisoners of war on April 19 and exchanged June 6, 1775. Cf. Frothingham, *Siege of Boston*, p. 112.
6. John S. Copley to Henry Pelham, Aug. 6, 1775, Copley, *Letters & Papers*, pp. 348-49.
7. Mackenzie, *Diary*, I, 30.
8. Barker, *British in Boston*, pp. 38-39.
9. French, *Taking of Ticonderoga*, pp. 43-44.
10. Allen, *Narrative*, pp. 14-15.

CHAPTER 4

1. Artemas Ward to the Massachusetts Congress, April 24, 1775, *American Archives*, 4th ser., II, 384.
2. Trumbull, *Autobiography*, pp. 18-19.
3. Peter Brown to his mother, June 28, 1775, Stiles, *Literary Diary*, I, 595.
4. *Ibid.*, pp. 595-96.
5. "A British Officer to a Friend in England," n.d., Mass. Hist. Soc., *Proc.*, XLIV (1910-11), 101-02.
6. John Burgoyne to "a Noble Lord," June 25, 1775, *New Eng. Hist. and Gen. Reg.*, XI (April, 1857), 125-26.
7. Robert Steele to William Sumner, July 10, 1825, MS letter, Samuel Swett Papers on Bunker Hill. N.-Y. Hist. Soc.
8. William Prescott to John Adams, Aug. 25, 1775, Frothingham, *Siege of Boston*, pp. 395-96.
9. Samuel B. Webb to Joseph Webb, June 19, 1775, Webb, *Correspondence and Journals*, I, 64-65.
10. John Chester to ———, n.d., Webb, *op. cit.*, I, 67-69. Captain Walter Sloane Laurie, who had commanded the British at the North Bridge in Concord, was detailed to bury the dead, and on June 23, 1775, reported: "Doctor Warren . . . I found among the slain, and stuffed the scoundrell with another into one hole and there he and his seditious principles may remain." French, *First Year of the American Revolution*, p. 263n.
11. "A British Officer to a Friend in England," n.d., Mass. Hist. Soc., *Proc.*, XLIV (1910-11), 102-03.
12. Thomas Gage to Lord Barrington, June 26, 1775, Gage, *Correspondence*, II, 686-87.

CHAPTER 5

1. Benjamin Franklin to William Strahan, Philadelphia, July 5, 1775, *Mag. Amer. Hist.*, IX (June, 1883), 438. On the same day Strahan in London wrote to Franklin urging him as a newly elected Delegate to the Continental Congress to use all his influence to effect a compromise and settle the dispute between England and her colonies. Strahan's letter is abstracted in Gt. Brit. Hist. Mss. Comm., *Manuscripts of the Earl of Dartmouth*, [I], 381.
2. Silas Deane to Elizabeth Deane, June 3, 1775, Deane, *Deane Papers*, I, 53-54.
3. Harrower, "Diary, 1773-1776," *Amer. Hist. Review*, VI (Oct., 1900), 100.
4. Roger Atkinson to Samuel Pleasants, Oct. 1, 1774, *Va. Mag. Hist.*, XV (April, 1908), 356.
5. Adams, *Works*, II, 415-16.
6. *Ibid.*, pp. 416-18.

7. U. S. Continental Congress, *Journals*, II, 92.
8. Washington to Martha Washington, June 18, 1775, Freeman, *Washington*, III, 452-54.
9. John Adams to Abigail Adams, June 23, 1775, Adams, *Familiar Letters*, p. 70.
10. "Extract of a Letter from a Clergyman in Maryland . . . Aug. 2, 1775," *American Archives*, 4th ser., III, 9-10.
11. "Extract of a Letter from a Gentleman in Virginia . . . Sept. 1, 1775," *American Archives*, 4th ser., III, 621.
12. Niles, *Principles and Acts of the Revolution*, pp. 305-06.
13. *New York Journal*, Nov. 23, 1775, as quoted in *Hist. Mag.*, 2nd ser., V (Jan., 1869), 57.

CHAPTER 6

1. Belknap, "Journal of my Tour to the Camp," Mass. Hist. Soc., *Proc.*, IV (1858-60), 82-83.
2. Washington to the Continental Congress, July 10, 1775, *WW-f*, III, 327.
3. Joseph Reed to his wife, Oct. 11, 1776, Reed, *Life and Correspondence of Joseph Reed*, I, 243.
4. Washington to Lund Washington, Aug. 20, 1775, *WW-f*, III, 433.
5. William Emerson to his wife, July 17, 1775, *WW-s*, III, 491. The original letter seems lost, but an incomplete copy is in the Bancroft Transcripts, Manuscripts Division, New York Public Library. The transcriber evidently made the copy from the original and Sparks's copy, for he omitted paragraphs published by Sparks and indicated errors Sparks had made in transcription.
6. *Loc. cit.*
7. Wright, "Revolutionary Journal," *Hist. Mag.*, VI (July, 1862), 209.
8. Fitch, "Journal," Mass. Hist. Soc., *Proc.*, 2nd ser., IX (1894-95), 53.
9. *Essex Gazette*, Nov. 2-9, 1775, as quoted in Essex Inst., *Hist. Coll.*, III (June, 1861), 137n.
10. Jesse Lukens to John Shaw, Jr., Sept. 13, 1775, *Amer. Hist. Record*, I, (Dec., 1872), 547-48.
11. Gt. Brit. Hist. Mss. Comm., *Manuscripts to Mrs. Stopford-Sackville*, II, 17-18.
12. Nathanael Greene to ———, Jan. 4, 1776, Greene, *Greene*, I, 126-27.

CHAPTER 7

1. "A Letter . . . from Mr. Grant, one of the Surgeons Attending the Military Infirmary at Boston, June 23 [1775]," *Farley's Bristol Journal*, Aug. 5, 1775, as quoted in Willard (ed.), *Letters*, p. 141.
2. Jonathan Sewall to Thomas Robie, July 15, 1775, Mass. Hist. Soc., *Proc.*, 2nd ser., X (1895-96), 414.
3. "Extract of a Genuine Letter from Boston . . . July 25, 1775," *Morning Chronicle and London Advertiser*, Sept. 11, 1775, as quoted in Willard (ed.), *op. cit.*, pp. 174-75.
4. Leach, "Journal," *New Eng. Hist. and Gen. Reg.*, XIX (July, 1865), 260.
5. Brooks, *Henry Knox*, p. 33.
6. Cooke, "Revolutionary Correspondence," Amer. Antiq. Soc., *Proc.*, XXXVI (Oct., 1926), 257.
7. Fitch, "Journal," Mass. Hist. Soc., *Proc.*, 2nd ser., IX (1894-95), 54-55.
8. Huntington, *Letters*, p. 22.
9. General Orders, Dec. 5, 1775, Kemble, *Kemble Papers*, I, 269-70.
10. Lord Rawdon to the Earl of Huntingdon, Oct. 5, 1775, Gt. Brit. Hist. Mss. Comm., *Report on the Manuscripts of the Late Reginald Rawdon Hastings*, III, 159-60.

11. General Orders, Jan. 3, 1776, Kemble, *op. cit.*, I, 288.
12. "Extract of a Genuine Letter from an Officer in the King's Army at Boston . . . Jan. 20 [1776]," *Gazetteer and New Daily Advertiser* (London), Feb. 27, 1776, as quoted in Willard (ed.), *op. cit.*, p. 258.
13. Peter Oliver, "Origin and Progress of the American Rebellion to the Year 1776 in a Letter to a Friend," (1781), British Museum, Egerton Manuscripts, 2671. (Copy in Gay Transcripts, Mass. Hist. Soc.) As quoted in French, *First Year of the American Revolution*, p. 344.

CHAPTER 8

1. Washington to the President of Congress, Nov. 8, 1775, *WW-f*, IV, 73.
2. Washington to the President of Congress, Nov. 11, 1775, *WW-f*, IV, 82-83.
3. Washington to Joseph Reed, Nov. 28, 1775, *WW-f*, IV, 124-25.
4. Lyman, "Journal . . . 1775," Conn. Hist. Soc., *Coll.*, VII (1899), 128-29.
5. Washington to the President of Congress, Dec. 11, 1775, *WW-f*, IV, 156-57.
6. Charles Lee to Benjamin Rush, Dec. 12, 1775, Lee, *Lee Papers*, I, 226.
7. White, *Narrative of Events*, pp. 5-6.
8. Henry Knox to Washington, Dec. 17, 1775, Sparks (ed.), *Correspondence*, I, 94-95.
9. Heath, *Memoirs*, pp. 27-28.
10. Washington to Joseph Reed, Jan. 4, 1776, *WW-f*, IV, 211.
11. Heath, *op. cit.*, pp. 32-33.
12. Trumbull, *Autobiography*, pp. 24-25.
13. Henshaw, *Orderly Books*, p. 101.
14. Josiah Quincy to James Bowdoin, Mar. 13, 1776, Bowdoin, *Bowdoin and Temple Papers*, I, 397.
15. Moore, *Diary*, I, 219-22.

CHAPTER 9

1. L. L. Hunt, "General Richard Montgomery," *Harper's New Monthly Mag.*, LXX (Feb., 1885), 353.
2. Allen, *Narrative*, pp. 27-28.
3. Washington to Philip Schuyler, Oct. 26, 1775, *WW-f*, IV, 46.
4. Jesse Lukens to John Shaw, Jr., Sept. 16, 1775, *Amer. Hist. Record*, I (Dec., 1872), 548. This letter was written over a period of several days, the part quoted here being dated Sept. 13.
5. Ware, "Expedition against Quebec," *New Eng. Hist. and Gen. Reg.*, VI (April, 1852), 129.
6. *Loc. cit.*
7. Senter, "Journal," in Roberts, *March to Quebec*, pp. 202-03.
8. *Ibid.*, pp. 205-06.
9. *Ibid.*, p. 207.
10. *Ibid.*, pp. 218-19.
11. Stocking, "Journal," in Roberts, *op. cit.*, pp. 555-56.
12. Morison, "Journal," in Roberts, *op. cit.*, pp. 525-26.
13. Senter, *op. cit.*, p. 219.

CHAPTER 10

1. Guy Carleton to William Howe, Jan. 12, 1776, *American Archives*, 4th ser., IV, 656.
2. Senter, "Journal," in Roberts, *March to Quebec*, pp. 230-31.
3. Stocking, "Journal," in Roberts, *op. cit.*, pp. 563-64.
4. Daniel Morgan to Henry Lee (?), n.d., *Hist. Mag.*, 2nd ser., IX (June, 1877), 379-80. An account by Morgan, differing in a few

phrases, was published in 1856 as "Fragment of a Sketch of Morgan's Military Career, Written by Himself," in Graham, *Life of General Daniel Morgan*, Appendix B, pp. 464-66.

5. Morison, "Journal," in Roberts, *op. cit.*, pp. 537-38.
6. Senter, *op. cit.*, pp. 234-35.
7. Henry Caldwell to James Murray, June 15, 1776, *Hist. Mag.*, 2nd ser., II (Aug., 1867), 101.

CHAPTER 11

1. Moore, *Diary*, I, 209-10.
2. Moultrie, *Memoirs*, I, 140-41. The date of Lee's arrival is given in Moultrie erroneously as June 4, and has been corrected here.
3. *Ibid.*, pp. 141-42.
4. *Ibid.*, p. 174.
5. *Ibid.*, p. 175.
6. *Ibid.*, p. 176.
7. *Ibid.*, p. 176, 176n.
8. *Ibid.*, p. 177.
9. *Ibid.*, pp. 178-79
10. "Diary of Captain Barnard Elliott," in Charleston, S. C., *Yearbook*, 1889, p. 222.
11. "A New War Song," Mass. Hist. Soc., *Proc.*, LX (1926-27), 239.

CHAPTER 12

1. Henry Knox to Lucy Knox, Jan. 5, 1776, Soc. of the Cincinnati, Mass., *Memorials*, pp. 108-09.
2. Peter Elting to Richard Varick, June 13, 1776, N. Y. Mercantile Lib. Assoc., *New York City during the American Revolution*, p. 97.
3. Loammi Baldwin to his wife, June 17, 1776, MS letter, Baldwin Papers, Harvard College Lib., as quoted in Freeman, *Washington*, IV, 85.
4. Henshaw, *Orderly Books*, p. 219.
5. *Ibid.*, p. 131.
6. William Eustis to ———, June 28, 1776, *New Eng. Hist. and Gen. Reg.*, XXIII (April, 1869), 208.
7. Serle, *American Journal*, pp. 30-31.
8. John Adams to Abigail Adams, March 19, 1776, Adams, *Familiar Letters*, p. 146.
9. Thomas Jefferson to Dr. James Mease, Sept. 16, 1825, *Potter's Amer. Monthly*, IV (March, 1875), 224.
10. Thomas Jefferson to Henry Lee, May 8, 1825, Jefferson, *Writings*, VII, 407.
11. John Adams to Abigail Adams, July 3, 1776, Adams, *op. cit.*, pp. 193-94.
12. John Adams to William Plumer, March 28, 1813, Adams. *Works*, X, 35-36.
13. Thacher, *Military Journal*, 2nd ed., p. 49.
14. Bangs, "Journal," N. J. Hist. Soc., *Proc.*, VIII (1856-59), 125.
15. *Massachusetts Spy*, July 24, 1776, as quoted in Amer. Antiq. Soc., *Proc.*, new ser., XXXV (Oct., 1925), 248-49.
16. Alexander Graydon to John Lardner, July 18, 1776, *Amer. Hist. Reg.*, No. 15 (Nov., 1895), 431.
17. Serle, *op. cit.*, pp. 28-30.
18. Washington to the New York Legislature, Aug. 17, 1776, *WW-f*, V, 444.
19. General Orders, July 13, 1776, *WW-f*, V. 268-69.
20. Henry Knox to Lucy Knox, July 15, 1776, Brooks, *Henry Knox*, p. 58.
21. Henry Knox to Lucy Knox, July 22, 1776, Brooks, *op. cit.*, p. 59.
22. Lord Rawdon to the Earl of Huntingdon, Aug. 5, 1776, *Gt. Brit.*

Hist. Mss. Comm., *Report on the Manuscripts of the Late Reginald Rawdon Hastings,* III, 179-80.

23. Long Island Hist. Soc., *Memoirs,* II (1869), 350.

CHAPTER 13

1. Lowell, *Hessians,* p. 61.
2. Stiles, *History of Ancient Windsor,* pp. 714n-715n.
3. Lord Rawdon to the Earl of Huntingdon, Sept. 3, 1776, Gt. Brit. Hist. Mss. Comm., *Report on the Manuscripts of the Late Reginald Rawdon Hastings,* III, 181.
4. Colonel von Heeringen to Colonel von Lossberg, n.d., Long Island Hist. Soc., *Memoirs,* II (1869), 433.
5. "Extract of a Letter from an Officer in General Frazier's Battalion, Sept. 3, 1776," *American Archives,* 5th ser., I, 1259-60.
6. Lewis Morris, Jr., to Lewis Morris, Aug. 28, 1776, N.-Y. Hist. Soc., *Coll.,* VIII (1875), 440.
7. Onderdonk, *Revolutionary Incidents,* pp. 147-48.
8. [Martin], *Narrative,* pp. 19-21.
9. Tallmadge, *Memoir,* pp. 11-12.
10. Account of General Edward Hand, *Penn. Archives,* 2nd ser., X, 308-09.
11. Tallmadge, *op. cit.,* pp. 12-14.
12. "Occupation of New York City by the British, 1776," *Penn. Mag. Hist.,* I (1877), 148.
13. "Extract . . . from the Journals and Original Papers of Sir George Collier," Long Island Hist. Soc., *Memoirs,* II (1869), 413-14.

CHAPTER 14

1. John Haslet to Caesar Rodney, Sept. 4, 1776, Rodney, *Letters,* p. 112.
2. Lewis Morris, Jr., to Lewis Morris, Sept. 6, 1776, N.-Y. Hist. Soc., *Coll.,* VIII (1875), 442.
3. Ezra Lee to David Humphreys, Feb. 20, 1815, *Mag. Amer. Hist.,* XXIX (Mar., 1893), 263-64.
4. *Ibid.,* pp. 264-65.
5. Washington to the President of Congress, Sept. 8, 1776, *WW-f,* VI, 28.
6. *Loc. cit.*
7. [Martin], *Narrative,* pp. 25-28.
8. George Weedon to John Page, Sept. 20, 1776, MS letter, Chicago Hist. Soc.
9. Thacher, *Military Journal,* 2nd ed., pp. 59-60.
10. Serle, *American Journal,* pp. 104-05.
11. Washington to the President of Congress, Sept. 16, 1776, *WW-f,* VI, 59.
12. Joseph Reed to his wife, Sept. 17, 1776, *Mag. Amer. Hist.,* IV (May, 1880), 370.
13. *Loc. cit.*
14. John Chilton to "My dear Friends," Sept. 17, 1776, MS letter, Keith Papers, Va. Hist. Soc.
15. Tench Tilghman to his father, Sept. 19, 1776, Tilghman, *Memoir,* pp. 138-39.

CHAPTER 15

1. Mackenzie, *Diary,* I, 59-61.
2. *Ibid.,* pp. 62-63.
3. Washington to Lund Washington, Sept. 30, 1776, *WW-f,* VI, 138.
4. John Chilton to "My dear Friends," Oct. 4, 1776, MS letter, Keith Papers, Va. Hist. Soc.
5. Heath, *Memoirs,* p. 55.

6. *Ibid.*, pp. 62-63.
7. Kemble, *Kemble Papers*, I, 95.
8. Heath, *op. cit.*, pp. 68-69.
9. Tallmadge, *Memoir*, pp. 17-18.
10. Heath, *op. cit.*, p. 70.
11. Wiederhold, "Capture of Fort Washington," *Penn. Mag. Hist.*, XXIII (1881), 95.
12. Mackenzie, *op. cit.*, I, 95-96.
13. Robert Auchmuty to the Earl of Huntingdon, Jan. 8, 1777, Gt. Brit. Hist. Mss. Comm., *Report on the Manuscripts of the Late Reginald Rawdon Hastings*, III, 190.
14. Wiederhold, *op. cit.*, pp. 96-97.
15. Lowell, *Hessians*, pp. 81-82.
16. Kemble, *op. cit.*, I, 100.
17. Mackenzie, *op. cit.*, I, 111-12.
18. Nathanael Greene to Henry Knox, Nov. 17, 1776, Soc. of the Cincinnati, Mass., *Memorials*, p. 117.
19. Joseph Reed to Charles Lee, Nov. 21, 1776, Lee, *Lee Papers*, II, 293-94.

CHAPTER 16

1. Moore, *Diary*, I, 350.
2. McMichael, "Diary," *Penn. Mag. Hist.*, XVI (1892), 139.
3. Bamford, "Diary," *Md. Hist. Mag.*, XXVIII (March, 1933), 18.
4. Moore, *op. cit.*, I, 357-58.
5. Anderson, *Personal Recollections*, p. 28.
6. Charles Lee to Horatio Gates, Dec. 12/13, 1776, Lee, *Lee Papers*, II, 348.
7. Stiles, *Literary Diary*, II, 106.
8. *Freeman's Journal*, Dec. 31, 1776, and January 14 and 21, 1777, as quoted in Moore, *Diary*, I, 361.
9. Kemble, *Kemble Papers*, I, 425.
10. Jones, *History of New York*, I, 716.
11. Stedman, *History of the . . . American War*, I, 242-43.
12. Thomas Paine, *American Crisis*, No. 1 [1776], page [1] reproduced in Monaghan, *Heritage of Freedom*, p. 27.
13. Samuel B. Webb to Joseph Trumbull, Dec. 16, 1776, Webb, *Correspondence and Journals*, I, 175.
14. Rush, *Autobiography*, pp. 124-25.
15. "Diary of an Officer on Washington's Staff," Stryker, *Battles of Trenton and Princeton*, pp. 361-64. This journal, asserts Douglas S. Freeman (*Washington*, IV, 310n) "has to be rejected as a forgery or later compilation." Stryker does not give the provenance of the journal, but historians have found it acceptable as from the hand of an eyewitness. Although it may be a later compilation it appears to be authentic and probably written by John Fitzgerald of Virginia.
16. "Battle of Princeton, by Sergeant R———," *Penn. Mag. Hist.*, XX (1896), 515.
17. *Ibid.*, pp. 515-16.
18. Henry Knox to Lucy Knox, Jan. 7, 1777, Soc. of the Cincinnati, Mass., *Memorials*, p. 122.
19. Washington to the President of Congress, Jan. 5, 1777, *WW-f*, VI, 468.
20. "Battle of Princeton, by Sergeant R———," *Penn. Mag. Hist.*, XX (1896), 516-18.
21. *Mag. Amer. Hist.*, IV (April, 1880), 310.

CHAPTER 17

1. William Harcourt to Simon Harcourt, March 17, 1777, Harcourt (ed.), *Harcourt Papers*, XI, 208.

2. Seybolt, "A Contemporary British Account of General Sir William Howe's Military Operations in 1777," Amer. Antiq. Soc., Proc., new ser., XL (April, 1930), 70-71.
3. Jones, History of New York, I, 170-71.
4. Robert Morris to Washington, March 6, 1777, Sparks (ed.), Correspondence, I, 348-49.
5. Martha Bland to Frances Randolph, May 12, 1777, N.J. Hist. Soc., Proc., LI (July, 1933), 151-52.
6. Jones, op. cit., I, 177.
7. Serle, American Journal, p. 195.
8. William Howe to George Germain, April 2, 1777, Anderson, Command of the Howe Brothers, p. 223.
9. Continental Journal and Weekly Advertiser (Boston), July 17, 1777.
10. London Chronicle, Sept. 27-30, 1777.
11. Cresswell, Journal, pp. 251-52, 257.

CHAPTER 18

1. McMichael, "Diary," Penn. Mag. Hist., XVI (1892), 146.
2. Ibid., p. 147.
3. John Adams to Abigail Adams, Aug. 24, 1777, Adams, Familiar Letters, p. 298.
4. "A Sermon Preached on the Eve of the Battle of Brandywine, Sept. 10, 1777, by the Rev. Joab Trout," Mag. Amer. Hist., XIII (March, 1885), 281.
5. Charles Cotesworth Pinckney to [William] Johnson, Nov. 14, 1820, Hist. Mag., X (June, 1866), 202-03.
6. William Darlington to Dr. A. L. Elwyn, Nov. 29, 1845, "Papers Relating to the Battle of Brandywine," Penn. Hist. Soc., Bulletin, I, No. 7 (1846), 58-59.
7. Jarvis, "An American's Experience in the British Army," Journal of Amer. Hist., I (Sept., 1907), 449.
8. George Weedon to John Page, Sept. 11, 1777, MS letter, with battle map, Chicago Hist. Soc.
9. "Battle of Brandywine," Penn. Mag. Hist., XX (1896), 421.
10. Anonymous letter, Sept. 11, 1777, Penn. Mag. Hist., XXIX (1905), 368.
11. Townsend, Some Accounts of the British Army, p. 26.
12. Morton, "Diary," Penn. Mag. Hist., I (1877), 3-4.
13. Ibid., pp. 7-8.

CHAPTER 19

1. "Extract from the Diary of General Hunter," Hist. Mag., IV (Nov., 1860), 346-47.
2. Timothy Pickering to ———, Aug. 23, 1826, North Amer. Review, XXIII (Oct., 1826), 427-28.
3. George Weedon to John Page, Oct. 8, 1777, MS letter, Chicago Hist. Soc.
4. [Martin], Narrative, pp. 53-54.
5. Thomas Paine to Benjamin Franklin, May 16, 1778, Penn. Mag. Hist., II (1878), 288-89.

CHAPTER 20

1. Cotton Mather Smith to his wife, July, 1775, Tuckerman, Life of General Philip Schuyler, p. 108.
2. William Duer to Philip Schuyler, June 19, 1777, Burnett (ed.), Letters, II, 385.
3. Thacher, Military Journal, 2nd ed., p. 86.
4. Samuel Adams to Roger Sherman, Aug. 11, 1777, Mass. Hist. Soc., Warren-Adams Letters, I, 353n.

5. John Adams to Abigail Adams, Aug. 19, 1777, Adams, *Familiar Letters*, pp. 292-93.

CHAPTER 21

1. John Burgoyne to George Germain, July 30, 1777, *The Remembrancer* (1777), p. 362.
2. Anburey, *Travels*, I, 219-20.
3. "A Scrap of Unwritten History," *Catholic World*, XXXVI (Dec., 1882), 348.
4. Peter Clark to his wife, Aug. 6, 1777, *New Eng. Hist. and Gen. Reg.*, XIV (April, 1860), 121-22.
5. Frederick Baume to John Burgoyne, Aug. 14, 1777, Burgoyne, *State of the Expedition from Canada*, Appendix, p. xxxxix.
6. "Account of the Battle of Bennington, by Glich, a German Officer," Vt. Hist. Soc., *Coll.*, I, 219-23.
7. Breymann, "Account," Vt. Hist. Soc., *Coll.*, I, 224-25.
8. Peter Clark to his wife, Aug. 29, 1777, *New Eng. Hist. and Gen. Reg.*, XIV (April, 1860), 123.
9. John Burgoyne to George Germain, Aug. 20, 1777, Burgoyne, *op. cit.*, Appendix, p. xxv.
10. Marinus Willet, "Narrative," Aug. 12, 1777, *Continental Journal and Weekly Advertiser* (Boston), Sept. 4, 1777.
11. Dwight, *Travels*, III, 196-98.

CHAPTER 22

1. Wilkinson, *Memoirs*, I, 237-38.
2. John Glover to J. Glover and A. Orne, Sept. 21, 1777, Essex Inst., *Hist. Coll.*, V (June, 1863), 101-02.
3. Digby, *British Invasion*, p. 274.
4. Anburey, *Travels*, I, 248-51.
5. Burgoyne, *State of the Expedition from Canada*, p. 124.
6. Richards, *Diary*, pp. 51-52.
7. Wilkinson, *op. cit.*, I, 267-69.
8. Mass. Hist. Soc., *Proc.*, III (1855-58), 273.
9. Riedesel, *Letters and Journals*, pp. 119-20.
10. *Ibid.*, pp. 125-27.
11. *Ibid.*, pp. 128-29.
12. *Ibid.*, p. 133.
13. Digby, *op. cit.*, pp. 319-20.
14. Wilkinson, *op. cit.*, I, 321-22.
15. *Continental Journal and Weekly Advertiser* (Boston), Jan. 14, 1779.
16. Hannah Winthrop to Mercy Warren, Nov. 11, 1777, Mass. Hist. Soc., *Warren-Adams Letters*, II, 451-52.

CHAPTER 23

1. Waldo, "Valley Forge, 1777-1778, Diary," *Penn. Mag. Hist.*, XXI (1897), 305.
2. *Ibid.*, pp. 306-07.
3. [Martin], *Narrative*, pp. 73-74.
4. General Orders, Dec. 17, 1777, *WW-f*, X, 167-68.
5. Waldo, *op. cit.*, pp. 309-10.
6. *Ibid.*, p. 312.
7. Marshall, *Extracts from the Diary*, pp. 152-53.
8. Waldo, *op. cit.*, pp. 312-13.
9. John Adams to Abigail Adams, Oct. 26, 1777, Adams, *Familiar Letters*, pp. 322-23.
10. Jonathan D. Sergeant to James Lovell, Nov. 20, 1777, MS letter, Samuel Adams Papers, New York Public Library.
11. Washington to Richard Henry Lee, Oct. 17, 1777, *WW-f*, IX, 388.
12. Washington to Thomas Conway, Nov. 9, 1777, *WW-f*, X, 29.

13. Thomas Conway to Washington, Nov. 5 [9 or 10(?)], 1777, MS letter, George Washington Papers, Library of Congress.
14. Washington to the President of Congress, Jan. 2, 1778, *WW-f*, X, 249.
15. Washington to Horatio Gates, Jan. 4, 1778, *WW-f*, X, 264-65.
16. Washington to Horatio Gates, Feb. 9, 1778, *WW-f*, X, 440.
17. Washington to Horatio Gates, Feb. 24, 1778, *WW-f*, X, 508-09.
18. Thomas Conway to Washington, July 23, 1778, *WW-s*, V, 517.

CHAPTER 24

1. Philip van Cortlandt to George Clinton, Feb. 13, 1778, N. Y. Governor, *Public Papers of George Clinton*, II, 843-44.
2. *Ibid.*, p. 844.
3. Washington to George Clinton, Feb. 16, 1778, *WW-f*, X, 469.
4. Baron von Steuben to Washington, n.d., Palmer, *General von Steuben*, pp. 114-15.
5. Baron von Steuben to Baron von der Goltz, n.d., Palmer, *op. cit.*, p. 157.
6. Baron von Steuben to Baron von Gaudy, n.d., Palmer, *op. cit.*, p. 157.
7. Alexander Scammell to John Sullivan, April 8, 1778, Palmer, *op. cit.*, pp. 154-55.
8. Du Ponceau, "Autobiography," *Penn. Mag. Hist.*, LXIII (April, 1939), 219.
9. Palmer, *op. cit.*, p. 157.
10. Ewing, *George Ewing*, p. 34.
11. John Laurens to Henry Laurens, April 1, 1778, Laurens, *Army Correspondence*, p. 152.
12. Du Ponceau, *op. cit.*, p. 208.
13. *Ibid.*, p. 209.
14. Waldo, "Valley Forge" (poem), *Hist. Mag.*, VII (Sept., 1863), 274.
15. Waldo, "Valley Forge, 1777-1778, Diary," *Penn. Mag. Hist.*, XXI (1897), 319-20.
16. Du Ponceau, *op. cit.*, p. 457.
17. Boudinot, *Journal*, p. 77.
18. *Ibid.*, pp. 77-78.
19. Waldo, "Valley Forge" (poem), *Hist. Mag.*, VII (Sept., 1863), 272.
20. *Loc. cit.*
21. Washington to John Banister, April 21, 1778, *WW-f*, XI, 291-92.
22. "Letter of a Soldier at Valley Forge, dated May 7, 1778," *Pennsylvania Packet*, May 13, 1778.
23. *WW-s*, V, 357n.
24. McMichael, "Diary," *Penn. Mag. Hist.*, XVI (1892), 158.

CHAPTER 25

1. Rebecca Franks to Mrs. William Paca, Feb. 26, 1778, *Penn. Mag. Hist.*, XVI (1892), 216-17.
2. "From a Lady in Philadelphia to Mrs. Theodorick Bland, Jr., n.d., Bland, *Bland Papers*, I, 92.
3. "Extract from a Letter dated Philadelphia, January 9," *Continental Journal and Weekly Advertiser* (Boston), Feb. 19, 1778.
4. "British Valour Displayed," *Continental Journal and Weekly Advertiser* (Boston), March 26, 1778.
5. "From a Lady in Philadelphia to Mrs. Theodorick Bland, Jr.," n.d., Bland, *op, cit.*, I, 94.
6. Lossing, *Two Spies*, pp. 57-59.

CHAPTER 26

1. William Bradford, Jr., to his sister, Rachel, May 14, 1778, *Penn. Mag. Hist.*, XL (1916), 342-43.
2. "From a Late Philadelphia Paper," *Continental Journal and Weekly*

Advertiser (Boston), July 30, 1778.

3. Alexander Hamilton to Elias Boudinot, July 5, 1778, *Penn. Mag. Hist.*, II (1878), 140-42.
4. [Martin], *Narrative*, pp. 92-93.
5. Testimony of Tench Tilghman, Court Martial of Charles Lee; Lee, *Lee Papers*, III, 81.
6. Custis, *Recollections*, pp. 413-14.
7. [Martin], *op. cit.*, pp. 93-96.
8. James McHenry to John Cox, July 1, 1778, Montgomery, "Battle of Monmouth," *Mag. Amer. Hist.*, III (June, 1879), 358-59.
9. [Martin], *op. cit.*, pp. 96-97.
10. Charles Lee to Washington, June 30, 1778, Lee, *op. cit.*, II, 435-36.
11. Washington to Charles Lee, June 30, 1778, *WW-f*, XII, 132-33.
12. Charles Lee to Washington, June 30, 1778, Lee, *op. cit.*, II, 437-38.
13. Anthony Wayne to Richard Peters, July 12, 1778, Stillé, *Anthony Wayne*, pp. 153-54.
14. Fisher, "Diary," in Godfrey, *Commander-in-Chief's Guard*, p. 280.

CHAPTER 27

1. Parke-Bernet Galleries, Inc., *James McHenry Papers*, II, 10.
2. Count d'Estaing to Congress, Aug. 26, 1778, *WW-ford*, VII, 114n.
3. Paul Revere to his wife [Aug. 1778], Mass. Hist. Soc., *Proc.*, XIII (1873-75), 251-52.
4. Washington to John Sullivan, Aug. 28, 1778, *WW-f*, XII, 369.
5. Nathanael Greene to Washington, Sept. 16, 1778, Greene, *Greene*, II, 143-44.
6. Moré, *Chevalier de Pontgibaud*, pp. 66-67.
7. Washington to John Sullivan, Sept. 1, 1778, *WW-f*, XII, 385.

CHAPTER 28

1. Clark, "Memoir, 1773-1779," Clark, *George Rogers Clark Papers, 1771-1781*, pp. 269-70.
2. *Ibid.*, p. 271.
3. *Ibid.*, p. 274.
4. Hamilton, "Report," Gt. Brit. Hist. Mss. Comm., *Manuscripts of Mrs. Stopford-Sackville*, II, 234.
5. Fellows, "Journal," N. Y. Sec. of State, *Journals of the Military Expedition of Major General John Sullivan*, p. 87.
6. Parker, "Journal," *Penn. Mag. Hist.*, XXVII (1903), 416.
7. Davis, "History of the Expedition against the Five Nations," *Hist. Mag.*, 2nd ser., III (April, 1868), 200.
8. Beatty, "Journal," N. Y. Sec. of State, *op. cit.*, p. 32.
9. Fogg, "Journal," N. Y. Sec. of State, *op. cit.*, p. 101.

CHAPTER 29

1. Nathanael Greene to James Varnum, Feb. 9, 1779, Greene, *Greene*, II, 168-69.
2. Washington to Gouverneur Morris, Oct. 4, 1778, *WW-f*, XIII, 21-22.
3. Washington to Benjamin Harrison, Dec. 18 [-30], 1778, *WW-f*, XIII, 466-68.
4. "Extracts from Interleaved Almanacs kept by John White of Salem," Essex Inst., *Hist. Coll.*, XLIX (Jan., 1913), 93-94.
5. Drake, *Life and Correspondence of Henry Knox*, pp. 60-61.
6. W. Croghan to Barnard Gratz, Mar. 4, 1779, *Hist. Mag.*, I (June, 1857), 180.
7. Nathanael Greene to Jeremiah Wadsworth, Mar. 19, 1779, *Mag. Amer. Hist.*, XX (Sept. 1888), 247.
8. Ebenezer Huntington to Joshua Huntington, May 3, 1779, Huntington, *Letters*, pp. 80-81.
9. Washington to Henry Lee, July 9, 1779, *WW-f*, XV, 388.
10. William Irvine to Anthony Wayne, July 10, 1779, Philips, *Historical Letters*, p. 11.

11. Stillé, Wayne, p. 181.
12. New York Journal, Aug. 2, 1779, as quoted in N. Y. Governor, Public Papers of George Clinton, V, 154n.
13. Henry W. Archer to Anthony Wayne, July 28, 1779, Penn. Mag. Hist., XL (1916), 298.

CHAPTER 30

1. Washington to Lafayette, Sept. 30, 1779, WW-f, XVI, 372.
2. Ibid., pp. 375-76.
3. Anthony Wayne to William Irvine, Dec. 14, 1779, Hist. Mag., VI (Oct., 1862), 322.
4. Thacher, Military Journal, 2nd ed., p. 181.
5. [Martin], Narrative, p. 124.
6. Thacher, op. cit., p. 183.
7. [Martin], op. cit., pp. 132-35.
8. Lafayette to Joseph Reed, May 31, 1780, Reed, Life and Correspondence of Joseph Reed, II, 207.
9. Washington to Joseph Jones, May 31, 1780, WW-f, XVIII, 453.
10. Thacher, op. cit., p. 196.
11. Simeon DeWitt to John Bogart, June 26, 1780, Bogart. John Bogart Letters, p. 26.

CHAPTER 31

1. Samuel Cogswell to his father, July 15, 1780, Hist. Mag., 2nd ser., VIII (Aug., 1870), 102.
2. Ebenezer Huntington to Andrew Huntington, July 7, 1780, Huntington, Letters, pp. 87-88.
3. Washington to the President of Congress, Aug. 20, 1780, WW-f, XIX, 412.
4. Joshua King to ———, June 9, 1817, Hist. Mag., I (Oct., 1857), 294.
5. Ibid., pp. 293-94.
6. Alexander Hamilton to Betsy Schuyler, Sept. 25, 1780, Hamilton, Works, IX, 207-08.
7. General Orders, Sept. 26, 1780, WW-f, XX, 95-96.
8. Benjamin Tallmadge to Jared Sparks, Feb. 17, 1834, Mag. Amer. Hist., III (Dec., 1879), 756.
9. Lamb, Journal, pp. 327-28.
10. "Colonel Tallmadge's Account of Major André," Hist. Mag., III (Aug., 1859), 230.
11. Thacher, Military Journal, 2nd ed., pp. 222-23.
12. Barber, Historical Collections, p. 303.
13. Ibid., pp. 303-04.
14. Lloyd's Evening Post (London), Dec. 11-13, 1780.
15. John Hugh Griffith to George Findley, Oct. 11, 1780, Mass. Hist. Soc., Coll., 4th ser., X (1871), 813.

CHAPTER 32

1. George Germain to Henry Clinton, Mar. 8, 1778, Gt. Brit. Hist. Mss. Comm., Manuscripts of Mrs. Stopford-Sackville, II, 99.
2. Moultrie, Memoirs, I, 412-13.
3. [Simms], South-Carolina in the Revolutionary War, p. 104.
4. Ibid., p. 115.
5. Tarleton, Campaigns, pp. 15-17.
6. [Hough], Siege of Charleston, pp. 85-86.
7. Moultrie, op. cit., II, 96-97.
8. [Hough], op. cit., pp. 129-30.
9. Moultrie, op. cit., II, 108.
10. John Mathews to Thomas Bee, June 9, 1780, Burnett (ed.), Letters, V, 204.

CHAPTER 33

1. Dr. Robert Brownfield to William D. James, n.d., James, *Marion*, Appendix, pp. 3-4.
2. Horatio Gates to Benjamin Lincoln, July 4, 1780, *Mag. Amer. Hist.*, V (Oct., 1880), 283.
3. Williams, "Southern army. Narrative of the Campaign of 1780," in Johnson, *Greene*, I, Appendix B, 487.
4. *Ibid.*, pp. 493-94.
5. *Ibid.*, p. 494.
6. *Ibid.*, pp. 494-95.
7. *Ibid.*, pp. 495-96.
8. Charles Magill to his father, n.d., *Mag. Amer. Hist.*, V (Oct., 1880), 279.
9. Williams, *op. cit.*, p. 496.
10. *Ibid.*, p. 497.
11. Senf, "Plan of the Battle near Camden," *Mag. Amer. Hist.*, V (Oct., 1880), 278.
12. Edward Stevens to Horatio Gates, Aug. 21, 1780, *Mag. Amer. Hist.*, V (Oct., 1880), 271.
13. *Royal Gazette* (New York), Sept. 16, 1780.

CHAPTER 34

1. Seymour, *Journal*, p. 7.
2. Horatio Gates to Washington, Aug. 30, 1780, Sparks (ed.), *Correspondence*, III, 67.
3. *New Jersey Gazette*, Jan. 31, 1781, as quoted in Moore, *Diary*, II, 352.
4. Patrick Ferguson to ———, n.d., Ferguson, *Two Scottish Soldiers*, pp. 66-67. Though the story sounds apocryphal, Washington did go personally on reconnaissance, Sept. 7. Cf. *WW-f*, IX, 195.
5. Isaac Shelby to William Hill, Aug. 26, 1814, Hamilton (ed.), "King's Mountain," *Journal of Southern Hist.*, IV (Aug., 1938), 374-75.
6. [Shelby], *Battle of King's Mountain*, p. 5.
7. [Collins], *Autobiography*, p. 52.
8. Chesney, *Journal*, p. 17.
9. Young, "Memoir," *The Orion*, III (Oct., 1843), 86-87.
10. [Shelby], *op. cit.*, p. 6.
11. [Collins], *op. cit.*, p. 53.

CHAPTER 35

1. Nathanael Greene to Catherine Greene, n.d., R.I. Hist. Soc., *Coll.*, XX (Oct., 1927), 106-07.
2. Du Ponceau, "Autobiography," *Penn. Mag. Hist.*, LXIII (July, 1939), 312-13.
3. Williams, "Southern army. Narrative of the Campaign of 1780," in Johnson, *Greene*, I, Appendix B, 510.
4. Nathanael Greene to Alexander Hamilton, Jan. 10, 1781, Hamilton, *Works*, Hamilton (ed.), I, 205-06.
5. Young, "Memoir," *The Orion*, III (Oct., 1843), 88.
6. *Ibid.*, p. 100.
7. McCall, *History of Georgia*, II, 357.
8. [Collins], *Autobiography*, p. 57.
9. Lee, *Campaign of 1781*, pp. 97n-98n.
10. Mackenzie, *Strictures on Lt.-Col. Tarleton's History*, pp. 100-01.
11. Moore, *Life of Gen. Edward Lacey*, p. 6n.

CHAPTER 36

1. Otho Williams to Daniel Morgan, Jan. 25, 1781, Graham, *Life of General Daniel Morgan*, p. 323.

2. Graham, *General Joseph Graham*, pp. 289-90.
3. Henry, *Narrative*, pp. 9-10.
4. *Ibid.*, pp. 10-11.
5. *Ibid.*, p. 11.
6. *Ibid.*, pp. 11-12.
7. Charles Cornwallis to George Germain, March 17, 1781, Stevens (comp.), *Campaign in Virginia*, I, 360.
8. Stedman, *History of the . . . American War*, II, 335.
9. Nathanael Greene to Washington, March 10, 1781, Sparks (ed.), *Correspondence*, III, 260.
10. St. George Tucker to Frances Bland Tucker, March 4, 1781, *Mag. Amer. Hist.*, VII (July, 1881), 38.

CHAPTER 37

1. Nathanael Greene to Thomas Jefferson, March 10, 1781, Jefferson, *Papers*, V, 112.
2. St. George Tucker to Frances Bland Tucker, March 13, 1781, *Mag. Amer. Hist.*, VII (July, 1881), 39.
3. Richard Harrison to Anne Harrison, March 15, 1781, *Amer. Hist. Reg.*, No. 10 (June, 1895), 1123.
4. Lamb, *Journal*, p. 361.
5. Lee, *Memoirs*, pp. 277-78.
6. St. George Tucker to Frances Bland Tucker, March 18, 1781, *Mag. Amer. Hist.*, VII (July, 1881), 40.
7. Lamb, *op. cit.*, p. 362.
8. Lee, *op. cit.*, p. 279.
9. *Ibid.*, pp. 279-80.
10. *Ibid.*, p. 280.
11. *Ibid.*, p. 286.
12. William Dickson to Robert Dixson, Nov. 30, 1784, Dickson, *Dickson Letters*, p. 15.

CHAPTER 38

1. Nathanael Greene to Washington, March 29, 1781, Sparks (ed.), *Correspondence*, III, 278-79.
2. Samuel Mathis to William R. Davie, June 26, 1819, *Amer. Hist. Record*, II (March, 1873), 106-09.
3. Otho Williams to Elie Williams, April 27, 1781, *Potter's Amer. Monthly*, IV (Feb., 1875), 103-04.
4. Lee, *Memoirs*, p. 332.
5. William Pierce to St. George Tucker, July 23, 1781, *Mag. Amer. Hist.*, VII (Dec., 1881), 436.
6. Otho Williams to ———, n.d., Tiffany, *Williams*, pp. 23-24.
7. Gibbes, *Documentary History*, III, 149-56.

CHAPTER 39

1. Charles Cornwallis to George Germain, April 23, 1781, Stevens (comp.), *Campaign in Virginia*, I, 420-22.
2. Charles Cornwallis to Henry Clinton, April 23, 1781, Stevens (comp.), *op. cit.*, I, 424.
3. Charles Cornwallis to William Phillips, April 10, 1781, Cornwallis, *Correspondence*, I, 88.
4. Charles Cornwallis to Henry Clinton, May 26, 1781, Stevens (comp.), *op. cit.*, I, 488.
5. Dr. Robert Wharry to Dr. Reading Beatty, July 27, 1781, *Penn. Mag. Hist.*, LIV (1930), 160.

CHAPTER 40

1. Denny, *Military Journal*, pp. 39-40.

2. Edward Hand to Jasper Yeates, Sept. 17, 1781, MS letter, Force Transcripts, Library of Congress.
3. [Martin], *Narrative*, p. 165.
4. "Diary of a French Officer, 1781," *Mag. Amer. Hist.*, IV (June, 1880), 445.
5. "An English Officer's Account of his Services in America, 1779-1781," *Hist. Mag.*, IX (Sept., 1865), 272.
6. Tucker, "Journal of the Siege of Yorktown, 1781," *Wm. and Mary Quart.*, 3rd ser., V (July, 1948), 380-81.
7. Duncan, "Diary," *Penn. Archives*, 2nd ser., XV, 748.
8. Denny, *op. cit.*, p. 41.
9. [Martin], *op. cit.*, pp. 166-68.
10. *Ibid.*, p. 168.
11. Duncan, *op. cit.*, p. 749.
12. "Diary of the Pennsylvania Line," Linn and Egle (eds.), *Pennsylvania in the War of the Revolution*, II, 694.
13. General Orders, Oct. 9, 1781, *WW-f*, XXIII, 203.
14. Van Cortlandt, "Autobiography," *Mag. Amer. Hist.*, II (May, 1878), 294.
15. Denny, *op. cit.*, p. 41.
16. Popp, "Journal, 1777-1783," *Penn. Mag. Hist.*, XXVI (1902), 41.
17. Tucker, *op. cit.*, pp. 386-87.
18. Deux-Ponts, *My Campaigns in America*, pp. 144-47.
19. [Martin], *op. cit.*, pp. 169-71.
20. Charles Cornwallis to Henry Clinton, Oct. 15, 1781, Stevens (comp.), *Campaign in Virginia*, II, 188.
21. Butler, "Journal," *Hist. Mag.*, VIII (March, 1864), 110.
22. *Va. Hist. Reg.*, V (Oct., 1852), 229.
23. Tarleton, *Campaigns*, p. 388.
24. Döhla, *Tagebuch eines Bayreuther Soldaten*, p. 148.
    The quotation is from a translation in the library of the Colonial National Historical Park, Yorktown, Va.
25. Denny, *op. cit.*, p. 44.
26. Tucker, *op. cit.*, p. 391.
27. [Balch], *Letters and Papers*, pp. 284-85.
28. Denny, *loc. cit.*
29. Dumas, *Memoirs*, I, 52n-53n.
30. Moore, *Diary*, II, 508n.
31. *Va. Hist. Reg.*, VI (Oct., 1853), 205.
32. Richard Butler to William Irvine, Oct. 22, 1781, Johnston, *Yorktown Campaign*, p. 202.
33. Moore, *op. cit.*, II, 518.

CHAPTER 41

1. Boudinot, *Journal*, pp. 38-39.
2. Moore, *Diary*, II, 527n.
3. Heath, *Memoirs*, p. 297.
4. Wraxall, *Historical Memoirs*, p. 246.
5. Ebenezer Hazard to Jeremy Belknap, Jan. 29, 1783, Mass. Hist. Soc., *Coll.*, 5th ser., II, 184.
6. Horatio Gates to Robert Morris, Oct. 25, 1782, Henkels, *Confidential Correspondence of Robert Morris*, pp. 108-09.
7. Samuel Shaw to Rev. Eliot, Mar. 23, 1783, Shaw, *Journals*, p. 103.
8. *Ibid.*, pp. 103-04.
9. [Martin], *Narrative*, pp. 202-04.
10. Tallmadge, *Memoir*, pp. 95-98.
11. Washington, "Address to Congress on Resigning his Commission," Dec. 23, 1783, *WW-f*, XXVII, 284.
12. *Ibid.*, pp. 284-85.
13. *Ibid.*, p. 285.

Bibliography

AS THE FOOTNOTES OF *Rebels and Redcoats* ARE CONFINED TO THE
QUOTATIONS IN THE TEXT, SO THE FOLLOWING BIBLIOGRAPHY LISTS
ONLY THE WORKS QUOTED.

BOOKS

ADAMS, JOHN, *Familiar Letters of John Adams and his Wife Abigail
Adams,* Charles Francis Adams, ed. New York, 1876.
————, *The Works of John Adams,* Charles Francis Adams, ed., 10 vols.
Boston, 1850-56.
ALLEN, ETHAN, *A Narrative of Col. Ethan Allen's Captivity,* 4th ed.
Burlington, Vt., 1846.
AMERICAN ARCHIVES, Peter Force, ed., 4th ser., 6 vols.; 5th ser., 3 vols.
Washington, [1837-53].
ANBUREY, THOMAS, *Travels through the Interior Parts of America,* 2
vols. Boston, 1923.
ANDERSON, ENOCH, *Personal Recollections of Captain Enoch Anderson,
an Officer of the Delaware Regiments in the Revolutionary War*
(Hist. Soc. of Delaware, *Papers,* XVI). Wilmington, 1896.
ANDERSON, TROYER S., *The Command of the Howe Brothers during the
American Revolution.* New York, 1936.
[BALCH, THOMAS], *Letters and Papers Relating Chiefly to the Provincial
History of Pennsylvania.* Philadelphia, 1855.
BARBER, JOHN W., *Historical Collections of the State of New York.*
New York, 1851.
BARKER, JOHN, *The British in Boston.* Cambridge, 1924.
BLAND, THEODORICK, *The Bland Papers,* Charles Campbell, ed., 2 vols.
Petersburg, 1840-43.
BOGART, JOHN, *The John Bogart Letters* (Rutgers College Publication,
2nd ser.). New Brunswick, 1914.
BOUDINOT, ELIAS, *Journal or Historical Recollections of American
Events during the Revolutionary War.* Philadelphia, 1894.
BOWDOIN, JAMES, *The Bowdoin and Temple Papers,* 2 vols. (Mass.
Hist. Soc., *Collections,* 6th ser., IX; 7th ser., VI). Boston, 1897-
1907.
BROOKS, NOAH, *Henry Knox, a Soldier of the Revolution.* New York,
1900.
BURGOYNE, JOHN, *A State of the Expedition from Canada.* London, 1780.
BURNETT, EDMUND C. (ed.), *Letters of Members of the Continental
Congress,* 8 vols. Washington, 1921-36.
CHESNEY, ALEXANDER, *The Journal of Alexander Chesney, a South
Carolina Loyalist in the Revolution and After,* E. A. Jones, ed.
(Ohio State University Studies, Contributions in History and
Political Science, No. 7). n.p., 1921.
CLARKE, GEORGE R., *George Rogers Clarke Papers, 1771-1781,* James A.
James, ed. (Illinois State Hist. Library, *Collections,* VIII). Spring-
field, Ill., 1912.
[COLLINS, JAMES P.], *Autobiography of a Revolutionary Soldier,* John
M. Roberts, ed., Clinton, La., 1859.
COPLEY, JOHN S., *Letters & Papers of John Singleton Copley and
Henry Pelham, 1739-1776* (Mass. Hist. Soc., *Collections,* LXXI).
Boston, 1914.
CORNWALLIS, CHARLES, *Correspondence of Charles, First Marquis Corn-
wallis,* Charles Ross, ed., 3 vols. London, 1859.

CRESSWELL, NICHOLAS, *The Journal of Nicholas Cresswell, 1774-1777.* New York, 1924.

CUSTIS, GEORGE W. P., *Recollections and Private Memoirs of Washington.* New York, 1860.

DAWSON, HENRY B. *Battles of the United States by Sea and Land,* 2 vols. New York, 1858.

DEANE, SILAS, *The Deane Papers . . . 1774-1790,* 5 vols. (New-York Hist. Soc., *Collections,* XIX-XXIII). New York, 1887-90.

DENNY, EBENEZER, *Military Journal.* Philadelphia, 1859.

DEUX-PONTS, WILLIAM D., *My Campaigns in America,* Samuel A. Green, trans. Boston, 1868.

DICKSON, WILLIAM, *The Dickson Letters,* James O. Carr, ed. Raleigh, 1901.

DIGBY, WILLIAM, *The British Invasion from the North,* James P. Baxter, ed. Albany, 1887.

DÖHLA, JOHANN C., *Tagebuch eines Bayreuther Soldaten.* Bayreuth, 1913. (Translation in the Library of the Colonial National Historical Park, Yorktown, Va.)

DRAKE, FRANCIS S., *Life and Correspondence of Henry Knox.* Boston, 1873.

DUMAS, MATHIEU, *Memoirs of His Own Time,* 2 vols. Philadelphia, 1839.

DWIGHT, TIMOTHY, *Travels in New-England and New-York,* 4 vols. New Haven, 1821-22.

EWING, THOMAS. *George Ewing, Gentleman, a Soldier of Valley Forge.* Yonkers, 1928.

FERGUSON, JAMES, *Two Scottish Soldiers,* Aberdeen, 1888.

FREEMAN, DOUGLAS S., *George Washington,* 6 vols. New York, 1948-54.

FRENCH, ALLEN, *The First Year of the American Revolution.* Boston, 1934.

———, *General Gage's Informers.* Ann Arbor, 1932.

———, *The Taking of Ticonderoga in 1775.* Cambridge, 1928.

FROTHINGHAM RICHARD, *History of the Siege of Boston,* 3rd ed. Boston, 1872.

GAGE, THOMAS, *The Correspondence of General Thomas Gage,* 2 vols. New Haven, 1931-33.

GIBBES, ROBERT W., *Documentary History of the American Revolution,* 3 vols. New York, 1853-57.

GODFREY, CARLOS E., *The Commander-in-Chief's Guard, Revolutionary War.* Washington, 1904.

GOSS, ELBRIDGE H., *The Life of Colonel Paul Revere,* 2 vols. Boston, 1891.

GRAHAM, JAMES, *The Life of General Daniel Morgan.* New York, 1856.

GRAHAM, WILLIAM A., *General Joseph Graham and His Papers on North Carolina Revolutionary History.* Raleigh, 1904.

GRAYDON, ALEXANDER, *Memoirs of His Own Time,* John S. Littell, ed. Philadelphia, 1846.

GREAT BRITAIN. HISTORICAL MANUSCRIPTS COMMISSION, *The Manuscripts of Mrs. Stopford-Sackville, of Drayton House, Northamptonshire,* 2 vols. London, 1904-10.

———, *Report on the Manuscripts of the Late Reginald Rawdon Hastings.* London, 1934.

———, *The Manuscripts of the Earl of Dartmouth,* 3 vols. London, 1887-96.

GREENE, GEORGE W., *The Life of Nathanael Greene,* 3 vols. New York, 1867-71.

HAMILTON, ALEXANDER, *The Works of Alexander Hamilton,* Henry C. Lodge, ed., 12 vols. New York, 1903.

———, *The Works of Alexander Hamilton,* John C. Hamilton, ed., 7 vols. New York, 1850-51.

HARCOURT, EDWARD W. (ed.), *Harcourt Papers*, 14 vols. Oxford, [1880-1905?].

HEATH, WILLIAM, *Memoirs of Major-General William Heath*, William Abbatt, ed. (new ed.). New York, 1901.

HENKELS, STANISLAUS V., *The Confidential Correspondence of Robert Morris.* (auction catalog). Philadelphia, 1917.

HENRY, ROBERT, *Narrative of the Battle of Cowan's Ford . . . and Narrative of the Battle of King's Mountain, by Captain David Vance.* Greensboro, 1891.

HENSHAW, WILLIAM, *The Orderly Books . . . October 1, 1775 through October 3, 1776.* Worcester, 1948.

[HOUGH, FRANKLIN B.], *The Siege of Charleston*, Albany, 1867.

HUMPHREYS, DAVID, *An Essay on the Life of the Honorable Major General Israel Putnam.* Boston, 1818.

HUNTINGTON, EBENEZER, *Letters Written . . . during the American Revolution* (Heartman's Historical Series, No. 2). New York, 1915.

IZARD, RALPH, *Correspondence . . . from the Year 1774 to 1804*, Vol. 1, New York, 1844.

JAMES, WILLIAM D., *A Sketch of the Life of Brig. Gen. Francis Marion.* Charleston, 1821.

JEFFERSON, THOMAS, *Papers*, Julian P. Boyd, ed., Vols. 1-12. Princeton, 1950-55.

———, *Writings*, H. A. Washington, ed., 9 vols. New York, 1853.

JOHNSON, WILLIAM, *Sketches of the Life and Correspondence of Nathanael Green*, 2 vols. Charleston, 1822.

JOHNSTON, HENRY P., *The Yorktown Campaign and the Surrender of Cornwallis, 1781.* New York, 1881.

JONES, THOMAS, *History of New York during the Revolutionary War*, Edward F. DeLancey, ed., 2 vols. New York, 1879.

KEMBLE, STEPHEN, *The Kemble Papers*, 2 vols. (New-York Hist. Soc., *Collections*, XVI-XVII). New York, 1884-85.

LAMB, ROGER, *An Original and Authentic Journal of Occurrences during the Late American War.* Dublin, 1809.

LAURENS, JOHN, *The Army Correspondence of Colonel John Laurens in the Years 1777-78.* New York, 1867.

LEAKE, ISAAC Q., *Memoir of the Life and Times of General John Lamb.* Albany 1857.

LEE, CHARLES, *The Lee Papers . . . 1754-1811*, 4 vols. (New-York Hist. Soc., *Collections*, IV-VII). New York, 1872-75.

LEE, HENRY [1787-1837], *The Campaign of 1781 in the Carolinas.* Philadelphia, 1824.

LEE, HENRY [1756-1818], *Memoirs of the War in the Southern Department of the United States*, Robert E. Lee, ed. New York, 1870.

LINN, JOHN B., and EGLE, WILLIAM H. (eds.), *Pennsylvania in the War of the Revolution, Battalions and Line, 1775-1783*, 2 vols. Harrisburg, 1880.

LOSSING, BENSON J., *The Two Spies: Nathan Hale and John André.* New York, 1886.

LOWELL, EDWARD J., *The Hessians and the other German Auxiliaries of Great Britain in the Revolutionary War.* New York, 1884.

McCALL, HUGH, *The History of Georgia*, 2 vols. Savannah, 1811-16.

MACKENZIE, FREDERICK, *Diary of . . . as an officer of the regiment of Royal Welch fusiliers during the years 1775-1781*, 2 vols. Cambridge, 1930.

MACKENZIE, RODERICK, *Strictures on Lt.-Col. Tarleton's History "of the Campaigns of 1780 and 1781."* London, 1787.

MARSHALL, CHRISTOPHER, *Extracts from the Diary . . . Kept in Philadelphia and Lancaster, during the American Revolution, 1774-1781*, William Duane, ed. Albany, 1877.

[MARTIN, JOSEPH P.], *A Narrative of Some of the Adventures, Dangers and Sufferings of a Revolutionary Soldier.* Hallowell, Me., 1830.

MASSACHUSETTS HISTORICAL SOCIETY, *Warren-Adams Letters* . . . *1743-1814,* 2 vols. (*Mass. Hist. Soc., Collections,* LXXII-LXXIII). Boston, 1917-25.

MONAGHAN, FRANK, *Heritage of Freedom.* Princeton, 1947.

MOORE, FRANK, *Diary of the American Revolution,* 2 vols. New York, 1860, 1859.

MOORE, MAURICE A., *The Life of Gen. Edward Lacey.* Spartanburg, S. C., 1859. (Reprinted, Rock Hill, S. C., 1933.)

MORÉ, CHARLES A., *The Chevalier de Pontgibaud, a French Volunteer,* 2nd ed. Paris, 1898.

MOULTRIE, WILLIAM, *Memoirs of the American Revolution,* 2 vols. New York, 1802.

NEW YORK. MERCANTILE LIBRARY ASSOCIATION, *New York City during the American Revolution.* New York, 1861.

NEW YORK. (STATE) GOVERNOR, *Public Papers of George Clinton,* 10 vols. New York, 1899-1914.

NEW YORK. (STATE) SECRETARY OF STATE, *Journals of the Military Expedition of Major General John Sullivan against the Six Nations of Indians in 1779.* Auburn, 1887.

NILES, HEZEKIAH, *Principles and Acts of the Revolution in America.* Baltimore, 1822.

NORTHUMBERLAND, HUGH PERCY, 2ND DUKE OF, *Letters of Hugh, earl Percy, from Boston and New York, 1774-1776,* Charles K. Bolton, ed. Boston, 1902.

ONDERDONK, HENRY, *Revolutionary Incidents of Suffolk and Kings Counties.* New York, 1849.

PALMER, JOHN M., *General von Steuben.* New Haven, 1937.

PARKE-BERNET GALLERIES, INC., *The James McHenry Papers,* 2 vols. (auction catalog). New York, 1944.

PHILIPS, GEORGE M., *Historic Letters from the Collection of the West Chester State Normal School.* Philadelphia, 1898.

REED, WILLIAM B., *Life and Correspondence of Joseph Reed,* 2 vols. Philadelphia, 1847.

RICHARDS, SAMUEL, *Diary of* . . ., *Captain of Connecticut Line.* Philadelphia, 1909.

RIEDESEL, FRIEDERIKE C., *Letters and Journals Relating to the War of the American Revolution,* William L. Stone, trans. Albany, 1867.

ROBERTS, KENNETH L., *March to Quebec,* 3rd ed. New York, 1940.

RODNEY, CAESAR, *Letters to and from Caesar Rodney, 1756-1784.* Philadelphia, 1933.

RUSH, BENJAMIN, *Autobiography* . . ., George W. Corner, ed. (Amer. Phil. Soc., *Memoirs,* XXV). Princeton, 1948.

SERLE, AMBROSE, *The American Journal* . . . *Secretary to Lord Howe, 1776-1778,* Edward H. Tatum, Jr., ed. San Marino, Calif., 1940.

SEYMOUR, WILLIAM, *A Journal of the Southern Expedition, 1780-1783* (Hist. Soc. of Delaware, *Papers,* XV). Wilmington, 1896.

SHAW, SAMUEL, *The Journals of Major Samuel Shaw.* Boston, 1847.

[SHELBY, ISAAC], *Battle of King's Mountain.* [n.p.], 1823.

[SIMMS, WILLIAM G.], *South-Carolina in the Revolutionary War.* Charleston, 1853.

SOCIETY OF THE CINCINNATI, MASSACHUSETTS, *Memorials,* by Francis S. Drake. Boston, 1873.

SPARKS, JARED (ed.), *Correspondence of the American Revolution,* 4 vols. Boston, 1853.

STEDMAN, CHARLES, *The History of the Origin, Progress, and Termination of the American War,* 2 vols. London, 1794.

STEVENS, BENJAMIN F. (comp.), *The Campaign in Virginia, 1781,* 2 vols. London, 1888. [Binder's title: *Clinton-Cornwallis Controversy.*]

STILES, EZRA, *The Literary Diary* . . ., Frankling B. Dexter, ed., 3 vols. New York, 1901.

STILES, HENRY R., *The History of Ancient Windsor, Connecticut.* New York, 1859.

STILLÉ, CHARLES J., *Major-General Anthony Wayne and the Pennsylvania Line in the Continental Army.* Philadelphia, 1893.

STRYKER, WILLIAM S., *The Battles of Trenton and Princeton.* Boston, 1898.

TALLMADGE, BENJAMIN, *Memoir,* Henry P. Johnston, ed. (Sons of the Revolution in the State of New York, *Publications,* I). New York, 1904.

TARLETON, BANASTRE, *A History of the Campaigns of 1780 and 1781, in the Southern Provinces of North America.* London, 1787.

THACHER, JAMES, *A Military Journal during the American Revolutionary War,* 2nd ed. Boston, 1827.

TIFFANY, OSMOND, *A Sketch of the Life and Services of Gen. Otho Holland Williams.* Baltimore, 1851.

TILGHMAN, TENCH, *Memoir . . . Secretary and Aid to Washington.* Albany, 1876.

TOWNSEND, JOSEPH, *Some Account of the British Army . . . and of the Battle of Brandywine* (Hist. Soc. of Pennsylvania, *Bulletin,* I, and No. 7). Philadelphia, 1846.

TRUE, HENRY, *Journal and Letters . . . Also an Account of the Battle of Concord by Captain Amos Barrett.* Marion, Ohio, 1900.

TRUMBULL, JOHN, *Autobiography, Reminiscences and Letters . . . from 1756 to 1841.* New York, 1841.

TUCKERMAN, BAYARD, *Life of General Philip Schuyler, 1733-1804.* New York, 1905.

U.S. CONTINENTAL CONGRESS, *Journals . . . 1774-1789,* 34 vols. Washington, 1904-37.

WASHINGTON, GEORGE, *Writings,* Worthington, C. Ford, ed., 14 vols. New York, 1889-93.

——, *Writings . . . 1745-1799* [prepared under the direction of the United States George Washington Bicentennial Commission], John C. Fitzpatrick, ed., 39 vols. Washington, 1931-44.

——, *Writings,* Jared Sparks, ed., 12 vols. Boston, 1834-37.

WEBB, SAMUEL B., *Correspondence and Journals,* Worthington C. Ford, ed., 3 vols. New York, 1893.

WHITE, JOSEPH, *A Narrative of Events.* Charlestown, Mass., 1833.

WILKINSON, JAMES, *Memoirs of my own Times,* 3 vols. Philadelphia, 1816.

WILLARD, MARGARET W. (ed.), *Letters on the American Revolution, 1774-1776.* Boston, 1925.

WRAXALL, NATHANIEL W., *Historical Memoirs of my own Time.* Philadelphia, 1845.

DIARIES AND JOURNALS

BAMFORD, WILLIAM, "Diary, the Revolutionary Days of a British Officer," *Md. Hist. Mag.* XXVII (Sept., 1932), 240-59 *et seq.*

BANGS, ISAAC, "Extract from the Journal of . . .," N.J. Hist. Soc., *Proc.,* VIII (1856-59), 120-25.

BEATTY, ERKURIES, "Journal of . . . of the 4th Penn Line," in N.Y. (State) Sec. of State, *Journals of the Military Expedition of Major General John Sullivan.* Auburn, 1887. pp. 15-37.

BELKNAP, JEREMY, "Journal of My Tour to the Camp," Mass. Hist. Soc., *Proc.,* IV (1858-60), 77-86.

BREYMANN, HEINRICH VON, "Account of his Part in the Affair near Wallorms-Kork, August 16, 1777," Vt. Hist. Soc., *Coll.*, I, 223-25.

BUTLER, RICHARD, "Journal of the Siege of Yorktown," *Hist. Mag.*, VIII (March, 1864), 102-12.

COLEMAN, GEORGE W., JR., "The Southern Campaign, 1781 . . . Narrated in the Letters from Judge St. George Tucker to his wife," *Mag. Amer. Hist.*, VII (July, 1881), 36-46.

COOKE, NICHOLAS, "Revolutionary Correspondence . . . 1775-1781," Amer. Antiq. Soc., *Proc.*, XXXVI (Oct., 1926), 231-353.

DAVIS, NATHAN, "History of the Expedition against the Five Nations," *Hist. Mag.*, 2nd ser., III (April, 1868), 198-205.

"Diary of a French Officer, 1781," *Mag. Amer. Hist.*, IV (June, 1880), 205-14 *et seq.*

"Diary of an Officer on Washington's Staff," in Stryker, William S., *Battles of Trenton and Princeton*. Boston 1898. pp. 360-64.

"Diary of the Pennsylvania Line, May 26, 1781-April 25, 1782," Linn, J. B. and Egle, W. H. (eds.), *Pennsylvania in the War of the Revolution, Battalion and Line, 1775-1783*, Vol. 2. Harrisburg, 1880.

DUNCAN, JAMES, "Diary of . . . of Colonel Moses Hazen's Regiment. In the Yorktown Campaign, 1781," *Penn. Archives*, 2nd ser., XV, 743-52.

DU PONCEAU, PETER S., "Autobiography," *Penn. Mag. Hist.*, LXIII (April, 1939), 189-227 *et seq.*

ELLIOTT, BARNARD, "Diary," in Charleston, S.C., *Yearbook, 1889*. Charleston, 1889. pp. 151-262.

FELLOWS, MOSES, "Journal," in N.Y. (State) Sec. of State, *Journals of the Military Expedition of Major General John Sullivan*, Auburn, 1887, pp. 86-91.

FISHER, ELIJAH, "Diary," in Godfrey, Carlos E., *The Commander-in-Chief's Guard, Revolutionary War*. Washington, 1904. pp. 275-92.

FITCH, JABEZ, "A Journal from August 5th to December 13th, 1775 . . . at the Siege of Boston," Mass. Hist. Soc., *Proc.*, 2nd ser., IX (1894/95), 41-91.

FOGG, JEREMIAH, "Journal," in N.Y. (State) Sec. of State, *Journals of the Military Expedition of Major General John Sullivan*. Auburn, 1887. pp. 92-101.

GLICH (a German Officer), "Account of the Battle of Bennington," Vt. Hist. Soc., *Coll.*, I, 211-23.

GRAHAM, SAMUEL, "An English Officer's Account of His Services in America, 1779-1781," *Hist. Mag.*, IX (Aug., 1865), 241-49 *et seq.*

HAMILTON, JAMES G. DE R. (ed.), "King's Mountain: Letters of Colonel Isaac Shelby," *Journal of Southern Hist.*, IV (Aug., 1938), 367-77.

HARROWER, JOHN, "Diary . . . 1773-1776," *Amer. Hist. Review*, VI (Oct., 1900), 65-107.

JARVIS, STEPHEN, "An American's Experience in the British Army," *Journal of Amer. Hist.*, I (Sept., 1907), 441-64.

LEACH, JOHN, "A Journal . . . during his Confinement by the British in Boston Gaol in 1775," *New Eng. Hist. and Gen. Reg.*, XIX (July, 1865), 255-63.

LYMAN, SIMEON, "Journal . . . Aug. 10 to Dec. 28, 1775," Conn. Hist. Soc., *Coll.*, VII (1899), 111-34.

McMICHAEL, JAMES, "Diary of . . . of the Pennsylvania Line, 1776-1778," *Penn. Mag. Hist.*, XVI (1892), 129-59.

MORISON, GEORGE, *"Journal,"* in Roberts, Kenneth, *March to Quebec*, 3rd ed. New York, 1940, pp. 501-39.

MORTON, ROBERT, "Diary," *Penn. Mag. Hist.*, I (1877), 1-39. "Papers Relating to the Battle of Brandywine," Penn. Hist. Soc., *Bulletin*, I, No. 7 (1846), 40-63.

PARKER, ROBERT, "Journal of . . . of the Second Continental Artillery, 1779." *Penn. Mag. Hist.*, XXVII (1903), 404-20 *et seq.*

POPP, STEPHEN, "Journal, 1777-1783," *Penn. Mag. Hist.*, XXVI (1902), 25-41 *et seq.*

R——, SERGEANT, "Battle of Princeton," *Penn. Mag. Hist.*, XX (1896), 515-19.

SENF, COL. [CHRISTIAN], "Plan of the Battle near Camden," *Mag. Amer. Hist.*, V (Oct., 1880), 275-78.

SENTER, ISAAC, "Journal," in Roberts, Kenneth, *March to Quebec*, 3rd ed. New York, 1940, pp. 193-241.

SEYBOLT, ROBERT F., "A Contemporary British Account of General Sir William Howe's Military Operations in 1777," Amer. Antiq. Soc., *Proc.*, new ser., XL (April, 1930), 69-92.

STOCKING, ABNER, "Journal," in Roberts, Kenneth, *March to Quebec*, 3rd ed. New York, 1940. pp. 543-69.

TUCKER, ST. GEORGE, "Journal of the Siege of Yorktown, 1781," *Wm. and Mary Quart.*, 3rd., ser., V (July, 1948), 375-95.

VAN CORTLANDT, PHILIP, "Autobiography," *Mag. Amer. Hist.*, II (May, 1878), 278-98.

WALDO, ALBIGENCE, "Valley Forge, 1777-1778. Diary." *Penn. Mag. Hist.*, XXI (1897), 299-323.

——, "Valley Forge" (poem), *Hist. Mag.*, VII (Sept., 1863), 270-74.

WARE, JOSEPH, "Expedition against Quebec," *New Eng. Hist. and Gen. Reg.*, VI (April, 1852), 129-45.

WHITE, JOHN, "Extracts from interleaved almanacs," Essex Inst., *Hist. Coll.*, XLIX (Jan., 1913), 92-94.

WIEDERHOLD, ANDREAS, "The Capture of Fort Washington," *Penn. Mag. Hist.*, XXIII (1899), 95-97.

WILLIAMS, OTHO, "Southern Army. A Narrative of the Campaign of 1780," in Johnson, William, *Sketches of the Life and Correspondence of Nathanael Greene*. Charleston, 1822. I, Appendix B, 485-510.

WRIGHT, AARON, "Revolutionary Journal . . . 1775," *Hist. Mag.*, VI (July, 1862), 208-12.

YOUNG, THOMAS, "Memoir of . . . a Revolutionary Patriot of South Carolina," *The Orion*, III (Oct., 1843), 84-88 *et seq.*

PERIODICALS

American Antiquarian Society, Proceedings, new ser., Vol. 1- , 1880- . Worcester, Mass., 1880- .

American Historical Record, Vol. 1-3; January, 1872- December, 1874. Philadelphia, 1872-74.

American Historical Register, Vol. 1-4; September, 1894- November, 1896; new ser., Vol. 1, March/May, 1897. Philadelphia, 1894-97.

American Historical Review, Vol. 1- , October, 1895- . New York, 1895- .

Connecticut Historical Society, *Collections*, Vol. 1-24; 1860-1932. Hartford, 1860-1932.

The Continental Journal and Weekly Advertiser, Vol. 1-10 (No. 1-591); May 30, 1776-June 21, 1787. Boston, 1776-87.

Essex Institute, *Historical Collections*, Vol. 1- , 1859- . Salem, Mass., 1859- .

Historical Magazine, Vol. 1-10, 1857-66; 2nd ser., Vol. 1-10, 1867-71; 3rd. ser., Vol. 1-3, 1872-75. Boston, 1857-75.

Journal of American History, Vol. 1- , January, 1907- . New Haven, 1907- .

Journal of Southern History, Vol. 1- , February, 1935- . Baton Rouge, La., 1935- .

Lloyd's Evening Post, December 11-13, 1780. London.
Long Island Historical Society, *Memoirs,* Vol. 1-4; 1867-89. Brooklyn, N. Y., 1867-89.
Magazine of American History, Vol. 1-30; January, 1877- September, 1893. New York, 1877-93.
Maryland Historical Magazine, Vol. 1- , March, 1906- . Baltimore, 1906- .
Massachusetts Historical Society, *Collections,* Vol. 1- , 1792-. Cambridge, 1792- .
———, *Proceedings,* Vol. 1- , 1791/1835- . Boston, 1859- .
New England Historical and Genealogical Register, Vol. 1- , January, 1847- . Boston, 1847- .
New Jersey Historical Society, *Proceedings,* Vol. 1- , 1845/46- . Newark, 1847.
New-York Historical Society, *Collections,* Vol. 1- , 1868- . New York, 1868- .
The Orion, Vol. 1-3; March, 1842-February, 1844. Penfield, Ga., 1842-44.
Pennsylvania. Historical Society, *Bulletin,* Vol. 1, 1845-47. Philadelphia, 1848.
Pennsylvania Archives, Vol. 1-Ser. 9, Vol. 10; 1852-1935. Philadelphia, 1852-1935.
Pennsylvania Magazine of History, Vol. 1- , 1877- . Philadelphia, 1877- .
Pennsylvania Packet, October 28, 1771-December 31, 1790. Philadelphia.
Potter's American Monthly, Vol. 4-19; January, 1875-September, 1882. Philadelphia, 1875-82.
The Remembrancer, 1775-84. London, 1775-84.
Rhode Island Historical Society, *Collections,* Vol. 1- , 1827- . Providence, 1827- .
Royal Gazette, September 16, 1780. New York.
Vermont Historical Society, *Collections,* Vol. 1-2; 1870-71. Montpelier, 1870-71.
Virginia Historical Register, Vol. 1-6; January, 1848-October, 1853. Richmond, 1848-53.
Virginia Magazine of History and Biography, Vol. 1- , July, 1893- . Richmond, 1893- .
William and Mary Quarterly, Vol. 1- , July, 1892- . Williamsburg, Va., 1892- .

MANUSCRIPTS

Samuel Adams Papers, New York Public Library.
Bancroft Transcripts, New York Public Library.
Miscellaneous Letters, Chicago Historical Society.
John Chilton Letters in Keith Papers, Virginia Historical Society.
Peter Force Transcripts, Manuscripts Division, Library of Congress.
Samuel Swett Papers on Bunker Hill, New-York Historical Society.
George Washington Papers, Manuscripts Division, Library of Congress.
George Weedon Papers, Chicago Historical Society.

Acknowledgments

The authors wish to thank the following publishers for permission to reprint material published by them:

The Dial Press, Inc., for passages from *The Journal of Nicholas Cresswell, 1774-1777*, copyright 1924, 1928, 1956.

Goodspeed's Book Shop, Inc., for passages from *The Letters of Hugh, Earl Percy*, edited by Charles K. Bolton.

Harvard University Press, for passages from *The British in Boston*, by John Barker; *The Taking of Ticonderoga in 1775: The British Story*, by Allen French; *The Mackenzie Diary*, by Frederick Mackenzie; copyright 1924, 1928, 1930.

Historical Society of Delaware, for passages from *Letters to and from Caesar Rodney, 1756-1784*, copyright 1933.

Houghton Mifflin Company, for passages from *The First Year of the American Revolution*, by Allen French, copyright 1934; *Travels through the interior parts of America*, by Thomas Anburey, copyright 1923; *Letters on the American Revolution, 1774-1776*, edited by Margaret W. Willard, copyright 1925.

Henry E. Huntington Library and Art Gallery, for passages from *The American Journal of Ambrose Serle, 1776-1778*, edited by Edward H. Tatum, Jr., copyright 1940.

Illinois State Historical Library, for passages from *George Rogers Clark Papers, 1771-1781*, edited by James A. James, copyright 1912.

Massachusetts Historical Society, for passages from *Letters & Papers of John Singleton Copley and Henry Pelham, 1739-1776*, copyright 1914, and *Warren-Adams Letters . . . 1743-1814*, copyright 1917, 1925.

The Graduate School, The Ohio State University, for passages from *The Journal of Alexander Chesney*, edited by E. A. Jones, copyright 1921.

Princeton University Press, for passages from *The Papers of Thomas Jefferson*, Volume 5, edited by Julian P. Boyd, copyright 1952; *The Autobiography of Benjamin Rush*, edited by George W. Corner, copyright 1948; *Heritage of Freedom*, by Frank Monaghan, copyright 1947.

Charles Scribner's Sons, for passage from *The Literary Diary of Ezra Stiles*, edited by Franklin P. Dexter, copyright 1901.

Sons of the Revolution, headquarters, Fraunces Tavern, New York, for passages from *Memoir of Colonel Benjamin Tallmadge*, edited by Henry P. Johnston, copyright 1904.

The University of Michigan Press, for passages from *General Gage's Informers*, copyright 1932.

Yale University Press, for passages from *The Correspondence of Thomas Gage*, Volume 2, copyright 1933.

Index

Abercrombie, Maj. Robert, 564

Acland, Maj. John Dyke, 321

Actaeon, 157

Active, 194

Acton, Mass., 31, 34, 42

Adams, Abigail, 73, 74, 80, 86, 168, 265, 293

Adams, Hannah, 39

Adams, John, described 73-74; nominates Washington Commander-in-Chief, 74-77; moves to adopt army at Cambridge, 76; on military discipline, 90, 265; on *Common Sense*, 167; member committee to draft Declaration of Independence, 169-172; on war in Northern Department, 293-294; on Washington, 337; mentioned 48, 80, 105, 265, 338, 340

Adams, Deacon Joseph, 39

Adams, Samuel, described, 20, 21, 22; leader of Boston Whigs, 15, 16, 17, 18, 19, 26; in Second Continental Congress, 73, 76, 77; on Schuyler, 293; mentioned 47, 58, 81, 87, 104, 149, 175

Admiral Warren Tavern, near Phila., 274

Alamance Creek, N.C., 509

Albany, N.Y., 125, 261, 287, 289, 292, 294, 299, 311, 312, 318, 328, 343, 346

Alexander, Lady Kitty, 356

Alexandria, Va., 79, 256

Allegheny Mountains, 230, 404

Allegheny River, 396

Allen, Andrew, 276

Allen, Ethan, 55, 124, 258; expedition to Ticonderoga, 51-54; assaults Montreal, 126-127

Allen, William, 276

Allentown, N.J., 378

Altenbrockum, Capt., 241

Amboy, N.J., 227, 244, 250, 252, 256, 259

American Crisis, The, 238

American fleet on Delaware, 284

American Turtle, 200-201

Amherst, Gen. Jeffrey, 124

Anburey, Lt. Thomas, 296, 317

Anderson, Capt., at Cowpens, 498

Anderson, Capt. Enoch, 233, 273

Anderson, John. *See* André John

Andover, Mass., 31, 44

André John, and the Mischianza, 369-371; meeting with Arnold, 437-440; captured and sentenced, 439-440, 443-444; objects to mode of death, 445; hanged, 446-447

Angell's Regiment, 430

Annapolis, Md., 257, 585

Annual Register, 148

Anspachers, 329

Apollo, 285

Appalachian Mountains, 395

Appletown (Indian town), 406

Appomattox River, 542

Aquackinack Bridge, N.J., 230

Archer, Edward, 254

Archer, Capt. Henry, 418

Armand, Col. Charles, 466, 469

Armstrong, Brig. Gen. John, 149, 267, 278

Armstrong, Maj. John, 323, 579

Arnold, Benedict, described, 50, 127; expedition to Ticonderoga, 50-54, 124; expedition to Canada, 127-145; misjudges distance to Quebec, 132-133; summons Quebec garrison, 137; assaults Quebec, 138-143, 451; wounded, 143-144; retires to Montreal, 144; sent to inspire New Englanders, 290; expedition to Fort Schuyler, 307-311; commands left wing Gates's army, 312; at Bemis Heights, 313-316; criticizes defense, 314; called "mad man" at Bemis Heights, 323; wounded, 323, 375; loses command, 320-321; quarrels with Gates, 320-321; military governor at Philadelphia, 375; declines command left wing Continental Army, 434; given West Point command, 434, 435; high living in Philadelphia, 436; profiteering, 436; court-martialed, 436; reprimanded by Washington, 436; treason of, 435-442, 446-447, 499; informs Clinton of Washington's whereabouts, 437; flees after André's capture, 441; deliberately weakened West Point, 442; unpopular with British, 447; as British general, 542; burnt in effigy, 575; mentioned, 130, 132, 133, 330

Arnold, Margaret Shippen "Peggy," 436, 437, 441

Arnold's Foot Guard, 144

Arnold's Tavern, Morristown, N.J., 250

Articles of Confederation, 407-408

Articles of War, 81, 105, 110

Ashley River, 150, 153, 453, 456, 457

Asia, 201

Assunpink River, 240, 246

Auchmuty, Robert, 225

Augusta County, Va., 231

Augusta, Ga., 450, 452, 462, 479, 524, 526, 529

Back Bay, Boston, 17, 100

Back Street, Boston, 18

"Backwater men." *See* Overmountain men

Balcarres, Maj., the Earl of, 322, 323

Baldwin, Col. Jeduthan, 445

Baldwin, Col. Loammi, 164

Ballard, Benjamin, 64

Baltimore, Md., 234, 243, 585

Bangs, Lt. Isaac, 172

Banister, John, 363

613

Other MENTOR Books of Special Interest

The American Presidency *by Clinton Rossiter.* A clear account of the history and evolution of the Presidency and the President's current duties and responsibilities.
(#MT454—75¢)

A Documentary History of the United States (expanded) *edited by Richard D. Heffner.* Important documents that have shaped America's history, with commentary.
(#MT605—75¢)

American Diplomacy: 1900-1950 *by George F. Kennan.* A trenchant appraisal of U. S. foreign relations by a distinguished diplomat.
(#MP360—60¢)

George Washington *by Marcus Cunliffe.* A masterful book which brilliantly separates Washington the man from Washington the myth.
(#MP536—60¢)

Jefferson (revised and abridged) *by Saul K. Padover.* Story of Jefferson as farmer, philosopher, architect, statesman, and President.
(#MP408—60¢)

America in Perspective (abridged) *edited by Henry Steele Commager.* Commentary on our national characteristics by 21 acute and perceptive foreigners from Tocqueville to Matthew Arnold and Denis W. Brogan. (#MT424—60¢)

American Essays (expanded) *edited by Charles B. Shaw.* A sampling of American thought up to the present, with essays by Emerson, Twain, Mencken, and others.
(#MP377—60¢)